PROPERTY AND WEALTH IN CLASSICAL SPARTA

Property and Wealth in Classical Sparta

Stephen Hodkinson

Duckworth
and
The Classical Press of Wales

First published in 2000 by
Gerald Duckworth & Co. Ltd.
61 Frith Street, London W1V 5TA
(sole distributor outside N. America)
and
The Classical Press of Wales

Distributor in the United States of America:
The David Brown Book Co.
PO Box 511, Oakville, CT 06779
Tel: (860) 945–9329
Fax: (860) 945–9468

Originated and prepared for press at
The Classical Press of Wales
15 Rosehill Terrace, Swansea SA1 6JN
Tel: 01792 458397
Fax: 01792 419056

© 2000

All rights reserved. No part of this publication may be reproduced, stored in a retrieval system, or transmitted, in any form or by any means, electronic, mechanical, photocopying, recording or otherwise, without the prior permission of the publisher.

ISBN 0-7156-3040-7

A catalogue record for this book is available from the British Library

Typeset by Ernest Buckley, Clunton, Shropshire
Printed and bound in the UK by Biddles Ltd., Guildford, Surrey

Hilariae meae

τῇ Στεφανοφόρῳ

CONTENTS

	Page
List of Figures	viii
Acknowledgements	ix
Abbreviations	xi
Introduction	1

PART I. SPARTAN PERCEPTIONS

1. Spartan economic egalitarianism and communitarianism in modern thought	9
2. The growth of the dominant egalitarian image in ancient thought	19

PART II. THE ANATOMY OF THE SPARTIATE PROPERTY SYSTEM

3. The ownership and inheritance of land - revisited	65
4. Helotage and the exploitation of Spartan territory	113
5. Movable wealth: ownership, acquisition and exchange	151
6. Public rights over private property	187

PART III. RICH CITIZENS AND THE USE OF PRIVATE WEALTH

7. Restrictions on the use of wealth in Spartiate life	209
8. Restrictions on the use of wealth: burial and funerary practice	237
9. Material and religious investment: bronze dedications at Sparta and abroad	271
10. Equestrian competition: participation and expenditure	303
11. The use of wealth in personal and political relations	335

PART IV. PROPERTY AND THE SPARTAN CRISIS

12. Spartiate household economies: towards an estimate of a balance-sheet	369
13. Property concentration and the emergence of a plutocratic society	399
Bibliography	447
Index	485

LIST OF FIGURES

1. Map of mainland and Aegean Greece (showing places mentioned in the text) xii/xiii
2. View over central and western parts of Sparta Valley 136
3. Map of Sparta Valley 137
4. Map of Lakonia 140
5. Map of Messenia 143
6, 7. Bronze figurines of hoplites 223
8. Lead figurines, from the sanctuary of Artemis Orthia 223
9, 10. Two sides of an Athenian victory monument, from the Acropolis 225
11. Drawing of terracotta relief amphora 241
12. Fallen Lakedaimonian soldiers buried in the Kerameikos 252
13. Figurine of a running figure (front and back), bronze vessel ornament 274
14. Drawing of inscribed bronze bell dedicated to Athena 277
15. Bronze figurine of Athena, from the Spartan Acropolis 283
16. Small votives from the sanctuary of Artemis Orthia 288
17. Inscribed miniature breastplate dedicated to Athena 292
18. Two parts of an inscribed marble victory stēlē dedicated by Damonon 304
19. Detail of the sculpted relief on the Damonon stēlē 304
20. Drawing of a Panathenaic amphora dedicated to Athena 309
21. Inscribed figurine of a bronze lion from the Heraion on Samos 343
22. Inscribed marble seat from the stadium at Olympia 343
23. Graph of family landholding 402
24. Graph of male landholding 403
25. Family tree of the Agiad house, later sixth and fifth centuries 411
26. Family tree of the Eurypontid house, fifth and fourth centuries 412

ACKNOWLEDGEMENTS

In the course of many years' study of classical Sparta I have accumulated debts to a great number of persons and institutions. My education in ancient Greek history began as an undergraduate in the 'Manchester History School', where I was inspired to work on Sparta by the teaching of Cosmo Rodewald and the writings of Geoffrey de Ste Croix. My postgraduate research at Cambridge was skilfully guided, initially by Sir Moses Finley, and latterly by Paul Cartledge, to whom I owe over two decades of personal encouragement and advice. Anthony Snodgrass too has since the late 1970s given consistent support to my work. I am especially indebted to him and to James Roy for their helpful comments as examiners of my doctoral dissertation, of which this volume is a distant descendant.

Most of the research and writing for this book was performed during my tenure of a Nuffield Foundation Social Science Research Fellowship and an award under the Research Leave Scheme of the British Academy Humanities Research Board. The University of Manchester provided a further semester of sabbatical leave and also, through the Faculty of Arts Recurrent Grant for Research, funding for invaluable teaching relief during the final months of writing. My capacity to undertake this research has been aided immeasurably by the excellent holdings of the John Rylands University Library of Manchester, supplemented where occasionally necessary by the efficient efforts of the Inter-Library Loans department. A fruitful month in the library of the British School at Athens enabled me to access numismatic material and work by Greek scholars not easily accessible in the UK. I also thank the editor of the BSA Studies Series, Dr W.G. Cavanagh, for permission to reproduce material from my contribution to vol. 4 in the series (Hodkinson 1998b) which forms a major part of chapter 9.

I am glad to express my gratitude to my colleagues (both academic and secretarial) in the School of History and Classics at the University of Manchester for their personal and practical support during the long gestation of this book. I am grateful to colleagues in the Department of Classics at the University of Nottingham, who generously offered me the honorary position of Special Lecturer, which has permitted my access to the University's library and computing facilities. David Taylor of the Department of Archaeology at Nottingham has kindly produced the volume's maps. One of the joys of working on Sparta today is the growing spirit of international cooperation among scholars from different nations. Many colleagues around the world have assisted me with specialist advice on particular aspects of my study. I have endeavoured to acknowledge

Acknowledgements

their help at appropriate points in the text; and I apologise here to any whom I have inadvertently omitted. Certain academic friends, however, merit special mention. Robin Osborne and Paul Cartledge have provided constructive criticism of several chapters, which have been materially improved by their comments. Noreen Humble generously volunteered to proof-read several chapters. Above all, Anton Powell, my editorial collaborator over many years, has contributed much expert academic and technical assistance. To his unstinting efforts and to the unrivalled typesetting skills of Ernest Buckley I am indebted for the prompt production and publication of this complex book.

My greatest debts, however, are personal ones. My children (Christopher, David, Rosemary, Peter and Joy) have learned, with the enviable flexibility of the young, to tolerate a father's constant preoccupation with a project seemingly without end. My wife Hilary Hodkinson has proof-read the entire volume and greatly improved my clarity of exposition. Her unswerving support has been a continual reminder that there are more important things in life than property and wealth. I dedicate this book to her.

The publication of this book has been assisted by
a grant from The Scouloudi Foundation
in association with the Institute of Historical Research

ABBREVIATIONS

Abbreviations of ancient sources generally follow the forms used in LSJ⁹ or OCD³; abbreviations of modern periodicals those in *L'Année Philologique*. In certain cases common and easily identified variants have been used. In addition, the following abbreviations should be noted:

BMC, Attica   British Museum. Department of Coins and Medals, *Catalogue of Greek Coins. Attica–Megaris–Aegina*, London 1888.
CEG   P.A. Hansen, *Carmina Epigraphica Graeca*, 2 vols., Oxford 1983–9.
CH   Royal Numismatic Society, *Coin Hoards*, London 1975–.
CID II   J. Bousquet, *Corpus des Inscriptions de Delphes. Tome II: Les comptes du quatrième et du troisième siècle*, Paris 1989.
CVA   *Corpus Vasorum Antiquorum*, 1925–.
FdD   *Fouilles de Delphes*
FGrH   F. Jacoby, *Die Fragmente der griechischen Historiker*, Berlin 1923–.
FHG   C. Müller, *Fragmenta Historicorum Graecorum*, Paris 1848.
IG   *Inscriptiones Graecae*, Berlin 1873–.
IGCH   M. Thompson, O. Mørkholm and C.M. Kraay (eds.) *An Inventory of Greek Coin Hoards*, New York 1993.
IvO   W. Dittenberger and K. Purgold, *Olympia: die Ergebnisse der von dem deutschen Reich veranstalteten Ausgrabung. V. Die Inschriften*, Berlin 1896.
LSJ⁹   H.G. Liddell, R. Scott and H.S. Jones, *Greek-English Lexicon*, 9th edition, Oxford 1968.
LSJ, Rev. Suppl.   P.W. Glare, *Greek-English Lexicon*, revised supplement, Oxford 1996.
ML   R. Meiggs and D.M. Lewis, *Greek Historical Inscriptions to the End of the Fifth Century*, revised edition, Oxford 1988.
OCD³   S. Hornblower and A. Spawforth (eds.) *The Oxford Classical Dictionary*, 3rd edition, Oxford 1996.
RE   A. Pauly, G. Wissowa and W. Kroll (eds.) *Real-Encyclopädie der classischen Altertumswissenschaft*, Munich 1893–.
SGDI   H. Collitz et al. (eds.) *Sammlung der griechischen Dialekt-Inschriften*, Göttingen 1884–1915.
SEG   *Supplementum Epigraphicum Graecum*, Leiden 1923–.
SIG   W. Dittenberger, *Sylloge Inscriptionum Graecarum*, 4th edition, Hildesheim 1960.

References to sub-sections of chapters in Plutarch's *Lives* follow those given in the Loeb Classical Library editions.

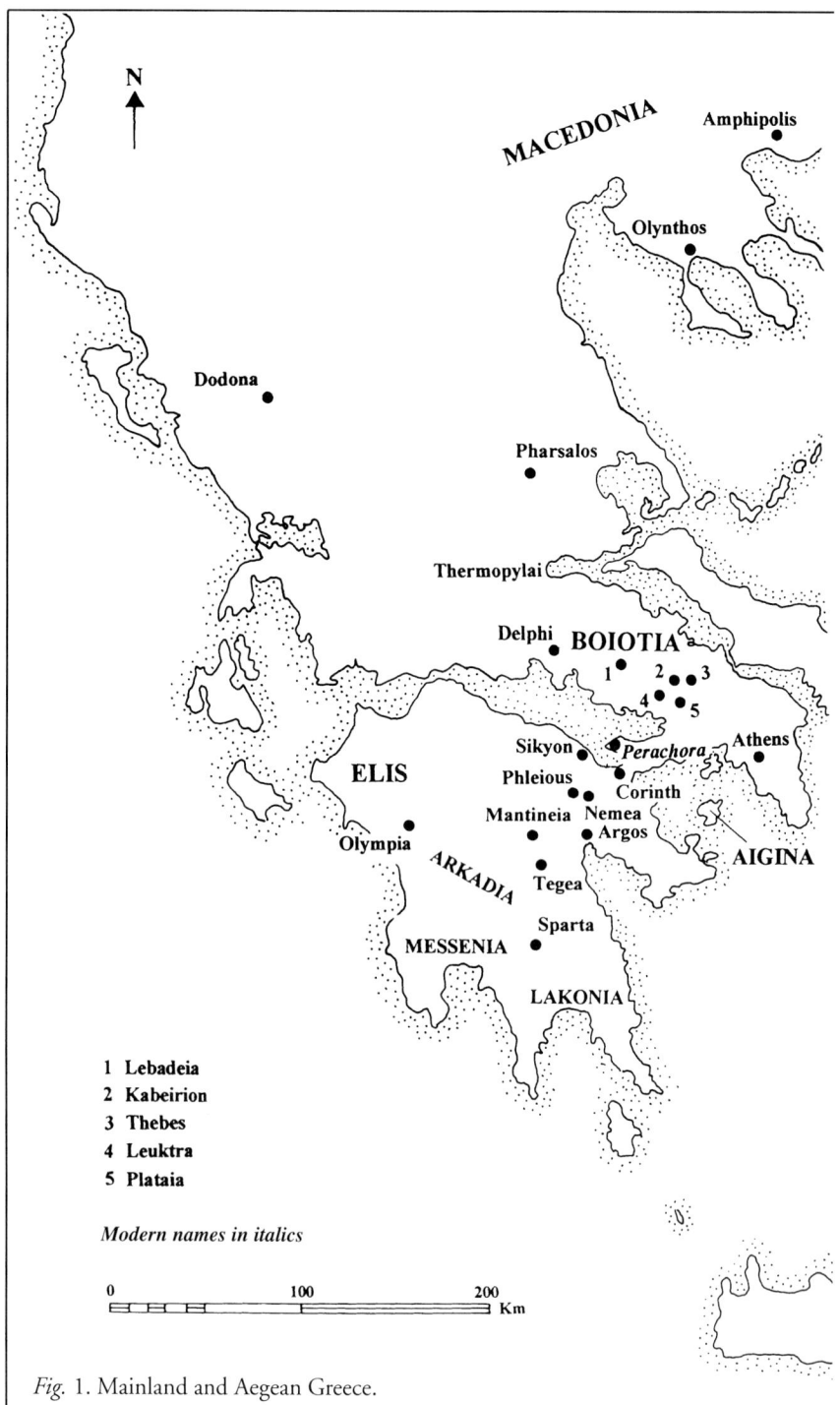

Fig. 1. Mainland and Aegean Greece.

INTRODUCTION

The aim of this book is to provide a systematic examination of a crucial aspect of classical Sparta, her system of property, and to analyse the role of private wealth within her society. Its publication coincides with the 200th anniversary of the first specialised modern history in this field, J.C.F. Manso's *Sparta*, whose first volume was published in 1800. In his preface Manso emphasized his decision to write a specialist study of Sparta rather than yet another general history of Greece, whose existing examples he criticised for their lack of thoroughness, their uneven degree of accuracy and their inadequacy of overall perspective. The history of Greece, he argued, would not prosper until it was founded upon critical, detailed studies of each of its constituent city-states (ibid. iii–iv). Two hundred years later, Manso's innovatory concept of specialised studies of particular Greek poleis has become well-established. Yet in Spartan scholarship his vision has been only incompletely realised. In some respects, Spartan studies currently stand in a similar problematic position to that which Manso outlined at the broader level of Greece as a whole. The twentieth century witnessed a plethora of books on Sparta;[1] but, instead of the detailed, in-depth discussions envisaged by Manso, most books on Sparta were briefer, rather generalised accounts. The consequence has often been a certain superficiality of analysis, a state of affairs which prompted Geoffrey de Ste Croix's scathing remark (1972, 89 n. 1): 'Books on Sparta are numerous and mostly bad.' Since Ste Croix wrote, the notable resurgence of Spartan studies during the last generation has produced several books of higher quality. Moreover, the prevalence of generalised accounts of Sparta in published books is partly counterbalanced by many excellent, recent specialist articles in academic journals and edited volumes. Nevertheless, there remains an important gap in scholarly approaches: there are comparatively few detailed monographs which provide a sustained and systematic analysis of specific Spartan institutions or practices in such a way as to shed new light upon the overall character of Sparta's society and historical development.[2] The purpose of this study is to attempt to close that gap. Through a comprehensive study of the role of property and wealth, I hope to confront and illuminate some of the central issues in our current understanding of Spartan society and historical development.

The essential challenge facing the historian of classical Sparta is to construct an analysis of Spartan society that can explain *both* her long-standing external success *and* her subsequent rapid decline. For nearly 200 years, from *c.* 550 until her defeat at the battle of Leuktra in 371 BC, Sparta was a (sometimes *the*) leading power in mainland and Aegean Greece; yet within a decade of

1

Leuktra she had declined to the rank of a second-rate Greek polis. Sparta's external power was rooted in her creation of a socio-economic and political structure whose key theme was the organisation of her citizens into a body of *homoioi* or 'Peers' known as the 'Spartiates'. Her lasting domination of her neighbours in the Peloponnese, and at times of poleis further afield, rested upon the extraordinary longevity and success of this singular structure. Likewise, Sparta's rapid international decline stemmed from a deep-rooted internal crisis which undermined the principles of her citizen organisation.

The origins of Sparta's citizen organisation in the classical period cannot be traced in detail, owing to the paucity of evidence from early Sparta. Yet there are sufficient indications that it emerged as a solution to civil crisis and strife which centred around issues of property and wealth (cf. van Wees 1999). The poet Tyrtaios, writing in the mid-late seventh century BC, reveals that Sparta was already a rich and powerful polis which – in addition to controlling her home region of Lakonia (ancient 'Lakedaimon') in the south-eastern Peloponnese – had two generations earlier also expanded westwards to conquer the fertile territory of neighbouring Messenia (fr. 5, West). Yet, despite her immense resources, there were severe inequalities among the Spartan population. Visual scenes on seventh- and sixth-century Lakonian artistic products depict an elite lifestyle of leisure and conspicuous consumption (A. Powell 1998). The Spartan poet Alkman, writing *c.* 600, makes an implicit contrast between those who eat 'sweet confections' and the common people who eat more ordinary food (fr. 17, Page). Another contemporary poet, Alkaios, quotes a saying of Spartan origin: 'man is what he owns; no poor man is good or honourable' (fr. 360, Campbell, *ap.* Schol. Pindar, *Isthmian* 2.17). The acquisitive behaviour of the Spartan elite, who so disdained their poorer compatriots, is expressed in the proverb, 'Greed will destroy Sparta, nothing else.'[3] These inequalities led to internal crisis when the conquered Messenians went into revolt, as we learn from Aristotle's citation of one of Tyrtaios' poems (fr. 1, West). According to Aristotle (*Pol.* 1306b36–1307a2) civil wars tend to break out

> when some are excessively poor and others excessively rich; and this happens especially during wars, and this occurred in Lakedaimon during the Messenian war – as is evident from the poem of Tyrtaios called *Eunomia*; for certain men, being reduced to straitened circumstances through the war, demanded a redistribution of the territory.

Neither was this the only occasion of civil strife. According to the Spartans' own traditions, foreign poets had several times been invited into their city during the seventh century at the command of an oracle to help cure internal dissension (van Wees 1999, 4–6). For Herodotus (1.65), the Spartans had once been the worst governed people in Greece. Thucydides too comments that they had suffered 'the longest known period of faction' (1.18).

Sparta's classical citizen organisation was a definitive response to this chronic state of crisis. Analytically, we can distinguish four essential strands. First, a military system according to which full citizenship was extended to all adult male members of the Spartan community, a body of men several thousand strong. Full citizenship entailed membership of a guild of full-time hoplite warriors who each, as a condition of membership, made a fixed contribution of foodstuffs to a mess group where they dined every day. Secondly, an economic system according to which each citizen had (in theory, at least) sufficient land and an accompanying helot labour force to enable him to meet his compulsory mess dues without personal engagement in manual labour. Thirdly, a political system, originally promulgated in the so-called 'Great Rhētra' (Plut. *Lyk.* 6), which gave the mass of citizens in assembly a formal role in decision-making, whilst retaining considerable influence in the hands of the kings and Gerousia (a council of Elders). Finally, a social and ritual system which marked out from birth to the grave a common, public way of life which every non-royal citizen was to follow.

As with its origins, the precise chronology of the implementation of this new citizen organisation is difficult to recover. After the archaic poets cited above, there is a gap of over 150 years before the advent of sustained literary evidence about Spartan society in the works of writers from the later fifth and early fourth centuries. In opposition to older studies which tended to view the entire structure as operative by the end of the seventh century or even earlier, more recent accounts have opted for somewhat lower dates. Some studies have suggested that many aspects of Sparta's classical organisation were introduced as late as the mid-fifth century (e.g. Thommen 1996). It is surely right to abandon myths of a 'fossilised' Sparta: I have long argued (Hodkinson 1983, 240; 1989, 95–108; 1997a, 86–7) that we should envisage continual development in Spartan institutions and practice. Yet, there is good reason to believe that the structure in its essentials was in place well before the fifth century. Our late fifth-century historical sources, Herodotus (1.65) and Thucydides (1.18), both portray Sparta's contemporary organisation as originating long before their time. Whilst we need not accept Thucydides' figure of 'more than 400 years', their evidence is incompatible with a structure created within their lifetimes. There are firm indications that the decisive changes had already been made by around the mid-sixth century. It was then that Croesus of Lydia approached Sparta for military assistance as the leading Greek polis (Hdt. 1.65–9), an approach later followed by several other states.[4] Shortly afterwards Sparta started to build her Peloponnesian league, a system of alliances which rested on the long-term reliance that her allies felt able to place upon Spartan military support. All this presupposes that by this time Spartan society had emerged from its chronic state of strife into an assured condition of internal stability. Another sign is Sparta's avoidance of the tyrannical regimes which affected many other leading sixth-century poleis (cf. Andrewes 1956). Although we cannot trace the exact chronology of the introduction of the key elements of Sparta's classical citizen

Introduction

organisation, Moses Finley was right, in his classic article on Spartan society (1986), to ascribe them loosely to a 'sixth-century revolution'. Consequently, whilst taking due account of specific changes within the period, I shall treat Spartan society from (approximately) the mid-sixth to the mid-fourth century as a single, coherent entity possessing an underlying continuity of socio-economic and political structure. (The shorthand term 'classical Sparta' used in my title and elsewhere in the volume hence signifies the period *c.* 550–*c.* 350 BC – the 'long classical period'. When distinguishing different parts of this period, however, especially when discussing changes in material culture, I shall sometimes use the traditional art–historical periodisation, referring to the period 550–480 BC as 'late archaic'.)

Issues of property and wealth were central to this new citizen organisation. Possession of Spartiate status depended upon membership of a common mess, and mess membership upon one's delivery of a fixed monthly contribution of foodstuffs (Arist. *Pol.* 1271a26–37). The operation of these mess dues rested upon each citizen's possession of sufficient land to grow the required produce. A sufficient landholding was necessary in any case to enable each Spartiate to live the life of leisure, free from manual labour, which permitted him to devote his entire time to civic and military affairs. Underpinning this economic system was Sparta's possession of a servile labour force, the helots, drawn from the subjugated populations of her home territory of Lakonia and neighbouring Messenia. Finally, the demands of the Spartiate common public way of life bore directly upon the material aspects of living, involving a degree of uniformity between rich and poor. In studying property and wealth, one is consequently penetrating into almost every facet of Spartiate life and tackling directly the fundamental questions posed above regarding the success and crisis of the classical Spartan polis. Yet, surprisingly, there has been no previous monograph-length study of this essential subject. Indeed, as will become apparent in this volume, many aspects of the subject have yet to be fully explored and many others are clouded in controversy, both ancient and modern.

This state of affairs has necessarily influenced the shape of my study. The volume falls into four parts. In Part I, *Spartan perceptions*, I shall outline certain misleading but highly influential images of Sparta's property system and attitudes to wealth which have prevailed since ancient times. Chapter 1 will sketch the prevalence of perceptions of Sparta as an economically egalitarian society in the works of key modern thinkers from the sixteenth to the eighteenth centuries – perceptions which have formed an influential backdrop to historical scholarship on Sparta during the last 200 years. Chapter 2 examines the creation and development of these images in antiquity under the influence of what is commonly known as the 'Spartan mirage': that is, 'the partly distorted, partly invented, image created by and for non-Spartans (with not a little help from their Spartan friends) of what Sparta ideally represented' (Cartledge 1987, 118).

Part II, *The anatomy of the Spartiate property system*, attempts to uncover the 'reality' obscured by these 'Spartan perceptions', focusing on the balance between private and public elements in Spartan property-holding. Chapter 3 analyses the nature of land-ownership and inheritance, emphasising – contrary to the pervasive images of egalitarian state control – the predominantly private character of land tenure. Chapter 4 examines the Spartiates' control over the servile helot population, focusing upon their relationship as landowners and cultivators, and the character and geographical extent of Spartiate agricultural exploitation of Lakonia and Messenia. Chapter 5 discusses private ownership and use of non-landed property, especially the controversial questions of Sparta's iron currency, the use of foreign coinage and the role of monetary wealth. Finally, chapter 6 examines certain public limitations on private property ownership, placing them in a broader historical perspective.

Part III, *Rich citizens and the use of private wealth*, analyses the extent to which rich citizens were able to make use of their private resources and the impact of those uses upon Spartiate society. Chapter 7 considers certain restrictions upon the deployment of private wealth in Spartan life; chapter 8 similar restrictions on burials and funerary practice. Chapter 9 investigates the sphere of religious dedications, assessing the degree to which it was marked by restrictions on the use of wealth or by its deployment for prestige displays. Chapters 10 and 11 discuss two particular spheres in which rich citizens were able to employ their surplus wealth with potentially significant socio-political consequences: through horse-rearing and engagement in equestrian contests, and through the establishment of personal and political relations of patronage and clientism at home and abroad. My overall thesis is that, despite manifold restrictions, their deployment of private wealth created a significant gulf between wealthy Spartiates and their poorer fellow citizens.

Part IV, *Property and the Spartan crisis*, pursues this point in examining the contribution of inequalities in wealth to the crisis of Spartiate society. Chapter 12 attempts the difficult task of quantifying the economic viability of 'ordinary' citizen households, suggesting that their productive capacity would normally have been sufficient to meet their material demands, as long as the distribution of land remained only moderately unequal. Finally, chapter 13 analyses the growth of excessive property concentration and the impoverishment of citizen households during the fifth and early fourth centuries. It also examines the impact of these developments on the crisis of Spartiate society, focusing especially on the growth of a plutocratic society, in which the dominance of wealthy citizens undermined the classical Spartan social order.

As will be evident from the above summary, this book is above all a study of the ruling group in Spartan society, the body of full citizens known as the 'Spartiates' (*Spartiatai* in Greek). The other human populations of classical Lakonia and Messenia – most notably the servile helot population and the free but non-citizen inhabitants known as the *perioikoi*[5] – will appear in my study in so far as their societies impinge on the understanding of Spartiate property

Introduction

and wealth. The restriction of my primary focus to the ruling Spartiates is simply for reasons of practicality: issues of Spartiate property and wealth are a sufficiently large and coherent subject in themselves. Current research rightly emphasizes the validity and importance of viewing the internal workings of helot and perioikic societies both in their own right and for the insights which the study of helot–Spartiate and perioikic–Spartiate interactions can offer to our understanding of the Spartiates themselves (e.g. Alcock forthcoming; Shipley 1997). The Spartiate perspective offered here should likewise be seen as complementary to these other perspectives, as a contribution to the understanding of the Spartan state as a whole, including both perioikic and helot societies.

This book represents the culmination of many years' study of Spartan society and economy, and perceptive readers will observe that some of my chapters discuss issues which I have already examined in earlier articles (see Bibliography). Chapter 3 is explicitly labelled as a 'revisit' to a subject first treated in 1986. I have devoted much thought to the question of how to cover topics on which I have published elsewhere. My decision has mostly been to cover each aspect of my subject with the thoroughness it deserves, regardless of the existence or otherwise of a prior publication. My reasons are several. First, this volume is intended as a systematic study: to skim over important aspects treated elsewhere would imbalance and distort my overall presentation. Secondly, my previous publications are scattered around a variety of journals and edited volumes. Some are unavailable in many libraries, and sometimes in entire countries; some are perhaps largely unknown, except among Spartan specialists. Thirdly, the pace of Spartan scholarship has quickened markedly during the 1990s. Several topics have received subsequent studies from other scholars which have led me to rethink my views, whether to modify them or to realise the need for further discussion. This volume, accordingly, presents an opportunity to revise certain of my earlier publications. Consequently, although specialists will recognise certain passages drawn from my earlier studies, they should also notice frequent changes of opinion and presentation. Fourthly, even on topics where my views have not changed, the context in which they appear in this book often differs from that of the previous publication. Hence, with the explicit exception of chapter 3 noted above, only chapters 1 and 9 appear in anything like the form of their original publication – and even there I have augmented my original study with substantial new sections.

The final reason for my re-presentation of earlier studies alongside newer discussions is that it permits the juxtaposition in a coherent setting of diverse approaches to different kinds of evidence which have hitherto appeared in separate studies: approaches via historiography and intellectual history, via comparative sociology, physical geography and geomorphology, via historical analysis of literary texts, via archaeological, epigraphic and numismatic evidence, via statistical analysis of the material record, and via the use of historical simulation. The basic ground for this diversity of approach is the need to paint a more rounded picture of Spartan society. Past studies have too often viewed Sparta in one-dimensional terms (for example, as merely an austere military camp), an approach which does insufficient justice to the complexity of Spartan society and the diverse contexts of Spartiate life. Each of these contexts displays the role of property and wealth in a subtly different light: one context cannot speak as a proxy for all. This variety of contexts needs approaching via diverse kinds of evidence and from the perspective of different academic disciplines. One important benefit of a more rounded depiction of Sparta is that it permits us, as I have advocated elsewhere (Hodkinson 1997a), to view her society not in isolation but in the context of other Greek poleis, and indeed of societies at other times and places. This comparative perspective will be an explicit or implicit theme throughout my study.

Notes

[1] e.g. Däubler 1923, Berve 1937, Lüdemann 1939, Meier 1939, Roussel 1939, Solari 1947, Cavaignac 1948, Chrimes 1949, Huxley 1962, Michell 1964, Jones 1967, Forrest 1968, Oliva 1971, Cartledge 1979, Hooker 1980, Clauss 1983, MacDowell 1986, Piper 1986, Link 1994.

[2] Honourable exceptions include Cartledge 1987, Ducat 1990a, Nafissi 1991, Kennell 1995, Thommen 1996, Richer 1998.

[3] The archaic origin of this proverb has been convincingly established by van Wees 1999, 3–4.

[4] Hdt. 3.46, 148; 5.49; 6.84; cf. 5.63.

[5] The official term for the Spartan state was 'the Lakedaimonians' (*hoi Lakedaimonioi*). The *perioikoi* were included, along with the Spartiates, among the Lakedaimonians. Hence they were not subjects but members of the Spartan (or, perhaps better, Lakedaimonian) state; but they were excluded from political decision-making, which was reserved to the Spartiates alone. For convenience, I use the word 'citizen' in this study to signify those who possessed the most complete citizen rights, i.e. the Spartiates. When referring to '(Spartan) citizenship', I mean full membership of the body of Spartiates, untinged by any loss of civic rights.

PART I

SPARTAN PERCEPTIONS

Chapter 1

SPARTAN ECONOMIC EGALITARIANISM AND COMMUNITARIANISM IN MODERN THOUGHT

To view Spartan society in broader, comparative context consciously goes against the dominant trend of modern thought since the rediscovery of classical antiquity during the Renaissance. Modern thought has often viewed classical Sparta as a unique society, somewhat different from other Greek poleis and, indeed, from most other civilised human societies. As Paul Cartledge (1987, 415–16) has noted, Sparta is 'the ultimate model and fountainhead of the entire western utopian tradition'. An important element in modern perceptions has been certain misleading but highly influential images of Spartan property arrangements and attitudes to wealth – images drawn especially from the writings of the ancient biographer Plutarch (c. AD 50–after 120) – whereby Sparta has been viewed as the embodiment of economic egalitarianism and communitarianism. To provide an intellectual context for my own study, it is important to outline the significant influence that these images have had within modern social and political thought,[1] an influence from which professional scholarship on Sparta during the last 200 years has not remained immune.

Appropriately enough, we can start with the influence of notions of Spartan property arrangements upon the first major utopian work of the modern era, Thomas More's *Utopia* (1516). The extent to which the *Utopia* is modelled on the depiction of the Spartan property system in the writings of Plutarch has been noted by Thomas Africa (1979, esp. 348). Like Plutarch's Spartans (see ch. 2), More's Utopians have equal property holdings, eat in common messes, disdain luxury, have no use for money and prefer iron to gold and silver.[2] More's image of Spartan property and wealth was shared by other sixteenth-century writers. According to the political philosopher, Jean Bodin, in his *Six Livres de la République* (first published in 1576), the Spartan lawgiver Lykourgos had banished the use of gold and silver and made an equal distribution of the lands. Bodin stresses the singularity of Lykourgos' arrangements by contrasting his success with Plato's supposed failure to persuade the Thebans and Phokians to accept similar proposals. Subsequently, however, 'the use of gold and silver was allowed in Lacedemon after the victorie of Lisander, and…the testamentarie law was brought in, the which was partly the cause of inequalitie of goods' (1606, 569–70). This account of the collapse of Lykourgos' measures comes straight from Plutarch's *Lives*.[3] Nicholas Cragius' antiquarian investigation into Spartan institutions, *De Republica Lacedaemoniorum* (1593), naturally cites a wider range of authorities. But Plutarch is again prominent, and Cragius' perception of Sparta's property system is fundamentally similar to More's and Bodin's, including equal property holdings, the avoidance of luxury, a ban on gold and silver and an iron currency.[4]

During the English revolution of the mid-seventeenth century, prompted by James Harrington's *The Commonwealth of Oceana* (1656), Sparta's property arrangements became central to political debate (cf. Rawson 1969, 191–7). Using his imaginary Oceana as a utopianised England, Harrington pictured his legislator Olphaus Megaletor (viz. Oliver Cromwell) imitating Lykourgos in introducing a mixed constitution with a substantial popular element, as at Sparta. The economic foundation for this political balance was to be a 'law fixing the balance in lands' (called an 'Agrarian') along the lines of Lykourgos' division of land. His account of Sparta's Agrarian once again follows Plutarch's *Lykourgos*, including a description of the fixed quantities of produce supplied to each citizen from his lot (*Lyk*. 8.3–4) and a reference to Lysander's ruining the commonwealth by importing previously banned money (30.1).[5] Harrington's invocation of Sparta provoked criticism from those of opposing political persuasions. None of them, however, challenged his account of her Agrarian. For the monarchist Matthew Wren, neither Lykourgos' Agrarian nor his prohibition of gold and silver had the purpose or the beneficial effects which Harrington claimed. He notes that inequality reigned as early as the Second Messenian war and that 'the Lacedaemonians began to cast amorous Glances upon Gold in the times of Croesus'. Wren explicitly accepts, however, the reality of Sparta's Agrarian.[6] Another critic, Henry Stubbe, provided a sketch of Sparta's constitutional development, insisting against Harrington that for most of her history Sparta was an oligarchy, a state ruled by a few men. But he readily agrees that Lykourgos 'divided the land into lots, and nulled the use of Money', with 'foreign commerce, Rhetorique and Learning, yea accumulation of riches being prohibited or prevented'. He, too, follows the account in Plutarch, *Agis* 5 for the subversion of this system by Lysander's introduction of riches and the testamentary law of Epitadeus, mentioning him explicitly as his source.[7]

Similar Plutarchean-based views persisted in political writings later in the century. According to Henry Neville's *Plato Redivivus* (1681), 'Lycurgus, the greatest politician that ever founded any government, took sure way to fix property, by confounding it and bringing all into common', dividing it into 9,000 lots, a provision which survived until 'the riches and luxury brought into their city by Lysander…destroyed the proportions of land allotted to each of the natural Spartans'.[8] So also in Walter Moyle's *An Essay upon the Lacedaemonian Government* (1698) Lykourgos' primary political act was to persuade the Spartans 'to come into a new and equal Division of Lands'.[9] Though they concurred with Harrington's account of Lykourgos' Agrarian, none of the above writers shared his expectation of the feasibility of a new lawgiver like Lykourgos; for them, as Rawson (1969, 197) notes, an Agrarian was merely a utopian measure.

The general assumptions about Lykourgos' measures regarding property which we have witnessed in early modern writings are also evident – with some important variations – in the moral and political debates about 'le luxe' in eighteenth century France. This comment applies equally to perceptions of Sparta as a somewhat alien society and to perceptions of the assumed substance of her economic practice.[10] For Montesquieu, Lykourgos was a legislator who set his people on a 'unique path', who divided wealth equally and 'seemed to remove all its resources, arts, commerce, silver, walls'. He even refused to 'tolerate the citizen's increasing the tax of the slave' (Montesquieu specifically cites Plutarch for this detail).[11] Similarly, the Marquis d'Argenson: 'l'égalité est le seul bien général et jamais législateur n'a eu plus de raison que Lycurgue sur ce point là'.[12] According to the Chevalier de Jaucourt, in an article in the *Encyclopédie*, Lykourgos persuaded the rich to renounce their wealth, divided Lakonia into equal portions, banned gold and silver, substituting an iron currency, and regulated the character of housing, furnishing and dress with a uniformity and simplicity which eliminated luxury.[13] The circulation of such ideas in the *Encyclopédie* gave them a wide diffusion and frequently uncritical reception (Grell 1995, i.480). Hence François Turpin's *L'Histoire du gouvernement des anciennes républiques* could assert Lykourgos' prohibition of the use of wealth, his equal redistribution of land and proscription of 'le luxe' without citing a single ancient source.[14] Sparta's equality of landholding, elimination of commerce, money and luxury were likewise taken as read in Helvétius' posthumously-published *De l'Homme* (1772).[15] The most concerted advocacy of such ideas, however, came from the distinguished laconiser, Gabriel Bonnot, abbé de Mably (Guerci 1979). Against the inequalities in wealth and the luxury of modern society, Mably's *Observations sur l'Histoire de la Grèce* (1766) opposed 'the perfect equality of wealth' established by Lykourgos which – along with the usual range of measures mentioned by other writers – stamped out the very germ of the love of wealth from the heart of Sparta's citizens.[16] In the heat of his debate with the Physiocrats, who argued that property was the cornerstone of the natural and social order,[17] Mably's claims for Lykourgos' work soon went one step further. Arguing in his *Doutes proposés aux philosophes économistes* (1767) that landed property was an arbitrary and dispensable human institution, Mably invoked the example of the Spartiates, who never knew landed property but had only the usufruct of the land – a claim later repeated in his *De la Législation* (1776) where he mentioned the Spartan 'communauté des biens' ('community of possessions') as an example of government in accord with nature.[18]

As in the parallel case of Harrington, the immediate Physiocratic critiques of Mably's *Doutes* attacked his invocation of Sparta (mainly on grounds of her oppression of the helots), but tended to accept his assertions about her property system, including her 'communauté des biens'.[19] Certain others, it is true, did deny the community of possessions (using, notably, the evidence of Aristotle) and even the existence of Sparta's equality; but the ground for the latter denial was the differential fertility of their equal-sized lots rather than scepticism about the reality of Lykourgos' division of lands.[20] Elsewhere there were some more sceptical stirrings. Already the more extreme notions prevalent among other laconophiles had been largely eschewed by the 'arch-priest of laconism', Jean-Jacques Rousseau.[21] Voltaire's *Ésprit des Lois* (1777) fluctuates between accepting that there was no property in Sparta and questioning the grounds of our knowledge of Lykourgos, since Plutarch lived much later;[22] his sceptical remarks were subsequently endorsed by Condorcet. Such scepticism reached its peak in the work of Corneille de Pauw, who argued that money had long circulated inside Sparta and denied the equality of wealth. But even Pauw did not doubt the equal division of Lakonian territory: his argument was rather that true equality of wealth was undermined by other factors (differences in soil fertility, family size and so on) and that Sparta's inheritance by primogeniture itself produced a mass of poverty-stricken younger sons.[23] However, as has been well remarked (Guerci 1979, 79), contemporary debates about Sparta were largely a dialogue among deaf men. During the Revolution Sparta continued to evoke 'above all else economic egalitarianism or even communism' (Rawson 1969, 269), whether among laconophiles or laconophobes, partly because the participants' acquaintance with ancient Greek literature was largely confined to Plutarch's *Lives* (H. Parker 1937, 16–21). Consequently, Spartan equality of landholding and austerity are praised or denounced by figures from as diverse political and intellectual standpoints as Desmoulins, Vergniaud, Saint-Just, Billaud, Lakanal and Babeuf.[24]

When we turn from social and political theorists to eighteenth-century histories of Greece, we find a general acceptance of Plutarch's account of Spartan property with none of the scepticism expressed by some social critics. The account of Lykourgos' economic legislation in Charles Rollin's *Histoire Ancienne* (1730–38) is little more than a paraphrase of Plutarch, *Lykourgos* 8–12.[25] John Gillies' *History of Ancient Greece* (1786) also largely follows Plutarch's evidence, though he does attempt to contextualise Lykourgos' measures. The latter's land division was a return to a primitive equality which existed in both ancient Greece and Germany. Iron was a common measure of exchange in heroic times and valuable too; hence its introduction as currency 'probably appeared not so violent a measure as later writers were inclined to represent it'. Sparta's property system thus appears as intelligible within early Greek terms, if still exceptional among later societies.²⁶ William Mitford's *History of Greece* (1784–1818) likewise avers that neither equality of landholding nor iron money was totally unknown elsewhere in Greece. His account, however, otherwise accepts Plutarch's evidence without query. In fact, by generalising from Xenophon's and Aristotle's evidence on the shared use of certain items of property (cf. ch. 6, below), he goes rather beyond Plutarch in claiming that 'private property thus was nearly annihilated'.²⁷ In early nineteenth-century Germany too, some historians of Greece simply followed intellectuals like Schiller in accepting at face value Plutarch's account of Lykourgos' equal redistribution of land.²⁸ Others, however, whilst accepting the basic fact of redistribution, sought to modify aspects of Plutarch's account.²⁹ For example, Manso's book on Sparta depicted Lykourgos as partially correcting a previous landed equality which had fallen into decline. Drawing upon earlier writers, especially Aristotle, he attempted to define the precise rules of transmission and inheritance within a system of state-controlled lots (1800–05, i.1.109–23; i.2.129–34). He thus stands at the head of a long line of such scholarly 'reconstructions' which we shall have occasion to mention in chapter 3. A similar approach was taken in Britain by Connop Thirlwall, who portrayed Lykourgos' redistribution as a limited provision to the poor of allotments unjustly seized by the rich (1835–44, i.344–7). Such half-measures provoked a fierce reaction from George Grote, whose *History of Greece* (originally published 1846–56) took the radical step of dismissing as later invention the entire notion of a Lykourgan redistribution.³⁰ For him, 'Lykurgus does not try to make the poor rich, nor the rich poor; but he imposes upon both the same subjugating drill' (1862, i.175).

Grote's work thus established the terms for the modern scholarly debate which has continued to the present day (see ch. 3). The most remarkable feature of this debate has been the tenacity – amidst increasing challenge – of the old notions of Spartan economic egalitarianism and communitarianism. Despite Grote, several of the 'majestic procession of [nineteenth-century German] historians' of Greece continued to follow this line.³¹ For Curtius (1858, 160), land belonged to the Spartan state and Plutarch's account of its division into 9,000 equal lots was a 'completely credible tradition'. Though rejecting the idea of landed equality, Gilbert (1872, 170–2) depicted the holdings of ordinary Spartiates as *ager publicus* allotted in fief from the state. Busolt (1893–1904, i.521) wrote of 'the principle of equality' and referred to Spartan territory as 'communal land'.³² In his account, as in other works, the decline of this Lykourgan system was still ascribed to the influx of foreign wealth and Epitadeus' testamentary law in the late fifth and early fourth century (ibid. iii.346). Limitations of space prohibit a full doxography of subsequent international scholarship, whose views will be considered in more depth in later chapters. But the notions that much, if not all, of Spartan territory was public land, that this land was held in equal lots (*klēroi*), and that Spartan citizens were merely life-tenants of these lots, which in principle reverted on death to the state, have remained current in the scholarship of many countries throughout the twentieth century.[33]

Sometimes these notions have been explicitly linked to powerful political ideologies. For Karl Marx, in his *German Ideology*, forms of property in the ancient world underwent a partial development from 'communal- and state-property' ('*Gemeinde- und Staatseigentum*') to private property.[34] The precise characteristics of Marx's *Gemeindeeigentum* were a matter of debate among Soviet and eastern European scholars (Andreev 1975, 75–6). For one school of thought, which identified it as property owned directly by the state, Sparta constituted the archetypal case of a backward polis marked (to quote the Czech scholar, Pavel Oliva) by 'survivals of the old Dorian tribal society' which had not yet developed private ownership of property. Hence 'Spartan citizens were tenants and not owners of their *kleroi*. Proprietary rights…were vested in the whole body of citizens.'[35] The most notorious example of ideologically-linked perceptions of Spartan property ownership, however, came from Nazi Germany. In his 1929 book *Das Bauerntum als Lebensquell der Nordischen Rasse* (*The Peasantry as the Life-source of the Nordic Race*), Walther Darré drew upon notions of Spartan land tenure in earlier German scholarship to construct a historical foundation for longstanding Germanic romantic traditions regarding the peasantry. These traditions underpinned the *Reichserbhofgesetz* (*State Law of Hereditary Entailment*) which he subsequently introduced in 1933 as *Reichsminister für Ernährung und Landwirtschaft*.[36] Darré's account of the Spartans as tenants of inalienable and indivisible state-owned lots is echoed in the content of the *Reichserbhofgesetz*, which established state control over peasant farms, turned the former owners into dismissable farm managers, introduced single-heir inheritance, restricted testamentary freedom and prohibited sale.[37] In the contemporary words of the leading ancient historian under the Third Reich, Sparta's landed property system was 'a phenomenon which in Germany today excites particular interest'.[38]

It is time, however, to turn to the ancient foundation for modern images of Spartan economic equality and communitarianism. Whether inspired by social theories or by more scholarly concerns, the Spartan perceptions traced above from the sixteenth to the twentieth centuries are largely rooted in the writings of one man whose name has recurred throughout this brief survey: Plutarch of Chaironeia. As we have seen, Plutarch's *Life of Lykourgos* supplies the essential basis for the key elements of modern images: the equal division of land; the allocation of lots to new-born Spartiates, which implies a system of life-tenure; the ban on gold and silver; the iron currency; the devaluation of wealth. His *Life of Agis* supplies the basis for many modern explanations of the decline of this property system: the influx of foreign coinage and wealth; and the testamentary law of Epitadeus. The impact of Plutarch on modern perceptions of Sparta is of course but one part of a much larger story, embracing his immense influence

Ch. 1. Spartan economic egalitarianism and communitarianism in modern thought

on images of antiquity and on modern thought in general – a story beyond the scope of this work.³⁹ In the following chapter my analysis will turn in a different direction. Plutarch is of course a relatively late source, who wrote some four centuries after the end of classical Sparta. Hence to assess his image of Sparta's classical property and wealth, and to prepare the ground for analysis of the system itself, we need to examine the sources of that image in ancient writers of earlier periods.

Notes

¹ Within the limited span of this chapter I can provide only a brief sketch of this influence, eschewing more systematic exploration of the connections between my theme and the broader history of the reception of Sparta, and of antiquity more generally, in modern thought: see further Rawson 1969; Bolgar (ed.) 1979; Christ 1986; Grell 1995, i.456–506.

² Thomas More, *Utopia*, in E. Surtz and J.H. Hexter (eds.) *The Complete Works of St Thomas More* (New Haven and London 1965), iv.103, 140, 150, 152.

³ *Lykourgos* 30.1, and especially *Agis* 5.

⁴ N. Cragii, *De Republica Lacedaemoniorum, libri IV*, in *Thesaurus Graecarum Antiquitatum*, contextus & designatus ab Jacobo Gronovio, *V. Attici Imperii amplitudinem ac mutationes, ut & Lacedaemoniis complexum* (Lugduni Batavorum 1699), 2496–2674, esp. pp. 2600, 2649–61.

⁵ James Harrington, *The Commonwealth of Oceana* and *A System of Politics*, ed. J.G.A. Pocock (Cambridge 1992), 12–13, 103–4, 110–11.

⁶ *Considerations on Mr Harrington's Commonwealth of Oceana* (1657), cited in Rawson 1969, 194–5; *Monarchy Asserted or the State of Monarchicall & Popular Government in Vindication of the Considerations upon Mr. Harrington's Oceana* (Oxford 1659), 24–5, 66–8, 139–43 (= *Early English Books 1641–1700*, UMI microfilm collection, Ann Arbor, Unit 45, Reel 1346:25).

⁷ H. Stubbe, *The Common-Wealth of Oceana put into the Ballance and found too light. Or an account of the Republick of Sparta, with occasional animadversions upon Mr James Harrington and the Oceanistical model* (London 1660), 4, 7–9 (= *Early English Books 1641–1700*, UMI microfilm collection, Ann Arbor, Unit 58, Reel 1623:16).

⁸ H. Neville, *Plato Redivivus or, a Dialogue concerning Government*, in C. Robbins (ed.) *Two English Republican Tracts* (Cambridge 1969), 61–200; quotations from pp. 95, 100; cf. also 91.

⁹ *The Whole Works of Walter Moyle, Esq.; that were Published by Himself* (London 1727), 49–77; quotation from p. 51. Moyle, however, follows Wren in arguing that the 'Golden Age at Sparta' declined 'so early as the time of Croesus' when the Lacedaemonians were corrupted by his gold 'and by that means lost their Barrier'.

¹⁰ As Rawson (1969, 268) notes, even to contemporary laconophiles, 'Sparta seemed a remote and extraordinary place and certainly no direct model for France.'

¹¹ A.M. Cohler, B.C. Miller and H.S. Stone (eds.) *Montesquieu, The Spirit of the Laws* (Cambridge 1989), 36–7, 98, 215; translation of *L'Esprit des Lois* (1748). On Montesquieu's reliance on Plutarch throughout the work, Howard 1970, 49–52.

¹² E.J.B. Rathéry (ed.) *Journal et Mémoires du Marquis d'Argenson* (1859), as quoted

in Rawson 1969, 231.

13 'Sparte ou Lacédémone', in *Encyclopédie ou Dictionnaire Raisonné des Sciences, des Arts et des Métiers*, XV (Neufchastel 1765), 428–34, at 433. Cf. Grell 1995, i.478–80.

14 F.H. Turpin, *L'Histoire du gouvernement des anciennes républiques* (Paris 1769), 8–12; cf. Grell 1995, i.480–3.

15 Claude-Adrien Helvétius, *De l'Homme, de ses Facultés Intellectuelles et de son Éducation*, II (London 1773), vi.12 (pp. 94–5), ix.2 (pp. 233–4); repr. Bristol and Taipei 1994. Cf. Grell 1995, i.483–6.

16 *Oeuvres Complètes de l'abbé de Mably* (Lyon 1792), iv.1–222, at 20. Although he traces the corruption of Lykourgos' work back to the Persian wars, like many earlier and later writers he follows Plutarch in attributing the full decline to Lysander's introduction of riches and greed (ibid. 101–3); cf. also his *Entretiens de Phocion sur le rapport de la morale avec la politique* (1763) = *Oeuvres Complètes* x.25–203, at 67–8, 117–18.

17 Cf. Mercier de la Rivière, *L'Ordre naturel et essentiel des Sociétés politiques* (London and Paris 1767).

18 *Doutes proposés aux philosophes économistes sur l'Ordre naturel et essentiel des sociétés politiques, Lettre I* = *Oeuvres Complètes de l'Abbé de Mably* (Lyon 1792), xi.1–28, at 6–7; *De la Législation ou Principes des Loix* = *Oeuvres Complètes* ix.1–399, at 73–5.

19 For an analysis of these critiques, published in the Physiocratic journal *Éphémérides du Citoyen* for 1767 and 1768, see Guerci 1979, 79–82.

20 J.-F. Vauvilliers, *Examen historique et politique du gouvernement de Sparte, ou Lettre à un ami sur la Législation de Lycurge, en réponse aux Doutes proposés par M. l'Abbé de Mably, contre l'Ordre naturel et essentiel des sociétés politiques* (Paris 1769); *Éphémérides du Citoyen*, 1767, I.97–160. Cf. Guerci 1979, 85–6; Grell 1995, i.505–6.

21 Quotation from Rawson 1969, 242. Rousseau's *Discours sur les Sciences et les Arts* (1750) mentions Lykourgos' banishment of arts and artists; and Sparta's iron money appears in his *Considérations sur le Gouvernement de Pologne* (1772). Otherwise, however, Sparta's property arrangements make little appearance beyond generalised praise of her austerity, largely because Rousseau advocated proportional rather than absolute equality (cf. Cartledge 1999, 327).

22 *Commentaire sur quelques principales maximes de L'Ésprit des Lois* (1777) = *Oeuvres Complètes de Voltaire* (Paris 1785), xxxix.353–437, at 368–9.

23 C. de Pauw, *Recherches philosophiques sur les Grecs* (1788), in *Oeuvres philosophiques de Pauw* (Paris 1795), vii.240–4, 252–9.

24 For references and more detailed discussion of the role of Sparta in the Revolution beyond the limited coverage possible here, Parker 1937 and Rawson 1969, 268–290.

25 *The Ancient History of the Egyptians…and Grecians*, 9th edn. (London 1795), iii.24–8. Cf. Howard 1970, 58: 'The *Histoire Ancienne*…is little more than a scissors-and-paste job accomplished on Plutarch.'

26 J. Gillies, *The History of Ancient Greece* (London, 1825 edn.) 32–3.

27 W. Mitford, *The History of Greece* (London and Edinburgh 1835) i.250–3.

28 F. von Schiller, *Die Gesetzgebung des Lykurgus und Solon* (1790), in K.-H. Hahn (ed.) *Schillers Werke, XVII. Historische Schriften* (Weimar 1970), i.414–44, at 415–17. On Schiller's 'abridgement' of Plutarch, Howard 1970, 117.

29 Convenient summaries of various early nineteenth-century studies in Grote 1862, ii.164 n. 1.

30 1862, ii.145–76. In this new edition he acknowledges (166, n. 2) his earlier ignorance

Ch. 1. Spartan economic egalitarianism and communitarianism in modern thought

of the fact that certain other scholars – Lachmann and Körtum – had also independently questioned the reality of the Lykourgan redivision.

[31] The phrase is from Rawson 1969, 327. Certain specialist studies in Germany adopted Grote's sceptical approach, but these were often overruled in the monumental works of *Griechische Geschichte* (e.g. Busolt 1893–1904, i.521–2, n. 5). Some histories were, however, more sceptical. Holm (1899, 179–80) doubted the Lykourgan redistribution. Beloch (1912–27, i.1.303–4) accepted the existence of standard lots, but thought that they could be accumulated through inheritance and that the nobility had larger estates.

[32] In his *Griechische Staatskunde* Busolt subsequently changed his views about the idea of communal land (Busolt and Swoboda 1920–26, ii.634 n. 2).

[33] One or more of these notions can be found in the following sample of twentieth-century studies: Pareti 1917, 197–200; Ehrenberg 1924, 48; Glotz 1925, 351–2; Ziehen 1933; Chrimes 1949, 286; Asheri 1961; 1963; Michell 1964, 205–11; Forrest 1968, 135; Oliva 1971, 32–8; David 1981, 46–50; Figueira 1984, 98; MacDowell 1986, 89–110; Ogden 1996, 246–7.

[34] 'The German Ideology', in Karl Marx, Friedrich Engels, *Collected Works*, 5. *Marx and Engels: 1845–47* (London 1976), 33; trans. of German original.

[35] Oliva 1971, 38; cf., similarly, the east German scholar, Detlef Lotze (1959, 77). I am grateful to Andrey Eryomin of Samara University for advice based on his first-hand knowledge of Soviet scholarship.

[36] Darré explicitly names Busolt's *Griechische Staatskunde* as the source of his depiction of the Spartan property system and subsequently cites Gilbert (presumably 1872, 170–2) for the idea of 'die Kleroi als Staatslehen' (Darré 1937, 162). Darré was not the immediate political mover in the precise formulation of the law, being formally outside the government until his appointment as *Reichsminister* in late June 1933; but he had been the Nazi party adviser on agriculture since 1930, was consulted on the law's content before its initial introduction in Prussia, and after his appointment as minister was instrumental in extending it to the entire Reich (Farquharson 1976, 17, 56, 107–9).

[37] Compare Darré's account of Sparta (1937, 162–3) with the text of the *Reichserbhofgesetz* – which he purposely added to the volume from the 5th edition onwards (ibid. 466–81). On Darré, see also Rawson 1969, 340–1; Losemann 1977, 23–4; Christ 1986, 51–3; on the *Erbhofgesetz*, see further Farquharson 1976, 63, 107–23.

[38] Berve 1941, 8. Two of the three German books on Sparta included in his review devoted considerable attention to Spartan land tenure: Meier 1939; Lüdemann 1939.

[39] See, for example, Hirzel 1912, 102–206; Ziegler 1951, 947–62; Berry 1961, 1–34; Howard 1970.

Chapter 2

THE GROWTH OF THE DOMINANT EGALITARIAN IMAGE IN ANCIENT THOUGHT

The previous chapter outlined the prevalent modern perceptions of the Spartan property system as essentially egalitarian, and even communitarian, in character and indicated the dependence of those views upon the image presented, above all, by Plutarch. This chapter will examine the growth of the egalitarian image in ancient thought. I shall argue that it is absent from the earliest contemporary evidence and trace the stages by which it developed into its ultimately pre-eminent position, in the process indicating how these developments reflected the role classical Sparta played in political and moral debates from classical times until the Roman imperial period. In doing so, I shall examine the role of particular writers and the relationship of their evidence to earlier writings, as a prelude to subsequent chapters in which the historical value of that evidence will be assessed.[1]

The original image

We start, as in all Greek historiography, with Herodotus. What is remarkable about his depiction of the role of wealth in Spartiate society is precisely how *unremarkable* it is. Herodotus highlights several noteworthy features of Sparta: her transformation from disorder to good order (1.65), her dual kingship (6.56–9), and the willingness of her citizens to fight to the death in obedience to their *nomos* (7.101–5). A distinctive attitude to property and wealth is not among them. In so far as the subject does appear, Sparta seems little different from other Greek states. There are inequalities of wealth (6.61; 7.134) and precious gifts are exchanged freely (6.62). Her citizens can privately accept – and plan to appropriate – deposits of foreign silver (6.86); and they are accused, as representatives of other Greeks, of cheating in the market-place (1.153). Her soldiers receive distributions of booty along with the other Greek soldiers at Plataia (9.81). There are also heiresses (6.57) whose very name, *patrouchos* ('holder of the patrimony'), implies the normal Greek system of private property (Ducat 1983, 148).

Recent studies have noted that Herodotus sometimes treats Sparta as the 'Greek Other', in a manner comparable to his treatment of non-Greeks, 'describing some of the Spartans' customs as if they might be as unfamiliar and outlandish to his audience as those of the Nasamones' (Cartledge 1993a,

80). This analysis does not apply to his treatment of property and wealth. It is true that Herodotus attaches more stories (eight in total) of potential, alleged and actual gift or receipt of bribes to Sparta than to any other Greek state; but five of these relate to the singular institution of the dual kingship about whose holders he has many tales to tell.[2] Although he has fewer juicy stories about leading men from other poleis, Herodotus makes it clear that they were no less susceptible to bribery than were Spartiates (e.g. 9.2, 41, 88). Moreover, the fact that he could plausibly associate stories of bribery with Sparta confirms that she was viewed no differently from other poleis as regards the valuation and use of wealth. Only at one point is there a hint of a more austere image, at 9.82 where the regent Pausanias contrasts a Spartan with a Persian meal. Even here, however, there is no contrast with other Greeks: Spartan austerity is treated as representative of the poverty of Greece as a whole. There is no trace in Herodotus of the image of Spartan property and wealth which dominated ancient perceptions in later periods.

The marginality of property and wealth to prevailing images of Sparta in the later fifth century is evident in other writers. As David Harvey (1994) has noted, a pun on the infamously distasteful 'black broth' in the common messes (*Knights* 278–9) is the nearest Aristophanes approaches to the material aspects of Spartiate life. William Poole's study of Euripides (1994) has demonstrated that, despite his highly negative portrayal of Spartan characteristics, the playwright's references to the material vices of luxury and extravagance were largely confined to Spartan women. Covetousness does appear among the list of accusations levelled at Spartan males by Andromache in her name play (451), but only after treachery, lies, guile, crooked thoughts and murder have all been wheeled out beforehand. The marginality of such issues persists too in certain early fourth-century writers. Sparta's arrangements regarding wealth are absent from Lysias' Olympic festival oration in 388 (33.7). The Spartans are justified as the legitimate leaders of Greece,

> both by their inborn merits and by their warlike gifts, since they are the only ones whose country was never ravaged by war, who live unprotected by walls, who are free from internal unrest, who were never conquered and always had the same customs.

There is no hint here that a distinctive attitude to wealth was a significant factor in Sparta's success.

In Thucydides we can detect the beginnings of a change. Like Herodotus, Thucydides describes several real or alleged incidents of bribery involving Spartiates (e.g. 1.109, 131; 2.21; 5.16; 8.83), but no more than those involving Athenians (e.g. 2.101; 3.11, 38–43; 4.65; 7.44, 46). Once again Sparta appears little different from other Greek states. Thucydides' very first statement about Sparta (1.6), however, strikes a new and different note: 'it was the Lakedaimonians who first began to dress simply...and in general those who had great possessions adopted a lifestyle that was as much as possible like that of the many'. Notably, Thucydides assumes, like Herodotus, that property was privately held and that there were differences in wealth. For him, however, an attempt to minimize the daily impact of these differences was a significant and unusual feature of Spartan society. Unfortunately, nowhere else in his work is this perception developed, not even in the speeches in Books One and Two which outline the characteristics of Spartan society. One might have expected a hint during the comparison of Athenian and Spartan practices in Perikles' Funeral Oration (2.35–46, esp. 37–40). Given the emphasis his oration places on Athenian lack of extravagance and proper, unboastful use of wealth (40.1), one might have expected him to contrast Athenian voluntarism with Spartiate compulsion, as he does with obedience to the law and courage in battle. But Thucydides/Perikles neglects to do so.

One general reason for this neglect may be that in Perikles' speech the central emphasis is on education and its capacity to provide a firm foundation for civic life (Hussey 1985, esp. 123–9). Since their divergent types of education were the determining factors behind the different character of Athenian and Spartan society, attitudes to property and wealth were necessarily secondary. Education as the key to virtue, and indeed to all social and political problems, was an essential tenet of much of the contemporary Sophistic movement (cf. Kerferd 1981, 131–62). This was not of course true of all thinkers. Some, such as Phaleas of Chalkedon, held that the correct regulation of property ownership was most important, since this was the source of political strife (Arist. *Pol.* 1266a37–9). Even Phaleas, however, emphasized equality of education as a necessity in his proposed state (1266b31–3). Accordingly, writers on Sparta, such as Xenophon, who were influenced by sophistic (including Socratic) thought tended to give prior emphasis to the Spartan upbringing in explanations of her distinctive character.

The early development of an ideal

Issues of property and wealth began, however, to receive more comment from the end of the fifth century as part of a general explosion of interest in Spartan society among leading men in the rest of the Greek world, not least among the upper classes in Athens. The underlying reason for this phenomenon is well known, namely the threat which the Athenian democracy posed to their power and privilege. A growing interest in the Spartan alternative – itself fuelled by the polarization of Greece into two camps during the Peloponnesian war – was given expression through the intensified enquiry into the theory of society, leading to a number of treatises on state forms, which developed as part of the Sophistic movement patronized by disgruntled members of the elite (Ollier 1933–43, i.164–8, 206–14; Tigerstedt 1965–78, i.153–6, 233–41).

The first known works on Sparta to issue from these developments are those of Kritias: two treatises entitled *Polity of the Lakedaimonians*, one in verse and one in prose. The surviving fragments include four references to

Spartan austerity and moderation.[3] Fragment 6 (*ap.* Athen. 432d) contrasts Spartan drinking habits in the common messes with those in Athens which, he claims, lead to drunkenness, loose talk, weak physique, undisciplined slaves and ruinous extravagance:

> It is a habit and established practice at Sparta to drink from the same wine cup and not to give toasts mentioning someone by name and not to pass it round, as is customary in Athens, moving to the right in a circle around the company… Lakedaimonian youths, however, drink only enough to direct the thinking of all towards cheery hopefulness and the tongue towards friendliness and temperate laughter… The way of life of the Lakedaimonians is evenly ordered: to eat and drink the appropriate amount to render them capable of thought and labour. No day is set aside for soaking the body through immoderate draughts.

This picture is elaborated in fragment 33 (*ap.* Athen. 463e), according to which, in contrast to practice in Chios, Athens and Thessaly, the Lakedaimonians drink each from his own cup and the wine-waiter pours only as much as each wants to drink.

In the above fragments Kritias provides the first extant idealization of the Spartiates' use of material goods and the first explicit contrast with the practice of other states. His presentation is reinforced in fragment 7 (*ap.* scholium on Euripides, *Hippolytos* 264), in which Kritias attributes the saying 'Nothing in excess' to the Spartan sage Chilon. Finally, fragment 34 (*ap.* Athen. 483b) contains praise of the practical, utilitarian nature of certain Lakonian products – shoes, cloaks and a special drinking beaker called the *kōthōn* – as appropriate to modest daily living.

Our lack of the complete text of Kritias' two Lakedaimonian polities limits our appreciation not only of his contribution to the development of images of Spartan property arrangements, but also of the historiographical context of Xenophon's *Polity of the Lakedaimonians*.[4] Like Kritias (fr. 32), Xenophon begins his treatise with the subject of procreation. He then moves on immediately (chs. 2–4) to the upbringing. The importance he ascribes to the Spartan educational process is shown by its early placing in his treatise. Only in chapters 5–7 are we presented with a sustained discussion of Spartan use of property. Note, however, that Xenophon's starting-point is not property itself but, in the vein of Kritias, the common meals. Moreover, the initial statement of their purpose is purely non-material in character: '[Lykourgos] established the public messes outside in the open, thinking that this would reduce disregard of orders to a minimum' (5.2). When the discussion does move on to the material plane Xenophon retains the moralizing theme of moderation evident in Kritias:

> The amount of food he [sc. Lykourgos] allowed was just enough to prevent them getting either too much or too little to eat…the table is never bare until the company breaks up, and never extravagantly furnished. Another of his reforms was the abolition of compulsory drinking, which is the undoing alike of mind and body; but

he allowed everyone to drink when he was thirsty, believing that drink is then most harmless and most welcome. Now, what opportunity did these common messes give a man to ruin himself or his household by gluttony or drunkenness? (5.3–4)

These kinds of comments were to be repeated by Plutarch (*Lyk.* 10.1–2); but Plutarch went a step further in claiming that the messes rendered wealth unusable. Xenophon does not take this road. In his account, besides extras supplied from hunting, rich men can deploy their greater landed resources by making additional donations of wheaten bread. It is indeed these extra donations which, for Xenophon, sustain the happy mean between meagre and extravagant fare quoted above.

Chapter 6 introduces the practice of communal sharing. Once again the opening is non-material in tone and content: Spartiate fathers share authority over one another's children 'because he [sc. Lykourgos] wished the citizens to benefit from one another without doing any harm' (6.1–2). Xenophon then moves on to the sharing of slaves (*oiketai*), hunting dogs, horses and caches of surplus food left by hunting parties (3–4). The common criterion given for the practice of sharing these items is one of *need*, and the nature of the sharing is limited by the extent of that need. A man can borrow other men's slaves in case of necessity. A man who falls ill or needs a carriage or has to get somewhere quickly may borrow another's horse; he uses it carefully and then duly restores it. Those in need of food while out hunting take what they need and leave the rest behind. Those who need hunting dogs invite the owner to join them in the hunt. Only if he is otherwise engaged do they get sole use of the dogs. The verb *deomai* ('need') is used no fewer than six times in the above examples, making a seventh and final appearance in Xenophon's concluding judgement: 'Thanks to sharing with one another in this way, even those who have but little receive a share of everything in the country, whenever they need something.' There is something rather extravagant about this judgement. Exactly how extravagant depends upon the intended scope of Xenophon's claim. Several writers, including myself, treating it as a comment on the sphere of property ownership in general (e.g. Ollier 1933–43, i.41–2; Moore 1975, 107–8; Hodkinson 1994, 192–3), have emphasized its naive exaggeration of the scale of resources made available to poor citizens. Recently, Noreen Humble has argued that the final phrase (πάντων τῶν ἐν τῇ χώρᾳ) should be regarded as referring merely to the aforementioned items of shared property (1997, 223). Even this reinterpretation, however, does not clear Xenophon of the taint of exaggeration, since to claim that helots, dogs, horses and hunting caches constituted 'everything in the country' – even within the limited terms of movable agricultural goods – is still a significant misrepresentation.

Xenophon's argument is developed in chapter 7, in which he introduces the Lykourgan prohibition of gainful activity (*chrēmatismos*). Its effectiveness, he claims, is proved by several points. First, the lack of incentive to accumulate wealth: equal contributions to the messes and an equal standard of living exclude the attraction of money to obtain luxury. Even cloaks require no expenditure, since adornment comes through one's bodily condition and physical work to help one's messmates is honoured over spending. Secondly, the disincentives against dishonest acquisition: the legal system of currency is too bulky for secret storage and searches are made for illegal gold and silver, with fines imposed on anyone detected in possession. Why should Spartiates indulge in making money when the pains of possession exceed the pleasure of using it? Once again, the chapter contains much special pleading. To make his case about wealth's uselessness and lack of attraction, Xenophon paints an idealised picture of contemporary Sparta, selectively privileging certain aspects and ignoring others, especially those related to the activities of his friend and patron, Agesilaos II. The supposed absence of spending on messmates has a hollow ring during the reign of a king who believed that 'the generous man is required also to spend his own in the service of others' (Xen. *Ages*. 11.8). The items of expenditure cited hardly exhaust the range of activities for which Spartiates might want to acquire wealth. In describing the punitive measures against illegal possession, however, Xenophon cuts through his own idealisation by implying that, despite the supposed absence of incentives, the desire to acquire wealth remained so strong that legal measures were necessary against owners of forbidden gold and silver (Humble 1997, 222–3).

A similar schism is apparent throughout much of the work. In its emphasis upon the sharing of certain goods, upon the prohibition and purposelessness of gainful activity, and upon the outlawing of gold and silver in favour of a more bulky form of currency, Xenophon's *Polity* provides our first surviving attestation of certain themes which were later to be important in the dominant idealised image of Spartan wealth. Indeed, the idealised character of Xenophon's own account comes out most clearly in his claim in chapter 10 that 'to all those who performed their legal duties he gave an equal share in the polis, without regard for deficiencies of body or of money' (10.7) – an extraordinary statement in view of the widespread loss of citizenship suffered by many Spartiates in his day for failure to pay their mess dues (Arist. *Pol*. 1271a26–37). There is, however, no trace of the supposed equality of property which appears in later writers. Xenophon is quite frank, not only about the existence of differences of wealth, but also about the fact that 'family prestige and wealth are still of concern to Spartans and are taken into account in the formulation of Lykourgan decrees' (Humble 1997, 214). Note, for example, his comments on the wife-sharing practices that, 'He gave his sanction to many such arrangements, for … the men want to get for their sons brothers who are members of the kin and share in its power but do not claim part of its property' (1.9). Given that his purpose is to highlight respects in which Spartan institutions diverged from those elsewhere, it is notable that Xenophon draws no attention to any difference in this regard, not even with reference to the better Lykourgan past referred to in chapter 14.

Ch. 2. The growth of the dominant egalitarian image in ancient thought

To this much-debated chapter 14 (15 in some editions), in which Xenophon inserts his criticisms of contemporary Sparta, we must now turn. In it he introduces another significant component of later images of Spartiate wealth.

> If someone were to ask me whether I think that the laws of Lykourgos still remained unchanged, I could not confidently say yes. I know that formerly the Lakedaimonians preferred to live together at home with moderate possessions rather than expose themselves to the corrupting influences of flattery as harmosts of various cities. I know too that in former days they were afraid to be seen in possession of gold; whereas nowadays there are some who even boast of its possession…

These comments have normally been interpreted as a contrast between the Spartiates' traditional disdain for wealth and their current high valuation of it. In the last sentence, however, as Humble (1997, 233–4) has pointed out, the contrast is not so much between the possession or otherwise of gold as between public denial and advertisement of its ownership. Harking back to his intimation in chapter 7 that some citizens possessed illegal gold, Xenophon contrasts their previous fear to be seen (φαίνεσθαι) in possession with their current boastful attitude. Nevertheless, Xenophon becomes the first writer to claim that a ban on private possession of gold was a traditional Lykourgan measure. Moreover, the topics of wealth and material possessions now take centre stage, when corruptions of the Spartan ideal and the decline of Spartan power are at issue, in a way that they had not previously done in accounts of the idealised Lykourgan system.[5] The notion of a declining Sparta polluted by the desire for wealth stands on the threshold of a long and influential history.

Before we consider, however, the development of this idea in other fourth-century writers, we must first take note of another of Xenophon's works. Recent years have witnessed renewed discussion concerning whether Xenophon's writing is biased towards Sparta, with the majority positive answer to that question coming under challenge from the revelation of a range of occasions on which he adopts a critical stance towards Spartiate policy or institutions.[6] The issue is complex, as we have seen in our discussion of the *Polity*, in which at one moment Xenophon appears to write as an apologist reflecting the rationalisations of contemporary Spartiate ideology, at another as a detached and critical observer of the Spartan system. There is, however, one work of Xenophon's which is, in keeping with the genre to which it avowedly belongs (Humble 1997, 247–53), undoubtedly and unashamedly apologist in tone: his encomium in praise of his dead friend and patron, Agesilaos.

Bias towards Agesilaos is of course not the same as bias towards Sparta. There are points in the work at which Xenophon portrays Agesilaos as possessing kingly virtues beyond the reach of Spartans in general (e.g. 6.4; 7.3; 8.1; 9.1–2, 7; 11.13). There are others at which these kingly virtues fit somewhat awkwardly with the image of wealth portrayed in the *Polity*. As already noted, it is references in the *Agesilaos* to the king's financial benefactions (4.1; 7.1;

25

11.8) which undermine the *Polity*'s image of the lack of personalised spending. There is even a remarkable account of how Agesilaos in Asia built up his clientele through the manipulation of booty, thereby enabling his friends to make a prodigious amount of money (1.17–19). In other respects, however, the king is portrayed as the model of disdain for the material things of life: as a man who disdained physical pleasures (5.1; 8.8), who dressed simply (11.11), and who was content with a modest house (8.6–7), the roughest of beds (5.2) and any kind of food or drink (9.3). He put manly virtue (*andragathia*) before wealth (9.6), refused foreign gifts (4.6) and never committed injustice for the sake of money (8.8). Even his benefactions are evidence of his indifference to personal gain (4.1–6). Xenophon represents all these material virtues as Agesilaos' personal qualities, without any implication that they should be generalised to other Spartiates. It is not until the hellenistic *Apophthegmata Lakōnika* that Agesilaos' personal virtues become representative of the society as a whole.

Material purity corrupted: the impact of Sparta's decline

Sparta's dramatic decline after 371 BC from leading power to local Peloponnesian wrangler had a major effect on the development of images of Spartan wealth during the fourth century. For purposes of analysis, we may distinguish three main types of image, which reflect three general approaches to Sparta's decline. In this section I shall consider the first two approaches; the third will be discussed in the following section.

First, some writers largely ignored Sparta's contemporary decline, continuing to stress the virtues of her traditional society (Fisher 1994). The evidence of fourth-century Athenian writings and public speeches (especially Isokrates' *Panathenaikos* 108–11) suggests the existence of a considerable number of lakonophiles who laid stress upon Sparta's educational system, her discipline and the cohesiveness of her citizen body. As in earlier periods, material matters seldom feature in this image. In his *Life of Phokion* (20.3) Plutarch cites one anecdote in which the Athenian general supposedly invoked Spartiate austerity in the common messes in his rebuke of the soft living of an opponent. As Fisher notes, however, the accuracy of the anecdote is uncertain, although the idea that Phokion associated his general opposition to luxury with traditional Spartan values is not implausible (1994, 360–1).

A second group of writers expatiated on Sparta's moral decline from her former state of good order. The main known exponents of the second approach were Isokrates and his pupils, Theopompos and, most of all, Ephorus. In their works issues of wealth play a central role. Of these three writers, the important role of wealth is least developed in the works of Isokrates. In those passages which speak favourably of Sparta the standard image of austerity typically receives mention among other virtues. In the *Archidamos* (59) the Spartans are said to possess good government, sober habits of life and willingness to fight to the death. The *Areopagitikos* (7) refers to their simple and warlike way of life; and there is a more generic reference to equality in the choice of officials, daily life and other institutions later in the same work (61).

When Isokrates writes of Sparta's decline, however, material factors become more prominent. In the *Peace* (95–103) he claims that due to their empire Spartan citizens abandoned their customs and succumbed to unjust ways, laziness, lawlessness and greed; and the polis, likewise, to contempt for its allies, covetousness of the possessions of other states and indifference to oaths and agreements. Although it has been suggested that Isokrates hints at some decline in the austerity of the messes (Fisher 1994, 379), it is primarily greed abroad which is in his mind. So also in the *Panathenaikos* (225): 'the Lakedaimonians always covet everything that belongs to others'. Similarly, the reference to greed in the *Busiris* (17) seems to relate to Spartiate relations with the helots rather than with one another. For Isokrates it was the misdeeds of her imperial rule which brought issues of wealth to the fore as a cause of her crisis.

The works of Ephorus and Theopompos represent a development from this position in emphasizing that Sparta's moral decline was not confined to her external activities. Admittedly, there are certain points of continuity. Ephorus echoes Isokrates' point that Sparta lost her empire due to her maltreatment of her subjects (cf. Diod. 15.1–5). Theopompos lays stress upon the corrupted personal lifestyles of Spartan commanders abroad (*FGrH* 115F192, *ap.* Athen. 536b–c; F232, *ap.* Athen. 536c–d). He comments on King Archidamos III that,

> Archidamos deserted the traditional mode of life and was accustomed to live in a foreign and effeminate manner; he was unable to endure the life at home, but on account of his incontinence he was eager always to live abroad.

Taken on its own, this passage appears to suggest a contrast between the corrupt life possible outside Sparta and a more austere life at home. Nevertheless, Theopompos also emphasized material corruption inside Sparta. In one fragment (F71) he mentions the advice given to the Spartans not to honour gold or silver. This reference is relevant to a passage in Plutarch's *Life of Lysander* (16–17) in which he cites both Theopompos and Ephorus as sources for his account of the debate in Sparta in 404 concerning the large amount of gold and silver coinage sent back by Lysander. According to Plutarch, it was decided to admit this coinage for public, though not for private, use; the decision, however, made individual citizens greedy to acquire this form of wealth. The passage implies that the admission of foreign coinage into Sparta was something entirely new. In the fourth century, therefore, there first appears the idea that before 404 foreign coinage had been prohibited not only from private possession (as Xenophon claims) but also from public use; and that the decision made about Lysander's coinage constituted a decisive change in policy which corrupted a *politeia* previously unsullied by a desire for wealth.

We must obviously exercise caution in distinguishing the authentic views of

Ephorus and Theopompos from those which Plutarch later injected. However, the evidence of Diodorus Siculus, who also drew upon Ephorus as his main source for this period, shows that the basic ideas in Plutarch's account were already present in Ephorus' writings. At 7.12.8 Diodorus comments that after 400 years' observation of Lykourgos' laws, the Lakedaimonians

> little by little began to relax each one of their institutions and to turn to luxury and idleness, and as they grew so corrupted as to use coined money and to amass wealth, they lost their leadership.

At 14.10.2 he is even more explicit. Referring to Spartan policy after the end of the Peloponnesian war, he claims that 'they also levied tribute upon the people they had conquered and, although before this time they had not used coined money, they now collected yearly from the tribute more than 1000 talents'. These passages confirm two points: first, that the notion that foreign coinage had traditionally been excluded from Sparta, and was only introduced for public use in 404, goes back to Ephorus; secondly, that this idea arose in the context of discussions regarding the reasons for Sparta's international decline.[7] Ephorus' judgement, as represented by the first quotation from Diodorus, does not blame coinage alone for Sparta's decline. For him use of coinage was part of a general trend towards luxury and idleness; but its part was significant because it permitted the accumulation of wealth. The theme of corruption through money was evidently prominent in Ephorus' thought, since he is also the probable source of most of the accounts of the peculation of Gylippos, the event which sparked off the coinage debate.[8] Unlike Isokrates, Ephorus promulgates the view that this corruption affected not just Spartiates abroad but also Sparta's internal society.

How did Ephorus' views originate? It was a general and longstanding Greek tendency to explain military defeat in terms of moral corruption caused by susceptibility to a lifestyle dominated by material wealth (de Romilly 1977, 16–18, 59; Flower 1991, 93–4). To link this corruption with Sparta's acquisition of imperial rule was an obvious step, since it was a further commonplace of Greek thought that 'hard' peoples such as the Persians and Spartans invariably lost their original national characteristics by acquiring the wealth of the 'soft' peoples whom they conquered (cf. Hdt. 9.122; Redfield 1985, 109–18; Austin 1993, 210–12). Yet it remains to be explained why, although several other writers invoked imperial corruption as the cause of her downfall, only in Ephorus do we get the specific assertion that the traditional Lykourgan *politeia* had enforced a total ban on coinage. Here we must consider a second source of Ephorus' account, one whose possibly significant influence on images of Spartiate wealth remains a tantalizing issue: the pamphlet on the laws of Lykourgos which the former Spartan king Pausanias wrote during his exile after 395 BC. Our sole explicit testimony to the pamphlet's existence is a sentence attributed to Ephorus himself by the geographer Strabo (8.5.5). The purpose of this pamphlet has long been a matter of controversy; but to my mind it has been convincingly argued that Pausanias' work was written in support of the traditional Lykourgan laws which he accused his political enemies at home of corrupting.[9] The pamphlet's influence upon subsequent writing about Sparta is evident in Plato and Aristotle, not least in the appearance of the idea that the ephorate was a post-Lykourgan creation by King Theopompos.[10] His citation of the pamphlet and the similarity of the two men's approach suggests that Pausanias' work exercised a considerable influence upon Ephorus (Barber 1935; David 1979a, 109–11). As Ephorus/Strabo tells us, Pausanias quoted the oracular responses given to Lykourgos by Delphi, and it is probable that he is the ultimate source of such basic 'documents' of Spartan history as the Great Rhētra (Plut. *Lyk.* 6) and various mythical Delphic oracles associated with the Spartan constitution (Parke and Wormell 1956, ii, nos. 216–22). One of these supposed oracles is of particular relevance: 'love of money (*philochrēmatia*) will destroy Sparta'. This saying, reminiscent of the warning cited by Theopompos, was repeated not only by Aristotle (fr. 544 Rose) and other, later writers (references in Parke and Wormell 1956, ii, no. 222), but also by Diodorus in the chapter clearly influenced by Ephorus (7.12.6).[11]

Beyond this point resort must be made to informed speculation; but it seems likely that Pausanias, a longstanding opponent of Lysander whose death had caused his condemnation, would have made accusations that Lysander's imperialist policies had corrupted the Lykourgan system. Pausanias would have known of course from his own personal experience that foreign coinage was in use in Sparta before the decision of 404 – see chapter 5, below; but he might plausibly have claimed that Lykourgos had once banned it altogether. This could then, in the mind of an uncritical writer like Ephorus, have slid into the notion that Lykourgos' prohibition had remained in force until 404. After all, was not Sparta's success due to the survival of Lykourgos' prescriptions?

A further respect in which Ephorus has often been viewed as an innovator appears in a passage written by Polybius in the second century BC (6.45).

> How could the most learned of the writers of earlier times – Ephorus, Xenophon, Kallisthenes and Plato – claim in the first place that it [sc. the constitution of Crete] was one and the same with that of the Lakedaimonians and, secondly, that it was worthy of admiration? Neither of these assertions seems to me to be true. One can judge from the following. To start with, let us consider its dissimilarity. The distinctive features of the Lakedaimonian *politeia*, they say, are, first, those concerning landed property, by which no citizen may own more than another, but all must possess an equal share of the citizen land (*politikē chōra*); secondly, those concerning the acquisition of money, which has no value among them: it follows that all competition regarding wealth is entirely eliminated from their city. Thirdly, among the Lakedaimonians the kings hold a permanent office, those known as the *gerontes* are chosen for life; by these and with these all the affairs of state are conducted.

What conclusions can we draw about Ephorus' views from this passage? The first essential question is: from whom did Polybius derive the assertions regarding the distinctive features of Spartan society in the second part of the passage? Whom, in particular, did he intend by the phrase 'they say' (φασι)? Many scholars have thought that he was referring to the four writers mentioned earlier in the passage (e.g. Ed. Meyer 1892–9, i.219 n. 2; Walbank 1957, 727; Cozzoli 1979, 18–21). Several writers – including myself in earlier works – have pointed out that, since neither Xenophon nor Plato refers to an equal distribution of land in historical Sparta, the views which Polybius records here must in reality be those of Ephorus alone (Walbank 1957, 727; Hodkinson 1986, 381; 1994, 199).[12] On this view, Ephorus was the first author (or at least the first non-Spartan author) to write of equality of landholding in Sparta.

There is, however, a difficulty with this view (Ducat 1983, 154–5). In the first part of the passage Polybius criticizes the named writers for treating the Cretan constitution as identical to the Spartan. Logically, therefore, the phrase 'they say', which prefaces his account of the distinctive features of Sparta, cannot refer to the same writers. One could of course argue that Polybius was mistaken in his claim that Ephorus identified the Cretan constitution with that of Sparta, but correctly recorded his account of Spartan equal landholdings. Certainly, he made an identical mistake regarding Xenophon's view of Crete;[13] yet the fact that none of Polybius' three distinctive features of Sparta corresponds to Xenophon's views makes a parallel with Xenophon a very insecure basis for ascertaining the views of Ephorus.[14] It is more likely that the phrase 'they say' is intended to refer not to the views of particular writers, but rather, in a far looser sense, to current opinions about the then-extinct traditional Spartan system. As Ducat (1993, 155) has noted, the first two of Polybius' distinctive features are repeated in the same order in Plutarch's *Life of Lykourgos* (chs. 8–9), a work which (as we shall see) is influenced by the propaganda of Sparta's late third-century revolution. To Ducat's argument one could add a further point: the exclusion of the ephorate from Polybius' third distinctive feature is precisely what one would expect from the revolutionaries, given the abolition of the ephorate during the revolution by Kleomenes III and his promulgation of the view that the ephors were not part of the original Lykourgan constitution (Plut. *Kleom.* 7–10).[15] Although the possibility cannot be entirely ruled out, there are, consequently, serious grounds for doubting that Polybius' evidence proves that the idea of equality of landholdings goes back beyond the third century revolution to Ephorus in the fourth century .

Critiques of the property structure

The third approach to Sparta's decline viewed Sparta's corruption as deriving from inherent failings in her traditional *politeia*. This approach is found in the works of the most serious fourth-century analysts of Spartan society, Plato and Aristotle. Despite many differences in the character and purpose of their respective works, they share a critical attitude towards both the tendency to eulogize Sparta and the approach which treated her fourth-century failings as the product of recent corruption.

Plato

In Book 8 of the *Republic* Plato describes four imperfect types of society and their corresponding types of individual. In the prologue to these descriptions he twice identifies his first type of society, 'timarchy' or 'timocracy' – a society dominated by motives of ambition – as corresponding to Spartan society (544c; 545a). In his description of the compromise by which the timarchic society is created, the very first feature relates to material possessions: the allocation of land and houses to individual ownership (547a). In the list of timarchy's resemblances to the 'ideal society' (547d) respect for authority comes first, but abstention from agriculture, manual crafts and gainful activity are mentioned second, with the maintenance of common messes third. In the following outline of timarchy's resemblance to oligarchy (548a–c) only one feature is mentioned: love of money. When Plato moves on to the timarchic individual (548d), he mentions initially a list of non-material characteristics; but then at 549b he returns to wealth: 'when he is young… he will despise money, but the older he grows the keener he will get about it. His nature has a touch of avarice (*philochrēmatia*).'

Two essential points emerge. First, Plato gives the nature of property ownership and attitudes to wealth a high profile in defining the character of his Spartan-based timarchy. Secondly, the comments on property and wealth cited above express the very essence of a timarchic regime. They do not relate to the corruptions of timarchy which he describes later and which may be associated with Sparta's fourth-century decline. For Plato individual property ownership, abstention from agriculture, manual crafts and gainful activity, and the vices of avarice and the secret love of money are all part and parcel of the successful, traditional Sparta whose pre-eminence qualified it for attention as one of the major alternative models of the Greek polis.

Plato's description of the corruption of timarchy begins only after this point, at 550d–551b, when he discusses how oligarchy originates from timarchy. The accumulation of personal wealth leads to extravagance, citizens and their wives stretch and disobey the law, and envious spying and rivalry ensue. Wealth eclipses *aretē* as the determinant of status, prestige and office are reserved for the rich, and the poor are despised. Finally, a property qualification for office is established through armed force, if terror will not work. Clearly, this is not (neither could it have been intended as) a straightforward description of the development of the crisis of early fourth-century Sparta. Nevertheless, as I have suggested elsewhere (Hodkinson 1989, 100), there are certain affinities, especially regarding the growing importance of wealth and the wealthy.[16] In so far as there is a reflection of contemporary Sparta, the key point is that the decline of timarchy results from the development of inherent weaknesses in its essential character, rather than from exogenous factors such as the influx of foreign wealth or abrupt changes of direction in policy or law. In this sense, Plato's description of Sparta in the *Republic* is a polemic against uncritical admirers who vaunted Sparta's traditional *eunomia* and treated her fourth-century crisis as a corruption of a previously perfect polis (Tigerstedt 1965–78, i.266).

Not surprisingly, the *Laws* presents different emphases. Since Plato's concern was to construct an entire *politeia* for his imagined Cretan colony of Magnesia, he dwells on matters of property as just one item among many. Previous discussions (Morrow 1960; A. Powell 1994) have indicated the extent of Spartan references, both positive and negative, in the work; but it is her educational system (Books 1–2) and balanced constitution (Book 3), rather than her system of property, that Plato follows. He proposes an equal allocation of land and the introduction of 'single heir' inheritance (745b–e; 923c–924a). There is no evidence, however, that Plato thought that an equal allocation of land was ever in force in historical Sparta.[17] His recommended system of unigeniture is equally unhistorical (Lane Fox 1985, 211–12); though, as we shall see, it subsequently had an important impact on the image of Spartiate inheritance promoted by the propagandists of the late third-century revolution. The laws regulating the economic activities of citizens, such as the prohibition of participation in handicrafts and trade, have more of a Spartan ring and the prohibition of private possession of gold and silver (742a–b) may reflect Spartiate practice after 404; but Plato hardly intended that the Magnesians should employ Sparta's bulky iron currency (Morrow 1960, 140)!

More explicit references to Spartiate practice regarding wealth are few and somewhat mixed. The austere life of Spartiate youths is briefly recounted with approbation – in fourth place out of a list of beneficial Spartan institutions (633b–c). At 696a Sparta is given credit for the fact that poverty and wealth, laity and royalty, are honoured and educated the same. The passage is placed in Plato's account of the failings of the Persian empire (693d–698a) which Anton Powell (1994, 295–8) plausibly suggests is intended as a reference to similar developments in Sparta. Plato's tale of how the luxurious female-dominated education of the other Persian kings came to replace the tough, simple upbringing of Cyrus and Darius, recalls his later comment that the Spartan lawgiver had let the females indulge in luxury, extravagance and disorderliness (806c; cf. 637c). Plato's account then turns into a dialogue in which the Athenian speaker expatiates to his Spartan interlocutor on the harm which results when, *inter alia*, wealth is promoted above other criteria of honour (696b; 697a–b; 697e–698a) and an imperial power attacks friendly nations (697d). Although Plato here moves closer to the moralizing view that the Spartan system was ruined by imperial success, the root of the problem, the characteristics of Spartan women, is for him a longstanding structural phenomenon, deriving from the lawgiver's original failure to extend to them the control established over the men.

Aristotle

Aristotle's attempt in his *Politics* to construct a theoretical *politeia* via a criticism of the institutions of Sparta and Crete is, as Eckart Schütrumpf (1994, 324–5, 328) has pointed out, largely based on Plato's project in the *Laws*. The major difference is that, whereas in Book 7 Aristotle precisely follows Plato's procedure in interspersing references to Sparta and Crete within the body of his discussion, in Book 2 he launches a separate critique of the two polities in their own right. Consequently, his account in chapter 9 constitutes the most systematic critical discussion of Sparta in any ancient source.

Despite this departure from Platonic method, Aristotle's remarks on Spartan women (*Politics* 1269b12–1270a14) follow closely those already made by Plato. His criticisms of the women come immediately after his opening salvo against the system of helotage and in them he draws even more explicit attention than did Plato to the connection with issues of wealth. The lawgiver, he says, has been negligent in failing to control the women, who

> live intemperately, enjoying every licence and indulging in every luxury. An inevitable result under such a constitution is that esteem is given to wealth, particularly in cases where the men are dominated by the women; and this is a common state of affairs in military and warlike races…this is why that state of affairs prevailed among the Lakonians, where in the days of their empire a great deal was managed by women… The poorness of the arrangements concerning women seems, as was said earlier, not only to create a sort of unseemliness in the constitution in itself, but also to contribute something to the greed for money (1269b21–32; 1270a11–14).

From here Aristotle moves on directly to criticize the unequal distribution of property. He ascribes it, first, to errors in the laws which permitted gift and bequest of land (1270a19–22). Furthermore, he states, about two-fifths of the land is possessed by women because heiresses are numerous and dowries are large. Again, the fault lies with the laws (or lack of them) on the marriage of heiresses (1270a25–9). Consequently, although the land could have supported a greater number of citizens, the number fell to below 1,000 and Sparta succumbed owing to a shortage of men. Referring to the tradition that the Spartiates used to open their citizenship to outsiders and hence did not suffer from manpower shortage, he comments that it is better to maintain numbers by equalising property. As before, he asserts, the blame lies with the law, which offers incentives for reproduction without provision for the poverty that results from increased division of the inheritance (1270a39–b6).

Further criticisms pertaining to property and wealth appear thick and fast later in the same chapter. Because the ephorate is open to all citizens, the poverty of many holders of the office lays them open to bribery (1270b8–13). The other Spartiates have so high a degree of austerity in their daily lives that they cannot endure it and secretly break the law (1270b33–5). The Elders also 'conduct much business by taking bribes and showing favouritism', since their affairs are exempt from scrutiny (1271a3–5). The rules made by the person who established the common messes are unsatisfactory and lead to the opposite of what the lawgiver intended. Poor men are unable to pay their contributions and join in the messes, yet the established regulation is that those who cannot pay them are excluded from citizenship (1271a26–37). Finally, public finance is badly handled. There is never any money in the treasury and the Spartiates are bad at paying their property taxes (*eisphorai*). Since they own most of the land themselves, they do not scrutinize one another's contributions (1271b10–15). This last comment leads Aristotle to conclude the chapter with a final ringing condemnation:

> and so a state of affairs has come about which is just the opposite of the happy conditions envisaged by the lawgiver: he has produced a state which has no money but is full of persons eager to make money for themselves (1271b15–17).

Issues of property and wealth also appear at other points in the work. Some are positive features. Earlier in Book 2, at 1263a35–7, Aristotle provides a compressed and somewhat distorted summary of the information in Xenophon's *Polity of the Lakedaimonians* (6.3–4) about the shared use of property as an example of the practicability of communal use in well-run states. In Book 4, among the democratic features of Spartan society which establish its merit as a mixed constitution, he includes the equal treatment of rich and poor in the upbringing, the messes and in daily dress (1294b21–7). Other references, however, resume a negative tone. In Book 5, in his discussion of faction arising in aristocracies due to wide inequalities in wealth, Aristotle cites the trouble from impoverished Spartans at the time of the (Second) Messenian war attested by Tyrtaios' poem *Eunomia* (1306b37–1307a2). Shortly afterwards, as an example of his proposition that 'as all aristocratic constitutions are inclined towards oligarchy, the notables grasp at wealth', he cites the increasing concentration of landed property in contemporary Sparta (1307a34–6).

Issues of property and wealth are clearly central to Aristotle's perception of the failings of the Spartan *politeia* and the causes of its crisis. Although not completely absent, they are less prominent in those parts of the *Politics* which focus on meritorious aspects of Spartan society. Aristotle's picture is of a society which, despite some notable moderating institutional provisions, was dominated by a concern to amass wealth – an image comparable with the more schematic account in Plato's *Republic*. Moreover, in his account the luxury of Spartan women is no longer, as in Euripides, an isolated phenomenon, but one with direct implications for the ambitions of Spartiate men who, under pressure from their wives, partake of the same apple of greed for wealth in spite of their more austere upbringing.

Aristotle's criticisms are directed at long-established characteristics of the Spartan *politeia* and at the mistakes of its lawgiver, who was responsible for the deleterious property arrangements and attitudes to wealth. As Schütrumpf has demonstrated (1994, 338–41), his criticisms are not directed at new corruptions only recently introduced since the end of the Peloponnesian war. As his citation of impoverishment at the time of Tyrtaios indicates, inequality of property and the resulting problems were for Aristotle not new factors in Spartan society. Even where his critical remarks refer to current practice (such as the bribery of ephors and Elders) or recent consequences (such as the full-blown development of manpower shortage or the female management of affairs during the period of empire), these are always traced back to the original errors of the lawgiver whose provisions or omissions led to the effects described.[18] Aristotle's critique, whilst not blind to the merits of Sparta's longstanding material provisions, thus constituted a vigorous response to other writers, such as those considered above, who presented an idealised image of Spartan property arrangements in the period before her imperial hegemony.

The return to a moralizing ideal

Although they agreed with other fourth-century writers that material factors played a critical role in Sparta's decline, Plato and Aristotle presented a picture according to which Sparta's property system, although distinctive in certain respects, shared common characteristics with arrangements in other Greek poleis. In the long run, their critiques were unable to stem the tide of idealizing and moralizing interpretations; but there is one enigmatic work which shares partly in their approach. This work is the dialogue *Alkibiades I*, which, although it has come down to us among the works of Plato, has been thought by many scholars to be a pseudo-Platonic work, probably deriving from one of Plato's immediate disciples in the so-called 'Old Academy', perhaps towards the end of the fourth century (Tigerstedt 1965–78, i.277). Its depiction of the presence of wealth in Sparta (122c–123b) is not too dissimilar to that of Plato. The possession of large amounts of property is presented as a distinctive feature of Spartan life. (The dramatic date is the later fifth century during the life of Alkibiades.) Spartiates have more land, slaves and livestock than any Athenian citizen; and certain individuals have more gold and silver in their possession than all the rest of Greece, since these have poured into Spartan territory for many generations. What is different from Plato's presentation, however, is the absence of any notion of *clandestine* enjoyment of a forbidden fruit. Wealth is presented as an additional boon to the Spartiates' noble ancestry and other qualities such as moderation (*sōphrosynē*), orderliness, magnanimity, discipline, courage and endurance. These other virtues make strange bedfellows for wealth from the angle of both the moralizing and the philosophic approaches of the previous century. The resulting picture seems almost to have come full circle to the Herodotean image of an outstanding but in most respects typical Greek polis.

Aristotle's intellectual successors within the Peripatos, however, soon abandoned his interpretation of the causes of Sparta's international decline. Whereas Aristotle blamed the traditional laws for the failings of Spartan society, his pupil, Klearchos of Soloi, lamented the lapse of contemporary Sparta from its ancient political order (fr. 39 Wehrli, *ap.* Athen. 681c). In fleshing out the details of the Peripatetic writers' presentation of Spartan property arrangements, we face the same problem as with Kritias. One suspects that their influence on subsequent images of Spartan wealth was considerable, but the fragmentary preservation of their works leaves us the most meagre of clues with which to prove it. The problem of incomplete survival obscures, first of all, the relationship between the image of property arrangements in Aristotle's *Politics* and in the surviving fragments of the Aristotelian treatise, the *Polity of the Lakedaimonians* (*Lak. Pol.*) – which we know only through excerpts made by a certain Herakleides, probably the second-century BC statesman and scholar Herakleides Lembos (Dilts (ed.) 1971). The *Lak. Pol.* was probably completed after Aristotle wrote his critique of Sparta in *Politics*, Book 2 (Keaney 1980; Schütrumpf 1991, 296–7). Given the apparently collaborative nature of the treatise, as part of the overall research project into the constitutions of Greek states organized by Aristotle but largely (if not wholly) carried out by his disciples, it may stand in many respects as a work of transition between Aristotle and his Peripatetic successors. Whatever substantive differences there may or may not be between the *Politics* and the *Lak. Pol.* (see ch. 3), there is, as I have argued elsewhere (Hodkinson 1986, 388), a divergence of presentation between the two works which is attributable to the difference between a compressed analytical critique and a collection of information. The wider range of details which the *Lak. Pol.* aimed to include, together with the tendency of its excerptor to highlight trivial details devoid of supporting context, has an effect upon its image of property arrangements. So, for example, one surviving fragment (Arist. fr. 13 Rose = Dilts 1971, 19 no. 13) dutifully records items such as the prohibitions on female ornamentation, the restrictions on food for the boys, the modest and uniform burials, and diet of barley meal instead of wheat. Although there is no reason to doubt the basic veracity of these details, the image implied by such an uncritical listing is necessarily one of unrelieved austerity; whereas, as noted above, the *Politics* depicts the Spartiates' austere life as too hard for them to live up to.

    Plutarch, we know, utilized the Aristotelian *Lak. Pol.* and it is likely that the work contributed to the idealized image of the role of wealth in his *Life of Lykourgos*. There is, however, good reason to think that much of Plutarch's detailed information about Spartan institutions came also from other Peripatetic sources, such as Dikaiarchos and Theophrastos (Aalders 1982, 64). Certain similarities between the Plutarchean and Peripatetic attitudes to Sparta would be compatible with this hypothesis. The Peripatetics seem generally to have taken a pro-Spartan stance, deriving from their hostility to Athenian democracy, which contrasted sharply with the balanced approach of Aristotle (Tigerstedt 1965–78, i.304–9). Of Dikaiarchos we are told that his treatise on the Spartan *politeia* so pleased the Spartans that they had it recited annually to their youths;[19] but its line on matters of wealth and property is unknown. The only part of his surviving oeuvre germane to our interests is a fragment from his *Tripolitikos* (fr. 72 Wehrli, *ap*. Athen. 141a–c) describing the meal served at the common messes and the contributions of produce which made up the mess dues. The content is factual in character (and the details of the mess contributions are corroborated by a separate source: see ch. 6 below), though with a tendency to emphasize the sparseness of the diet.

Theophrastos' approach to Spartan property and wealth and its subsequent impact is somewhat clearer. One of Plutarch's works, his *Praecepta Gerendae Rei Publicae*, seems to have been influenced by Theophrastos' *Politika pros tous Kairous* (Aalders 1982, 64); and it seems likely that his views on Sparta also owed much to the relevant parts of the latter's *Nomoi*, a large work in 24 books on the laws of different peoples. Theophrastos' moralizing interests are shown by his relation of an episode in which King Agesilaos in Egypt declined the gifts of sweetmeats in favour of more ordinary fare.[20] Most suggestive, however, is his comment cited by Plutarch in his *Lykourgos* (10.2) that in Sparta wealth was 'an object of no desire' (ἄζηλον: fr. 78 Wehrli). The context in which Theophrastos made this remark is unknown; but, taken at face value, it represents the fullest assertion yet made of Spartan disdain for wealth, the earliest indication of the emergence of the extreme image of Spartan wealth later expressed in its fullest form in the writings of Plutarch.

The development of the dominant ancient image: problems of the sources

With the loss of her political importance and the reversion away from the political analyses of her *politeia* by Plato and Aristotle, the image of Sparta moved away – as the remark of Theophrastos shows – from that of a political ideal whose merits could be argued and debated to that of a moral ideal whose merits were regarded as indisputable. It has been claimed that 'at the end of the fourth century BC, the legend of Sparta had on essential points assumed its final shape' (Tigerstedt 1965–78, ii.14). That judgement, however, underestimates the significant contribution of post-classical writers, whose works were to shape the precise contours of subsequent images of Sparta's property system. Consideration of the full range of surviving post-classical evidence lies beyond the scope of this survey; but it is essential to examine the main outlines of the development of these images. The history of its elaboration is also important for the historian who, in assessing the evidence of the post-classical sources, needs to appreciate the processes through which their views were formed and the relationship of their testimony both to one another and to the evidence of earlier sources.[21]

It is precisely on this point, however, that we encounter a cluster of long-disputed issues. The problem centres around the fact that the works of most post-classical writers about Sparta no longer survive. Indeed, the vast bulk of the surviving post-classical evidence concerning Spartan society has come down to us in the writings of Plutarch (c. AD 50–after 120). Plutarch's best known writings on classical and earlier Sparta are his *Lives* of the historical Spartan individuals, Lysander and Agesilaos, and above all his *Life of Lykourgos*, in which he describes the social and political system which the legendary lawgiver supposedly created. Also relevant is his combined *Life* of the later-third-century Spartan kings Agis IV and Kleomenes III, which includes comments on the earlier, classical society which the kings claimed to restore. Finally, among Plutarch's *Moralia* there is a section relating to Sparta which was classified in antiquity under a single heading, as the *Apophthegmata Lakōnika* ('Lakonian Sayings'). Though clearly conceived of as a unity (Ziegler 1951, 865), it also comprises three distinct parts which Stephanos of Byzantion and, following him, most modern editors have classified separately: (i) the *Apophthegmata Lakōnika* proper (*Mor.* 208a–236e), a series of anecdotes about and gnomic sayings ascribed to individual Spartan men, some named, others anonymous; (ii) the *Instituta Laconica*, a description of ancient Spartan institutions and customs (236f–240b); and (iii) the *Lakainōn Apophthegmata*, 'Sayings of Lakonian women', again both named and anonymous (240c–242d).[22]

The question is the nature of this material in the *Moralia* and its relationship to Plutarch's *Lives*. Their close relationship is not in question. Chapters 8–30 of the *Life of Lykourgos* contain many of the anecdotes and sayings connected with Lykourgos in the *Apophthegmata Lakōnika* (*Mor.* 225f–229a) and several of the institutions and customs described in the *Instituta Laconica*. Moreover, these sayings and customs, whose contents are mutually complementary rather than overlapping, appear in the *Lykourgos* in an alternating sequence which, although somewhat irregular, largely mirrors their order of appearance in the other two works.[23] Likewise, the majority of the apophthegms ascribed to Agesilaos and Lysander in the *Apophthegmata Lakōnika* appear also in their respective *Lives*, once again in identical sequences (Ziegler 1951, 273; Fuhrmann 1988, 133).

Scholars have interpreted these parallels in diverse ways. Most earlier scholars thought that the *Lives* constituted the original versions, and that the *Apophthegmata Lakōnika* and *Instituta Laconica* were compiled later, either by Plutarch himself or by a subsequent excerptor who extracted parts of the *Lives* for this purpose.[24] This hypothesis, however, has serious problems. The *Apophthegmata Lakōnika* and *Instituta Laconica* are both poorly prepared works lacking the finished polish of Plutarch's *Lives*. The former, for example, contains several sayings which are ascribed to more than one Spartan (Tigerstedt 1965–78, ii.90–1). Both contain grammatical infelicities, and also the occurrence of hiatus, not found in the *Lives*.[25] It is hard to envisage either that Plutarch constructed such disordered and poorly written works out of his Spartan *Lives* or what purpose he had in doing so. Similar considerations apply to the hypothesis of a later excerptor. In particular, why should he have constructed two separate sequences of *apophthegmata* from the *Life of Lykourgos*?

Finally, if the *Instituta Laconica* and *Apophthegmata Lakōnika* were compiled out of the *Lives*, whence came the various customs in the *Instituta* and the sayings relating to Lykourgos, Agesilaos and Lysander in the *Apophthegmata* which do not appear in their respective *Lives* – not to mention the great body of apophthegms which are ascribed to the large number of Spartans, both named and anonymous, who were never the subject of Plutarchean biography?

These considerations have led to a current consensus that the *Apophthegmata Lakōnika* and *Instituta Laconica* (and presumably also the *Lakainōn Apophthegmata*) were the primary works, from which the parallel passages in the *Lives* were drawn.[26] The obvious explanation for their appearance among the Plutarchean corpus is that they represent a collection of material used by Plutarch in the composition of his Spartan *Lives*. It is probable, given that the contents share an identical order of appearance, that the selection of this material was performed by Plutarch himself. The *Apophthegmata* and *Instituta* constituted his working notes, of the sort which – as he himself states (*Mor.* 464e–f; cf. 457d) – he was in the habit of collecting during his compendious reading of earlier writers.

From which sources, however, did Plutarch assemble this material? To pose the question in its starkest form: did Plutarch assemble this collection passage by passage from his direct reading of primary sources, or did he excerpt the passages from an existing collection of *Lakōnika*? We must inevitably discuss this question against the background of the unfortunate tendency in much older scholarship to deny to Plutarch the credit for either independent research or any significant degree of personal creativity in the composition of his works; indeed, to treat the contents of his *Lives* as the outcome of uncritical compilation from postulated (but now lost) hellenistic and early Roman originals. Theories of this sort have now, thankfully, long since been discredited. Plutarch's commitment to and capacity to undertake a wide range of personal reading and research are now firmly re-established in current scholarship.[27] Certainly, in his Spartan *Lives* Plutarch gives evidence of having directly consulted a wide range of classical and hellenistic authors whose writings could have informed his collection of apophthegms. Some sayings in the *Apophthegmata Lakōnika* are very close to passages in writings of classical authors;[28] and some so-called apophthegms are not sayings at all, but extracts which Plutarch may well have taken from diverse historical sources.

Nevertheless, it is hard to believe that Plutarch could personally have assembled, one by one from separate sources, each of the 500 passages of the *Apophthegmata Lakōnika*, *Instituta Laconica* and *Lakainōn Apophthegmata* (Santaniello 1995, 13–19). We should not, in an understandable desire to avoid the errors of the past, blind ourselves to genuine evidence for the existence of collections of Spartan material upon which Plutarch could have drawn (Nachstädt 1935; Santaniello 1995, 8–9). It seems clear (to focus for the moment solely on the *apophthegmata*), that already in the fifth and fourth centuries there was widespread interest in that special type of saying associated with Spartans whose typical characteristic was a brief and arresting encapsulation of human wisdom, often in retort to a question or adverse comment or in response to a challenging situation (cf. Thuc. 4.40). It has been suggested that collections of Spartan sayings were made initially by sympathizers elsewhere in Greece (Fuhrmann 1988, 138). Certainly, sayings ascribed to figures from Sparta's past are quoted by Plato (*Phdr.* 260e) and by Aristotle (*Pol.* 1313a26; *Rhet.* 1389b4), who elsewhere refers to 'Lakonian apophthegms' as a distinct category of utterance.[29] In these circumstances it is unlikely that no ancient author before Plutarch should have essayed a collection of such apophthegms. Indeed, the very character of Greek intellectual enquiry in the later fourth and third centuries tells against such a proposition, since the systematic, empirical collection of data was a fundamental procedure of Peripatetic and other post-Aristotelian philosophy (Jaeger 1948, 324–41). Aristotle, the inventor of this new methodology, himself laid the foundation for a collection of gnomic sayings (Jaeger 1948, 129–30; cf. Gemoll 1924, 38) in which Lakonian apophthegms may well have featured. Although the specific contribution of particular schools of thought is debated, there is widespread agreement among the experts that the collection of apophthegms was one of the many projects engaged in by hellenistic philosophers, stimulated no doubt by their evident interest in 'traditional' Spartan morality.[30]

It is more than probable that the widely-read Plutarch would have consulted and drawn working notes from these collections during his research for his intended Spartan writings (Ziegler 1951, 866; Fuhrmann 1988, 138). To assert this is no slur upon the independence of his research or upon the creativity of his composition, as we shall see presently in examining his use of this material in his Spartan *Lives*. Besides these general considerations, there are particular reasons for thinking that Plutarch drew most of his apophthegms from a larger collection (or collections) of Spartan sayings current in hellenistic times.[31] Tigerstedt's study of the temporal location ascribed to the Plutarchean apophthegms (1965–78, ii.25–7) has revealed that, apart from one example relating to the death of Agis IV in 241 BC (*Mor.* 216d), none of the apophthegms concerns any event later than Pyrrhos' invasion of Lakonia in 272. Apart from that one case, the period of the 'third-century revolution' from the late 240s onwards is especially conspicuous by its absence. This suggests that Plutarch did not assemble the bulk of his Lakonian apophthegms by personally abstracting notable sayings from his primary reading of earlier writers. Otherwise, the *Apophthegmata Lakōnika* would surely have included apophthegms from the revolutionary period, whose dramatic events and speeches could have furnished many notable sayings. It indicates, rather, that he drew largely upon a collection (or collections) of apophthegms which was largely complete by the mid-third century. Further support for this argument is provided by the character of the underlying moral attitudes in the *Apophthegmata Lakōnika*. Although generally redolent of post-Platonic and post-Aristotelian philosophical thought, including a critical attitude towards the influence of wealth, they lack the sharp sense of political or economic egalitarianism which (as we shall see below) pervades surviving accounts of the third-century revolution.[32] The sole exception to this generalisation is a small number of apophthegms (31 in total) ascribed to Lykourgos. However, several of the Lykourgan 'apophthegms' are not sayings at all and derive from a different kind of source. Hence they will receive separate discussion in a later section of this chapter.[33]

The influence of third-century philosophy: the *Apophthegmata Lakōnika*

In this section I shall consider the Plutarchean *Apophthegmata Lakōnika* (excluding the Lykourgan *apophthegmata*) as an indication of the development of images of Spartan property and wealth down to the mid-third century BC. First, we must establish the characteristics of these sayings. The term *apophthegma* comes from the verb ἀποφθέγγομαι, 'to make a decisive riposte' (del Corno 1996, 30) and an apophthegm proper invariably centres on a verbal response which a speaker makes to a comment or question from another person or to the situation facing the speaker. Consequently, the core of the apophthegm is the saying itself. In contrast, the context of a particular saying often varies both in substance and also in the person to whom it is attributed. Hence, although many apophthegms are attached to particular personages or events, only in a minority of cases can these attributions be regarded as historically sound. There is a particular tendency for famous Spartan individuals to attract sayings which are otherwise – and were probably originally – ascribed to anonymous or lesser-known Spartans. In addition, several apophthegms are attached to early Spartan kings of dubious historical authenticity. What the apophthegms tell us, as Tigerstedt has rightly said, 'is not what the Spartans really were but what they were believed to be' (1965–78, ii.18). 'Believed to be', that is, from a predominantly hellenistic perspective: for whilst some apophthegms simply repeat sayings from earlier sources, a greater number present either a perceptible development from former images, or a distinct change of presentation, or even an image which is entirely new. In what follows I shall examine these three phenomena in turn.

The development of former images sometimes comes through a more explicit assertion of values implicit in earlier representations. Thus at 210a (*Agesilaos* 21) the king's supposed assertion, that through plain clothing and food 'we reap a harvest of liberty', develops the association of the Spartan lifestyle with liberty already made by Xenophon (*Lak. Pol.* 7.2; 11.3), but links them more directly with the practice of austerity. Sometimes this development appears in the form of small but significant alterations of details. The apophthegm at 210c (*Agesilaos* 24), for example, is adapted rather freely from a fragment of Theopompos concerning the Thasians' offer of costly foodstuffs to the king

(*FGrH* 115F22, *ap.* Athen. 657b–c; cf. Flower 1988, 124). Whereas the original text specifies that Agesilaos accepted the sheep and cattle but rejected the pastries and sweetmeats, in the version in the *Apophthegmata* the only foodstuff he would accept was barley flour (*alphita*).³⁴ Agesilaos is thus made to conform to the strict diet of the common messes (on which see below, ch. 6) and the gap is widened between Spartan austerity and the diet of other Greeks. This alteration is accompanied by a change in Agesilaos' concluding justification of his passing the rejected foods to his helots. The simple justification in Theopompos' account, that it was more appropriate that the helots be corrupted than the Lakedaimonians, is expanded in the *Apophthegmata* to a programmatic statement that gormandizing is incompatible with manly virtue (*andragathia*) and that servile allurements are alien to free men.

One example of a distinct change of presentation concerns the chronic emptiness of the Spartan public treasury. Whereas Thucydides (1.80) and Aristotle (*Pol.* 1271b10–15) present it as a weak point of Spartan affairs associated with individual citizens' evasion of their taxes, at 217b (*Anaxandros*) it is presented as deliberate policy, 'so that those made guardians of it may not become corrupt'! Another presentational change concerns the Spartans' habit of sporting long hair. The first classical reference to this practice (Hdt. 1.82) relates it to their victory at the battle of Thyrea c. 545. In Xenophon's *Polity of the Lakedaimonians* (11.3) it acquires the rationalising purpose of making the Spartiates look taller, more free and more terrifying. In two separate, and differently worded, apophthegms (230b = *Nikandros* 2; 232d = *Charillos* 6), however, the practice acquires a new material connotation through the explanation that long hair is the most inexpensive form of personal adornment.³⁵

The second of these passages also characterizes adornment through long hair as 'natural' (*physikos*). This image of the 'natural' character of the Spartan attitudes to the material world is a new one. It also comes across vividly elsewhere in the *Apophthegmata*, in the first attested criticism of the use of squared timbers in house construction (210e = *Agesilaos* 27):

> Seeing in Asia a house roofed with square beams, he asked the owner if timber in that country grew square. And when the man said, 'No, but round,' he said, 'Well, then, if they were square, would you finish them round?'

It is hard not to suspect a philosophical influence behind these last passages and behind several other apophthegms to do with attitudes to wealth. It is certainly evident in a saying attributed to an early Spartan king (216f = *Alkamenes* 3), who justifies his living a modest life despite owning adequate property with the comment that, 'it is a noble thing for one who possesses much to live according to reason (*logismon*) and not according to his desire (*epithymian*)'.³⁶ It is apparent too at 224f (*Leon, son of Eurykratidas* 1) where King Leon's recipe for security in a state is 'Where the inhabitants shall possess neither too much nor too little, and where right shall be strong and wrong shall be weak.'³⁷ The precise nature of the philosophical influences behind these sayings is much debated, with different scholars championing the impact of various schools of thought from the Peripatetics through Cynicism to Stoicism.[38] Unfortunately, the sparse and late nature of the evidence prevents a clear conclusion and it may be that the intellectual sources of the apophthegms were both many and varied. It is clear, however, that they represent a further stage in the idealisation of the Spartan approach to property and wealth.

Egalitarian Sparta: the impact of the third-century revolution
Plutarch's *Lives of Agis and Kleomenes*

We have already noted the considerable transformations which images of the role played by property and wealth during the heyday of Spartan power underwent, both during the classical period itself and during the early hellenistic period down to *c.* 250. We must now consider the impact on those images of the sustained period of internal turmoil within Sparta during the second half of the third century BC, the series of events loosely but conveniently known as the 'third-century revolution'. The essential elements of this 'revolution' were a range of fundamental social and economic changes which were attempted initially by King Agis IV (244–241) and then, following his execution, implemented more successfully by King Kleomenes III (236–222), before he himself was forced into flight from Sparta by the forces of Macedon and the Achaian league. Our perception of the impact of these events on images of Spartan property arrangements depends mainly on the account of the revolution given three centuries later in Plutarch's lives of the two Spartan kings.[39] Plutarch is not the earliest source to reflect the new images that resulted from the revolution – as we shall see shortly, that honour belongs to Polybius; but he provides by far the fullest description. His account, which is almost uniformly favourable to the revolutionaries, is based upon the lost writings of contemporary propagandists of the revolution, most notably the historian Phylarchos (Gabba 1957). It indicates that the revolutionaries sought to justify their programme of reforms by portraying them as a restoration of the original provisions of the lawgiver Lykourgos, which (so the revolutionaries claimed) had been abandoned during Sparta's period of imperial hegemony. Hence Plutarch's *Lives of Agis and Kleomenes* present us with a clear idea of how men closely connected with the revolution portrayed the role of property and wealth both in Sparta's idealised past and during the period of crisis and decline in the early fourth century.

The main points of the revolutionaries' programme were the redistribution of land, the abolition of debts, the replenishment of the citizen body with suitable *perioikoi* and foreigners, and the restoration of the austere Spartan discipline and way of life (Fuks 1962a, 118). Although none of these elements was entirely new within the repertoire of Greek political thought, only the idea of material austerity can definitely be said to draw upon notions of Lykourgan Sparta current before the revolution. Nevertheless, each element was explicitly advertised by the revolutionaries as a return to the measures introduced by Lykourgos (*Agis* 5.1; 9.3; *Comp. Agis-Kleom.-Gracch.* 2.3). Apparently, only the Lykourgan pedigree of King Agis' proposal to abolish debts was challenged by opponents of the revolution through their main spokesman, King Leonidas (*Agis* 10.2). Although the lawgiver's adoption of this measure was reaffirmed by Agis in his response to Leonidas (10.2–3), and the ascription reappears without question in the *Life of Kleomenes* (18.2), the notion of a Lykourgan abolition of debts certainly does not occur in any of our surviving evidence from earlier times. It is relevant that, in defending its Lykourgan origin, Agis links it with the well-established idea of Lykourgos' prohibition of coinage, claiming that he had 'banished borrowing and lending from the polis along with coinage'. Although such an association is not illogical, it is perhaps a sign that Agis (or, at least, the pro-revolutionary sources of our accounts) realised the weakness of his case. It is notable that, with one exception to be considered shortly, abolition of debt does not reappear in any of the accounts of Lykourgos' reforms which post-date the eventual failure of the revolution.

Other innovatory images articulated by propagandists of the revolution were, however, more successful. The most important image was of course the idea that Lykourgos had redistributed land. As we have already seen, the grounds for attributing this idea to fourth-century writers, even to Ephorus, are extremely flimsy. Yet it is notable that Leonidas apparently did not challenge the Lykourgan pedigree of this measure – or at least he was not represented as doing so, according to the pro-revolutionary accounts which dominate Plutarch's *Life of Agis*. Why? Recent studies have noted the important influence which the works of Plato exercised over the ideas of the revolutionaries (e.g. Schütrumpf 1987); and the similarity of the Lykourgan single-heir inheritance system described in Plutarch, *Agis* 5 to that advocated in Plato's *Laws* is undeniable (cf. Ducat 1983, 150, 166). It may be that the combined precedent of Plato's theoretical plan and of his assertion that there had once been equality in Sparta after the initial Dorian invasion was sufficient to establish as unchallengeable – at least for the authors of pro-revolutionary accounts – the notion of a Lykourgan redistribution of land.

The invention of tradition concerning the Lykourgan redistribution was not, however, confined to generalities. The variations in the numbers of lots (9000, 6000 or 4500) which Lykourgos supposedly distributed – according to the account in Plutarch's *Life of Lykourgos* (8.3) – as well as the notion of a subsequent distribution (of either 3000 or 4500 lots) by King Polydoros, have been shown to reflect the efforts of propagandists to harmonize Lykourgos' efforts with the different numbers (4500 and 6000) involved in the respective projects of Agis and Kleomenes.[40] Another invention was the revolutionaries' depiction of the development of landed inequality after the Peloponnesian war due to the rhētra of Epitadeus – a depiction which later made its way into Plutarch's *Life of Agis*, chapter 5. As Eckart Schütrumpf (1987) has convincingly demonstrated, the account of the breakdown of the Lykourgan equality of landholding through the *rhētra* of Epitadeus is a fiction closely derived from the account in Plato's *Republic* of the breakdown and overthrow of oligarchy through the accumulation of property by a few.[41] Above all, the distinctively new contribution of the propaganda surrounding the revolution, with its combination of landed equality and abolition of debts, was an overwhelming emphasis upon equality. The concept is referred to no fewer than four times in the chapters of the *Life of Agis* (5–9) which outline the state of Spartan society and Agis' plans.[42]

The Lykourgan sayings in the *Apophthegmata Lakōnika*
This emphasis upon equality appears with even greater force in the Lykourgan apophthegms which have come down to us among the Plutarchean *Apophthegmata Lakōnika* (*Mor.* 225f–229a). Their thoroughly egalitarian character, which marks them – or at least some of them – as influenced by the third-century revolution, is a prime reason for separating the Lykourgan apophthegms from the other apophthegms in the collection, whose emphasis instead upon the themes of liberty and austerity strikes a markedly different, pre-revolutionary tone (Tigerstedt 1965–78, ii.85).[43] Another reason is the form of some of the Lykourgan apophthegms, which differ from other *apophthegmata* in that they contain no saying.[44] Several of the opening apophthegms are indeed primarily a description of Lykourgos' purported reforms. The precise nature of the work from which the Lykourgan apophthegms were drawn is not precisely known. Tigerstedt's suggestion (1965–78, ii.243) that they comprise extracts from a biography of the lawgiver is not implausible; though, as we shall see below, signs of a lack of homogeneity within the group of apophthegms raise the possibility of more than a single source.

Whatever the precise nature of the source(s), several of the Lykourgan apophthegms share – as intimated above – the emphasis upon equality evident in the *Life of Agis*. The second part of apophthegm no. 1 (*Mor.* 226a–b), a story of how differential training turned a house dog into an effective hunter and a hunting dog into a useless one, concludes with the assertion,

> 'So also in our case, fellow-citizens, noble birth, so admired by the multitude, and descent from Herakles, bestows no advantage, unless we do the sort of things for which he was manifestly the most glorious and most noble of all mankind, and unless we practise and learn what is good all our life.'

Other apophthegms extend this egalitarian tendency to the sphere of property. No. 2 (226b) stresses Lykourgos' equal division of land. According to no. 3 (226b–d), he abolished debts (this is the only post-revolutionary source to perpetuate this notion) and even tried to divide up all household possessions too, in order to do away with all inequality. Most extraordinary of all, however, is Lykourgos' reported saying in no. 4 (226d–e) that he had established the common messes,

> '…also that there may be for all an equal portion of food and drink, and so that not only in drink or food, but in bedding (*strōmnē*) or furniture (*skeuesin*) or anything else whatsoever the rich man may have no advantage at all over the poor man.'

A similar, though not entirely identical point, occurs in no. 9 (227b–c), in which Lykourgos gives his reason for ordaining that Spartans should use only axe and saw in constructing, respectively, the roofs and doors of their private houses: 'So that the citizens may be moderate in regard to all things which they bring into their houses, and may possess none of the things which are the cause of rivalry among other peoples.' No. 27 (228e) provides a different link between equality of wealth and the absence of rivalry through the saying that the Spartans could prevent enemy invasion, 'If you remain poor, and none of you desires to be more important than another'.

Aside from their striking egalitarian emphasis, two general points emerge from this collection of passages. One is a certain lack of homogeneity. In apophthegm no. 4, for example, the comments concerning equality in bedding and furniture, as Tigerstedt (1965–78, ii. 357 n. 274) has noted, do not logically belong to the context of the establishment of the common messes; and they sit rather oddly with the content of no. 3 where Lykourgos is said to have given up the attempt to equalize household possessions. Similarly, in no. 3 the account of Lykourgos' failed attempt at dividing household possessions is succeeded, without explanation of the logical connection between the two, by an account of his replacement of gold and silver coinage with the iron currency. Furthermore, within this latter account a series of overblown rhetorical generalisations about the effects of the measure ('all wrongdoing was banished from Lakedaimon…no merchant, no public lecturer, no soothsayer or mendicant priest, no maker of fancy articles ever made his way into Sparta') is followed by extraordinarily precise detail of the exact relationship between the value and weight of the former iron currency ('in weight one Aiginetan mina, in value four chalkoi'). It appears that a nugget from a serious earlier treatise (such as the Aristotelian *Polity of the Lakedaimonians* or a work by Dikaiarchos) has somehow become embedded in a matrix of hellenistic moralizing. Likewise, in no. 1 the canine story mentioned above is preceded by a different version which, although it shares the emphasis upon the importance of training, omits the denigration of birth by making the two dogs puppies of the same litter. Whether the presence side by side of these variant versions results from Plutarch himself drawing upon different sources, or whether they were already together in his hellenistic source, we cannot tell. The presence of divergent elements within a single apophthegm in nos. 3 and 4 perhaps suggests the latter. Support for the former alternative might, however, be sought in apophthegms 9 and 10. No. 9 (noted above) represents, with its direct reference to use of only axe and saw, a new form of reference to the simplicity of Spartan domestic architecture, together

Ch. 2. The growth of the dominant egalitarian image in ancient thought

with a new moral conclusion regarding the avoidance of internal rivalry through limitation of household possessions. No. 10, on the other hand, simply harks back to the pre-revolutionary criticism of squared timbers outside Sparta (210e = *Agesilaos* 27), suggesting that Plutarch may have inserted the passage himself due to its loose association with the theme of no. 9.

The second general point is the novelty of many of the images presented of Lykourgos' work. Several of these novel images go beyond even those claimed – at least according to Plutarch's *Lives* – by the revolutionaries themselves. As Tigerstedt (1965–78, ii.80–1) has remarked, 'Philosophers and reformers may have expressed ideas that no responsible politician was able or willing to realize'. In apophthegm no. 3 the idea that Lykourgos had intended to divide all household possessions appears for the first time in our extant sources. Apophthegm no. 4 goes still further in implying a real equality of bedding, furniture and so on. Another novel measure appears in the latter part of apophthegm no. 3, in the form of an assertion that the lawgiver 'brought about the banishment of everything not absolutely necessary'. The bare bones of this assertion are given some flesh in apophthegms nos. 18 and 19 (*Mor.* 228b), which claim that Lykourgos banished perfume, the art of dyeing and all those whose business was the enhancement of personal beauty. This last measure is mentioned also in no. 15 (227f). Its main theme, however, introduces another novelty: the claim – which appears also around the same period in the writings of Hermippos (fr. 87, *ap.* Athen. 555c), who was himself probably influenced by the propaganda of the revolution (cf. Marasco 1978a, 120) – that Lykourgos had prohibited the giving of dowries. This claim conflicts, notably, with the evidence both of Aristotle (*Pol.* 1270a25) and of an apophthegm in the pre-revolutionary *Lakainōn Apophthegmata* (anon. no. 24 = *Mor.* 242b), which had stressed instead the moralizing point that family virtue could serve as an alternative to a propertied dowry. Another instance of a new approach which runs counter to the pre-revolution apophthegms is the Lykourgan apophthegms' stress on the value of poverty. Apophthegm no. 27, quoted above, which emphasizes that the Spartans should remain poor, marks a clear development from the non-Lykourgan sayings, in which the emphasis is merely on moderation of wealth (224f = *Leon* 1; 232b = *Teleklos* 4). Similarly, of the three passages in the *Apophthegmata Lakōnika* which address the issue of spoils from the enemy dead, only the Lykourgan apophthegm (no. 31) claims that spoliation was forbidden so that the Spartans 'may keep to their poverty as well as to their post'. The non-Lykourgan apophthegms (224b = *Kleomenes, son of Anaxandridas* 18; 224f = *Leotychidas, son of Ariston* 4) both assume that spoliation was permitted, and that only the dedication of spoils was forbidden because they were taken from cowards.

Two further innovations also merit attention. One comes in no. 22 (228d), which produces the first assertion of the inexpensive nature of Spartan sacrifices, a claim absent from previous extant sources.[45] The other is a generalization of larger significance. In no. 5 (226e–f) Lykourgos is said to have made wealth 'an object of no desire' (*adzēlon*), a comment which repeats the statement attested of Theophrastos. He then, however, goes on to remark, 'What a good thing it is, my friends, to show in actual practice the true characteristic of wealth, that it is blind.' This is the first attested application of the idea of 'Blind Wealth' to Sparta. It clearly bears a different connotation from the standard personification of Blind Wealth found in literature of the classical period, not least in Aristophanes' *Ploutos* and more generally in Athenian popular morality, a representation which expressed the idea 'that there is no correlation between possessions and merit' (Dover 1974, 110). The idea here (expressed, admittedly, implicitly rather than explicitly) is rather that Wealth is blind because it is useless: 'since nobody could make any use or show of it', as the apophthegm itself says. Once again, this appears to be a new development, one which encapsulates the entire image of wealth in the Lykourgan apophthegms. It is no wonder that Plutarch himself was later to pick up this image and develop it in his own description of Lykourgos' material reforms.

Other post-revolutionary perspectives

The *Instituta Laconica*

I turn now to the remaining Spartan work among Plutarch's *Moralia*, the so-called *Instituta Laconica* (*Mor.* 236f–240b). The *Instituta*, as mentioned above, comprise a purported description of ancient Spartan institutions and customs traditionally divided by editors into 42 short entries. They are clearly distinct from the Lykourgan and non-Lykourgan *Apophthegmata* in both character and content. They contain not a single saying; and not only is there very little overlap of material with the *Apophthegmata*, they are also wholly unrhetorical in nature and their philosophic character is rather different (Tigerstedt 1965–78, ii.89–90; Kennell 1995, 106–7; Santaniello 1995, 19–21). As already indicated, the *Instituta* as we currently possess them are part of Plutarch's working notes; but what about the source(s) of those notes? It is certain that Plutarch's immediate source wrote sometime after Rome's establishment of her hegemony over Greece in 146 BC, which is mentioned in the final entry; and we can be reasonably sure from the character of the entries that the ultimate source was a work on the Spartan *politeia*. Beyond this point there is room for debate. Two points should be noted at the outset. First, the *Instituta* provide only partial coverage of Spartan social institutions. Secondly, although the first 17 entries are logically connected, the remainder appear to leap from topic to topic with no obvious underlying rationale (Tigerstedt 1965–78, ii.90; Kennell 1995, 22). The normal interpretation of these features is that Plutarch collected the material in the *Instituta* from a work on Sparta's *politeia* written after 146; but that this work was itself excerpted from an earlier treatise whose coverage was more systematic. Kennell (1995, 21–3; 102–7), however, has argued, on the basis of certain grammatical anomalies and signs of altered tenses, along with the disorder of the later entries, that the work from which Plutarch made his collection was itself a compilation of material from diverse earlier sources.[46] In particular, he argues that the coherent opening 17 chapters, which largely cover the upbringing, are imbued with elements of Stoic philosophy which suggest that they derive from the work on the Spartan *politeia* by a pupil of the founder of Stoicism, the philosopher Zeno: possibly Persaios of Kition (*c*. 306–*c*. 243 BC), but more probably Sphairos of Borysthenes, the tutor of King Kleomenes III. The prevailing uncertainty whether we are dealing with a late third- or a late second- (or possibly even early first-) century perspective on Sparta clearly hinders an examination of the contribution of the *Instituta* to the development of images of property and wealth. It does not, however, preclude consideration of the work's perspective on classical Sparta *per se*. Since the *Instituta* were an important source for Plutarch's *Life of Lykourgos*, which we shall examine presently, their perspective is important for an assessment of his contribution to the dominant ancient image.

Whatever the work's relation to Sphairos, the atmosphere is often quite unlike that of other works stimulated by the third-century revolution. Stress is laid upon the austerity and simplicity of Spartiate life. Entry no. 2 emphasizes the sparse diet in the messes; no. 3 moderate drinking. The subjects of nos. 5 and 6 are the sparse clothing and bedding of the youths. There is, however, no emphasis upon equality, no hint of the egalitarian social measures ascribed to Lykourgos in Plutarch's *Life of Agis* and in the Lykourgan apophthegms. Similarly, in the account of Sparta's corruption in no. 41, there is the standard criticism of the introduction of gold and silver and the association of her decline with greed and love of wealth; but there is no reference to any resulting inequalities among the citizens such as is foregrounded in the revolutionary propaganda reflected in Plutarch's *Life of Agis*.

Likewise, in contrast to the *Apophthegmata*, the *Instituta* draw more heavily and explicitly upon earlier accounts of Sparta's *politeia*, especially those of Xenophon and the Aristotelian school.[47] There is less outright novelty in the work, at least as regards issues of property and wealth. In some entries the version given is largely faithful to the original source, as in no. 23 (238f), a reasonable summary of Xenophon's remarks (*Lak. Pol.* 6.4) on the sharing of slaves, dogs, horses and caches of food for hunters. The remarks on the simplicity of Spartiate burials in the Aristotelian *Polity of the Lakedaimonians* (*ap*. Herakleides Lembos fr. 373.13 Dilts) probably also lie behind the content of no. 18.

There is less straight reportage, however, in other entries. The account of the youths' legitimized stealing and sparse diet in *Instituta* nos. 12 and 13 (*Mor*. 237e–f), for example, is clearly based upon Xenophon's *Polity of the Lakedaimonians* (2.5–9). The order of presentation, however, is reversed from that of Xenophon and, as Kennell (1995, 104) has pointed out, the justification given for the sparse diet is different. Xenophon's plain-spoken 'nourishing bodies to keep them slender would be more conducive to height than distending them with food' is replaced by an explanation couched in medical-philosophical terminology: 'They think that…thin and spare constitutions are apt to be subtle in articulation, whereas over-fed ones resist due to their heaviness.' In no. 2 (236f–237a) the time-honoured subject of the infamous black broth is spiced with the first appearance – at least to our knowledge – of the anecdote of the foreign ruler who hired a Spartan cook but recoiled from the broth's disgusting taste. We shall also have cause to note later (ch. 7) how Xenophon's account of the boys' clothing (*Lak. Pol.* 2.4) is altered in *Instituta* no. 5, thereby exaggerating its sparseness. The manipulation of earlier source material is not, however, confined to these early entries. The first part of no. 41 (239d–e) combines ideas which go back to Xenophon (*Symp.* 8.35; *Lak. Pol.* 7.1–2) regarding the prohibition of engagement in banausic occupations and money-making with Theophrastos' aforementioned claim that wealth was an object of no desire. There then follows an important innovation on this subject, the claim that,

> The helots tilled the soil for them [sc. the Spartiates], paying the tribute (*apophora*) set down in the past. A curse was laid upon anyone who charged more, in order that they [sc. the helots] might serve gladly because they were making a profit and [the Spartiates] themselves might not try to get more.

As has been noted (Ducat 1990a, 56–8; Hodkinson 1992a, 125–6; cf. ch. 4 below), the notions of fixed helot rents and of a 'contract of servitude' between master class and helots are indissolubly linked to ideas of Spartiate landed equality, especially those promulgated during the third-century revolution.[48] So too – I shall argue in ch. 3 – is the final part of no. 22 (238e–f), concerning sale of the so-called *archaia moira*, or 'ancient portion'. In these two passages alone is there evidence of the impact of the revolution upon the content of the *Instituta*, although even here the consequent equality between Spartan citizens is implicit rather than explicit.

Polybius

The other major hellenistic source for the Spartan *politeia* to be only partially affected by the propaganda of the third-century revolution is Polybius (*c.* 200–*c.* 118 BC). As a citizen of Megalopolis, member of the Achaian league, and heir to the anti-Spartan policies of Aratos, Philopoimen and his own father Lykortas, Polybius was naturally hostile to the revolutionaries' aim of restoring Sparta's external power. As an upper-class property owner, the revolution's egalitarian socio-economic reforms were for him the embodiment of all evils; and this is how they are represented in his account of hellenistic politics in his *Histories*. Yet in his famous exposition of the character of Roman institutions in Book 6 it is the traditional Spartan *politeia*, as first established by Lykourgos, which he sets up as the model, well-ordered Greek society fit to be compared with Rome. As we saw earlier in our discussion of Ephorus, at the start of his

Ch. 2. The growth of the dominant egalitarian image in ancient thought

account (6.46) Polybius singles out as two distinctive features of the Spartans' *politeia* their equal division of citizen land and contempt for the acquisition of money. Indeed, for him the key to the Spartans' internal harmony lay in their attitude to wealth:

> For, there being two things to which a state owes its preservation, bravery against the enemy and concord among its citizens, Lykourgos, by doing away with the lust for wealth, did away also with all civic discord and strife.

These comments are developed shortly after, at 6.48, where the moderation of the citizens' private lives and the absence of strife within the community is ascribed to 'the equal distribution of landed property and the simple and common way of living'. In this way Sparta's economic arrangements are judged to have made a major contribution to what Polybius agrees, from the perspective of the attainment of autonomy and liberty, to have been an unrivalled polity.

In the field of foreign relations, however, Polybius identifies a major weakness of Sparta's system. Her ambitious and aggressive nature is criticized both in itself and – more relevantly to our purposes – in that once the Spartans' warfare extended beyond the Peloponnese,

> it became clear that neither their iron currency nor the exchange of their crops for the commodities they lacked could provide for their needs so long as they remained confined by Lykourgos' economic legislation, since these enterprises required a currency which was in universal circulation and a supply of goods from foreign sources… They were compelled to recognize that if they retained the Lykourgan system, it would be impossible to exert any important influence on affairs, let alone achieve the hegemony of Greece (6.49).

Hence, in Polybius' opinion, the inferiority of the Spartans' *politeia* to that of Rome: when they did attempt to gain hegemony in Greece, they came in danger of losing their own liberty (6.50).

Polybius' relation to the egalitarian propaganda of the third-century revolution is, consequently, a complex one. Owing to the non-survival of the revolutionaries' original writings, he is the earliest surviving, securely-datable, source to assert Sparta's Lykourgan equality of landholding. He is also significant as an illustration of the widespread impact of the revolutionaries' propaganda. Though opposed to their attempt to introduce economic equality in their own day, Polybius swallowed their myth of Lykourgos' ancient division of lands.

Likewise, Polybius' account of Sparta's weakness is an intriguing mixture. On the one hand, it presents a penetrating criticism of her modes of economic exchange which in method recalls the approach of Aristotle – especially in its revelation of a structural weakness in Sparta's arrangements which became evident over time. On the other hand, unlike Aristotle, Polybius uncritically accepts the notion of an economically primitive Sparta, isolated from foreign transactions (see further, ch. 5). Also, unlike Aristotle's critique, his comments are concerned, not with the impact of the structural weakness upon Sparta's internal affairs, but rather with the inadequacy of her rudimentary modes of exchange for foreign campaigning. He shows a singular lack of interest in the domestic consequences of the conflict between internal property arrangements and foreign ambitions. The main consequence which interests him is that the Spartans' attempt at empire, unlike that of the Romans, failed and even almost lost them their liberty. Although the final sentence of the passage quoted above notes the Spartans' recognition that they could not succeed abroad if they retained the Lykourgan system, Polybius has nothing to say about any alterations to, or corruptions of, the system which resulted from the Spartans' attempt to achieve an imperial hegemony. He eschews comment on the unequal socio-economic situation in third-century Sparta which provided justification for the sweeping revolutionary reforms to which, as a member of the propertied class, he was ideologically opposed.

The culmination of the dominant egalitarian image: the contribution of Plutarch

Having thus far traced the development of images of Spartan property and wealth century by century from the fifth to the second (or possibly early first) century BC, we must now – with one exception – leap forward in time until the later first and early second centuries AD, to the writings of Plutarch. Whilst a complete study of the legend of Sparta would require due consideration of the intervening period, this is not necessary for our current purpose of tracing the development of the dominant view which antiquity has conveyed to the modern world. For, to quote one who *has* studied the Spartan legend throughout this period, 'The literature of the Principate would lack any decisive importance to the legend of Sparta if it did not include Plutarch' (Tigerstedt 1965–78, ii.226) – a comment that applies equally, in the case of our subject, to the period of the late Roman Republic. During these eras the socio-economic aspects of Spartan society receive occasional mention, but they are hardly prominent in contemporary assessments. With the declining interest in Sparta as a political model, Lykourgos and his laws became of less significance (both to contemporary Spartans and to others, both Greeks and Romans) than Sparta's role in the Persian wars. The so-called 'restoration' of ancient Spartan customs and institutions during the Roman period focused upon the upbringing, not upon matters of property: 'The inhabitants of Sparta enjoyed, or aspired to, the level of material comfort widespread among the urban communities of the time: no sign here of the well-known austerities of classical Sparta.'[49] Their aristocratic local magistrates had no interest in the idea of landed equality which had dominated images of Spartan society in hellenistic thought.

The fact that these hellenistic images have survived as the predominant image conveyed by antiquity to modern times is almost entirely due to the lasting impact of Plutarch's *Parallel Lives*. I say 'almost', since there is one other post-hellenistic work which is occasionally cited in early modern accounts of

Ch. 2. The growth of the dominant egalitarian image in ancient thought

Sparta: Justin's epitome of the *Philippic Histories* of Pompeius Trogus written (probably) in the Augustan period. Trogus' account of the work of Lykourgos appears to have been brief, a mere two chapters in Justin's epitome; but it encapsulates several of the key themes of hellenistic historiography which were subsequently elaborated by Plutarch. Issues of property and wealth evidently held a prominent place in Trogus' perception of Lykourgos' legislation. After a brief reference to obedience and just government, his account moves straight on to Lykourgos' injunction of frugality and his prohibition of monetary transactions (3.2). There is no mention of the iron currency; instead (perhaps a Polybian touch?) purchases were to be made through exchange of commodities. But the prohibition of gold and silver is clearly stated. The start of the following chapter (3.3) interestingly anticipates the order of presentation in Plutarch's *Lykourgos*. Comments on Sparta's political institutions are followed by an account of Lykourgos' equal division of land ('that equality of possession might leave no one more powerful than another') and his institution of the common messes as a measure against splendour and luxury. Avoidance of luxury is also given as the reason for a restriction of the youths to one garment per year and for a prohibition against anyone wearing finer clothing or eating more sumptuously. There then follow further remarks on the upbringing which emphasize its toughness, austerity and avoidance of highly-seasoned food. The account then concludes with the prohibition of dowries and a generic comment that 'the highest respect should be paid, not to the rich and powerful, but to the old'. In sum, Trogus provides an egalitarian account of the laws of Lykourgos which derives from the third-century revolution, combined with an emphasis upon austerity and the avoidance of luxury stemming from more general hellenistic perspectives upon Sparta.

Relevant as Trogus' account (through the agency of Justin) was to certain modern writers, it is from Plutarch, as we have seen (ch. 1), that most modern images of Spartan property and wealth derive. This is not just because his surviving Spartan *Lives* preserve in much fuller detail information and ideas which would otherwise have been lost. It is as much due to the vivid and influential picture of Spartan society created by Plutarch's creative literary artistry. Plutarch's ideas on Sparta were not startlingly original; all take their origins from, or were anticipated by, earlier writings. Nevertheless, recent scholarship is agreed (in opposition to former views of him as a mere compiler of earlier works) that in writing his *Lives* Plutarch actively adapted and altered his source material, sometimes reshaping its contents, sometimes transferring material to different contexts, sometimes simplifying complex information, at other times adding made-up detail, all with the aim of the plausible reconstruction of past actions and events.[50] Often, too, material from one source was enlarged upon through use of material from other sources or through Plutarch's own personal reflections. This approach is evident in his Spartan lives, particularly in his *Life of Lykourgos*. The result is the powerful amalgam of images which has dominated modern perceptions. The survival of the *Apophthegmata Lakōnika*, the *Instituta Laconica*, and certain earlier works, especially Xenophon's *Polity of the Lakedaimonians*, presents us with a good opportunity to use the *Life of Lykourgos* to detect Plutarch's precise impact on, and contribution to, this dominant view.

As with Trogus, issues of property and wealth are central to Plutarch's image of Spartan society – so much so that he placed Lykourgos' redistribution of land second among the lawgiver's measures, behind only his establishment of Sparta's famous political institutions. In his comparison between Lykourgos and Numa, Plutarch describes the equality which resulted from the redistribution as 'the foundation and base of the polity' (*Comp. Lyk.-Num.* 2.6). This and other socio-economic issues, especially those to do with sumptuary legislation, crop up in no fewer than 10 of the 31 chapters of the work. The very first of these (chapter 8, on the redistribution of land itself) illustrates the way in which Plutarch combines material from diverse sources into a mixture which is all his own. It begins with a description of pre-Lykourgan Sparta as marked by inequality and the indigence of the masses, a depiction which has clearly been transferred from the account of conditions in the mid-third century as taken from Phylarchos (Plut. *Agis* 5.4). Lykourgos' intentions to end these conditions are then described in phrases modelled on a speech which Plutarch elsewhere ascribes to Kleomenes III (*Kleom.* 10.4). However, his account of the purpose of the redistribution, (that the citizens should 'live with one another on a basis of entire uniformity and equality in the means of subsistence, seeking pre-eminence through virtue alone…'), appears to be Plutarch's own. As Cozzoli (1978) has noted, the dual principles of equality (*isotēs*) and virtue (*aretē*) are for Plutarch the two constituent principles of the Lykourgan *politeia* which he stresses throughout the work. There follows an account of the redistribution in which the figures for the number of lots are based, as we saw earlier, on those distributed by Kings Agis and Kleomenes. Accompanying this are details of the amounts of produce supposedly produced by each lot which, if they have any historicity, also relate to the third-century revolution. The chapter ends, however, with an apophthegm deriving from a different source, one of the Lykourgan sayings among the *Apophthegmata Lakōnika* (no. 2). Although this stems from a source influenced by the revolution, it contains one element which diverges from the description of Lykourgos' land measures in the *Life of Agis* (5.1). On seeing the stacks of grain at harvest standing parallel and equal to one another, the lawgiver is reported as saying that all Lakonikē looked as if many brothers had recently divided it. Unless this statement was intended as irony by its originator, its reference to the standard Greek practice of partible inheritance squares awkwardly with the revolutionaries' conception of inheritance under the Lykourgan system, under which each lot was inherited by only a single son.

Chapter 9 draws heavily upon another Lykourgan apophthegm (no. 3) concerning the lawgiver's failed attempt to equalise movable property, his introduction of an iron currency and exclusion of unnecessary crafts; but there are significant alterations. First, Plutarch omits the apophthegm's reference to the abolition of debts: that supposed measure plays no part in his account. Secondly, after the statement concerning the introduction of the new currency, he inserts some remarks on its high weight in relation to its value which are closely based, though with minor modifications, on Xenophon's *Polity of the Lakedaimonians* (5.5). In doing so, he reorganises the order of presentation in the Lykourgan apophthegm, for (as we have seen) the latter had included a precise statement on the relationship of weight to value, placed not here but at the very end of the apophthegm. Plutarch's preference for the Xenophontic material is probably for reasons of dramatic presentation, for Xenophon's exclamation that even 10 minas would fill a huge space and require a wagon for transport provided a more vivid image than the apophthegm's dry arithmetical details. He returns briefly to the apophthegm, recapitulating with some alterations and turning into a rhetorical question its remarks about the impossibility of theft, bribery or fraud. But he then adds an assertion, new to us, regarding treatment of the iron currency with vinegar to render it useless for other purposes. Thirdly, he now moves on to the banishment of unnecessary and superfluous arts and crafts (*technai*). On this subject the comments in the Lykourgan apophthegm were relatively brief. Plutarch reorders, modifies and expands those comments into a more elegant presentation. He adds, in particular, the claim (which prepares the ground for an important assertion in the following chapter) that 'luxury…died away of itself, and men of large possessions had no advantage over the poor because their wealth found no public outlet, but had to be stored up at home in idleness'. He also adds comments regarding the excellence of Spartan functional household items, including a reference explicitly derived from Kritias (fr. 34) to the Lakonian *kōthōn*.

Chapter 10, on the introduction of the common messes, opens by repeating the purpose for this measure given in Lykourgan apophthegm no. 4, to attack luxury and remove the pursuit of wealth; but the rest of the apophthegm, with its claim of equality of all household possessions, is then ignored. Instead, Plutarch comments rhetorically upon the beneficial moral consequences of the messes. Then, after citing Theophrastos' comment that wealth was 'an object of no desire', he develops the point about the blindness of wealth which we have already seen in apophthegm no. 5. However, whereas the apophthegm merely asserts that wealth is blind and only implicitly indicates that it is blind because it is useless, Plutarch goes so far as to call wealth 'unwealth' (*plouton…aplouton*) and makes the link between its blindness and its uselessness explicit:

> For the rich man could neither use nor enjoy nor even see or display his abundant means, when he went to the same meal as the poor man; so that it was in Sparta alone, of all the cities under the sun, that men could have that far-famed sight, a Ploutos blind and lying as lifeless and motionless as a picture.

As I have noted elsewhere (Hodkinson 1994, 183), this statement, coming at the culmination of his description of Lykourgos' economic and sumptuary measures, encapsulates Plutarch's vision of the role of wealth throughout Spartiate life. The chapter then ends with a reaffirmation of the point in the context of the messes, obtained by extracting the first half of yet another Lykourgan apophthegm (no. 6), which stated that the rich man could not even dine beforehand at home since he would be reviled for not eating the food in the mess.

Plutarch returns to the messes in chapter 12 after a digression in chapter 11 on the opposition to Lykourgos' reforms. Although parts of it stray somewhat beyond our subject, the chapter provides an especially good example of the diversity of sources – good and bad – upon which he drew and of the way he combines, and sometimes modifies them, within a framework which is all his own. He commences with a discussion in the present tense of the Spartans' current name for the messes in his own day (cf. Kennell 1995, 24, with 178 n. 123). He then reverts to the past tense with details of the compulsory mess contributions which clearly relate to the classical messes, since they concur with similar details given by Dikaiarchos (fr. 72 Wehrli, *ap.* Athen. 141a–c). Dikaiarchos, however, cannot have been the source of Plutarch's information, since (as we shall see in ch. 6) Dikaiarchos has translated the contributions into Attic measures, whereas Plutarch gives them in the authentic Lakonian measures. The most plausible hypothesis is that Plutarch's information here comes directly from the Aristotelian *Polity of the Lakedaimonians*. There then follow certain details about extra contributions to the mess from sacrifices and hunting. Although hunting as a source of foodstuffs is mentioned in earlier sources (Xen. *Lak. Pol.* 5.3; Sphairos, *ap.* Athen. 141d), the material relating to sacrifices is new to us, as also is the information that delays caused by either activity constituted the only valid excuse for non-attendance at the mess.

At this point Plutarch introduces a story about King Agis (presumably II) taken from the second half of Lykourgan apophthegm no. 6, the first half of which he had used in chapter 10. Note, however, how he manipulates the form of the story. In the apophthegm the story is introduced as an illustration of the rule that a fine was laid upon anyone who failed to consume his mess rations because he had already dined at home. Agis refuses to attend the mess on return from a long campaign and demands that his allowance of food be sent to his home. The polemarchs refuse to send it and, when the episode is disclosed on the following day to the ephors, they fine Agis. In the *Lykourgos* Plutarch introduces the story, as we have seen, in the slightly different context, not of failure to eat at the mess, but of compulsory attendance. His version of the story follows the apophthegm up to the point of the polemarchs' refusal; but then it is only when Agis on the following day omits in his anger the customary sacrifice that the ephors impose a fine. Plutarch has clearly altered the version in the apophthegm to meet the different context in which he uses the story.

Part of the reason may be that in the apophthegm the story does not actually match its supposed context, since Agis had not gone to the mess too full to eat his rations: he was willing to eat them, but wanted to do so at home. Plutarch is known in his other biographies to alter key elements in earlier versions of episodes when they seemed not to make proper sense.[51] His version of the Agis story is modified to match its context exactly, since the polemarchs' refusal to send Agis' mess ration affirms the fact that he has broken the rules concerning attendance; and the ephors' fine is punishment for his unjustified protest at the polemarchs' decision. Furthermore, unlike the version in the apophthegm, Plutarch does not introduce his story as an illustration of the circumstances in which a fine was imposed – he does not claim that non-attendance at the mess incurred a fine; hence the ephors' fine, quite logically, is imposed only in response to Agis' subsequent offence.

The remainder of chapter 12 continues with comments regarding the socializing aspects of the mess for boys which are loosely derived from Xenophon (*Lak. Pol.* 5.5), but with a moralizing emphasis upon characteristics such as *sōphrosynē* (self-control, moderation) and freedom which are absent from the original.[52] Plutarch then inserts – somewhat unconnectedly with what precedes or follows it – the contents of the first entry of the *Instituta Laconica* regarding secrecy within the messes. He then provides a substantial and detailed account from an unknown, but authoritative-sounding, source of the procedures for electing new members. Then, again rather unconnectedly, he turns back to the contents of the meal; or, rather, not to the standard foodstuffs mentioned earlier in the chapter, but to the (in)famous black broth. His account here is based upon entry no. 2 of the *Instituta*, which recounts how a foreign ruler purchased a Spartan cook but, on expressing his disgust at the broth's taste, was told that to enjoy it one needed first to have exercised in the Lakonian manner and bathed in the River Eurotas. Again, however, though the substance is the same, Plutarch introduces minor modifications, dropping the reference to exercise and changing the ruler's identity from Dionysios of Syracuse – who also appears in Cicero's account of the anecdote (*Tusculan Disputations* 5.34.98) – to an unnamed king of Pontos. The emphasis upon austerity of eating in this entry, which claims that the older men ate nothing but the broth, is then developed as Plutarch concludes the chapter by repeating *Instituta* no. 3, which refers to the Spartiates' moderate drinking and walking (home) at night without a torch.

Other references to property issues in the *Lykourgos* are drawn from a similar hotchpotch of sources. In chapter 13 Plutarch's comments on domestic simplicity commence with the opening part of the Lykourgan apophthegm no. 9 on the restriction to use of axe and saw, but omit its actual saying in favour of rhetorical comments on the role of simple domestic architecture in precluding extravagant interior possessions – comments derived from a similar apophthegm in his *Sayings of Kings and Commanders* (*Apophthegmata Basileōn kai Stratēgōn*,

Lykourgos 3 = Plut. *Mor.* 189e). The section then concludes with another Lykourgan apophthegm (no. 10), the one citing King Leotychidas' criticism of squared interior woodwork, which, as we saw earlier, goes back to the pre-revolutionary, non-Lykourgan *Apophthegmata Lakōnika* (210e = *Agesilaos* 27). In chapter 16, as I shall argue later (ch. 3, below), his reference to an infant boy's being assigned one of the 9,000 lots of land is attached as extraneous addition to a description of the elders' physical scrutiny of infant boys stemming from an unknown but credible and sober source. In chapter 19, in contrast, Plutarch repeats, with little change, two Lykourgan apophthegms (nos. 22 and 27) concerning the inexpensive nature of sacrifices and the value of poverty for warding off enemy invasions.

The blending of sources in chapter 24, which treats the character of the Spartiates' daily lives, is especially complex. The chapter opens with general remarks on the continuance of their civic duties into adulthood which are loosely reminiscent of Xenophon's message in his *Polity of the Lakedaimonians*. There also appears the analogy of Spartan society as a military camp found in Isokrates (6.81) and Plato (*Laws* 666e). Plutarch then borrows almost word for word the contents of *Instituta Laconica* no. 41 concerning the Spartiates' life of leisure and their prohibition from banausic and money-making activities. He also quotes most of the first sentence of the *Instituta*'s comments (quoted above) on the fixed rent (*apophora*) paid by the helots, but towards its end makes a crucial change in the words qualifying the *apophora* itself. The *Instituta*'s 'rent which was settled from the start (ἀποφορὰν τὴν ἄνωθεν ἰσταμένην/ἑσταμένην)' is altered to read 'rent mentioned above (ἀποφορὰν τὴν εἰρημένην)', thus linking the *apophora*, in a way that the *Instituta* does not, to the quantities of produce from each land lot detailed in chapter 8. He then omits, as irrelevant to his present concern, the remainder of the *Instituta*'s entry regarding the Spartiate-helot 'contract of servitude'. Subsequently, he introduces an apophthegm not attested elsewhere contrasting the Spartan life of leisure with a fine for idleness supposedly levied on an Athenian. From this apophthegm Plutarch draws his own conclusions, again loosely based on Xenophon and Polybius, concerning the Spartans' disdain for crafts and money-making. The chapter then concludes with further comments from Plutarch himself regarding the lack of lawsuits in the absence of coinage, the Spartiates' 'equality in well-being' (an idea surely influenced by the third-century revolution) and their simple needs and wholesome social activities.

It will be evident from the foregoing account that, although the *Lykourgos* takes the form of a biography of its founding lawgiver, the work often deviates into an account of the supposed social and political practices of historical Spartan society. For Plutarch, the measures introduced by Lykourgos constituted the essential laws and customs under which the historical Spartiates lived, with only minor modifications, down to the end of the fifth century BC, as he himself emphasizes in chapter 29. Chapter 30, however, is devoted to the breakdown of Lykourgos' *politeia*. Following Ephorus, he ascribes the primary role to the influx of gold and silver currency, and with it greed and a desire for wealth, which filled Sparta with a love of riches and luxury. This picture is effectively an abridged version of his longer disquisition on the effects of the influx of foreign currency which we have already viewed in the *Life of Lysander*, ch. 17. It constitutes the basis upon which, in the *Life of Agis*, he added the corrupting impact of the law of Epitadeus concerning gift and bequest of land. For Plutarch, problems of wealth are as central to the decline of the Spartan *politeia* as Lykourgos' provisions regarding property were to its successful establishment.

The magnitude of Plutarch's personal contribution to the prevailing image of property arrangements in classical Sparta will be apparent from the preceding survey. Throughout the *Lykourgos* we can detect him drawing upon a variety of sources from all periods of antiquity to create a coherent picture of a lawgiver whose social institutions systematically minimized the role of private property and both prohibited and disdained any kind of display or use of wealth. It is this coherence which has no doubt given his picture such a powerful hold over modern views.

Recent work on Plutarch's methods in his *Lives*, whilst not denying his predominantly biographical and moral rather than strictly historical perspective, has done much to establish his credibility as an intelligent and critical interpreter of the Graeco-Roman past.[53] The coherence of his interpretation of Lykourgan Sparta is strong testimony to the merits of this approach. Yet behind this apparent coherence, as we have seen, is a mass of disparate material produced by writers from various periods who held widely differing views of the role of property and wealth within Spartan society. Plutarch himself admits awareness of this point at the very start of the work in his comment that 'Concerning Lykourgos the lawgiver in general nothing can be said which is undisputed, since there are different accounts of his birth, his travels, his death and, above all, of matters regarding his laws and the *politeia*' (1.1). As in his other *Lives* (Pelling 1990), Plutarch is by no means uncommitted to seeking some form of truth from this mass of controversy. Indeed, he announces his attempt to apply some plausible criteria of reliability by following in his narrative 'those authors who are least contradicted, or who have the most notable witnesses for what they have written about the man' (1.3). This procedure, however, does not prevent him from utilizing as sources several writers whose historical perspectives and interest in historical authenticity were strictly limited. Indeed, the first of his stated criteria – to give priority to those authors least contradicted – was bound to induce him to follow the dominant political and philosophical interpretations which had developed during the hellenistic period and to utilize earlier, more contemporary sources only in so far as they agreed with these later images. Hence he relies primarily upon writings which he must have known were produced long after Lykourgos' measures, on his own account, ceased to be in force. As Pelling has noted, such imperfect critical rigour regarding his source material is a common feature of his lives of figures 'who had become enveloped in the sort of tradition which made it difficult to write a more "historical" biography' (1990, 30). Certainly, despite his references to variant versions of the lawgiver's dating and descent in the *proemium* to the work (1.1–4), the main body of *Lykourgos* contains almost no discussion of the huge differences among his sources regarding the content of his reforms and the resulting character of Spartan society.[54] Instead, Plutarch navigates his own personal route through the maze, tacitly reordering and reworking the core of earlier material within a matrix of his own devising.

We have seen that the image of Sparta as a state with a distinctive property system and radically different attitudes to wealth is largely absent from the earliest classical sources. It began to develop at the end of the fifth century under the combined influences of upper-class disenchantment with democratic Athens, the polarization effected by the Peloponnesian war and the upsurge of philosophic enquiry into the nature of the ideal society. It was further stimulated in the fourth century by Sparta's internal crisis and international decline, along with the leakage of 'information' about the laws of Lykourgos in the pamphlet of Pausanias. Moralizing explanations of these events, especially in the influential work of Ephorus, contrasted a corrupt contemporary Sparta with an idealized past society whose success had been founded upon the suppression of certain types of private property ownership for the good of the polis. Plato and Aristotle attempted to debunk such interpretations, portraying Sparta's property arrangements as both similar to those of other Greek states and fundamentally flawed from the start; but the powerful attraction of the mirage of a pure and pristine society, unsullied until comparatively late by the claims of Mammon, proved irresistible. With the decline of Sparta's political importance, images of her past society took on a more purely moral conception, impregnated with the ideas of hellenistic philosophy, which gave birth to notions of an austere Spartiate lifestyle in which material possessions were held in disdain. The propagandists of the third-century revolution developed these ideas still further, transforming them with their concept of a thoroughly egalitarian society. Finally, this mass of competing images was transformed by Plutarch into a coherent amalgam made up from a combination of fourth-century moralizing, early hellenistic moral philosophy and revolutionary egalitarian propaganda. In this way the Spartiates were transformed in ancient thought into something akin to the Noble Savages of early antiquity, the archetypal Others whose virtues of disdain for material possessions and restraint from expenditure on luxuries were admirable but inimitable within the context of contemporary civilized society. The task of the remainder of this volume will be to confront and challenge such images by examining the reality of the classical Spartan property system which they have done so much to obscure.

Ch. 2. The growth of the dominant egalitarian image in ancient thought

Notes

¹ For an earlier version of this chapter, restricted to classical writers, Hodkinson 1994. For a similar enterprise, focused on Spartiate land tenure, Ducat 1983.

² Hdt. 5.51; 6.50, 66, 72, 82; those involving other Spartiates are 3.56, 148; 8.5.

³ Frs. 6, 7, 33, 34, Diels-Kranz; translations in Sprague (ed.) 1972, 251–2, 262.

⁴ I accept the standard attribution of the work to Xenophon (cf. Momigliano 1936), which has been reaffirmed by the most recent studies (Humble 1997, 39–40, 257–9; Rebenich (ed.) 1998, 14–15).

⁵ Note also that in his description of the invasion of Lakonia in the *Hellenika* (6.5.27) Xenophon notes that the Spartiates' plundered houses were full of many valuable things.

⁶ The main recent challenges to the standard view have come from Christopher Tuplin's works on the *Hellenika* and *Cyropaedia* (1993; 1994) and Noreen Humble's re-examination of the *Anabasis, Hellenika* and *Polity of the Lakedaimonians* (1997; 1999).

⁷ The fact that Polybius, Book 6, which is often thought to draw upon Ephorus does not mention the notion is no obstacle to this view since, as Lévy (1987, 64–71) has demonstrated, Polybius here makes no allusion at all to the corruption of Spartan institutions. For doubts about Polybius' dependence upon Ephorus, see further below.

⁸ Alessandrì 1985, 1081–9. The accounts in question are Poseidonios, *FGrH* 87F48c = fr. 240.24–7 Edelstein and Kidd, *ap.* Athenaios 233f–234a; Diod. 13.106.7–10; Plut. *Lys.* 16; *Per.* 22; *Nik.* 28.

⁹ David 1979a, with references to earlier scholarship.

¹⁰ Plato, *Laws* 691d–692a; Arist. *Pol.* 1313a26–33; cf. Tigerstedt 1965–78, i.110–11; Oliva 1971, 123–5; David 1979a.

¹¹ As van Wees has argued (1999, 3–4), this warning was probably originally a snatch of archaic poetry which the singer gave not in his own voice but as if from an oracle.

¹² Cozzoli (1979, 18–21) also accepts this attribution, but believes that Polybius has misrepresented Ephorus.

¹³ According to Xenophon, Spartan institutions were unique; and he says nothing of any Cretan origin or connection (*Lak. Pol.* 1.2; cf. 8.5).

¹⁴ Polybius' second distinctive feature bears some resemblance to Xenophon's view in *Lak. Pol.* 7; but Xenophon never claimed that wealth was entirely eliminated. Moreover, the third feature – the dominance of the kings and *gerontes* – contradicts Xenophon's emphasis upon the tyrannical power of the ephors (*Lak. Pol.* 8.3–4).

¹⁵ Admittedly, one might equally view this feature as in line with the views of Ephorus, since the non-Lykourgan origin of the ephorate probably goes back to King Pausanias.

¹⁶ This section (550d–551b) should be distinguished sharply from the subsequent section (555b ff.) concerning the decline of oligarchy. Despite the fact that this latter section came, as we shall see, to influence third-century portrayals of the Spartan crisis, Plato himself did not intend it as such (Schütrumpf 1987, 451–2).

¹⁷ *Contra* Morrow 1960, 107–8. The equal distribution to which Plato refers at 684e–685a applies to the period of the original Dorian conquest of Argos, Lakonia and Messenia and has no bearing on historical Sparta. MacDowell (1986, 89) claims that when Plato says that Argos and Messene later destroyed their *politeia* and laws with only Sparta remaining steadfast, 'this appears to imply that equality of landholdings in Sparta still obtained in Plato's time'; but Plato's phraseology gives no indication of how long he thought it persisted.

¹⁸ In the case of the corruptibility of the ephors, Aristotle explicitly states that it had

occurred frequently in earlier times (πρότερον); cf. Schütrumpf 1994, 345 n. 53.

[19] Suda, s.v. Dikaiarchos = fr. 1 Wehrli. The date of the original source of this information is unknown. Tigerstedt (1965–78, i.586 n.651) suggests that it pertains to the archaizing Sparta of the Roman Imperial period rather than to the decadent Sparta of Dikaiarchos' own time, as Chrimes (1949, 7) has proposed. It is not so certain that early hellenistic Sparta was so uniformly neglectful of its traditional *politeia* as Tigerstedt supposes; but, even if his argument is correct, it still marks the work out as eulogizing in character.

[20] Fr. 142 Wehrli = Fortenbaugh et al. 1992, frs. 512A, 605; *ap.* Plut. *Ages.* 36.6.

[21] My own previous work is often insensitive to the diverse layers of post-classical evidence within the Plutarchean corpus discussed below.

[22] Preceding the *Apophthegmata Lakōnika* is another collection of apophthegms, the *Apophthegmata Basileōn kai Stratēgōn*, 'Sayings of Kings and Commanders' (*Mor.* 172a–194e), which includes sayings by Spartan kings and generals, most of them identical to the Lakonian apophthegms. Tigerstedt (1965–78, ii.298–9 n. 4) lists a number of other ancient collections of gnomic sayings which include apophthegms relating to Sparta; but they lack satisfactory modern critical editions. For the purposes of this historiographical survey, I shall focus on the material in the *Moralia*, since it is most directly relevant to my consideration below of Plutarch's *Lives*.

[23] See esp. the table of parallels in Nachstädt et al. 1935, 166–7; cf. also Ziegler 1951, 273; Fuhrmann 1988, 132–3.

[24] References to this early scholarship in Fuhrmann 1988, 134 n. 2; Santaniello 1995, 10 n. 5.

[25] Examples in Nachstädt et al. 1935, 208 (critical apparatus); Fuhrmann 1988, 136 n. 2; cf. Ziegler 1951, 866.

[26] Nachstädt 1935; Ziegler 1951, 866; Fuhrmann 1988, 133–5; Santaniello 1995, 13–19; del Corno 1996, 33–5.

[27] For references to the controversy, Tigerstedt 1965–78, ii.230–1, with bibliography at 509–11, nn. 783–9.

[28] Fuhrmann 1988, 137, with detailed notes ad loc.

[29] *Rhetoric* 1394b33; cf. del Corno 1996, 30–2.

[30] For scholarly disagreement concerning which philosopher merits being accorded the priority in this field, see the refs. in Tigerstedt 1965–78, ii.303 n. 103.

[31] I say 'most of them' because Plutarch's collection also includes some epigrams which, being the literary work of poets, are not properly apophthegms. Many of them date from the later third century, but their subject matter is typically based on apophthegms which were in circulation before the mid-third century (Tigerstedt 1965–78, ii.27).

[32] This sense is absent even from the single apophthegm concerning Agis IV (*Mor.* 216d), which relates purely to his noble acceptance of death.

[33] A final piece of evidence for Plutarch's use of a collection is the fact that among the *Lakainōn Apophthegmata* the alphabetically-arranged sayings ascribed to named individual women terminate abruptly at the letter Delta. Although the sayings of these named women do not come quite at the very end of the *apophthegmata* (they are followed by the sayings of unnamed women), this termination is surely related to the fact that the overall number of passages is limited to 500. The restriction of the named women to the letters Alpha to Delta surely indicates use of a collection up to the prescribed limit, since had Plutarch drawn the female apophthegms from his own diverse reading they would surely

Ch. 2. The growth of the dominant egalitarian image in ancient thought

have been spread around the alphabet.

34 The foodstuffs rejected are said to comprise geese, sweetmeats, honey-cakes, other foods and drinks. The reference to geese suggests that the version in the *Apophthegmata* was influenced by the similar account, also in Theopompos (F106–8), of Agesilaos' similar response to foodstuffs offered to him on his arrival in Egypt. Even here, however, there seems to have been some adaptation of Theopompos' text, for in both the version recorded by Plutarch (*Ages*. 36.6) and that by Nepos (*Ages*. 8) the king accepts a variety of foods: *alphita*, cattle and geese, according to Plutarch; veal, bread and fish, according to Nepos.

35 Cf. also the similar version in the *Apophthegmata Basileōn kai Stratēgōn* 189f (*Charillos* 3). Note, however, that at 189e (*Lykourgos* 1) the same work also includes a different non-material development of Xenophon's explanation, that long hair makes handsome men more comely and ugly men more frightful. This version appears also among the Lykourgan sayings in the *Apophthegmata Lakōnika* (228f = *Lykourgos* 29) and is repeated in Plut. *Lyk*. 22.1.

36 The antithesis between *epithymia* and *logismos* is drawn by Aristotle (*EN* 1119b5–10).

37 Cf. also the eschewal of *kerdos* ('gain') at 216e (*Alkamenes* 1) and the attribution of a similar saying to Thales in Plutarch's *Dinner of the Seven Wise Men* (*Mor*. 154e).

38 Tigerstedt 1965–78, ii.13–48. Cf., most recently, Santaniello 1995, 21–6, who suggests a primary influence of Cynic ideas, amidst diverse other influences.

39 On other independent attestations of the revolutionaries' programme, see Fuks 1962a.

40 Plut. *Agis* 8.1; *Kleomenes* 11.1–2; 23.1; 28.5; for more detailed discussion, Marasco 1978a; Hodkinson 1986, 382; and ch. 3 below.

41 For further discussion, ch. 3 below. For the purposes of my discussion, the question of precisely who invented the account of Epitadeus – Phylarchos, Sphairos or another writer – is immaterial.

42 At 5.1 and 9.3 it is used to describe the essential character of the laws of Lykourgos; at 6.1 and 7.2 it is announced as Agis' own aim. Cf. also *Kleom*. 18.2, where the king is said to be imitating Lykourgos (and Solon) in his equalisation of landed property.

43 Further support for this separation comes from the fact that very few sayings attributed to Lykourgos appear among the other, non-Plutarchean collections of apophthegms (Tigerstedt 1965–78, ii.361 n. 321).

44 Apophthegms without sayings: nos. 3, 6, 7, 18, 19.

45 The claim, admittedly, appears earlier in [Plato] *Alk. II* 149a; but there it appears as a comparison with expensive Athenian practice and seems to relate to public sacrifices. The claim also appears in a more worked-up, non-apophthegmatic form in the dedicatory preamble to Plutarch's *Apophthegmata Basileōn kai Stratēgōn* (172c) and also in his *Commentary on Hesiod's Works and Days*, fr. 47. For the argument that the *Apophthegmata Basileōn kai Stratēgōn*, often regarded as spurious, contains Plutarch's personal reworking of apophthegms collected during the course of his researches, Fuhrmann 1988, 3–9.

46 He does not consider the argument that the disorder might also be due to Plutarch's reorganisation of the excerpts according to his planned order of composition (Gomme 1945–81, i.78, n. 1; Tigerstedt 1965–78, ii.233). This hypothesis is suggested by the fact that the passages throughout the *Apophthegmata* and *Instituta* appear largely in the same order as in the lives in which they are used. Although slightly more than half of the passages in the *Instituta*, and especially those in the second half, do not appear in

the *Life of Lykourgos*, their current order may still reflect Plutarch's intentions at an early stage of planning the *Life*.

⁴⁷ Xenophon's *Lak. Pol.* lies, either wholly or in part, behind *Instituta* nos. 3, 7, 10, 11, 12, 13, 19, 20, 23, 24, 41; the Aristotelian *Lak. Pol.* behind nos. 12, 13, 18, 19.

⁴⁸ It is possible that a fixed helot rent was actually introduced along with the equal *klēroi* introduced by Kleomenes III (Cartledge and Spawforth 1989, 52). The idea of a 'contract of servitude', though not necessarily of a fixed rent – the word used is not *apophora* but *moira*, which may indicate a proportional rent – appears also in a fragment of Myron of Priene (*FGrH* 106F2, *ap.* Athen. 657d). Myron's date, however, is uncertain. He is normally dated by reference to his fr. 6 (*ap.* Rutilius Lupus, *De Fig.* 1.20, who quotes him to illustrate points of rhetoric), in which he appears to mention his friendship with a certain 'Cremonides', probably the prominent Athenian politician Chremonides (*floruit c.* 270–240). Pearson (1962, 411) notes, however, that it does not necessarily follow that the two men were contemporaries, since the passage may be a purely academic oration or an illustration in a rhetorical handbook. Myron could have lived at any time in the late third or second century, since the only certain *terminus ante quem* appears to be the citation of a Myron in the Lindos temple chronicle of 99 BC (fr. 4–5); even this depends upon the (plausible) assumption that the two Myrons are the same man.

⁴⁹ Cartledge and Spawforth 1989, 200; see their ch. 14 on the 'image of tradition' in imperial Sparta, especially on the Persian wars and the *agōgē*. For in-depth analyses of these two subjects, see now Spawforth 1994; Kennell 1995.

⁵⁰ The classic recent study of Plutarch's use of his sources is Pelling 1980 (see also the convenient digest in Pelling 1988, 33–6); but similar ideas, specifically directed at the Spartan lives, are already expressed in Tigerstedt 1965, ii.232–3.

⁵¹ Cf. D.R. Shipley 1997, 79–95, on his alteration of Xenophon's account of the accession of Agesilaos II due to its apparent weaknesses.

⁵² On Xenophon's deliberate omission of *sōphrosynē* as a virtue characteristic of Sparta, Humble 1999.

⁵³ e.g. Pelling 1980; 1988; 1990; D.R. Shipley 1997, 2–9.

⁵⁴ The one partial exception is in his discussion of the *krypteia* (ch. 28) where he expresses his reluctance to follow Aristotle in ascribing the institution to Lykourgos. Even this, however, is not a question of balancing one source against another, since he cites no earlier writer for what seems to be a purely personal judgement that the harshness of the *krypteia* was incompatible with Lykourgos' mildness and justice.

PART II

THE ANATOMY OF THE SPARTIATE PROPERTY SYSTEM

Chapter 3

THE OWNERSHIP AND INHERITANCE OF LAND – REVISITED

Part I of this volume considered ancient and modern perceptions of the role of property and wealth in Spartiate society. Part II (chapters 3–6) will move beyond those perceptions to study the reality which they have often obscured. This chapter will commence with the most fundamental form of property – land.

The problem of Spartiate land tenure

As we saw in chapter 2, from the third century BC onwards there developed the idea that landed property had been divided equally among Spartan citizens by the laws of Lykourgos and that this equality had survived until the period after the Peloponnesian war, sometime in the early fourth century. Thanks to Plutarch this idea became the dominant image of Spartiate land-ownership conveyed by antiquity to the modern world. As we also saw, however, even in the earliest sources in which the idea of landed equality appears, the period during which this equality is said to have existed is always in the past. No writer ever claims that such equality existed in his own day. In particular, the historical sources from the classical period, during which landed equality supposedly existed, attest the presence of considerable differences of wealth among Spartan citizens.

Consequently, it is no surprise that among modern scholarship the question of the character of Spartiate land tenure has been, in the words of Frank Walbank (1957, 728), 'one of the most vexed in the obscure field of Spartan institutions'. Academic controversy surrounding this subject, which goes back to the early nineteenth century, reached fever pitch in the late 1970s and early 1980s with the publication of several widely divergent accounts.[1] It was in this context that I published my own original contribution to the debate (Hodkinson 1986), in the hope that 'through the introduction of a new perspective it may be possible to advance our understanding of the subject' (ibid. 378). My argument was that, in contrast to the dominant ancient image of Spartiate land-ownership outlined in chapter 2 – one of inalienable, publicly-controlled, equal landholdings – the system in operation throughout archaic and classical Spartan history was in reality one of unequal, private estates transmitted to one's heirs by partible inheritance, lifetime gift or testamentary bequest. I also argued – both in that article and in a subsequent discussion (Hodkinson 1989) – that Spartiate women possessed considerably greater landholding rights than previously recognised and that female land-ownership was throughout our period a more important feature of Spartan society than had been allowed for in previous accounts.

This new reading of the ancient evidence has been largely accepted by many Spartan specialists, some of whose views were already moving independently in the same direction as my own.[2] Since 1986, moreover, the specialist debate has moved on regarding certain key issues. Since the question of the nature of land tenure forms the foundation for broader interpretations of the overall character of Spartiate property ownership, this chapter will provide a full re-examination of the issues under debate. Although the overall shape of this chapter follows the outline of my earlier study, my discussion has been restructured and updated at many points to take account of more recent views.

In the first part of this chapter I shall review several influential scholarly theories concerning the nature of Spartiate land tenure and inheritance, examining their feasibility and the reliability of the evidence upon which they are based. I shall then begin to construct a more plausible alternative account based upon more trustworthy evidence. Finally, I shall discuss what until recently has been a comparatively under-emphasized aspect of the topic, the property rights of Spartiate women, which suggests, I shall argue, a rather different interpretation of the character of land tenure and inheritance from those more usually adopted.

Some standard views of land tenure and inheritance

Much of the controversy surrounding Spartiate land tenure concerns how far landholdings in the hands of individual citizens were publicly or privately controlled. Every Spartan citizen, we know, held (at least in theory) an estate sufficient to support his family and provide his means of paying the contributions to the common messes necessary for the maintenance of his citizen status. Some citizens held considerably more than that. What private rights did the individual Spartiate have over his landholdings? How did he personally come into their possession? And, beyond that, by what processes had the historical distribution of landholdings among the Spartiate citizen body taken shape?

Until recently at least, the majority opinion has argued in favour of a considerable degree of public control over Spartiate landholdings. This view usually gives prominence to the late evidence of Plutarch, who in his *Life of Lykourgos* (8.3)

Ch. 3. The ownership and inheritance of land – revisited

claims, as we have seen (ch. 2), that the mythical Spartan lawgiver,

> persuaded his fellow citizens to make one parcel of all their territory and divide it up anew, and to live with one another on a basis of entire uniformity and equality in their means of subsistence… Suiting the deed to the word, he distributed the rest of the Lakonian land to the *perioikoi* in thirty thousand lots, and that which belonged to the city of Sparta, in nine thousand lots (*klēroi*), to as many Spartiates. Some say, however, that Lykourgos distributed six thousand and that afterwards Polydoros added three thousand; others, that Polydoros assigned half of the nine thousand and Lykourgos the other half.

Later (16.1) he adds that

> a child was not reared at the will of the father, but was taken and carried by him to a place called *Leschē*, where the elders of the tribes officially examined the infant; and, if it was well-built and sturdy, they ordered the father to rear it, and assigned it one of the nine thousand lots of land.

However, in his biography of King Agis IV, the third-century reforming king, Plutarch gives a somewhat different account when writing of the decline of Sparta in the early fourth century.

> Since, however, the number of households instituted by Lykourgos was still preserved in the transmission of lots (*klēroi*), and father left to son his inheritance, to some extent the continuation of this order and equality sustained the polis in spite of its errors in other respects. But when a certain powerful man, Epitadeus by name, who was headstrong and of a violent temper, came to be ephor, he had a quarrel with his son and introduced a law (*rhētra*) permitting a man during his lifetime to give his household (*oikos*) and lot (*klēros*) to any one he wished, or to bequeath it in his will (5.1–2).

Those scholars who emphasize this Plutarchean evidence differ among themselves concerning the degree of reliance to be placed upon one or other of the above passages. Some, stressing the evidence of *Lykourgos* 16, envisage a Spartiate as being merely the life tenant of his *klēros* which reverted to the state on his death.[3] Others follow *Agis* 5 in arguing that the *klēros* passed down hereditarily from a man to his eldest son. Some of those who hold the latter view (e.g. Ziehen 1933; Asheri 1961; 1963) incorporate the evidence of *Lykourgos* 16 to the extent of postulating a state-controlled reserve of *klēroi* available for distribution to younger sons who did not inherit their fathers' lots. Others (e.g. Busolt and Swoboda 1920–26, ii.633–5; Hooker 1980, 116–18; David 1981, 46–50) dismiss *Lykourgos* 16 and the notion of the state endowing a young Spartiate with a *klēros*, except as an occasional measure when a citizen died heirless or needed to adopt an heir before his death – in which case, according to this hypothesis, a landless younger son could be nominated to succeed. Despite their differences, common to all these views is the belief that the transmission of land on a Spartiate's death was governed by (variously defined) strict state-enforced rules which were designed to ensure that the estate remained undivided and which denied the individual landholder any power of alienating any part of his land, whether by gift, sale or testament.

Those scholars who adopt the view that the *klēros* was transmitted hereditarily to the eldest son but who do not believe in a regular public reserve of land do, it is true, sometimes distinguish two types of land.[4] In doing so, they draw upon two passages found in hellenistic sources. The first passage is an excerpt from the second-century BC writer, Herakleides Lembos (373.12 Dilts), which is thought to derive ultimately from the Aristotelian *Polity of the Lakedaimonians* (fr. 611.12 Rose):

> To sell land is considered shameful by the Lakedaimonians, but from the ancient portion (*archaias moiras*) it is not permitted.

The other passage occurs in the hellenistic *Instituta Laconica* (no. 22 = Plut. *Mor.* 238e) and refers to 'the anciently established portions (*archēthen…moiras*); it was not permitted to sell'. Some scholars (e.g. Pareti 1917, 197–200; David 1981, 46–8) would identify these 'ancient portions' with land in the *politikē chōra* which appears in a passage from the second-century BC historian, Polybius (6.45.1–3). Referring to the constitution of Crete, he remarks

> How could the most learned of the writers of earlier times – Ephorus, Xenophon, Kallisthenes and Plato – claim in the first place that it [sc. the constitution of Crete] was one and the same with that of the Lakedaimonians and, secondly, that it was worthy of admiration? Neither of these assertions seems to me to be true. One can judge from the following. To start with, let us consider its dissimilarity. The distinctive features of the Lakedaimonian *politeia*, they say, are, first, those concerning landed property by which no citizen may own more than another, but all must possess an equal share of the citizen land (*politikē chōra*)…[5]

It is suggested that Polybius' *politikē chōra* is identical with the 'ancient portion' mentioned above and that the firm state controls described earlier applied only to this category of land, which – it is argued – should be identified with the *klēroi* allotted in the Lykourgan redistribution. In addition to these state-controlled equal *klēroi*, it is maintained, many Spartiates held varying amounts of other landholdings which were less subject to state interference. According to proponents of this view, the landed inequality attested by contemporary historical writers can thus be squared with the evidence of Plutarch that the most fundamental category of land was owned equally and subjected to strict regulation.

Critique of the standard views
The lateness of their sources
The above views can be criticized on a variety of counts. One general weakness is the reliance placed upon the evidence of later writers like Polybius and Plutarch at the expense of alternative earlier accounts, particularly that of Aristotle's *Politics*, consideration of which is often relegated to the tail-end of modern

Ch. 3. The ownership and inheritance of land – revisited

discussions.[6] A related problem is that the sources of information upon which these later writers drew are not such as to inspire confidence. This point can be seen most clearly if we trace the sources of the three main elements of Spartiate land tenure in these late accounts: first, the ascription of an equal redistribution of *klēroi* to Lykourgos (sometimes also to King Polydoros), which is common to all accounts;[7] secondly, the claim that this equality was maintained into classical times, explicitly stated in Plutarch's *Agis* and implicit in the *Lykourgos* and in Polybius; and, thirdly, the description of a system of land tenure and inheritance supposedly responsible for the maintenance of this equality.

The first element, the idea of an equal redistribution of *klēroi* by Lykourgos, is clearly the basis upon which the other elements rest. Yet, as we saw in chapter 2, the evidence suggests that it did not originate until a comparatively late period. There is no sign of it in fifth-century writers. It was not known to Hellanikos, who attributed the whole Spartan polity not to Lykourgos but to Kings Eurysthenes and Prokles (fr. 91, *ap.* Strabo 8.5.5, 366c); nor is it mentioned in Herodotus' account of Lykourgos' reforms (1.65–6). In the fourth century, it is absent from Xenophon's *Polity of the Lakedaimonians*, which claimed instead that Lykourgos' measures were designed to ensure that the poor were not in want and the rich not able to employ their wealth (6.4–7.6). Plato (*Laws* 648d) and Isokrates (*Archidamos* 20) wrote of an equal distribution of land in a much earlier era after the original Dorian conquest of Lakonia, but never hinted at any later similar measure.[8] Indeed, Isokrates (*Panathenaikos* 259) denied that there had been any subsequent redistribution in Spartan history. Aristotle not only does not mention the idea in his discussion of Spartan society, but states (*Pol.* 1266a39–40) that Phaleas of Chalkedon was the first to propose equality of landholding, thereby excluding the idea of a Lykourgan redistribution at Sparta.

It is not until Polybius (6.45) in the second century BC (in the passage quoted above) that the idea of equality of landholdings first appears in our surviving sources. Polybius may also have believed that this equality survived into the classical period, to judge from the fact that it is mentioned immediately before such longstanding elements of Spartiate life as denigration of money-making and the offices of kings and *gerontes*. As we have already seen in our earlier study of that passage (ch. 2), it is far from clear that Polybius intended – as many scholars, including myself, have previously suggested – to ascribe the idea of landed equality to the four authors whom he mentions earlier in the passage: Ephorus, Xenophon, Kallisthenes and Plato. The likelihood is rather that he was reflecting the propaganda of the late third-century revolution. But, even if Polybius did so intend, it is clear in the case of Xenophon and Plato that he was misrepresenting their views. Only in the case of Ephorus is there any possibility that he was the source of Polybius' comments on landed equality, and even in this case we cannot rule out, as Cozzoli (1979, 18–21) has argued, that Polybius has been guilty of misinterpretation. This would not be the only occasion when he ascribes to a classical writer a view which did not originate until hellenistic times.⁹ Whichever view one takes of the source of Polybius' account, the passage cannot be used as evidence that several classical writers believed in an authentic equality of land.

Just as the views of Polybius probably derive from the late third-century revolution, so do the details of the alleged Lykourgan reform given in Plutarch, *Lykourgos* 8. The work of Gabriele Marasco (1978a; 1979; 1981, i.248–50; ii.584–5; cf. Manfredini and Piccirilli 1980, 246–9) has shown that none of the three versions which Plutarch cites concerning the precise number of lots antedates the third century BC. The supposed Lykourgan distributions of 4,500 and 6,000 lots reflect the attempts of propagandists of the late-third-century Spartan revolution to justify, respectively, the numbers involved in the projected reform of King Agis IV and the size of the citizen body finally achieved by King Kleomenes III (Plut. *Kleom.* 11.2, 23.1, 28.8). The inventors of both versions also added a subsequent Polydoran distribution to bring the figures into approximate relationship with the 8,000 and 10,000 Spartiates mentioned by Herodotus (7.234) and Aristotle (*Politics* 1270a36–8).¹⁰ Finally, it seems from Plutarch's wording that his account of the different versions came from a single source, possibly the late third-century writer Hermippos of Smyrna, who, noting the agreement on the total figure of 9,000 *klēroi*, simplified matters by ascribing them all to Lykourgos.¹¹ He probably also doubled the number of 15,000 perioikic *klēroi* projected by Agis IV, in order to bring them into apparent agreement with the 30,000 potential hoplite population referred to by Aristotle (*Politics* 1270a29–30).

Plutarch's two separate descriptions of a system of tenure and inheritance supposedly responsible for the maintenance of landed equality, are similarly the products of late invention. It has been argued that, since his description in *Lykourgos* 16 of the procedure by which an infant Spartiate was assigned a *klēros* on passing his examination by the elders appears in a different context from the account of the Lykourgan and Polydoran redistributions in chapter 8 of the same work, it may derive from a different – and earlier – source from the third-century ones behind the latter account (Cozzoli 1979, 23). Since Plutarch's description of this procedure implicitly assumes the maintenance of landed equality, this might be thought to suggest a late classical origin for the idea. Indeed, it has been suggested independently that much of Plutarch's information in the *Lykourgos* may derive from the early Peripatetic writers of the late fourth and early third centuries (Tigerstedt 1965–78, i.304–6; Aalders 1982, 64). Although it is not impossible that a Peripatetic source may inform part of Plutarch's account, it is unlikely to be responsible for the notion that *klēroi* were assigned to infants. Plutarch's account here, in common with the rest of the *Lykourgos* (see ch. 2), is an amalgam of material drawn from different sources. The bulk of the passage concerning the physical examination of the infant by the elders reads like a coherent description from a reliable source of an authentic classical Spartan process, which logically concludes with the elders' decision that a sturdy infant should be reared. Onto the end of this coherent account, however, is attached the artificial and extraneous claim that the elders also assigned the successful infant one of the 9,000 *klēroi* (cf. Cartledge 1979, 167). As we have seen (ch. 2), the equality of landholding implied by the procedure runs counter to Peripatetic and other post-Aristotelian approaches to issues of Spartan property, which differed greatly from the egalitarian tone of later sources which were affected by the late third-century revolution. Hence, even if Plutarch's account of the elders' scrutiny of male infants comes from a Peripatetic source, the additional detail regarding their supposed allocation of a *klēros* is unlikely to do so. This discrepancy, together with the established late third-century origin of the figure of 9,000 for the number of lots, suggests that the notion of the elders' allocation of an equal *klēros* was post-classical in origin.

Also of post-classical origin is Plutarch's account in the *Life of Agis* of a system of land tenure and inheritance according to which each father passed down his *klēros* intact to a single son over a period of centuries. This system of inheritance by unigeniture is integral to the propaganda of the late third-century revolution. To validate their attempts to sweep away the existing system of unequal, private land-ownership and replace it with a scheme of equal *klēroi*, the revolutionaries claimed that their plans were a return to the landed equality established by Lykourgos, which had been maintained by the practice of unigeniture until that practice was undermined by the *rhētra* promulgated by the ephor Epitadeus sometime after the end of the Peloponnesian war. This is the historical reconstruction given in the passage cited earlier from Plutarch's *Agis*, which reflects the ideology of the revolution as described by the partisan Phylarchos.[12]

Some scholars have tried to date this system of unigeniture to the classical or even archaic periods. It has been argued that the system is attested by the fact that various writers on Spartan affairs, including classical authors, use terms such as *despotēs*, *desposynos* and *hestiopamōn*, all of which – it is claimed – 'clearly allude to the practice of a "single heir"' (Asheri 1963, 5; cf. 1961, 66). Most of the passages in question, however, tell us nothing about land tenure or inheritance.[13] The passages cited from Tyrtaios (frs. 6–7 West) and Plutarch (*Lyk.* 28.5) refer only to Spartiate mastership over the helots. Those from Pollux (1.74, 10.20) show only that each household had just one master. Finally, the reference cited from Xenophon (*Hell.* 3.3.5) indicates no more than that on each estate there was only one master, which would equally be the case under another system such as partible inheritance; the other persons on each estate will have been helots.[14]

A different attempt to ascribe the Spartan system of unigeniture to a classical source has been made by Marasco (1978b), who claims that Plutarch derived his account of land tenure in the lives of Agis and Kleomenes from information in the largely lost Aristotelian *Polity of the Lakedaimonians* whose contents are reflected in Aristotle's *Politics* (1270a15–b6). The supposed similarities between the *Politics* and the two lives (Marasco 1978a, 174) do not, however, stand up to scrutiny.[15] Despite the oft-repeated assertion that the wording of Plutarch's description of freedom of gift and bequest (*Agis* 5.2: ἐξεῖναι τὸν οἶκον αὐτοῦ καὶ τὸν κλῆρον ᾧ τις ἐθέλοι καὶ ζῶντα δοῦναι καὶ καταλιπεῖν διατιθέμενον) resembles that of Aristotle (*Pol.* 1270a21: διδόναι δὲ καὶ καταλείπειν ἐξουσίαν ἔδωκε τοῖς βουλομένοις),[16] there is no real correspondence in terminology between the two passages, apart from their unsurprising common use of the verbs διδόναι ('to give') and καταλείπειν ('to bequeath'). Above all, there is little similarity between the sophisticated analysis in the *Politics*, in which the concentration of land and decline in manpower are explained in terms of a variety of contributory factors, and the simplistic account in the *Life of Agis* which ascribes the bulk of the responsibility to a single person. As we shall see in more detail below (cf. also ch. 2), the Phylarchan–Plutarchean tradition derives not from Aristotle but from a fictional account inspired by Plato's theoretical discussion of the breakdown and overthrow of oligarchy in the *Republic* (555c–e).[17] Not that Plato himself would have recognised this fictional account as reflecting Spartan reality. It is indicative that when he proposed a system of indivisible *klēroi* for his imaginary Cretan colony (*Laws* 740a–741a), he did not point to a Spartan precedent. As Cynthia Patterson (1998, 250 n. 12) has commented, 'Plato's silence on any such Spartan system of indivisibility and inalienability of *kleros* while setting up just such a system in the *Laws* (in the presence of a Spartan) is strong evidence that there was none'. The alleged Spartan system of unigeniture described in Plutarch's *Agis* is, consequently, not attested in any source before it was included in the reconstruction of Spartan history effected by the third-century revolutionaries.

The impracticability of the standard views

The sources of these late accounts are therefore not of the highest quality. One's misgivings about their reliability are not allayed when one examines the inherent practicability of the systems of tenure and inheritance which they describe or which scholars have built upon them. First of all, the property systems described in Plutarch's separate accounts in *Agis* and *Lykourgos* are, as they stand, incompatible (cf. Busolt and Swoboda 1920–26, ii.636 n. 3). According to the former, one son inherited the *klēros* of his father; according to the latter, each son was assigned a *klēros* by the state. The two systems are radically different in character. Whereas the latter implies public ownership of the land, the former is a restricted form of private ownership (Ducat 1983, 150–1). The two accounts are reconciled only by modern invention, such as the claim that the state allocation in the *Lykourgos* applied (contrary to what Plutarch says) only to younger sons whom the inheritance system in *Agis* left without land. This supposed reconciliation distorts the evidence of both accounts. Since Plutarch either did not appreciate or was unconcerned that his accounts were incompatible, a saner approach would be to doubt the reliability of his evidence.

Taken separately, however, both systems are impracticable. It is highly improbable that the Spartan state possessed the bureaucratic machinery necessary to keep the records required to administer a state-controlled system of several thousand *klēroi* which were subject to continual reallocation, such as is implied by the account in *Lykourgos* 16 (Toynbee 1969, 302; Buckler 1977, 258; Link 1991, 78). Moreover, the system in its own right contains several inherent points of implausibility (cf. Cozzoli 1979, 28; Ducat 1983, 145–6). First, it would have necessitated an unlikely reserve of *klēroi* to ensure that there were sufficient available to match the unpredictable birthrate of Spartiate boys. Secondly, the allocation of *klēroi* to infants would have entailed a large number of holdings in the hands of children; hence the number of warriors would have been considerably fewer than the available number of *klēroi*. Indeed, since boys under age 20 typically account for a third or more of the male population under Mediterranean pre-industrial conditions, even on the assumption that all 9000 *klēroi* were taken up, only some 5,500–6,000 *klēroi* would have been available to adult citizens.[18] Yet, according to Herodotus (7.234), there were as many as 8,000 Spartiates in 480 BC. Thirdly, the effect of automatically providing each male with economic security in infancy would have been to relieve parents of all concerns for their children's material well-being and would surely have led to a high rate of reproduction – the opposite of what happened in reality. In view of these inherent problems, it is not surprising that several scholars who have wished to retain the evidence of *Lykourgos* 16 have felt compelled to argue that what was allocated to each successful infant was not the current possession of an actual *klēros*, as Plutarch states, but merely the right to inherit a holding at some future date (e.g. MacDowell 1986, 94; Lupi 1997, 142). However, although such a solution would obviate the first two difficulties mentioned above, it would not remove the third, since under the alleged system of publicly-controlled equal *klēroi* it would still provide an absolute guarantee of economic security for a Spartiate in his adult life.

To say all this is not to doubt the reality of the scrutiny of infant boys, which forms the core of the passage and shows little sign of the taint of later propaganda or idealisation. As mentioned above (ch. 2), I suggest rather that Plutarch has elaborated his description of an authentic Spartiate practice by appending the entirely spurious detail that it was at this point that the future citizen was allocated his *klēros*. In support of this suggestion, I would note that the five words of Greek with which Plutarch mentions this allocation in *Lykourgos* 16 (κλῆρον αὐτῷ τῶν ἐνακισχιλίων προσνείμαντες·) constitute the sole evidence in the whole of ancient literature for the entire modern theory that the Spartiate was merely a life tenant of his holding, which reverted to the polis on his death. Polybius' account of landed equality, for example, clearly assumes individual rather than collective ownership of land (Ducat 1983, 143–4).[19] Even in Plutarch's own account of the Lykourgan/Polydoran distribution of *klēroi* in *Lykourgos* 8 there is nothing to suggest the system of public ownership implied in *Lykourgos* 16. But for those five words in *Lykourgos* 16, scholars would have assumed that in *Lykourgos* 8 Plutarch was describing the origins of the system of single-heir inheritance outlined in the *Life of Agis*.

Not that, taken on its own, the inheritance system described in *Agis* 5 is any more viable. The difficulty with the account is that, although Plutarch insists that landed equality was maintained for several centuries, he does not explain how younger sons were catered for or what arrangements were made under a regime of hereditary transmission to prevent accumulation of land by kinsmen or others when there was no son to inherit or no children at all. The lack of reality behind Plutarch's description of the system is highlighted through a comparison with the similar system of unigeniture in Plato's *Laws*. Cognizant of the many practical difficulties which could arise, Plato spends several pages (923c ff.) laying down detailed legislation for a variety of potential situations in which the smooth transition of holdings from father to son might be disrupted or in which the accumulation of unequal landholdings might occur; and, ultimately, his provisions for dealing with the problem of additional sons rely upon a factor rarely available to historical Spartiates – state schemes for their emigration from the polis. In contrast, the inheritance system in *Agis* 5 is made workable only through the liberal application of modern conjecture outlined above: by the forced 'reconciliation' with the account in the *Life of Lykourgos*; by the unsupported speculation that uninherited estates were always diverted to landless younger sons; or by the claim that, although he fails to say so, Plutarch is referring only to one of the two categories of land supposedly mentioned by Herakleides Lembos.[20]

This last conjecture illustrates the problems of relying upon the *Life of Agis*. On the one hand, modern studies are compelled to modify Plutarch's evidence in order to remedy the fact noted above, that the complete equality of landholding assumed in his account is inconsistent with the testimony of all the historical sources from the sixth to the fourth centuries. On the other hand, their claim that, besides the equal *klēroi*, there was other land of a more private nature which was owned unequally contradicts the idea of strict equality in Plutarch's account.[21] Furthermore, one of the main supporting arguments for this view, the suggestion that the 'ancient portions' of Herakleides and Plutarch's equal inheritances are identical with the equal shares in the *politikē chōra* referred to by Polybius, involves a misrepresentation of Polybius' evidence. Polybius does not distinguish two types of land.[22] The implication of his equal shares in the *politikē chōra* is that this meant complete equality in landholding, a point repeated shortly afterwards (6.48.3), and that the *politikē chōra* was the only type of land available to citizens. The *politikē chōra* means not 'civic land', in contrast to another type of citizen-held land more private in character, but simply the 'land divided among the citizens' (Busolt and Swoboda 1920–26, ii.634 n. 2; Walbank 1957, 728–31; Cartledge 1979, 166; Ducat 1983, 143; Link 1991, 82). Polybius, therefore, is not describing the same system as that which some scholars have conjecturally extrapolated from the account in Plutarch's *Agis*.[23] His remarks do not offer any support for their attempts to rescue its evidence. Polybius' own account is merely one of complete equality, itself offered without explanation as to how that equality was sustained.

Explanatory weaknesses of the standard views
The final major weakness of these late accounts and of modern studies which accept their evidence is that they do not adequately explain the serious decline in Spartiate numbers in the classical period which, whatever one's precise explanation of its causes, was in some way connected with the increasing concentration of land in a few hands and the impoverishment of many citizen households. Although the exact rate of the decline in different periods is the subject of debate, there is sufficiently wide agreement that it was a long-term process which had begun by the mid-fifth century at the latest.[24] Plutarch's *Lykourgos* provides no framework at all for explaining these developments. Those studies which rely upon its evidence, since they cannot explain the decline in terms of inherited poverty, are forced, rather implausibly, to account for it in terms of either widespread personal mismanagement and misfortune or a general increase in luxurious living which supposedly led to extensive poverty and consequent failure to reproduce (Michell 1964, 207–9, 228–32; Forrest 1968, 136).

Plutarch's *Agis* does attempt to provide an explanation of the concentration of land and widespread poverty. Following the passage already quoted (p. 67, above), he continues:

> This man, then, satisfied a private grudge of his own in introducing the law (*nomos*); but his fellow citizens welcomed it out of greed, made it valid, and so destroyed the most excellent of institutions. For the men of power and influence at once began to acquire estates without scruple, ejecting the rightful heirs from their inheritances; and speedily wealth streamed into the hands of a few and poverty ruled the polis…

This explanation, however, covers only the period after some unspecified time following the end of the Peloponnesian war. It provides no explanation of the decline in citizen numbers before that time, when equality of landholding supposedly still prevailed.[25] Those studies which follow this version, in so far as they do not simply ignore the earlier decline in the number of Spartiates, are able to explain it only by the poverty of deprived younger sons, who then supposedly became a drain on the *klēros* of the eldest son, or by the natural extinction of citizen families.[26] The manifest inadequacy of these explanations has already been pointed out by Buckler (1977, 259). It is indeed impossible to reconcile the evidence for citizen population decline with the testimony of the *Life of Agis*, since Plutarch insists that until the law of Epitadeus the number of households instituted by Lykourgos remained undiminished.

Towards an alternative account: unequal and private land-ownership

It is possible to provide a more satisfactory explanation of the decline in citizen numbers upon the basis of a different system of land tenure and inheritance according to which the landholdings of individual Spartiates were private property and distributed unequally among the citizen body. This point of view has been argued in the past by a number of scholars;[27] but in the light of the continuing debate it is necessary to develop the argument somewhat further than has previously been attempted. This alternative system can be founded more securely upon the evidence of contemporary and more reliable sources than the theories already discussed.

The earliest evidence comes from Tyrtaios, writing around the mid- or late seventh century. As we saw at the start of chapter 1, Aristotle (*Pol.* 1306b36–1307a2) cites Tyrtaios in support of his proposition that civil wars may arise 'when some are excessively poor and others excessively rich'; 'and this', says Aristotle, 'occurred in Lakedaimon during the [Second] Messenian war – as is evident from the poem of Tyrtaios called *Eunomia*, for certain men, being reduced to straitened circumstances through the war, demanded a redistribution of the territory' (fr. 1 West). As previous commentators (Cozzoli 1979, 34–5; Ducat 1983, 147) have noted, the evidence of Tyrtaios' poem implies that the territory of Lakonia was unequally divided; otherwise how could some Spartiates have been reduced to poverty by the temporary loss of Messenia, and what would have been the point of demanding a redistribution of land? The tone of the passage also implies private rather than public ownership of land.

Some scholars assume that the demand for redistribution attested by Tyrtaios was actually put into effect (e.g. Singor 1993, 38); but there is no evidence that it was and good reason to doubt this idea. Rather than redistribute land in Lakonia, the Spartan response was to reconquer Messenia. What was done with Messenian territory after the reconquest – indeed, what had been done after the initial conquest – is unknown. The passage above suggests that some citizens who possessed relatively little land in Lakonia owned other, perhaps somewhat larger, estates in Messenia. Certainly, it is likely that the newly-conquered Messenian territory was parcelled out among those who had participated in the original conquest, as was later planned when the Spartiates hoped to conquer Tegea (Hdt. 1.60). There is, however, no certainty – whatever one thinks of the reality behind the enigmatic episode of the Partheniai[28] – that every single citizen shared in it (cf. Link 1991, 80). After the Second Messenian war there was doubtless pressure to ensure that every citizen held at least a basic competence of land. The subsequent remodelling of Spartan society over the following generations, which established each citizen as a full-time hoplite warrior freed from economic activity, made it necessary that all Spartiates should possess sufficient land to enable them to contribute the set amount of produce to the common messes which was a condition of their citizenship. Any distribution of land carried out in such a context, however, would have been very different from the wholesale equal redistribution of land described by Plutarch and does not imply the kind of state control envisaged in his accounts (Toynbee 1969, 301 n. 1). There is no reason why Messenian landholdings distributed among the citizenry should not from the very start have been regarded as private property.

The unequal and private character of land-ownership – as of property ownership in general – is, indeed, the overwhelming impression given by our late archaic and classical sources. The poet Alkaios, writing around 600 BC, cites a saying by a certain Aristodemos in Sparta: 'man is what he owns; no poor man is good or honourable' (fr. 360, Campbell, *ap.* Schol. Pindar, *Isthmian* 2.17). Herodotus' use of the term *patrouchos* (literally, 'holder of the patrimony') to describe the Spartan heiress (6.57) suggests that she inherited her property – of which land was no doubt the major part – privately from her father. The implied ownership and inheritance of land by women also contradicts the Plutarchean picture of publicly-controlled, male-owned *klēroi*. In the story which Herodotus (6.61) tells concerning the childhood of the future wife of the mid-sixth-century king Ariston, the girls' parents are described as 'prosperous people' (ἀνθρώπων τε ὀλβίων). This tale indicates how Herodotus' fifth-century Spartiate sources viewed the property structure of their society in earlier times, probably in reflection of the situation in their own day. Similarly, the two citizens, Sperthias and Boulis, who volunteered to give their lives to atone for the murder of some Persian heralds, are said (7.134) to have been 'of good family and in wealth among the first' (…καὶ χρήμασι ἀνήκοντες ἐς τὰ πρῶτα). This information is likely to be accurate, since the sons of these citizens were well-known men in Sparta who had recently (in the year 430) been in the news as ambassadors captured by the Athenians and put to death (7.137; Thuc. 2.67).

Thucydides too – in a passage (1.6) already quoted early in ch. 2 – looks back into the Spartan past to the time when the Spartans began to dress simply and those who had great possessions (οἱ τὰ μείζω κεκτημένοι) adopted a lifestyle as much as possible like that of the many. He implies that both the common lifestyle and differences in wealth remained in his own day. The picture of the unequal distribution of wealth in sixth- and fifth-century Sparta indicated by the above writers is supported by other evidence, not least by the numerous *xeniai* (guest- or ritualised friendships) which certain Spartiate lineages maintained with leading families from other states, a relationship which necessarily entailed the possession and disposal of considerable amounts of wealth.[29] Although neither Herodotus nor Thucydides specifies the nature of the wealth owned by the rich men whom they mention, it would be extraordinary if it were confined to non-landed property. Indeed, both writers mention other specific Spartan individuals whose wealth must undoubtedly have consisted of large amounts of landed property: Euagoras, Damaratos and Lichas, all of them owners of victorious Olympic chariot-race teams (Hdt. 6.70, 103; Thuc. 5.50). Other evidence indicates that these individuals were just a few of a larger number of Spartiates in the fifth and fourth centuries whose engagement in chariot racing indicates their possession of wide areas of grazing land for teams of horses (see ch. 10).

This evidence for the private and unequal character of land-ownership during the fifth century and earlier is especially important, since it ante-dates the period after the Peloponnesian war when, according to Plutarch (*Agis* 5), the law of Epitadeus undermined the equality of Spartan landholdings and the strict controls over inheritance. It thereby undermines the major objection often adduced against the hypothesis of a private and unequal system of landholdings: namely, that the detailed references to such a system by certain well-informed fourth-century writers (especially by Aristotle) refer to a corrupted system which had only recently developed.

In truth, although the evidence of the best-informed fourth-century sources is more detailed than that of earlier writers, it conforms in all essential details to the picture of Spartiate land-ownership already evident before 400. We can see this most clearly from the evidence of Xenophon. Writing in the early/mid-fourth century, he refers both to 'the rich' who were able to make additional contributions of wheaten bread to the messes (*Lak. Pol.* 5.3) and to 'the very rich' who reared horses for the Spartan cavalry (*Hell.* 6.4.10–11). Both references not only clearly refer to wealth in land but also provide indications of continuity with the period before 400. The first reference indicates that the rich men in question possessed larger than average estates, on which they were able to cultivate not only the barley crop required for their compulsory mess dues but also a higher-quality, but more risky (because less drought-tolerant), wheat crop. It connects with another passage in which Xenophon himself suggests that the capacity of certain men to produce surplus foodstuffs on larger than normal estates was not merely a new phenomenon of the fourth century. In his *Memorabilia* (1.2.61) he recalls that the aforementioned Spartan named Lichas won enduring renown for his entertainment of foreigners staying in Sparta during the festival of the Gymnopaidiai, no doubt using produce from his large estates. Similarly, the second reference mentioned above links up with the evidence of Herodotus and Thucydides that there was a group of the very wealthiest men who possessed extensive land for grazing horses. Indeed, the fact that Sparta's cavalry originated in the year 424 (Thuc. 4.55) provides further confirmation that the considerable landholdings of the citizens who reared war horses were not the product of the alleged fourth-century corruption of a supposedly previous system of equal landholdings. Further evidence of continuity linking Xenophon's early fourth-century evidence with that from earlier periods comes in his reference to two particular individuals who owned more land than other citizens: namely, the kings of the Agiad and Eurypontid royal houses, who, he says, possessed choice land in the territories of many of the perioikic poleis (*Lak. Pol.* 15.3). Xenophon portrays this land-ownership as part of the original contract between king and polis, explicitly said to be unchanged since the time of the (legendary) lawgiver Lykourgos (15.1). Whatever one may think of the precise origins and supposed immutability of this arrangement between kings and polis – one must always beware of the phenomenon of the 'invention of tradition' (cf. Hodkinson 1997a, 84–5) – it is highly unlikely that the kings' possession of estates in perioikic territories was a new feature of the Spartan property system introduced only in the early fourth century.

Xenophon's testimony regarding Spartiate land-ownership undeniably assumes that land was, and always had been, private property. We shall consider shortly his detailed evidence regarding its inheritance and the specific rights of Spartiate landowners. For the present it is sufficient to note that his account gives no hint that there had ever existed a system of equal publicly-controlled *klēroi*. As we saw in chapter 2, Xenophon describes several aspects of the communal use of property among Spartan citizens (*Lak. Pol.* 6); indeed, he rather inflates their overall significance. The assumed background to this communal use, however, is that the property in question was private in character. As Jean Ducat has perceptively noted (1983, 149), given Xenophon's intention throughout his *Polity of the Lakedaimonians* to stress the respects in which Sparta's Lykourgan institutions differed from those of other poleis, the fact that he gives no hint of anything distinctive regarding the ownership of land is a sure sign that it was fundamentally similar in character to land-ownership elsewhere in Greece. Moreover, the fact that land-ownership is not mentioned in the infamous chapter 14 as one of the spheres in which the laws of Lykourgos had been abandoned indicates that for Xenophon land-ownership in Sparta had always been private.

A similar picture emerges from the description of Spartiate landholdings in the late fourth-century pseudo-Platonic dialogue *Alkibiades I* (122d):

> You have only to look at the wealth of the Lakedaimonians, and you will perceive that our [sc. Athenian] riches here are far inferior to theirs. Think of all the land that they have both in their own country and in Messene. Not one of our estates could compare with theirs in extent and excellence, not in ownership of slaves, especially the helot class, nor of horses, nor of the other livestock that graze in Messene.

The evidence from earlier sources cited above indicates that the picture painted in the *Alkibiades I* was no new phenomenon but an accurate reflection of Spartiate land-ownership throughout the late archaic and classical periods. Indeed, as noted in chapter 2, this depiction is very much akin to that portrayed by Herodotus. The specific context of the depiction, however, is particularly significant. Whereas the other sources cited above are writing solely about Sparta, the description here of Spartiate land-ownership is made as part of an explicit comparison with (and denigration of) the propertied resources available to the wealthy Athenian, Alkibiades. The description in the *Alkibiades I* thus explicitly confirms the implication of earlier sources that the landed property of Spartan citizens was every bit as much their private property as that of Alkibiades or other wealthy Athenians. Neither is this presented as a new phenomenon of a corrupt fourth-century Sparta. The literary context of the work is the lifetime of Alkibiades in the late fifth century. Like Xenophon, the author of the dialogue assumes that Spartiate land-ownership in fifth-century Sparta had been private.

Finally, there is the source which provides our most detailed account of Spartiate land tenure, the discussion of Aristotle in Book II of his *Politics* (1270a15–b6).

> The defects of the arrangements concerning women seem, as was said earlier, not only to create a sort of unseemliness in the constitution itself, but also to contribute something to the greed for money; for, after the points just made, one could attack practice in respect of the uneven levels of property. For we find that some have come to possess far too much, others very little indeed; hence the land (*chōra*) has fallen into the hands of a few. This matter has been badly arranged through the laws too. For while he quite rightly made it dishonourable to buy or sell land in someone's possession, he left it open to anyone, if they wished, to give it away and bequeath it; and yet this inevitably leads to the same result, both in this case and in the other. Moreover, approximately [or 'nearly'] (σχεδόν) two-fifths of all the land is possessed by women, both because of the many heiresses (*epiklēroi*) that appear, and because of the practice of giving large dowries. Now it would have been better if it had been arranged that there should be no dowry, or a small or even a moderate one. But, as it is, one may give an *epiklēros* in marriage to any person one wishes; and, if a man dies without making a will, the man he leaves as *klēronomos* gives her to whomever he likes. As a result, although the land was sufficient to support 1,500 cavalry and 30,000 hoplites, their number was not even 1,000. The sheer facts have shown that the provisions of this system served them badly: the polis withstood not one single blow, but collapsed owing to the shortage of men. It is said that in the time of their early kings they used to give others a share in their constitution, so that in spite of their being at war for a long time, a shortage of men did not then occur; and they say that at one time the Spartiates had as many as 10,000. Nonetheless, whether these statements are true or not, it is better for the polis to have plenty of males through a levelling of property. But the law on the begetting of children militates against this reform. For the lawgiver, intending that the Spartiates should be as numerous as possible, encourages the citizens to make their children (*paides*) as numerous as possible; for they have a law by which the father of three sons is exempt from military service, and the father of four from all taxes. But it is obvious that, if many are born and the land has been divided accordingly, many inevitably become poor.

Like the other classical sources cited above, Aristotle explicitly attests the unequal ownership of landed property in his comment that 'the land has fallen into the hands of a few'. Although he uses the perfect tense (συμβέβηκε) to suggest that land-ownership had become more unequal in the recent past, there is no suggestion that he views the rules of land-ownership which caused this inequality as a recent phenomenon, since (as already indicated in chapter 2) throughout the *Politics* Aristotle's criticisms are directed against long-established characteristics of the Spartan *politeia* which were the consequence of the original errors of the lawgiver. (For a more detailed argument that the lawgiver in question was not Epitadeus, see below.) Indeed, in contrast to the account in Plutarch's *Agis*, Aristotle's explanation of landed inequality and the consequent decline in citizen numbers does not rely on a single cause but provides a sophisticated analysis which lays stress on a variety of contributory factors: the rights of gift and bequest, the number of heiresses and lack of controls over their marriages, the size of dowries, the failure to extend citizen rights to outsiders, the law on procreation and the system of partible inheritance. He thereby offers a reasoned discussion of the causes of the concentration of land and of widespread impoverishment which, when linked with his further remark (1271a26–36) that those who were too poor to contribute their *syssitia* dues were excluded from citizenship, provides an account of the long-term decline in Spartiate numbers whose explanatory power far exceeds that provided by Plutarch or by those modern scholars who rely upon Plutarch's evidence.

The operation of the classical system of private land tenure

Above all, Aristotle's account supplies important details concerning the system of private land tenure which amplify the less systematic evidence of other classical writers. In this section I shall reconstruct the operation of the classical Spartan system of private land tenure as it is attested by the fifth- and fourth-century sources discussed above – with the exception of one important aspect, female ownership and inheritance of land, which will be examined in detail in a later section. For clarity of exposition, I shall also reserve for subsequent discussion one objection which has often been made against my reconstruction, namely, that the fourth-century evidence upon which it partly relies is describing not the original classical land tenure system but the altered system following the law of Epitadeus. In the previous section I have already adduced arguments demonstrating the evident continuity between the accounts of the fourth-century sources and those from the fifth century. This continuity provides ample justification for the procedure in this section, whereby the evidence from the two centuries is combined into a homogeneous description of a uniform system of classical land tenure.

The first and foremost element in the operation of Spartiate private land-ownership was that land was transmitted hereditarily within the lineage from one generation to the next by means of the normal Greek system of partible inheritance, that is, by dividing it among one's heirs.[30] This is directly attested by Aristotle's statement that, 'if many are born and the land divided accordingly, many must inevitably become poor'. His remarks are confirmed by Xenophon's account (*Lak. Pol.* 1.9) of the contemporary Spartan practice of wife-sharing. He explains that the reason why Spartiate men were willing to lend their wives to produce children by other men is that they 'want to get for their sons brothers who are part of the kin and share in its power but do not claim part of its property (*tōn chrēmatōn*)'.[31] The implication is that the property would be inherited by and divided among the man's natural sons (with the brothers in question themselves inheriting from *their* own father).

Indeed, this very custom of wife-sharing should be interpreted as a method of reducing the excessive division of estates inherent in the system of partible inheritance. Polybius (12.6b.8) implies as much in his remark – probably derived from an earlier source uninfected by his notion of equal *klēroi*, since it occurs in a different part of his work – that it was when a man had begotten enough children by his wife that he would give her to a friend. The man who borrowed the wife could also of course use this custom as a means of limiting the number of his heirs.[32] In the light of the evidence of the first-century AD Jewish scholar, Philo (*On Special Laws* 3.4.22), that the Spartiates allowed marriages between uterine half-siblings (*homomētrioi*, i.e. children of the same mother but different fathers), it has been noted that this cooperation could then be continued through the intermarriage of the sons and daughters of the two men, thus concentrating their properties for the benefit of the succeeding generation.[33] In the passage mentioned above Polybius mentions another practice that had the same purpose of concentrating properties which would otherwise be divided: the practice of adelphic polyandry, that is, of several brothers sharing a single wife. Polybius states that it was a longstanding custom and quite usual for three, four or even more brothers to have one wife.[34] The practices of wife-sharing, uterine half-sibling marriage and polyandry all make sense on the supposition that land was transmitted hereditarily by means of partible inheritance.

The second element of the classical Spartan system of private land tenure was, however, that individual landowners possessed considerable latitude to modify the natural process by which their property would pass down within the lineage. As in other Greek poleis, a landowner who had no surviving natural son could adopt a male from another family who would henceforth become heir to his adoptive father's property. The evidence for such adoptions is provided by Herodotus (6.57.5), whose account of the prerogatives of the kings includes the statement that 'if anyone wishes (ἤν τις…ἐθέλῃ) to adopt a child, he must do it in the presence of the kings'. The role envisaged for this procedure of adoption by scholars who follow the account in Plutarch's *Agis* (e.g. MacDowell 1986, 95–8) is one whereby the kings ensured that the person adopted was a landless younger son without an inheritance, with apparently little attention being paid to the wishes of the adopter. As Grote (1862, ii.174–5 n. 1) pointed out, however, the passage of Herodotus lends no weight at all to this interpretation. Its phraseology 'if anyone wishes…' emphasizes the voluntary nature of the adoption and the initiative and wishes of the adopter. The passage contains no suggestion of the kind of state intervention envisaged above. It affords no grounds for assuming that the kings determined whom the man was to adopt. It was normal practice that an adoption should take place before official witnesses such as the kings, since it might have the effect of depriving the adopter's nearest relatives of a potential inheritance. An official witness was imperative in case of a subsequent legal challenge to the adoptive son's right to inherit. The kings' role as witnesses suggests no more than official confirmation of an otherwise private transaction and there is no implication that they interfered with the choice of adoptee to ensure that the property went to an unrelated landless son. This interpretation concurs with the results of recent research on classical Athens, which has likewise concluded that the polis did not intervene actively in adoptions. In Athens too the initiative was left entirely up to private individuals (Rubinstein 1993). As Lacey (1968, 201) has remarked, 'the right to adopt a son is…characteristic of a family-based society, a society which thinks in terms of inheritance through the family'. The right to choose a successor through adoption is a powerful indicator of the right of the individual Spartiate to control the disposal of his own estate.

Whether or not there were sons, a landowner also had the right to alienate his estate by other, more direct means. Aristotle is explicit that any landowner who wished had the right to give away his land or bequeath it by will. His evidence is corroborated, as regards freedom of gift, by Xenophon's account of the first action taken by King Agesilaos II at the start of his reign at the very beginning of the fourth century.

> Now when the polis pronounced him heir to all the property of Agis, he gave half to his mother's kinsfolk because he saw that they were in want (Xen. *Ages*. 4.5; cf. Plut. *Ages*. 4.1).

This passage, one should note, disproves the historical reconstruction in Plutarch's *Agis*. According to the chronology of that account, the Spartan state began to suffer corruption soon after the end of the Peloponnesian war in 404, and then there was a period of unspecified length during which the traditional system of land inheritance preserved the social order before it was ruined by Epitadeus' law, which first introduced freedom of gift and bequest. It is hardly possible, however, for all this to have happened before Agesilaos' accession, which took place most probably in 400 (Funke 1980, 36 n. 31), only four years after the end of the war![35] Xenophon's evidence, therefore, refutes the idea that it was the law of Epitadeus which instituted freedom of gift.[36] The combined testimony of Aristotle and Xenophon suggests that the right of landowners to alienate their estates by gift or bequest was a longstanding feature of the classical Spartan property system.

The other potential means by which a landowner might alienate his land was by sale. On this question the extant evidence is considerably more controversial. Aristotle, as we have seen, attests that the purchase or sale of land was dishonourable (οὐ καλόν) and he indicates that it was not through sale but through gift or bequest that land had fallen into the hands of a few. His account is perfectly intelligible since, although an action's being dishonourable is not strictly the same as its being illegal, in a close-knit, authoritarian society like Sparta the power of social pressure and sanction was probably such as to prevent any citizen from selling his land, except in the most extreme circumstances. There are certain ancient sources, however, who have been viewed as providing somewhat conflicting evidence to that of Aristotle. The first, a classical source, will be considered in this section; the other, hellenistic, sources, will be discussed in the following section. The classical evidence is Thucydides' description (5.34) of the sanctions officially imposed in 421 upon the soldiers who had surrendered on Sphakteria. Thucydides states that the Spartans 'made them *atimoi*; their deprivation (*atimia*) meant that they could neither hold office nor have the authority to buy or sell anything'. Ducat (1983, 148) has recently revived an old argument by Fustel de Coulanges (1891, 108 n. 1) that this right to buy and sell was the equivalent of the Roman *ius commercii*, under which deprivation of *commercium* applied – in Fustel's view – only to non-movable property, i.e. land. On this argument, the right to buy and sell land was at the time of Thucydides an integral part of the rights of Spartan citizenship. Ducat (1983, 159) suggests that between the time of Thucydides and that of Aristotle there was a reaction against this right, perhaps in an attempt to halt the concentration of landed property to which freedom of sale gave rise; hence Aristotle's statement that sale was dishonourable.

This interpretation of Thucydides possesses some explanatory power. The existence of the right to buy and sell land would certainly help explain the rapid decline of Spartiate numbers in the fifth century. Moreover, this would not be the only instance in which the Spartiates' property rights were subsequently subjected to increased restrictions. (I have argued elsewhere that the prohibition of private ownership of foreign coinage was a new measure introduced in 404: Hodkinson 1993, 151; 1996, 87–9; ch. 5 below). Such increased restriction might also account for the fact that in Aristotle's day sale of land was dishonourable rather than illegal, on the hypothesis that the authorities were able to apply sufficient propaganda against purchase and sale of land to render it shameful without being able entirely to abrogate a longstanding privilege of citizenship. Indeed, such propaganda might explain one peculiarity of Aristotle's formulation: that it was not merely sale of land that was dishonourable (one can readily envisage that having to sell one's landholding would be a source of dishonour) but its purchase too. The social pressure against purchase would be explicable if the authorities' concern was to restrict the acquisitive behaviour of wealthy citizens.

However, it remains uncertain that Thucydides' reference to the right of buying and selling should be interpreted as relating to landed property. Thucydides himself does not specifically mention land; and the parallel with Roman law adduced by Fustel de Coulanges is somewhat uncertain.[37] There is, moreover, an alternative analogy which suggests a different reading of Thucydides' evidence. The *atimia* imposed upon the Sphakterians recalls the conditions applying to the *hēbōntes*, the young Spartiates between age 20 and 30. The Sphakterians were deprived of two privileges: the right to hold office and the right to buy and sell. They were not apparently deprived of other rights, such as membership of a mess or service in the army. This was exactly the situation of the Spartiate youths, the *hēbōntes*. They too belonged to a mess and fought in the army but could not hold office, since that right was limited to men over age 30. The *hēbōntes* also suffered a particular economic disability. According to Plutarch (*Lyk.* 25.1), 'those under thirty years of age did not go into the *agora*, but had their household needs (ἀναγκαίας οἰκονομίας) supplied by their relatives and lovers'. In other words, the *hēbōntes*, like the Sphakterians, could not engage in buying and selling. As described by Plutarch, their economic disability related not to landed property but to everyday market transactions for household necessities, i.e. to movable property. It seems unlikely that Plutarch has misunderstood or misreported the scope of the disability, since it is improbable that *landed* transactions on behalf of *hēbōntes* would have been shared by the unusual combination of relatives and lovers, rather than by a single guardian. On this analogy, the deprivation of buying and selling applied to the Sphakterians related only to movable property and says nothing about the right to alienate landholdings. Thucydides' evidence cannot be adduced as evidence that fifth-century Spartiates had the right to buy and sell landed property. The only certainty is that in Aristotle's day purchase and sale of land were regarded as so dishonourable that he could discount them as having any significant impact on the concentration of land.

Nevertheless, even without the right of sale, the picture of Spartiate land tenure in the classical sources, spanning both fifth and fourth centuries, is of a considerable degree of private rights. A citizen landowner could pass his property to his children through partible inheritance; if he lacked direct heirs, he could adopt a son for that purpose. He could also re-direct the normal flow of inheritance by passing on his land to anyone he wished through either a lifetime gift or a testamentary bequest. I use the masculine pronoun 'he', restricting my phraseology to what has thus far been established. In a later section, however, I shall argue that the correct pronoun could equally well have been 'she'.

Objections to a uniform classical system of private land tenure

Before that, however, we must deal with two objections to the homogeneous picture of private classical Spartiate land tenure which I have presented.

Two categories of land?: the 'ancient portion'

The first objection is that there was not one single category of land but rather two types of land, one of which was subject to a greater degree of public control. The purported evidence for a second category of land is the passages from Herakleides Lembos (fr. 373.12 Dilts) and the *Instituta Laconica* (no. 22 = Plut.

Mor. 238e–f) quoted earlier in this chapter, which refer to the *archaia moira*, or 'ancient portion'. The more important passage, that from Herakleides, is worth quoting again, along with the original Greek text:

> To sell land is considered shameful by the Lakedaimonians, but from the ancient portion (*archaias moiras*) it is not permitted.
>
> πωλεῖν δὲ γῆν Λακεδαιμονίοις αἰσχρὸν νενόμισται. τῆς ἀρχαίας μοίρας οὐδὲ ἔξεστι.

This passage has been accepted as reliable because it has been thought to derive from the lost Aristotelian *Polity of the Lakedaimonians* (*Lak. Pol.*, = fr. 611.12 Rose). Here, it is argued, is unambiguous classical evidence for the existence of two separate categories of land: one more private in character whose sale was permissible (albeit shameful); and another, more ancestral form of land, the ancient portions, which was subject to tighter public control and whose sale was strictly forbidden.

That the passage appears to contradict, or at least modify, Aristotle's statement in the *Politics* (which gives no hint of formal prohibition) has given rise to several divergent explanations. One explanation, deriving from evidence that *Politics*, Book 2, was composed before the *Lak. Pol.* (Keaney 1980; Schütrumpf 1991, 296–7), is that Aristotle only learned about the ancient portions after writing Book 2. This, however, is not entirely satisfactory. It is true that certain of Aristotle's comments on Sparta in Book 2 are imprecise compared with those in later books, which may have been written after the publication of the *Lak. Pol.*. That Book 2 predated the *Lak. Pol.*, however, does not mean that it was written in total ignorance of specific details about Spartan society, especially such a supposedly basic element of land-ownership as the ancient portions.[38] Aristotle's statement that nearly two-fifths of the land lay in female hands and his knowledge of the rules applying to the marriage of heiresses are testimony to some such exact information. Another proposed explanation is that Aristotle knew about the ancient portions, but that in the *Politics* he deliberately ignored them, 'discussing only one category of land, legally alienable property' (Cartledge 1979, 166). My own preferred explanation in my original study of this problem (Hodkinson 1986, 388) likewise assumed that Aristotle knew about the prohibition on sale of the ancient portions, but that for brevity – in keeping with the compressed character of the *Politics* – he simply stressed the dishonour attached to the purchase or sale of *any* land: such an all-embracing statement being sufficient (without distracting qualifications about the ancient portions) for his contrast with the lack of restrictions on gift and bequest.[39]

Hence I too accepted Herakleides' evidence for the existence of a special category of land called the 'ancient portion', the right to alienate which – at least by sale – was subject to public control. If one accepts the reality of the ancient portions, however, one must face the problem of what distinguished them from the other type of land. Older studies typically viewed the ancient portions as *klēroi* in the original Spartiate heartland of the Eurotas valley distributed among the whole citizen-body, as distinct from land which some citizens acquired elsewhere;[40] and, as noted earlier, they have often been equated with the *politikē chōra* of Polybius and the equal *klēroi* of Plutarch. The error of this identification with such fictional entities of land has, however, already been demonstrated. Alternatively, they have been linked to landholdings allocated in Messenia, either after the initial conquest or following the seventh-century reconquest, which might have been regarded as the original citizen portions of newly-incorporated poorer families (cf. Cartledge 1979, 135, 168). Yet another school of thought disassociates the ancient portions from a historical land distribution, viewing them in contemporary terms, with the ancient portion simply being land thought of as having passed down within the family from of old as opposed to land more recently acquired (Jones 1967, 43; Cozzoli 1979, 8; Lupi 1997, 151–2).

Given such prevailing uncertainties, my own interpretation of the nature and significance of the ancient portions was guilty – as subsequent scholars have pointed out – of a certain degree of ambiguity and contradiction (cf. Link 1991, 93 n. 150; Lupi 1997, 140 n. 9). Whilst accepting the existence of this second category of land, I concluded from Aristotle's discussion of the deleterious effects of partible inheritance and the rights of gift and bequest that – apart from the legal prohibition on purchase or sale – the ancient portions must either have been subject to the same rules as other land or they must have comprised so small a fraction of citizen landholdings that they did not affect Aristotle's generalizations (Hodkinson 1986, 391, 394, 404–5). As Schütrumpf (1991, 311) has noted, however, it remains somewhat problematic to treat the information in the *Politics* as covering a category of land (the ancient portions) of whose existence Aristotle there shows no knowledge. Moreover, if either the differences or the extent of the ancient portions were so minuscule as I suggested, why do the ancient sources – and why should modern scholars – trouble to distinguish them from the generality of land? As my own comment (p. 404) that 'some uncertainties remain, especially concerning the enigmatic ancient portions' indicates, the ancient portions were the one aspect of Spartiate land tenure which I conceded was not properly resolved.

Fortunately, however, two recent studies have now, I believe, solved many of the interpretational problems described above by demonstrating that the passage of Herakleides does not provide solid evidence for the existence of a separate category of land called the 'ancient portion'. As Stefan Link (1991, 93–40) has noted, there is something suspicious about the statement of Herakleides. The first part (πωλεῖν δὲ γῆν Λακεδαιμονίοις αἰσχρὸν νενόμισται) is in perfect agreement with Aristotle's *Politics* that it was shameful to sell land. There is no qualification that this applied only to one of two categories of land. Taken on its own, the statement should surely be interpreted as referring to *all* land. Indeed, the statement could very well stand on its own without need for further qualification. The text of the second part of the statement (τῆς ἀρχαίας μοίρας οὐδὲ ἔξεστι) connects very poorly with the first part both grammatically and syntactically. The lack of a syntactical link has led certain editors to create one by inserting an additional δὲ(δ') between τῆς and ἀρχαίας; but this of course is entirely artificial modern intrusion. Moreover, whereas the word γῆν ('land') in the first part stands in the accusative, in the second part τῆς ἀρχαίας μοίρας ('the ancient portion') appears as a partitive genitive, despite supposedly depending upon the same verb πωλεῖν ('to sell'). Far from deriving from a reference to two types of land in the Aristotelian *Polity of the Lakedaimonians*, the second part reads like a later addition to what was originally a perfectly coherent statement in its own right. The addition need not have been the work of Herakleides himself, since what we possess in the manuscripts from which this statement comes is not the text of Herakleides' original work but excerpts from that work by a later copyist. This would not be the only occasion on which the excerpts differ from the original Aristotelian *Politeiai* (Lazenby 1995, 88).

The source of this addition can in fact be detected through the evidence of the closely parallel passage in the other source which mentions the ancient portions, the *Instituta Laconica*, which dates at the earliest to the late third century.

τῆς ἀρχῆθεν διατεταγμένης μοίρας· πωλεῖν δ' οὐκ ἐξῆν.

the anciently established portions; it was not permitted to sell.

Interpretation of this passage is impeded by a probable lacuna in the text immediately beforehand (cf. Fuhrmann 1988, 240 n. 6; Santaniello 1995, 411 n. 527); but the previous portion of surviving text concerns the admission of foreigners to the citizenship in accordance with the prescription of Lykourgos. This was of course a major element in the programme of the late third-century revolution (Plut. *Agis* 8.2; 10.2–3). We have already seen in chapter 2, first, that the *Instituta* were heavily influenced by the revolution's ideas on issues to do with the land; and, secondly, that several statements in the work draw upon information from classical sources, including the Aristotelian *Polity of the Lakedaimonians*, whilst making significant modifications to their precise content. Pulling all these threads together, it is apparent that the statement regarding the prohibition on sale of the ancient portion in the text of Herakleides represents a late hellenistic addition, influenced by the propaganda of the late third-century revolution, to the original text of the Aristotelian *Lak. Pol.*, whose content simply echoed that of Aristotle's *Politics* in saying that sale of land was dishonourable. The further implication is that the ancient portion itself is a late hellenistic, not a classical, element of Spartan land tenure.

This argument receives support, in my opinion, from a recent study by John Lazenby (1995) which makes a strong case that the 'ancient portion', or *archaia moira*, was not land at all but a somewhat different item connected to land-ownership.[41] The statements in Herakleides and the *Instituta Laconica* are not the only occasion on which the word *moira* appears with reference to

Sparta. The hellenistic writer Myron of Priene (*FGrH* 106F2, *ap*. Athen. 657d) also uses the word in saying that the Spartans, 'handing over the land to them [sc. the helots], fixed a *moira* (ἔταξαν μοῖραν) which they should always render to them'. As Lazenby notes, Myron's verb ἔταξαν is cognate with the participle διατεταγμένης used in the *Instituta Laconica*. The most economical hypothesis is that all three sources which refer to this *moira* are referring to the same thing; hence the 'ancient portion', or *archaia moira*, was not land, as scholars have previously thought, but the tribute in kind from the land paid by the helot farm workers to each Spartiate landowner. This hypothesis is corroborated by another passage in the *Instituta Laconica* (no. 41 = 239d–e) which also refers to the helot tribute. Although the tribute is called by a different name (*apophora*), it is described by a similar phrase – the *apophora* 'set down in the past' (ἄνωθεν ἱσταμένην) – to the phrase 'anciently established' (ἀρχῆθεν διατεταγμένης) used to describe the *moirai* in *Instituta* no. 22.[42]

The hypothesis that the ancient portions refer not to land but to the helot tribute fits well with several features of this topic mentioned above. First, it accords with the context of the admission of *perioikoi* to the citizenship in *Instituta* no. 22, since the receipt of tribute from helot labourers was an essential privilege of Spartan citizens and enabled them to pay their mess contributions, which were a requirement of citizenship. Secondly, it makes perfect sense of both the content and the grammatical and syntactical structure of the passage of Herakleides. The statement that the sale of land was dishonourable can stand as it appears, as a complete and accurate statement applying to all Spartiate land. This helps explain why, when the second part of the passage was added later, it was not connected syntactically or harmonised grammatically with the first part, since it was not a qualification of the preceding statement; on the contrary, their respective subjects were different. The hypothesis also removes one particular difficulty with the passage as it is normally interpreted. Whilst, in terms of strict legal theory, there is a difference between sale being shameful and its being expressly forbidden, in such a controlled society as classical Sparta one would not expect such an explicit distinction to be made between law, on the one hand, and social sanction and custom, on the other (Ducat 1983, 159–60). Indeed, as we have already seen, Aristotle's *Politics* suggests that the dishonour attached to purchase and sale of land in itself meant that they were not practised. By separating both the subject matter of the two parts of the passage and the period in which each was developed, this difficulty is removed.

Finally, the hypothesis that the ancient portions refer to the helot tribute fits with the argument that the ancient portions were a hellenistic not a classical phenomenon. The idea that Spartiates were prohibited from selling the produce they received from the helots fits very badly with the classical reality of unequal landholdings, in which the helot rent was a proportion of the total produce and rich citizens would have received very large quantities of produce (Hodkinson

1992a), some of which they would surely have disposed of by sale. It fits ideally with the notion of a fixed, and therefore limited, helot rent which – as recent scholarship (Ducat 1990a, 56–8) has noted – is indissolubly linked to ideas of Spartiate landed equality promulgated during the third-century revolution. As I shall argue in more detail later, it is in this late and revolutionary context, in which each citizen was allocated a fixed, limited and inalienable *klēros* and a fixed amount of rent, that there existed a *dirigiste* state authority which would most likely have intervened to ensure that Spartiates did not sell any of their produce and thereby risk their citizen status.

The alleged *rhētra* of Epitadeus

The second objection to a homogeneous picture of private classical Spartiate land tenure is that the private character of land tenure which I have advocated did not apply throughout the classical period but only after the passing of the law of Epitadeus in the early fourth century. As we have already seen, the sole reference to the law of Epitadeus is in Plutarch's *Life of Agis*. According to Plutarch, the equality of landholdings which had been preserved through the Lykourgan system of single-heir inheritance was ruined at some indefinite point after the Peloponnesian war when the ephor Epitadeus introduced his law permitting lifetime gift and testamentary bequest. The influence of this passage has been considerable. Although a number of scholars have questioned the historical authenticity of Epitadeus,[43] many others have used the passage as the fundamental key to developments in Spartiate land tenure and to the interpretation of the contemporary classical sources, especially the evidence of Aristotle. There has even been a tendency in some modern accounts to go beyond the strict terms of the evidence in the passage by claiming it as support not just for the alleged introduction of gift and bequest but for other alleged changes, such as the change from the single-heir system of inheritance to the partible inheritance attested by Xenophon and Aristotle.[44]

In earlier sections of this chapter I have already adduced a number of reasons for thinking that there is no significant gulf separating the picture of landed property in the fifth-century sources from that portrayed by early fourth-century writers. We have also seen evidence that the right of gift supposedly introduced by Epitadeus was already in operation at the time of the accession of King Agesilaos II at the very start of the fourth century, before the earliest possible date for Epitadeus' legislation. It is also hard to see how the purported introduction of gift and bequest would have brought about a system of partible inheritance. David (1981, 102–3; 1982/83, 87) suggests that families used the new freedom of bequest to divide their estates among all their sons and that this became common practice, with deleterious effects on the heirs, who each inherited too little land to remain citizens. This view, however, involves the implausible view that families throughout Spartiate society abandoned a system of single-heir inheritance, which David believes had been operating perfectly

Ch. 3. The ownership and inheritance of land – revisited

satisfactorily, and voluntarily adopted a new inheritance practice, even when it was detrimental to their heirs. Moreover, it runs counter to the alleged effects of Epitadeus' law as stated by Plutarch himself. For Plutarch, the ensuing problem was not the partition of landed properties among a man's heirs, but rather their acquisition by powerful men outside the family who 'began to acquire estates without scruple, ejecting the rightful heirs from their inheritances'.

The main ground on which scholars have given credence to Plutarch's account of the law of Epitadeus is, however, its supposed correspondence with the evidence of Aristotle's *Politics*. The argument takes two forms, one generic, the other particular. The generic argument is that Aristotle's criticisms of Sparta, written in the later fourth century, are directed, like those in Plutarch's *Agis*, not against the Lykourgan regime as such but against recent corruptions of Lykourgan institutions (e.g. David 1982/83). The particular argument is that the lawgiver to whom Aristotle ascribes the permissibility of gift and bequest whose deleterious effects he criticises is none other than Epitadeus himself, and hence that Aristotle's evidence reinforces Plutarch's account.[45]

Neither argument holds water. As we saw in chapter 2, Aristotle's criticisms are not directed at new corruptions only recently introduced since the end of the Peloponnesian war. Even where his critical remarks refer to current practice or recent consequences, these are always traced back to the original errors of the lawgiver whose provisions or omissions led to the effects described. As Eckart Schütrumpf's commentary on the *Politics* (1991, 295–6) has demonstrated, the notion that he intended to differentiate between the original character of the Spartan constitution and its contemporary flawed condition is incompatible with Aristotle's text (cf. esp. 1260b29; 1269a30 ff.; 1270b11; 1271a26 ff.).[46]

Similarly, there is no good reason to believe that Aristotle's comments on the freedom of gift and bequest are intended as a reference to the alleged recent law of Epitadeus. Let us recall the precise structure of the relevant passage of the *Politics* (1270a18–21).

> This matter has been badly arranged through the laws too. For while he quite rightly made it dishonourable to buy or sell land in someone's possession, he left it open to anyone, if they wished, to give it away and bequeath it.
>
> τοῦτο δὲ καὶ διὰ τῶν νόμων τέτακται φαύλως· ὠνεῖσθαι μὲν γὰρ ἢ πωλεῖν τὴν ὑπάρχουσαν ἐποίησεν οὐ καλόν, ὀρθῶς ποιήσας, διδόναι δὲ καὶ καταλείπειν ἐξουσίαν ἔδωκε τοῖς βουλομένοις·

There are two key points to note about this passage. First, Aristotle's remarks about purchase, sale, gift and bequest are included within the same sentence; and the regulations on these subjects are all ascribed, through the use of the verbs ἐποίησεν and ἔδωκε, to the same person. Secondly, the identity of that person is not specified, since the verbs in question are not attached to any corresponding subject.

To start with the second point, since the person's identity is not specified in the sentence in question, one can reasonably expect that it is to be found earlier. There are two relevant earlier passages in this chapter of the *Politics*: 1269b19–22 and 1270a6–8. The former passage states that 'the lawgiver' neglected to control the women; the latter reports the tradition that Lykourgos tried to bring them under control but abandoned his attempt. It is apparent that Lykourgos and 'the lawgiver' are to be equated. It seems likely, therefore, that the unspecified individual responsible for the regulations concerning purchase, sale, gift and bequest, in what is the next comparable context, must also be Lykourgos.[47] This inherent likelihood is strengthened by the fact that Aristotle's remarks on women and landed property are closely linked. He concludes his comments on the lack of control over women by saying that their status contributes to the love of money. He then moves straight on to the comments on the inequality of property and the errors in the laws on gift and bequest, at the end of which he discusses female ownership of the land. It is improbable that such closely linked comments could contain a major shift of reference from the original founding lawgiver Lykourgos to a 'Johnny-come-lately' like Epitadeus. As Schütrumpf (1987, 447 n. 37) has noted, it is hardly likely that Aristotle would have regarded Epitadeus, who merely proposed a bill passed by the Spartans, as a *nomothetēs* in the same category as Lykourgos.

Consideration of other parts of Aristotle's account also favours this conclusion. Throughout the remainder of the section devoted to Sparta he refers to 'the lawgiver' on seven different occasions, at least four of which refer to Lykourgos, since they concern fundamental aspects of the Spartan system which all ancient traditions attributed to him.[48] The only apparent contrary example is 1270b19, where 'the lawgiver' responsible for the ephorate is often thought to be King Theopompos, to whom the creation of the office is ascribed in Book 5, at 1313a25–33. The latter passage, however, may well represent a change of opinion from that in Book 2, reflecting the fruits of subsequent research for the Aristotelian *Lak. Pol.* That Aristotle has Lykourgos in mind as the Spartan lawgiver in Book 2 is suggested by his remark at 1273b32–5 that Lykourgos framed the Spartan laws and constitution of which he has already spoken.[49] His normal practice of avoiding mentioning the lawgiver by name seems to follow that of Plato (*Laws* 806c; cf. 692a) and carries no implication that he is thinking of anyone other than Lykourgos. But, even if (for the sake of argument) one grants the case of the ephorate as an exception to Aristotle's ascription of Sparta's institutions to Lykourgos, it concerns an institution founded several hundred years previously and constitutes no parallel to the supposed reference to Epitadeus' recent law.

A more effective counter-argument, against a positive identification of the lawgiver responsible for freedom of gift and bequest as Lykourgos, is to be made not by asserting the claims of Epitadeus, but through the argument that the phrase 'the lawgiver' is used not to specify a particular individual but more generically to denote simply the author, whoever it may be, of whatever law Aristotle is discussing at the time.[50] However, although this formulation does not formally exclude the possibility that in discussing gift and bequest Aristotle may be referring to a recent law, equally it does nothing to advance that possibility. In particular, it does not alter the cardinal point that, since Aristotle ascribes the disapproval of purchase or sale and the freedom of gift and bequest to the same unspecified person, they must *both* in his view be either longstanding rules or recent innovations. Since the disapproval of purchase and sale of land was for Aristotle a characteristic of archaic states (*Pol.* 1266b17–21; 1319a10–11), it is unlikely that he believed it was a recent innovation in Sparta. It is impossible to maintain, as David (1982/83, 82) tries to do, that for Aristotle the law on purchase and sale was an archaic attitude but that the law on gift and bequest was a product of an early fourth-century change of law.[51] As Schütrumpf (1987, 448) points out, the idea of decadence and corruption with which freedom of gift and bequest is associated in Plutarch's *Agis* is unknown to Aristotle, who does not contrast the fourth century with an earlier period when Sparta enjoyed sounder conditions, but instead praises the stability of the Spartan system. Consequently, whether or not he intended to attribute it specifically to Lykourgos, Aristotle must have regarded freedom of gift and bequest as a traditional right, not as a recent innovation introduced by Epitadeus.

With the removal of the alleged corroboration of Aristotle, the last prop supporting the claimed historicity of the law of Epitadeus on gift and bequest is effectively removed. The question remains, however, how this unhistorical episode came to be invented. This question has recently been answered by Schütrumpf's demonstration (1987; cf. 1991, 312) that Plutarch, *Agis* 5 derives from a fictional account adapted in the third century, possibly by Sphairos, from Plato's *Republic* (especially 555c–e). The derivation is clear from the almost exact parallelism in motifs (conflict between father and son, legally conceded rights, voluntary alienation of land and opposition between rich and poor), in psychological qualities, in the technique of individualization and even in the order of exposition. In one respect only does Plutarch's account depart significantly from its ultimate model, in that rights of gift and bequest are substituted for Plato's emphasis on rights of purchase and sale. This change was made no doubt because the propagandists who invented the episode, in order to explain the demise of the supposedly Lykourgan system which they wanted to restore, could plausibly attribute it to the misuse of gift and bequest in a way they could never to purchase and sale, whose practice had long been inhibited by the associated dishonour. The artificiality of this substitution is indicated by the fact that the *Laws* (922e–923a) shows that Plato viewed the concession of the right of bequest as a failing not of recent lawgivers but of those of earlier times (Schütrumpf 1987, 449). The substitution should also dispel any thoughts that the relevant section of Plato's account might itself constitute a sound basis for authentic comment on Sparta's decline, since there are no grounds for ascribing that decline to rights of purchase and sale. Indeed, Plutarch, *Agis* 5 derives not from the portion of the *Republic* Book 8 which may genuinely be modelled on Sparta, the discussion of timarchy and its decline (547c–552e), but from Plato's theoretical account of the breakdown and overthrow of oligarchy in its transition to democracy. The chosen model is singularly inappropriate to the conditions of early fourth-century Sparta, in which oligarchy was in fact becoming more entrenched (Cartledge 1987; cf. ch. 13, below). As Schütrumpf (1987, 447) rightly remarks, 'the account in *Agis* 5 is a mere fiction in a Platonic spirit and is therefore historically useless'.

The property rights of Spartiate women

It is clear then on all counts that throughout the classical period Spartiate land tenure was fundamentally private in character, with the only significant restriction being on alienation by purchase and sale. Thus far we have considered only land-ownership by men; but Aristotle's analysis in particular stresses that a large proportion of landed property – nearly two-fifths – was owned by Spartiate women. In contrast, female inheritance is absent from the account of classical Spartan land tenure by those later sources who write of equal *klēroi*, appearing only in the description of the supposedly degenerate third-century system described in Plutarch's *Life of Agis*. For Aristotle, however, the role of women as landowners, both as heiresses and as the recipients of landed dowries, was a crucial part of the traditional system, as is shown by the fact that he portrays it as an important factor in the decline in the number of male citizens.

Women as heiresses

In many classical Greek states the position of daughters whose fathers had died without male issue was governed by special regulations specifying who had the right to marry them (Schaps 1979, ch. 3). Three texts inform us about the position of such women in Sparta. The earliest text forms part of Herodotus' list of royal prerogatives (6.57.4):

> The kings are the sole judges of these cases only: concerning an unmarried heiress to whom it pertains to have [her], if her father has not betrothed her… (πατρούχου τε παρθένου πέρι, ἐς τὸν ἱκνέεται ἔχειν, ἢν μή περ ὁ πατὴρ αὐτὴν ἐγγυήσῃ).

Three points require attention. First, the heiress is called by the term *patrouchos*, a combination of πατρῷα and ἔχειν, meaning 'holder of the patrimony'. It seems to correspond to the term *patrōiōkos* in the law code of Gortyn. A *patrōiōkos* in Gortyn, as long as she conformed to the laws specifying whom she was to marry, remained the legal owner of her father's property throughout her life, in contrast with the Athenian heiress, the *epiklēros*, who ceded the property to her son when he came of age.[52] The similarity of terms suggests that the Spartiate *patrouchos* enjoyed legal rights of ownership over the patrimony comparable to those of her Gortynian counterpart. This is illustrated by the case of Lysander's daughters in 395 BC (Plut. *Mor.* 230a; *Lys.* 30.6; Aelian, *VH* 6.4; 10.15). The fact that they were courted when their father was thought rich, but deserted when on his death his poverty was revealed, suggests that they were heirs to Lysander's property.[53] Accordingly, when Herodotus gives Leonidas I's marriage to Kleomenes I's only child, his daughter Gorgo, as one reason why he succeeded to the throne *c.* 490 (7.205.1; cf. 5.48.7, 7.239.4), the most likely explanation is that the marriage bolstered Leonidas' claim because Gorgo had inherited Kleomenes' property.

Secondly, the kings' jurisdiction applied only to the case of an unmarried *patrouchos* not already betrothed by her father. An heiress already married or even merely betrothed was apparently permitted to retain her existing or intended spouse instead of having to marry her next-of-kin.[54] This is confirmed by the case of Lysander's daughters. On their father's death the men to whom they were betrothed, far from being expected to give way to the next-of-kin, were fined when they disowned the girls. This contrasts with the law in both Athens and Gortyn, where the next-of-kin had the right to marry the heiress unless she was married and already had a son (in Athens) or child of either sex (in Gortyn).[55] There was evidently less control in Sparta over the father's right to pass on his estate to descendants of other lineages by marrying his heiress outside the kin. This fits perfectly with the landowner's freedom of gift and bequest attested earlier in this chapter.

Thirdly, there is the question of the nature of the kings' jurisdiction. It is sometimes assumed (e.g. Asheri 1961, 61; 1963, 18; Cozzoli 1979, 7) that their role was to allocate the heiress to a landless citizen. On the contrary, however, the verb ἱκνέεται denotes that the potential husband had some right to the heiress' hand and was not selected upon the arbitrary initiative of the kings.[56] It seems likely that, as in other Greek states, the right to marry an heiress who came within the kings' jurisdiction belonged to the nearest male relative. The circumstance of an old man with a young wife discussed by Xenophon (*Lak. Pol.* 1.7; cf. Plut. *Lyk.* 15.7) was surely typically the outcome of just such a marriage between an heiress and her father's brother.[57] The situation was apparently so common that there was a special officially-sanctioned arrangement by which the elderly husband could introduce a younger man to beget children on his behalf. The kings' role was probably to adjudicate between the competing claims of different kinsmen to the position of next-of-kin, as did the *dikastērion* of the eponymous *archōn* at Athens.[58]

The next text is the testimony of Aristotle: 'but, as it is (νῦν), one may give an *epiklēros* in marriage to any person one wishes; and, if a man dies without making a will, the man he leaves as *klēronomos* gives her to whomever he likes'. This text is often regarded as indicating a change in the law from that referred to by Herodotus. I shall argue, however, that the differences between the two sources are more apparent than real. First, on the question of ownership of the paternal estate, Aristotle calls the heiress by the Athenian term *epiklēros* and mentions a person called the *klēronomos*, presumably the next-of-kin, who had control over her marriage when her father died intestate. The word *klēronomos* often means 'heir';[59] but Aristotle clearly believed that the heiress herself was the legal owner of her father's estates, not just the temporary holder until her sons reached majority (as was the Athenian *epiklēros*), since he specifies the number of heiresses as one reason why approximately two-fifths of the land was owned by women.[60] Aristotle's use of the term *epiklēros* appears, therefore, to be a case of loose, untechnical phraseology (Wolff 1957, 166–7; Cartledge 1981, 97). As for the *klēronomos*, although the term often means the 'taker of the lot' – or 'he to whom the lot is distributed' (from *nemein*) – other, weaker interpretations are also possible. It could mean 'he who has the management of the lot' (from *nemesthai*) or, on analogy with the official called the *paidonomos* who supervised the upbringing of Spartiate boys, 'he who (shep)herds the lot'. Either of these latter meanings would tie in with Aristotle's statement that the *klēronomos* decided whom the unbetrothed heiress should marry, and thus into which lineage the parental property would ultimately descend. This would be compatible with the view that the heiress retained all the property in question.

Secondly, Aristotle's evidence concurs with that of Herodotus regarding the freedom with which an heiress could be married outside the kin. His statement that an heiress could be given in marriage to anyone (in the context this means by her father) echoes that of Herodotus. His following remark that, if a man died intestate, the person left as *klēronomos* gave the heiress to whomever he likes, appears to indicate that a father could validly betroth his heiress not only during his lifetime but also in his will.[61] This right may already be implicit in the evidence of Herodotus, although the latter's testimony is insufficiently specific to permit certainty.

Aristotle's remarks concerning the *klēronomos* have led many scholars to conclude that he is reporting important changes in law and practice since the time of Herodotus. It is argued, first, that the kings had lost their jurisdiction over the unbetrothed heiress, who now automatically came under the guardianship of her male next-of-kin; secondly, that the rules governing the marriage of the heiress had been relaxed so that the next-of-kin could freely give her in marriage outside the kin. These changes are often viewed as a loosening of the law corresponding to the corruptions of the system of land tenure allegedly introduced by Epitadeus.[62]

The laws described by Herodotus and implied by Aristotle may not, however, be as different as these views suggest.[63] In comparing their testimony one must take into account the different nature of the two sources. Herodotus' account is a record of the legal prerogatives of the kings which, as Pierre Carlier (1984, 249–52) has demonstrated, draws without comment upon a more or less official Spartiate source which itself portrayed the law as traditional and uncontroversial without detailed reference to its practical impact. Aristotle's sharp criticisms, in contrast, highlight controversial aspects of Spartiate practice, focusing upon their impact without specifying the precise legal procedures. Their seemingly divergent evidence may result as much from their totally opposite standpoints as from significant differences in either law or practice.

Indeed, Aristotle's testimony does not prove that the kings' adjudicatory role had disappeared. He says nothing about the precise procedures followed when the father died intestate. There will surely have remained a need for adjudication between competing claimants to the position of *klēronomos*, which was probably much sought after because of the potential for personal advantage and patronage afforded by control over the marriage of the heiress. Neither is it clear that the role of the heiress' next-of-kin differs greatly between the two passages. Herodotus' brief statement of the official procedure does not specify the exact obligations upon the man to whom an heiress was adjudicated. Nothing in his evidence says that the next-of-kin was obliged to marry her himself, rather than betrothing her to another citizen. Equally, nothing in Aristotle's evidence says that the *klēronomos*, although free to dispose of the heiress' hand, could not choose to marry her himself.[64] It is perhaps significant, given Aristotle's Athenian frame of reference, that the sole attested Athenian example of a man being called a *klēronomos* in a case involving an *epiklēros* concerns a relative who expected to marry the girl himself (Menander, *Aspis* 85; cf. MacDowell 1986, 108).

There are, therefore, no grounds for the hypothesis that there was a change in the laws regarding the marriage of heiresses between the time of Herodotus in the later fifth century and the period of Aristotle in the later fourth. Indeed, the final piece of evidence, from the later third century – Plutarch's description of King Leonidas II's treatment of Agiatis, widow of King Agis IV whom he had executed in the year 241 – shows signs of continuity with the evidence from earlier periods.

> Leonidas took his [Agis'] wife, who had a new-born child (*paidion*), from her home and compelled her to marry his son, Kleomenes, who was not quite at the age of marriage. He did not want to give the woman to anyone else because Agiatis was an *epiklēros* of the large estate of her father, Gylippos... (*Kleomenes* 1.1).[65]

The one difficulty with this passage is the legal status of the action of King Leonidas. On the death of her husband, although clearly no *parthenos* (virgin), did Agiatis revert to the status of an unmarried, unbetrothed heiress, whose remarriage therefore came legitimately within Leonidas' jurisdiction? Was Leonidas using, and of course abusing, the kings' still extant traditional role of adjudicating the right to marry an heiress? Or was he simply acting arbitrarily, entirely outside the law, in compelling a rich widow to marry his son? The revolutionary character of the times, in which many traditional political practices were simply flouted or ignored, makes it impossible to tell.

In terms of family and inheritance law, however, as opposed to political practice, Agiatis' position seems no different from that of classical heiresses.

Her current status as heiress at the time of this incident implies that her father Gylippos had died some unspecified time previously and that she was already in possession of her inheritance. Whether she had already been in possession at the time of her marriage to Agis is unknown; but, whichever was the case, she stands as a classic example of an heiress who married outside her lineage, as in the time of Herodotus and Aristotle. Also like classical heiresses, she owned her father's property in her own right. It is implied in the episode that any sons born of her remarriage would have a claim to the inheritance alongside that of her child – a son, as we learn elsewhere – by her first marriage.[66] Like classical Spartiate heiresses, she was not merely the vehicle for passing on the paternal property to the son(s) of the man whom her father had chosen as her husband.

Dowries and female inheritance

The other factor which Aristotle identified as responsible for the great extent of female land-ownership was the prevalence of large dowries (*proikes*). Some later writers claimed that dowries were officially prohibited in 'Lykourgan' Sparta, and this notion has exercised a remarkable hold upon modern scholarship (e.g. Asheri 1963, 14; MacDowell 1986, 81–2; Singor 1993, 36). None of the evidence is, however, of any great reliability. As we saw in chapter 2, the earliest reference to a ban on dowries comes from two sources influenced by the propaganda of the third-century revolution: the Lykourgan sayings among the *Apophthegmata Lakōnika* (no. 15 = Plut. *Mor.* 227f) and Hermippos (fr. 87, *ap.* Athen. 555c). The supposed ban on giving any property to women through dowry is clearly part and parcel of the system of equal, publicly controlled *klēroi* passed down intact from father to a single son which we have already identified as an invention of revolutionary propaganda.[67] The reason given for the ban in the Lykourgan saying is heavily infected with that propaganda's characteristically egalitarian tone: 'So that none may be left unmarried because of poverty or sought eagerly because of affluence'. Hermippos' reference to the ban is part of his incredible portrayal of the supposed custom whereby youths gained their brides by capturing them unseen in a dark room. This procedure is not supported by the classical evidence. Although matrimonial rites may have included a symbolic marriage by capture (Plut. *Lyk.* 15.3), which was on one infamous occasion exploited by King Damaratos, who carried off the woman betrothed to his kinsman Leotychidas (Hdt. 6.65), the passages of Herodotus and Aristotle regarding heiresses considered in the previous section indicate that it was Leotychidas' method of acquiring a wife which was the norm and that marriages were typically preceded by a betrothal arranged by the bride's parents or next-of-kin.

Other post-classical sources which are sometimes cited as evidence for the absence of dowries in fact testify to their presence, except perhaps among the very poor. According to an apophthegm in the pre-revolutionary *Lakainōn*

Apophthegmata (anon. no. 24 = *Mor.* 242b), 'A poor girl, being asked what dowry she brought to the man who married her, replied, "The family *sōphrosynē*"'. The implication of the question is surely that bringing a dowry was the norm. In Plutarch's account of the love story of Damokrita (*Mor.* 775c–e), the same implication follows from the confiscation of her exiled husband's property so that his two daughters might not be provided with dowries. Aelian (*VH* 6.6) claims that those who married undowried women were relieved of all public duties. The implication again is that marrying without a dowry was the exception not the rule.

The testimony of Aristotle is sufficient evidence that in the classical period a girl on her marriage received a significant transfer of land from her parents. Although Aristotle is the first source to refer to dowries, there are no grounds for thinking that this was a new practice in the fourth century. The case studies below of sixth- and fifth-century brides who brought great wealth to their husbands will demonstrate otherwise. These land transfers need not, however, have been exactly the same as the institution of dowry as it operated in classical Athens. As with his reference to the *epiklēros*, Aristotle may be using the term *proix* in a loose, untechnical sense to describe an analogous but not identical social practice (Schaps 1979, 85–7, with Appendix II). It is not necessary, therefore, to believe that any property thus transferred came under the management of the bride's husband as at Athens (A.R.W. Harrison 1968–71, 52–4; Schaps 1979, 75). The fact that Aristotle saw dowries as partly responsible for female possession of two-fifths of the land suggests that the bride retained control of the gift just as the *patrouchos* did of her inheritance. This is the interpretation of Cartledge, who argues that 'what Aristotle calls "large dowries" were really…marriage-settlements consisting of landed property together with any movables that a rich father (or mother) saw fit to bestow on a daughter' (1981, 98).

The issue raised by this formulation is whether the amount of property transferred was solely at the discretion of the bride's parents or whether it was predetermined in any way. The Gortyn Code, for example, also refers to the transfer of property to a bride by her father and indicates that, as in Sparta, it remained under her control (6.9–12; Willetts 1967, 20; Schaps 1979, 88). The property in question, however, was not merely a voluntary gift but an anticipation of the daughter's rightful inheritance. If it was not given to her at marriage, she would receive it ultimately on her father's death (4.37–5.9). A daughter was entitled to share in the inheritance of all her father's (and mother's) property, apart from certain specified items (town houses, the contents of untenanted country houses and livestock), even when there were surviving brothers. Her portion was half that of a son (4.39–43). This amount could be given to her on marriage: 'if the father, while living, should wish to give to a daughter upon her marriage, let him give as prescribed, but no more' (4.48–51). The evidence of the Code is corroborated by Ephorus' statement (*FGrH* 70F149, *ap.* Strabo 10.4.20) that 'the dowry (*phernē*), if there are brothers, is half of a brother's portion'.⁶⁸ The question is whether a Spartiate daughter had the same rights of (anticipated) inheritance as her Gortynian counterpart. If she was not a *patrouchos*, was the amount of property transferred to her on marriage dependent solely upon the generosity of her parents and the strength of their desire to secure a desirable husband for her? Or did the settlement reflect her right to inherit a portion of the parental estates, even in the presence of surviving brothers?

The normal assumption has been that Spartiate women did not have any rights of inheritance in the presence of brothers. There is, however, one important indication to the contrary. Aristotle states that approximately (or 'nearly': σχεδόν) two-fifths of the land was in the possession of women. This statement has to my knowledge never been satisfactorily explained. Is it possible to explain how or why this particular proportion of land should have been in female hands? Now, a system of inheritance like that at Gortyn, according to which a daughter is entitled to a landed inheritance half that of her brother, will tend to produce a distribution of land between the sexes such that the proportion owned by women is nearly 40%. The reason is that the 33.3% of land inherited by females in households with both surviving sons and daughters (on the assumption of an equal sex ratio across the population as a whole) is increased several per cent, by the fact that in households with surviving daughters only the female inheritance is treble the normal share, whereas in those with only surviving sons, the male share is increased only one and a half times.⁶⁹ The existence of such an inheritance system at Sparta would, consequently, explain Aristotle's figure. I have described this system by the phrase 'universal female inheritance' (Hodkinson 1989, 82), inasmuch as all women gain some inheritance, whether they have brothers or not.

Here it is necessary to correct a misunderstanding of my theory which has surfaced recently in an article by Ducat (1998, 393). He correctly notes that Aristotle explains female landed wealth in terms of two mechanisms, dowry and inheritance as a sole heiress. Next, however, he mistakenly asserts that, judging that these two practices would be insufficient to explain female possession of two-fifths of the land, I am proposing to add a third mechanism, 'universal female inheritance'. This is to misinterpret my argument. 'Universal female inheritance' is not an additional mechanism by which women could acquire land. Rather, the phrase unites Aristotle's two mechanisms into a single system. On my theory, all daughters inherited some land. (In the case of a daughter with brothers my hypothesis is that this was half of a son's share.) My suggestion is that what Aristotle calls 'dowries' were in reality a *pre-mortem* inheritance given on a daughter's marriage and that the size of those dowries was influenced by what the daughter would expect to receive ultimately on her parents' death. Taken together in this way, Aristotle's two mechanisms are sufficient to explain female possession of about two-fifths of the land (as is demonstrated by the calculations in n.70), without the addition of any further mechanisms for its acquisition. Ducat criticises my suggestion of universal female inheritance on the grounds that, had it existed, Aristotle would have mentioned it in his criticisms of the failings of the Spartan *politeia*. The point, however, is that Aristotle does not explicitly mention it because his account of the property rights of Spartiate women, though perceptive, describes them not in authentic Spartan terms but in terms drawn from the rather different situation in contemporary Athens with which he was more familiar. Just as he uses the Athenian term *epiklēros* to describe the Spartiate *patrouchos*, so also he uses the Athenian term *proikes* ('dowries') to describe *pre-mortem* allocations of a girl's inheritance at the time of her marriage. My hypothesis, although not capable of definitive proof, has at least the merit of offering a complete explication of Aristotle's text, in that it offers the only explanation (to my knowledge) in modern scholarship of the precise figure given by Aristotle for the proportion of land in female hands. It also has the merit of explaining another puzzle ignored by many scholars, namely, why Spartiate parents gave such large amounts of land to their daughters on marriage, in spite of that practice's deleterious diminution of the family landholdings.

Furthermore, Aristotle's remarks concerning Sparta's system of partible inheritance (*Politics* 1270b1–6) are not incompatible with the thesis of universal female inheritance. His statement (lines 5–6) that, 'if many are born (πολλῶν γινομένων) and the land has been divided accordingly' appears to refer back to lines 2–3, where he comments that the lawgiver encouraged the citizens 'to beget many children' (ὅτι πλείστους ποιεῖσθαι παῖδας). There is no indication here that only sons inherited. It may be significant that Aristotle uses terms which carry no obvious differentiation between the sexes when he writes about division of the inheritance, despite the fact that he could easily have indicated such a differentiation. Although in lines 3–4 he mentions the alleviation of public duties which was granted to fathers of three or more sons, he does so only in order to illustrate his general remark about the lawgiver's intentions. He does not continue this explicit reference to sons into the following sentence in which he discusses division of the inheritance.

There are also several historical instances which suggest universal female inheritance. Some concern marriages to close consanguineous kin contracted by members of the royal houses.[70] Take the mid-sixth-century marriage between King Anaxandridas II and his sister's daughter (see *Fig.* 25, on p. 411). The king refused to dissolve this union, despite his wife's initial childlessness and the ephors' insistence that he divorce her and remarry to perpetuate the royal lineage (Hdt. 5.39–41). Only when he was permitted to retain her as well, did Anaxandridas agree to take another wife. Although he was reportedly devoted to his niece, material considerations were probably also involved. Had he divorced her, she would have taken her property away. Even after his second wife had borne him a son, Anaxandridas still ensured that his niece subsequently bore him children (three sons) to inherit her property. All this suggests that she was of some wealth. There are several unknowns in this case which hinder a full interpretation, in particular whether the girl was a *patrouchos*. Under the hypothesis of universal female inheritance, however, her property would have included at least part (and possibly all) of the estates which had formerly belonged to Anaxandridas' parents, land which the king had had to share with his sister, the girl's mother. Anaxandridas' desire to recover for his descendants the remaining portions of his parents' estates would explain both the initial marriage to his niece and his subsequent determination to retain her and beget children. This episode makes perfect sense on the thesis of universal female inheritance.

A second example is the early fifth-century marriage between the future King Archidamos II and his step-aunt, Lampito (Hdt. 6.71; see *Fig.* 26, on p. 412). This match originated from the two marriages of King Leotychidas II. His first marriage produced an only son, Zeuxidamos, who in turn fathered Archidamos before dying prematurely without further issue. Lampito was the only child of Leotychidas' second marriage to a certain Eurydamē. Eurydamē herself was not a *patrouchos*, since she had a brother named Menios. Since Archidamos' succession to the throne was not in doubt, the purpose of the match, which was arranged by Leotychidas himself, was surely to concentrate and add to the royal property. This marital manoeuvre would be understandable under the hypothesis of universal female inheritance, since Lampito would have been a very rich bride. First, having only one step-brother, she would be due to inherit one-third of Leotychidas' estates. Secondly, she would have inherited further property from her mother Eurydamē, who would herself have inherited up to a third of the estates of her parents.[71] Such an inheritance would also explain why Leotychidas chose Eurydamē as his second wife. Note that without the operation of universal female inheritance neither Lampito nor her mother Eurydamē would have been guaranteed such considerable levels of wealth.

A third example concerns Kyniska, daughter of Archidamos II (*Fig.* 26). She was not a *patrouchos*, since her father had two sons, Kings Agis and Agesilaos. Yet she owned sufficient land and other resources to breed horses to gain two victories in the Olympic four-horse chariot race (Xen. *Ages.* 9.6; Moretti, 1957, nos. 373 and 381) and to commission a grandiose victory monument.[72] It seems more likely that her great wealth stemmed from a right to inherit a fifth of the estates of Archidamos than that she was voluntarily given a dowry of such great proportions.[73] Neither was Kyniska alone. According to Pausanias (3.8.1, 17.6), Olympic chariot-race victories were subsequently won by several Spartiate women, such as Euryleonis, victrix in the two-horse chariot race, probably in 368 (Moretti 1957, no. 418). In view of the evidence regarding Kyniska's position, it would be special pleading to claim that these women must all have been *patrouchoi*. That these women owned such considerable amounts of land adds further strength to the thesis of universal female inheritance.[74]

Cumulatively, these examples lend support to the thesis that a daughter inherited a portion of her parents' landed property even in the presence of surviving brothers. I would suggest that by the time of the fourth century the knowledge that a daughter would ultimately expect to receive a significant portion of her parents' estates by way of inheritance exercised a pronounced influence upon the size of marriage-settlements. That was why Aristotle named large dowries as one of the two reasons for the ownership by women of approximately two-fifths of the land.

Even if one rejects my hypothesis of universal female inheritance and prefers to view landed dowries as voluntary gifts, it is apparent that by the fourth century marriage-settlements were often large. They were obviously designed not merely to provide support for the bride in her new household, but to settle either the whole or the bulk of her claim to her parents' estates, thus ensuring that a significant part of the parental property was ultimately passed on to her own children.[75] It is clear therefore that the Spartiate inheritance system operated on the basis of what is known as a diverging pattern of devolution, that is, one in which the property of an individual (in the Spartiate case, either male or female) was distributed to children of both sexes and hence diffused outside the kin (Goody 1973; 1976a, 6–7). Indeed, the characteristics of Spartiate marriage patterns, such as uterine half-sibling marriage and royal unions with other close blood relations, closely parallel those found in other societies in which diverging devolution operates (Hodkinson 1989). Such societies often have a high level of endogamy and other forms of in-marriage as a means of restricting diffusion of property outside the kin (Goody 1973, 27). Adelphic polyandry, another practice evidenced in Sparta, is also associated in many societies with property ownership by women as well as by men (Leach 1955). This combination of ethnographic parallels with the evidence of royal marriage manoeuvres going back to the mid-sixth century provides a firm indication that the system of diverging devolution and the significant amount of female land ownership to which it gave rise were basic aspects of Spartiate land tenure and inheritance throughout late archaic and classical Sparta.

Developments in the distribution of land

The picture of Spartiate land tenure and inheritance suggested in this chapter is markedly different from those postulated by Plutarch and his modern followers. In place of a schema governed by public controls and dominated by indivisible, inalienable, male-owned and equal *klēroi*, with reversion back to the state at death or succession by primogeniture, we have witnessed a system in which individual citizens had indefinite possession of private landholdings which were transmissible to both sons and daughters by means of partible inheritance and were open to alienation through lifetime gifts, testamentary bequests and the betrothal of heiresses.

Owing to the paucity of evidence, we have been able to view the system of land tenure and inheritance only in its crudest outlines, without the possibility of considering the many subtleties and complexities of law and practice to which the variety of individual circumstances no doubt gave rise in everyday life – complexities which appear prominently in the more complete evidence from contemporary Athens (Cox 1998). Indeed, the existence of the various types of marriage practices mentioned above, along with the availability of adoption and freedom of gift and bequest, suggests that different individuals and families adopted a variety of strategies for coping with a diverse range of personal circumstances.

This variety of voluntary strategies reminds us that, although the laws governing Spartiate land tenure and inheritance remained – as I have argued – largely unchanged throughout the classical period, and certainly did not undergo radical corruption and change in the early fourth century, there is no reason to believe that the responses of Spartiate families to those laws remained unchanged throughout this period or that the economic context which informed those responses was uniform from one century to the next. Certainly, there were major changes in the distribution of land during our period. Although there was never the wholesale redistribution of land described in Plutarch's *Lykourgos*, there must at some point in the seventh or sixth centuries have been some significant allocation of land, possibly in newly-acquired territory, to poorer citizens, in order to sustain them viably as full-time hoplite warriors who did not support themselves by working for their own living. Although there was never a system of equal *klēroi* – at least before the third-century revolution – and there were always some wealthy families, the overall distribution of land was surely more evenly spread at the start of our period than at the end. The decline of Spartiate citizen numbers in the fifth and fourth centuries was surely grounded in increasing inequalities of wealth. Aristotle seems to imply as much in his comment that 'the land has fallen into the hands of a few'.

Thus the conclusions of this chapter direct us to two basic and related contradictions within Spartiate society: first, between the façade of a seemingly stable society marked by an unchanging system of government and property laws and the reality of a changing economic context involving continual shifts in the fortunes of a declining number of citizen households; and, secondly, between the narrowly political demands of the male-centred hoplite polis, which overtly minimized the importance of material considerations, and the fundamental economic needs of households, a significant proportion of whose property lay in female hands. I shall return to these findings in my final chapter (ch. 13), which will discuss the changing economic context – especially the increasing concentration of property and the extent to which it was resisted or fuelled by family inheritance strategies – as part of a broader examination of the contribution of issues of property and wealth to the crisis of Spartiate society.

Notes

¹ For an example of nineteenth-century controversy, Grote 1862, ii.156–76, with references to earlier views. For the 1970s and 1980s, see Cartledge 1979, 165–70; Cozzoli 1979, 1–58; Hooker 1980, 116–18; David 1981, 46–50; Marasco 1981, i.204–23; Ducat 1983; Figueira 1984; 1986; MacDowell 1986, 89–110. For references to other discussions, Walbank 1957, 731; Michell 1964, 205–32; Oliva 1971, 32–8, 48–54, 188–93.

² Largely accepted: e.g. Spawforth 1990; Link 1991, 69–105; Mossé 1991, 150 n. 3; Nafissi 1991, 32–4; Singor 1993; Blundell 1995, 155–7; Lazenby 1995, 87 n. 1; Lupi 1997, 139–40; Patterson 1998, 73–9, 101–2. Moving in a similar direction: Cozzoli 1979, 1–38; Cartledge 1979, 165–70; 1987, 166–74; I would draw particular attention to the perceptive study of Ducat 1983, of which I was unaware until after the publication of my article.

³ e.g. Michell 1964, 205–11; Oliva 1971, 36–8; Forrest 1968, 135–6; Figueira 1984, 96–7. Both Michell and Oliva, however, waver somewhat in their accounts, saying that a man's *klēros* must often have been passed on by the state to his eldest son.

⁴ See the works cited by Tigerstedt 1965–78, i.566 n. 412.

⁵ Cf. 6.48.3, where this equality is attributed to Lykourgos.

⁶ This procedure, denounced already by Grote (1862, ii.172, note) in the last century, is most obvious with regard to belief in the indivisibility of the Spartiate *klēros*. Some examples: i) Michell (1964) accepts the evidence of Plut. *Lyk.* 16 on pp. 207 ff., without mentioning Aristotle's account, which is not introduced until p. 219. Aristotle's crucial comment on the divisibility of Spartiate estates (*Politics* 1270b4–6) is not quoted until p. 229 and is then ignored in the subsequent discussion. ii) Hooker (1980) pronounces on p. 116 that estates were indivisible, does not quote Aristotle until pp. 142–3, and ends the quotation one sentence before Aristotle's comment upon divisibility. iii) David (1981, 46–9) conducts his discussion without a reference to Aristotle in the main text, mentioning his testimony only in later sections (68–9, 102–5) as evidence for the supposed new system allegedly introduced by the law of Epitadeus.

⁷ In addition to those cited above, cf. Plut. *Comp. Lyk.-Num.* 2.6; *Solon* 16.1; *Kleom.* 18.2; *Mor.* 226b; Justin 3.3.3.

⁸ Against MacDowell's claim (1986, 89) that Plato's remarks 'imply that equality of landholdings in Sparta still obtained', see ch. 2, n. 17. MacDowell is equally cavalier in his assertion (1986, 92) that the idea that equality of landholding was invented in the late fourth or third century 'can be dismissed at once, because we have already seen that it goes back as early as the time of Plato'. He ignores the fact that Plato's equal distribution, unlike that ascribed to Lykourgos, is not located in the historical period (cf., recently, Link 1991, 69).

⁹ Cf. Plb. 6.5.1, where 'the *anacyclosis*, which is probably the work of some writer of the third or second century, is said to have been set forth by "Plato and certain other philosophers"' (Walbank 1957, 727).

¹⁰ And possibly also with the 9,000 strong citizen body achieved in Athens in 322 by a limitation of the franchise, which was portrayed as a return to the ancestral constitution (Diod. 18.18.5; Plut. *Phokion* 27.5) and may have been viewed as the archetype of a balanced constitution.

¹¹ This explanation of Plutarch's first version seems preferable to the alternative argument that the 9,000 citizen *klēroi* represent an arbitrary doubling of the *klēroi* in

Agis' projected reform designed to reflect Sparta's former control of Messenia (see the references in Marasco 1981, i.115 n.1, to which add Cartledge 1979, 169–70), since the tradition about Lykourgos uniformly places him before the conquest of Messenia. The opposite theory, that Plutarch's first version was in existence before the third century and was halved by the revolutionaries (Ehrenberg 1924, 44; Ziehen 1933, 223), fails to explain the 30,000 perioikic *klēroi*. Since there is no reason to believe that the Spartiates (re)distributed, or were thought to have (re)distributed, perioikic land before the third century, the revolutionaries' figure for the perioikic, and therefore also for the Spartiate, *klēroi* must have existed first (Jones 1967, 40; Cartledge 1979, 169–70). MacDowell's assertion (1986, 28) that Plutarch's statement about the perioikic *klēroi* does not imply a systematic distribution is hard to credit, since their allotment is covered by the same verb (*eneime*) as the allotment of citizen *klēroi*.

12 Cf. Africa 1961; Starr 1965; Tigerstedt 1965–78, ii.49–85; and ch. 2, above.

13 Asheri's additional references to privileges within the royal houses deriving from primogeniture (Hdt. 6.52; Paus. 1.1.4) are no support for a supposed system of indivisibility. Indeed, his general perspective (for which, cf. also 1966, 71, 77), which involves the claim that primogeniture was the traditional practice of moderate constitutions, is fundamentally mistaken. Partible inheritance was the invariable practice throughout Greek antiquity. The unique regulations of Plato's *Laws* (740b–d, 923c–d) and the frequently misunderstood advice of Hesiod concerning the desired number of sons (*Works and Days* 376–80) offer no support to Asheri's view. Cf. Lane Fox 1985, 211, 216.

14 Cf. also the criticism of Asheri's interpretation of this last passage by Cozzoli 1979, 7 n. 2.

15 e.g. (i) the reference to conflict between kings and ephors in Plut. *Agis* 12.2 goes far beyond Arist. *Pol.* 1271a24–6, especially the idea that the two kings together could outweigh the ephors. (ii) in *Agis* 9.1, 11.1, despite the fact that an assembly was called when the Gerousia was divided, it was still the Gerousia which made the final decision, not the assembly as in *Pol.* 1273a6 ff. – whichever one prefers of the two possible interpretations of Aristotle's evidence suggested by Saunders 1981, 156 n. 3. (iii) in *Kleom.* 10.2–3 the ephors gradually usurp power after initially being assistants to the kings, whereas in *Pol.* 1313a25 ff. and in Plut. *Lyk.* 7.2 they are a check on royal authority from the start. This last example demonstrates the error of Marasco's general assumption that Plutarch's sources for the lives of Agis and Kleomenes were the same as those for the life of Lykourgos. Plutarch's use of Aristotle in the *Lykourgos* does not prove that he was a significant source for the other lives.

16 Marasco 1978b, 179, with references to earlier works; David 1982/83, 80.

17 Schütrumpf 1987, whose study contradicts David's implicit claim (1981, 59–66) that the remarks of Plato, *Republic* 547d–552e on the decline of (Spartan) timarchy and the evils of oligarchy corroborate the account of Phylarchos. The link which Schütrumpf has established between Plutarch's *Agis* and Plato's *Republic* does not relate to this part of Plato's work, in which Plato says nothing of changes in the nature of land tenure. His general statement that under an oligarchy a man is allowed to sell all he has to another and become a pauper (552a–b) is unlikely to be a reference to such a measure as the supposed law of Epitadeus, which concerned not sale but gift and bequest.

18 On an appropriate model life table, such as Coale and Demeny's Model South, Mortality Level 3, males under 20 account for some 33.17% of the population under a population growth rate of -10. This figures increases to 36.98% on a growth rate of -5

and 40.86% on a static growth rate (Coale and Demeny 1983, 449).

19 Justin's abridgement (3.3.3) of Pompeius Trogus' account of Lykourgos' equal division also, in its reference to the uniformity of '*patrimonia*', seems to assume a system of private property.

20 The most recent example of arbitrary conjecture is that of MacDowell (1986, 95), who is compelled to postulate the existence of no fewer than three different unattested laws in order to explain how Plutarch's lots were passed on in approximately the same number over the generations.

21 For this claim, see e.g. Michell 1964, 207–9; David 1981, 46–8; Marasco 1981, i.211; MacDowell 1986, 93–4. Marasco attempts to avoid this contradiction by claiming that Plutarch's account is not one of complete equality. He argues that the phrase ἁμῶς γέ πως in *Agis* 5.1 indicates that the equality was only partial. For this to be so, however, one would expect the phrase to be placed either before or after διαμένουσα. As it stands, the more natural interpretation of the meaning of the sentence is that other defects in the state were partially corrected by the complete equality.

22 Indeed, we shall see later that even Herakleides' apparently indisputable reference to two types of land is by no means as securely based at it might first seem.

23 Hence MacDowell's attempt (1986, 91) to use Plut. *Agis* 8 – the description of the boundaries within which Agis IV proposed to carve out his 4,500 *klēroi* – to clarify the meaning of the *politikē chōra* must be ruled out of court.

24 e.g. Andreades 1933, 53–7; Jones 1967, 134–7; Ste Croix 1972, 331–2; Cartledge 1979, 307–11; Forrest 1968, 134–7; Cawkwell 1983, 385–90; Lane Fox 1985, 221–2.

25 It is no defence to argue, as does Marasco (1981, i.209–10), that Plutarch was concerned not with the concentration of land but with the freedom to alienate the *klēros* which led the poor into destitution. Plutarch himself states that equality existed before Epitadeus' law and that concentration of land and widespread poverty were its consequences.

26 Poverty of younger sons: David 1981, 48; both he (at p. 92) and Hooker (1980, 143) fail to discuss the question of manpower decline before the battle of Mantineia in 418. Natural extinction: Marasco 1981, i. 211; the implausibility of this explanation is increased by the fact that it is supposed to account for the entire manpower decline down to the 360s, since Marasco believes that each Spartiate possessed by right of birth a lot sufficient for his maintenance until the law of Epitadeus, which he dates after the loss of Messenia (p. 214).

27 References to older works in Toynbee 1969, 301 n. 1; cf. more recently Cartledge 1979, 165–70; 1987, 166–74; Cozzoli 1979, 1–38; Ducat 1983, and other works referenced in n. 2, above.

28 For which we are dependent on the divergent evidence of late sources (listed in Michell 1964, 85 n. 1). On the fictional, fourth-century origins of our accounts of the episode, see now Nafissi 1999, 251–58.

29 Herman 1987; Mitchell 1997, see further ch. 11 below.

30 On partible inheritance as the general Greek pattern, cf. Lane Fox 1985.

31 MacDowell's claim (1986, 95) that *tōn chrēmatōn* 'probably refers to other forms of property' than land is extremely forced. Why should we think that Xenophon means to exclude the most important form of property, land?

32 For other references to wife-sharing, *Lakainōn Apophthegmata* no. 23 = Plut. *Mor.* 242b; Plut. *Lyk.* 15.13; *Comp. Lyk.-Numa* 3.3.

³³ Cartledge 1981, 103 n. 118; Lane Fox 1985, 223. The reliability of Philo's evidence is confirmed by the accuracy of his accompanying statements that the Athenians permitted marriage between non-uterine half-siblings and the Egyptians full brother-sister marriage (cf. A.R.W. Harrison 1968–71, i.22-3; Hopkins 1980). His evidence has been doubted on generic grounds by Vérilhac and Vial (1998, 94); but they display no awareness of the many studies of Spartiate marriage in the last 15 years which have demonstrated the close inter-connection of uterine half-sibling marriage with the practice of wife-sharing.

³⁴ I have adopted the interpretation of this passage by Lane Fox (1985, 222), who suggests that the clause ἀδελφοὺς ὄντας should be taken with all the preceding accusatives. On the relevance of polyandry to the concentration of property, Kunstler (1983, 475, 593 n. 990), who, along with Lane Fox (1985, 223), stresses that avoidance of division was as much a strategy of the rich as of the poor. This is, indeed, suggested in the context of wife-sharing by Xenophon's reference to the power (*dynamis*) of the kin.

³⁵ The earliest date at which most scholars who accept the authenticity of Epitadeus would place his law is the mid-390s: e.g. David (1981, 67), who supposes that it was enacted towards the end of Pausanias' reign in 395, or shortly afterwards. Other scholars place Epitadeus as late as after the battle of Leuktra: e.g. Marasco 1980, 132. Attempts, like that of MacDowell (1986, 105), to date his law before 404 or to equate Epitadeus with the commander Epitadas, who died on Sphakteria in 425 (Thuc. 4.8, 31, 33, 38), violate the chronology of Plutarch's account upon which they rely and are justly criticized by David 1981, 211 n. 88.

³⁶ The fact that Xenophon's evidence concerning Agesilaos' gift was repeated by Plutarch in his own biography of the king (*Ages*. 4.1) further demonstrates the latter's lack of awareness of contradictions between his accounts in different biographies and casts additional doubt upon the veracity of the account in the *Life of Agis*. Note that Agesilaos' freedom to alienate this land was not restricted by the fact that his son, Archidamos, was probably already alive at the time. Since Archidamos' *paidika*, Kleonymos, was at least 14 in the year 378 (he had just come out of the *paides*: Xen. *Hell*. 5.4.25; cf. Kennell 1995, 32, 117), he must himself then have been 22 or older (there was normally at least 8 years between *erastēs* and *paidika*: Hodkinson 1983, 245, 251 n. 28) and will therefore have been born, or at least expected, in 400 BC.

³⁷ Fustel cites no sources in support of his claim concerning the deprivation of *commercium*; I have not been able to gain any enlightenment on the point from standard modern handbooks of Roman law. Even if Fustel is correct, the claimed parallel between Spartan and Roman law remains uncertain.

³⁸ Schütrumpf himself notes elsewhere (1987, 448–9) that Book 2 was 'based on some source material, probably local chronicles'. Indeed, although it was composed earlier than the *Lak. Pol.*, it is perfectly possible that the account in Book 2 could have drawn upon unpublished research material for the latter work.

³⁹ In support of this argument I cited, for comparison, *Pol*. 1263a35–7, a truncated summary of the details in Xen. *Lak. Pol*. 6.3–4.

⁴⁰ See esp. Pareti 1917, 197–200; Ehrenberg 1924, 45–9; further references in David 1981, 200–1 n. 13.

⁴¹ I say 'in my opinion', since Lazenby himself thinks that the *moira* was mentioned in the Aristotelian *Polity of the Lakedaimonians*, though he agrees that its meaning was misinterpreted or misrepresented by Herakleides or his excerptor.

⁴² The difference in terminology between *moira* and *apophora* is at first sight puzzling,

Ch. 3. The ownership and inheritance of land – revisited

but it may reflect the diverse sources from which the *Instituta* originate. The two terms also reflect different aspects of the helot tribute: the latter its fixed amount, the former its character as payment in kind (Ducat 1990a, 57).

43 e.g. Meyer 1892–99, i.258 n. 3; Busolt 1893–1904, i.523; Jones 1967, 41; Forrest 1968, 137; Cartledge 1979, 167–8; Cozzoli 1979, 6; Hodkinson 1986, 389–91; Schütrumpf 1987.

44 Asheri 1961, 66; 1963, 5; David 1981, 102, 221–2 n. 49; 1982/83, 87.

45 Ehrenberg 1929, 1402; Asheri 1961, 45–7; 1963, 12; Fuks 1962b, 251 = 1984, 237; Oliva 1971, 191; Christien 1974, 201–2; David 1981, 68–9; 1982/83, 81–3; Marasco 1981, i.179–80.

46 Note that *Rhetoric* 1398b17–18, which David (1982/83, 85–7; 1981, 69 with 213 nn. 98, 100–1) cites to underpin his argument that the objects of Aristotle's criticisms were departures from Lykourgos' laws, not the laws themselves, will hardly bear the weight placed upon it. The statement that the Spartans were happy as long as they obeyed the laws of Lykourgos appears merely as a commonplace saying cited as an example of argument by induction, a counterpart to the vague statement that the Athenians were happy as long as they observed Solon's laws and the ascription of Theban success to their leaders' becoming philosophers. It is not even certain that the statement is by Aristotle himself, rather than a continuation of the quotation from Alkidamas which precedes it (Cope 1877, ii.233).

47 Cf. also Schütrumpf 1987, 447; 1991, 312. Marasco (1981, i.179) claims that the phrase διὰ τῶν νόμων indicates that Aristotle is referring not to the original Lykourgan constitution but to the contemporary situation. This is far from clear, however, especially since at 1270a7 he uses the phrase ὑπὸ τοὺς νόμους with reference to Lykourgos' attempt to control the women. (I owe this last point to Professor J.F. Lazenby.)

48 The four references are: 1270b42, concerning the elders; 1271a13, ambition; 1271a32 (cf. 26–8), the common meals; 1271b13, intention to instil disdain for money. The other references are: 1270b1; b19; 1271a22.

49 The fragment from the *Lak. Pol.* (Dilts 1971, fr. 9), which implicitly criticizes those who attributed the whole Spartan *politeia* to Lykourgos, bears no necessary implications for Aristotle's view in the *Politics* (*pace* David 1982/83, 81), since it could be another instance of a change of opinion following the composition of Book 2 (Keaney 1980, 52).

50 Von Holzinger 1894, 61; Weil 1960, 244; MacDowell 1986, 103–4.

51 His attempt (1982/83, 86) to evade this point by arguing that, because the law was passed several decades before the *Politics* was written, Aristotle already regarded it as an integral part of the Spartan law code, is unconvincing. For an almost identical argument to that in the text, Schütrumpf 1987, 447 n. 37.

52 *Gortyn Code* 7.52 ff.; 9.8 ff.; text and English trans. in Willetts 1967. On the Athenian *epiklēros*, A.R.W. Harrison 1968–71, i.132–8; Schaps 1979, 25–42. See also Patterson 1998, 91–103. The discussion of this issue by Karabélias (1982, 476) is vitiated by his view that a Spartiate held only a life tenure over an inalienable *klēros* until the time of Epitadeus (ibid. 471 n. 7).

53 There is no evidence that Lysander had any sons. The episode in which Dionysios of Syracuse offered him a gift for his daughters (Plut. *Mor.* 141f, 190e, 229a; *Lys.* 2.7–8) suggests that they were his only children, though the historicity of the episode has been questioned (Sansone 1981).

54 Cf. Karabélias 1982, 474. Note that the passage lends no weight to the interpretation

The anatomy of the Spartiate property system

of Lacey (1968, 203) that marriage extinguished a girl's claim to her father's estate. It merely specifies which *patrouchoi* came within the kings' jurisdiction.

55 A.R.W. Harrison 1968–71, i.11–12 and Appendix I; Schaps 1979, 28; *Gortyn Code* 8.20 ff. At Gortyn a childless heiress was allowed to avoid the obligation only if she ceded half the inheritance to her next-of-kin (7.52 ff.).

56 Karabélias 1982, 473 n. 14; 474–5; Grote 1862, ii.174–5 n. 1; Roussel 1939, 122; cf. the usages of ἱκνέομαι recorded by J.E. Powell 1960, 171. Patterson (1998, 101) over-interprets Herodotus' evidence in asserting that 'the king's decision was apparently not governed by set rules'. The fact that 'Herodotus specifies no formally defined group of candidates from which the king would choose' tells us nothing, since the passage is concerned with the king's role, not with the specifics of inheritance law.

57 Cf. Ollier 1934, 23; Karabélias 1982, 479. MacDowell (1986, 97) argues that there were other criteria besides proximity of relationship. These criteria, however, such as the non-ownership of a lot of land, are his own inventions designed to make Herodotus' evidence fit that of Plutarch.

58 A.R.W. Harrison 1968–71, i.10–11. I would not deny that the kings may often have exercised partiality in their adjudications. King Kleomenes' marriage of his daughter and heiress Gorgo to his brother Leonidas may have been designed to avoid the adjudication of competing claims to be Gorgo's nearest kinsman (and, by implication, the new king) being made by the king of the other royal house. Leonidas had a twin brother, Kleombrotos, who could have mounted a serious challenge and – depending on the date of the marriage – the other king at the time may well have been Kleomenes' inveterate enemy, Damaratos! It remains, however, that the adjudicating king had to select a close relative with a plausible claim of proximity; he could not arbitrarily select anyone he wished.

59 Cf. the usages cited in LSJ⁹, s.v.

60 The possible existence at Sparta of the *kyrieia* (the legal guardianship of a female by her male next-of-kin; cf. Cartledge 1981, 99–100) does not as such effect the question of female *ownership* of property.

61 Karabélias 1982, 478; cf. the translations of this phrase by Newman (1887–1902, ii. 329: 'without having disposed of her hand by will') and by Asheri 1963, 19.

62 See e.g. Asheri 1961, 62; 1963, 19; Jones 1967, 135; Lacey 1968, 204–5; Cozzoli 1979, 7; David 1982/83, 88–9; Carlier 1984, 271; MacDowell 1986, 107; Vérilhac and Vial 1998, 111–12.

63 Note that the adverb νῦν used by Aristotle signifies not a contrast between present and past laws but the antithesis between the actual state of the law and that which Aristotle himself deemed more expedient (Grote 1862, ii.171 note).

64 Unlike Schütrumpf (1991, 313), I can see nothing in Aristotle's phraseology to forbid the possibility of marriage between *klēronomos* and heiress. Aristotle focuses upon the giving of the heiress outside the kin because his subject is the concentration of land. He does not provide a full statement of alternative courses open to the *klēronomos*, including marrying the heiress himself, because it is not the concern of his argument.

65 Like Aristotle, Plutarch mistakenly uses the Athenian term *epiklēros*.

66 Paus. 2.9.1; 3.10.5. According to Pausanias, the son was named Eurydamidas; but cf. Bradford (1977, s.v.), who notes that Pausanias may have mistaken his name; cf. Marasco 1981, ii.347–8.

67 Justin's assertion of no dowries (3.3.8) is also connected with the false notion of Lykourgan landed equality.

68 Gortyn is not the only place where a 2:1 ratio between male and female inheritance is found. Note the inheritance division originally agreed by claimants to the estate of Dikaiogenes II in late fifth-century Athens, whereby the adopted son was given one-third and four sisters shared the remaining two-thirds (Isaios 5.6).

69 Take, for example, the demographic calculations of Goody and Harrison (1973, 16–18) = Goody (1976a, 133–4), which they deem to correspond most closely with the situation in pre-industrial societies. According to their calculations, in a self-reproducing 'natural fertility' population marked by high mortality, averaging six children ever born per family, and with only a one in three chance of a child surviving its father, roughly 41% of families would have both son(s) and daughter(s), 21% son(s) only, 21% daughter(s) only and 17% no surviving heirs. The resulting proportion of land inherited by females would be 38.91% [(41 × 1/3) + (21 × 1) + (17 × 1/4)]. (The figure used for calculating the proportion deriving from heirless families is conservative, bearing in mind the prior claim to inherit of the brother(s) of an heirless person.)

The exact proportion of land in female possession will of course vary according to the precise percentage of households with, respectively, both surviving sons and daughters, surviving children of one sex only and no surviving children at all. But even quite significant changes in these percentages do not lead to deviations far from the figure of 40%. Take the extreme case of the calculations given by Goody and Harrison which postulate the greatest degree of continuity in family succession, assuming a population marked by low mortality, averaging six children ever born per family, but with more than a two in three chance of a child surviving its father. According to these calculations, roughly 74% of families would have both son(s) and daughter(s), 10% son(s) only, 10% daughter(s) only and 6% no heirs. The resulting proportion of land inherited by females would still be as high as 36.16% [(74 × 1/3) + (10 × 1) + (6 × 1/4)].

70 Unlike the kings of ancient Persia and Egypt, who were monarchs distanced from their subjects and whose marriage customs were exceptional within their societies (Hopkins 1980, 306–7), Spartiate kings were more like leading citizens. Their marriage strategies are likely to have been accentuated versions of practices prevalent among Spartiates generally, rather than radically different.

71 We do not know whether she had any other siblings than Menios. Note that her family may have been very wealthy. Her father, Diaktorides, may be the Olympic four-horse chariot victor of 456 BC (Moretti 1957, no. 278).

72 On Kyniska's victories and monument, and the expense of chariot racing, see ch. 10.

73 The sources are silent on whether she was indeed married. Her mother was probably Archidamos' second wife, Eupolia, rather than Lampito, since the sources (Xen. *Ages.* 9.6; Plut. *Ages.* 20.1) call her sister of Agesilaos. The fact that on Agis II's death, Agesilaos, as step-brother, inherited all his property (Xen. *Ages.* 4.5; cf. Plut. *Ages.* 4.1), with Kyniska, as step-sister, apparently not sharing in the inheritance, does not contradict the thesis of universal female inheritance. In the Gortyn Code, in the absence of sons or daughters, a person's property went first to any brothers, next to their children or grandchildren, and only in the absence of all these to any sisters (5.9–22).

74 In the original publication of this chapter (Hodkinson 1986, 402–3) I also discussed the case of Agesistrata and Archidamia, the mother and maternal grandmother of the mid-third-century king, Agis IV. According to Plutarch (*Agis* 4.1), these women owned more property than anyone in Sparta, including Agis and Agesistrata's wealthy brother, Agesilaos. Utilizing Bradford's reconstruction of the Eurypontid family tree (1977,

Appendix 6), I suggested how this statement could be accounted for on the thesis of universal female inheritance. Recently, however, McQueen (1990) has advocated a different configuration of Eurypontid family relationships which would deflate the landholdings of the two women in relation to those of Agesilaos and Agis. McQueen's arguments against Bradford's reconstruction – the improbability of the cross-generational marriages of Kings Eudamidas I and II to Archidamia and Agesistrata, respectively – are by no means certain, given the evidence for similar royal marriages in earlier periods. Since, however, definitive reconstruction of the family tree currently lies beyond our reach, I have omitted the case study from this discussion.

75 These different functions of dowry are clearly distinguished by Saller 1984, following the work of Goody 1973, 17–19.

Chapter 4

HELOTAGE AND THE EXPLOITATION OF SPARTAN TERRITORY

This chapter extends the examination of Spartiate land-ownership to two interrelated aspects of the economic exploitation of their estates. The first part of the chapter will discuss the Spartiates' relationship to their helot servile labour force. I shall examine the character of Spartiate mastery over the helots, the relationship of the Spartiates and helots as landowners and cultivators, and the organisation of the agricultural tribute which the helots paid to their masters. The second part of the chapter will consider the geographical location and extent of Spartiate landholdings within Spartan territory.[1]

Spartiates and helots

A fundamental feature of Spartan society was that the Spartiate citizen elite lived as rentier landowners supported economically by a servile population, the helots, who worked their estates. The Spartiates themselves inhabited a cluster of villages towards the northern end of the Sparta plain (see *Fig.* 3, p. 137).[2] Their landholdings, in contrast, were extensive. During most of the archaic and classical periods, when Spartan territory covered the entire southern Peloponnese, Spartiate estates farmed by helot cultivators were to be found in both its constituent regions, Lakonia and Messenia. Following Sparta's loss of Messenia in 370/69, the helots continued to be the predominant labour force on citizen estates in Lakonia until at least the second century BC.[3] Agricultural labour was *the* distinctive feature of helot servitude. Although some helots were employed in other sectors such as service in Spartiate households and in the messes (and as batmen on campaigns), the essential servile function of the vast majority of helots was to work their masters' lands. Although there are hints in the evidence of some use of chattel slaves on wealthy estates, they were a small minority in agricultural production as a whole.[4] The helots were, consequently, the indispensable mainstay of the Spartan property system. Yet, although scholars have been considerably exercised by the political relationships between Spartiates and helots, especially the extent of the threat posed by the helots and the brutal Spartan response, there has been little investigation of citizen–helot relations from the perspective of Spartiate land-ownership and agrarian economy.

Helot status: collective servitude or private slavery?
The precise status of the helots has perplexed commentators since antiquity,

owing to the mixture of communal and private elements in their servitude. The most common modern approach has been to regard the helots as collectively owned by – or at least in a position of collective servitude to – the Spartan polis. This perspective has been expressed in various ways: from 'collective slavery' (Lotze 1959), through 'intercommunal servitude' (Garlan 1988, 93–8) to the definition of helots as 'state serfs' (Ste Croix 1981, 149–50; Cartledge 1988a, 39). These views are founded on Strabo's statement (8.5.4) that the Lakedaimonians possessed the helots 'as, in a way, public slaves' (τρόπον...τινα δημοσίους δούλους) and Pausanias' designation of them (3.20.6) as 'slaves of the community'. Strabo also cites the classical historian Ephorus as stating that the helots were 'condemned to slavery on certain conditions' laid down by the polis (*FGrH* 70F117): only the polis could manumit helots, not an individual Spartiate master; and there were restrictions on private sales. Indeed, Spartiate–helot relations were governed by a variety of communal measures. The ephors made an annual declaration of war against the helots (Arist. fr. 538 Rose, *ap.* Plut. *Lyk.* 28), signifying their position as public enemies against whom the citizens waged a truceless fight. In keeping with this ideology, the youths who took part in the *krypteia* could kill helots with impunity and without reference to their Spartiate holder (Herakleides Lembos 373.10 Dilts = Aristotelian *Polity of the Lakedaimonians* fr. 611.10 Rose). A Spartiate also had to let other citizens make use of his helots in case of need (Xen. *Lak. Pol.* 6.3; Arist. *Pol.* 1263a35–7). Furthermore, the polis supervised the personal appearance of helots, putting to death those who exceeded the vigour proper to a slave's condition and fining their masters for failing to prevent their growth (Myron of Priene, *FGrH* 106F2, *ap.* Athen. 657d). Individual citizens were thus personally responsible to the authorities for the condition of their helots.

For all the collective elements in their servitude, however, most helots were, at any given time, in the service of one particular Spartan individual or household. Every Spartiate landowner had a particular set of helots working his or her landholdings. Indeed, there is a minority but longstanding modern view that the helots were not publicly owned but the private property of individual Spartiates (e.g. Diesner 1953/4; Cozzoli 1979, 158–62). This view has received recent support from Jean Ducat's examination of the textual evidence (1990a, 19–29), which argues that the fact that the helots were typically viewed as a collectivity does not necessarily mean that they were collective *property*. As Ducat notes, the idea of the helots as public slaves appears only in late sources like Strabo (born 64 BC) and Pausanias (fl. *c.* AD 50), who were writing after the late third-century revolution. This idea, he argues, was indissolubly linked to the revolution's redistribution of private Spartiate estates into a system of state-controlled equal *klēroi*, which meant a real change in status for the helots working the *klēroi*, who now likewise became public property.

In contrast, there is no hint of collective ownership of helots in the classical sources. Xenophon (*Lak. Pol.* 6.3), when describing the right to use someone else's helots ('he [Lykourgos] also gave permission, if someone needed, to use other persons' *oiketai*'),[5] does not refer to them as communal property. He lists them along with other privately-owned possessions – horses, dogs and foodstuffs – which were also subject to communal use. Aristotle's reference to these same measures places them even more unequivocally in the context of private property, though moderated by communal use:

> …while property should in a certain sense be communal, in general it should be private… Even now, this sort of arrangement exists in some states in an outline form…and in the well-run ones particularly it exists in part and in part might come about. For although each individual does have his own private property, he makes available some things to be used by his friends, while he has the use of others communally. For example, in Lakedaimon they use each other's slaves practically as their own, and horses and dogs too.

Similarly, although Ephorus (as noted earlier) describes certain conditions of helot servitude laid down by the polis, the form in which those conditions are presented is as a modification of the normal rights of a master regarding manumission and sale.

The exclusive capacity of the polis to liberate helots, mentioned by Ephorus, is sometimes used as an argument for public ownership, especially since on several occasions when we know the mechanism by which such liberations were effected the Spartiate holders of those helots are conspicuously absent from the transaction. In 425 when the Spartans needed persons to convey food to their soldiers trapped on the island of Sphakteria (Thuc. 4.26), in winter 370/69 when they desperately needed new troops to defend against enemy invasion (Xen. *Hell.* 6.5.28–9; Diod. 15.65.5), and in the infamous episode of uncertain date when they wanted to eliminate the most spirited helots (Thuc. 4.80), the method of selecting those helots who were to receive their freedom was an official call for volunteers. In theory, at least, this method placed the initiative in the hands of the helots themselves and was a direct transaction between polis and helots, with no role for the Spartiate master. As Ducat (1990a, 26) points out, however, such mass liberations without reference to the owner are also known from poleis where chattel slavery predominated, such as Athens and Chios.[6] Neither is the absence of any hint of compensation for Spartiate owners significant, since there is no evidence at Athens either for compensation in the case of public manumission of groups of chattel slaves.

In the classical sources, then, the helots appear in some senses as the private property of their Spartiate holders, but also as subject to various forms of communal intervention. Moreover, the significance of this communal intervention should not be underestimated. The range and importance of the measures mentioned above indicate that public intervention was exercised far more strongly over the helots than over the private landholdings of Spartan citizens. The helots were thus in a real sense in a condition of 'double dependence on the individual holder and on the state' (Diesner 1953/4, 222), a situation which meant that Spartiate masters did not possess rights of mastery as full as owners of chattel slaves.

In this chapter I shall explore the socio-economic aspects of this combination of private ownership with lack of full rights of mastery. What were the characteristics of Spartiate agrarian exploitation of the helot population? I shall argue that Spartiate landowners were able to decide and vary the ways in which they utilized their labour force; but that they did so within a context of collective domination and communal intervention which gave the helots some limited rights vis-à-vis their individual owners. Furthermore, from the collective perspective of the Spartan citizen body, the helots were a self-reproducing population upon whose continued exploitation depended the entire Spartiate way of life. The range of public measures considered above indicates that the polis was anxious to preserve the integrity of, and to perpetuate, that population. Hence, in contrast to chattel slaves, helots enjoyed 'all the normal human institutions except their freedom' (Finley 1985, 63). Not the least of these institutions was family relationships which were recognised by the polis: when the helot rebels were given safe conduct out of servitude at the end of the 460s revolt, they were allowed to depart 'with their children and wives' (Thuc. 1.103).

The effect, I submit, was to create, in the sphere of agricultural production, an exploitative but nevertheless interdependent relationship between Spartiate masters and helot cultivators which we can fruitfully study from the comparative perspective not just of other slave societies but also of other systems of dependent labour. I stress this last point, since the value of this perspective has been challenged by Paul Cartledge (1993b, 132; cf. 1998, 13) who has criticised my earlier study (Hodkinson 1992a) of Sparta's economic exploitation of the helots, on the grounds that 'the use of "peasant" (or "sharecropping tenant", as in Hodkinson 1992) seems to me unusually inappropriate and rather grossly misleading, since ...the Helots were also in official Spartan parlance "slaves"...'. It is true that the helots are labelled ἡ δουλεία – the collective noun cognate to *douloi*, 'slaves' – in the Sparto-Athenian treaty of 421 (Thuc. 5.23). The context, however, is both heavily propagandistic (the treaty was prominently displayed in major sanctuaries in both poleis) and politicised, in that Athens was agreeing to aid Sparta against the helots, in abandonment of her previous policy of promoting their liberation as free 'Messenians'.[7] To view such official rhetoric as providing an exclusive or comprehensive statement of the helots' position is to read their history solely from the masters' viewpoint (cf. Alcock, forthcoming). In any case, it has never been my purpose to *describe* helots as 'sharecropping tenants', as Cartledge implies, simply to illuminate critical features of their position through comparative evidence from other types of labour systems. As I stated in my study, my concern 'is not to deny the primary phenomenon of helot servitude...but simply to recognize that complete analysis of the complex nature of the helots' position requires the application of a variety of approaches. No single model can claim a monopoly of insights or of truth' (Hodkinson 1992a, 125). This should not be a matter of controversy. After all, the comparative study of different types of labour systems – whether involving peasants, dependent tenants, serfs or slaves – has been successfully practised for many years in the field of modern socio-economic history (e.g. Hoch 1986; Kolchin 1987).

Helots, Spartiates and the land

The first important issue concerning the agricultural exploitation of the helots by Spartiate landowners is the exact relationship of the helots to the landholdings they worked. The degree to which a dependent farming population possesses effective security of cultivation of particular landholdings or can be shifted around at the wish of the landowner is invariably a major determinant of interaction between landowner and cultivator. In the region of Tuscany in post-unification Italy, for example, tenants' rights were weak. The landlord's control was ensured by terms of contract which specified that the labour capacity and subsistence needs of the tenant's family should match the labour requirements and size of the holding. To achieve this balance landlords were able to disperse members of their tenants' families elsewhere or order the adoption of living-in help, could give or withhold permission for marriage, could vet the appointment of new heads of households and could ensure that tenant families never amassed sufficient saleable surplus to achieve independence (Gill 1983, 147).

How secure was the position of the helots? The most informative evidence is the passage of Strabo (8.5.4) cited above:

> Ephorus says...[that] the Heleians, the inhabitants of Helos, revolted and were forcibly subdued by a war and condemned to slavery on certain conditions, namely that it was not permitted for the holder either to liberate them or to sell them outside the boundaries; and that this was called the war against the helots. In effect, it was Agis [I, son of Eurysthenes] and his associates who instituted the helotage which lasted down to the time of the Roman supremacy; for the Lakedaimonians possessed these as a kind of public slaves, fixing for them certain places of residence and particular duties (κατοικίας τινὰς αὐτοῖς ἀποδείξαντες καὶ λειτουργίας ἰδίας).

At first sight, the final clause of this passage might seem to prove that helots in the classical period possessed a strong degree of security in the cultivation of particular landholdings; but it is essential to distinguish different layers of evidence within the passage. The passage begins with a quotation from the classical historian Ephorus, but this lasts only till the end of the first sentence. The following sentence, which includes the statement that helotage lasted down to the time of Rome's supremacy, cannot come from Ephorus, since Rome's supremacy came long after his death. This sentence, including the statement that the helots had fixed residences and particular duties, must come from Strabo himself. Hence the statement does not constitute contemporary evidence for helotage in classical times. Its close linkage to Strabo's previous statement that the Lakedaimonians possessed the helots as quasi-public slaves marks it out as late evidence, connected with the conditions of the third-century revolution, which has nothing to do with conditions in the classical period. The idea that the polis intervened directly to fix specific residences and duties – indeed the notion of the helots performing *leitourgiai* (public services) – is incompatible with the classical evidence viewed above.

The sole classical evidence in the passage is Ephorus' statement that it was not permitted for the Spartiate holder either to liberate helots or to sell them outside the boundaries. Both the precise meaning of this statement and its import for the extent of the helots' security of cultivation are open to interpretation. The passage is usually interpreted as signifying that a Spartiate landowner had no right to alienate his or her helots, whether by sale or manumission (cf. Finley 1985, 63). This would not necessarily entail their full security of tenure, since some landowners might still be able to move helots between their various holdings; but it would apply a certain limitation on the landowners' capacity to augment or reduce their labour force to match fluctuating labour needs. Of course, the passage does not state categorically that sale was completely forbidden, merely that it was not permitted 'outside the boundaries (ἔξω τῶν ὅρων)'. These 'boundaries' are normally interpreted as the borders of Spartan territory, thus leaving open the possibility of sale between Spartiates. MacDowell (1986, 35), however, argues that the reference is rather to the boundaries of particular landholdings, signifying that 'the Spartiate could not sell a helot and thus remove him from his land'. Even among scholars who follow the normal interpretation of the phrase, it is frequently argued (e.g. Jeanmaire 1939, 478) that Ephorus' reported words do not constitute a complete statement of the ban on sale and that, owing to its juxtaposition with the prohibition of private manumission, the ban should be viewed as applying inside as well as outside Spartan territory.

Against this last argument, a number of scholars have insisted that Ephorus' evidence should be read as it stands. They argue, in particular, that a complete ban on sale would have marked a clear distinction between helots and chattel slaves which Ephorus could not have failed to mention (Ducat 1990a, 21–2; cf. Kahrstedt 1919; Klees 1975, 146). The implication of this argument is that one must either follow MacDowell's interpretation of the boundaries as signifying those of particular landholdings or accept that the ban on sale only applied to external transactions. Against MacDowell's interpretation, moreover, Ducat has urged the comparable case of the Mariandynoi of Herakleia Pontika, whose status is frequently compared to that of the helots. According to certain post-classical sources (Poseidonios fr. 60, Kidd, *ap*. Athen. 263c–d; Strabo 12.3.4), the Mariandynoi accepted a state of servitude under the Herakleiots on condition that they could be sold inside but not outside the territory of Herakleia. Ephorus' statement, it is claimed, with its reference to the helots' being condemned to slavery 'on certain conditions', embodies a similar idea of a 'contract of servitude' between Spartiates and helots.

It is unclear, however, whether this parallel with the Maryiandynoi is truly apposite to the interpretation of Ephorus' text. The evidence regarding the Mariandynoi comes from post-classical passages written at a time when the notion of a quasi-voluntary contract of servitude had become well-established (Ducat 1990a, 70–6). A similar notion may be detectable in the post-classical sources for the helots (e.g. Myron of Priene *FGrH* 106F2, *ap.* Athen. 657d; *Inst. Lac.* no. 41 = Plut. *Mor.* 239d; Plut. *Lyk.* 24.3).[8] These, however, are sources affected by the third-century revolution, in contrast to the earlier evidence of Ephorus. Ephorus' statement does not stem from the notion of a contract of servitude. On the contrary, the basis of his statement is the helots' revolt and forcible enslavement and the implicitly harsh conditions imposed upon them. The references to the ban on private liberation and sale abroad are intended to signify, not advantages for the helots, but rather the Spartiates' determination to ensure their permanent enslavement through the impossibility of escape from helotage by private manumission. It is therefore unsurprising that Ephorus says nothing about sale inside Spartan territory. It is irrelevant to his concerns, since internal sale did not entail the end of helot status. His lack of reference to a ban on internal sales, consequently, cannot be treated as a sign that such sales were permissible.

The evidence of Ephorus and Strabo is therefore inconclusive.[9] In assessing the extent of the helots' security of tenure, one must consequently turn to general considerations. On this issue, it is notable that even Ducat, who advocates the permissibility of private sale, explicitly abjures the idea of helot 'markets'. Indeed, he envisages rather that sales were personal transactions which took place when land under helot cultivation was transferred from one citizen to another, so that the helots would remain attached to the land they were cultivating. Consequently, even on Ducat's view, most helots would have effective security of tenure, regardless of changes of Spartiate owner, even if that security was not legally defined.

Indeed, such an arrangement fits well with our understanding of the origins of helotage. This is especially so in the case of the Messenian helots, who were subjugated by conquest (Tyrtaios fr. 5, West). After their conquest most Messenian working farmers presumably became servile cultivators of the same fields they had farmed before the conquest. Concerning the origins of Lakonian helotage there is more dispute (cf. Ducat 1978, 5–13), but almost all theories accept that most of those thus enslaved were working farmers, who in their new state of servitude simply continued to farm their former landholdings for the Spartiates' benefit.

The nature of the helots' position as a self-reproducing group with their own families also suggests a population with a stable existence and subsistence derived from secure cultivation of particular landholdings, rather than one subject to continual movements from estate to estate as the property holdings of their individual masters' lineages altered through the generations.[10] The latter arrangement would have produced an extraordinary level of disruption for the helot population under the Spartiate inheritance system, which operated, as we saw in chapter 3, on the basis of division of the parental property among all their children, including daughters. When not only men inherit land but women also, and those women receive at least a portion of their inheritance on marriage, land changes hands both down the generations and between the sexes at almost every adult death and at every marriage (Goody 1976b, 10). The ownership of specific holdings is drastically reorganized every generation and continually reallocated from one patriline to another. Given such ongoing perturbation of Spartiate land-ownership, self-perpetuating helot families could hardly have maintained themselves over several centuries, unless they had been a fixture on the land who normally changed ownership along with the holdings they cultivated.

The drastic effects that Spartiate inheritance laws would have had on the helots, if they were not normally fixed to the land but had to follow their masters, is well illustrated by Singor (1993, 47–8), who believes that this was indeed the helots' fate. As he notes, when a piece of land worked by a helot family was divided among two Spartiate heirs, either one heir would have had to take over the helot family with half the land, or the family would have had to be broken up, a practice feasible only if it possessed an adult son. As Singor acknowledges, 'we have to assume that very often at partitions of inheritance one of the heirs got land without helots, while another got both land and helots... In the second instance a helot family would see its plot of land drastically reduced. Unless their Spartan master had other pieces of land that could be reassigned to them, their future as a household was in peril.' Singor suggests various possible 'solutions' to this difficulty: the permanent loan of family members to another master, subsistence help from better-off helots, adoption of children into other helot families, flight and a consequent life of brigandage. He concludes, however, that 'it was the helots who suffered first when ...the property within a Spartan family line diminished while the number of helots attached to that family remained the same or at least did not go down proportionately'. These consequences would have ensued from a sizeable proportion of all inheritance divisions in every generation, especially as many Spartiate families fell into increasing poverty in the later fifth and fourth centuries (see further below). In my view, the continual large-scale disruption to, and impoverishment of, helot farmers implied by Singor's theory is irreconcilable with the reality evident in our sources, which attest a thriving and numerous servile population whose farming sustained both itself and its Spartiate masters over a period of several centuries.[11] Indeed, some helots were apparently even able to amass a disposable surplus, as in the case of 6,000 Lakonian helots in the year 223 BC who had accumulated wealth to the value of five minas (500 drachmas), with which they purchased their freedom (Plut. *Kleom.* 23).[12]

The *de facto* security of tenure which I am suggesting does not of course mean that helot cultivators were never transferred from their original holdings when the latter passed into different ownership. Likewise, Spartiate landowners may sometimes have intervened to rearrange the personnel working on their estates. No doubt such factors as the changing requirements of agricultural exploitation, the varying demands of Spartiate households and the diverse demographic histories of helot families sometimes made it a practical necessity. The successful self-reproduction of the helot population over several centuries suggests, however, that this intervention was not employed on such a widespread or disruptive scale as to interrupt the fundamental security of cultivation of most helot families. The resulting intimate knowledge of the local terrain, with its diverse microclimates and specialised ecological niches, acquired by stable helot families was surely a valuable asset for absentee Spartiate landowners concerned to maximise the productivity of their estates, especially given the frequent movement of holdings from one citizen lineage to another.

If helot families normally remained farming particular landholdings regardless of changes of Spartiate owner, some significant implications follow for the relationship between landowners and cultivators. The post-classical sources (*Inst. Lac.* no. 41 = Plut. *Mor.* 239d–e; Plut. *Lyk.* 24.3; cf. 8.4) – influenced by the third-century revolution with its vision of equal, inalienable *klēroi* – conjure up a simple image of an enduring relationship between an unchanging group of helot farmers and a single Spartiate owner. The classical reality will have been a more fluid situation involving a complex web of relationships in which changing helot personnel owed their obligations to a number of different Spartiates. To appreciate this situation more fully, a brief discussion of the impact of inheritance customs and demographic factors is necessary.

First of all, on the Spartiates' side, the identity of the owner of a given piece of land will have changed constantly as portions of the parental estates were handed over to daughters on marriage and divided among the surviving heirs on the owner's death. Demographic studies of pre-industrial societies have observed that, even given varying rates of fertility and mortality, only a small minority of families – typically some 10–20% – produce just a single heir or heiress; the remaining 80–90% produce either no heirs or multiple heirs.[13] Even if we take account of the tactic of adoption (Hdt. 6.57), which many heirless parents may have practised in order to ensure a single direct heir, a sizeable majority of parental estates will have been subject to some level of division. The precise impact of this division upon the relationship with the helot farmers will have varied according to circumstances. One should assume that the estates of most Spartiate households were split into different holdings scattered throughout Spartan territory. This has been the typical pattern of landholding in peasant societies the world over and is attested also among the wealthy elite in other regions of ancient Greece (Osborne 1987, 37–40; Gallant 1991, 41–5). At Sparta it was built into the property system, since both husband and wife brought their own separate landed property to the household. In principle, then, division of inheritance could have been managed in some cases by allocating each of the heirs one or more discrete, intact holdings. In such situations the helot cultivators will simply have experienced a change of owner. In other cases, however, the division of inheritance will have operated at the deeper level of the splitting of individual holdings. In these situations the impact upon the landowner–cultivator relationship will have been more significant, leading to the separation of the helot farmers between the newly-split parts of the former holding.

Is it possible to estimate the relative extent of these alternative possibilities? The issues are complex and much-debated (cf. Bentley 1987, esp. 35–40). In some societies, such as modern Greece, systems of partible inheritance have been responsible for the widespread fragmentation of individual fields, especially when strict equity between siblings or considerations of risk management, crop scheduling or use of multiple ecozones have been overriding considerations for the heirs (Herzfeld 1980, esp. 93–7). This is not, however, a universal phenomenon. In other societies this outcome has been avoided, at least below a certain 'minimum threshold size', when absolute sameness of inheritance and claims for tiny shares of small fields have not been insisted upon. This happens more frequently in areas of minimal environmental diversity, where there is less value in possessing scattered holdings to reap the benefits of exploiting different agricultural niches. It might be thought that Spartiate landholding falls into this category, since many of their landholdings were concentrated in the central plains of Lakonia and Messenia. As I shall argue below, however, the agricultural environments of these plains were themselves by no means completely uniform and Spartiate estates probably spread also into other locations, especially the diverse rolling hill country of western Messenia.

Some studies have suggested that overpopulation may be a more potent factor than partible inheritance in leading to fragmentation, and one study has employed a mathematical model to demonstrate that without population growth land becomes no more fragmented over time (McCloskey 1975). The critical factor here is whether a family owns sufficient discrete fields to distribute without requiring internal fragmentation: when the number of fields is fewer, equitable division without splitting becomes more difficult. The crucial issues are therefore the distribution of property among the Spartan citizen body and the size of Spartiate estates. Unfortunately, we have no statistics either for the overall size of Spartiate estates or for the size of individual plots. Moreover, as we saw in chapter 3, global generalisation is impossible, since land was always unequally distributed among Spartan citizens. Nevertheless, the position of the citizens as full-time hoplite warriors freed from economic activity made it necessary that all should possess a sufficient competence of land. The fact that they had to support not only Spartiate subsistence needs and mess contributions but also the helot cultivators suggests that during the heyday of the property system, down to the early fifth century, Spartiate estates will have been significantly larger than the holdings of ordinary citizens in other poleis, such as the 4.5–5.4 hectare plots apparently regarded elsewhere as standard-sized hoplite farms (Burford Cooper 1977/8; Gallant 1991, 86–7). I shall suggest later (ch. 12) that the mean size of landholding owned by 'ordinary' Spartiates was of the order of 18 ha. If this is right, Spartiate landholdings will have fallen comfortably into the upper bracket of estate sizes attested across different times and places in the Mediterranean region (Gallant 1991, 82–86, esp. fig. 4.7). It may be, then, that during the archaic and early classical periods the splitting of individual plots could often be avoided, if it was felt desirable to do so. During the later fifth and fourth centuries, however, there developed an increasing number of poor citizen families whose overall landholdings – and, presumably also, number of discrete plots of land – were much more limited. In these circumstances the splitting of plots was probably a more frequent occurrence.

It is true, as Lane Fox (1985) has pointed out, that for such families there existed various means of delaying or modifying this kind of fragmentation. One of these was temporary or permanent fraternal cohabitation and there is evidence for the practice in Sparta of adelphic polyandry (Plb. 12.6b.8). This tactic itself, however, substituted a corporate for a single landlord and would not have prevented some portion of the land going to any sisters. It was perhaps for the latter reason that close-kin marriage and the combination of wife-sharing with uterine half-sibling marriage were also practised in classical Sparta.[14] In the latter arrangement two brothers could produce by the same woman children who could then intermarry to reunite their paternal grandparents' original properties. But even this manoeuvre, though it concentrated overall property holdings, did not eliminate boundary alterations and changes of ownership between the sexes, as regards either the paternal grandparents' holdings or the property belonging to the shared wife. It is uncertain, moreover, that these marital manoeuvres were practised primarily by poorer families who were most likely to split their landholdings. In other societies polyandry has often been a tactic of the wealthy concerned to conserve their property and social position (Leach 1955; Kunstler 1983, 475, 593 n. 990); and the attested cases known from other regions of ancient Greece relate primarily to better-off families (Lane Fox 1985, 222–3). For poorer families, in contrast, faced with the risk of insufficient production for their essential needs, fragmentation of landed property is often viewed more positively as a means of spreading that risk, so that disasters to plots in one region do not affect their holdings elsewhere. We should therefore envisage a particularly complex web of relationships between Spartiate owners and helot farmers on the landholdings of poorer families. Many of their rather small individual plots will have been insufficient to support an entire helot family off the latter's share of the produce. Consequently, helot households farming several tiny holdings belonging to multiple poorer landowners may have been a common occurrence.

We must also take account of the impact of frequent changes of ownership between the sexes as daughters inherited from their fathers and sons from their mothers. The ownership of land by women, together with Sparta's comparatively loose regulation of the marriages of heiresses, meant – as we saw in chapter 3 – a high level of transference of land between lineages. This factor, when combined with a high failure rate to produce a surviving male heir (about 40% of marriages in most pre-industrial societies), will have meant that only a minority of holdings were passed down within the male line from father to son over a number of generations. Only in a small proportion of cases, therefore, will there have been an enduring relationship between a Spartiate lineage and the helot family farming its estates.

In sum, helot farmers will have experienced considerable and continuous changes in the identity and number of the Spartiate masters or mistresses for whom they worked. There was probably also considerable variation in the numbers of helots on different landholdings. On larger holdings, particularly as property concentration advanced from the fifth century onwards, there will have been several helot families. This is exemplified in Xenophon's account of the conspiracy of Kinadon in the early 390s, when the latter pointed out to the informer that each master on the estates near to Sparta itself was outnumbered by many helots (*Hell.* 3.3.5). On the other hand, the phenomenon of plot fragmentation and the increasing number of landowners who, as either poor Spartiates or Inferiors,[15] owned comparatively little land, probably meant that many helots were farming for more than one master. Some helot families may even have cultivated more land than their masters owned.[16]

In considering these effects of Spartiate demography and inheritance, we should not forget the impact of similar factors within the helot population. Even if a helot family remained attached to its plot of land when Spartiate ownership changed, that family was itself not a static entity but an ever-changing unit subject to the normal household life cycle resulting from the birth and marriage, the ageing and death of its constituent members. The number of able-bodied cultivators on each holding will have been constantly fluctuating. In addition, helot households will in each generation have experienced differing demographic histories, with the usual range of permutations of single male heirs, several surviving sons and no sons at all. We have no direct evidence for how the cultivation of specific holdings was passed on through the generations. However, there must have been some arrangements for the devolution of *movable* property which helots are attested as owning (Hdt. 9.80; Thuc. 4.26; Plut. *Kleom.* 23). Some degree of negotiation with the Spartiate landowner was no doubt necessary. But, given that the helots apparently had family relationships comparable to those of free Greeks, it is logical to believe that the cultivation of one's holding was normally passed to one's descendants through some system akin to the partible inheritance found throughout the rest of Greece – with agnatic kinsmen perhaps having the usual residual claims in the case of sonless or heirless families.

Allowance should also be made for the varying conditions of cultivation. Helot households working together on larger Spartiate holdings may often have intermarried in order to benefit from spreading the extremes of variable fertility and child mortality over several families, with those households with several children taking up the slack from those without sons. These intermarrying families may even have resided together, forming multiple family households such as is attested among sharecropping households in regions of modern central Italy (Kertzer 1984). The existence of such co-residential arrangements might find some support from archaeological evidence that the settlement pattern in archaic and classical Messenia was more nucleated than in other parts of mainland Greece.[17] Through such arrangements the usual problem of partibility – the fragmentation of holdings for descendants in subsequent generations – might often have been avoided. In contrast, for helot households working on their own on smaller holdings or on land which embraced the properties of more than one Spartiate, the situation may have been more fluid. In the absence of other families with an interest in mutual co-operation, such households may have faced a less predictable pattern of marriage alliances and possessed less insurance against the reproductive problem that faces any individual farming household: namely, the difficulty of avoiding either leaving no (male) heirs or having too many surviving sons to share a holding that formerly supported a single household.

Whatever the details, it is a plausible assumption that differential reproduction and mortality and diverse conditions of cultivation led to the development of inequalities among the helots in their access to land. There is a hint of such socio-economic differentiation in an emended gloss of Hesychios (μ 1626, ed. Latte, ii.676) which mentions certain 'leaders of the helots'.[18] On the other hand, since it seems likely, given the exigencies of a servile labour force, that the devolution of cultivation 'rights' would *not* normally pass down to women, transfers of possession were presumably less frequent and division less severe than in the case of Spartiate ownership. Consequently, although – given the constraints of demography – few helot lineages will have had an unbroken ancestral association with the plots to which they were tied, their links with those plots will generally have been more continuous than was the case for their masters. The three-way relationship between landed property, its Spartiate owners and its helot cultivators was clearly far from straightforward.

Economic exploitation: fixed rent or sharecropping?

I turn now to examine the nature of the economic support which the Spartiates extracted from the helots. It is clear that the helots had to provide a tribute in kind from the produce of the Spartiates' estates. The details of this tribute, however, are controversial, since the ancient sources disagree about whether the Spartiates extracted a *proportional* or a *fixed* share of the crops.

The post-classical sources typically refer to the extraction of a fixed share.[19] According to the hellenistic *Instituta Laconica* no. 41 (= Plut. *Mor.* 239e),

> the helots worked the land for them, paying over the tribute (*apophora*) set down in the past. A curse was laid on anyone who charged more, in order that they might serve gladly because they were making a profit and [the Spartiates] themselves might not try to get more.

The term *apophora* is often used of fixed sum payments.[20] Plutarch repeats it twice in his *Life of Lykourgos*. At 8.4 it describes the 70 and 12 *medimnoi* of barley and proportionate quantity of tree crops supposedly produced annually for, respectively, a Spartiate and his wife by each of the 9,000 equal Lykourgan (and Polydoran) *klēroi*. At 24.3 Plutarch refers back to these amounts, saying that the helots paid 'the *apophora* mentioned above'.[21]

There is, however, reason to doubt that such fixed rents operated in the classical period. Their authenticity cannot be separated from that of the Lykourgan/Polydoran *klēroi* from which Plutarch says they were produced; but, as I have argued (ch. 3), these equal *klēroi* reflect not classical reality but the work of the third-century revolution. The same conclusion necessarily follows for the idea of a fixed rent.[22] There is indeed an air of unreality in the account in the *Instituta Laconica*. There is the naive assumption of the helots' willing service, which Ducat (1990a, 57–9) has identified as an element of the hellenistic notion of a 'contract of servitude' that sought to give helotage a favourable image. There is also the equally naive assumption of profit by the helots, with no hint of the subsistence risk which is inherent in a system in which the master takes a fixed amount of produce regardless of the amount harvested. The operation of a single rent fixed globally by the state is, moreover, incompatible with the private holdings of variable size owned by classical Spartiates (cf. Cozzoli 1979, 162–3). How was such a rent apportioned between different plots among a Spartiate's holdings? What rent was due when the landowner was not an adult male Spartiate with a wife, but a woman or a minor? Could wealthier landowners receive no more rent from their larger estates than could ordinary citizens from theirs? And if so, how can one reconcile this with their known additional expenditures (see chs. 9–11)?

What then of the evidence for a proportional (or sharecropping) quota? The earliest evidence is a fragment of Tyrtaios from the seventh century (fr. 6, West):

> Like asses oppressed with heavy burdens;
> bringing to their masters (δεσποσύνοισι) under grim compulsion,
> half… of what the soil bears as fruit;
> (ἥμισυ πάνθ' ὅσσων καρπὸν ἄρουρα φέρει).

This passage is quoted by Pausanias (4.14.4) in his account of the conditions suffered by the Messenians after their initial conquest; and most scholars accept this as an accurate reading of its context.[23] Both Pausanias and Aelian (*VH* 6.1) interpret Tyrtaios as saying that the Messenians had to render half the produce to their Spartan masters; and this too is the sense adopted by most historians.[24]

There is one apparent difficulty with this interpretation. Our manuscripts are defective at the critical phrase ἥμισυ πάνθ' ὅσσων and the word πάνθ' has been judged ungrammatical (cf. MacDowell 1986, 33). Textual critics have suggested various emendations which preserve Pausanias' interpretation of the passage's meaning, such as ἥμισυ παντός and, most frequently, ἥμισυ πᾶν, 'an entire half'.[25] The emendation, however, which remains closest to the manuscript readings is ἥμισυ πᾶν θ', which gives a slightly different sense: 'half and all' or 'half and the whole' (Allen 1936, 202; Rocha-Pereira (ed.) 1973, ad loc.). MacDowell, interpreting this to mean that 'some helots handed over half and some the whole of their produce', suggests that it is poetic rhetoric which makes it 'doubtful whether the passage can be used as evidence that a half was a legal figure'. He argues that Tyrtaios is saying that a fixed rent in practice often amounted to a half.

Although this last argument introduces an element of uncertainty, it is far from conclusive. First, Allen, the originator of this emendation, admitted that it was, to his knowledge, a singular usage. Secondly, the interpretation given by Pausanias and Aelian should be given some weight. As Habicht (1985) has demonstrated, Pausanias was a careful researcher whose accurate verbatim copying and interpretation of hundreds of inscriptions, often written in unfamiliar alphabets and dialects, is abundantly substantiated. Moreover, he probably had a better text than the defective ones in our manuscripts. Thirdly, claiming half the movable goods was common practice in archaic Greek wars (*Iliad* 18.509–12; 22.114–121; Singor 1993, 43). The extraction of half the produce is simply an extension of that practice to a situation of permanent conquest. Even if one prefers Allen's reading and MacDowell's translation, however, the passage is still reconcilable with the idea of a proportional share. Sharecropping arrangements frequently contain different provisions for different crops (e.g. Warriner 1962, 27; Reid 1973, 118, 128–9; Delano Smith 1979, 79; Valensi 1985, 109) and the passage could reflect a situation in which staple crops were shared equally, but non-subsistence foodstuffs went entirely to the Spartiate owner. There is therefore no good reason to doubt that the evidence of Tyrtaios attests the operation of a sharecropping arrangement between Spartiates and the conquered population of Messenia.

What relationship do these terms of economic exploitation imposed upon early Messenia bear to the situation in Lakonia and Messenia in the later archaic and classical periods? There is no hard evidence on the point; but there is nothing to suggest that within Messenia itself the initial terms of servitude were significantly altered in later centuries or that the same terms of exploitation did not apply in both Messenia and Lakonia. As Cartledge (1979, 97) has noted, 'there is nothing in the ancient literary sources to suggest that the status of the Lakonian helots differed from that of the Messenians'. It is *a priori* likely that Spartiates would have assimilated the Lakonian and Messenian helots to a single set of conditions. Hence it seems more probable than not that the sharecropping arrangement described by Tyrtaios constituted a condition of helotage throughout our period (cf. Singor 1993, 43).

Some scholars have, admittedly, claimed that at the time of Tyrtaios the Messenian helots had not been fully helotised, a process which they insist took place only after the Second Messenian War (Kiechle 1959, 57–62) or the revolt of the 460s (Ducat 1990a, 60–1, 141–4). On this view, the sharecropping arrangement is characteristic of a semi-independent people only partially enslaved, not of the full state of helotage. There are, however, difficulties with this interpretation. The idea of a semi-independent Messenia depends largely upon Pausanias' portrayal of her as a vassal state which had accepted an oath of loyalty to Sparta (4.14.4). In contrast to the issue of agricultural tribute, he is unable to cite a passage of Tyrtaios to support the notion of an oath. On this point Pausanias' account is heavily influenced by the pseudo-historical Messenian tradition which developed after her liberation in 370/69. The idea that they remained semi-independent after the original conquest is a means by which the Messenians created an 'early history' for themselves; as historical reality it is highly suspect (Pearson 1962; Oliva 1971, 111). There is no support for this idea in the archaic or classical evidence. In the surviving fragments of his poems Tyrtaios clearly portrays the relationship of the Messenians to the Spartans as one of enslavement: the Spartans are described twice as their 'masters' (*desposynoi* and *despotai*: frs. 6.2, 7.1, West).[26] Ducat argues that Herodotus consistently treats the Messenians as a separate entity whom he never confuses with the helots. Whitby (1994, 94–5), however, has shown that Herodotus' references to 'helots' are not restricted to Lakonians; and that his use of the term 'Messenian(s)' is, with one mythical exception (6.52), confined to the context of military conflict with Sparta (Hdt. 3.47; 5.49; 9.35, 64).[27] Herodotus used the specific term 'Messenian(s)' where it was appropriate, otherwise the generic term 'helot(s)' embracing both Lakonians and Messenians. He provides no grounds for believing that the Spartans treated the Messenians as a separate entity. As Figueira (1999) has demonstrated, the main inspiration for the evolution of a separate Messenian identity – which took place relatively late during her period of subjugation to Sparta, after the 460s revolt – was external Athenian propaganda, which was firmly resisted by the Spartans. This is not to deny that there *were* certain distinctive features of communal organization and local consciousness among the Messenian helots, as exemplified by their religious dedications (Ducat 1990a, 142–3) and capacity to revolt (Cartledge 1985a). But these are better explained in terms of the differential operation of common terms of helotage in Messenia and Lakonia, due mainly to differences in their proximity to Sparta.[28] There is therefore no reason to believe that the sharecropping arrangement attested by Tyrtaios was merely an ephemeral phase in the early history of Messenia rather than an essential element of helot servitude in both Messenia and Lakonia.

Sharecropping has been termed 'probably the most widespread form of economic organization in the world' (Warriner 1962, 59). It is therefore worth considering its practical impact and suitability for Sparta's exploitation of the helots in the light of comparative evidence from other societies. Some scholars have thought a 50% quota too large to be a regular levy; but it has been common practice elsewhere, as is indicated by the etymology of the standard French and Italian terms for sharecropping, *métayage* and *mezzadria*.[29] Sharecropping quotas are attested historically as varying considerably, with landlords taking between 10% and 80% of the main crop (Delano Smith 1979, 79; Valensi 1985, 107–8), depending on a variety of factors, such as density of population, alternative employment opportunities, quality of land and especially the relative proportions of the factors of production supplied by landlord and tenant. The situation on Spartiate estates fulfilled several of the conditions favouring higher quotas: a high population density, a captive labour force and high-quality land.[30] The one uncertain aspect is the relative production inputs of Spartiates and helots. The Spartiates provided the land and the helots the labour; but who supplied the seed, draught animals and equipment such as ploughs, pressing beds and milling installations? No direct evidence exists and it may be rash to expect a single answer, owing to the considerable inequalities in access to landed resources among both Spartiates and helots and the significant differences in distance from Sparta between plots in the central Lakonian plain and those in remoter parts of Messenia. The Spartiate landowners depicted by Xenophon as supervising their nearby large estates containing numerous helots are likely to have been interventionist and proactive in supplying higher-quality livestock and materials to maximise production. On distant Messenian smallholdings there was probably greater reliance upon local inputs from more self-sufficient helot households. The system as a whole was well designed to combine a degree of security for poorer Spartiates with a proportionate return for richer landowners. However few production inputs poorer Spartiates could contribute, they were guaranteed half the produce. Richer, more proactive owners, on the other hand, would share in the increased harvests produced by the extra inputs which they had supplied.

Sharecropping also provided a degree of security for the helots – certainly far more security than the system of fixed rents described in the post-classical sources. When the landowner extracts a fixed rent, the cultivator reaps the profits of potential crop surpluses (as the passage from the *Instituta Laconica* implies), but he also has to bear all the risks of crop failure – a point the passage conveniently ignores. A sharecropping arrangement provides a more equitable distribution of both profit and risk. As James Scott's classic study of the 'moral economy' of peasants in southeast Asia (1976, esp. 7 and 46–9) amply demonstrates, subsistence farmers typically prefer to avoid fixed rents in favour of sharecropping, even if the former are more profitable in most years, precisely in order to escape the risk that in bad years the fixed rent will leave them with little or nothing to live on. These considerations are equally relevant in conditions of Mediterranean farming, which are marked by a high interannual variability of weather conditions, leading to considerable fluctuations in crop yields. Recent studies have suggested that 'the vast majority of communities of the [ancient] Mediterranean were endemically vulnerable to food crisis' (Garnsey 1988, 45; cf. Gallant 1989; 1991). Besides sharing the risk, sharecropping may also contribute to overall risk *reduction* by permitting a more flexible agricultural response than is possible under fixed rent to the emerging and variable conditions of each year (Reid 1975/6).[31] Of course, Scott's 'moral economy' approach does not in itself explain Sparta's employment of sharecropping. We need not credit the Spartiates with any philanthropic concern for the helots' well-being. Their needs would have been of little avail had sharecropping not also suited the 'political economy' of the Spartiates, to borrow the phrase adopted by Popkin (1979) in his critique of Scott's peasant-centred approach. The uninterrupted maintenance of helot production was crucial to their own position. Sharecropping was consequently the most secure arrangement in the Spartiate–helot relationship, characterized as it was by a long-term mutual interdependence between landowner and cultivator.

At the same time, sharecropping is not ineffective in producing surpluses. Sharecropping has traditionally suffered criticism from neoclassical economists for its inefficiency, in that a cultivator who receives only half the crop has an incentive to stint his efforts when the marginal product of his labour is still twice as high as the marginal costs, whereas the owner-cultivator will labour on until the costs are as high as the product. These criticisms, however, have been undermined by studies within both the neoclassical and Chayanovian schools of thought.[32] Marginal productivity under sharecropping can be as high as, if not higher than, under alternative regimes. It is often employed by landlords as a means of maximizing labour input, total productivity and surplus, particularly when the holding worked is relatively small. The 'whip of hunger' forces the sharecropper to work as hard and long as is necessary to ensure survival.[33] This effect counteracts the Marshallian principle that sharecropping is inefficient where there is 'practical fixity of tenure' (such as the helots possessed) because the landlord has no instrument for increasing the output of labour. Long tenures can in fact lead to increased productivity because they encourage improvements (R.A.C. Parker 1955/6, 158; Herring 1983, ch. 9). The considerable difference in population between helots and Spartiates worked to the latter's advantage here. In providing their own subsistence, the numerically superior helots will necessarily have produced abundant surpluses for their masters. Only the increasing disparity in land between rich and poor Spartiates ultimately ruined this system by diverting too much of this surplus into too few hands.

Sharecropping was, accordingly, an effective means of sustaining the long-term economic relationship between Spartiates and helots. It was also well-suited to prevailing political conditions, permitting the Spartan polis to control and regulate citizen-helot relations. By maximizing labour input, it kept the helots occupied with farming at the expense of subversive activities. The global imposition of a standard proportion also enabled the polis to limit the acquisitiveness of its citizens in years of poor harvests, thus safeguarding helot subsistence and the essential foundation of Spartan society. The sharing of produce also fitted with the responsibility of citizens for the personal condition of their helots. Citizens were in a better position to influence cultivation choices and to control the foodstuffs available for helot consumption. Finally, sharecropping eased the problem of extracting tribute from distant parts of Spartan territory in years of crop failure. Tenants faced with rents which would take the bulk of the crop often simply appropriate whatever is needed for their subsistence (Scott 1976, 124–46). As the younger Pliny complained of his distant fixed-rent Italian tenants, 'they even seize and consume the produce of the land in the belief that they will gain nothing themselves by conserving it' (*Letters* 9.37). The sharing of reduced harvests will have minimised the growth of grievances and increased the likelihood of helot compliance. From all perspectives, therefore, the interests of the 'political economy' of the Spartiates and of the 'moral economy' of the helots coincided to make sharecropping the most effective means of economic exploitation.

The economic geography of Spartiate-helot landholdings
The character of agricultural exploitation

The geographical location and extent of citizen landholdings cultivated by the helots are important matters in their own right and for their implications for the character of Spartiate-helot agriculture and the size of individual citizen estates. Yet, partly due to the paucity of written evidence, these are questions of considerable controversy and uncertainty.

There are wide differences in modern estimates of the amount of land occupied by citizen estates in Lakonia and Messenia (TABLE 1). These divergences stem from different approaches to several key variables. The highest estimates in older studies stemmed from an over-simplified reliance upon gross topography which assumed that all valley areas were equally suitable for arable cultivation, without attention to local geology, geomorphology or soil type; Bölte's more cautious estimate was the first serious attempt to take these factors into account. Some early studies were also significantly over-pessimistic or over-optimistic in their estimates of productivity.[34] More recent differences stem from disagreement over two further issues. The first is the geographical distribution of Spartiate landholdings, in particular whether they were confined to the main arable

The anatomy of the Spartiate property system

TABLE 1. Estimates of the area of citizen landholdings (in hectares).

	Lakonia	Messenia	Total
Busolt–Swoboda (1920–26, ii.641–2)	120,000		
Kahrstedt (1919, 280–1)			200–250,000
Jardé (1925, 112–13)	90–100,000	126–140,000	216–240,000
Cartledge (1987, 173)	50–75,000		
Figueira (1984, 102–3)		92,500	
Ehrenberg (1924, 47)	60,000		
Bölte (1929a, 1339–40)	<50,000		
Jameson (1992, 137)	21,000		
Roebuck (1945, 151, 156–7)		20,000	

NB. In the cases of Kahrstedt and Jardé the different figures given represent their estimates of Spartiate land exclusive and inclusive of land devoted to arboriculture (which Jardé appears to believe was not divided among individual citizens).

plains or spread more widely. The widely varying estimates for citizen estates in Messenia, for example, derive from the fact that Jardé and Figueira view them as covering a significant portion of Messenian territory, whereas Roebuck would restrict them to the eastern plains (Stenyklaros and Makaria) and the adjoining Soulima valley (see *Fig.* 5, p. 143). The second issue is the interrelated question of the character of agricultural exploitation. Jameson's very low estimate for Lakonia, based on his belief that Spartiate land was restricted to the main valleys of the Sparta basin and Helos plain (see *Fig.* 4, p. 140), is allied to his assumption of a conservative agricultural regime based upon extensive cultivation of subsistence crops, especially cereals, and a low level of production for sale. In his opinion, Sparta's 'serf system worked well only on large estates of the best land' (1992, 137), in contrast to the diversified, specialised, intensive and more market-oriented farming in parts of Greece where agriculture was based upon chattel slavery (cf. Jameson 1977/8). The resulting differences between the extent of Spartiate landholding estimated by various scholars are quite radical, since the combined figure of a mere 41,000 ha produced by Jameson's and Roebuck's figures for Lakonia and Messenia, respectively, is many times fewer than the generous 200,000+ ha proposed by Kahrstedt and Jardé and less even than Bölte's conservative figure of <50,000 ha for Lakonia alone.

We are, consequently, presented with a stark choice between two fundamentally different images of the geography of Spartiate landholding. To decide between them we should first assess the plausibility of the interpretations of the character of Spartiate–helot agriculture with which they are associated. In what follows I shall argue, first, that, although the broad outlines of Jameson's view are correct, certain important qualifications should be entered regarding the supposed low degree of intensification of the agrarian regime; secondly, that these and other factors suggest that Spartiate landholdings were not as geographically restricted as Jameson and Roebuck propose.

In some respects the Spartiates' exploitation of their estates was clearly geared towards subsistence crops. The primary purposes of each citizen's holdings were to feed his family and to supply his required contributions to the common mess. The foodstuffs demanded for the mess were basics of life: barley meal, wine, cheese and figs (Dikaiarchos, *FHG* 2.242, fr. 23, *ap.* Athen. 141c; Plut. *Lyk.* 12.2). Indeed, evidence that the quantity of mess dues demanded of each citizen was higher than he can personally have consumed (Figueira 1984, 91) indicates that state intervention pushed Spartiate landowners in the direction of an even greater orientation towards subsistence crops. Citizen estates, moreover, also had to supply the subsistence needs of the helot labour force. This orientation towards subsistence crops, however, was not complete, nor need it imply a low degree of diversification, intensification or even of market production. As we have seen, the sharecropping system produced abundant surpluses for many Spartiates. As Jameson himself acknowledges (1992, 137), 'the elite used the surplus they controlled to acquire personal possessions… The market was probably always a restricted but not insignificant element in the economy.' Wealthy landowners also used their large estates for non-subsistence crops, such as wheat for the high-status bread that they contributed voluntarily to the messes (Xen. *Lak. Pol.* 5.3).

Wealthy Spartiate estates, moreover, were not merely arable prairies but included a significant level of animal husbandry that reportedly put Athenian estates to shame:

> Not one of our estates could compare with theirs in extent and excellence, not in ownership of slaves, especially the helot class, nor of horses, nor of the other livestock that graze in Messene ([Plato] *Alk. I* 122d).

Note that the contrast made between Spartan and Athenian estates is one of size and quality, not of contrasting types of agricultural practice. (It is even envisaged that wealthy Spartiates would employ not only helots but also some chattel slaves, thus opening up further possibilities for intensification of farming.) A similar picture of Spartiate farming is presented by Euripides (*ap.* Strabo 8.5.6), who describes Messene as,

> watered with countless streams, furnished with good pasture for both cattle and sheep, being neither very wintry, nor yet made too hot by the chariots of Helios.

As Euripides emphasizes, Messenia possessed an ideal environment and climate for the practice of diversified agriculture with a substantial pastoral element. Recent studies have emphasized that animal husbandry at anything above subsistence level typically involves a significant degree of involvement in market transactions as a means of exchanging the wide range of secondary products deriving from pastoral activity (cf. Khazanov 1984, 202; Whittaker (ed.) 1988, 4;

Forbes 1995, 338). Wealthy Spartiates needed to engage in such exchanges to fund the variety of expenditures demanded by their elite lifestyles (see further chs. 5, 9–11.) From this angle too, the agricultural practices of wealthy Spartiates appear more complex than those of an unintensive subsistence regime.

Furthermore, we should not draw too firm a line between the agricultural activities of the rich and of ordinary Spartiates. The range of compulsory mess contributions indicates that farming on the holdings of ordinary citizens was diverse in its scope, involving not only arable culture but also viticulture, arboriculture and animal husbandry. Scholars often envisage these diversified activities as operating in marginal settings divorced from areas of cereal production. Jardé (1925, 112–13) thought that land devoted to arboriculture was not divided among individual citizens. Jameson assumes that 'the considerable amount of hilly and rough country adjoining the Spartiates' *kleroi* was used by helots for grazing, while small patches of cultivable land in these marginal areas were used for vines, fruits and field crops' (1992, 137 n. 12). According to Roebuck (1945, 151), Messenia was exploited through 'cereal production on the Spartan *kleroi* in the plains and…stock-raising in the hills'. This supposed separation of activities, however, runs counter to current understandings of the practice of Greek arboriculture and animal husbandry. Arboriculture frequently included the intercropping of trees and cereals (Gallant 1991, 38–41) and animal husbandry typically involved the integration of arable and pastoral activities, often including a degree of on-farm husbandry (Hodkinson 1988; Forbes 1995).

Nor should we think of production on ordinary citizen estates as necessarily unintensive or isolated from the market. The year-round requirement upon every household to supply the specified mess contributions probably created an ongoing demand for these products as households sought to obtain particular foodstuffs of which they were (temporarily) in short supply, balancing their acquisitions where possible through the disposal of items in surplus. Whether these transactions took place through the market or through more personalised exchange does not affect the boost given to production for surplus. The increasing poverty of many Spartiate households from the fifth century onwards probably also led to increased intensification in an effort to maintain production of the mess dues from smaller holdings.

Further intensification of cultivation stemmed from subsistence pressures on the helot cultivators. The size of the helot population is uncertain, even for the better-attested periods of the fifth and early fourth centuries, with modern estimates varying between 140,000 and 375,000.[35] (For further discussion, see ch. 12.) No doubt it was not static, and it probably adhered to the general population increase evident throughout archaic and classical Greece (Sallares 1991, 50–107). Most scholars, however, whatever their precise figures, would subscribe to Cartledge's proposition (1987, 174) that 'most helots could have been living at or near the margin of subsistence'.[36] Far from a regime of extensive cultivation, we should arguably envisage on many estates a considerable degree of intensification as helot families struggled hard, making high labour inputs to ensure their subsistence. Even with such intensive farming, it would have been a major struggle for even a mere 140,000 helots to live off half the produce of Roebuck's and Jameson's projected 41,000 ha, at an effective population : farmland density of almost seven persons per ha. In fact, not all helots did live on the subsistence margin. We saw reason earlier to postulate considerable differentiation within the helot population, with some households cultivating sizeable landed properties capable of surplus production. Although the mechanisms by which surpluses might be disposed of are unclear, there are intimations in both the literary and archaeological record that means existed by which helots could engage in exchange and constructively employ their surplus resources.[37] For better-off helots too there were good reasons for practising more intensive cultivation.

We should conclude, therefore, that the depiction of Spartiate–helot agriculture as a system of unintensive cereal cultivation which worked well only on large estates of the best valley land is altogether too simple. Indeed, Jameson himself acknowledges the existence of systems of serf labour elsewhere in other regions of Greece – at Sikyon and Lokris – which were less suited to large-scale extensive cultivation (1992, 138–9). In Sparta too the system of partible inheritance embracing both sons and daughters probably meant that the landholdings of most households were fragmented into individual plots of modest size. Hence even the estates of wealthier citizens will have been an aggregation of smaller-scale units of cultivation.

Agricultural potential and the spread of Spartiate landholdings

The implication of these preceding remarks for the location of Spartan estates is surely to dissolve the sharp distinction between the agricultural exploitation of the plains and of other land which dominates much scholarly discussion. In the light of this observation, let us consider the regions of Lakonia and Messenia in turn.

Lakonia

The pressures towards intensification discussed above suggest that one would expect Spartiate landholdings in Lakonia, especially in the parts closest to Sparta, to spread beyond the Eurotas valley, westwards and eastwards up the hill sides towards the Taygetos and Parnon ranges, to occupy every available niche. The plausibility of this expectation is confirmed by study of the area's agricultural potential. Although definitive assessment is problematic in the absence of systematic geomorphological surveys, some provisional comments can usefully be made.[38]

We can start with the area most easily accessible for Spartiate exploitation, the Eurotas valley close to Sparta itself (*Figs.* 2–3). The precise chronology of the fluvial sequences which contributed to the formation of this landscape is as

The anatomy of the Spartiate property system

yet unknown. From the available studies, however, it seems clear that land in the valley bottom in antiquity was not always markedly superior to the adjacent hill land. The present-day soil cover in the valley bottom itself varies considerably in character and fertility and has been formed in different periods by a diverse range of processes.[39] The modern landscape comprises a dissected chain of low hillocks running down the length of the valley (shown in the foreground of *Fig.* 2), consisting of light, fertile Neogene marls, conglomerates and sands. This chain is flanked, to the west, by a broad, shallow alluvium-filled depression, which itself gives way to less fertile piedmont fans characterised by red soils at the foot of Mt Taygetos. (Both features are evident in the background of *Fig.* 2.) To the east, the chain of hillocks is flanked by a lower terrace of fertile alluvial soils which runs along the banks of the River Eurotas.

As regards the valley in antiquity, recent studies, based especially upon magnetic data, suggest that the mid-Holocene (Neolithic and later) landscape also comprised distinct subdivisions containing soils of diverse fertility (Pope 1995). The following description moves across the valley from west to east (see *Fig.* 3).

First, on the valley's western margin, the piedmont fans mentioned above were still active with deposition, causing them to extend towards the interior of the basin. The upper fan surfaces were relict landforms, although the soils developing on them were susceptible to erosion which removed the A-horizon and exposed the less fertile underlying B-horizon. Secondly, the aforementioned broad alluvial depression probably experienced intermittent erosion by occasional run-off from the Taygetos range which in turn partly truncated the soils developing on the surface.

Fig. 2. View over central and western parts of Sparta valley, looking towards Mt Taygetos (photo courtesy of Deutsches Archäologisches Institut, Athens). Note, in the foreground, the chain of hillocks and, in the distance, the shallow alluvial depression and piedmont fans.

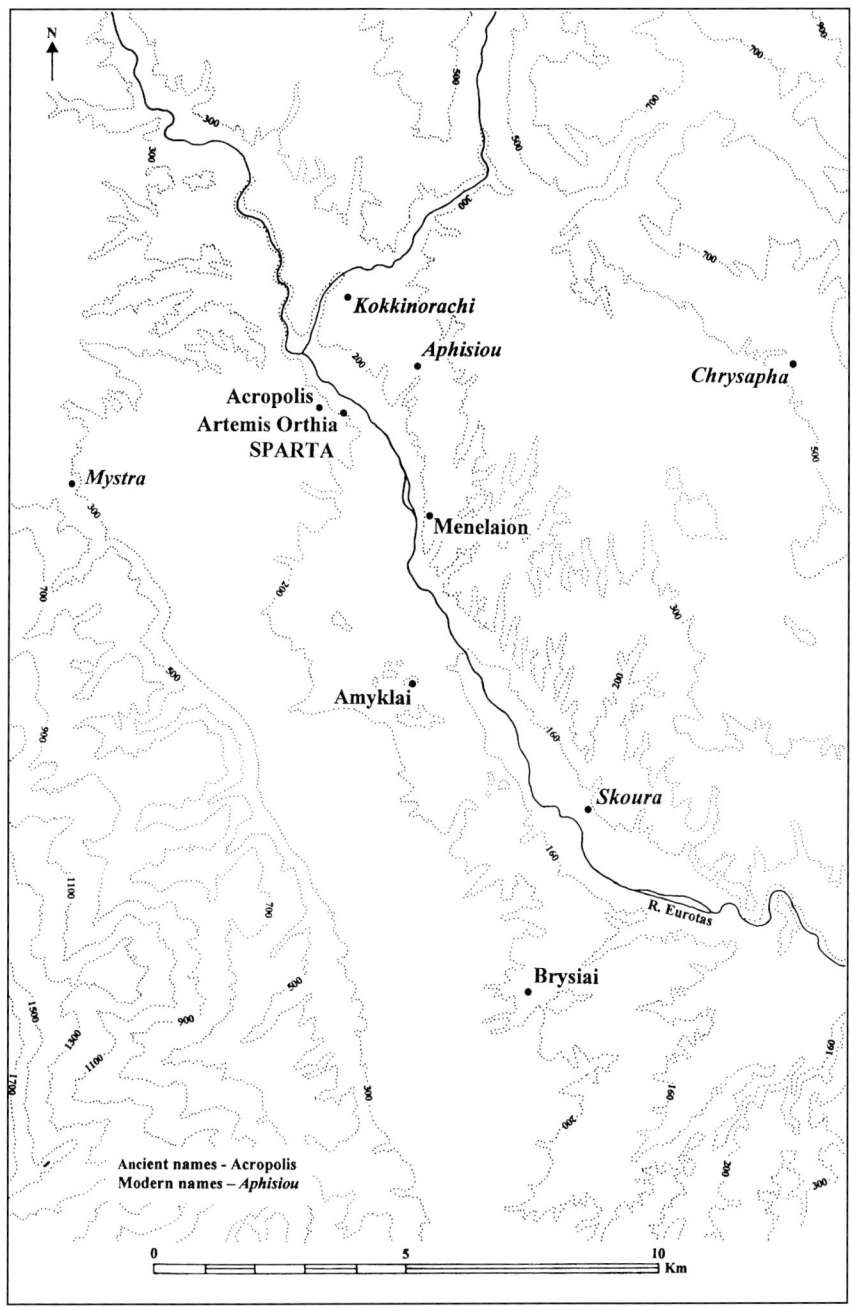

Fig. 3. Sparta Valley.

Thirdly, the low Neogene hillocks were by this period largely a relict landscape formed by erosion of the initial Neogene landscape and subsequent dissection, probably during the middle Pleistocene; in consequence, *in situ* weathering of Neogene deposits provided material for soil formation. Fourthly, due to this erosion, material was transferred to the central parts of the basin, where fertile soils evolved from reworked Neogene deposits. Bore-hole data suggests that reworked Neogene now underlies the alluvium and alluvial soils developing in the area adjacent to the present-day River Eurotas.

Finally, down the basin's eastern side soils were developing on Holocene fluvial sediment deposited by the River Eurotas. However, many of the current fertile soils which have developed on the alluvium are probably of post-classical date. The thesis of Vita-Finzi (1969) and Bintliff (1977) that the alluvial soils known as the 'Younger Fill' were not deposited until after AD 400 as a consequence of Mediterranean-wide climatic change is nowadays heavily disputed (Wagstaff 1981; van Andel et al. 1986). Current theories emphasize instead the impact of human cultivation and the differential timing of deposition in different locations. Nevertheless, Wagstaff (1981, 250 table 1) accepts a late Roman date for alluviation at Limnai in Sparta itself. Geomorphological studies of the north-eastern part of the Eurotas valley for the British School at Athens Laconia Survey have dated the later phase of alluvial fan deposits and basin fill to the late classical/hellenistic period and the current river terraces to the last 200–700 years.[40]

Overall, therefore, it seems that before the widespread deposition of alluvial soils, which took place largely after our period, certain parts of the Sparta plain in antiquity were significantly poorer in quality than they are today. In classical times soils developing on the Neogene were probably more extensive within the Eurotas basin and probably constituted the prime agricultural land. These soils, however, were not confined to the valley bottom. Even today fertile soils developing on Neogene extend into the foothills north-west of Sparta and north of Mystra. They are extensive also to the east of Sparta, on the plateau above the valley bottom. Although nowadays this region is heavily dissected and eroded, substantial areas of Neogene-derived soils still remain north-east of Sparta between the modern villages of Kokkinorachi and Aphisiou, around the sanctuary of the Menelaion and (further south) near the village of Skoura. Further areas are found in the south of the Sparta basin and at the northern end of the Helos plain (Bintliff 1977, ii.374–5, 382–3, 389 and 445 fig. 3; Cavanagh et al. 1996, 362). Geomorphological studies within the Laconia Survey area have concluded that, as in the Eurotas basin, the soils developing on Neogene on the plateau east of Sparta were deeper and more extensive in antiquity. It is *a priori* likely, therefore, that during the expansion of their territorial control Spartiate households took the opportunity to acquire these nearby high-quality areas of Neogene, which may have been superior to some valley land. This hypothesis is supported by the fact that they contained the greatest amount of classical surface archaeological material within the Survey area (Cavanagh et al. forthcoming, ch. 2).

The evidence from the Sparta valley, consequently, provides further indications that citizen landholdings in Lakonia as a whole were spread more diffusely than is usually thought. Traditionally, Spartiate landholdings in Lakonia are envisaged as having been located in discrete blocks clearly separated from the territories of the *perioikoi* (Bölte 1929a, 1321–40). This view is founded almost exclusively upon the passage of Plutarch, *Agis* (8.1) which describes King Agis IV's proposals for a complete redistribution of land in the 240s. According to these proposals,

> the land should be divided up, that which lay between the water-course at Pellene, Taygetos, Malea, and Sellasia, into 4,500 *klēroi*, that which lay outside into 15,000; and this latter should be apportioned among those of the *perioikoi* who were capable of bearing arms, that inside to the Spartiates.

As has already been demonstrated (ch. 3), Agis's proposals, though presented as a return to Sparta's glorious past, were a radical departure from previous practice. Hence there is no surety that the precise demarcation between areas of Spartiate and perioikic landholdings reflects the classical situation. Although it made sense for Agis to use the existing perioikic poleis of Sellasia and Pellene for fixing his northern boundary, there is no evidence that this stemmed from the presence of a similar boundary between Spartiate and perioikic private estates in classical times.[41] The specification of the Taygetos range and Malea peninsula as the other boundaries in fact contradicts classical arrangements, since the huge area thus delimited embraces certain probable classical perioikic sites. (It also includes far more territory than just valley land, thus offering no support for notions that Spartiate landholdings were confined to the plains.)

In contrast to Agis's proposals, the organisation of Spartan-perioikic relations in classical Lakonia was not the result of systematic planning. The increasing in-filling of the landscape revealed in the archaic and classical archaeological record shows that the establishment of perioikic communities took place over several centuries and must have sprung from a variety of circumstances.[42] Consequently, we should not expect strict demarcation between areas of Spartiate and perioikic landholdings. Indeed, we know that the kings held land within many perioikic territories (Xen. *Lak. Pol.*15.3). The location of certain perioikic settlements, such as Brysiai and Krokeai, in the Sparta and Helos plains also suggests a patchwork of Spartiate and perioikic farms;[43] and Graham Shipley (1992, 217–19) has suggested several other cases outside the central valleys (Geronthrai, Chrysapha and the plain south of modern Molaoi) where this may have applied. This intermingling of farms would help explain the markedly dispersed character of perioikic settlements (G. Shipley 1992, 223).

Where does this leave the question of the extent of Spartiate landholdings in Lakonia? The considerations discussed above suggest that Jameson's estimate

The anatomy of the Spartiate property system

of a mere 21,000 ha of Spartiate land is too low. As he notes, the Greek National Statistical Service's 1961 Agriculture-Livestock Census recorded 47,153 ha of cultivated land within the modern administrative unit, the Eparchia Lakedaimonos, which covers the Sparta valley and adjacent areas, including part of the Helos plain. To bolster his argument that the Spartiates themselves exploited less than half of this area, Jameson not only excludes the

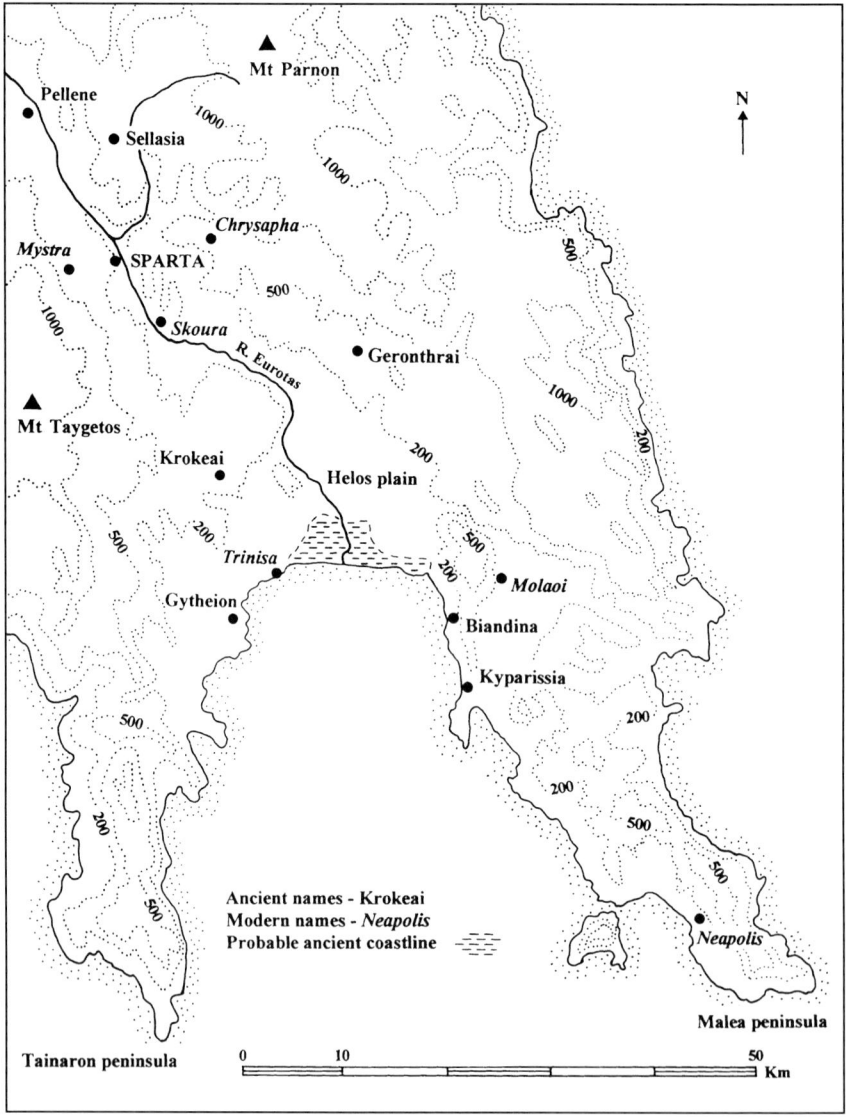

Fig. 4. Lakonia.

non-plains areas but also argues for a further reduction of the area within the Eparchia available for Spartiate landholdings, on the grounds that the ancient Helos plain was considerably smaller before post-classical alluviation (1992, 137 n. 14). In fact, however, the Eparchia Lakedaimonos includes only about one-third of the plain's post-classical alluvial areas: those located in the plain's south-western sector.[44] Most of the recent alluvium falls outside the Eparchia Lakedaimonos, within the neighbouring Eparchia Epidaurou Limiras. Hence more of the cultivable land within Sparta's immediate region was available for cultivation than Jameson acknowledges. Indeed, the Eparchia Epidaurou Limiras itself also includes about 5,000 ha of non-alluvial cultivated land in the eastern part of the Helos plain, which should be added to the area available for Spartiate estates.[45]

There were probably also Spartiate–helot farms further south-east, in the Malea peninsula (see *Fig.* 4). In 415 the Athenians established a fort at the southern end of the peninsula opposite the island of Kythera, probably by the bay of modern Neapolis, 'so that the helots might have a place to which they could desert' (Thuc. 7.26; cf. Gomme et al. 1945–81, iv.399–400). The fort was abandoned in winter 413/12 (8.4); but in just two and a half years it attracted a sizeable number of deserters, since Xenophon (*Hell.* 1.2.18) states that in winter 410/09 'the Lakedaimonians let go under treaty the helots who had revolted and fled from Malea to Koryphasion [sc. Pylos in western Messenia]'. The Malea fort was obviously close to a region of helot-worked estates. The nearby plain of Neapolis is one obvious candidate for the location of these estates; another is the large plain of high-quality Neogene soils south of modern Molaoi. Certain scholars have argued that the owners of these helot-worked estates in this region were *perioikoi* (Hampl 1937, 24; G. Shipley 1997, 203). The issue of whether perioikoi could possess helots, however, is a vexed one which has divided modern scholarship: the sources permit no clear-cut conclusion.[46] Even if one grants the possibility of perioikic ownership, it is noteworthy that there is no definite archaeological evidence for the presence of a significant classical perioikic settlement in the Neapolis plain (G. Shipley 1992, 220) and the plain of Molaoi also lacked perioikic sites east of the coastal settlements of Kyparissia and Biandina (ibid. 219). Hence the helot-worked farms in these two regions may well have been Spartiate-owned, or perhaps a mixed patchwork of Spartiate and perioikic holdings. If so, they will have constituted a significant addition to the area of Spartiate land-ownership, since the cultivated area of the plain of Molaoi on its own totalled over 9,000 ha, including adjacent non-plains land, in the 1971 Agriculture-Livestock Census.[47]

Clearly, the modern figures cited above provide only a generic indication of the amount of land available for Spartiate farms in antiquity; but together they suggest an area significantly larger than Jameson's 21,000 ha and surely closer to the maximum of 50,000 ha suggested by Bölte.

Messenia

The case of Messenia, as noted earlier, presents similar differences of opinion concerning the geographical extent of Spartiate landholdings (see *Fig.* 5). Many scholars believe that Spartiate estates worked by helots were restricted to the two eastern plains: the upper Messenian plain known in antiquity as Stenyklaros and the lower plain by the Messenian gulf, known as Makaria. According to this view, non-perioikic land elsewhere in central and western Messenia was not divided into private arable estates but used for pastoralism and other activities.[48] Other scholars, however, envisage Spartiate holdings as being spread over a much wider area of the region's territory (Jardé 1925, 112–13; Figueira 1984, 102–3). This latter view is supported – as we have seen – by the considerations urged above regarding the character of Spartiate-helot agriculture.

The two eastern plains, separated by Mt Ithome, were undoubtedly the central focus of Spartiate landholdings. Their acquisition had been the objective of the original Spartan conquest (Tyrtaios, fr. 5 West). Spartiate estates occupied the whole of the upper Stenyklaros plain and the western part of the lower Makaria plain. A fragment of Euripides (*ap.* Strabo 8.5.6; 366c), which indicates that the River Pamisos (which flows north–south through the lower plain) formed the border between Lakonikē and Messenia, is normally interpreted as signifying that the river divided Spartiate territory to the west from the territories of perioikic settlements along the eastern edge of the plain and the eastern coast of the Messenian Gulf (Ernst Meyer 1978, 253–4). In his poem referring to the original Spartan conquest, Tyrtaios refers to 'Messene, good to plough and good to sow'; but we should not regard the eastern plains as devoted solely to arable culture. As we saw earlier, Euripides calls the same region 'rich in produce, watered with countless streams, furnished with good pasture for both cattle and sheep'. His evidence indicates a mixed arable and pastoral regime and his description of the watery landscape nicely fits the Makaria plain and the 'Five Rivers' region around the northwestern head of the Messenian Gulf. As a modern agricultural economist has commented, 'the floodplains and coastal lowlands must have served as grazing grounds for large animals' (van Wersch 1972, 181), not least the horses mentioned in the passage from [Plato], *Alkibiades I* quoted earlier.

Conversely, although the regions of central and western Messenia no doubt also witnessed much pastoral activity, to dismiss them as merely grazing and hunting land is to ignore their immense arable potential. Van Wersch's modern study (1972, 186) has noted 'the suitability for grain production of the sizeable plateau lands and the rolling hill country' of inland Messenia. The region contains many promising arable environments: well-drained, gently-sloping alluvial slopes; fertile Pliocene terraces with terraceable slopes and flattish valleys; upland kampos and dissected Pliocene hill lands characterised by moderately fertile, non-calcareous soils; also regions of dissected kampos and ridges, more marginal cropland, to which barley, however, with its lower moisture

Ch. 4. Helotage and the exploitation of Spartan territory

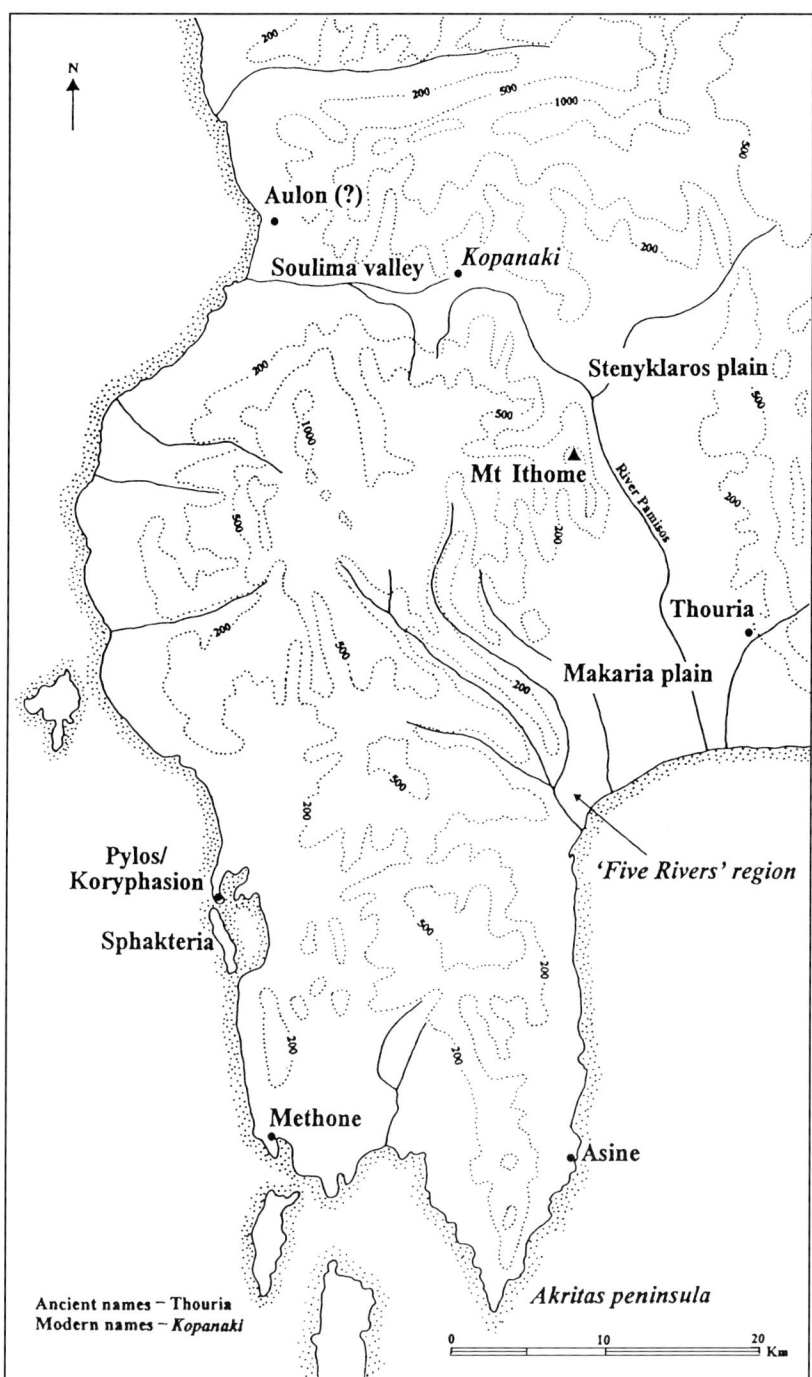

Fig. 5. Messenia.

The anatomy of the Spartiate property system

requirements, is well adapted.[49] Settlement evidence from eras as diverse as the Middle and Late Helladic, Roman, medieval, early and late modern periods indicates the capacity of these non-plains regions to support a broad scatter of villages and hamlets.[50] Even in 1971, after much recent population loss and land abandonment, the combined cultivated area of the Eparchiai Pylias and Triphylias, which together cover the bulk of southern and western Messenia, amounted to over 70,000 ha.[51]

There is good reason to believe that in our period too the fertile regions of central and western Messenia were utilised for mixed farming and supported a healthy settled population. Despite the paucity of archaeological study of archaic and classical Messenia, there is sufficient evidence to indicate that agrarian exploitation went beyond specialised herding operations – which typically leave little trace in the archaeological record. The site catalogue of the Minnesota Messenia Expedition records a significant number of archaic and classical sites, despite the Expedition's primary concentration on Bronze Age remains.[52] Similarly, the recent survey in western Messenia by the Pylos Regional Archaeological Project suggests that during the archaic and classical periods this region, although not densely populated, contained significant clusters of nucleated settlements.[53] A late archaic and early classical habitation site excavated at Kopanaki in the Soulima valley contained a range of domestic pottery (including food preparation, cooking and storage items) comparable to those found in the Laconia Survey area, which suggests the rounded exploitation of local farmland.[54] Finally, the evidence of archaic and classical tomb cult at several locations in inland Messenia attests an attachment of inhabitants to their local territories indicative of a settled farming life.[55] It is unlikely that much of this archaeological evidence relates to the *perioikoi*, since there are only three attested classical perioikic settlements in central and western Messenia: Asine (modern Korone) and Methone at the south-east and south-west points of the Akritas peninsula, respectively, and Aulon near the northern border with Elis.[56] Hence the probability is that most of the attested settlements were inhabited by helots farming Spartiate estates. In addition, Thucydides' reference (4.26) to helot boat owners who sailed from various parts of the Peloponnese suggests that there were helots inhabiting the coastal areas of Messenia as of other regions under Spartan control.

We can conclude that Spartiate landholdings were dispersed over the vast bulk of Messenian territory. A huge swathe of Messenian territory was available for Spartiate agricultural exploitation, stretching eastwards from the Stenyklaros and Makaria plains across to the west coast, northwards to include the Soulima valley and southwards down the Akritas peninsula as far as Methone and Asine. If we add the 30,000 ha of cultivated land, recorded for the modern Eparchia Messinis (which covers the Stenyklaros plain, the Makaria plain west of the River Pamisos and adjacent terrace and rolling hill land to the west) in the 1971 Agriculture-Livestock census, to the more than 70,000 ha from the

Ch. 4. Helotage and the exploitation of Spartan territory

Eparchiai Pylias and Triphylias, the overall total of available land comes to over 100,000 ha.[57] Deduction of land around the few attested perioikic sites and of extraneous territory in northern Triphylia brings this figure close to other modern estimates, such as Figueira's figure of 92,500 ha (which was derived from the 1961 census, when the region had a slightly higher overall cultivated area) and Roebuck's estimate of 87,500 ha for the cultivated area of the region during its independence after 369 (1945, 162 n. 91).

We may envisage the area of Spartiate-helot landholdings then as totalling somewhat less than 50,000 ha in Lakonia and approximately 90,000 ha in Messenia. These relative proportions accord with Thucydides' comment (1.101) that most of the helot population was Messenian and with other evidence for the critical significance of Messenia. Although these figures are only approximate guides, they provide an order of magnitude whose implications for the size of citizen estates will be pursued in chapter 12.

Notes

[1] The section on the organisation of agricultural tribute is a reworking of my discussion in Hodkinson 1992a. In this chapter I shall discuss the listed issues primarily from the angle of the Spartiate property owners. I hope to approach them from the helots' viewpoint in a subsequent study.

[2] Standard opinion is that there were five citizen villages: the four central villages at Sparta itself (Pitane, Mesoa, Limnai and Kynosoura) plus Amyklai, 5 km to the south. Kennell (1995, 162–9), however, has recently challenged the Amyklaians' status as Spartiate citizens in classical times.

[3] On the end of helotage, Ducat 1990a, 193–9.

[4] Helot agricultural labour: Arist. *Pol.* 1271b40–1272a2; Livy 34.27.9; Plut. *Lyk.* 24.3; Aelian, *VH* 13.19; Slaves on wealthy estates: [Plato], *Alk. I* 122d; cf. Plut. *Comp. Lyk.-Num.* 2.4. Modern discussions: Kahrstedt 1919, 288–9; Ducat 1978, 14–15, 38–9; 1990a, 53–5; MacDowell 1986, 37–9.

[5] As Ducat (1990a, 21 n. 9) notes, *oiketai* doubtless here signifies either helots or, if there were also chattel slaves in Sparta, the ensemble comprising these and the helots together.

[6] After the battle of Marathon: Paus. 7.15.7; after Arginusai: Xen. *Hell.* 1.6.24; Aristop. *Frogs* 694, with Schol. (Hellanikos, *FGrH* 323aF25). Chios: L. Robert 1938, 118–26.

[7] Although the label is normally regarded as Spartan-inspired, one purpose may be to ease Athenian difficulties in abetting the subjugation of people whose claims to freedom they had previously accepted. On the fifth-century Athenians' role in the creation of the 'Messenian' identity, Figueira 1999.

[8] Even Ducat, however, concedes that no source alleges that the helots were enslaved by agreement (1990a, 73).

[9] So too is the evidence of the Tainaron manumission inscriptions from the late fifth and fourth centuries (*IG* v.1.1228–33). With the exception of *IG* v.1.1231, which concerns an Epeirote owner, presumably of a chattel slave, there are no firm grounds

for deciding whether the manumittees were slaves or helots and their owners Spartiates or *perioikoi* (cf. Ducat 1990b).

¹⁰ Cf. Finley 1985, 63. The fact that some helots were taken off the land from time to time, to serve in a Spartiate's household, for example, does not invalidate the general proposition in the text.

¹¹ Singor does, it is true, suggest that some impoverished helots were procured by Spartiates whose holdings had increased without a proportionate increase in their helot cultivators; but that would barely alleviate the degree of disruption described above. He also raises the question of helot residence, suggesting that they lived in villages rather than in isolated farmsteads and implying that their residential separation from the land went with their not being bound to the soil. As commentators have noted, the textual evidence is ambiguous concerning helot residence, though recent archaeological research (see n. 17, below) suggests that settlement in western Messenia, arguably helot-farmed territory, was in village-like groupings rather than in dispersed, isolated dwellings. However, the issues of helot residence and cultivation rights are not the same; helot village residence need not imply insecurity of tenure.

¹² The significance of this episode is not affected by evidence that the sum of five minas was a standard price paid by chattel slaves for their liberation in the third century (Ducat 1990a, 64).

¹³ Cf. Wrightson and Levine 1979, 96; R.M. Smith 1984, 308–9; Osborne 1988, 308–9.

¹⁴ Xen. *Lak. Pol.* 1.8–9; Philo *On Special Laws* 3.4.22; Cartledge 1981, esp. 99, 103; Lane Fox 1985, 222–3; Hodkinson 1989, 90–3.

¹⁵ There is no evidence that when Spartiates were degraded to Inferior status through (*inter alia*) failure to produce their mess contributions they ceased to own land. Given the private nature of Spartiate land tenure, it is unlikely that the polis intervened to take away their remaining holdings. The fact that Inferiors continued to serve in the army (Xen. *Hell.* 3.3.7) implies that they retained their former means of support.

¹⁶ Cf. the statement of Archemachos of Euboia (*ap.* Athen. 264b), *fl.* first half of the third century BC, that many Penestai were richer than their Thessalian masters. Although 'many' is no doubt an exaggeration and the passage is distorted by an over-favourable image of the institution (Ducat 1990a, 70–1), the phenomenon should not be entirely dismissed.

¹⁷ This evidence comes from the results of recent intensive survey by the Pylos Regional Archaeological Project (Davis et al. 1997, 455–7; A.B. Harrison and Spencer 1998, 158–62; Alcock et al. in prep.); from the mean size of sites noted in the older University of Minnesota Messenia Expedition and in more localised survey in the hinterland of Nichoria (Alcock forthcoming; cf. McDonald and Rapp (eds.) 1972, 264–321; Lukermann and Moody 1978); and from the evidence of the large late archaic and early classical house (some 30 x 17 metres) discovered at Kopanaki in the Soulima valley in northern Messenia (Kaltsas 1983).

¹⁸ The original text μονομοιτῶν Εἰλώτων ἄρχοντες has been plausibly emended to read μνῳονόμοι· τῶν Εἰλώτων ἄρχοντες. Despite Wilamowitz's view (1924, 273), followed by Talbert (1989, 30 n. 51), that this passage relates solely to Crete since the term *mnōia* is otherwise found only there, the mention of helots must indicate that the reference is to Sparta, as Gschnitzer (1964–76, ii.81 and n. 117) and Ducat (1990a, 63) have noted.

¹⁹ Greek texts and translations (which I have largely followed below) of the main sources are conveniently presented by MacDowell 1986, 32–3.

²⁰ e.g. Aeschines 1.97; Plut. *Theseus* 23.3. It was the regular word in classical Athens for the payments which a slave working independently delivered to his master.

²¹ As seen in ch. 3, the hellenistic writer Myron of Priene (*FGrH* 106F2, *ap.* Athen. 657d) refers to the helot tribute by the term *moira*. Although this term is less suggestive of a fixed amount than of a 'portion', it would be unwise to press this point too hard, since the main idea conveyed by the word may be that the tribute was in kind rather than cash (Ducat 1990a, 57).

²² Cf. Kessler 1910, 38–40; Lotze 1959, 29; 1971, 69–70; Jones 1967, 9; Cartledge 1985a, 43; Ducat 1990a, 57–9. As Singor (1993, 53) has noted, fixed rents were a levelling measure. However, they were not, as he suggests, a fifth-century measure designed to counteract growing inequalities, but part of the egalitarian measures of Agis and Kleomenes.

²³ Chrimes (1949, 290–1) argues that the 'masters' in the passage are the Messenian aristocracy. Den Boer (1954, 73–4) interprets it as a warning to the Spartans of their fate if defeated. These hypotheses have been refuted by several scholars: e.g. Diesner 1953/4, 220 n. 7; Kiechle 1959, 13, 62–6; Lotze 1959, 33; Oliva 1971, 109; Figueira 1984, 104 n. 54; Ducat 1990a, 60.

²⁴ e.g. Busolt and Swoboda 1920–26, ii.641; Lotze 1959, 28; Jones 1967, 9; Figueira 1984, 103–4.

²⁵ Cf. the emendations listed in Prato (ed.) 1968, 27; West (ed.) 1972, 153; Gentili and Prato (eds.) 1979, 23.

²⁶ Ducat's suggestion that this servile vocabulary is added on, perhaps in a figurative sense, to an essentially mild form of subjection seems implausibly forced.

²⁷ Ducat's picture of early fifth-century Messenia is of 'un peuple en guerre quasi permanente avec Sparte' (1990a, 141). But this view is achieved only by separating the battles of the Isthmos and Stenyklaros from their most probable context within the 460s revolt and by over-reliance upon the reported argument of Aristagoras (Hdt. 5.49, a piece of advocacy, not a dispassionate statement) that the Spartans should suspend their wars against the equally-matched Messenians in order to campaign against Persia. As Whitby notes, although the dramatic context of Herodotus' passage is the year 499, the argument probably reflects the fighting of the 460s; it does not provide evidence of continual conflict in the later sixth century.

²⁸ I hope to discuss the specific characteristics of Messenian helotage and community organisation, with especial reference to religious cult, in my proposed study mentioned in n. 1.

²⁹ Anton Powell (1988, 249) notes some scholars' doubts. For citation of a range of societies in which 50% is the norm, Hodkinson 1992a, 129 n. 26.

³⁰ On helot population density, see later this chapter. The Spartiates appropriated the best lands, on whose fertility see Euripides, *ap.* Strabo 8.5.6; [Plato], *Alkibiades I* 122d; Plb. 5.19.7; Thiersch 1833, i.303–4.

³¹ Reid has questioned the superiority of sharecropping over pre-agreed rent as a means of risk *sharing*; but his critique relates to situations in which percentage shares and levels of rent are mutually and competitively determined by the ability of landlords and tenants to seek alternative labourers or masters or to opt for alternative contractual arrangements. Neither of these situations applied between Spartiates and helots.

The anatomy of the Spartiate property system

32 Marshall (1890) defines the traditional neoclassical position. For the neoclassical revision, Cheung 1969; Reid 1973; 1975/6; 1977. For the Chayanovian interpretation, Herring 1984.

33 The phrase is from Herring 1984; cf. also Sen 1981 and the essays in Byres (ed.) 1983 by Byres, Bhaduri and Caballero, with Lehmann 1984, 264. Note that in my discussion *productivity* is used as a measure of *efficiency* because, although the latter should technically and properly be defined by relating returns to costs, in land reform policy literature, which dominates modern economic debate of sharecropping, inefficiency usually means low returns per unit of land, i.e. low yields (Herring 1984, 145 n. 1).

34 Kahrstedt 1919, 280–1, misinterpreting Plutarch's figure of 82 *medimnoi* in *Lyk.* 8.3–4 as the total barley production of the holding rather than just the helot tribute, calculated annual productivity at only 400 kg per ha, assessing Spartan productivity in terms of the least developed contemporary European agrarian systems. Jardé (1925, 11–12), criticising Kahrstedt's figure as excessively low, advocated the much higher figure of 1600 litres per ha (or 1,200 kg, at a weight-volume ratio of 0.75 kg per litre: cf. Foxhall and Forbes 1982, 76). The statistics for yields between 1911 and 1950 assembled by Gallant (1991, 77; table 4.7) fall in between these extremes, with an average productivity of 627.7 kg per ha in Lakonia and 650.9 in the region of Kalamata in Messenia.

35 Details and references in Oliva 1971, 53 n. 3.

36 Cartledge accepts an estimate of 175–200,000, near the lower end of the range. For more detailed calculations of the extent of this subsistence pressure, ch. 12.

37 Cf. the helots' sale of stolen booty after Plataia (Hdt. 9.80); the rewards of *argyrion* ('silver', in coins or bullion?) promised to them, and the insurance valuations of their boats, during the Sphakteria episode of 425 (Thuc. 4.26). Note the imported as well as local pottery among items of classical tomb cult at Nichoria (Coulson and Wilkie 1983, 334–5).

38 I am glad to acknowledge my debt in the following remarks to unpublished work by Drs Richard Pope and Keith Wilkinson. See also Pope 1995; Wilkinson 1998.

39 Wilkinson 1998, esp. 150 fig. 14.1, replacing Bintliff 1977, ii.371–450, esp. 445 map 3.

40 I am grateful to Bill Cavanagh for giving me access to the land evaluation chapter of vol. 1 of the Survey (Cavanagh et al. forthcoming, ch. 2) before publication.

41 In 403 Sellasia appears twice as a place where the ephors interrogated Athenian envoys before deciding whether to allow them into Sparta itself (Xen. *Hell.* 2.2.13, 19). The former text is sometimes interpreted as indicating a state border; but the key words may well be interpolated (Krentz 1989, 184). Sellasia's use as a place to keep enemy ambassadors at arm's length during sensitive negotiations carries no implication of a rigid boundary between Sellasian and Spartiate landholdings.

42 Cartledge 1979, 98; G. Shipley 1992, 214. Compare the period-specific maps in G. Shipley 1996, 268–70.

43 On the location of perioikic Bryseai, at Agios Vasileios in the south-west of the Sparta basin, and Krokeiai, probably at Krikiles in the Helos plain, G. Shipley 1992, 217, 219; 1996, Sites GG101, JJ120.

44 See the geomorphological maps in Bintliff 1977, ii.493; Cartledge 1979, 20.

45 National Statistical Service of Greece 1978, i.216–18. This land lies in the Koinotites Ambelochoriou, Apidea, Asteriou, Glykovrisis, Gouvon, Myrteas, Peristeriou and Vlachiotis.

46 In favour: Hampl 1937, 35–9; G. Shipley 1997, 203. Against: Ehrenberg 1924, 40; Kiechle 1963, 107–11; Cartledge 1979, 179; 1987, 178. Agnostic: Ducat 1990a, 189–91.

47 National Statistical Service of Greece 1978, i.218.

48 Roebuck 1941, 28–31; 1945, 151; Toynbee 1969, 189–90; Lotze 1971, 64–5; Ernst Meyer 1978, 253–5; Jameson 1992.

49 Loy 1970; Van Wersch 1972, 180–3, with Pocket Maps 3.7, 11.20, 11.21. Graded as 'land quality classes I–IV', these soil types accounted for 64% of the area covered by the Minnesota Messenia Survey and formed the location for 94% of their archaic sites. (The survey area covered a wider region than inland Messenia, including high-quality land in southern Elis but also poor-quality terrain in Triphylia and the north-western Mani.)

50 McDonald and Rapp (eds.) 1972, Pocket Maps 1.1, 5.8, 5.9, 8.13, 8.14, 8.18.

51 National Statistical Service of Greece 1978, i.422–6. These Eparchiai include upland and mountainous areas of the Tetrazion and Lykaion ranges which lie outside our area, but exclude much fertile Messenian territory immediately west of the eastern plains.

52 McDonald and Rapp (eds.) 1972, 310–21: Register B; also Pocket Maps 8–17.

53 Cf. refs. in n. 17, above.

54 Kaltsas 1983; R. Catling 1996, 34, 86. Catling would lower the excavator's date for the pottery assemblage from *c*. 475–60 to the second half of the fifth century.

55 *Praktika* 1960, 199; 1961, 170; Coldstream 1976, 10–11; Lukermann and Moody 1978, Appendix; Coulson and Wilkie 1983; Alcock 1991, nos. 3, 5, 6, 23, 26; 28, 30.

56 Asine: Hdt. 8.73; Thuc. 4.13; 6.93; cf. Xen. *Hell.* 7.1.25. Methone: Thuc. 2.25; Diod. 11.84.5; 12.43.2. Aulon: Xen. *Hell.* 3.3.8. Aulon's exact location is uncertain; its population included Aulonitai, helots and visiting Lakedaimonians. (The helots need not be native inhabitants; as Krentz 1995, 180 notes, they could be servants of a Spartan garrison.) Other ancient settlements around Messenia's coast which some scholars have deemed perioikic are first attested only after the end of Spartan domination. Korone, on the east coast of the Akritas peninsula, was founded during the liberation of 370/69 (Paus. 4.34.5). Cartledge (1979, 193) suggests the same of Kolonides, further south (Paus. 4.34.8) – though classical and hellenistic graves have been found at one possible location for the site (Kastelia-Vounaria: McDonald and Rapp (eds.) 1972, 312–13 no. 507). On the west coast, Koryphasion (around the Bay of Pylos) and Kyparissia are first attested in 365, when they were taken by the Arkadians (Diod. 15.77.4). In 425 Koryphasion had been uninhabited (Thuc. 4.3, 9; cf. 13).

57 National Statistical Service of Greece 1978, i.224.

Chapter 5

MOVABLE WEALTH: OWNERSHIP, ACQUISITION AND EXCHANGE

In this chapter I shall extend the analysis to the sphere of movable wealth. The initial aim will be to ascertain the Spartiates' rights of ownership over various kinds of movable wealth. I shall then investigate the extent to which the acquisition of movable wealth was a permissible activity and the relative roles of monetary, market and other forms of exchange. As in the case of Spartiate land tenure, these investigations will lead into areas of controversy whose origins lie in the distortions introduced by the Spartan mirage and the Spartiates' own invention of tradition.

The ownership of movable wealth

Livestock

As we saw in chapter 4, animal husbandry was an important element of Spartan agriculture (Euripides, *ap.* Strabo 8.5.6; [Plato], *Alkibiades I* 122d). Indeed, it was a practical necessity, since each citizen had to deliver a monthly quantity of five minai of cheese as part of his compulsory mess dues (Plut. *Lyk*. 12.2). Besides this official requirement, however, the keeping of productive animals will have made economic sense both for wealthy Spartiate landowners and for poorer citizens and their hard-pressed helot cultivators (cf. Hodkinson 1988, 59–66; Forbes 1995, 329–32). Animals enable farmers to utilise both the large proportion of the Greek landscape unsuitable for cultivation and the significant quantities of inedible crop residues, while improving soil fertility through their manure. For poorer citizens and for helot farmers, the milk products supplied by small flocks will have provided an invaluable nutritional resource and the animals themselves an emergency food store in time of famine. For wealthier landowners, rapidly-reproducing ovicaprine herds formed a potential means of income-generation through the sale of cheese or wool and of dispensable surplus animals for meat and/or sacrificial purposes (Hodkinson 1990; 1992b). The significance of productive herds is attested by religious dedications of animal figurines (e.g. Cartledge 2000, 62). Plough oxen presumably also featured on many estates, although no doubt some poor helot households had to resort to more intensive cultivation by hand.

For wealthy Spartiates, there were also powerful socio-political reasons for keeping animals. All adult Spartiates were expected to engage in hunting, and citizens without dogs could borrow them from richer citizens; there were similar arrangements too for the borrowing of horses (Xen. *Lak. Pol.* 4.7; 6.3; Arist. *Pol.* 1263a35–6). After Sparta's introduction of a cavalry force in the late fifth century, the warhorses were provided by the very rich (Xen. *Hell.* 6.4.11). King Agesilaos II, ever-mindful of the advantages of being seen to use his wealth for the needs of the polis, stocked his estate with many hounds and war-horses (Xen. *Ages.* 9.1). He also evidently kept oxen too, since – even more mindful of his personal influence – he used to give an ox to newly-elected members of the Gerousia (Plut. *Ages.* 4.5). Other wealthy citizens maintained teams, and sometimes entire studs, of chariot- and race-horses for participation in equestrian contests (see further ch. 10). This evidence suggests that ownership of productive animals was ubiquitous throughout the citizen body – though no doubt there was considerable variation in numbers owned – but that ownership of non-productive 'prestige' animals was dominated by the very rich. The ramifications of these inequalities will be considered further in chapters 10 and 11.

Valuables

In contrast to the ownership of animals, there is considerable controversy about other types of movable property. The source of disagreement is the programmatic statements by various writers, outlined in chapter 2, which express the idea that the simplicity and austerity of Spartiate life involved the prohibition of (or at least abstention from) ownership of certain kinds of material possessions taken for granted by other Greeks.

There is no question, of course, of the prohibition of *all* non-agricultural forms of movable property. Even Plutarch (*Lyk.* 9.1–5) concedes that Lykourgos abandoned any attempt to divide up the Spartiates' movable property. He insists, however, that the lawgiver took two particular steps to restrict ownership. First, Lykourgos is said to have withdrawn gold and silver coinage and substituted an iron currency – a question discussed below. Secondly, by securing the elimination of superfluous crafts, Lykourgos supposedly ensured that luxury atrophied and only practical household objects were made. Later, describing a supposed Lykourgan *rhētra* concerning simplicity of domestic architecture, Plutarch comments that no-one would bring silver-footed couches, purple bedspreads or gold drinking-cups into a plain, common house (13.3–4). For Plutarch, accordingly, Spartiate society was marked by the absence of privately-owned valuables.

As we saw earlier (ch. 2), these ideas were not original to Plutarch. His comments in *Lykourgos* 9 are a re-presentation of notions already evident in a Lykourgan saying in the hellenistic *Apophthegmata Lakōnika* (no. 3 = Plut. *Mor.* 226d). Likewise, Plutarch's remarks in *Lykourgos* 13 are presaged by two similar apophthegms attributed to Lykourgos: one in the *Apophthegmata Lakōnika* (*Lykourgos* 9 = Plut. *Mor.* 227c), the other among the *Sayings of Kings and Commanders* (*Apophthegmata Basileōn kai Stratēgōn, Lykourgos* 3 = Plut. *Mor.* 189e). As already outlined, these Lykourgan apophthegms bear the stamp of the egalitarian propaganda of the third-century revolution.

Ch. 5. Movable wealth: ownership, acquisition and exchange

At the end of *Lykourgos* 9, when stressing the manufacture of practical objects, Plutarch does cite one classical writer, Kritias, concerning the utilitarian Spartan drinking-cup known as the *kōthōn*. A fuller version of Kritias' remarks is preserved by Athenaios (*Deipnosophistai* 483b = fr. 88B34, Diels–Kranz):

> Apart from those things, the smallest details of their daily life [*sc.* are commendable]: Lakonian shoes are the best; their cloaks are the most pleasant to wear; the Lakonian *kōthōn* is a drinking-vessel most suitable for military service…

Plutarch's text was probably also influenced by another fragment of Kritias (fr. 88B35 = Athen. 486e) usually ascribed to one of his Lakedaimonian polities: a brief reference to 'a Milesian-made couch (*klinē*) and Milesian-made stool (*diphros*), a Chian-made couch (*klinē*) and a Rheneian-made table (*trapeza*)'. Kritias may have contrasted these items with plainer Spartan furniture (Ollier 1933–43, i.172 n. 4; Freeman 1946, 410), an argument which gains force from Plutarch's reference to Spartan couches, stools and tables. Already in the late fifth century, therefore, the plainness of certain Spartiate possessions was a subject of praise in Lakonophile circles and presumably reflected some real element of simplicity in Spartan life. Kritias' remarks, however, even if taken at face value, are a far cry from later claims that ownership of valuables was prohibited or disdained. Kritias' comments cover only items in everyday use, not valuables among the household's stores. The evidence of other classical sources suggests that Kritias' comments, as we should expect from a partisan source, were only part of the truth about Spartiate movable possessions.

Several passages of Herodotus are instructive. First, there is the exchange between King Ariston and his friend Agetos (Hdt. 6.61), whereby each agreed to swap one item chosen from one another's possessions. The items intended for exchange were *keimēlia* ('treasures'), a word used of the stored valuables of Homeric *basileis* (*Iliad* 6.47; 23.618; *Odyssey* 1.312; 2.75). Rare in classical prose, it appears in Herodotus on only one other occasion: at 3.41, when the tyrant Polykrates considers which of his *keimēlia* he should lose to avert the gods' envy and selects an emerald seal-ring set in gold. Secondly, when Maiandrios of Samos solicited help from Sparta around 516 BC (3.148), his attempts to persuade Kleomenes I included displaying his silver and gold drinking cups and inviting the king to take whatever he wished. Kleomenes declined and, 'thinking that if he made the same offers to others he would get the aid he sought', advised the ephors to expel Maiandrios, lest the latter 'persuade either him or other Spartiates to do wrong'. The wrongdoing mentioned is not that of acquiring an illegal object – there is no sense of the illegality of the cups themselves – but rather of taking a bribe. Thirdly, there is the distribution of booty to the Greek forces after Plataia in 479, including the luxurious contents of the Persian camp (9.80–1). After setting aside tithes for the gods, the Greeks,

> divided the remainder, and each man received according to his deserts from the concubines of the Persians and the gold and silver and the rest of the wealth and the

beasts of burden… And tenfold of everything was set apart and given to Pausanias: women, horses, talents, camels, as of the other wealth.

There is no reason to doubt that the Spartiate soldiers shared in this distribution. Moreover, the full range of booty (multiplied tenfold) was given to Pausanias, a Spartiate who was not king but merely regent. Nowhere is there the slightest hint that Spartiate soldiers were debarred or discouraged from receiving these valuables.

Confirmation of Herodotus' picture appears in Xenophon's account of the invasion of Lakonia in 370/69. The enemy approached from the north but, instead of crossing the bridge over the Eurotas to attack the centre of Sparta, marched southwards, burning and plundering houses east of the river which were 'full of many valuable things' (*Hell.* 6.5.27).[1] On reaching a point opposite the outlying Spartiate village of Amyklai, they crossed the river and again plundered local houses (6.5.30). This depiction of the contents of Spartiate households and their attractiveness to enemy looters confirms their possession of the kinds of valuables recorded by Herodotus.

The evidence from classical historians, then, indicates that Spartiate households were not lacking in valuable movable possessions. Although their everyday belongings may have avoided ostentatious display, Spartiate households also possessed valuables in their domestic stores, some apparently in considerable quantities.

Coinage and currency

If Spartan citizens could possess a range of valuables, including gold and silver vessels and jewellery, what was the situation regarding precious metal currency in the form of coinage and bullion? Unlike many Greek poleis, Sparta minted no coinage of its own until the 260s or 250s (Grunauer–von Hoerschelmann 1978; Mørkholm 1991, 149–50). As we saw in chapter 2, several sources from the fourth century onwards claim that gold and silver coinage issued by other states was excluded by Lykourgos and that this prohibition remained in force until 404 when the booty sent to Sparta by Lysander was admitted for public use. After 404, it is claimed, the ban on private ownership was officially retained, although increasingly ignored in practice. Throughout the classical period the only legal currency, according to these sources, was the bulky and impractical iron currency specially instituted by Lykourgos to inhibit the desire for wealth. My earlier discussion of the origin and development of these ideas (ch. 2) intimated that they were *post hoc* constructions created at a time of political controversy and developed under the influence of moralising explanations of Sparta's decline. Here I shall attempt a more systematic review of the evidence and arguments concerning their authenticity.[2]

The literary evidence
We should begin with the evidence of the earliest sources, from the fourth

century BC. According to Xenophon (*Lak. Pol.* 7.5–6), Lykourgos

> instituted currency (*nomisma*) of such a type that neither master nor servant could ever be unaware of even 10 minai going into a house: indeed, this would require much space and a cart for transport. Searches are made for gold and silver (*chrysion…kai argyrion*); and should any come to light anywhere, its possessor is punished.

Later in the same work (14.3), in his chapter on contemporary corruptions of the 'traditional' Spartan regime, Xenophon somewhat qualifies his earlier remarks:

> And I know that in the past they were afraid to appear to have gold (*chrysion*), whereas nowadays there are some who even pride themselves on possessing it.

Secondly, there is Plato's description (*Republic* 547b–548b) of the decline of his ideal state into his Spartan-inspired timarchy. This decline takes place during strife between different elements in the ruling class, whom he characterises by identifying them with various metals:

> Once internal strife has started, the two types of elements pull in opposite directions: the Iron and Bronze towards the acquisition of wealth (*chrēmatismos*) and the possession of land and houses, gold and silver (*chrysiou…kai argyrou*); the others, the Golden and the Silvern, having true riches in their own hearts, towards excellence and the traditional order of things.[3] The violence of their opposition is resolved in a compromise under which they distribute land and houses to private ownership…

The implication of Plato's account is that under this compromise gold and silver remain prohibited. Nevertheless, he continues, a significant feature of the timarchic state,

> will be its love of money (*chrēmata*). There will be a fierce and secret passion for gold and silver, now that there are storehouses and private treasuries to hide it in, and also the enclosures of their private houses…

Thirdly, there is the evidence of Ephorus and Theopompos, as reflected by Plutarch (*Lysander* 16–17; *Nikias* 28.3) and Diodorus (13.106.8–9). According to these sources, before his return to Sparta following his victory over Athens, Lysander sent home under the guardianship of Gylippos some 1000 or 1500 talents.[4] Gylippos, however, stole part of this sum (30 talents according to Plutarch; 300 according to Diodorus), mainly in the form of Athenian coinage. When this theft was detected,

> the wisest of the Spartiates, being led by this instance, in particular, to fear the power of coinage (*tou nomismatos*)…reproached Lysander and called upon the ephors to purify the city of all the silver and gold (*to argyrion kai to chrysion*) as imported curses. And it was Skiraphidas, according to Theopompos, or Phlogidas, according to Ephorus, who declared that they ought not to admit gold and silver coinage (*nomisma chrysoun kai argyroun*) but to use that of the country. Now this was of iron and was dipped in vinegar as soon as it came out of the fire, so that it might

not be worked over but be made brittle and intractable by the dipping. Besides, it was very heavy and troublesome to carry and a great weight of it had little value. It seems likely that it was all originally of this kind and that, instead of coins, men used spits (*obeliskoi*) made of iron or bronze. For this reason many small coins are known to this day as *oboloi*, and six obols are called a drachma, since this was the largest number that could be grasped in one hand.

But, since Lysander's friends opposed this measure and insisted that the wealth (*chrēmata*) remain in the polis, it was decided that this coinage (*nomisma*) could be imported for public use, but that if any private person should be found in possession of it, he should be punished with death – as if Lykourgos had feared the coin (*nomisma*) and not the greed produced by the coin (*epi tō nomismati*). And this vice was not removed by not allowing private individuals to possess it, so much as encouraged by permitting ownership by the polis, its use thereby acquiring dignity and honour… So they merely set fear and the law to guard the houses of the citizens, that coinage (*nomisma*) might have no entrance there. But they did not make their spirits insensible and impervious to silver (*argyrion*); they rather inspired them all with a passion to acquire wealth as something exalted and noble (Plut. *Lys.* 17.1–6).

Subsequently, one leading commander, Thorax, was found in possession of silver (*argyrion*) and executed (*Lys.* 19.4).

We must exercise caution in distinguishing the authentic views of Ephorus and Theopompos from those injected later by Plutarch into the above account. Much of the lengthy sermon in the latter part, after the narration of the decision itself, appears to be Plutarch's own. That the essence of the passage genuinely reflects Ephorus' views is, however, shown by two passages of Diodorus (7.12.8; 14.10.2), quoted in chapter 2 (p. 28), which refer in general terms to the Spartans' beginning to use coined money. The second of these passages concurs in placing this development at the end of the Peloponnesian war, as also do two brief passages in Plutarch's *Lykourgos* (30.1) and *Agis* (5.1).

Fourthly, there is a passage in the hellenistic *Apophthegmata Lakōnika* (*Lykourgos* no. 3 = Plut. *Mor.* 226c–d):

> he [Lykourgos] decreed that gold and silver currency (*chrysoun kai argyroun nomisma*) should in future have no value, and ordained that the people should use only one of iron. He also limited the time within which it was lawful to exchange their present holdings for this… For he permitted no convenient currency (*nomisma*) to circulate among them, but instituted the iron [currency] exclusively, which in weight constituted one Aiginetan *mina*, but in value four *chalkoi*.

As already noted (ch. 2), except for certain rhetorical elaborations and alterations of detail, especially concerning the treatment of the iron with vinegar to render it useless, Plutarch's account in his *Life of Lykourgos*, ch. 9, derives essentially from this passage.

The final substantive passage regarding the prohibition of currency comes from the hellenistic philosopher Poseidonios (c. 130–50 BC), as cited in Athenaios' *Deipnosophistai* (233e–234e = fr. 240 Kidd = *FGrH* 87F48c):

> Although the Lakedaimonians, as Poseidonios records, were forbidden by custom from importing into Sparta or acquiring silver or gold (*argyron kai chryson*), they nonetheless acquired it; but they deposited it for safe-keeping with their neighbours the Arkadians. They then proceeded to make enemies of them, when once they were friends, in order that through this enmity their disobedience should be unaccountable for scrutiny. It is recorded, to be sure, that the gold and silver (*chryson kai argyron*) which had previously been in Lakedaimon was dedicated to Apollo at Delphi, but that Lysander brought it into the polis for public use, and so became the author of many evils. There is a story, at any rate, that Gylippos, the liberator of Syracuse, starved himself to death because he had been convicted by the ephors of having embezzled some of the funds (*chrēmatos*) sent by Lysander. It was not easy for a mere mortal to regard as of small value the gold which had been dedicated to the god and acknowledged, it would appear, as his honour and possession.

The reference to Spartiates making deposits with the Arkadians is often linked to a mid-fifth-century inscription on a bronze plaque from Tegea recording financial deposits made in favour of a certain Xouthias, son of Philachaios, and his heirs, whose order of succession is carefully defined.[5] The identity of the depositor is not indicated, though it may be Xouthias himself. His ethnic is unspecified, but some scholars see him as a Spartan evading the law in the manner claimed by Poseidonios. Lysander's alleged deposit of booty from his victory at Aigospotamoi in the treasury of the Akanthians at Delphi (Plut. *Lys.* 18.1, citing Anaxandrides of Delphi) is sometimes adduced as evidence of similar behaviour.

Besides these sources, there are other authors who mention Sparta's iron currency.[6] The pseudo-Platonic dialogue *Eryxias* (400a–b) – probably from the third century BC (Souilhé 1962, 87–8) – asserts that,

> In Lakedaimon they use as money weights of iron (σιδηρῷ σταθμῷ νομίζουσι), and these in a useless form: he who possesses a large weight of this iron is thought to be rich; elsewhere, however, this property is worth nothing.

There are also the comments of Polybius (6.49):

> So long as their ambitions extended only to ruling over their neighbours or the inhabitants of the Peloponnese, they [sc. the Spartans] found the supplies and resources which their own country could provide were sufficient... But once they had begun to make expeditions by sea or to fight campaigns outside the Peloponnese, it became clear that neither their iron currency nor the exchange of their crops for the commodities they lacked, as permitted by the legislation of Lykourgos, could provide for their needs, since these enterprises required a currency in universal circulation and a supply of goods from foreign sources.

Note that, although he mentions no formal prohibition, Polybius assumes the absence of any precious metal currency in Sparta.[7] Indeed, he refers earlier to the singular nature of the Spartans' view of money-making: 'for money being esteemed of no value at all among them, the jealous contention due to the possession of more or less is utterly done away with'.

In referring to the iron currency, Polybius uses the term *nomisma*, as does Pollux (*Onomastikon* 9.79) in the second century AD. Elsewhere, however, Pollux refers, among a list of synonyms, to 'iron spits (*obeloi*), the iron currency (*nomisma*) of the Lakedaimonians and Byzantines' (7.105). Also of note is a gloss in the lexicon of Hesychios which reads πέλανορ· τὸ τετράχαλκον. Λάκωνες ('pelanor: the *tetrachalkon*. Lakonians'), indicating that in Lakonia the term *pelanor* signified a *tetrachalkon*, a unit of currency worth four *chalkoi*.[8]

Scholars are divided in their reactions to this evidence. Many modern accounts accept the sources' claims concerning the prohibition of foreign gold and silver coinage. Hooker states that 'it is recorded as a fact that an iron currency was the only one tolerated at Sparta' (1980, 134). David agrees that private possession of foreign coinage was illegal before 404 (1981, 175 n. 11). So does Mørkholm: 'according to the Lycurgan constitution the possession and use of coinage was forbidden within Sparta's frontiers' (1991, 149). Burelli Bergese (1986) takes the prohibition as the assumed starting-point for her discussion of how the Spartans overcame the potentially isolating effects of this situation. Equally, however, several studies have dismissed the sources' claims as erroneous. Huxley thinks that 'the Spartan government certainly needed coinage of its own from time to time', and even possessed 'state balances of foreign currency' (1962, 63). Cawkwell agrees (1983, 396) that 'Sparta must always have held some money in a form acceptable to the rest of the Greeks'. Some scholars also dismiss the prohibition of private possession of coinage. For Michell 'that Lycurgus ever forbade the use of any money other than the iron pelanors is a pure fairy tale' (1964, 303; cf. 1947, 43). MacDowell (1986, 119) too argues that 'Plutarch makes clear that the ban imposed about 404 was a new one'. This controversial subject is clearly in need of full reconsideration.

Sparta's abstention from coining
It is important to consider the issues from a broad perspective, starting with the fact that, unlike many other poleis, including several members of her own Peloponnesian league,[9] Sparta did not issue her own precious metal coinage. What inferences should we draw from this fact? Some of the sources quoted above portray Sparta's abstention as a purposeful part of her singular disdain for things material: as a measure consciously designed to isolate her citizens from external economic transactions and from a divisive means by which individuals might accumulate and deploy personal wealth. However, whilst it would be rash to deny any connection between coinage and the use of personal wealth, this superficially attractive thesis is hard to sustain – at least in its strongest form.

First, Spartan practice in not coining was far from unusual. It has been estimated that at least 50% of poleis never coined at all (Ruschenbusch 1978, 6). Several other Greek poleis issued no precious metal coinage for a considerable period of time after its inception. Some of these long-term abstainers were no doubt remote and insignificant poleis; but by no means all. Argos did not coin until *c.* 475 (Kraay 1976, 96–8). Byzantion and Chalkedon, which were well-placed to exact tolls on marine trade due to their strategic locations on the sea route between the Aegean and the Black Sea, issued no precious metal coinage until around 400 (Head 1911, 266–7; Kraay 1976, 259).[10] Locri Epizephyrii, in southern Italy, issued no coins before the fourth century (Rutter 1997, 70, 78). In addition, many other poleis, after a period of coinage, subsequently ceased minting for considerable lengths of time.[11] It follows that the number of poleis coining in any given century will have been a distinct minority. As one illustration, only around 60 of the 205 states which paid tribute to Athens coined between 480 and 400 BC. Even among the larger tribute-paying states, one-third lacked their own mints (Nixon and Price 1990, 156).

Secondly, the fact that so many Greek states never coined ties in with recent research which indicates that poleis normally needed strong reasons to do so. It has been suggested that the minting of coinage was closely linked to the emergence of liturgies and the development of benefactions by wealthy citizens and tyrants which moved beyond localised largesse to outlays touching the wider citizen body (Martin 1996). Other scholars have emphasized that the decision to coin typically depended upon the state's need to make or extract financial payments for purposes such as military expenditure, payment of officials or taxation. Even this factor, however, was not always enough, as is indicated by the large majority of non-coining poleis in the Athenian Empire, poleis which presumably made their payments in foreign coinage or bullion. Studies of states which ceased coining suggest causes such as a lack of silver due to financial impoverishment or a lack of need for local minting due to the circulation of a neighbouring widely-accepted coinage (Martin 1985). Conversely, Barello's study (1993) of several Greek poleis which abstained from minting in precious metals for lengthy periods of time after the first appearance of coinage (Sparta, Locri Epizephyrii, the Ozolian Locrians, Argos, Thessalian Larissa and Byzantion) notes the significance of certain common factors, especially a primarily agrarian society dominated by a landed elite whose servile labour force comprised an indigenous population bound to the soil rather than chattel slaves acquired through private commercial exchange.

These considerations suggest that, whilst the emergence of coinage was undoubtedly implicated in the increasing personal deployment of wealth, whether or not a polis issued coins was determined by structural factors as much as, indeed perhaps more than, by conscious policy. From this perspective, Sparta's lack of native coinage is neither unusual nor difficult to comprehend, since the Spartan state displays many of the characteristics which inhibited other poleis from coining and lacks those which promoted it. Her abstention from coining reflects the character of her underlying socio-economic structure, with a landed agrarian elite, an indigenous servile population, a conscripted hoplite army, a largely non-monetary system of taxation, unpaid officials, a lack of liturgies, an impoverished public treasury, no access to silver mines, and access to the widespread Aiginetan currency.[12] Hence although Sparta's lack of native coinage may be connected with the absence of opportunities for personalised largesse, there is no necessity to invoke a specific policy of isolating her citizens from transactions involving coined metals. Indeed, the evidence from other Greek states suggests that lack of a native coinage did not necessarily imply isolation from coined wealth. As already noted, some states abstained from issuing their own coinage precisely because of the availability of coinages of neighbouring states. Foreign coinage even penetrated into certain poleis which abstained longest from minting their own coins. Locri Epizephyrii was making use of foreign coinage at least as early as the fifth century (Barello 1993, 107). Byzantion must have extracted tolls in foreign coinage long before it first minted around 400 BC.

A final consideration is that the notion that the issuing of coinage increased the openness of a polis' internal economy to the outside world is far from certain. As Kroll (1998) has recently noted, monetary exchange across political boundaries through the use of uncoined, weighed silver was well established long before the creation of silver coins. Many polis coinages contributed little to the integration of local transactions within a wider economic sphere, being largely local in circulation. All coinages were overvalued in relation to their bullion value (Carradice and Price 1988, 90–1; Martin 1996, 259). Most were not widely acceptable outside the territory of the issuing state; recipients of such coinage were thereby compelled to spend the money locally (Osborne 1996, 256). Hence in certain respects coinage may have acted as a hindrance to inter-polis exchange. Indeed, sometimes the issuing of coinage led to a purposeful increase in barriers between a polis and the outside world, since some poleis insisted that both citizens and foreigners use local coinage in official transactions, thereby establishing control over the currency circulating within their territories – precisely the motive often ascribed to Sparta in her retention of an outdated iron currency!

The iron currency

Is it true, however, that Sparta's iron currency did serve this purpose? Once again, we should view Sparta's situation in broader context. In human history a wide range of objects has been used as 'primitive money'. The use of weighed amounts of metal as items of payment and exchange is known from the ancient Near East. Similarly, early Roman monetary transactions were conducted through the use of uncast lumps of bronze (the so-called *aes rude*) or of bronze currency bars with a heavy admixture of iron (*aes signatum*), which were chopped into smaller pieces as needed (Burnett 1976, 3, with pl.1.1). It has been suggested that iron performed a similar monetary function in southern Greece during the early Iron Age before the advent of silver currency (Kroll n.d.). It is noteworthy that Aristotle, in his account of the development of natural exchange (*Pol.* 1256b40–1257a41), included iron along with silver and other metals as 'a useful commodity easy to handle in use for general life' (1257a37) which men used as currency as an alternative to simple barter.

There is, therefore, nothing inherently implausible in the consensus among the sources that classical Sparta operated some system of iron currency (cf. Nenci 1974).[13] The sources' claims concerning the circumstances of its creation should, however, be dismissed as unhistorical invention, especially the anachronistic claim in the *Apophthegmata Lakōnika*, repeated by Plutarch (*Lyk.* 9.1), that Lykourgos substituted it for a pre-existing gold and silver coinage! Unlike the sources, we should view it not as a new introduction but as the traditional form of currency maintained from an earlier period. There is, indeed, some evidence to suggest that before the controversy of 404 BC this was how the Spartiates themselves viewed it; and that the attribution of the currency to Lykourgos, first attested by Xenophon, was a post-404 invention developed in the context of attempts to explain and justify its use as the only form of currency permitted to private citizens.[14] In the 404 debate the reported words of the opponents of Lysander's foreign currency, as given by Theopompos and Ephorus, refer to the iron currency not as Lykourgan but simply as 'that of the country' (τῷ πατρίῳ). Had the Lykourgan origin of the iron currency been a current idea, one would have expected Lysander's opponents to stress it in the debate. Clearly, we should reject the idea that the Sparta's classical iron currency was introduced at a stroke as a radical egalitarian measure, rather than developing from an earlier use of iron as proto-money. Sparta's maintenance of her iron currency was probably influenced by two factors in particular: first, the underlying socio-economic character of the polis outlined above, which entailed only a modest degree of involvement in long-distance exchange; secondly, Sparta's possession of unusually extensive workable sources of iron ore within Lakonia.[15] An apposite parallel is the case of the use of bronze currency by mid-Republican Rome (Nenci 1974, 651–2). Note that, as in the Spartan case, Rome's bronze currency, though originally adopted for practical reasons, came in later centuries to be associated with her supposed former austerity by way of contrast to the luxury associated with contemporary use of silver and gold (cf. Nenci 1968).

Comparative support for the existence of a Spartan iron currency comes from the fact that Sparta was not the only classical Greek state to use iron as currency in some form or other. A number of iron coins (19 in total) survive from the classical period, deriving mainly from various Peloponnesian communities (Argos, Tegea, Heraia), along with Phokis in central Greece.[16] Scholars are currently divided about the role of these coins. Some have viewed them as serving a genuine currency use, as predecessors of the bronze coinages which emerged in the late classical period. Others, noting the provenance of several examples in sanctuary contexts, see them as special festival issues, of perhaps only token use. Comparative evidence from the study of lead 'currencies' suggests, however, that the distinction between such usages is not always stable or clear-cut (Morrisson 1993, 85–6). Besides this archaeological evidence, several classical writers of comedy refer to units of currency at Byzantion known as *sidareoi* (a term derived from the word for iron), references which later antiquarian writers regarded as evidence for an iron coinage.[17] The existence of a Byzantine iron coinage has been challenged by Crawford (1982), who argues that the term *sidareos* was simply the local name for a (silver) obol, explaining the use of a term referring to iron as deriving from the early form of money in iron spits, *sidareoi oboloi*. Some of the references to the *sidareoi*, however, date from before the earliest attestation of silver coinage in Byzantion; and the claimed derivation of the name *sidareoi* from the iron spits of early Greece is somewhat uncertain, given recent doubts cast upon their alleged monetary role (see below). The fact that a word referring to iron was used as a term of currency remains suggestive, even if the Byzantine currency did not consist of coins. Finally, there is fourth-century evidence from Klazomenai for an emergency temporary issue of iron coins which their owners were able to use for internal transactions (Ps.-Aristotle, *Oikonomika* ii.1348b).

The form which Sparta's iron currency took is uncertain. It has long been argued (e.g. Svoronos 1906, 192–202) that early Greek iron currency took the form of the roasting spit, or *obelos*: hence, as claimed by various ancient writers, the subsequent use of the related term *obolos* in southern Greek coinage systems.[18] Indeed, numerous dedications of iron or bronze spits are attested at several Greek sanctuaries, mostly from the late eighth to the early sixth centuries (Strøm 1992; Melville Jones 1993, nos. 35–45); at least some of these, according to one school of thought, were intended as proto-monetary dedications (Brown 1950, 191–2; Courbin 1959, 223–4). These ideas, however, have come under challenge. The dedicated spits' proto-monetary role has been doubted because of difficulties in establishing a weight standard, given the corroded state of the finds (Furtwängler 1980); and it has been asserted, more generally, that 'there is no indication that *oboloi* circulated in a clearly defined area in which their value was standardised and granted by higher authority' (von Reden 1997, 160).

At Sparta finds of iron spits at the sanctuary of Artemis Orthia span the Geometric period down to the early third century BC (Dawkins 1930, 299, correcting Woodward in Dawkins (ed.) 1929, 391). The timing of their cessation may appear to suggest a link with the minting of Sparta's first silver coinage, thus implying their function as currency. This suggestion, however, receives little support from the literary evidence. The earliest sources are remarkably vague concerning the nature of Sparta's traditional currency. Xenophon specifies neither its form nor even the metal of which it consisted. Most of the subsequent sources concur that it was of iron; but none of the hellenistic sources (the *Apophthegmata Lakōnika*, the pseudo-Platonic *Eryxias* or Polybius) specifies its precise form. Not until Plutarch's *Lysander* do we get our first reference to spits; and even then they are mentioned not with direct reference to Sparta but rather as the universal form of early currency. The nature of this reference suggests that Plutarch's (fourth-century) sources contained only generic statements, rather than a precise ascription of the use of spits to Sparta. This hypothesis gains support from the absence of any reference to the form of the currency in his *Life of Lykourgos*. Only in the late evidence of Pollux's *Onomastikon* do we find our sole explicit statement that Sparta's currency (along, note, with that of Byzantion) was in the form of spits.

What about possible alternative forms? Laum's theory (1925) that the iron sickles dedicated at Artemis Orthia were a survival of the iron currency has been discredited by subsequent studies (Blinkenberg 1926; Michell 1947, 42). None of the sickles is earlier than the fourth century BC and most are of Roman date. Although, as noted above, classical iron coins are attested from other Peloponnesian communities, there is no particular evidence for iron coinage in Sparta.[19] It has been suggested, drawing upon the term *pelanor* which Hesychios uses of Spartan currency, that the units of currency were shaped like *pelanoi* or flat, round cakes used as sacrificial offerings.[20] This is not impossible; but, on the basis of current evidence, the vague formulation of the third-century pseudo-Platonic *Eryxias* (quoted above), that the currency consisted of weights of iron, is as far as we can reasonably go.

Although Sparta's use of an iron currency is intelligible in terms of the maintenance of traditional forms, this need not exclude specific acts of intervention by the polis to modify the precise terms of its operation. As Aristotle noted, iron's role as a form of currency in early Greece was related to its intrinsic value as a metal. Yet several of the sources for Sparta's iron currency suggest that its value was not intrinsic but based upon official convention (Nenci 1974, 646–51). The *Eryxias* and (in more detail) Plutarch's *Lysander* claim that the iron used as currency was deliberately rendered useless for other purposes. The *Eryxias* specifically comments upon the discrepancy between its high value inside Sparta and its worthlessness elsewhere. The existence of a conventionalised value does not depend upon the doubtful metallurgical feasibility of the alleged practice of rendering iron useless through the use of vinegar (cf. Michell 1964, 301). An officially standardised value is stated explicitly in the weight:value ratio specified in the *Apophthegmata Lakōnika* and is implicit in Xenophon's comment on the weight and volume of ten Aiginetan minas' value of the iron currency.

The information which the post-classical sources provide about the currency's value possesses some consistency. According to the *Apophthegmata Lakōnika*, one Aiginetan *mina*'s weight of the iron currency had the value of four *chalkoi*. The significance of this latter figure is confirmed by the glosses of Hesychios quoted above, both of which refer to local Lakonian terms – *pelanor* and *hipp(op)or* – describing a unit of currency which was equivalent to a *tetrachalkon*, or four *chalkoi*. The *chalkous* was a unit of bronze currency. In areas such as

Sparta where – as the *Apophthegmata Lakōnika* indicates – the Aiginetic standard prevailed, it was reckoned at one-twelfth of a silver obol. One Aiginetan mina's weight of the iron currency with a value of four *chalkoi* will therefore have been worth one-third of a silver obol (Tod 1946). At the rate of 600 obols (100 drachmas) to the mina,[21] this is equivalent to an iron:silver value ratio of 1:1800.[22] In other words, the ratio between the value of a given weight of the iron currency and that of an equivalent weight of Aiginetan silver currency was 1:1800.

At what period did this 1:1800 ratio apply, and how longstanding was it? The source of the information in the *Apophthegmata Lakōnika* is uncertain. I suggested in chapter 2 that the mismatch between these precise details and the rhetorical generalisations in the rest of the apophthegm is an indication that the information about the currency's weight:value ratio probably goes back to an earlier treatise, perhaps a work by Dikaiarchos or even the Aristotelian *Polity of the Lakedaimonians*. If so, the 1:1800 ratio may relate to the late fourth century; but this must remain uncertain. The 1:1800 ratio is reasonably close to the iron:silver ratio of about 1:2000 suggested by Courbin (1959) from calculations of the original weight of excavated iron spits from the archaic period. However, the form in which the ratio is expressed – through the value of four bronze *chalkoi* – cannot go back this far; it was probably not current before the fourth century, when bronze coinage first entered into widespread use (Price 1968; Picard 1989). Moreover, it is not easy to square a 1:1800 ratio with Xenophon's remark that ten minai of the currency would require much space and a cart for transport. Xenophon's reference to ten minai is to the currency's *value* (Cozzoli 1979, 38–9). Since an Aiginetan *mina* weighed around 630 g (*OCD*³, 1621), the quantity of iron currency whose value was equivalent to ten minai of Aiginetan silver coinage would – at the ratio of 1:1800 – have weighed 11,340 kg! On the basis of evidence from the contemporary building accounts at Epidauros, which suggests that the capacity of a cart-load drawn by a single yoke of oxen was a little over 1,000 kg (Burford 1969, 187–8), this quantity would have required not one but at least 10 carts. Clearly, we should not press Xenophon's evidence too hard for strict mathematical accuracy; but the considerable discrepancy between the value of the currency implied by his evidence and the value specified in the *Apophthegmata Lakōnika* suggests that the conventional value was modified periodically by the polis to take account of fluctuations in the relative values of iron and silver.[23] Xenophon's evidence suggests that in the early fourth century the iron currency was valued considerably higher than a ratio of 1:1800. This would fit with the recent influx of plentiful quantities of silver during Sparta's imperial hegemony, which will have caused its relative value to fall. The polis may also have been keen to reflect the comparatively low value of silver in its official valuation, as part of its efforts against attempts by leading Spartiates to evade the prohibition on private ownership introduced in 404 BC (see further below).

I asked earlier whether classical Sparta's iron currency entailed the exclusive use of local currency within her territory and, more generally, erected a barrier between Sparta and the outside world. A negative answer is suggested by the fact that it represented, not a new political measure of austerity, but a development from an earlier currency system. Indeed, the very existence of an accepted conversion rate, between Sparta's iron currency and foreign silver currencies operating on the Aiginetic standard, indicates that the iron currency did not in principle entail isolation from the outside world. It implies that there was nothing in the operation of an iron currency *per se* that was incompatible with the parallel use of silver currency inside Sparta. Such parallel usage surely applied in other poleis who used iron (for however temporary or limited a purpose) as a form of currency. Indeed, the low value of Sparta's iron currency may positively suggest a system based upon parallel usage, since transactions beyond a certain value would have been very difficult, if not unmanageable, in iron currency alone. Larger transactions surely required the use of precious metals, whether in the form of bullion or of foreign coinage.

The sources for the alleged prohibition of gold and silver currency
What, then, of the evidence which claims that gold and silver currency was entirely prohibited until 404 BC, when the ban on private possession was reaffirmed but public use permitted for the first time? In this section I shall outline certain weaknesses in the sources responsible for this historical depiction.

An initial question to examine is the exact scope of both the alleged Lykourgan prohibition and that decided in 404: did they embrace coinage only or also bullion? The post-classical sources (the *Apophthegmata Lakōnika*, Diodorus, Plutarch's *Lysander* and *Lykourgos*) write explicitly of gold and silver coinage, *nomisma*. Xenophon (*Lak. Pol.* 7.6; 14.3), however, uses terms, *chrysion* and *argyrion*, which could refer equally to uncoined gold and silver. Since the sentence preceding the first of Xenophon's references deals with Sparta's traditional currency, some scholars believe that the reference must be to gold and silver coinage (Finley 1986, 168). At 14.3, however, Xenophon again refers only to gold, with no mention of either silver or coinage. Similarly, Plato writes of *chrysion* and *argyron* and uses the generic term *chrēmata*. Certainly, Xenophon's and Plato's formulations are in tune with normal contemporary variations in forms of currency, since coinage and uncoined silver or gold bullion were normally used interchangeably in monetary contexts in archaic and classical Greece.[24] The prohibition of private possession decided in 404 surely covered bullion since, as Michael Flower has noted, it could otherwise have been used as a means of circumventing the law through melting down illegal coinage.[25] That the other sources, who insist on the original Lykourgan prohibition, talk of coinage as the sole form of currency is a sign of anachronism in their accounts.

Divergence between the sources is evident also in their different representations of the situation after 404, when public but not private possession of gold and silver currency was permitted. Xenophon represents the post-404 situation as reflecting the intentions of Lykourgos. In contrast, the Ephoran viewpoint, as given in Plutarch's *Lysander* and in Diodorus, represents it critically as a deleterious change from traditional practice. I have argued elsewhere that these radically different interpretations derive from the divergent political standpoints of, respectively, the established king, Agesilaos II, staunch defender of the status quo, and the exiled former king Pausanias, fierce critic of the policies of Lysander which had led to the decision in 404.[26] As I hope to have shown, both representations are contemporary 'inventions of tradition' created amidst contemporary political controversy. Note also that they imply a different view of the position regarding public possession of foreign currency before 404: on the Ephoran viewpoint it had been banned, whereas Xenophon's focus purely on private ownership carries no such implication.

The early fourth-century origin of these invented traditions is further suggested by two particular points. First, the notion that Sparta had formerly applied a complete prohibition of gold and silver currency appears only in fourth-century sources who refer to its supposed breakdown; there is no contemporary evidence for the prohibition in the period before 404 when it supposedly applied. Secondly, the earliest sources evince signs of the embryonic nature of these traditions. Although Xenophon explicitly ascribes the traditional iron currency to Lykourgos, when he describes the penalties for possession of gold and silver he switches from past to present tense to avoid a direct attribution to the lawgiver. He wishes to portray the penalties as in tune with Lykourgos' intentions, but cannot pretend that they were instituted by Lykourgos himself. Lykourgos is even more conspicuously absent from the account of the 404 debate in Plutarch's *Lysander*, which comes ultimately from Theopompos and Ephorus. As noted above, the reported arguments of the opponents of foreign currency omit any claim that they were defending the laws of Lykourgos. Indeed, Lykourgos receives no mention at all in the report of the actual debate. His name appears only in Plutarch's own comments on the debate's outcome. This suggests that the notion of specific Lykourgan currency arrangements did not exist in 404 and began to develop only subsequently as the different sides started to justify their stances towards the decision. By the time of Xenophon's *Polity of the Lakedaimonians* the traditional iron currency could be ascribed to Lykourgos, but not the measures enforcing the prohibition of gold and silver. Not until the hellenistic *Apophthegmata Lakōnika* do we get the first attested attribution of this prohibition to Lykourgos.

These invented accounts of a traditional prohibition of foreign currency appear to have affected even the otherwise perceptive account of Plato. As already noted (ch. 2), Plato attempts to represent the essential characteristics of Spartan society, not merely its current form. However, the atmosphere of secrecy regarding private ownership of foreign currency that he invokes shows that he too has been taken in by contemporary portrayals of a situation which, as we shall see, had existed only since 404. Yet even Plato, beguiled as he was into believing that a ban on private ownership was a fundamental feature of Spartiate society, contradicts the notion in Plutarch's *Lysander* that the compromise decision of 404 had the deleterious effect of stimulating the desire for private possession of gold and silver coinage. In his *Laws* (742a) he positively recommends the same compromise – public use, private ban – for his Cretan state, something hardly credible had that compromise had the disastrous consequences claimed by Plutarch. For Plato, Spartiate susceptibility to gold and silver was due not to recent changes but to ingrained weaknesses of her *politeia*.

Similarly, we cannot use the account of Poseidonios to prove the illegality of Spartan ownership of foreign currency. Poseidonios' account is 'not history as such, but moral anecdote, topped off with a gnomic generalisation' (Kidd 1988, 839). His claim that the Spartans made enemies of their Arkadian friends to conceal their illegal deposits of foreign currency bears no relation to our knowledge of Spartan–Arkadian relations. There is no independent evidence for any such Spartan deposits at Delphi before the time of Lysander or for the alleged starvation of Gylippos. Nor does the Xouthias inscription offer any solid support to Poseidonios' claims. The identity of the depositor is uncertain and, even if it was Xouthias himself, there is no evidence that he was a Spartiate. Attempts to adduce a Spartiate identity from the name of his father Philachaios (Carvalho Gomes 1995) are inconclusive, since any Peloponnesian family connected with Sparta might have grounds for advertising its 'Achaian' allegiances. Moreover, even if we assume (for the sake of argument) that Xouthias was a Spartiate depositing money abroad, there is no proof of illegality. Someone making illegal deposits would hardly announce them on a prestigious bronze plaque, which must have been given considerable visibility (probably at Tegea's main sanctuary of Athena Alea) to act as testimony to its meticulous stipulation of the order and age of inheritance. Similarly, there is no evidence that Lysander's alleged Delphic deposit, even if authentic, was in itself illegal; the shady element was rather that his deposits were made from dubiously appropriated public property.

State ownership of precious metal currency before 404 BC
Contrary to the programmatic statements in the literary sources, a range of evidence indicates official possession and use of precious metal currency before 404. The polis must long have possessed stores of 'a currency in universal circulation' (as Polybius put it) for its dealings abroad, such as for the use of its ambassadors (Cawkwell 1983, 96; Cartledge 1987, 88; Flower 1991, 92). Historical sources, indeed, assume the Spartan polis' use of a currency acceptable to foreigners early in the fifth century, in her attempt to bribe the seer Teisamenos (Hdt. 9.33) and in her donations to the enemies of Themistokles (Diod. 11.54.4, following Ephorus). It is during the Peloponnesian war, however, that Spartan use of precious metal currency becomes most apparent.

The anatomy of the Spartiate property system

From the 420s onwards the Spartans had to pay mercenary soldiers, as in 424 when Brasidas recruited 1,000 troops for his northbound expedition by means of pay (μισθῷ πείσας: Thuc. 4.80). Currency was used too in other military contexts: for example, in the ransom agreement with Athens in 408/7 when, after an equal exchange of prisoners, the remaining prisoners were ransomed for one mina each (Androtion, *FGrH* 324F44). Some form of universally accepted currency was even more necessary for Sparta's naval activity. It was used in ship construction, as in 413/12 when representatives of the satrap Pharnabazos brought 25 talents with which the polis equipped 27 triremes (Thuc. 8.8, 39). It was also needed for the ships which Sparta herself contributed to the Peloponnesian fleet, since these contained a sizeable proportion of mercenary rowers (cf. Xen. *Hell.* 7.1.12). During the Ionian war the Spartans also had to secure pay for the fleet as a whole, a requirement which involved them in regular receipt of financial contributions from both Persia and other Greek poleis (e.g. Thuc. 8.28–9, 44, 101; Xen. *Hell.* 1.5.2–7, 6.12). Although many of these transactions were dealt with by local commanders, the home authorities were also necessarily involved. In 406, for example, the admiral Kallikratidas clearly expected the home government to have appropriate currency at its disposal when he sent to Sparta for funds (Xen. *Hell.* 1.6.9).[27] Neither were Spartan naval efforts confined to the late fifth century: witness her expedition against Samos *c.*525 and her contribution to the Greek fleet in 479 (Hdt. 3.47, 54–6; 8.1).

What form of currency was used in these transactions? Since the sources rarely specify the precise medium involved, several of them could, strictly speaking, have been conducted through the use of silver bullion rather than foreign coinage. The fact, however, that coinage and uncoined bullion were normally used interchangeably in monetary contexts suggests that a similar mix probably applied in the above transactions, especially in the case of financial contributions received from other states. In one case, in particular, the three 'fortieths' given by the Chians for each of their citizens in the fleet of Mindaros (Thuc. 8.101), the payment was almost certainly in coins (schol. ad loc.; Figueira 1998, 158–9; Gomme et al. 1945–81, v.346–7). As regards transactions in which the home government was directly involved, some numismatists have suggested that early in the war the Peloponnesians agreed to use a common coinage on the Aiginetic standard already used by most of the allies, except Corinth; and that this decision explains the sudden shift from Corinth to Sikyon as the major regional coin producer (Carradice and Price 1988, 55, 77; cf. Kraay 1976, 82–5, 99). If so – the theory has been criticised (Mattingly 1989, 230–1) – Sparta presided over a remarkable measure of currency co-ordination which contradicts her image as a state ignorant of foreign coinage.

More solid evidence is provided by the well-known inscription (*IG* v.1.1 = ML 67; cf. Loomis 1992) – a list of contributions to the Spartan war fund, probably to be dated sometime during the Peloponnesian war.[28] Since the inscription was erected at Sparta by the home authorities, the contributions recorded were surely received into the public treasury, rather than simply passing through the hands of local commanders, especially as the donors come from diverse regions of the Greek world. The information from the fragmentary inscription is presented below in tabular form (TABLE 2).

Although the inscription records a most eclectic range of contributions, the majority are contributions of currency. The manner in which these donations are recorded suggests that several were payments in coin. The diverse range of currencies – both Persian and Greek – indicates that the donations came in the form most convenient for the donors, not in a form imposed by the Spartan authorities. The fact that even the contributions in Greek currency are not described in uniform fashion (one in minas and staters, another in staters alone) also suggests that we are not dealing with uniform donations all in bullion. It is interesting, moreover, that three of the donations are singled out from the rest as consisting of silver (*argyrio*). If, as Loomis (1992, 79) suggests, this is a signal that these donations were uncoined, the logical deduction is that the remaining currency contributions were in coin. Indeed, the contributions in Persian darics are surely a reference to the Persian gold coin; if the donors had wanted to donate in bullion, they would surely have used silver, which would have been described on a Greek weight standard. The Aiginetans too surely contributed in their own widespread currency.

Further evidence for the polis' possession of coinage is provided by Sparta's special arrangements for the disposal of war booty (Pritchett 1974–91, v.404–16). Sparta's armies are the only ones attested as accompanied by official booty-sellers, the *laphyropōlai*. Booty was regularly sold on campaign; what came home to Sparta was not the objects of booty, but the proceeds from their

TABLE 2. Contributions to the Spartan war fund (*IG* v.1.1).

Donor	Donation
The ...	400 darics
The Aiginetans	14 minas, 10 staters
The ...oi	...?... darics
Som...ophon of Olenos in Achaia	trireme ...?... and 32 minas of silver
The exiles of the Chians	1000 Aiginetan staters
...non	4000 ...?...; another [4–9]000 and of raisins ... talents
The ...?...	...?... many and 800 darics and ...?... talents
...?...	...?... 30 minas and [2 or 3]000 medimnoi and [30-90] ... and 60 ...?...
The Ephesians	1000 darics...
The Melians	20 minas of silver
Molokros	1 talent of silver
The Melians	...?...

sale. It seems unlikely that these proceeds were always in the form of bullion, never in coin. Indeed, as Pritchett notes (ibid. 408–9), much of the coinage sent back by Lysander in 404 (of which the 'owls' stolen by Gylippos were a small sample; cf. Alessandrì 1985) was the proceeds from booty gained at Aigospotamoi. Ironically, therefore, the influx of foreign coins which provoked such outcry at Sparta was the outcome not of new initiatives but of longstanding official policy. What differed was the scale of the booty proceeds, some 1000 or 1500 talents (Plut. *Nik.* 28.3; Diod. 13.106.8–10). The shockwaves produced by this huge amount can be appreciated by contrast with the level of foreign currency with which Sparta was used to dealing – the 25 talents from Pharnabazos or the minuscule cash donations revealed in the 'war fund' inscription. It was the disturbing impact of this immense amount of foreign coinage, inflamed by the peculation of Gylippos, that provoked the controversy which has led to so much subsequent misrepresentation and confusion.

Private ownership of precious metal currency
There is also evidence, both direct and indirect, for the possession and use of precious metal currency in both bullion and coin by individual Spartiates in the period before 404. It has, indeed, been suggested that the 'war fund' inscription may provide direct evidence for private ownership of bullion, on the presumption that one of the donors of silver, a certain Molokros, was a Spartiate, since he is introduced without an ethnic (Loomis 1992, 53–4, 81). This tantalising assumption, however, remains uncertain.[29] One strand of indirect evidence (to be examined in detail below) comprises the involvement of citizens in various private transactions – buying, selling, lending, making contracts – which, whilst not strictly requiring the use of silver or gold currency, may well imply it. Another strand relates to financial transactions between citizens and polis. The state's possession and use of both bullion and coinage makes it more probable that these were the media for transactions between polis and citizen, such as those which lay behind the private debts owed to king and state (Hdt. 6.59) or levies of *eisphorai* (Arist. *Pol.* 1271b11–18; cf. Thuc. 1.80) – especially as the latter concerned war finance.

In two spheres of financial transaction between citizen and polis the amounts are actually specified in common Greek currency. One sphere is official fines. In 446 King Pleistoanax was reportedly fined 15 talents, or 90,000 drachmas (Ephorus, *FGrH* 70F193, *ap.* schol. in Aristop. *Clouds* 859). A fine of 100,000 drachmas was imposed upon Agis II in 418, though it was subsequently withdrawn (Thuc. 5.63). A non-royal commander, Phoibidas, was fined the same amount in 382;[30] and the much smaller sum of 1,000 drachmas was imposed on his son Isidas in 362 (Plut. *Ages.* 34.8). This is not conclusive evidence, however, for private possession and use of foreign coinage. The specification of the fines in terms of common Greek currency could simply be as a measure of value, with the fine being due in uncoined valuables. Secondly, with the exception of Isidas' modest fine, it is possible that the huge amounts involved were intended as ruinous fines, designed to drive the victim from Sparta, and hence never intended to be paid.[31] This suggestion might appear to gain some force from the apparent contradiction involved in the specification of Phoibidas' fine in monetary terms at a date a mere 22 years after the prohibition of private ownership of precious metal coin and bullion in 404, when the ban might be expected still to have been current.[32] On the other hand, it is arguable that Phoibidas' fine is a sign of the prohibition's rapid demise. Certainly, the more plausibly-sized fine imposed on Isidas adds to other evidence – to be considered shortly – that the ban introduced had only a limited lifespan.

The other sphere in question is the compulsory mess dues, which included a monthly contribution per member of 'about ten Aiginetan obols' for procuring the side-dishes called the *opsōnia* (Dikaiarchos, *ap*. Athen. 141c). That this was a genuine monetary payment is suggested by the specification of the monetary standard and confirmed by Plutarch's statement (*Lyk*. 12.2) that it comprised a small amount of coinage (*nomismatos*). This payment would have required about 10.5 gm of silver per person per month. Although Dikaiarchos' evidence dates from the late fourth century, there is no reason why such silver payments should not have been feasible throughout our period. The question is in what form of silver these payments were made. Payment in Aiginetan coinage itself or in another coinage on the Aiginetic standard is not impossible. The latest numismatic research suggests that significant quantities of 'fractional' coins (of an obol and below) were produced from the earliest days of Greek silver coinage (Kim 1994; cf. Howgego 1995, 6–7). The first series of Aiginetan obol coins commenced as early as 550/540 and were produced in good quantity from the start (Kim 1994, 16–22); even smaller denominations (hemiobols and tetartemoria) were also produced. Aiginetan coins continued to circulate throughout the Peloponnese down into the fourth century (Oeconomides 1992). Alternatively, payment could have been made in uncoined silver. Dikaiarchos' imprecision ('*about*' ten obols) can be interpreted in different ways. It could reflect either the use of small silver scraps of variable weight, such as appear in archaic coin hoards,[33] or the possibility of payment in coins on other weight standards, or the normal marginal difference between the weight of ten obols' worth of uncoined silver and the slightly lighter weight of ten obols of Aiginetan coins.

In the transactional spheres discussed above the evidence clearly suggests private use of precious metals in the form of uncoined bullion, but is less conclusive regarding foreign coinage. More certain evidence for private possession of both kinds of precious metal currency comes from Herodotus. First, he relates the cautionary tale of the Spartan, Glaukos, who appropriated from its rightful heirs a large sum of silver which a Milesian had left in his guardianship (6.86). The story is doubtless apocryphal and is located temporally some three generations before its alleged narration by King Leotychidas in the late 490s.

It speaks volumes, however, for the perceptions of Herodotus' fifth-century Spartan sources. Glaukos' crime was the deceit of the Milesian's heirs; there is no hint that his possession of silver was illegal *per se*. The story does not indicate the form of the silver in Glaukos' possession; but another Herodotean passage is unequivocal. His account of the distribution of Persian booty to the Spartans and other Greek troops after Plataia indicates that the distribution included 'talents', which he had earlier described as consisting of gold coins as well as unminted gold and silver (9.81, cf. 41).

Further indications that Spartiates owned both forms of precious metal currency in the period before 404 BC come from numerous references in the sources to alleged incidents of Spartiates' accepting or giving foreign bribes (Noethlichs 1987). The essential point is not the historical authenticity of these incidents (some allegations are patently tendentious and few capable of definitive proof), but the very fact of their attribution to Spartiates. The sources include contemporary writers – Herodotus, Thucydides, Aristophanes (cf. Harvey 1994) – who had visited Sparta or were well-informed about Spartiate life and would have known of any official prohibition on ownership. Yet no source exhibits any doubts that such bribery could plausibly have taken place or conveys any hint that bribes to or from a Spartiate had to be in uncoined form. On the contrary, Spartiates are portrayed as no different from other Greeks in their perceived openness and access to all forms of silver and gold.

Another important point is that these contemporary sources never express any doubt that Spartiate recipients of bribes could utilise their ill-gotten gains. This issue is particularly relevant to two incidents whose historicity is not in doubt: the theft committed by Gylippos which sparked off the 404 debate and Thorax's subsequent execution for possession of silver. The scale of Gylippos' theft was immense, 30 talents, about twice the ruinous fines discussed above.[34] It must have dwarfed any other Spartiate's holdings of movable wealth. Note, moreover, that the silver stolen by Gylippos was in the form of coinage: Athenian 'owls'. For what purpose did he steal this foreign coinage? This question surely prompts the answer that, unless he intended to keep it uselessly in storage, there must already have been legitimate means for its employment. Moreover, to use such a large amount without suspicion implies that he was someone already known to be rich in silver coin. It is relevant that Gylippos had already had an independent spell abroad in Sicily in 414–13, during which he had been denounced by the Syracusans for his avarice.[35] Similarly, Thorax's suicidal possession of silver – presumably acquired on his foreign commands between 406 and 403[36] – makes sense if he was the victim of a recent policy change, whereby wealth which was legitimate when he acquired it suddenly became punishable by death through a measure passed during his absence abroad. His return to Sparta with such incriminating goods implies his expectation that they could continue to be used, that the potential gains from their possession outweighed the risk.

We can, indeed, identify one sphere in which, by the time of Gylippos and Thorax, certain wealthy Spartiates had long been legitimately committing considerable sums to what were almost certainly monetary expenditures. In the later fifth century several Spartiate victors in the Olympic four-horse chariot race commissioned life-size bronze statues to celebrate their successes (see further, ch. 10). In the case of at least one victor (and probably also in others) the sculptor was a foreign artist, the celebrated Myron of Athens (Paus. 6.2.2), who was surely paid in silver coinage or bullion.

There are then many grounds for believing that before 404 BC precious metal coin and bullion were both legal property and tender for Spartan citizens. This conclusion is supported by the fact that these items were certainly held by, and were therefore surely in circulation among, Sparta's non-citizen populations. After Plataia the helots sold stolen booty to the Aiginetans, presumably getting Aiginetan currency in return. In 425 a reward of silver was offered to volunteers who smuggled food to the troops trapped on Sphakteria (Hdt. 9.80; Thuc. 4.26).[37] In 424 the Athenians imposed a tribute of four talents on the island of Kythera (Thuc. 4.57). From Kythera too comes a coin hoard dated 525–500, containing one or more silver staters of Seriphos (*IGCH* no. 4). In his account of the conspiracy of Kinadon *c.* 398 BC Xenophon depicts the *agora* in Sparta as filled with more than 4,000 non-Spartiates intermingling with the Spartiates present (Xen. *Hell.* 3.3.5). If the non-citizen stallholders and purchasers were using silver currency in their transactions, Spartan citizens can hardly have been isolated from its possession and use.

Mention of the Kythera coin hoard might appear to raise an objection to the arguments for Spartiate use of foreign coinage: namely, the extreme paucity of coin finds attested from Sparta itself. I say 'extreme paucity', rather than 'absence', since an archaic Aiginetan stater is recorded from the village of Anogeia in the eastern foothills of Mt Taygetos. Moreover, a largely overlooked entry in Tod and Wace's old *Catalogue of the Sparta Museum* notes a find of silver coins made 'on the right bank of the stream running north of Sparta', comprising three Athenian tetradrachms and an Argive diobol.[38] Autopsy of the coins themselves has not proved possible. Tod and Wace, however, ascribe the Athenian coins to the fifth century; and their catalogue descriptions would appear to support this date.[39] Their date of production of course does not inform us about the date at which they were brought into Sparta: whether they circulated in Sparta during the fifth century or formed part of the booty sent back by Lysander. Uncertainty about the history of their use is compounded by the fact that the Argive coin, which apparently should have been identified as tetrobol rather than a diobol, probably belongs to a large series conventionally dated from the mid-fourth to the third century.[40] It is unclear, however, whether or not the four coins were found together as a hoard. Without direct study of the wear of the coins, no reliable inferences about the historical implications of these coins are currently possible.

In any case, the absence of coin hoards from Sparta would hardly be a major obstacle to my arguments. The 1973 *Inventory of Greek Coin Hoards* records a mere 23 archaic or classical hoards from the entire Peloponnese, despite the existence of several significant mints. The record from other parts of Spartan territory is virtually blank.[41] Similarly, the hellenistic period, when Sparta coined in abundance (Grunauer–von Hoerschelmann 1978), has produced only one hoard from Sparta (*IGCH* no. 181). Hence the absence of coin hoards cannot prove the absence of coins. As for individual coin finds, although none of the 71 identifiable Greek coins found in the excavation of Artemis Orthia (Woodward, in Dawkins 1929, 393–8) appears to date before 404 BC, this is hardly surprising, since the numbers of coin finds increase significantly through time (4 possibly late classical; 38 hellenistic; 108 Greek and Roman Imperial; 160 Byzantine/Frankish/Venetian). The uncertain relationship between the finds and the presence of coinage is indicated by the complete absence of any local Spartan coins from the hellenistic period. The absence of archaic or early classical coins is in fact compatible with the view that silver coinage, though permitted, was mostly owned on a comparatively modest scale before 404, with Spartiates owning most of their silver in the form of bullion.

The prohibition of private ownership introduced in 404, then, was a new measure: not a relaxation, but a restriction of previous practice. It was passed due not to the novelty of foreign currency entering Sparta but to its immense increase in scale (David 1979b). How effective was the prohibition? The execution of Thorax shows that initially it was implemented with severity. Xenophon's reference to searches for gold and silver (*Lak. Pol.* 7.6) also indicates determination to ensure compliance. His comments, however, imply that some were flouting the ban; and his later remark (14.3) that some even boast of their possession of gold indicates that such evasion was becoming overt. The timing of these developments is uncertain, connected as it is with the intractable problem of dating Xenophon's *Polity of the Lakedaimonians*. There are clear indications, however, that by the late 360s the prohibition had been officially abandoned. In addition to the 1,000 drachma fine imposed upon Isidas, there is a body of evidence which has rarely, to my knowledge, been exploited by historians of Sparta – the inscriptions from Delphi recording financial donations made by states and individuals to the fund of the Naopoioi, the officials responsible for rebuilding the temple of Apollo following its destruction in 373/2 (*CID II*, nos. 1–30).

TABLE 3 lists the recorded monetary donations to the Delphic fund made by individual Spartan men (and one woman – Philostratis) who visited the sanctuary in particular biannual periods. The list is very incomplete. Although the fund commenced in spring 366, possibly even in 371, the first surviving inscription relates only to the year 362/1 (the eleventh round of contributions) and most of the subsequent inscriptions are lost or survive only in fragmentary state; only those recording the donations for spring 361 and spring–autumn

TABLE 3. Private Spartan donations to the fund of the Naopoioi at Delphi (on the Aiginetic standard).

Date	Donor(s)	Amount	Reference CID II
Spring 361	Andokos	6 dr.	1 II, 10–12
	Nausiadas	1 dr.	13–15
Spring 360	Andokos	2 dr.	4 I, 33–34
	Philostratis	0 dr. 3 obols	55–6
Spring 358	P[lou]tos and Megyllias	0 dr. 4 obols	5 I, 16–18
Autumn 336	(name missing)	1 dr.	24 II, 1–3
	Charmos	2 dr.	3–5
	Menon	1 dr.	5–8
	Butis	1 dr.	8–10
	Timeas	0 dr. 3 obols	10–13

360 are practically intact. Even this incomplete record, however, provides incontrovertible evidence of individual Spartans utilising silver coinage on the Aiginetic standard from 361 onwards. That the Spartan donors made their gifts in silver coins is well-nigh certain, since their contributions are recorded in precisely the same manner as donations by other Greeks. The inscriptions are generally assiduous in recording non-standard gifts, such as donations in Attic coinage or in kind; but they give no indication of anything unusual about the Spartan donations.

The Spartan donations may look modest; but this does not constitute evidence that personal cash holdings were more limited than elsewhere, since the amounts are similar to donations by citizens of other poleis. Indeed, Andokos' 6 drachma gift in spring 361 is three times the next highest private donation for that season; and even his 2 drachma gift the following year is higher than most other offerings. Similarly, in autumn 336 Charmos' 2 drachmas are the highest recorded private donation and the remaining Spartiate gifts of ½–1 drachma fall within the standard range of private donations for that year.

These gifts are, indeed, probably only a mere fraction of total Spartiate private donations, since they relate only to persons who actually visited the sanctuary. The inscriptions also record official contributions made by the Lakedaimonians as a polis: 2,542 drachmas in spring 361, another 7,120 drachmas 2½ obols in autumn 360, a further 32 drachmas in 358, and finally 510 drachmas in spring 336.[42] Although in theory the contributions between 361 and 358 were specified by a tax imposed by the Delphic Amphiktyony and calculated on a capitation basis, in practice many donor states appear to have contributed whatever they could raise through local collections (*CID II*, p. 10) – hence the variable amounts and odd numbers of obols and even half-obols in the

Lakedaimonian and other contributions. During the years in question the Spartan public treasury was desperately short of funds to finance the payment of mercenaries for its efforts to recapture Messenia after abstaining from the Common Peace of 362/1 (Xen. *Ages.* 2.28–31; Plut. *Ages.* 36–40). The official Spartan dues to Delphi were probably, therefore, gathered by private contributions, whether as tax or donations. And gathered they were on an impressive scale, since Sparta's total recorded contributions, at over 10,000 drachmas, are almost three times those attested for any other state.[43] Indeed, there is another case of even more substantial private funding attested at precisely this period, when, to finance Sparta's warfare, King Agesilaos had to draw loans and contributions (δανείζεσθαι καὶ συνερανίζεσθαι) from his friends in the polis (Plut. *Ages.* 35.3).

This evidence for significant amounts of foreign currency in Spartiate hands is conclusive proof of the demise of the ban on private possession. Its comparatively short-lived existence is yet further evidence that, far from a traditional measure, the prohibition of 404 was a new introduction which never took root in Spartiate practice and quickly withered once the initial impetus for its implementation, the growth of overseas imperialism, had ended. By the late fourth century the pseudo-Platonic dialogue *Alkibiades I* (122e) could state that 'there is more gold and silver privately held in Lakedaimon than in the whole of Greece, for during many generations it has been passing in to them from every part of Greece and often also from the barbarians'. The short-lived prohibition had evidently been forgotten.

Movable and monetary wealth: acquisition and exchange

We have seen that the Spartiate property system, although grounded in citizen ownership of land, also embraced the legitimate possession of various forms of movable wealth. The fact that the compulsory mess contributions included small quantities of silver coinage or bullion demonstrates that even monetary forms of wealth were integrated into the functioning of Spartiate society. These findings exemplify and support the conclusions of recent research on the role of money in ancient Greece. Although criticised by ancient writers and perceived by modern analysts as inimical and threatening to aristocratic society and values (Seaford 1994, 199–206; 222–6; Kurke 1995; cf. von Reden 1995, 182–7), there was nothing inherent in money or coinage which precluded their development and usage within the established order (von Reden 1997, 154–5). Yet it remains to examine the significance of the role played by monetary and other forms of movable wealth within Spartiate society. Spartan citizens could legitimately possess such forms of wealth. How far, however, could they engage in the full range of activities by which movable wealth might potentially be acquired or generated? To what extent could they participate in market or other exchange? How far did money and coinage penetrate into various spheres of Spartiate life?

Ch. 5. Movable wealth: ownership, acquisition and exchange

The acquisition and generation of monetary wealth

As a counterpoint to the Spartan situation, it is helpful first to consider the position in classical Athens, the polis which demonstrates the maximum extent of citizen involvement in the generation and utilisation of mobile wealth (Osborne 1991). Wealthy Athenian property owners engaged in income generation on a significant scale, using a variety of means: production of cash crops from arable farming and arboriculture, market-orientated pastoral production (Hodkinson 1990, 146–51; 1992b), exploitation of woodland resources, hiring out slaves, ownership of slave workshops, letting urban multiple dwellings, and monetary loans. These profit-generating activities were stimulated by rich citizens' need to produce large amounts of cash to meet public liturgies and taxes, as well as private obligations such as cash dowries and funeral expenses. They were sustained by the existence of the large mining region of Laurion and the even larger urban markets of Athens and the Peiraieus, whose capacity to pay for agricultural produce was itself sustained by the democratic redistribution of the public resources provided by the rich. The entire system involved a high degree of monetisation and liquidity in both the household economies of wealthy Athenians and the economy of the polis as a whole.

Clearly, major differences between Spartan and Athenian public economy and society meant a much lower degree of liquidity in Spartiate household economies. The more communal character of the servile labour force precluded hiring helots out for profit. The agrarian character of Spartan society precluded not merely the existence of multiple urban dwellings but, more fundamentally, such an intense level of market demand for agricultural products as existed at Athens. Above all, the different nature of her socio-political system entailed, as we shall see in chapter 7, a minimal level of public demands or private obligations requiring cash expenditures. Apart from the mess contribution of 10 obols per month, Spartiates could satisfy the requirements of citizenship simply through the extraction of agricultural produce from the helots. Compared with Athens, therefore, many of the opportunities and requirements for market exchange and the generation of mobile wealth were eliminated or considerably reduced.

According to some sources, these structural factors were reinforced by a specific prohibition against gainful activity or employment.

> In other poleis, I suppose, all men make as much money (χρηματίζονται) as they can. One man farms, another owns a ship, another trades, and others live from crafts (*technōn*). At Sparta, however, Lykourgos forbade the freemen to engage in anything to do with money-making (*chrēmatismos*). He insisted on their regarding as their own concern only those activities which make for civic freedom (Xen. *Lak. Pol.* 7.1–2).

Xenophon's primary concern here is financial gain. Elsewhere, however, in a passage clearly describing Sparta in his *Oikonomikos*, the focus shifts to the prohibition of engagement in *technai* (crafts) as such: 'in some poleis, and especially in those reputed warlike, it is not even lawful for any of the citizens to work at *technai*' (4.3). Earlier, Herodotus (2.167) had written of the Spartans as being the most contemptuous of all Greeks towards manual crafts. Plato, outlining his Spartan-based timarchy, combines these two concerns in portraying the soldier class as abstaining from agriculture, manual crafts and *chrēmatismos* (*Repub.* 547d). Statements asserting prohibitions against banausic and/or gainful activity are repeated by several later sources.[44]

Scholars have generally accepted this evidence as proof of an official prohibition on citizen participation in money-making and manual occupations. Indeed, the Spartiates' position as leisured rentier landlords and full-time hoplite warriors might appear to presuppose their abstention from such activities without need for formal prohibition.[45] Paul Cartledge (1976) has in fact drawn attention to certain evidence – a number of famous early Spartiate sculptors and two late archaic craftsmen's inscriptions bearing aristocratic names discovered on monumental works in Lakonian sanctuaries[46] – which suggests that there was no absolute prohibition on craft activity before the classical period.[47] It is unlikely that many Spartiates ever engaged in such crafts; but it seems that in the archaic period, at least, talented artists may have been permitted to follow their crafts, especially at religious sanctuaries.[48] If this is right, then we should assume that a formal prohibition of such activity was subsequently imposed during classical times. Cartledge (1976, 119) suggests that the decision to introduce this prohibition should be ascribed to the progressive decline of Spartiate manpower, as part presumably of an increasing focus on military affairs. An alternative possibility is that an increasing number of Spartiates whose landholdings had become insufficient or barely sufficient to sustain their citizen status turned to banausic activities as a means of supplementary support; and that a formalised prohibition ensued as part of a consequent definition of citizenship requirements and a drawing of boundaries between citizens and Inferiors.

A prejudice or prohibition against *chrēmatismos* or banausic occupations, however, does not necessarily signify a lack of desire for, or an inability to generate, monetary gain. As seen in chapter 2, Xenophon supports his statement of the prohibition of *chrēmatismos* by listing several reasons why Spartiates had no need of wealth. As observed there, however, the items for which he claims personal expenditure was unnecessary (food, clothing and gifts to messmates) hardly exhaust the range of activities for which Spartiates might want to acquire monetary wealth. Moreover, his subsequent revelation of searches and penalties for those in possession of gold and silver implies that their acquisition was still sought after. Similarly, the range of so-called money-making activities in other poleis which Xenophon implies were absent from Sparta – farming, shipowning, trading, craftsmanship – hardly exhausts the options open to wealthy men in search of profit. Indeed, it barely addresses the options for wealthy men at all, since these activities were ones which men would undertake in person as their livelihoods. The means by which the leisured elite in other poleis generated their wealth, not through personal labour but through the agency of others, are largely ignored.

In fact, there were ways that Spartiates could generate monetary gains without incurring the taint of banausic activity or of money-making as a livelihood. Spartiate landowners directing the work of their helot cultivators (Xen. *Hell.* 3.3.5) could hardly be accused of *chrēmatismos*. Yet we have seen (ch. 4) that Spartiate-helot sharecropping arrangements probably produced considerable agricultural surpluses for the Spartiate masters, some of which could have been used in market exchange. As already noted, the year-round requirement to supply specified foodstuffs for the mess contributions probably created an ongoing market demand as households (temporarily) ran short of particular items. Similarly, as we saw at the start of this chapter, the large animal herds owned by rich citizens formed another potentially significant means of income-generation. Besides the private demand for cheese for the mess contributions and wool for clothing, the polis also needed plentiful supplies of sacrificial animals.[49] Some scholars have argued that Spartiates could also engage in manufacture and trade, evading charges of *chrēmatismos* and banausic activity by operating through the agency of others: for example, through the ownership of workshops manned by helots or slaves.[50]

Gift, market and monetary exchange
This picture of state control over, but not complete exclusion of, monetary acquisition is paralleled in the sphere of exchange. At first sight the archetypal form of Spartiate exchange would appear to be the intended exchange of treasures between Ariston and Agetos – a transaction marked, at least initially, by generosity between friends and involving non-monetary valuables. Similarly, when Maiandrios of Samos wanted to persuade King Kleomenes, he offered him not money but a choice of his gold and silver drinking cups. Gift-giving in non-monetary form and within a context of sociability is evident in various spheres of Spartiate life. In the messes citizens were supposed not to spend money on their messmates (Xen. *Lak. Pol.* 7.4); instead, the rich donated wheaten bread and hunters their spoils, and the kings honoured other Spartiates with their second portion (Xen. *Lak. Pol.* 5.3; 15.5). King Agesilaos regularly gave an ox and a cloak to newly-elected members of the *gerousia*; and his reign commenced with his greatest gift of all, as he donated to his mother's kinsfolk half his inheritance from his half-brother Agis (Xen. *Ages.* 4.5; Plut. *Ages.* 4.1). An atmosphere of willing generosity is again conveyed by Xenophon's characterisation of Agesilaos as 'one who delighted to give away his own for the good of others' (*Ages.* 4.1). The same atmosphere of sociable giving is said to have pervaded the communal right of citizens to share use of each other's property (cf. ch. 6). Would-be borrowers of hunting-dogs invited the owner to join their hunt; but, if he were otherwise engaged, he gladly sent the hounds (Xen. *Lak. Pol.* 6.3).

The anatomy of the Spartiate property system

To these examples of non-monetary gifts we can add the evidence of social contexts in which monetary payments, common in other states, were absent from Sparta. The absence of monetary liturgies will be discussed in chapter 7. Monetary and other material rewards were commonly offered by other poleis to victorious athletes (von Reden 1995, 164–7); but not in Sparta, where the sole reward for Olympic victors was the honour of fighting in the king's bodyguard (Plut. *Lyk.* 22.4; *Mor.* 639e; Hodkinson 1999, 168–9). Likewise, 'matrimonial transactions were clearly cash affairs in the classical period' (von Reden 1995, 164); but less so in Sparta, where the large dowries complained of by Aristotle consisted of land rather than money (*Pol.* 1270a23–5; quoted on p. 80).

The prevalence of gift-giving and sociable transactions is, however, only part of the story. There is also evidence for regular citizen engagement both in market transactions (whether monetary or non-monetary) and in monetary transactions (whether within or outside a market context). Such transactions were not merely officially sanctioned by the polis. Thucydides' statement (5.34) regarding the men who surrendered on Sphakteria – that the Spartans 'made them *atimoi*; their deprivation (*atimia*) meant that they could neither hold office nor have the authority to buy or sell anything' – indicates that the right to buy and sell was an integral part of Spartan citizenship. This evidence is reinforced by Plutarch's comment (*Lyk.* 25.1), that 'those under thirty years of age did not go into the *agora*, but had their household needs (ἀναγκαίας οἰκονομίας) supplied by their relatives and lovers'. The other restriction on youths under 30 was that, like the Sphakterians, they could not hold public office (Xen. *Lak. Pol.* 4.7). The right to buy and sell and to enter the *agora* to participate in market exchange was, therefore, a central privilege of Spartiate life, on a par with office-holding, accorded only to Spartiates who possessed the fullest degree of citizenship.[51] Sparta did not separate civic and market activity, unlike the Thessalian 'free *agora*' from which market activity, artisans and farmers were strictly excluded (Arist. *Pol.* 1331a30–b4). On the contrary, the rhythms of civic and market activity moved in parallel. On the death of a king, when normal citizen life was suspended for public mourning, not only were there no assemblies or elections of magistrates (Hdt. 6.58), but also 'nothing is sold for three days and the *agora* is sprinkled with chaff' (Herakleides Lembos, fr. 373.10, Dilts = [Arist.] *Lak. Pol.* fr. 611.10, Rose). Xenophon's description of a scene in the Spartan *agora*, during his account of the conspiracy of Kinadon, depicts the state magistrates (kings, ephors and *gerontes*) conducting civic business, alongside 40 other Spartiates and more than 4,000 non-Spartiates (*Hell.* 3.3.5), most of whom were presumably engaged in market transactions.

The impression Xenophon gives of the Spartan *agora* as a bustling, regional market is reinforced by his subsequent reference to the 'iron market' (*sidēros*: 3.3.7; cf. Lazenby 1997, 443–4), whose existence suggests a level of commercial activity sufficiently large to justify the separation of stalls into separate zones for different kinds of products, precisely as occurred in other poleis like Athens.

As the passages cited above suggest, we should not envisage Spartan citizens as standing aside from these commercial exchanges. Plutarch's evidence implies that citizens would need to enter the market regularly to supply their household needs. As has already been suggested, the requirement upon each Spartiate to render a specified amount of various foodstuffs every month for his mess dues probably engendered a deal of market exchange as some citizens endeavoured to make good specific seasonal shortfalls and others to profit from the demand by off-loading surplus crops from store. Indeed, Spartiates had access to a suitably wide range of currency for engaging in such exchanges. It is frequently commented that most silver denominations, even the smaller ones of fractions of an obol, were of comparatively high value for small everyday transactions. Consequently, during the classical period several Greek poleis introduced a base metal coinage, normally in bronze, for small transactions (Howgego 1995, 7–8). In Sparta, in contrast, the extremely low monetary value of the iron currency surely made it a convenient medium of currency for small transactions.

Consequently, when the Persian king Cyrus reportedly directed his famous criticism of Greek market activity (Hdt. 1.153) – 'I have never yet been afraid of any men who have a set place in the middle of their polis where they come together to cheat each other and forswear themselves' – at a Spartiate herald, his jibe was not misplaced but directed at a polis for whose citizens such activity was a regular experience. Although Herodotus' comments extend the scope of Cyrus' jibe to the Greeks as a whole, he does not indicate any incongruity that it was aimed at a Spartan. The existence of disputes among Spartan citizens, and of official procedures for settling them, is intimated by other sources. According to Aristotle (*Pol.* 1275b9–10), 'individual ephors try different cases of agreements' (*symbolaia*). An anecdote in the *Apophthegmata Lakōnika* (221b) mentions the ephors' trying cases concerning *symbolaia* every day. The term *symbolaion* is a generic one which 'can be used of any relationship between persons in which one has a liability to another' (MacDowell 1986, 130). The above mentioned 'agreements' do not refer specifically to market or monetary exchanges, but they surely embrace them. Even Plutarch (*Lyk.* 13.2) concedes the existence of 'money contracts' (*chrēmatika symbolaia*).

Indeed, as we have already seen, there were several spheres of monetary exchanges outside the context of buying and selling in the *agora*. Each month every Spartiate contributed his 10 obols to the mess. There was monetary taxation (see further, ch. 6) and monetary fines could be imposed in legal cases. Individual citizens could make private donations to Delphi. There is also the entire realm of lending and borrowing, of personal credit, whose pervasive link with social relationships within the Athenian polis has been emphasized in recent research (Millett 1991). In third-century Sparta personal debt had become a major socio-economic problem which elicited revolutionary programmes of debt cancellation (Plut. *Agis* 6.4; 13.2–3; *Kleom.* 10.6). For our period, Herodotus' mention of debts owing to the kings, a reference to

The anatomy of the Spartiate property system

the Spartans' use of tally-sticks as a record of loans (Dioskourides, *ap.* Photios *Lexikon*, s.v. *skytalē*) and Agesilaos' raising of military loans from his friends (Plut. *Ages.* 35.3) provide tantalising hints of an important sphere of sociable monetary exchange.[52]

As these examples demonstrate, monetary transactions spanned both the public and private spheres, involving a range of compulsory, commercial and sociable contexts. The overall position is nicely characterised in an undated episode recorded in the pseudo-Aristotelian *Oikonomika* (2.2.9; 1347b):

> The Lakedaimonians, when entreated by the Samians for money (*chrēmata*) to enable them to return to their country, voted that they and their household slaves (*oiketai*) and their beasts of burden should fast for one day, and that the expenses each one thus saved should be given to the Samians.[53]

We witness here a citizen body lacking in financial reserves, but arranging a voluntary monetary gift via a self-imposed public levy, provided by individual private households through an act of personal sacrifice. There is also the implication that citizen households would possess currency and that the expenses of feeding humans and animals could be calculated in terms of monetary costs. The interconnectedness of these different transactional contexts, the evidently low level of liquidity, and yet the degree of penetration of money into both public and private spheres, were characteristic of the role of movable wealth in Spartiate society.

Notes

[1] Xenophon does not specifically label the houses as Spartiate, but it seems probable on several grounds. First, Xenophon's gratuitous reference to valuables suggests a veiled comment on the Spartiates' attachment to wealth, which he criticises explicitly in *Lak. Pol.* 14. Secondly, although the bulk of Spartiate houses lay west of the Eurotas, some probably spread over onto the plain east of the river. Despite difficult survey conditions, the Laconia Survey discovered several classical habitation sites here (Cavanagh et al. 1996, 362–8, 380–9: esp. site nos. J369, M171–2; M174; M328–9). Thirdly, the proximity of the plundered houses to the heart of Sparta is demonstrated by the shocked reactions of Spartan women at seeing the smoke from their burning. Their shock may indeed stem from the destruction of their property. The location of the bridge which the enemy declined to cross is disputed: one view placing it SE of Sparta (Armstrong et al. 1992, 295, 306), another to the NE, near the modern road bridge (Stibbe 1994, 63–8). The latter appears more compatible with Xenophon's account, especially since the women's reaction would seem less plausible if the plundering occurred after the enemy had already passed by the centre of Sparta.

[2] I must acknowledge the advice which I have received from several numismatic experts: Jennifer Cargill-Thompson, Nicholas Hardwick, Christopher Howgego, Henry Kim and Keith Rutter. They are not, however, responsible for the views expressed here.

[3] It is important to distinguish in this passage the *physical gold and silver* desired by the Iron and Bronze elements in the ruling class from the *Golden and Silvern elements*

of the ruling class whose characteristic is that they abhor the possession of physical gold and silver!

4   1,500 talents of silver (*argyriou*), according to Diodorus; 1,000 talents, according to Plutarch (*Nik.* 28.3, citing Timaios, *FGrH* 566F100b).

5   *IG* v.2.159. Text and recent discussion in Thür and Taeuber 1994, 1–11.

6   I leave aside the references to a leather currency in Seneca, *De Beneficiis* 5.14.4 and in Nik. Dam., *FGrH* 90F103, Z.8 (on which, see Nenci 1974, 643–5) and to a bronze currency by Olympiodoros, *In Plato Gorgiam Commentaria* 44.2; *In Plato, Alk. I* 164.10.

7   In contrast, note the comments of Justin (3.2), who regards the Spartans' employment of commodity exchange rather than money as due to the laws of Lykourgos.

8   Another gloss of Hesychios reads ἵππ(οπ)ορ· τόν τε ἵππον, καὶ τὸν τετράχαλκον. …Λάκωνες: 'Hipp(op)or. The horse and the *tetrachalkon*…Lakonians'. Once again there is an association of the Lakonians with the meaning signifying a *tetrachalkon*.

9   Aigina, Corinth, Elis, Mantineia, Sikyon and Tegea all coined in the period before 480 BC (see the convenient collection of data in Osborne 1996, 252–5, esp. fig. 66 and table 6).

10   Byzantion also participated in the inter-state ΣΥΝ coinage, which is now normally dated to the end of the fifth century (Karwiese 1980; Ashton 1993).

11   Carradice and Price 1988, 48; for some examples, Kraay 1976, 95, 99, 110, 135.

12   We may add a further, religious factor. Von Reden (1995, 175) suggests that 'the introduction of coinage indicates a shift of authority over social justice from the gods to the *polis*'. Spartans, in contrast, retained a strong faith in divine justice and the power of religious ritual (Hodkinson 1983, 273–6).

13   Note also Morrisson's study (1993) of the monetary role in diverse historical societies of another base metal, lead.

14   A similar process of myth-making has been suggested by Picard (1980), though he believes that the 404 debate concerned a proposal to mint silver coinage and that the iron spits were portrayed for the first time as Sparta's native currency by opponents of this proposal.

15   Daimachos, *FGrH* 65F4; Kayser et al. (eds.) 1964, no. 401; cf. Cartledge 1979, 90.

16   Chantraine 1956, 70–6; Oeconomides 1993, with references to earlier studies.

17   Classical comedians: Aristop. *Clouds* 247–9; Plato Comicus, fr. 95, Kock; Strattis, fr. 36, Kock. Later writers: Aristeides 46.145.15; Schol. on Aristop. *Clouds* 249; Pollux 9.78, 105; Hesychios, s.v. *sidareos*.

18   Pollux 9.77, citing Aristotle; Orion, *Etymologikon* s.v. *obolos*, citing Herakleides Pontikos (and ultimately from the Aristotelian *Lak. Pol.*?). It is unclear whether the statement in Plut. *Lys.* 17.3 is from an Aristotelian source or derives independently from Ephorus or Theopompos. Note, however, that the belief that a handful (*drax*) of spits gave its name to the drachma is now disputed (Carradice and Price 1988, 91–3).

19   Huxley (1962, 63) suggests that, although the 'old spit money continued in use… a kind of iron coinage was introduced for state purposes'. His supporting reference to iron *obeliskoi* (Xen. *Hell.* 3.3.7), however, concerns not coins but objects in the iron market with which potential rebels could arm themselves.

20   Svoronos 1906, 191–2; cf. Hesychios, s.v. *pelanor*; Photios s.v. *pelanos*; Suidas s.v. *pelanoi*.

21   The question of the number of drachmas and obols to the mina within the Aiginetan currency is a controversial issue. I am persuaded, however, by the arguments of Figueira

(1993, esp. 74–7) for a mina of 100 drachmas and 600 obols. Arguments for a 70-drachma mina are founded on Solon's alleged substitution of a 100-drachma mina in Attica for a supposedly earlier Pheidonian mina of 70 drachmas (*Ath. Pol.* 10; Androtion *FGrH* 324F34, *ap.* Plut. *Solon* 15.4) and on the appearance of Aiginetic minas reckoned in 70-drachma units in Delphic fourth-century accounts. As Figueira argues, however, the details of our fourth-century accounts of Solon's reforms and of the currency system which preceded them, are vitiated by their infection with classical Athenian hostility to Aigina. The Delphic 70-drachma mina is probably a secondary, local accounting practice 'intended to facilitate treasurizing and tallying Aiginetan talents when the Attic standard had come to predominate'. An inscription from Delphi itself attests an Aiginetic mina of 100 drachmas (*FdD* 3.1.294). Further confirmation comes from the probability that the late fifth-century Chian tetradrachm was termed '*tesserakostē*' (Thuc. 8.101) because it was equivalent to a fortieth of an Aiginetan mina (cf. Xen. *Hell.* 1.6.12; Figueira 1998, 158–9, with references to earlier studies). A 100-drachma mina is also attested for the related Aiginetic weight standard (Pollux 9.86; cf. Hero, *Geometrika* 23.55, 59).

[22] Svoronos (1906, 191) treats the weight:value ratio in the *Apophth. Lak.* as the equivalence accepted by later Greeks, arguing that the true Lykourgan ratio was 1:600 on the basis of the scholion to a passage from the *Alexipharmaka* of the second-century BC poet Nikandros of Kolophon (5.488), which, it is claimed, equates a *pelanos* to a silver obol. There is, however, no indication in either text that their evidence bears a Spartan reference, in contrast to the explicit Spartan reference in the glosses of Hesychios. (Note that *pelanos* also appears in other places such as Argos and Delphi as a measure of weight: LSJ⁹, s.v.). In any case, the scholion equates the *pelanos* with an obol in weight, not in value (πελάνου βάρος, ἀντὶ τοῦ ὀβολοῦ ὁλκήν. οὐ γὰρ μόνον τὸ πέμμα, ἤγουν τὸ ἕψημα, πέλανος λέγεται, ἀλλὰ καὶ ἡ τοῦ ὀβολοῦ ὁλκή).

[23] I am grateful to my economic historian colleagues, Drs A. Marrison and T. Balderston, for their advice on the economics of exchange rates in situations of bimetallism.

[24] Cf. the evidence assembled in Howgego 1990; 1995, 89–90; von Reden 1997, 161–2, 165–6; and the inventories from Athens and Attica in Melville Jones 1993 (e.g. nos. 136, 140, 145–50, 181). The near-universal use by the sources of the phrase 'gold and silver' to refer to the prohibited currency reflects literary convention (Rutter 1987). It is not an indication that gold currency was used more than silver.

[25] Flower 1991, 92, who informs me that in his published text the words 'former' and 'latter' have been mistakenly transposed, giving the unintended implication that bullion could be melted down into coinage.

[26] Hodkinson 1994, 193–4, 200–1, 212; 1997a, 92–4; cf. ch. 2 above.

[27] Note also the fine of 2,000 minai imposed upon the polis by the Eleans in 420 BC (Thuc. 5.49).

[28] The inscription has been dated between the 420s and the 380s, but Loomis (1992, 56–76) has shown that a setting after 404 is unlikely. The most recent study has argued for a date during the Ionian war (Piérart 1995).

[29] See further ch. 7, n. 2.

[30] Plut. *Pelop.* 6.1; cf. *Mor.* 576a; Plb. 4.27.4; Diod. 15.20.2; Nepos *Pelop.* 1.2–3.

[31] Ste Croix 1972, 135 n. 123; MacDowell 1986, 149. Pleistoanax did indeed go into exile on being unable to pay; and in another case, in 379, a certain Lysanoridas likewise departed after being heavily fined (χρήμασι πολλοῖς ζημιωθείς: Plut. *Pelop.* 13.2). Phoibidas, in contrast, remained in Sparta due to the efforts of his patron Agesilaos, who

Ch. 5. Movable wealth: ownership, acquisition and exchange

is said to have 'saved Phoibidas' (Plut. *Ages.* 23.7). It is uncertain whether this means that his fine was actually paid or simply shelved.

32 Note, however, that the apparent references to official fines in Xenophon, *Lak. Pol.* (4.6; 7.6; 8.4; 9.5; 10.6), do not, as might first be thought, contradict Xenophon's assertion that possession of gold and silver was prohibited. Although modern translators frequently translate the verb ζημιόω and noun ζημία in the above passages as referring to fines, in each case they are better interpreted as bearing the generic sense of (non-monetary) punishments. The same applies to the ζημίαι imposed on citizen households in Hdt. 6.58.

33 e.g. *CH* i.3, from late sixth-century Kolophon, which contained about a quarter kilo of uncoined silver scraps, mostly under 3 g in weight.

34 Timaios, *FGrH* 566F100b, *ap.* Plut. *Nik.* 28.3. The incredible 300 talents claimed by Diodorus (13.106.10) should surely be dismissed.

35 Timaios, *FGrH* 566F100b, *ap.* Plut. *Nik.* 28.3.

36 He was continuously abroad from the nauarchy of Kallikratidas until the end of his harmostship at Samos, which began only in autumn 404. Career and references in Poralla 1985, no. 380.

37 Note the presence of classical coins recently discovered among unpublished finds from Blegen's excavations at the nearby Palace of Nestor: *JHS, AR* 45 (1998–99) 53.

38 *BSA* 16 (1909/10) 65; Tod and Wace 1906, no. 695.

39 I am grateful to Dr Christopher Howgego and Professor Jack Kroll for their advice concerning the catalogue description of these coins. Their most diagnostic feature is the frontal eyes of Athena, which suggest a mid-century date, along with Tod and Wace's comparison with *BMC, Attica* nos. 46–61.

40 J.H. Kroll, pers. comm.

41 Apart from the Kythera hoard, there is only one dubious example, a hoard dated 450–425 whose reported provenance is the very margins of Spartan territory, the environs of modern Kyparissia (*IGCH* no. 23) in the borderland between Sparta and Elis. The fact that this hoard and another hoard (*IGCH* no. 24), recorded as from the environs of Pyrgos in Elean territory, may in fact be part of the same hoard and the nature of the contents – silver staters of Elis – throw doubt on its location within Spartan territory.

42 *CID II* 1 II, 35–9; 4 II, 48–54; 5 II, 28–31; 24 I, 15–22.

43 See the convenient summary tables in *CID II*, pp. 10–11. Admittedly, major states like Athens and Thebes are missing from the surviving inscriptions and we do not know whether the Lakedaimonian contributions included payments from *perioikoi*.

44 *Apophth. Lak.* 214a–b (Agesilaos 72); 230b (Nikandros 3); *Inst. Lac.* 239d–e (no. 41); Nikolaos Damaskos fr. 114 [Müller, *FHG* iii, p. 458]; Josephus, *Against Apion* 2.229; Plut. *Ages.* 26; Polyainos, *Strategemata* 2.1.7; Athen. 657d; Aelian, *VH* 6.6; Stobaios 3.23.8.

45 Cf. Isokrates' comments that 'lacking none of the necessities of life…none engage in any other *technai*, but all devote themselves to arms and warfare' (*Busiris* 18).

46 Paus. 3.17.2, 18.8; 5.17.2, 23.7; 6.4.4, 9.4, 19.14; *IG* v.1.823; *SEG* xi.638 = Jeffery 1990, 200 no. 32; 201 no. 43.

47 The excavation of a potter's kiln in the ancient Spartan village of Mesoa, enclosed within a tumulus in apparent association with four cist-graves and a late seventh-century terracotta relief amphora, was once thought to support this suggestion (Christou 1964a). However, the dating of the graves has subsequently been judged to be far more recent

⁴⁸ (Steinhauer 1972, 244 n. 15) and the association between the kiln and the archaic amphora appears far from certain. See further, ch. 8, pp. 239–40.

⁴⁸ The professions of herald, piper and cook held hereditarily by certain Spartiate families (Hdt. 6.60; 7.134; cf. Berthiaume 1976) are irrelevant to this issue, since they were an honorific privilege (*geras*), not practised as an occupation or for profit.

⁴⁹ e.g. Hdt. 6.56–7; Xen. *Lak. Pol.* 13.2–3, 8; 15.2–3; cf. Jameson 1988.

⁵⁰ MacDowell (1986, 117), partly disagreeing with Cartledge (1976, 118; 1985b, 239), who appears to restrict such Spartiate involvement to the sixth century on the grounds that it would count as *chrēmastikē*. A further suggested avenue for monetary gain is the sponsorship of foreign trade, following the thesis of Benedetto Bravo (1974; 1977; 1984) that much archaic Greek maritime trade was sponsored by aristocrats operating through 'agent traders'. It has been suggested that wealthy Spartiates participated in this trend by sponsoring the widespread foreign distribution of sixth-century Lakonian pottery, exploiting bonds of *philia* and *xenia* with their counterparts in places such as Samos, where it appears in abundance (Nafissi 1989, 73; 1991, 259). Though accepted by some scholars (e.g. Reed 1984), Bravo's general thesis has proved controversial (Cartledge 1983; cf. 1982, 252–4, regarding Samos). Even its proponents generally accept, moreover, that this mode of trade waned in classical times, when most maritime trade was conducted by independent traders.

⁵¹ Plutarch adds that it was disreputable for elderly men to loiter in the *agora*, though he does not indicate that they were banned. The *gerontes* were present in their official capacity in the Kinadon conspiracy episode discussed below.

⁵² Note also the reference to borrowing money to pay official fines in the *Apophthegmata Lakōnika* (Plut. *Mor.* 221f); cf. Cicero, *Tusc. Disp.* 1.42 (100).

⁵³ Isager (1988) argues that *Oikonomika* Book 2 was written towards the end of the fourth century by a pupil of Aristotle and the authenticity of the incidents it records is normally accepted. Plutarch (*Mor.* 64b) gives a variant version in which the people aided were the citizens of Smyrna and the aid given was grain rather than money. Polyainos (1.46) gives a very different version in which King Agis ordered fodder to be withheld from oxen with the army for purposes of military strategy rather than the saving of resources.

Chapter 6

PUBLIC RIGHTS OVER PRIVATE PROPERTY

In chapters 3–5 I argued that the Spartiate property system was considerably more private in character than has often been thought. Spartiate landholdings were privately owned and could be privately alienated. Citizens could, except during a brief period after 404, possess, acquire and dispose of all kinds of movable wealth, including foreign currency. Even the helots, though in a position of collective servitude, appear in some senses as the private property of their holders. We have also seen that there were certain limits to private property rights. There were social sanctions against purchase or sale of land. Certain kinds of gainful activities were prohibited. The polis liberated and liquidated helots without reference to their Spartiate holder. It also limited the proportion of produce citizens could draw from their estates.

This chapter will extend my analysis of the public aspects of the Spartiate property system by considering various ways in which material resources in the possession of citizen families could be drawn upon either by the polis or by other members of the community. I will organise my discussion under four headings: taxation of citizen property; levies upon agricultural produce, especially via the common mess dues; communal rights to the use of private property; and the legitimised practice of theft by Spartiate boys.

Taxation of property

In ancient Greek poleis – in contrast to modern industrialised states, which typically also use them for social and economic regulation – systems of taxation had as their primary purpose the raising of revenue to meet state expenditures. Hence the extent of taxation in Sparta, as elsewhere, was linked to levels of communal spending, themselves largely a function of the degree of the state's complexity, its military commitments and the extent of its public services (cf. Littman 1988). A full review of Spartan public finances lies beyond the scope of this book (cf. Andreades 1933, 37–78). It is clear, however, that although the polis had certain currency needs (cf. ch. 5), state expenditure was mostly at a relatively low level, compared with other leading poleis, in the key spheres of warfare, internal administration, and food supply. With only occasional small-scale naval operations, a land army operating through requisitioning and personal service and no specialised police force or fortifications to maintain, Sparta's military requirements before the Peloponnesian war were financially modest. Only with continuous long-term warfare after 431, involving considerable use of mercenaries and naval campaigning, did military costs significantly escalate. Regarding internal administration, a certain level of regular expenditure was required for the public maintenance of the kings' mess and the sacrificial duties of the kings (Hdt. 6.56–7); but the modest extent of public building (Thuc. 1.10) and the absence of public salaries kept running costs generally low. Finally, in a state well endowed with good agricultural land, there was no requirement for expenditure on external food supplies.

Conversely, there were significant limitations upon Sparta's capacity to raise revenues. The Spartans presumably operated indirect taxation through market taxes and customs duties, as did other poleis. But, although Sparta itself may have functioned as a regional market (Xen. *Hell.* 3.3.5), the volume of revenue generated by sales of non-precious agricultural and craft products was probably low. Moreover, given a largely self-sufficient regional economy, it is unlikely that significant income derived from taxes on imports or exports. Furthermore, unlike more cosmopolitan cities, Sparta had no sizeable metic population to whom direct taxation could be applied; and, although tribute was paid by the *perioikoi*, it went to the kings not the public treasury ([Plato], *Alk. I* 122e).[1] To what extent did the Spartan polis supplement its limited tax-raising capacity by direct taxation of its citizens? This question has an ideological as well as a financial dimension, for it is commonly held that in classical Greek poleis regular direct taxation of citizens and their property was regarded as an intolerable mark of degradation and tyranny, and hence typically avoided (Andreades 1933, 126–30; Finley 1985, 95–6). This orthodoxy has, however, come under considerable challenge.[2] It is largely founded not on contemporary evidence but on comments by the late second-century Christian apologist Tertullian (*Apologeticus* 13.6). Criticising the contemporary pagan practice of using the state gods as sources of income, he remarks that,

> Fields burdened with taxation (*agri tributi onusti*) are cheaper and persons subject to a poll-tax (*hominum capita stipendio censa*) are of less esteem. On the other hand, gods who have a greater tax on them are of greater sanctity; rather, one might say, the greater the sanctity, the greater the tax.

Tertullian's remarks provide little support for the prevailing orthodoxy. They relate to the circumstances of the Roman Empire, not those of the classical polis. The politically- and geographically-distant relationship between taxing authority and taxpayer in Tertullian's day differed markedly from the relationship involved when citizens of a polis agreed a self-imposed tax for the community's benefit. Indeed, Tertullian's comments make no reference to a community's attitude towards direct taxation. His world is one in which taxation is applied only to some sections of the community (doubtless the lower classes) and his reference to diminished esteem expresses not the attitude of taxpayers but their status in the eyes of more fortunate sections of society.

The social attitudes described by Tertullian differed greatly from those of the classical polis, in which any differential imposition of direct taxation normally fell upon wealthier citizens, who did not thereby incur loss of esteem. Contemporary evidence from archaic to hellenistic times suggests that the acceptability of direct taxation varied according to local circumstances and social class. Aristotle (*Pol.* 1320a20–2) notes the unpopularity of direct taxation among wealthy Greeks; but there is no evidence for universal abhorrence on the grounds of its incompatibility with the principle of citizenship. In classical Athens the capital tax, the *eisphora*, from which poorer citizens were exempt, was regarded as an exceptional means of raising extraordinary military revenue. Nevertheless, when circumstances demanded, an annual *eisphora* was maintained continuously from 347/6 until the end of Athenian independence in 323/2 (Thomsen 1964, 238–42). Admittedly, in the pseudo-Aristotelian *Oikonomika* direct taxes on land and produce are mentioned only in the section on satrapal administration, not in the section on the polis (2.2.4–5). The same source, however, subsequently undermines that schematisation in citing the case of Mende (2.2.21). At Mende capital taxation was apparently a permanent affair:

> the people of Mende…refrained from collecting the tax on land and houses but kept a register of the owners, and when the state needed funds they collected the arrears.

The account suggests that the Mendaians were unusual, not in levying capital taxes, but rather in their method of collection. The Spartan evidence should therefore be viewed within a context in which direct taxation of citizens was an available option whose feasibility varied between poleis according to the relative strength of rich and poor and of public and private interests.

Evidence for the taxation of Spartan citizen property is both brief and unsatisfactory in its lack of detail.

> Public finance is also badly regulated by the Spartiates: they are obliged to undertake large-scale wars, but there is never any money in the public treasury; they pay *eisphorai* (εἰσφέρουσί) badly, for as most of the land is the property of the Spartiates themselves, they do not enquire too closely into one another's *eisphorai* (Arist. *Pol.* 1271b11–15).

Aristotle clearly viewed *eisphorai* in Sparta as similar in character to *eisphorai* in Athens: as an occasional war tax assessed on the capital value of private property.[3] Given her modest military requirements in earlier periods, it is probable that, as in Athens, *eisphorai* were introduced during the Peloponnesian war to finance Sparta's imperial ventures.[4] Whether Spartan *eisphorai* were identical in all respects to the Athenian institution is unclear. In Athens the tax was assessed on all property – land, houses, slaves, and movable property, including money (Jones 1974, 154) – and poorer citizens whose property fell below 25 minai or 2,500 drachmas were exempt. In contrast, in the above passage Aristotle mentions only land and he makes no mention of any exemptions. Aristotle's comments on the Spartiates' evasion of *eisphorai* will be discussed more fully in chapter 13; but two points are worthy of remark here. First, the comment that 'most of the land is the property of the Spartiates themselves' indicates that the scope of the tax included other land besides that belonging to the Spartiates themselves. The implication is that *eisphorai* fell on all those who were classed as Lakedaimonians, including the *perioikoi*. Secondly, the fact that the Spartiates were apparently able successfully to evade full payment provides a notable insight into the limited extent to which a public tax was able to encroach upon the sphere of private landholding.

Other references to taxation of Spartan citizens are more vague. Aristotle (*Politics* 1270b3–5) states that fathers of four sons were exempt from all taxes (ἀτελῆ πάντων). According to Plutarch (*Ages*. 35.2), the descendants of Antikrates, the man who killed the Theban general Epaminondas, were granted perpetual exemption from taxes (ἀτέλειαν). These accounts imply that there were taxes other than the *eisphorai* which were collectively of sufficient weight for exemption to be a significant incentive or reward; but their precise nature is unclear.[5] The solution may lie in the fact that Aristotle (*Politics* 1271a36–7) refers to the contributions to the common messes as a tax (τέλος). If tax exemption did indeed include the waiving of mess contributions, it constituted a significant measure of economic relief, as we shall see.

Levies upon agricultural produce: the common mess dues[6]

Aristotle's account of citizen contributions to the common messes strikes a very different tone from his criticisms of the ease with which Spartiates could evade full payment of *eisphorai*:

> Unsatisfactory also are the rules about the common messes called *phiditia* made by the person who first established them. The gathering ought rather to be run at public expense, as at Crete. But among the Lakonians every individual has to contribute, though some of them are very poor and unable to meet this expenditure, so that the legislator finds that the result is the opposite of his chosen aim. For he intends the arrangement of the common meals to be democratic; but under rules such as these it becomes very little democratic: it is not easy for the very poor to participate, yet this is their traditional way of delimiting the citizenship – to exclude from it anyone who is unable to pay this due (*Pol*. 1271a26–37).

Every Spartiate had, as a criterion of citizenship, to belong to a common mess, in which he dined, barring certain minor exceptions, every evening of his adult life (Plut. *Lyk*. 12.2). As Aristotle indicates, mess membership required each messmate to pay an equal contribution of foodstuffs, regardless of his wealth (Xen. *Lak. Pol*. 7.3). Those who could not pay were excluded from the mess, and hence from citizen rights. Unlike the *eisphorai*, the mess dues were

Ch. 6. Public rights over private property

a permanent element of taxation which could not be evaded, being assessed per (adult male) head rather than on amount of property and supported by the severest of sanctions.

A tax on agricultural produce was far from unique within ancient Greece (Isager and Skydsgaard 1992, 139–41). Herodotus' report (6.46) that the Thasians were 'exempt from any tax on crops' (*ateleis karpōn*), due to the magnitude of their other revenues, implies that this tax was regular in less fortunate states – as indeed it became on Thasos after the Athenians deprived them of their mainland territory and mines (*IG* xii, Suppl. 349; Salviat 1986, 152–3, 181). An annual tithe of produce is also attested in hellenistic Thespiai (Roesch 1982, 298–9). There are even indications of such a tax (in the form of a *pentekostē*, a fiftieth part) in classical Athens, although the scope of its application is unclear.[7] The closest parallel to the Spartan system, in which a produce tax funded common messes, is the situation in Crete (Arist. *Pol.* 1272a12–27). However, whereas at Sparta each citizen provided an equal contribution from his own resources, on Crete the messes were supplied from a public pool of produce and livestock which – Aristotle seems to imply – was sustained from private contributions based, not on a fixed amount, but on a tithe of each citizen's produce.[8] In Aristotle's opinion, the Cretan system was better in that it provided a subsidy for the participation of the poor.

Two sources detail the monthly quantities of produce due from each Spartiate: the late fourth-century philosopher, Dikaiarchos, *Tripolitikos* (*FHG* 2.242, fr. 23, *ap.* Athen. 141c) and Plutarch (*Lyk.* 12.2). Their evidence is summarised in TABLE 4. Despite the apparent differences in the recorded quantities (measured by volume) of *alphita* and wine, the two accounts are fundamentally in agreement. The quantities can be reconciled on the reasonable assumption that Dikaiarchos has converted them to the Attic standard of measures (as is explicitly stated in the case of the *alphita*), whereas Plutarch records them in the Spartans' own measures, which were greater in volume, being based upon the Aiginetan standard (Hultsch 1882, 500, 533–5; Viedebantt 1917, 69–70; Cartledge 1979, 170–1; Figueira 1984, 89). This hypothesis is supported by two considerations. First, there is a consistent ratio of approximately 3:2 between the quantities given by Dikaiarchos and by Plutarch for both *alphita* and wine.[9] Secondly, the quantities of foodstuffs given by Plutarch

TABLE 4. The monthly mess dues.

	Dikaiarchos	*Plutarch*
Barley flour (*alphita*)	About 1½ Attic *medimnoi*	1 *medimnos*
Wine	11 or 12 *choes*	8 *choes*
Cheese	(Amount unspecified)	5 *minai*
Figs	(Amount unspecified)	2½ *minai*
For the *opsōnia*	About 10 Aiginetan obols	A small amount of coinage

are precise figures, as one would expect of the authentic Lakonian measures; whereas Dikaiarchos' figures contain a degree of latitude consonant with the fact that, when translated into a different system, they did not produce whole numbers of Attic measures. Comparison of the figures for the quantities of wine indicates, in fact, that the precise ratio of Attic to Lakonian measures was *a little less* than 3:2.[10] This suggests that the exact ratio of Attic measures to Lakonian/Aiginetan measures was identical to the 10:7 ratio between the Euboic-Attic and Aiginetan standards of weights and coinage.[11] That would explain why Dikaiarchos havers between the figures of 11 and 12 *choes* of wine, since on this ratio eight Lakonian *choes* is equivalent to 11.43 *choes* in Attic measures. The correspondence of Plutarch's figures with the testimony of Dikaiarchos, a pupil of Aristotle, indicates that, unlike other statistical evidence in his *Lykourgos*, his account of the mess dues constitutes genuinely fourth-century evidence. Probably both accounts derive from the Aristotelian *Polity of the Lakedaimonians* (Figueira 1984, 88–9).

The striking feature of the mess dues is that they are remarkably high in relation to ration figures from elsewhere in Greek antiquity and to modern estimates of human energy requirements. A monthly due of one Lakonian *medimnos* of barley meal (*alphita*) would, on a 30-day month, provide 1.6 Lakonian *choinikes* (2.48 litres) per day. The most plausible assumptions concerning the modern weight and energy values of ancient grain crops suggest that this would supply 5,294 daily calories.[12] This figure far exceeds, not only the 2,803 calories of the ancient Greek 'standard' ration of one Attic *choinix* of wheat per day,[13] but even the generous modern FAO recommended energy requirement of 3,822 calories per day for an 'exceptionally active' adult male. Moreover, the figure takes no account of the other foodstuffs among the compulsory dues, which together would add over 1,100 more calories;[14] nor does it include the *opsōnia* or the *epaiklon* (extra voluntary donations of wheaten bread and prepared dishes containing game and olive oil).[15] Even without the *opsōnia* and *epaiklon*, the daily calorific value of the mess dues comprised some 6,429 calories. Each citizen was hence required to contribute a large surplus of foodstuffs over what he needed for his personal consumption.

TABLE 5. Ancient Greek measures
(with modern litre equivalents, according to Lakonian/Attic measures).

Dry measures	Liquid measures
1 *medimnos* (74.54/52.18 litres) = 48 *choinikes*	
	1 *metrētēs* (55.54/38.88 litres) = 12 *choes*
	1 *chous* (4.63/3.24 litres) = 12 *kotylai*
1 *choinix* (1.55/1.087 litres) = 4 *kotylai*	
1 *kotylē* (0.39/0.27 litres)	1 *kotylē* (0.39/0.27 litres) = 2 *hemikotylia*
	1 *hemikotylion* (0.19/0.14 litres)

The mess dues were, therefore, in part a levy on the agricultural produce Spartiates received from their estates.

The size of the mess rations
How large was the surplus of each citizen's contribution over the food he actually consumed in the mess? The evidence suggests that there was a specified ration laid down by the polis – at least as regards the main staple, grain. Xenophon (*Lak. Pol.* 5.3) comments that 'the amount of *sitos* he [sc. Lykourgos] allowed them was just enough to prevent them getting too much or too little to eat'. (*Sitos* here means either 'grain' or 'food' as opposed to 'drink'.) It is *a priori* likely, on political grounds, that the polis would want to ensure equality of basic consumption between messes, rather than leaving consumption at the discretion of each mess. Furthermore, the evidence of Herodotus cited below suggests familiarity with the practice of providing fixed rations in peacetime, at least for the kings.

Unfortunately, no source provides a direct statement of the size of a citizen's daily ration. There are, however, two sources from which it might be deduced. The first is Herodotus' statement (6.57.3) concerning the prerogatives of the kings:

> If the kings do not come to the meal (*deipnon*), each has sent to him at his house two *choinikes* of *alphita* and a *kotylē* of wine; when they are present, they are given double of everything (παρεοῦσι δὲ διπλήσια πάντα δίδοσθαι).[16] And they are honoured the same when they are invited to a meal at a private house.

The second source is Thucydides' statement (4.16) that the daily rations permitted under terms of truce to the Spartan troops trapped on the island of Sphakteria in 425 comprised two Attic *choinikes* of *alphita*, two *kotylai* of wine and some meat.

The Herodotus passage is sometimes interpreted to mean that the king's mess ration was double the quantity of food he received when staying at home, i.e. that in the mess he received four *choinikes* of *alphita* and two *kotylai* of wine (Figueira 1984, 91; Murray 1991, 91; cf. Michell 1964, 289). According to this interpretation, the differential rations were intended as a penalty for absence and an incentive for attendance, in the form of a second portion with which to honour another citizen (Xen. *Lak. Pol.* 15.4; Cartledge 1987, 108). Since we know that a king's portion at the mess – as also at public sacrifices and even when entertained at a private house – was double that of other citizens (Hdt. 6.57.1, 3; cf. 7.103; Xen. *Lak. Pol.* 15.4), this interpretation would imply that the daily mess ration for ordinary citizens was two *choinikes* of *alphita* and a *kotylē* of wine, the same as the king's home ration.

This interpretation however, fails on the grounds that two *choinikes* per day is impossibly high. Since Herodotus' account of the kings' prerogatives, as we have already seen (ch. 3), draws upon a more or less official Spartiate source and followed its wording closely, the measures he gives are surely authentic Lakonian measures.[17] The postulated ration therefore exceeds the daily mess contribution of 1.6 Lakonian *choinikes*, implying the impossible conclusion that each Spartiate consumed more *alphita* than he contributed. Furthermore, since the mess dues themselves exceeded any plausible food ration, one can hardly believe that each Spartiate consumed a still larger quantity.

Superficially, it might seem attractive to suggest that Herodotus' figures are expressed not in Lakonian but in Attic measures. This mess ration would be identical to the two Attic *choinikes* of *alphita* permitted to the troops on Sphakteria (Thuc. 4.16); and, at 2.174 litres, it falls within the daily contribution of 1.6 Lakonian *choinikes* (2.48 litres). The suggestion is implausible, however, on several grounds. First, it does violence to Herodotus' text in implying that he translated Lakonian measures into Attic, but neglected to inform his readers. Secondly, 2 Attic *choinikes*, at a ratio of 7:10, does not translate into a meaningful number in Lakonian measures (2.857 Lakonian *choinikes*). Thirdly, at 4,641 calories per day, without adding the other foodstuffs, it still constitutes an unrealistically high level of regular peacetime calorie consumption. Fourthly, the circumstances on Sphakteria, where 2 Attic *choinikes* constituted a whole day's ration (with only wine and meat in addition) for besieged troops with no backup resources, were vastly different from those at home, where the mess ration covered only the evening meal and the messmates also consumed a wide range of additional foods. The rations on Sphakteria can, I shall argue later, offer a guide to Spartiate mess rations, but not as an exact equivalence.

The notion that the king's mess ration was double his home ration, and therefore that the mess rations of ordinary Spartiates were identical to the king's home ration, is therefore untenable. There is, however, a better way of understanding Herodotus' text, and especially the critical phrase διπλήσια πάντα ('double of everything'). To what precisely does the phrase refer? The phrase appears a little earlier (6.57.1) in a more complete formulation, referring to the king's rations at the meal following a public sacrifice: διπλήσια νέμοντας ἑκατέρῳ τὰ πάντα ἢ τοῖσι ἄλλοισι δαιτυμόνεσι ('each having twice as much of everything as the other guests'). Here the king's double ration is contrasted with the single ration received by other Spartiates, not with a different context in which he received only a single portion. The shorter version, διπλήσια πάντα, at 6.57.3 should mean the same: simply that in the mess (and when entertained privately) the kings received double the portions of other Spartiates. As Macan noted over a century ago (1895, i.317), the word διπλήσια describes the relationship between the kings' rations and those of other citizens, not that between the kings' rations at the mess and at home. Herodotus' text, however, clearly intends some contrast between home and mess. The key, I suggest, lies in the second word of the phrase, πάντα, 'everything', which is also stressed in the more complete formulation at 6.57.1. Herodotus' contrast is between the limited range of foodstuffs (staple items only, *alphita* and wine) which the kings received at home and the full range of rations (cheese, figs, *opsōnia* and *epaiklon*) they received in the mess. This interpretation retains the idea of an incentive to attend the mess, since the wider, more attractive range of foodstuffs enhanced not merely the kings' personal diet but also their capacity to honour others through their second portion.

What implications does this reading of Herodotus' text have for the size of the mess rations of the kings and of ordinary Spartiates? There are two alternatives. From the lack of contrast made between the size of the kings' rations at home and in the mess, one could argue either (i) that the rations of *alphita* and wine were identical in both situations, or (ii) that the passage permits no deduction about the size of mess rations. On the first argument, the kings' mess rations would be two *choinikes* of *alphita* and a *kotylē* of wine, as at home. Hence the mess ration of ordinary Spartiates would be a *choinix* of *alphita* and a *hemikotylion* (half a *kotylē*) of wine. How plausible are these figures?

The figure of one *choinix* for the ordinary citizen *alphita* ration is certainly reasonable. It fits well within the 1.6 *choinikes* contributed per day. It is also plausible in relation to ancient and modern estimates of human energy requirements. A Lakonian *choinix* (1.55 litres) of *alphita* would supply around 3,309 calories, above the 2,803 calories of the ancient Greek 'standard' daily ration, but just below the FAO recommended energy requirement of 3,337 calories for a 'very active' adult male. Even when the wine, cheese and figs are added, the diet, at 3,690 calories, falls below the 3,822 calories for an 'exceptionally active' adult male. A mess ration of 1.55 litres also fits with the *alphita* ration on Sphakteria. At two Attic *choinikes*, or 2.174 litres, the latter was almost exactly 40% higher, as was appropriate for an entire day's supply without backup resources.

The figure of a *hemikotylion* (only 0.19 litre) for the wine ration, however, is more problematic. It is a minuscule amount compared with consumption rates elsewhere. Even when diluted with water at the common ratios of 1:2½ or 1:3 (Athen. 426b–427c), it amounts to only 0.665–0.76 litres. (Compare the 3 litres per person which can perhaps be inferred from the fourth-century comedian Euboulos' description of a relatively temperate *symposion*.)[18] Admittedly, Spartiate messes were noted for their abstemiousness (Kritias frs. 6, 33, Diels-Kranz; Xen. *Lak. Pol.* 5.4–7; Plato, *Laws* 637a, 639d–e; Fisher 1989, 27–31). However, a *hemikotylion* per day is only 1¼ *choes* per month out of the monthly dues of 8 *choes*; it seems unlikely that barely 15% of the dues was consumed in the mess. It is also improbably small compared with the wine ration on Sphakteria which, at 2 Attic *kotylai* (0.54 litre) per day, was nearly three times larger.

There is, in fact, good reason why, unlike the *alphita* ration, the ration of wine that the king received when dining at home should bear no relation to the ration in the mess. The structure of commensality at the mess involved a clear distinction between the communal meal, which was taken first (no doubt with a little wine), and a subsequent session of drinking and eating various lighter foods (Dikaiarchos, *Tripolitikos*, *ap.* Athen. 141a–c; Murray 1991, 92). The latter session was the Spartan version of the *symposion* of other poleis.[19] When dining at home, a king was not participating in male sympotic sociability. Hence he received neither his full ration of wine nor the other light foods characteristic of the *symposion*. In contrast, his double *alphita* ration, not being part of the sympotic session, was given in full. Hence, just as the absence of cheese and figs from a king's rations at home contrasts with their presence in the sympotic sociability of the mess, so the size of the wine ration in the mess cannot be deduced from the small quantity provided for a king at home.

In view of this conclusion, two possibilities remain regarding the size of the wine ration of ordinary Spartiates. One possibility is that it can be deduced from the size of the ration on Sphakteria. I have already suggested that the Sphakteria *alphita* ration exceeded the normal mess ration by some 40%. If the Sphakteria wine ration of 2 Attic *kotylai* (or 1.4 Lakonian *kotylai*) was also 40% higher, the wine ration at the mess will have been precisely one Lakonian *kotylē*. It would be logical that the size of both *alphita* and wine rations at Sphakteria were calculated at the same ratio to the normal mess rations; and it may be no mere coincidence that this ratio produces mess rations of exactly one Lakonian *choinix* of *alphita* and one Lakonian *kotylē* of wine.[20] Moreover, the figure of one *kotylē* (0.39 litre) is more realistic for Spartan circumstances. Although still, comparatively speaking, rather low, in keeping with the Spartan ethic of sobriety, it is not a negligible alcoholic intake, representing at standard Greek dilution ratios approximately 1.4–1.6 litres, the equivalent in terms of both liquid intake and alcoholic strength of almost 3 pints of modern beer (cf. Murray 1991, 91, 101 n. 24).

The other possibility is that there was no fixed limit to the amount of wine a Spartiate could drink at his mess. According to Kritias (fr. 33, Diels-Kranz), 'the Lakedaimonians drink, each, the cup placed at his side, and the wine-pourer <pours in> just so much as he <wishes> to drink'. Xenophon (*Lak. Pol.* 5.4) too comments that Lykourgos 'allowed each person to drink when he was thirsty'. Both writers imply a degree of individual discretion; but this operated within a setting which imposed strict social sanctions against excessive drinking. Even without a fixed limit, it is therefore unlikely that an average intake would have much exceeded 2 litres, about half a litre or 1¼–1½ *kotylai* of undiluted wine.

Use of the surplus levy of produce

We can now assess the quantity of surplus produce levied through the compulsory mess dues. The *alphita* dues were 1 Lakonian *medimnos* (48 Lakonian *choinikes*) per month, or 1.6 *choinikes* per day. A mess ration of one *choinix* per day left a surplus of 0.6 *choinikes* (0.93 litre) per day, or 18 *choinikes* (27.9 litres) per month. The surplus levy therefore made up 37.5% of the total dues.

The wine surplus was probably even higher. The dues were 8 Lakonian *choes* (96 Lakonian *kotylai*) per month, or 3.2 *kotylai* per day. A ration of one *kotylē* per day would have left a surplus of 2.2 *kotylai* (0.86 litre), or 5½ *choes* (25.6 litres) per month, some 56% of the wine dues. A daily consumption of 1½ *kotylai* would have left a surplus of 1.7 *kotylai* (0.66 litre). Whether the cheese and fig dues and the 10 obols for the *opsōnia* also included a levy element is uncertain. The daily amounts involved (105 g of cheese, 52½ g of figs and one-third of an obol) are so modest that it is perhaps unlikely. The mess dues therefore involved a surplus levy per citizen per month of around 28 litres of *alphita* and some 20–26 litres of wine – the equivalent of over 2,500 calories per day, around three-quarters the energy requirements of a very active adult male. In *alphita*, the most important staple, each messmate contributed a surplus of over half (0.6) his daily ration. Even if we allow for deterioration and wastages in food storage, the surplus levies could still have fed a number of men roughly half the size of the entire citizen body: supplying for each mess of about 15 men (Plut. *Lyk*. 12.2) another 7½ daily rations.

Were these surpluses used within the mess or treated as a common fund for the polis? The polis probably took at least part. The mess rations of some citizens were provided at public expense: the kings, the four Pythioi (Hdt. 6.57.2; Xen. *Lak. Pol*. 15.4–5) and probably also the five ephors, whose special mess also entertained foreign ambassadors (*Apoph. Lak., Anon*. no. 13 = Plut. *Mor*. 232f–233a; cf. Plut. *Kleom*. 8.1). In addition, on the first and seventh days of every month each king was given from the public treasury a *medimnos* of *alphita* and a *tetartē* of wine for use in their ritual duties. These demands, however, will have consumed only a fraction of the available surplus. For example, the total peacetime requirement from these sources of about 582 *choinikes* of *alphita* could have been met by the surplus contributions from 33 citizens.

Another public demand was supplies for the army. During campaigns the king's staff was maintained by the state: the polemarchs (up to six in number in the early fourth century), the three tent-companions, and an unspecified number of seers, doctors, *aulos*-players and volunteers (Xen. *Lak. Pol*. 13.1, 7). Spartan armies also used to carry at least some supplies for ordinary soldiers (Thuc. 2.10, 23; 3.1; cf. Xen. *Lak. Pol*. 11.3; Lazenby 1994, 11). The source of these supplies, however, is unclear. At Athens soldiers were expected to provide their own supplies for the first few days of a campaign, but afterwards were either issued rations or given pay to buy food (Lazenby 1994, 11–12). Centralised provision of rations is also suggested for the Lakedaimonian army in Xenophon's reference to 'those who carried provisions for the *mora*' during its attack on Peiraion in 390 (*Hell*. 4.5.4). Any food provided centrally would surely come from the surplus levy. So too, in part, may any supplies which Spartiate soldiers provided themselves: since campaign rations, as on Sphakteria, were probably larger than at home, individual soldiers perhaps drew upon their mess dues over and above their normal rations. At times the polis also needed to supply non-Spartiate soldiers, such as the majority of the troops on Sphakteria (Thuc. 4.38). This surely became increasingly common as non-Spartiates (such as *perioikoi*, *hypomeiones* and *neodamōdeis*) formed a growing part of Spartan armies in the late fifth and early fourth centuries. We should also recall the need to feed helot batmen: on Sphakteria they were provided for at half the soldiers' rations. Military provisioning may, consequently, have been at times a significant drain on the surplus levies, although given the normally brief duration and seasonal character of most campaigns it is unlikely to have accounted for anything like the entire produce available.

A further potential source of public demand suggested by some scholars is the supply of food for the boys' messes in the public upbringing (e.g. Kahrstedt 1919, 284; Michell 1964, 288; Fisher 1989, 34). The available evidence, however, does not support this idea, but suggests rather that each citizen family was responsible for providing for its boys. The only passage which directly mentions the provision of rations in the upbringing is inconclusive.[21] But our information regarding the category of boys known as *mothakes* – sons of poor or disfranchised citizens who were sponsored through the public upbringing by being adopted as the foster-brothers of sons of wealthy families (Phylarchos, *FGrH* 81F43, *ap.* Athen. 271e–f; Aelian, *VH* 12.43) – indicates that the material support of these wealthy families was an essential element without which the *mothakes*' participation in the upbringing would have been impossible (Hodkinson 1997b, 55–62). This suggests that the provision of subsistence for boys in the upbringing was a private not public responsibility.

What about possible uses of the surplus dues within the mess itself? One use was surely for the meals of invited guests. Messes which contained leading Spartiates probably often received foreign visitors, especially guest-friends, including regular visitors from allied Peloponnesian poleis and exiles (such as Alkibiades) on lengthy stays.[22] A more regular category of invitees, who will have attended every mess not just those of the elite, was teenage youths. Xenophon treats the presence of *paidiskoi* at the mess as normal practice (*Lak. Pol.* 3.5; cf. Plut. *Lyk.* 12.4). Their attendance was probably part of the scrutiny which youths underwent before the vote on their admission to full membership at age 20 (Plut. *Lyk.* 12.5). Boys were probably normally introduced into their future mess, starting as early as age 15.[23] Since the maintenance of a mess of 15 men aged 20–59 requires a new recruit about every three years, each mess probably normally contained two invited youths, hence accounting for two of the postulated 7½ surplus rations.

It has been suggested that certain members of Sparta's subordinate populations also received food from the mess (Figueira 1984, 97, 106–7; Fisher 1989, 34–6). The brigading of non-Spartiates, such as *perioikoi* and *hypomeiones*, into the Lakedaimonian army from the late fifth century may have prompted messes to select some of these comrades to share their commensality. This would apply particularly if non-Spartiates fought in the same *enomōtiai* as citizens; but we lack details of precisely how they were integrated. Another, more radical, suggestion is that the surplus mess dues were distributed to certain helots, especially each messmate's helot personal attendant. Certainly, helots are attested at the mess. The wine-pourer who filled each Spartiate's separate cup (Kritias fr. 33, Diels-Kranz, *ap.* Athen. 463e) may have been a helot.[24] Helots presumably also performed the menial tasks involved in servicing the mess. Finally, helots were forced to drink strong wine and then exhibited in the messes (Plut. *Lyk.* 28.4). This practice may help explain the large wine surpluses revealed earlier, although the frequency of the procedure is obscure.[25] The idea that the surplus produce went to helot personal attendants could be supported by analogy with the situation on Sphakteria, where the batmen also received a ration. Indeed, the proportion of their ration – half the soldiers' ration – if applied to the mess rations, would account for most (0.5 out of the 0.6 *choinikes*) of the daily surplus of *alphita*. Despite these arguments, however, there is no hard evidence that the bulk of the surplus levy did go to such helots. The provision of rations at Sphakteria, where there was no alternative means of supply, is not an exact analogy; and the very fact that an equivalent ration would consume such a high proportion of the surplus *alphita* makes the thesis hard to reconcile with the other attested claims to its use. Even if each messmate was personally attended by his own helot servant – a point by no means certain – it need not imply that these helots were fed from the resources of the mess, rather than from the private resources of their masters. Whether helots were substantial consumers of the surplus dues, other than as enforced drunkards, must remain uncertain.

A full solution to the destination of the surplus mess dues is clearly not possible. It is noticeable, however, that of the various potential uses suggested above, there is no hint of any redistributive purpose. Indeed, some of the above uses – the funding of the royal messes and of the meals of visiting guest-friends of leading Spartiates – benefited the richest citizens. Other uses would have been economically and socially neutral. But there is no suggestion in our evidence that the surplus foodstuffs were used to fund the mess dues of poor citizens who were experiencing difficulty in producing their compulsory contributions.

Communal use of private property

Besides taxes on landed property and levies upon agricultural produce, there were also circumstances in which a citizen's remaining property and resources might be liable to communal use. The most detailed discussion of this practice is provided by Xenophon (*Lak. Pol.* 6.3–4).

> He [sc. Lykourgos] made it possible for someone to use another man's servants in case of need; and he made hunting dogs common property to this extent, that those who need them invite their owner to the hunt; and if he does not have the time

himself, he sends them gladly. And they make use of horses in a similar manner: for a man who falls ill or needs a carriage or wishes to get somewhere quickly, if he sees a horse anywhere, takes it, uses it and returns it in good condition. He [Lykourgos] also put into effect a practice which is not the custom elsewhere. For in cases when hunters out late are in need of food but have none prepared, he prescribed that those who have provisions should leave their surplus behind and those who are in need, having broken the seals and taken what they needed, should leave the rest behind after re-sealing it. Thanks to sharing with one another in this way, even those who have but little receive a share of everything in the country (μετέχουσι πάντων τῶν ἐν τῇ χώρᾳ) whenever they need anything.

Xenophon presents these measures as a general right for every citizen to use certain belongings of other citizens. How valid is this presentation? Ollier (1934, 40–1), as we have seen (ch. 2), has suggested that Xenophon's supposed communal rights of use were an exaggeration of typical soldierly sharing with comrades (cf. also Link 1998, 93). The implication is that they took place largely between messmates and close friends rather between citizens in general, and that a certain degree of permission was required. Although there are no evidential grounds for this claim,[26] the extravagant nature of Xenophon's conclusion was noted above. His instances of shared use hardly provided poor citizens with 'a share of everything in the country'. With the trivial exception of provisions for hunting expeditions, the poor were not given access to the large amounts and range of produce owned by wealthy landowners. None of the measures involved any element of redistribution or surrender of resources by the rich. Moreover, the instances cited are of very different levels of significance. The arrangements for reserve supplies when hunting were a matter of safety and convenience rather than of genuine property-sharing; similarly with the right to use another's helots, since all citizens already possessed helot household servants. In contrast, by no means all citizens owned hunting dogs and horses, and the ability to use a wealthy man's animals may have helped to soften a significant status divide. Even here, however, there are important differences. The borrowing of horses appears as an impersonal matter, involving no prior arrangement between the two parties; moreover, the purposes mentioned are of purely private concern. The borrowing of hunting dogs, on the other hand, was a social affair, with a personal approach from the borrower involving an invitation to a shared hunting expedition. Hunting, moreover, was not just a private pastime, but an officially-recommended activity for mature Spartiates to maintain their military fitness and one of the few justifiable excuses for missing the common mess (Xen. *Lak. Pol.* 4.7; Plut. *Lyk.* 12.2).

These practices of shared use are also mentioned by Aristotle (*Pol.* 1263a30–39) in a discussion of property arrangements in which he advocates a system of private ownership combined with communal use:

> Even now, this sort of arrangement exists in some states in an outline form, which implies that it is not impossible; and in the well-run ones particularly it exists in

part and in part might come about. For, although each individual does have his own private property, he makes available some things to be used by his friends, while he has the use of others communally. For example, in Lakedaimon they use each others' slaves practically as their own, and horses and dogs too; and if they need food on a journey, they turn to the fields across their territory ([ἐν] τοῖς ἀγροῖς κατὰ τὴν χώραν). Clearly then it is better for property to be private, but for its use to be communal.

Aristotle's comments mostly follow those of Xenophon in both order and content, but there are certain divergences. For Xenophon's details regarding the co-operative arrangements for provisioning hunting expeditions, Aristotle substitutes a more generalised right on any journey to take produce from anyone's fields. It is unlikely that Aristotle is reporting authentic information omitted by Xenophon. The latter would surely have mentioned this right, had it existed, as justification for his extravagant conclusion. The fact that part of Aristotle's description (κατὰ τὴν χώραν) echoes the words of Xenophon's conclusion (πάντων τῶν ἐν τῇ χώρᾳ) suggests that Aristotle has loosely treated Xenophon's unsubstantiated claim as a statement of fact. A similar procedure is evident in his summary statement regarding slaves, horses and dogs – which transforms the specific circumstances of borrowing detailed by Xenophon into the loose assertion that 'they use each others' slaves practically as their own'. Aristotle's imprecision derives from his use of Spartan arrangements to illustrate his thesis concerning the practicability of communal use of private property; in the process he simplifies them to the point of being misleading. However, even Aristotle concedes that these arrangements fell short of a proper system of communal use, for Sparta appears as his example of a well-run state in which such a system currently existed only in part. Thus interpreted, the evidence of Aristotle concurs with our earlier conclusion concerning the limited nature of the provisions for communal use of private property and their symbolic rather than material significance.

The theft of food by Spartiate boys

Another practice of symbolic importance for the assertion of public rights over private property was the practice of theft by Spartiate boys. This practice is mentioned by several sources. The main classical description is given by Xenophon (*Lak. Pol.* 2.6–9) at the end of his account of the meagre rations given to the boys:

> On the other hand, to prevent them suffering from hunger, although he did not allow them to take what they wanted without effort, he did permit them to steal some things to relieve their hunger. I imagine everyone is aware that he did not let them get food by trickery because he was unable to provide for them. Clearly, a would-be thief must stay awake at night, and by day must practise deception and lie in wait, as well as have spies ready if he is going to seize anything. So clearly it was Lykourgos' wish that by training the boys in all these ways he would make

them more resourceful at feeding themselves and better fighters. Someone might ask then, if he considered theft a good thing, why on earth did he inflict many lashes on the boy who was caught? My answer is because – as in every other branch of instruction – people chastise anyone who does not respond satisfactorily. So they [sc. the Spartans] too punish those who are caught as being incompetent thieves. And after making it a matter of honour for them to snatch as many cheeses as possible from Orthia, he commanded others to whip them, wishing to demonstrate thereby the point that a short period of pain may be compensated by the enjoyment of long-lasting prestige.

In this passage Xenophon presents two practices: the theft of foodstuffs to alleviate hunger, which he presents as a regular activity, and a specific ritual at the sanctuary of Artemis Orthia involving the seizure of cheeses. Note that these are clearly separate phenomena, between which Xenophon moves in a rather loose chain of thought.

Xenophon mentions the theft of foodstuffs elsewhere, in his *Anabasis* (4.6.14–15), in a speech in which he himself addresses the Spartan Cheirisophos.

For, as I hear, Cheirisophos, you Lakedaimonians, at least those of you who belong to the *homoioi*, practise stealing even from childhood and count it not disgraceful but honourable to steal whatever is not forbidden by law. And in order that you may steal with all possible skill and may try not to be caught at it, it is the law among you that, if you are caught stealing, you are flogged.[27]

The practice is also singled out by Isokrates in his criticism of reprehensible Spartan customs.

If I mention only a single one – one which they cherish most and by which they set most store – I think that I can put before you their whole manner of life. For every day they send out their boys, from the very cradle, as it were, with such companions as each may prefer, ostensibly to hunt, but in reality to steal the property of the people who live in the fields. In this practice, those who are caught are punished with fines and blows, while those who have accomplished the greatest number of thefts and have been able to escape detection enjoy a higher esteem among their fellow youths than the others, and when they reach manhood, provided they remain true to the ways which they practised in youth, they are in line for the most important offices (*Panathenaikos* 211–12; cf. 218–19).

The final classical reference appears in a passage of Herakleides Lembos (fr. 373.13, Dilts), which derives from the Aristotelian *Polity of the Lakedaimonians* (*Lak. Pol.,* = fr. 611.13, Rose).

They bring up their children on empty stomachs to train them to be able to endure hunger. They also train them to steal and they beat whoever is caught, in order that from this treatment they should be able to work hard and be alert among the enemy.

This passage parallels Xenophon's treatment in its stress on the connection with military training; but it differs in its reference to an active training in stealing rather than the more neutral permission to steal referred to in Xenophon's *Lak. Pol.*

The practice also appears in two later sources. According to the late hellenistic *Instituta Laconica* (no. 12 = Plut. *Mor.* 237e):

> The boys steal whatever provisions they can, learning to make their raids adroitly upon people who are asleep or keeping guard carelessly. The penalty for getting caught is a beating and no food. For the dinner allowed them is meagre, so that through coping with want by their own initiative, they may be compelled to be daring and cunning.

The final source is Plutarch's *Life of Lykourgos* (17.3–4). Plutarch states that the *eirēn* in charge of the boys,

> has them serve him in his meals like servants. The burlier boys he instructs to bring wood, the slighter ones to collect garden-herbs. They steal what they fetch, some of them entering gardens, others slipping into the men's messes with a fine mixture of cunning and caution. If a boy is caught, he receives many lashes of the whip for proving to be to be a clumsy, unskilled thief. The boys steal whatever provisions they can, learning to make their raids adroitly upon people who are asleep or keeping guard carelessly. The penalty for getting caught is a beating and no food. For the dinner allowed them is meagre, so that through coping with want by their own initiative, they may be compelled to be daring and cunning.

Note that the second half of this passage repeats word for word the text of the *Instituta Laconica*. Plutarch subsequently continues with a discussion of the purposes of the boys' spare diet. He then recounts an anecdote drawn from the *Apophthegmata Lakōnika* (Anon. no. 35 = Plut. *Mor.* 234a–b) of a boy who, in his efforts to conceal a stolen fox cub, allowed the animal to tear out his bowels rather than have his theft detected, concluding the story with the statement that 'this tale is not incredible, judging from the ephebes today. I have witnessed many of them dying under the lashes they received at the altar of Orthia.'

Like Xenophon, Plutarch links his discussion of the regular acts of stealing with description of a ritual at Artemis Orthia; and, as in Xenophon's account, the two are clearly separate phenomena. It has long been established that the flagellation ceremony witnessed by Plutarch was a Roman-imperial institution fundamentally different from the classical cheese-stealing ceremony mentioned by Xenophon (e.g. Rose 1929; 1941, 2; Kennell 1995, 79). So too Plutarch's account of the regular acts of stealing describes contemporary practice which differed in important respects from the practice in classical times. His description is given entirely in the present tense, which he normally reserves for practices current in his own day (Kennell 1995, 24). In Xenophon's account the purpose of the boys' theft was to augment their own meagre rations, and this same general line is followed by the passage from the hellenistic *Instituta Laconica*. Although in the second part of the passage quoted above Plutarch repeats the exact words of the *Instituta*, the first part describes thieving with a somewhat different purpose. His opening remarks concern thefts of wood and garden-herbs, not for the boys' own provisioning, as in all the earlier sources, but for a meal which the boys served to the *eirēn*.[28] Furthermore, whereas the thefts described in earlier sources were undertaken through the personal initiative of each boy, the thefts in the first part of Plutarch's account were ordered by the *eirēn*. This opening part of the passage is clearly a description of current practice within the Spartan upbringing of Plutarch's own day, to which he then appends the account of the *Instituta*, which in its original form related to classical upbringing. The two parts of the passage are not even properly integrated, since each contains a separate description of the punishment given to boys who were caught. In studying the practice of classical times, we must therefore disregard Plutarch's evidence, which has nothing new or authentic to add.

All the classical sources describe the boys' theft of food as a regular occurrence; Isokrates even says that it took place every day. Although most scholars accept this description,[29] some doubt whether the thefts were as regular and significant as the sources imply (Ollier 1934, 28; Kennell 1995, 122–3). Kennell argues that they were a purely ritual activity which occurred only during religious festivals, citing the cheese-stealing contest as an example. Xenophon, however, portrays that contest as distinct from the normal practice of theft. According to Kennell, Xenophon's evidence is contradicted by the anecdote in the *Apophthegmata Lakōnika* about the boy who died concealing the stolen fox cub. This source states that the theft took place 'when the time came for free children, according to custom, to steal whatever they could', thereby implying that the theft was not part of everyday life. The anecdote and its contents, however, are dubiously relevant to classical practice. The stealing of a fox, a non-food item, bears no relation to the hunger-relieving thefts described by the classical sources. Moreover, the anecdote's typically Stoic emphasis upon endurance under extreme circumstances suggests its invention in hellenistic times among the early Stoa. It cannot be used to overturn the unanimous evidence of earlier sources.

Neither is it plausible, as Kennell suggests, to dismiss Xenophon's and the Aristotelian school's association of these thefts with military training as an unwarranted 'rationalisation' of ritual practice. Rather, their accounts accurately represent the process of conscious, rational transformation towards military ends which was applied to all Spartan institutions during the late archaic and classical periods (cf. Murray 1990, 9–10). As for Isokrates' evidence, it is not, as claimed by Ollier (1934, 28), simply derivative upon Xenophon's accounts. It contains original elements, such as the rural location of the thefts and the association of success at stealing with public esteem and future promotion, the last insight showing a perceptive comprehension of the impact of personal achievement in the upbringing. Although Isokrates' evidence contains certain exaggerations, as one would expect from partisan criticism, these do not justify dismissing his testimony.[30] The evidence of the Aristotelian *Lak. Pol.*, too, is independent testimony, which – as we have seen – does not simply repeat Xenophon. Given this diverse range of independent evidence, we should regard the legitimate, regular stealing of foodstuffs by Spartan boys as authentic classical practice.

There remains, nevertheless, a reluctance to accept this conclusion on the grounds of the practice's alleged impracticability or threat to social order. Ollier argues that it would have prompted such security measures by other citizens that thefts became well-nigh impossible. Modern experience shows, however, the difficulties of preventing juvenile theft – even with the greater security offered by modern buildings and intruder detection systems – when stealing becomes a part of youth culture, let alone when it is sanctioned by adult society and successful thieves receive official approbation. Kennell, in contrast, thinks that 'either the city would have degenerated into anarchy or the act of stealing would have become a counterfeit, with food set aside especially for boys to filch'. It is unclear, however, that petty pilfering of foodstuffs would have had such a dramatic effect on Spartan society, especially if Isokrates is right that it was focused on (helot and perioikic) farmers in the countryside. Kennell's argument seems over-dependent on modern norms of social order and the boundaries of tolerable behaviour. Moreover, he ignores the fact – twice stressed by Xenophon – that the practice was carefully regulated through restrictions on which items which could legitimately be stolen (MacDowell 1986, 59). The boys' thefts were limited to 'some things' (ἔστιν ἅ) which would relieve their hunger (*Lak. Pol.* 2.6); they could steal only 'whatever is not forbidden by law' (*Anab.* 4.6.14). Hence, although the practice constituted another symbol of communal rights over private possessions, its practical impact was, like the other rights of communal use, surely limited in scope.

In this chapter we have seen that the Spartan polis drew upon the private property of its citizens through a variety of measures. Collectively, these measures established a certain level of public and communal rights. Yet, with one exception, they had little effect on the unequal distribution of property. The mess dues were symbolically important in confirming and justifying the Spartiate's right to share the common meal which signified his membership of the citizen body. They also imposed a significant material burden, going beyond what was necessary for personal consumption. This surplus levy, however, applied equally to every citizen, rich or poor, and some of the foodstuffs went to wealthy citizens such as the kings and the hosts of foreign guest-friends. The sharing of access to helots and hunting provisions and the pilfering of foodstuffs by Spartan boys were also symbolically significant in establishing rights of communal use; but they did not have any redistributive effect. Only the communal use of horses and hunting dogs operated one-sidedly in favour of poor citizens; but even this involved no material loss to their wealthier owners. One can understand, therefore, the strong resistance when *eisphorai* were introduced in the late fifth and early fourth centuries. For the first time, wealthy Spartiates were hit by a progressive tax which, being based on landed property, fell heavily on them in comparison with poorer citizens. Unsurprisingly, to judge from the evidence of Aristotle, the imposition of *eisphorai* did not work. It ran too much against the grain of Spartiate practice, which was too strongly founded upon private and unequal property holding.

Notes

[1] The text of Hdt. 6.59 ('When a king dies…the new king forgives every Spartiate the debts he owes either to the king or to the public treasury') makes a clear distinction between the resources of the king and *to dēmosion*.

[2] Lewis 1959, 243–4; Pleket 1973, 251–2; Roesch 1982, 298–9; Isager and Skydsgaard 1992, 135–43.

[3] Thomsen (1964, 38–44), noting the existence of *eisphorai*, almost invariably a capital tax, in several poleis.

[4] It could, admittedly, be argued that Aristotle mentions the obligation to undertake large-scale wars as simply one example of public expenditure and that his evidence is not formally incompatible with the notion that Spartan *eisphorai* were a regular tax, even in peacetime. More probably, however, Aristotle, writing after the collapse of Sparta's empire, intended his audience to interpret her *eisphorai* as war taxes whose under-payment contributed to her military failure.

[5] The pseudo-Platonic dialogue *Alkibiades I* (123b) does mention a 'royal tribute of no slight amount which the Lakedaimonians pay to their kings'; but whether this applied to Spartiates or only to perioikoi is uncertain.

[6] This section of the chapter has benefited greatly from the advice of Lionel Scott. I am also indebted to him for allowing me advance sight of part of his commentary on Herodotus recently submitted for a PhD at the University of Leeds.

[7] Cf. the comment of Lewis 1959, 244: 'we are too easily inclined to think that a produce-tax disappeared from Attica with the Peisistratids'.

[8] For this interpretation of Aristotle's text, Isager and Skydsgaard 1992, 139; Saunders 1995, 159–60. Aristotle's ascription of a uniform system to the many Cretan poleis has prompted doubts about the authenticity of his information; but there is some independent evidence for such a system in certain Cretan poleis (Isager and Skydsgaard 1992, 139).

[9] Foxhall and Forbes (1982, 58 n. 55) fail to perceive the correspondence between the two accounts. Michell (1964; 287) makes the erroneous claim that Dikaiarchos was using Lakonian measures and Plutarch Attic.

[10] Dikaiarchos' higher figure of 12 *choes* of wine produces an exact 3:2 ratio, but his lower figure of 11 *choes* one of only 1.375:1 (2.75:2).

[11] Johnston 1934, 181. See the Delphic inscription detailing contributions in spring 360 BC (*CID* II, no. 4 I, 21–3 = Tod 1948, no. 140). The inscription offers an impressive parallel to Dikaiarchos' conversion of Lakonian into Attic measures since, whereas the 10:7 ratio is used to convert larger contributions of Attic drachmas into Aiginetan currency, smaller amounts under five drachmas are converted using the more approximate but simpler 3:2 ratio (ibid. 57–66), just as Dikaiarchos does for the *alphita* contributions.

[12] Foxhall and Forbes suggest that a litre of barley flour equates to 0.643kg; and they adopt the FAO figure of 3,320 calories per kg as the most appropriate energy conversion (1982, 44, 46). Hence the daily calorific content of a Spartiate's *alphita* dues was 2.48

x 0.643 x 3,320 = 5,294 calories. This result differs from the calorific content given by Foxhall and Forbes (1982, 58 and table 3, on pp. 86–7), who propose a calorific content of only 3,146 calories per day. Failing to appreciate the correspondence between the accounts of Dikaiarchos and Plutarch, they ignore the former's evidence and, using only Plutarch's figures, treat them as expressed in 'normal' Greek measures (1 *choinix* = 1 litre) rather than on the Aiginetan–Lakonian standard.

13 This 'standard' ration has been interpreted as a 'rule of thumb' grain allowance designed to cover the heaviest individual consumption requirements required in unforeseen circumstances (Foxhall and Forbes 1982, 51–7).

14 Foxhall and Forbes (1982, table on p. 58) calculate, on the basis of FAO studies, that the wine would have provided approximately 568 calories daily, the cheese 106 and the figs 140, making a total between them of 814 calories per day. Their calculations concerning the wine, however, are subject to the same underestimation identified above concerning the *alphita*. The monthly contribution of 8 Lakonian *choes* of wine equates to 37.2 litres = 1.24 litres per day (not 24 litres and 0.8 litre, as in their table); hence its approximate daily calorific content was not 568, but 880.

15 There is no unanimity about the food content of the *opsōnia*. Foxhall and Forbes (1982, 58) regard it as 'salt, olives, relishes, etc.'. In contrast, the Loeb translators of Dikaiarchos/Athenaios and Plutarch render *eis opsōnian* as 'to procure the meat' and 'for such relishes as flesh and fish'. This is to beg the question, since in normal Greek usage *opsa* embraces all non-farinaceous foods. Hence in classical Athenian sources the word *opsōnia* likewise bears only a generic meaning (Antiphanes fr. 184 Kock, *ap.* Athen. 358d; Alexis, fr. 186.2 Kock, *ap.* Athen. 117c–d). As Figueira comments, the *opsōnia* was probably a catch-all item, which might include any of a range of foods, including (but not only) the piece of boiled pork – with the accompanying famous black broth – which Dikaiarchos (*ap.* Athen. 141b) terms the *opson*.

16 At first sight, the word *deipnon* here might appear to refer not to the ordinary mess, but to the meal following a public sacrifice mentioned at 6.57.1. That the text has here changed subject to the daily royal mess is, however, indicated by the immediately preceding sentence, which refers to the Pythioi being fed with the kings at public expense (cf. Xen. *Lak. Pol.* 15.4–5; How and Wells 1912, ii.86). Note that Herodotus' evidence is not vitiated by the incident involving King Agis (probably Agis II, reign 427–400/398 BC), when the polemarchs refused to send him his portions at home (Plut. *Lyk.* 12.3), which suggests that the kings' choice about whether to attend the mess soon ceased to exist. Herodotus is recording traditional privileges from the past.

17 His specific reference to a Lakonian *tetartē* just earlier, at 6.57.2, also suggests that he is using local measures.

18 Euboulos fr. 94 (Hunter), *ap.* Athen. 36b–c. The *symposion* is said to have consumed 3 kraters of wine. I assume a *symposion* of 14 persons (two persons per couch in a standard small *andrōn* containing seven couches: cf. Alkman, fr. 19 Page; Bergquist 1990, 37) and a krater containing 14 litres. I am grateful to Roger Brock for his advice concerning these calculations.

19 I have argued elsewhere (Hodkinson 1997a, 90–1) that the Spartan messes arose in the sixth century as a local transformation of the *symposion*; cf. Bowie 1990, 225 n. 16.

20 The issue is, admittedly, complicated by the fact that the stated Sphakterian rations represent not solely the Spartans' own calculations but were agreed in negotiation with the Athenians. Their specification in Attic measures, which do not translate into round

Lakonian measures, suggests that the Athenians decided their precise size. However, I suggest that these Attic measures were themselves based upon the rations the Spartans themselves had previously supplied before their troops' entrapment. The rations permitted under the truce were, I have argued, 1.4 times the normal mess rations. I suggest that the Spartans had originally supplied their troops with rations 1½ times the normal mess ration, i.e. 1.5 Lakonian *choinikes* of *alphita* and 1.5 Lakonian *kotylai* of wine. Since these translate to 2.14 Attic *choinikes* and 2.14 Attic *kotylai*, respectively, the Athenians simply rounded both rations down to 2 Attic *choinikes* and 2 Attic *kotylai*.

21 According to Xenophon (*Lak. Pol.* 2.5), σῖτόν γε μὴν ἔταξε τοσοῦτον ἔχοντα συμβολεύειν (συμβουλεύειν ABM) τὸν εἴρενα (codd. ἄρρενα), ὡς… ('As for food, he [sc. Lykourgos] required the *eirēn* (*codd.* 'male') to contribute ('recommend' *ABM*) such an amount that they should not be burdened by over-eating'). Notwithstanding the possible use of the word συμβολεύειν, 'contribute' (which, despite its preference by modern editors over the alternative συμβουλεύειν, appears only in the inferior MSS), this passage clearly refers to the daily distribution of foodstuffs to the boys and says nothing about the responsibility for their supply.

22 Cf. the reported attendance at the mess by the philosopher Hekataios of Miletos (*Apoph. Lak.*, Archidamidas no. 2 = Plut. *Mor.* 218b; cf. *Lyk.* 20.2).

23 Cf. Xen. *Hell.* 5.4.25–8, where Kleonymos, who had only recently graduated out of the *paides*, converses with his lover Archidamos in the mess. I accept Kennell's arguments (1995, 32, 117) that the *paides* covered the age range 7–14, not 7–18 as I previously suggested (Hodkinson 1983, 242, 251).

24 An alternative interpretation would see him as an adolescent boy: Bremmer 1990, 137. Kritias' term (ὁ δὲ παῖς ὁ οἰνοχόος) permits either interpretation.

25 At *Demetrios* 1.4 Plutarch states that the enforced drunkenness took place at festivals; but, as Fisher points out (1989, 34 n. 43), the messes did not operate at the major festivals (e.g. Athen. 138e–139b) and the practice cannot have been restricted to those occasions.

26 Ollier points to *Instituta Laconica* no. 23 = Plut. *Mor.* 238f, which describes the borrowing as dependent upon whether 'the owners required them for their own use'. However, it is unlikely that the late hellenistic compiler of this notice had an independent source of information; though clearly drawing upon Xenophon, he goes on to misrepresent what the latter says about provisions for hunting parties by stating that they were privately owned.

27 According to Ollier (1934, 28), *Cyrop.* 1.6.31–2 is a further reference. The reference here, however, includes several ways of cheating and deceiving, of which stealing from one's friends (note, not from other persons in general) is merely one instance. There is no reason to associate the method of education described here with Sparta; against the common idea that the *Cyropaedia* presents a blueprint of Spartan society, cf. Tuplin 1994.

28 Kennell 1995, 16–17, argues that the name and position of *eirēn* are themselves a post-classical creation.

29 References in Kennell 1995, 208 n. 43.

30 Compare his comments (*Panathenaikos* 177–81) on the subjection of the *perioikoi* which, although exaggerated, are grounded in reality (Mossé 1977).

PART III

RICH CITIZENS AND THE USE OF PRIVATE WEALTH

Chapter 7

RESTRICTIONS ON THE DEPLOYMENT OF WEALTH IN SPARTIATE LIFE

In Part II it was argued that the Spartiate property system, though containing some limited public elements, was largely private in character. Part III (chapters 7–11) will analyse the extent to which citizens were able to make use of their private resources and the impact of those uses upon Spartiate society. This chapter will begin by considering certain structural limitations upon the deployment of private wealth. I shall then examine certain spheres of citizen life and of the lives of Spartiate women in which the exploitation of wealth was specifically restricted. One important issue will be the extent and effectiveness of those restrictions.

That the lawgiver Lykourgos aimed systematically to restrict the deployment of wealth is a sentiment asserted, as noted earlier (ch. 2), in several post-classical accounts, most notably in his 'biography' by Plutarch. Lykourgos is credited by Plutarch with a range of measures which supposedly rendered Ploutos (Wealth) blind and lifeless, including a ban on superfluous *technai*, the introduction of common messes, a prohibition of extravagant domestic architecture, austerity in the upbringing, inexpensive sacrifices and simplicity of burials (*Lyk*. 9–10; 13.3–5; 16.6–7; 17.4; 19.3; 27.2). Although, as we have seen (ch. 2), several of these alleged measures were late accretions to the Lykourgan legend, the essential idea of special restrictions on the use of wealth was common currency in classical times – and not just in Lakonophile circles. It appears not only in Xenophon (*Lak. Pol.* 7.3–4), who claims that an equal standard of living and unostentatious clothing removed the possibility of spending for indulgence, but also in more dispassionate writers. Commenting upon the fact that many people described Sparta as a democracy, Aristotle (*Pol.* 1294b21–7) acknowledges that she possessed certain democratic features, such as uniformity between rich and poor in the upbringing, in the messes and in dress, all spheres in which the possession of wealth brought no advantage. Thucydides, almost a century earlier, presents a similar picture in his statement that 'in general those who had great possessions adopted a lifestyle that was as much as possible like that of the many' (1.6). This varied testimony suggests that, whatever the later inventions or elaborations, we are dealing with an authentic phenomenon of Spartiate property relations.

Restrictions imposed by the socio-political structure of the polis

Before discussing specific aspects of Spartiate life, we should consider certain general respects in which the socio-political structure of the polis restricted certain uses of wealth which were common practice in other poleis. The most significant of these practices was the deployment of material patronage by rich families towards poorer citizens, a phenomenon rooted in the landed poverty of ordinary citizens. Recent research suggests that in many poleis a sizeable proportion of citizen households typically lived on the margin of subsistence (Garnsey 1988; Gallant 1991). Given the limited capacity of help from immediate kinsmen, neighbours and friends, such households ultimately had no option but to seek assistance from wealthier citizens. By providing 'subsistence insurance' wealthy men were able to establish ties of clientage over poorer citizens (Gallant 1991, 159–66). For much of our period the potential for such material exploitation was limited in Sparta because the landholding position of ordinary Spartiates differed crucially from that of citizens elsewhere. As noted in chapter 3, the remodelling of Spartiate society in the archaic period made it necessary that all citizen households should possess sufficient land to supply their mess contributions and to free them from the need for manual labour. Initially, even the poorest Spartiate households would have possessed landholdings greatly in excess of that held by poor citizens in other poleis. Although many of these landholdings became reduced over subsequent generations, they must for some considerable period have supplied even the poorest citizens with an ample surplus over and above the level of subsistence and a consequent material independence of wealthier Spartiates.

Wealthy Spartiates were also restricted from engaging to any significant degree in 'community, or communal, patronage', namely, 'large-scale private expenditure… for communal purposes' (Finley 1985, 35; Gallant 1991, 148–9). This was in part a further consequence of the Spartiate property system. In most areas of the Greek world subsistence crises would strike, at some time or other, not merely individual poor families but whole communities. On such occasions wealthy citizen *euergetai* ('doers of good things') could display their generosity by giving grain or selling it at below market prices, giving or lending money or procuring supplies from external sources. The epigraphic record from the period 400–150 BC supplies at least 30 examples of official decrees voted in honour of such public benefactors (Herman 1980–81; Gallant 1991, 183). The scale of landed resources controlled by the Spartiate citizen body, however, ensured that – at least before the mid-fourth century – the bulk of the citizen community remained largely immune from subsistence crisis, even when its poorest members fell into difficulties.[1] Moreover, the fact that the compulsory mess dues were higher than a citizen's personal consumption requirements (see ch. 6) probably meant that a Spartiate would normally lose citizen status through defaulting on his contributions before severe subsistence crisis struck his entire family. By definition, only men already degraded to Inferior status could suffer the full plight of famine experienced by citizens of other poleis.

The consequent restriction of scope for generalised benefactions was a matter not just of historical circumstance but also of policy. In the episode from the pseudo-Aristotelian *Oikonomika* (2.2.9; 1347b) recounted in chapter 5, in which the Lakedaimonians wanted to raise funds for the Samians, they did so not through benefactions from wealthy citizens but through a shared effort of abstinence from food and a pooling of the expenses thus individually saved.[2] Although Sparta is sometimes compared to Rome in discussions of patronage (e.g. Ste Croix 1972, 354), there is no evidence for anything comparable to the private financing of games evidenced at Rome from the third century onwards, or to the donation of public feasts or monuments such as Aristotle recommended as sound practice for the preservation of oligarchic regimes (*Pol.* 1321a31–42). There is some evidence that certain individuals might offer additional private entertainment during festivals. A certain Lichas gained international repute for his lavish hospitality to visitors to the festival of the Gymnopaidiai (Xen. *Mem.* 1.2.61; Plut. *Kimon* 10.6); and Xenophon (*Ages.* 8.7) mentions the entertainment offered by King Agesilaos on days of sacrifice. The festivals themselves, however, were publicly-funded; and, as Herodotus' list of royal privileges (6.57) indicates, the animals consumed at regular sacrificial meals were supplied by the state. Doubtless, Sparta was not the only polis which wanted at times to retain the provision of public facilities within the realm of public financing and control. The illuminating 'Springhouse decree' from late fifth-century Athens (*SEG* x.47; trans. Crawford and Whitehead 1983, no. 152) shows the Athenian *demos* declining an offer by the family of Perikles to fund work on the public water supply and jealously insisting that the expenditure should come from its own resources. The practice of poleis like Athens, however, was never consistently opposed to such community patronage. Note, for example, the activities of Kimon, who used his resources to beautify the city of Athens and 'turned the Academy from a waterless, parched place into an irrigated grove, furnished by him with clear running tracks and covered shady walks' (Plut. *Kimon* 13.8). Although the absence of firm information about the financing of Spartan public utilities should dictate caution, it is hard to believe that the activities of a Kimon would have been conceivable. It is suggestive that in the one tract in which the use of wealth by Spartan citizens is a live issue, namely Xenophon's *Agesilaos*, the emphasis is solely upon Agesilaos' private benefactions. Community patronage receives no mention, either as a beneficial practice by Agesilaos or a deleterious practice by his rivals.

This impression of a state monopoly over the provision of public services is reinforced by the virtual absence of liturgical expenditures. The phenomenon of 'liturgies', as exemplified most notably in classical Athens, represents the compulsory, institutionalised form of voluntaristic acts of communal patronage. The term *leitourgia*, according to one recent account, 'encompasses the idea, deep-rooted in antiquity…that wealthy individuals had an obligation to spend part of their wealth and time on some service to the community' (Gabrielsen 1994, 7). The devotion of time – indeed the entire life of the citizen – and effort to civic concerns was thoroughly enshrined in Spartan practice; but the expenditure of wealth was not. In contrast to other poleis, Spartan ideology seems not to have included the expectation that wealthy men should be munificent on the community's behalf. Lykourgos 'made it more respectable to help one's fellows by physical labour than by spending money, pointing out that the former is the work of the *psychē*, the latter the work of wealth' (Xen. *Lak. Pol.* 6.4). This attitude is exemplified by an incomplete passage of Hesychios, s.v. *karneatai*, referring to the *leitourgia* of Apollo Karneios, which was held by five unmarried youths for four years. As Robert Parker comments (1989, 164 n. 7), the word *leitourgia* here relates to the performance of the rites of Apollo's festival, not to their financing, especially since unmarried youths under age 30 were not even permitted to engage in financial transactions to supply their own households (Plut. *Lyk.* 25.1).

As in ideology, so in practice. With one late exception, we hear of nothing comparable to the liturgies of classical Athens, whereby the wealthiest citizens were required by law to fund the costs of performances at public festivals or share the expenses of crewing, maintaining and equipping a trireme, in the process acquiring honour and prestige.[3] The consistent impression given by the sources is that in Sparta such services were obtained in more public ways. Performances at Spartan festivals depended upon the unpaid participation of citizens, as, for example, in the races of boys at the Karneia, the songs and dances of citizen girls at the Hyakinthia, and the choirs of men and boys both there and at the Gymnopaidiai (R. Parker 1989, 148–9). Every Spartiate was grouped into one of three choirs according to age (Plut. *Lyk.* 21.2); even kings and cowards were included (Xen. *Ages.* 2.17; *Lak. Pol.* 9.5). Common participation in choruses, subject to the discipline of the choirmaster, was a central feature of citizen life and a context in which ranking was defined according to one's allocated place. It was also, as Plutarch's text makes clear, a locus for competition between the different age groups. Spartan festivals were arenas of rivalry revolving around, not the expenditure of wealthy Spartiates, but the personal participation of the entire citizen body.

Concerning the financing of Sparta's navy, we lack explicit evidence; but several factors suggest that it left little room for the private deployment of wealth. There is no evidence in the early history of Spartan naval campaigning for private citizens' participating with their own ships and crew, as did the Athenian

Kleinias, who at Artemision in 481/0 'distinguished himself campaigning with 200 men, whom he provided with his own means, and on his own ship' (Hdt. 8.17; cf. Plut. *Alk.* 1.1). Similarly, the expedition made *c.* 510 by Dorieus, son of King Anaxandridas II, was joined by Philippos of Kroton, who provided a trireme and crew at his own expense (Hdt. 5.47). Dorieus' own men, however, and no doubt his ships, were supplied officially by the Spartan polis.[4] In the classical period, although triremes from Lakonia itself were commanded by Spartiates whom the sources call 'trierarchs' (e.g. Thuc. 4.11; Xen. *Hell.* 7.1.12), there is no evidence that their responsibility extended to financing the payment of the crew or the equipping and maintenance of the ship (Gabrielsen 1994, 230 n. 12; *pace* Gomme et al. 1945–81, iii. 448). Sparta's engagement in naval warfare, moreover, was sporadic until the Peloponnesian war; and even after 431 the number of ships supplied or maintained by Sparta herself was a small minority in the Peloponnesian fleet.[5] Furthermore, a large proportion of her rowers were helots (Xen. *Hell.* 7.1.12; cf. 5.1.11; Myron *FGrH* 106F1), who would have required no pay beyond the supply of adequate provisions. The minimalist character of Sparta's naval commitment does not suggest a sphere in which private outlay played any part. In this the Spartans were following established procedures for the land army: Xenophon's account of its mobilisation depicts a system in which manpower and goods were procured through public requisitioning rather than private liturgies.[6]

The only apparent exception to the absence of liturgies concerns the cavalry, which was not created until 424. We do not know how it was raised in its early years; but in 371, when it was probably 720 strong, the horses were provided by the very rich (οἱ πλουσιώτατοι: Xen. *Hell.* 6.4.11; cf. Lazenby 1985, 11–12). King Agesilaos, moreover, is said purposely to have bred war horses on his estates rather than the chariot horses of some other leading citizens (Xen. *Ages.* 9.6). Whether the provision of cavalry horses was compulsory for all large landowners is unclear. The tenor of Xenophon's remarks on Agesilaos' behaviour suggests a voluntary service to the community, but he may be deliberately obscuring the fact that the king was simply fulfilling a fixed obligation. We should, however, note the limits of the liturgy, if such it was. At Athens the obligation extended to personal military service (Bugh 1988; Spence 1993); in Sparta the wealthy citizen supplied the horse, but the cavalryman was an unconnected person appointed by the state.[7] Furthermore, in the different pastoral environment of Attica the requirement for cavalry service stretched down the social scale to embrace many families outside the normal horse-breeding elite, and sometimes even below the ranks of the liturgical class. At Sparta, in contrast, with its considerable pastoral resources (ch. 4), the liturgy probably fell only upon those whose large estates were already partly devoted to horse breeding. This partial exception to the general absence of liturgies applied, as Xenophon says, only to the very richest citizens.

Restrictions on the use of wealth in citizen life

Besides the foregoing structural restrictions, the deployment of wealth was also controlled in various areas of citizen life. The following discussion will focus on certain especially important areas of control (the upbringing of citizen boys; food and feasting; dress and equipment) for which we possess contemporary evidence from the archaic or classical periods. Other controls which are attested only in post-classical sources – such as the alleged simplicity of domestic architecture, interior decoration and ornament or the inexpensiveness of sacrifices (cf. ch. 2) – are omitted owing to their unverifiability.[8]

The upbringing of Spartiate boys

The first of these important areas of control was the upbringing of Spartan boys, as was recognised by many contemporaries:

> Many people try to describe it [sc. the Spartan *politeia*] as a democracy, because the system has a number of democratic features: first, the rearing of children, under which the sons of the rich are reared in the same way as the sons of the poor and receive an education which the sons of the poor could also receive (Arist. *Pol.* 1294b20–4).

Although Aristotle adopts a neutral position towards the view that Sparta's overall *politeia* was democratic (he subsequently explains why others termed it oligarchic), he accepts the existence of uniformity in the upbringing.

The uniform upbringing was an important institutional constraint upon the influence of wealth, as is evident by comparison with education elsewhere, especially in Athens (Beck 1964, 80–5; Golden 1990, 62–4). In other poleis, although education outside the home probably existed from the later sixth or early fifth century, schooling was not compulsory and schools were privately run. Consequently, the nature and extent of each boy's schooling rested entirely on family initiative and varied with wealth and social class. At Athens, schoolmasters were relatively poorly paid: hence most Athenian citizen boys could afford to receive some schooling in letters. Poorer boys, however, typically attended for fewer years than their wealthier peers; and their training often focused primarily upon reading and writing and less upon training in music or physical education. Wealthier parents, moreover, could influence the character of their children's upbringing. Sometimes richer boys went to more exclusive schools. Sometimes they were taught in neighbourhood schools along with poorer boys; but in such schools well-off families always had an advantage due to the presence of their agent and extension of their authority, the slave *paidagōgos*, who accompanied his charge into class. Consequently, as Aristotle comments, wealthier boys tended to refuse to submit to school authority (*Pol.* 1295b15).

The Spartan upbringing contrasted markedly in several respects, as can be seen, at least implicitly, through Xenophon's account in his *Polity of the Lakedaimonians*.[9] At Sparta the upbringing was compulsory and uniform for every boy – with the exception of the immediate heirs to the dual kingship (Plut. *Ages.* 1.2). Its duration was determined by state provision and control of its content was vested in a public official, the *paidonomos* (*Lak. Pol.* 2.2). There is some evidence that boys could be accompanied by personal helot servants (see ch. 11), but no evidence that the latter exercised any influence on proceedings. Indeed, family interests were explicitly obstructed. Even in public the possibility of an exclusive relationship between father and son was prevented: all citizens, regardless of wealth, were given common authority over the boys and youths (2.10; 4.6; 6.1–2). The poorest citizen therefore had, at least in theory, the right of authority over boys from the wealthiest families; the sons of these families were not privileged with a lighter discipline. A similar intention is evident in the respect and obedience due from boys towards officials and in the supervisory role exercised by elderly men (Plut. *Lyk.* 16.5; 17.1; 25.1–2). The rewarding of personal merit, another counter to the influence of wealth, was fundamental to the upbringing. The 'keenest of the Arrens' were given charge of younger boys (*Lak. Pol.* 2.11). The *hippagretai*, who selected the elite squad of 300 *hippeis* from among the 20–29 year-olds, announced publicly their reasons for choosing some and rejecting others (4.3–4). Youths successful in the cheese-stealing contest at the sanctuary of Artemis Orthia gained lasting prestige (2.9). Successful practitioners of clandestine theft, if they continued to display their merits in later years, were prime candidates for office (Isok. *Panathenaikos* 212).

Equality of treatment regardless of family wealth was also evident in the material aspects of the upbringing: the restricted food rations, prohibition of sandals and the limited range of clothing allowed to each boy (Xen. *Lak. Pol.* 2.4–5). The precise nature of this last regulation is often misunderstood due to mistaken reliance on the evidence of Plutarch. According to him (*Lyk.* 16.6), the boys over the age of 12 'went without a *chitōn* (tunic), wearing one *himation* (cloak) for the year, with their bodies dirty, and they did not experience baths or massages, except for a few days a year'. As Kennell (1995, 32–4) has pointed out, Plutarch's claim derives from the hellenistic *Instituta Laconica* (no. 5 = Plut. *Mor.* 237b). and differs from the evidence of Xenophon. Xenophon says that Spartan practice did not follow that of other Greeks, who made their children's bodies delicate with changes of *himatia* (*Lak. Pol.* 2.1); instead 'he required them to become used to a single *himation* all the year round, the idea being that they would thereby be better prepared for both cold and heat' (2.4). Unlike Plutarch, Xenophon does not say that the *himation* was the boys' only garment. They were made tough not by going without a *chitōn*, but by not changing between thinner and thicker *himatia* in different weather; hence his emphasis on their withstanding both cold *and heat*. The version of the *Instituta Laconica* and Plutarch's *Lykourgos* is hellenistic invention, possibly based on philosophical associations, since 'a *himation* without a *chitōn* was considered virtually a philosopher's uniform'.[10] In short, classical Spartan practice prohibited use of a wardrobe of clothing such as was used by sons of wealthy families elsewhere.

The necessary pre-condition for uniformity of upbringing was the freedom from engagement in agricultural labour which was guaranteed to all citizen boys by the rentier status of Spartiate families.[11] In return, as noted in chapter 6, all Spartiate families were probably required to supply food rations for their boys. Given the attested meagreness of these rations, this may not have been more burdensome than maintaining the boys at home. For most of our period the requirement was surely no bar to the participation of boys from ordinary citizen families.[12] The situation may, however, have differed in the late fifth and fourth centuries, with the increasing poverty of such families. We shall see in chapter 11 that the boys in the upbringing known as *mothakes* probably included sons of impoverished Spartiate families whose participation depended upon patronage from wealthier citizens.

Food and feasting

Another realm of Spartiate life which witnessed restrictions upon the deployment of wealth was that of food and feasting. Following upon the meagre rations imposed on all boys in the upbringing, adult Spartiate commensality was dominated by the common messes, the *syssitia*, in which every citizen dined each evening except when delayed by sacrifice or hunting (Plut. *Lyk.* 12.2). There were, admittedly, occasions for other types of commensality in connection with religious festivals and cults. Shared meals for specific groups of worshippers may have accompanied the guild, clan and hero cults attested by literary and archaeological evidence.[13] Private feasting was permitted during the festival of the Gymnopaidiai (Xen. *Mem.* 1.2.61; Plut. *Kimon* 10.5). The restriction of such private commensality to cultic contexts, however, confirms the dominance of the public messes in everyday life.

Compulsory attendance at the messes precluded the wide range of voluntary commensal groups, involving only a (self-)selected part of the citizen population, which existed in most other poleis (Fisher 1988; Murray (ed.) 1990; Gallant 1991, 157, 171–4). Of these, the most notable was the *symposion*, or drinking party. As the prime locus for the practice of voluntaristic, reciprocal commensality among private groups of peers, the *symposion* was associated above all with the wealthy elite. It 'became in many respects a place apart from the normal rules of society, with…its own willingness to establish conventions fundamentally opposed to those within the polis as a whole' (Murray (ed.) 1990, 7). As such, the *symposion* was frequently used for the promotion of the political interests of sections of the upper classes, becoming the basis for bands of young, aristocratic *hetaireiai*, as in archaic Lesbos and in late fifth-century Athens when they twice conspired to overthrow the democracy (Fisher 1988, 1176–7, 1184–5). Even without such conspiracies, *symposia* were a source of luxury, distinction and privilege for the rich and a potential cause of envy and division.

In the early archaic period Sparta displayed as wide a variety of occasions of private conviviality as did other contemporary Greek states (Nafissi 1991, 206–224; Hodkinson 1997a, 90–1). The poems of Alkman are particularly illuminating. One fragment (fr. 17, Page) attests a shared meal in which one person acted as host. A relict of such everyday personal hospitality may be present in Herodotus' list of the traditional privileges (*gerea*) of the kings, which refers to the double portion they received at private dinners (Hdt. 6.57).[14] The same fragment refers to the 'sweet confections' which wealthy Spartiates ate at such meals. Another fragment (fr. 19, Page) provides the earliest literary description of the physical scene of a *symposion*. These literary references find support from depictions on sixth-century Lakonian pottery and other media showing luxurious *symposia* (for one example, see the jacket illustration to this volume) and *kōmoi* – processional revels following the *symposion* which were often accompanied by drunkenness and violence.[15] It seems clear, as Ewen Bowie has remarked (1990, 225 n. 16), that 'Sparta will have had *symposia* comparable to those in other Greek states…and these will have been refashioned into messes of *homoioi* in the sixth cent[ury]'.

Although, as seen in chapter 6, the classical *syssition* retained a strong sympotic element, the radical nature of this refashioning cannot be over-emphasized, especially in the restrictions which the extension of the messes to the entire citizen body imposed on the wealthy elite. Whereas in other poleis a citizen established his social identity through membership of a variety of commensal groups, the status and identity of an adult Spartiate were defined entirely through his *syssition*, whose practices and customs were uniform with those of other messes. Whereas *symposia* were held in private houses, the *syssitia* were located along the public space of the Hyakinthian Way (Xen. *Lak. Pol.* 5.2, 7; Demetrios of Skepsis, *ap.* Athen. 173f; cf. Polemon, *ap.* Athen. 39c). Whereas members of the *symposion*, who were often age peers, were chosen at the invitation of the host, each *syssition* comprised Spartiates of widely differing ages who were chosen at age 20 by the entire mess and, once chosen, were members for life.

The food in the *syssitia*, as seen in chapter 6, may not have been as moderate in quantity as claimed by some ancient sources (e.g. Xen. *Lak. Pol.* 5.3); but it was the same for all, rich or poor (Arist. *Pol.* 1294b25–7). The primary meal, moreover, consisted mainly of subsistence foodstuffs, especially cereals, with the delicacy of *opsōnia* restricted to a mere 10 obols' worth per month and meat dependent on the voluntary (and no doubt variable) contribution of game. Moreover, the basic cereal was not the wheaten bread preferred by rich Greeks elsewhere but the humbler *alphita*, or barley meal, the staple of subsistence peasants, eaten as an unleavened 'cake' or *madza* (Plut. *Kleom.* 16.5). Hence the slightly exaggerated late classical comment that 'No-one bakes among them, for they do not harvest wheat but eat *alphita*' (Herakleides Lembos, fr. 313.12 Dilts = Aristotelian *Lak. Pol.*, fr. 611.13 Rose). Wheaten bread was not completely absent, but it was confined to the voluntary contributions of the *epaiklon*

(Xen. *Lak. Pol.* 5.3). The plainness of this fare underlay Herodotus' tale (9.82) of the two meals prepared after Plataia, which contrasted the poverty of the Spartan meal with the luxury of the Persian; and the reputed prosecution of Naukleidas, the ephor of 403 and opponent of Lysander, for obesity and luxury (Agatharkides, *ap.* Athen. 550d–e; Aelian *VH* 14.7). The unappealing character of the food in the *syssitia* has been symbolised, above all, in both ancient and modern thought by the infamous, distasteful black broth;[16] though, since it was probably part of the voluntary extras rather than the compulsory contributions, it has been suggested that its consumption was typically limited to poorer messes (Link 1998, 100–1).

The heavy emphasis upon the eating of food as opposed to the drinking of wine marks another difference from *symposia* elsewhere. As seen in chapter 6, the ration of wine per person (probably of the order of 0.39–0.55 litres) was not negligible: mixed with water at a dilution ratio of 1:2.5 or 1:3, total personal consumption would have been of the order of 1.4–2.2 litres. A variety of means was employed, however, to ensure that excessive drinking and the kind of hybristic behaviour indulged in by rich young men elsewhere were strictly controlled (Fisher 1989). In the mess itself there were no toasts, challenges or competitive, obligatory rounds of drinking (Kritias fr. 6 Diels-Kranz, *ap.* Athen. 432d; cf. fr. 33, *ap.* Athen. 463e). After the meal there was no room for drunken *kōmoi*: each man 'must take good care not to stumble under the influence of drink…and they must do in the dark what they do in the day; indeed, those who are still in the army are not even allowed a torch to guide them' (Xen. *Lak. Pol.* 5.7). Indeed, *kōmoi* were prohibited at all times, even during festivals: 'not one of us would not impose the severest penalties on anyone we saw engaged in a drunken *kōmos*, not even if he had the Dionysia as his excuse would we let him off', says the Spartan speaker in Plato's *Laws* (637a). This prohibition may be reflected in the disappearance *c.* 500 BC of depictions of musicians, dancers and satyrs from the popular lead figurines dedicated at Artemis Orthia (T.J. Smith 1998, 79).

We shall see later (ch. 11) that there were opportunities for richer messmates to use their extensive landholdings to gain prestige through making extra donations of special foodstuffs to their messmates for consumption in the additional course, the *epaiklon*. The criteria for engagement in such donations, however, were not exclusively those of wealth, as many donations derived from hunting, an activity open to all Spartiates through the system of communal sharing (Xen. *Lak. Pol.* 5.3; 6.3). Hence rich and poor messmates could each act as both donor and recipient, with every gift being shared by all. Fisher (1989, 45 n. 24) rightly notes how this 'envy-reducing mechanism of reciprocal gifts, *philotimia* and *charis* [was] designed to bind rich and poor mess-mates together'.

Dress and military equipment

State control over eating and drinking was matched by similar regulations which imposed a basic uniformity of clothing and equipment for all citizens. In his general study of Spartiate dress, David (1989) suggests that we can identify three distinct types of uniform in different contexts of Spartiate life: the civic uniform of everyday life, comprising a simple, coarse cloak known as the *tribōn*; the uniform of nudity used in athletic exercise and religious festivals; and the military uniform of a red cloak. The following discussion will examine each of these contexts in turn.

Civic dress
The masking of socio-economic differences in the everyday civic dress of Spartan citizens began, as we have seen, within the upbringing, and it continued into adult life. According to Thucydides, 'it was the Lakedaimonians who first began to dress simply and in accordance with modern taste' (1.6). Aristotle acknowledges the fact that 'the rich wear clothing which any poor man could afford' (*Pol.* 1294b26–9). Xenophon offers an interpretation of the underlying ideology: 'Besides, there is no point in making money even for the sake of cloaks (*himatiōn*), since they adorn themselves not through the costliness of their clothes but through the good condition of their bodies' (*Lak. Pol.* 7.3).

Although the principle of uniformity of civic dress is clear enough, the details are less certain. One uncertainty concerns the date of its introduction. On this question, Thucydides' statement is less helpful than might first seem. It appears as part of his discussion of the evolution of Greek dress, which is itself a digression within his outline of the development of Greek society. Within this digression Thucydides presents the Spartan innovation as the third and final stage in an evolutionary sequence from a period of insecurity when men had to carry weapons, through a time 'not long ago' when men could go unarmed and dressed in luxurious clothing, to the contemporary period which was marked by simplicity of dress. Thucydides here followed an established tradition which assigned the period of luxury to the years down to the early fifth century (McDonnell 1991, 189), a dating which finds some support in Athenian vase paintings (Gomme et al. 1945–81, i.103). He thereby implicitly dates the Spartans' introduction of simple dress – and indeed the entire equality of lifestyle – to this comparatively recent period. This implication is apparently confirmed by his following remarks on the Spartans' introduction of athletic nudity in place of the wearing of loincloths, a practice which he claims had ended 'not many years' ago. As McDonnell (1991, 190) has demonstrated, however, we should not accept this arbitrary scheme of material progress, which can be disproved in the case of athletic nudity (see further below), and which artificially forces Spartan developments into an Athenian chronological sequence. There are no grounds to suppose either that Thucydides had any hard evidence for the timing of the Spartans' introduction of simplicity of dress or that it occurred as late as the changes of dress in early fifth-century Athens.

Another point of uncertainty concerns the alleged status of the word *tribōn* as the standard term for the Spartans' everyday cloaks.[17] No classical source specifically uses this term for a cloak worn by a Spartiate. Xenophon uses the standard Greek term *himatiōn*. The nearest classical reference is Demosthenes 54.34, in which the speaker refers to certain Athenians 'who put on sour looks and pretend to play the Spartan and have *tribōnes* (λακωνίζειν φασὶ καὶ τρίβωνας ἔχουσιν) and wear single-soled shoes'. Since, however, *tribōn* is more frequently used in Attic literature to describe threadbare cloaks worn by Athenians and others in entirely non-Spartan contexts,[18] the word here probably simply indicates the state of clothing worn by Lakonophiles in imitation of the Spartiates' eschewal of changes of cloaks, without any implication that it was an authentic Spartan term. Indeed, it was not even an invariable term for the dress of Lakonophiles. Plato's description of their clothing (*Protagoras* 342c) makes no mention of the *tribōn*, referring instead to their short mantles (*anabolai*). It is not until Duris of Samos (*FGrH* 76F14, *ap.* Athen. 535e) in the early third century that we get the first attested mention of 'the ancestral *tribōn*' as the archetypal Spartiate dress.[19] The idea of the *tribōn* (or, sometimes, *tribōnion*) as typifying the austerity of Spartiate life was developed especially by Plutarch (*Ages.* 14.2, 30.3; *Agis* 14.2; *Kleom.* 16.5; *Lyk.* 18.1, 30.2). Even in the Roman imperial period, however, use of the term was not universal: Aelian (*VH* 9.34) refers instead to the simple Lakedaimonian *exōmis*, a term we shall encounter below regarding military dress. Although the Spartiates' everyday clothing in classical times was doubtless both inexpensive and reasonably uniform, there is no evidence that they themselves gave it a specialised name different from those in use elsewhere in Greece.

Nudity

In the eyes of some Greeks the dress of nudity was particularly associated both with Sparta and with her equality of lifestyle. For Thucydides (1.6), as already noted, nudity during athletic exercise was a Spartan innovation.

> They [sc. the Lakedaimonians] too were the first to exercise nude and strip openly to rub themselves with oil after exercising. In ancient times, even at the Olympic games, athletes competed wearing loincloths over their genitals, and it is not many years ago that they ended the practice.

This passage has caused headaches for commentators (cf. Gomme et al. 1945–81, i.106; Hornblower 1991, 27–8) due to the apparent conflict with various late traditions which credit the innovation to earlier athletes of the late eighth or seventh centuries.[20] The difficulties are compounded by Plato's claim (*Repub.* 452c) that nude exercising was a recent Cretan innovation which was followed by the Lakedaimonians. Various means of reconciling the differences of both innovator and chronology have been proposed. As McDonnell (1991, 183–5) has demonstrated, however, whatever one thinks of the reliability of these late traditions, there is abundant archaeological evidence for the existence, indeed prevalence, of athletic nudity by the sixth century at the latest; and there is no solid evidence for a subsequent return to using loincloths.[21] As noted above, Thucydides' dating of the Spartiates' introduction of athletic nudity, attached as it is to their introduction of simple dress, is part of an arbitrary developmental schema whose chronology should not be treated as historical reality. Plato's claim is based on Thucydides' statement, with the addition of the common tradition – espoused by the Spartans themselves (Hdt. 1.65) – that Sparta's reforms were derived from Crete (McDonnell 1991, 190–3). There is, consequently, no reason to believe that in the late fifth century the Spartiates had only recently started nude exercise;[22] but, equally, no special reason to believe that athletic nudity was a Spartiate innovation. What we can draw from the passage, however, is Thucydides' association of Spartiate athletic nudity with the simplicity of dress which he adduces as an important factor in their egalitarian citizen lifestyle.

An integral element of this association, it has been argued (David 1989), was that Spartiate nudity was not confined, as in most poleis, to athletic exercise. Certainly, nudity was also evident during the festival of the Gymnopaidiai in the choral dance called the *gymnopaidikē*, which was apparently performed by the mature men and elders, as well as the boys (Aristoxenos, *ap.* Athen. 630d–631b; Pettersson 1992, 42–56). David suggests (1989, 6) that, since Spartan rituals were adapted to serve political functions, this ritual nudity 'could stress the principles of simplicity, uniformity and equality among the *homoioi*'. Pettersson's recent study of the festival, however, argues that the state of nudity did not reflect the realities of everyday life, but was part of a liminal period of transition which stood in opposition to the normal order of society. Moreover, the infrequency of nudity in other Spartan festivals undermines the idea that it was the standard festive uniform.[23] Although citizen nudity may have been rather more frequent in Sparta than elsewhere, it is unclear that it played a qualitatively different role from its function in other poleis.

Military dress and equipment
Regarding military dress and equipment, we are on firmer, though still not altogether solid, ground. The question of the uniformity of military clothing and equipment is closely connected with the issue of supply. It is often argued that Spartiate arms and armour were procured and supplied centrally by the polis.[24] Literary evidence from the late fifth century onwards offers some support for this hypothesis. It is suggestive that Xenophon (*Lak. Pol.* 11.3) sandwiches details of the Spartans' military uniform between his descriptions of the procurement of military equipment and of the organisation of the army; and there is explicit evidence that Spartiate cavalrymen were issued their horse and their arms by the polis (Xen. *Hell.* 6.4.11). Moreover, it is precisely in this period, as we shall see, that there is evidence for the standardisation of dress and weapons which one would expect from centralised supply (Cartledge 1977, 12–15).[25] Whether we

should extrapolate these arrangements back into earlier periods is more doubtful. In the early archaic period there was probably – as in other poleis – a greater reliance on individual acquisition of military equipment. Tyrtaios indicates a marked difference between heavily-armed and light-armed soldiers within the citizen ranks (fr. 11, West; cf. Snodgrass 1967, 66–7). Even the Lakedaimonian army at Plataia in 479, when the *perioikoi* fought in a separate contingent (Hdt. 9.11, 28), was a very different institution from the army of the late fifth century onwards, in which *perioikoi* were brigaded in Spartiate regiments which also contained other non-citizens, including men without landed property such as *neodamōdeis* and mercenaries. Centralised supply of equipment may have been prompted by the need to provide for these latter troops and to incorporate the *perioikoi* on equal terms with the Spartiates.

Our knowledge of Spartan hoplite dress and equipment in the archaic period depends almost entirely upon artistic representations, in particular a series of Lakonian hoplite figurines in bronze and lead, the latter mainly from the sanctuary of Artemis Orthia.[26] The bronzes date mainly to the second half of the sixth century. Although some depict their subject in a state of semi-nudity wearing only helmet, bronze cuirass and greaves, others show various kinds of tunics worn under the cuirass. Although some of these clothed hoplites share a general similarity of dress, there is also substantial diversity of apparel. (See *Figs.* 6 and 7.) There are marked differences in the crests on the helmets, and in the shapes and degree of decoration on the tunics where they show below the cuirass. Some cuirasses also show considerable decoration, whereas others are plain. Moreover, although the helmets show few signs of elaboration, the potential for personal ornamentation here too is demonstrated by the famous early fifth-century marble torso of a hoplite, often named 'Leonidas', found near the Spartan Acropolis, the cheekpieces of whose helmet are decorated with the heads of a dog and a ram.[27] Few of the bronze hoplite figurines retain their shields, but shields are well represented on the lead figurines. From the later seventh century onwards the shields present a variety of designs. (See *Fig.* 8). In Leads I and II (650–580 BC) they are limited to rosettes, whirling patterns and wheel types. In Leads III and IV (580–500 BC) blazons bearing animal devices appear: water-birds, doves, lions, scorpions, oxheads, cocks, boars and gorgoneia.[28] The blazoned shields continue into Lead V (500–425 BC), but die out in Lead VI (425–250 BC), when there are relatively few warrior figurines and they bear only simpler, though still varied, shield patterns. Although caution is appropriate in extrapolating from artistic representation to military reality, the consistent picture from both the bronzes and the leads makes it hard to avoid the conclusion that during the archaic and early classical periods the dress and equipment of Spartan hoplites, although uniform in its basic character, exhibited considerable diversity of decoration by which citizens proclaimed their personal identities and differentiated themselves from their peers.

Ch. 7. Restrictions on the deployment of wealth in Spartiate life

Figs. 6 and 7. Bronze figurines of hoplites, from the sanctuaries of Zeus at Dodona, *c.* 535–525 BC (Ioannina Museum 4914) and Apollo Korynthos, Longa, Messenia, *c.* 540–525 BC (National Museum, Athens 14789); photographs courtesy of Deutsches Archäologisches Institut, Athens. Note the different styles of armour, dress and hair.

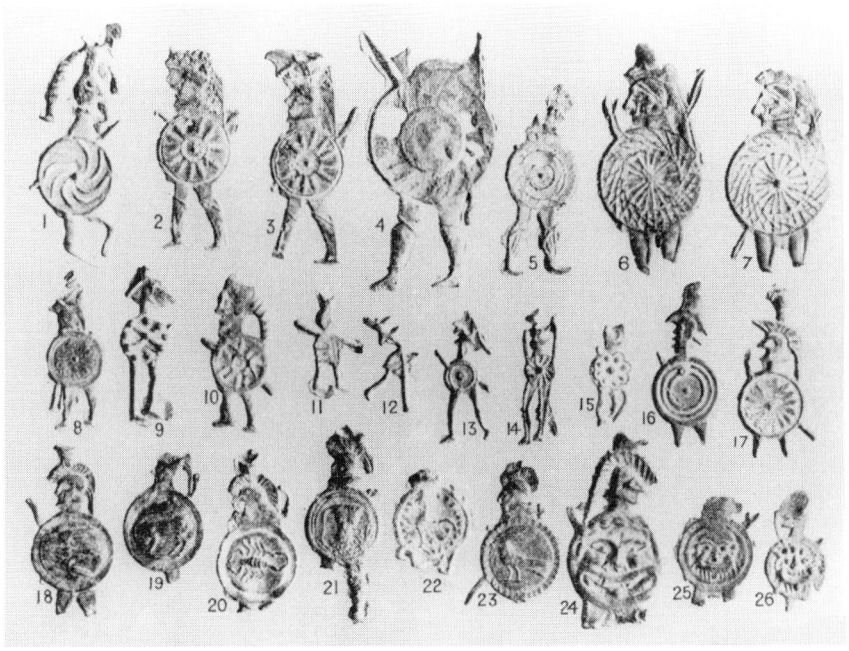

Fig. 8. Lead figurines, from the sanctuary of Artemis Orthia, Leads III–IV: 580–500 BC (reproduced with permission of the British School at Athens). Note the variety of shield designs.

This artistic evidence from the sixth century contrasts somewhat with the evidence of the late fifth- and early fourth-century literary sources. The most striking visual feature of the Spartan army around the time of the Peloponnesian war and afterwards was that all its hoplites, regardless of rank, wore a standard crimson uniform, the *phoinikis*, augmented by their long hair specially combed and garlanded on occasion of battle.[29] The earliest mention of the crimson garment comes in Aristophanes' *Lysistrata* (1138–40), produced in 411 BC, referring to the visit to Athens of the Spartan envoy Perikleidas to request military assistance during the Messenian revolt of the late 460s. Whether this backdated reference (which is, strictly-speaking, to a non-military context and is introduced for dramatic contrast with the face of the envoy, white with desperation and fear) is genuine, and how long the crimson uniform had been in existence, are both uncertain. The metal figurines discussed above do not reveal the colour of the tunics worn under the bronze cuirass. Indeed, the precise nature of the garment in question is obscure.[30] Nevertheless, the uniform wearing of the *phoinikis* is a clear mark of equality, since in late fifth-century Athens it was apparently reserved for commanders (Aristop. *Peace* 1172–6).[31] In contrast, the dress of Spartan officers apparently bore no distinguishing marks. When King Agesilaos visited Egypt, admittedly in command of a Spartan mercenary contingent, but with a formal entourage of thirty Spartiate counsellors, he was laughed at for his coarse, poor cloak (Plut. *Ages.* 36.5).

Other aspects of classical Spartan military equipment show similar characteristics of uniformity which are both obscured and illuminated by major changes in hoplite dress which took place throughout Greece in the fifth century. The most notable changes were the discarding of the cuirass and of the older metal helmet which enclosed much of the face. In their place came a corslet made of quilted linen or leather and the *pilos*, a lighter cap, made of stiffened felt, or sometimes of bronze, which covered just the top of the head (Snodgrass 1967, 90–5; Anderson 1970, 21–33; Sekunda 1998, 29–30).[32] The evidence from this period for Spartan practice varies. The hoplites on Sphakteria in 425 were already wearing *piloi*, presumably made of felt since they could not keep out the enemy's arrows; but they were probably still wearing metal cuirasses, since when they were hit with spears the shafts broke and stuck in their armour.[33] Evidence for the adoption of the lighter corslet comes, however, from a partially preserved late fifth-century Athenian monument, shown in *Figs.* 9 and 10. Two adjacent sides of the monument each contain a scene depicting a victory trophy (the 'symbolic representation of an opponent defeated in battle') in the form of a tree stump chopped and pollarded to give the impression of a man with raised arm.[34] In this period, as Anderson (1970, 33) notes, the defeated enemies depicted on these trophies are surely Spartans; hence the clothing of the figures symbolically represented on the monument probably depicts Spartan military dress. Both scenes show the defeated enemy wearing a leather or linen corslet

Ch. 7. Restrictions on the deployment of wealth in Spartiate life

and a conical *pilos*. The scenes also show another newish garment, an *exōmis*. One scene (*Fig.* 9) shows it being worn over the corslet and fastened over the left shoulder, leaving the right arm free. On the other scene (*Fig.* 10) the *exōmis* is held in the hand of a winged figure of Victory, who is about to place it on the corsleted enemy. The Spartan identity of these soldiers and the elements of their dress are confirmed by two late fifth-century Attic tombstones, which depict Athenian hoplites about to spear fallen opponents.[35] On both tombstones the latter attempt to defend themselves with short swords which, as we shall see below, securely identify them as Spartans. Both Spartans are depicted without body armour and, as on the victory monument, wear a *pilos* and *exōmis*.[36]

Although the Spartans' changes to their military clothing means that there is no such entity as 'the standard Spartan military dress' applicable throughout our period, the essential point is that these fifth-century changes were made systematically and uniformly across the entire army. In Athens, it seems, such changes took place unsystematically and 'probably as the result of personal preferences rather than official policy' (Anderson 1970, 41). In Sparta personal preference had no place. Thucydides' account implies that on Sphakteria all the Lakedaimonian troops, both Spartiate and non-Spartiate, were dressed alike. Similar co-ordinated changes are evident with the shield. By the late fifth century the normal hoplite shield, usually of wood with a bronze rim, had in Sparta been uniformly modified so that it was faced with a bronze sheet.[37] By the same period each shield also bore the official alphabetic badge of state, the letter Λ for 'Lakedaimonioi'.[38] Although the Spartans may not have been first to adopt a common shield symbol – the Mantineian trident, representing their guardian god Poseidon was already mentioned earlier by Bacchylides (fr. 21, Snell, *ap.* Schol. on Pindar, *Olympian XI* 83) – the use of the initial letter may have been their innovation (Anderson 1970, 18–19). Puzzlingly, however, the symbol does not appear on the – admittedly few – lead hoplite figurines from

Figs. 9 and 10. Two sides of an Athenian victory monument, from the Acropolis, late fifth century BC (Athens, Acropolis Museum 3173; photographs courtesy of Deutsches Archäologisches Institut, Athens). The 'trophies' are dressed as Spartan warriors.

this period, which show only ornamental patterns. Another distinctive element of classical Spartan arms was an unusually short, straight-edged sword attested in both iconographical and literary evidence.[39]

To summarise: whether or not the artistic record considered above should be interpreted as valid evidence for an earlier diversity, by the late fifth century the uniformity of Spartan military dress, arms and armour contrasted starkly with circumstances in many other poleis, which witnessed considerable variety of equipment and apparel, involving much rivalry and personal display (Hanson 1989, 58–9). In classical Sparta, unlike in contemporary Athens, there was no Nikias fighting with a shield whose exterior bore 'a design of gold and purple, elaborately inlaid and interwoven' (Plut. *Nik.* 28.5), no armourer like Pistias selling ornamented and gold-plated breastplates (Xen. *Mem.* 3.10.14). As Cartledge (1977, 27) has remarked, with only a little exaggeration, 'If we can give a concrete sense to the self-styled Spartan 'homoioi' (peers), it is to the uniformity of their hoplite equipment and training…that we should primarily look'.

Hair

A final levelling aspect of Spartiate personal appearance was uniformity of hair (David 1992). All citizen boys had their hair closely cropped; in contrast, all full-status men wore long hair with beards. Both practices are attested in the late archaic iconographic evidence as well as in classical and later literary sources.[40] This was more than just a question of common practice. The classical Spartan informants of our written earliest source, Herodotus (1.82), regarded it as a matter introduced by collective decision; and the ephors, on entering office, ordered all citizens 'to shave their moustaches and observe the laws' (Arist. fr. 539, Rose, *ap.* Plut. *Kleom.* 9.2). The occasion for beautifying one's long hair – during preparations for battle – was a state event (Hdt. 7.208–9; Xen. *Lak. Pol.* 13.8). The iconographic evidence of archaic bronze figurines of Spartiate warriors suggests that, in the sixth century at least, there was room for variations in precise hair styles (compare *Figs.* 6 and 7, above); and there is also evidence that they changed over time (Sekunda 1998, 24–5). Nevertheless, adult citizens in good standing were united by their long hair, which distinguished them from the boys, from cowards (who had half their beards shaved off: Plut. *Ages.* 30.3), and from the helots (whose servile status was marked by the wearing of a cap: David 1992, 17–19).

Restrictions on the use of wealth in the lives of Spartiate women

In chapter 3 I argued that Spartiate women enjoyed considerably greater landed property rights than their counterparts in certain other Greek states, especially in classical Athens. It was partly due to these rights that Spartiate women were often depicted by ancient writers as being exempt from the regulations over lifestyle and the use of wealth to which their menfolk were subjected. According to Aristotle (*Pol.* 1269b21–3), the Spartan lawgiver 'has been wholly negligent in the case of the women; for being under no constraint whatever they live unconstrainedly, and in luxury'. Euripides had earlier depicted the Spartan Hermione's love of beautiful clothing and costly ornaments (*Andromache* 147–53). This is not the place for a full-scale discussion of the negative representations of Spartan women by male, non-Spartan writers. Recent research, however, has demonstrated the distortions inherent in such images which have their origins in Athenocentric representations of the Spartan 'Other' (Greenstein Millender 1996, 215–86; 1999; Cartledge 1981). Although our information about the lives of the wives and daughters of Spartan citizens is scanty, we can nevertheless detect traces of similar restrictions upon the deployment of wealth to those observed in the lives of Spartan men.

Upbringing

Although Spartan girls, like their counterparts elsewhere, resided in their family homes until marriage, with consequent inequalities of access to food and possessions from one household to the next, in two respects their upbringing was more uniform and less susceptible to the influence of wealth. The first arose from the rentier status of all Spartiate families. Whereas the domestic upbringing of girls in other poleis varied considerably according to family wealth and status, every Spartiate household possessed a servile labour force which performed services for both its male and female members, thus permitting the latter freedom from domestic labour.[41] Unusually, female servile labour is said to have freed Spartan girls from the tasks of wool-working and making clothing, which were common roles even in leisured families elsewhere (Xen. *Lak. Pol.* 1.3–4; Plato, *Laws* 805e–806a; cf. Xen. *Mem.* 2.7; *Oik.* 7.5–6). That at least was the theory. One wonders, however, whether in practice poorer citizen households could always maintain sufficient domestic staff to cover every time-consuming household task, and whether their females did not sometimes turn their hands to activities avoided by their wealthier peers.[42]

The second respect was that all girls, rich or poor, underwent a uniform, public physical training. The precise nature of this training is controversial. The classical sources depict it as a comparatively limited affair: Euripides (*Andromache* 597–600) writes of participation in racing and wrestling.[43] Xenophon too writes (*Lak. Pol.* 1.4) of races and trials of strength, Plato (*Laws* 806a) of gymnastics and music. The post-classical sources expand this into a full range of contests in running, wrestling, the discus and javelin (*Apophth. Lak.* = Plut. *Mor.* 227d; *Lyk.* 14.2–3; Cic. *Tusc. Disp.* 2.15, [36]; Schol. to Juvenal 4.53), and even engagement in the *pankration*, boxing, hunting and warfare (Propertius 3.14.1–20)! Plutarch's *Lykourgos* also includes their participation in naked processions and dancing and singing in public festivals attended by the rest of the citizen body. Much of this post-classical evidence, however, lacks credibility (Hodkinson 1999, 150–1). Moreover, although some scholars (e.g. Nilsson 1912; Scanlon 1988) regard the above activities as a complete public upbringing parallel to that of Spartan boys, that is surely to over-interpret the evidence, which mentions nothing substantive beyond the physical and ritual elements to compare with the wide-ranging process of socialisation undergone by the boys. On the other hand, to suggest that the athletic and other physical activities had purely 'a ritual, rather than secular, character', as part of 'a complex series of prenuptial initiation rituals' (Greenstein Millender 1996, 259–60), seems excessively reductionist. Quite apart from the somewhat artificial nature of the supposed secular/ritual distinction, the eugenic aim of fitness for childbearing – on which Kritias (Diels-Kranz 1959, 88B32, *ap.* Clement *Miscellanies* 6.9), Xenophon and Plutarch all insist – must have required sustained physical training which cannot have been confined to religious festivals or transitional periods of prenuptial initiation.[44] It is important to emphasize the uniqueness of this public training. Female athletic contests are attested elsewhere, for example, at the sanctuary of Artemis at Brauron and in the festival of Hera at Olympia.[45] Spartan practice, however, appears unique in the incorporation of girls' athletic competition not just into religious ritual but as a regular part of their upbringing and in its extension to all girls of citizen households. Moreover, the sheer act of gathering the girls together in public to engage in collective activities in which their performances were judged on merit must have acted as a counterweight to evaluations of their eligibility for marriage in terms of their prospective inheritances.[46]

Whether merit was indeed the main determinant of the girls' performance in the physical training is, however, potentially open to challenge. Since women ate all their meals within the household, their diet was dictated by the range of foodstuffs produced on the family estates. In his comments on Spartan girls, Xenophon (*Lak. Pol.* 1.3) implies that they had a better diet than Greek girls elsewhere, including the consumption of wine and larger quantities of *opson* (i.e. foods other than grain). The implication is presumably, not that all girls ate equally well, but that they shared more fully in whatever foodstuffs were available within the household. The diet of Spartan women probably varied considerably, with those from wealthier families enjoying the wider range of non-subsistence crops which those households were able to grow. We should also no doubt envisage – in contrast to Xenophon's optimistic picture – that women from the poorest households whose menfolk were in difficulties meeting their mess dues may have suffered from food shortage as an increasing proportion of the household's foodstuffs were diverted to the mess. Girls from poorer households may therefore have been at a disadvantage in the physical training required of them. Moreover, the diverse nutritional status of Spartan girls was surely highly visible in a culture in which they spent much time in public, and often scantily-clad.

Dress and appearance
Spartan girls, of course, were notorious for the scantiness of their dress: for

the 'revealingly slit mini-chiton', worn while exercising and for their nakedness during festivals.[47] Such minimisation or absence of dress was clearly a levelling factor. It is often suggested that the clothes of married women too were similarly uninhibiting, but the late sources cited in evidence (*Lakainōn Apophthegmata* no. 4 = Plut. *Mor.* 241b; Teles, *ap.* Stob. *Flor.* 108.83) do not constitute proof.[48] The anecdote of the Spartan mother pulling up her clothing to shame her cowardly sons says nothing about how much of the body it normally covered or revealed, as is shown by the ascription of identical behaviour to Persian women (*Gynaikōn Aretai*, *Persides* = Plut. *Mor.* 246a), whose full covering is not in question. Moreover, there is certainly no hint of nudity in the representations of long female dresses among the lead figurines at Artemis Orthia.

How much room did the dress of married women leave for distinctions of wealth? By way of background, one should note that most Greek female clothing was typically simple in character, allowing little room for variation in basic design (Evans and Abrahams 1964; Granger-Taylor 1996). It was in decoration, hairstyle, make-up and jewellery that differentiation was possible. Certainly, the archaic evidence suggests plenty of scope for individuality and the use of wealth. Alkman's reference in his *Partheneion* (1.67–8, Page) to Lydian headgear provides evidence for foreign imports. The ornateness of the dress and textile patterns on the leads at Artemis Orthia suggests that female dress in ritual contexts in archaic Sparta was both rich and distinctive (cf. Foxhall 1998, 304–5; Foxhall and Stears 2000). Moreover, the Doric form of female dress, which – unlike the Ionian – required the use of dress fastenings (Hdt. 6.87), thereby gave potentially more scope for ornamentation. Early jewellery finds at Spartan sanctuaries, especially from the Geometric and Lakonian I–II periods, show a variety of ornamented brooches (*fibulae*) and other jewellery items in gold, silver and bronze (e.g. Droop 1929; Dawkins 1929b). The problem in interpreting this evidence is the difficulty of knowing whether such rich clothing and ornamentation was confined to ritual contexts or whether women were dedicating items connected with their everyday lives.

The classical evidence stands in stark contrast. The archaeological evidence is meagre or non-existent.[49] Finds of model textiles end after *c.* 580, the bronze jewellery finds dry up after *c.* 550, and the same is true of gold and silver items. This development does not in itself prove the introduction of sumptuary legislation specific to Sparta, since a decline of jewellery dedications is shared by sanctuaries throughout mainland and Aegean Greece. Nevertheless, according to the late fourth-century Aristotelian *Polity of the Lakedaimonians* (*ap.* Herakleides Lembos 373.13, Dilts), Spartan women were not permitted to wear ornaments, to let their hair grow long, or to wear gold.[50] Hence the polis did apparently act to prevent the possibility of displays of wealth through female appearance. The element of public display was of course the essential distinction between this sphere and that of differential consumption of food, which was confined to the privacy of the household. We shall explore in chapter 10 another sphere, that of chariot racing, in which wealthy families could engage in an activity not available to ordinary citizens but in which there were restrictions on public display.

Wedding ritual

The reference to women's short hair brings us to a final female-connected sphere in which public display was avoided, namely weddings: for the cropping of a girl's hair to symbolise her transition to woman and wife was part of the wedding ritual. In other poleis weddings were typically events involving the community at large, as can be seen in the earliest descriptions in the Homeric poems (*Il.* 18.490–6; *Od.* 4.15–19). Wedding rituals from contemporary Athens gave ample scope for richer families to use their wealth for special display: through the preparatory sacrifices and offerings; through the especially lavish clothing and perfume worn by bride and groom; through the decoration of family houses; through large and expensive feasts; through the bride's public procession to the groom's house accompanied by torches, music and dancing; through the singing of nuptial hymns (*epithalamia*) outside the couple's bedroom; and through the presentation of gifts to bride and groom (Oakley and Sinos 1993; Vérilhac and Vial 1998, 281–370). The length of wedding celebrations could be extended over several days for greater social impact.

From archaic Sparta there is evidence for the singing of *epithalamia* (Griffiths 1972, 10–11). In the classical period, in contrast, the wedding ceremony was a mute affair, involving a secretive ritual seizure following a privately arranged betrothal.

> When a woman was seized, the so-called bridesmaid (*nympheutria*) received her, and she shaved her head, dressed her in a man's cloak and shoes, and laid her on a pallet alone without a light. The bridegroom, not intoxicated or enervated, but sober, after dining in his mess as usual, would slip in, loose her belt, lift her and carry her to the bed. After spending a short time with her, he went away in an orderly manner to sleep in his usual quarters, with the other young men; and so he went on, passing his days and his rest with men of his own age, and visiting his bride secretly and cautiously, being ashamed and afraid that someone in the house might see him (Plut. *Lyk.* 15.3–4).

The essentials of this late account are corroborated by classical sources: by Herodotus' account (6.65) of how King Damaratos used the ritual to seize the woman betrothed to Leotychidas, and by Xenophon's comments (*Lak. Pol.* 1.5) on the shame of a newly-married man seen approaching or leaving his wife. Clearly, Spartiate weddings gave no room for the public display of wealth.

Notes

[1] Theopompos (*FGrH* 115F178, *ap.* Schol. Aristop. *Birds* 1013) apparently mentioned a food shortage at Sparta in Book 33 of his *Philippika*, which probably dealt with events after the Peace of Philokrates in 346; but this was after the loss of Messenia.

² Some scholars have suggested that in the inscription *IG* v.1.1 = ML 67; Loomis 1992 – a list of contributions to the Spartan war fund, dated sometime between the 420s and the 390s – one or more of the individual contributors who are given no ethnic may be Spartan citizens (Boeckh 1828, no. 1511; Loomis 1992, 47 and 53–4; cf. Crawford and Whitehead 1983, 347 n. 7). The prime candidate is the man named Molokros (Side, ll. 15 in Loomis' edition; ll. 8–9 in ML), who donated a talent of silver and whose name recalls the Spartan Molobros of Thuc. 4.8.9. There is also a certain …non (Front, l. 13 in Loomis' edn.), who also seems to lack an ethnic, to judge from the limited number of letters missing from the stone after his name. Loomis argues that the absence of an ethnic in these two cases, in contrast to its specification in the case of Som…ophon of Olenos in Achaia (Front, l. 7), indicates donors well-known locally. Although it is clearly possible that these men may be Spartiates, the argument is by no means conclusive. Loomis himself concedes that they could equally well be *perioikoi*. Moreover, detectable variations in other aspects of the entries (Loomis 1992, 40) mean that one should not necessarily expect complete consistency of nomenclature in the entries recording different contributions, especially if Matthaiou and Pikoulas (1989) are correct in suggesting that the entries were inscribed over an extended period.

³ The modern literature on the subject is considerable; cf. Davies 1967; 1981, xx–xxiv; Rhodes 1982; and the convenient summary in Sinclair 1988, 61–5. The definitive study of the trierarchy is now Gabrielsen 1994.

⁴ Hdt. 5.42, using the word *leōs*, a term he uses elsewhere (4.148) to signify the participants in an official colony; cf. Malkin 1994, 192–3.

⁵ e.g. in winter 413/12 the Spartans agreed to construct only 25 of the allied fleet of 100 (Thuc. 8.5). Shortly afterwards they agreed to despatch ten ships out of 40, but subsequently reduced their contingent to five (8.6). Astyochos brought out only four more in summer 412 (8.23 and 33); and Hippokrates only one in a contingent of twelve in early winter 412/11 (8.35). 27 Spartan ships were sent out later the same winter (8.39), but these were exceptional since their construction had been funded by the Persian Pharnabazos. By Arginusai in 406 the normal (im)balance of naval commitments had been restored: only 10 Spartan ships out of 120 (Xen. *Hell.* 1.6.26, 34).

⁶ *Lak. Pol.* 11.2: 'The ephors issue a proclamation stating the age limit fixed for the levy, first for the cavalry and hoplites, and then for the craftsmen… All the implements that an army may require in common are ordered to be assembled…' As noted in ch. 5, to finance Sparta's warfare in the late 360s, Agesilaos had to draw loans and contributions (δανείζεσθαι καὶ συνερανίζεσθαι) from his friends in the polis (Plut. *Ages.* 35.3); but this reads like an exceptional and semi-private arrangement.

⁷ The polis probably also supplied the cavalryman's arms, although Xenophon's text is unclear on this point.

⁸ Xenophon's reference (*Ages.* 8.6–7) to the simplicity of the doors of Agesilaos' house, which forms part of a contrast with the ways of the Persian king, is unhelpful in this regard. Certainly, the idea that citizen houses contained no valuable possessions is demonstrably false (e.g. Hdt. 6.62; Xen. *Hell.* 6.5.28, 30). The reference to simplicity of sacrifices in [Plato], *II* 148d–149c) appears to relate to public sacrifices.

⁹ Xenophon himself draws *explicit* contrasts with practice outside Sparta only in respect of certain aspects relevant to our discussion (control of *paidagōgos*/control of *paidonomos*; wearing of sandals/barefootedness; changes of cloaks/a single cloak only; unlimited food/moderate diet). The limited range of his explicit contrasts reflects his

concern to contrast the Spartan upbringing with the best education elsewhere, which was generally available only to wealthier boys. Hence he does not comment explicitly on the elimination of differences between rich and poor, though this emerges implicitly from his account.

[10] Kennell (1995, 180 n.29), citing D. Chr. *Or.* 72.2. The philosophical association is intensified by the possibility (ibid. 102–7) that the passage from the *Inst. Lac.* may come from a lost work of Sphairos.

[11] Contrast the Persian education system 'described' in Xenophon's *Cyropaedia* (1.2.15), which is said to be open only to 'non-producing' children (*paidas argountas*). Kennell (1985, 43; 133–4) mistakenly views this system as based on Spartan practice, misinterpreting the passage as a statement of the costs of the upbringing. On the considerable 'factual differences' between Xenophon's accounts of the Spartan and Persian educational systems, Tuplin 1994, 150–61.

[12] There is no basis for Kennell's claim (1995, 134) that 'only the propertied families [had] the resources to allow their sons to join the *ilai* and contribute food'. For most of our period all Spartiate families were sufficiently propertied to do so.

[13] Hdt. 4.149; 7.134; cf. 6.60; Wide 1893; Andronikos 1956; R. Parker 1989, 144, 147; Hibler 1992; 1993; Salapata 1993.

[14] This may be one of several instances of practices in Herodotus' traditional list which were obsolete by his day.

[15] Pipili 1987, 71–5; A. Powell 1998, 122–34; T.J. Smith 1998. Note, however, that there are no *symposion* scenes on vases found in Lakonia itself and a recent study suggests that these scenes reflect cult-meals at the Heraion on Samos (Pipili 1998, esp. 90).

[16] Aristop. *Knights* 278–9; cf. Harvey 1994, 36; *Inst. Lac.* 236f; Plut. *Lyk.* 12.7; Athen. 138d; Hesychius, s.v. *bapha*; Pollux 6.57.

[17] None of the sources which David cites (1989, 4 n.8; 5 n.18) to support this attribution mentions the term.

[18] e.g. Aristop. *Ach.* 343; *Ec.* 850; *V.* 1131; Pl. *Prt.* 335d; *Smp.* 219b6; Isaios 5.11; Thphr. *Char.* 22.13; Eub. fr.68, Hunter, *ap.* Athen. 307f and the references in LSJ, Rev. Suppl., s.v. I am grateful to Roger Brock for performing an electronic word-search on my behalf.

[19] The fact that Duris wrongly designates Pausanias as king hardly inspires confidence in his testimony.

[20] The most well-known tradition attributes it to Orsippos of Megara in Ol.15 = 720 BC (cf. scholiast *ad loc.*; Paus. 1.44.1; the Hadrianic copy of his epitaph sometimes attributed to Simonides, Hicks and Hill 1901, no. 1); but other traditions credit it to Akanthos of Sparta or an unknown Athenian athlete (cf. McDonnell 1991, 183 and n. 2, with refs.).

[21] McDonnell shows convincingly that the loincloths worn by athletes on some of the Perizoma Group of vases represent the practice of their Etruscan consumers (1991, 186–8).

[22] Instone (1989, 256), cited with approval by Hornblower (1991, 28), suggests that Thucydides' reference to recent change refers only to practice at Olympia. 'The force of the first καί in the second sentence is probably to imply that in the past loincloths were worn in the Olympic games too, as well as when training; only recently has *that* practice stopped, though the practice of wearing them continues for training.' This interpretation, however, runs counter to the archaeological evidence which, apart from a minority of

Ch. 7. Restrictions on the deployment of wealth in Spartiate life

vases in the Perizoma Group, shows no indication of the wearing of loincloths in training in Thucydides' time. It would also be odd if the previous sentence about the Spartiates' introduction of nudity during exercise, which implies that the practice had been followed in other poleis, were immediately followed by a statement implying that the practice had since been abandoned everywhere, including at Sparta.

23 The report in Lucian, *Anacharsis* 38, that Spartan youths were nude during their whipping at the altar of Artemis Orthia, relates to the Roman ritual (Kennell 1995, 73), not the very different classical rite.

24 Finley 1986, 166–7; Pritchett 1974–91, i.4 n. 3; Cartledge 1977, 27. The state surely supplied the equipment of helots and *neodamōdeis* in its service (cf. the comments of Gomme et al., 1945–81, iii.548).

25 In one of the *Lakainōn Apophthegmata* (Anon. no. 17 = Plut. *Mor.* 241f) a mother gives to her son the shield formerly used by his father; but, as Ducat (1999, 162–4) has shown, these hellenistic female anecdotes have little to do with reality. Sekunda (1998, 20–1) envisages military clothing being made by the warriors' wives and mothers; but there is no precise evidence for this in a Spartan context, where functional textile production was primarily the task of helot servants (Xen. *Lak. Pol.* 1.4).

26 Bronze hoplite figurines: Bloesch 1959; Jost 1975; Herfort-Koch 1986, nos. 127–45, with pl. 18–20. Lead hoplite figurines: Wace 1929.

27 *BSA* 26 (1924–25) 253; Fitzhardinge 1980, 87–9; Steinhauer n. d., 58–9.

28 Note also the personal blazon mentioned in *Apophth. Lak.*, Anon. no. 41 = Plut. *Mor.* 234c; the date to which the anecdote applies is unknown.

29 On the crimson uniform, cf. esp. Xen. *Lak. Pol.* 11.3; Arist. fr. 542, Rose; *Inst. Lac.* 24 = Plut. *Mor.* 238f; plus further refs. in Cartledge 1977, 15 n. 38. Spartan dress also influenced early fourth-century mercenary armies (Xen. *Anab.* 1.2.16; *Ages.* 2.7). On Spartiate hair, see further below. I am grateful to Dr Nicholas V. Sekunda for his advice on matters of military uniform.

30 The problem derives from the fact that the sources mostly call it simply by the colour term *phoinikis*. Xenophon elaborates a little, calling it a '*stolēn…phoinikida*'; but the term *stolē* is itself imprecise, usually carrying the generic meaning of clothing or apparel (LSJ⁹, s.v.). Scholars often refer to the *phoinikis* as a cloak; and Cartledge (1977, 15), adopting this interpretation, distinguishes it from the *chitōniskos*, or tunic worn against the skin. Anderson (1970, 39), however, thinks that the *phoinikis* was the tunic; whereas Lazenby (1985, 32) and Sekunda (1998, 20–2) suggest that both tunic and outer cloak were crimson. This last idea perhaps best fits the evidence of the sources: first, with their suggestion that the red outfit both created a striking visual impact (which implies external visibility) and concealed the presence of blood from wounds (which implies something worn against the skin); secondly, with the fact that Spartan troops wore different clothing in different weather conditions (cf. Xen. *Hell.* 4.5.4). The issue also requires setting in the context of the changes in military dress discussed in the main text, especially the wearing of the garment called the *exōmis* over the corslet. If the soldiers depicted on the Boiotian gravestones discussed below (n. 36) are indeed Spartans, that would solve part of the problem, since the *exōmides* which they wear are coloured crimson; as noted there, however, their Spartan identity seems unlikely.

31 Aristop. *Peace* 1172–6; cf. Kromayer and Veith 1928, 51.

32 Cf. Leonymos the Lakonian, who was killed by an arrow which pierced through his shield and leather *spolas* (Xen. *Anab.* 4.1.18).

33 Thuc. 4.34. On the material of the *piloi* at Sphakteria, Anderson 1970, 32–3; on the Spartans' metal cuirasses, Hanson 1989, 82–3.

34 The quotation is from Pritchett 1974–91, ii.247, citing Janssen 1957; cf. Anderson 1970, pl. 11.

35 (i) Grave stēlē of Stratokles: Museum of Fine Arts, Boston, 1971.129; *AJA* 76 (1972) pl. 74; Comstock and Vermeule 1976, 44 no. 64; Sekunda 1998, pl. on p. 6. (ii) Anderson 1970, pl. 10; Sekunda 1998, pl. on p. 16; G.M.A. Richter, *Catalogue of the Greek Sculptures of the Metropolitan Museum of Art*, no. 82.

36 It has been suggested that certain gravestones from Boiotia depicting hoplites with shortish swords, *piloi* and *exōmides* are also Spartans (Chrimes 1949, 364–8). Their Spartan identity has, however, been questioned (Anderson 1970, 32). The sword is not as short as on the Athenian example and the *exōmis* was by no means purely a Spartan garment. Moreover, the inscription bears only the deceased's name, as would be natural for a citizen buried in his own polis; in contrast, the Lakedaimonian grave monuments at Athens and Thespiai discussed in ch. 8 (van Hook 1932; *IG* vii.1904) specify the ethnic of the deceased.

37 Cf. Xen. *Lak. Pol.* 11.3 and the surviving example of a shield captured from the troops on Sphakteria (Shear 1937a and 1937b, 347–9).

38 Photius, Lexikon, s.v. *Lambda* and Eustathius *In Iliada* i.293.39–43, both citing Eupolis fr. 359, Kock.

39 For the iconographical evidence, see *Figs*. 9 and 10; for the literary evidence, *Apophthegmata Basileōn kai Stratēgōn* (= Plut. *Mor.* 191e); *Apophth. Lak.* (= *Mor.* 216c; 217e); *Inst. Lac.* (= *Mor.* 241f); Plut. *Dion* 58.3; *Lyk.* 19.2.

40 Boys: Plut. *Lyk.* 16.6. Men: Hdt. 1.82; Xen. *Lak. Pol.* 11.3; *Apophthegmata Basileōn kai Stratēgōn* (= Plut. *Mor.* 189e); *Apophth. Lak.* (= *Mor.* 228f); Plut. *Lyk.* 22.1; *Lys.* 1.2. Iconographic evidence: references in David 1992, 12–15, with nn. 7, 16–18.

41 Besides references to the servants of prominent individuals (e.g. Hdt. 6.63; Xen. *Hell.* 5.4.28; Plut. *Lys.* 16.2), note the generic references in Xen. *Lak. Pol.* 1.4; 6.3; 7.5.

42 Dedications of leads depicting ornate model textiles at the sanctuary of Artemis Orthia are most plausibly interpreted as representations of items of clothing made by their female dedicants (Hodkinson 1998b, 58; Foxhall and Stears 2000). But one should distinguish women's engagement in the production of such valuable clothing for socio-religious purposes from the routine labour of making everyday clothing. These textile motifs cease after the end of period 'Lead II' (i.e. after *c.* 580 BC), though this may reflect general developments in votive practice rather than a withdrawal from textile production.

43 This passage is sometimes interpreted (e.g. by Cartledge 1981, 91) as signifying that the girls actually wrestled with the boys; but all Euripides says is that they shared the same racetracks and palaistras.

44 Whether there was an intellectual content to the girls' public training is uncertain. References to the intellectual achievements of certain Spartan women in various Athenian sources (Cartledge 1981, 92–3, with references), even if they are to be taken seriously, need not imply that they were the product of public rather than home-based education.

45 Kahil 1977; Scanlon 1988; Sourvinou-Inwood 1988; Paus. 5.16.2–4.

46 I omit consideration of the lesbian pederastic relationships which allegedly existed between Spartan women and girls (Plut. *Lyk.* 18.4). If this was authentic practice, and not just late invention, its significance in terms of the influence of wealth is unclear, since the

selection of a partner might have been made either on grounds of physical and emotional attraction or on grounds of wealth and the formation of influential connections.

47 Scanty dress: Cartledge 1981, 91–2, with refs. to the literary sources and a number of Lakonian bronze figurines; cf. Herfort-Koch 1986, nos. K48–50; Scanlon 1988, 191–203. On festival nakedness, Plut. *Lyk.* 14.2–4; Stewart 1997, 108–14, with a catalogue of naked female bronzes (Appendix, pp. 231–4).

48 For the suggestion, Ollier 1933–43, i.34; Oliva 1971, 32; Cartledge 1981, 91 n. 45. It is disputed by Greenstein Millender 1996, 255–63.

49 The following remarks are outlined in more detail in chapter 9.

50 The prohibition of long hair is implied also by Lucian, *Fugitivi* 27 and (probably) by Xenophon of Ephesos 5.1.7.

Chapter 8

RESTRICTIONS ON THE DEPLOYMENT OF WEALTH: BURIAL AND FUNERARY PRACTICE

Recent years have witnessed vigorous debate concerning whether the factors governing Greek funerary behaviour were primarily religious, cultural or socio-political.[1] At first sight a study of the role of wealth in funerary behaviour might seem most closely aligned with a socio-political approach. As a recent study notes, 'a costly, elaborate and well-attended Greek funeral…provided a perfect showcase for the display of family wealth, power and prestige' (Garland 1989, 2). Nevertheless, even proponents of cultural interpretations would acknowledge the relevance of wealth and social status to the character of Greek funerary behaviour (cf. Sourvinou-Inwood 1995, 289). Similarly, whilst funerary legislation laid down by a number of poleis was undoubtedly directed at ensuring proper ritual behaviour for the burial of the city's dead and at limiting the incursion of mortuary rites into community life, it also aimed at restricting funerary expenditures and the divisive display and promotion of family interests (Garland 1989).[2] Religious and socio-political concerns went hand-in-hand. I would, consequently, align my study with recent approaches to Spartiate funerary practice and legislation (e.g. Cartledge 1987, 331–43; Nafissi 1991, 277–341) which give due weight to both their religious and cultural aspects and their socio-political aspects. In what follows I shall consider first the burial of non-royal citizens, then that of Spartan women, and finally the funerary customs for Spartan kings.[3]

The burial of non-royal citizens
Before 550
The evidence of Tyrtaios
To view the classical situation in context, it is necessary to begin with the evidence from the archaic period. The earliest literary evidence comes from the poetry of Tyrtaios in the late seventh century. He gives a clear impression that funeral rites in seventh-century Sparta were highly visible affairs. Fragment 7 (West) indicates that one of the obligations of the Messenian helots was that,

> …they bewail their masters, they and their wives,
> when the mournful fate of death strikes one of them.[4]

The most plausible interpretation of this passage is that each Spartiate was mourned by his own helots. By implication, therefore, wealthier landowners would receive a grander send-off from a greater crowd of mourners than less prosperous citizens.⁵

Further evidence for prominent funeral rites in this period is provided by two ivory fibula plaques from the third quarter of the seventh century found at the sanctuary of Artemis Orthia.⁶ Both show *prothesis* scenes. The more complete plaque depicts the deceased – a bearded male – laid out on a bier, behind which stand two wailing female mourners and another bearded man. The deceased and a standing male are also visible on the other, more fragmentary, plaque. Since such decorated ivories were surely prestige objects accessible only to the rich, they probably depict the funerary behaviour of wealthier families.

Another fragment of Tyrtaios (fr. 12) suggests that the polis made a conscious attempt to manipulate such visible private funeral rites for state purposes. In a poem praising the virtues of the hoplite soldier, Tyrtaios devotes several lines (27–34) to the burial of a fallen warrior:

> Then young and old alike lament his death
> and all the people mourn his grievous loss.
> His tomb is greatly honoured (ἀρίσημοι) among men, as are his sons
> and sons' sons and his lineage evermore.
> Neither his glorious reputation nor his name ever die,
> he still lives on, though laid beneath the ground
> if he stood firm and fought courageously
> for land and children till furious Ares struck him down.

As has long been recognised, Tyrtaios places the ideology of the heroic death of the individual evident in the Homeric poems into the new context of military service and death on behalf of the community. The fallen Spartiate warrior is offered magnificent public funeral rites on a par with those practised privately by wealthy families. He is promised the reward of heroisation (Fuqua 1981; Bockisch 1981, 43), with active community involvement in the funerary lamentations, honour within the polis for his tomb and for his descendants, and the perpetuation of his memory for time immemorial.

Excavated burials

How does this evidence correlate with the archaeological record? Any hopes that the prominent funeral ceremonies attested by the literary and iconographical sources would be matched by a series of equally prominent burials are sadly disappointed. The record of the earliest burials at Sparta is noticeably thin. Rescue excavations have produced four modest (ninth-century?) inhumations without grave goods, found under layers of Protogeometric pottery in the region of the ancient Spartan village of Limnai to the east of the Acropolis. Three of the tombs were found together, along with stray bones possibly from a secondary burial; they may have formed a small family cemetery.⁷ From Amyklai there is

Ch. 8. Restrictions on the deployment of wealth: burial and funerary practice

also a similarly early cist-grave (an inhumation in a box-shaped structure made of stone slabs set on edge). As one moves later in date, the burials become richer in content. We have evidence of five pithos cremations (burials in which the ashes were deposited in clay containers known as pithoi): four from Limnai (again), the other from just south of the Acropolis in the area of the ancient village of Mesoa. Three of these cremations, which date to the late Geometric period, contained metal grave goods such as bronze plain and spiral rings, pins, cylinders and disks. One of the Limnai pithoi appears to be a warrior burial, complete with iron sword and fragments of three daggers. Another pithos shows some signs of a stone mound over the grave.[8] Finally, there is an undated cremation covered by a terracotta slab which possessed a grave marker in the form of a plain slab and contained a few fragments of gold strips.[9]

As one approaches the period of Tyrtaios in the late seventh century, however, evidence for these prosperous burials dies away. Indeed, there is only one securely dated burial that is approximately contemporary to the literary and iconographical evidence. A cist-grave inhumation, once again from Limnai, is dated by two Lakonian II lakainai to the late seventh or early sixth century; but it apparently contained no metal grave goods.[10] Other candidates for burials in this period are marked by a degree of uncertainty.[11] A group of seven early seventh-century Proto-Corinthian aryballoi, now in the Ashmolean Museum, and said to be from Sparta, may come from a burial; but firm information about the circumstances of their find is lacking.[12] Rescue excavations in the early 1990s on the north slope of a small hill about 200 m south of the Acropolis uncovered a two-storey building from the early sixth century (Raftopoulou 1998b, 127, 134–5 and figs. 12.18–19). The building was surrounded by extensive water-control works, including a system of channels made of roof tiles, on one of which was placed a set of 22 pieces of Lakonian black-figure pottery from a symposiastic meal. The only report yet available treats the building as a tomb which later became a heroon; and it is true that other burials were found in this area. However, the report makes no mention of funerary remains in the building; and, although the pottery deposit is not given any date, its appearance (ibid. fig. 12.19) indicates that cult activity had already commenced during the sixth century. Although it is tempting to view the building in question as the tomb of a fallen warrior accorded continuing honour after his death, further details are awaited before the original funerary use of the building can be confirmed.[13]

The only other candidate for an archaic burial is also controversial. An excavation in the ancient village of Mesoa revealed a low wall, some 40 cm high, retaining a tumulus formed of ashes and animal bones (notably horses, oxen and boars). Within the tumulus was a burial group of four cist graves (two men, one woman and one child). There were no grave goods, apart from a small bone horse statuette in the female grave. Lying on its side among the graves was a terracotta amphora, decorated with a figured relief on its visible,

239

upwards-facing side, which the excavator dated to c. 600 BC or slightly later. Although it had a stone slab across its mouth, the amphora had no contents and was clearly not a burial container. Close by the graves was a pottery kiln and also the remains of a house wall.[14] Although originally hailed as an authentic archaic grave group, the dating of this burial assemblage has been challenged. The only artefact securely datable to the archaic period is the relief amphora;[15] yet its connection with the burials is uncertain. It is improbable that the amphora functioned as their grave marker, since its highest point stands only 10 cm above the covering stones of the graves and one of its handles was partly underneath one of the covering slabs (*BCH* 85 (1961), 684; cf. Christou 1964a, 143 fig. 1 and pl. 74). The burials are now seen not as archaic but as much more recent (Steinhauer 1972, 244 n. 15).

The terracotta relief amphoras
One category of contemporary excavated artefact constitutes an exception to the general paucity of funerary evidence for the late seventh and early sixth centuries. The archaic terracotta relief amphora found in the burial tumulus discussed above is not unique, but is matched by a further twenty or so similar amphoras found elsewhere in Sparta, mainly in fragmentary form (see *Fig.* 11).[16] Their chronological range is usually thought to cover the period from c. 625 to c. 550, though some would limit their time span to the early sixth century.[17] Scholars have generally regarded them as funerary in purpose (e.g. Christou 1964b; Fitzhardinge 1980, 52; Sourvinou-Inwood 1995, 220–1, 256, 276–8). One apparent difficulty with this interpretation is that several amphoras were found in or close to sanctuaries: in the Heroon by the River Eurotas; in the vicinity of the so-called Great Altar, about 100 m further north;[18] on the Acropolis; and at the sanctuary of Artemis Orthia.[19] However, the exact find spots of many of the amphoras are only loosely indicated and do not always reflect their original locations: one amphora found in the Roman theatre had been re-used within the theatre to store water, and fragments of at least one other have turned up both at the altar by the Eurotas and on the Acropolis.[20] Furthermore, funerary purpose and sanctuary context are not necessarily incompatible. There is literary testimony (considered below) for funerary monuments close to sanctuaries and archaeological evidence for the association of shrines (especially hero-shrines) with places of burial.[21] Indeed, most of the sanctuaries mentioned above lay in the burial regions of Limnai and Mesoa, and the fact that most of the amphoras were found in these regions is further argument for their funerary function. Whilst this evidence is not conclusive, there is a good case for viewing the amphoras as funerary objects. If so, the evidence for their subsequent re-use implies that these amphoras were not buried inside a mound but were used as markers above ground. Indeed, the fact that all the amphoras are decorated only on one side suggests that they were intended to be lain on their side with the decorated relief visible to passers-by.[22]

Ch. 8. Restrictions on the deployment of wealth: burial and funerary practice

Fig. 11. Drawing of terracotta relief amphora, from the Heroon by the R. Eurotas – with the addition of a fragment from the Cabinet des Médailles, Paris (reproduced with permission of the British School at Athens).

The size of these amphoras is noteworthy: the height of the two complete examples is some 670 and 700 cm, respectively. So too is the character of their relief decoration (see *Fig.* 11). It is spread over three horizontal zones. The decoration of the lowest zone is limited to large rosettes placed between abstract patterns. In the middle, shoulder zone, however, the extant amphoras bear similar reliefs, consisting of scenes depicting a chariot and charioteer followed by a hoplite on foot, who is sometimes shown in the process of mounting the chariot. The decoration of the upper zone around the neck displays three distinct chronological phases. On the earliest amphoras, decoration is limited to patterns of tongues and grooves. The second phase is marked by friezes of animals and mythical beasts. In the third phase, however, the neck receives the principal figured representation of the amphora, with lively scenes of hunting or battle. (*Fig.* 11 provides a good example of this last phase.)

The iconography of the amphoras matches the ideology proclaimed by Tyrtaios in several respects. Warfare and warriors are clearly a central theme, as is the hoplite infantryman who appears on the shoulder zone of every amphora. Yet the social persona of the hoplite is depicted in an overtly aristocratic manner (cf. Sourvinou-Inwood 1995, 220–1, 225–6, 273). By placing him in association with a chariot, these scenes – and especially those in which the warrior is actually mounting the chariot – give him a 'heroic' image akin to Tyrtaios' ascription of Homeric qualities to the fallen hoplite. The lions which sometimes appear on the neck in its second decorative phase may also suggest a connection with heroes through their strength and perceived pre-eminence in the animal world; lions appear too among the slaughtered game in the hunt scene from the tumulus amphora. Finally, the warrior scenes which appear in the third phase depict not regular hoplite battles but the kind of combat described in some of Tyrtaios' poems, in which the soldiers are supported by light-armed troops slinging stones, and even by archers.[23] The warriors' shields are not uniform as in hoplite combat, but comprise various styles, including the so-called figure-of-eight 'Dipylon shield', whose depiction was 'the standard "property" for artists who wished to depict a heroic scene' (Snodgrass 1967, 45). The archaizing atmosphere of the amphoras is further emphasized by the fact that they are significantly later in date than similar series known from elsewhere (the Cyclades, Crete, Rhodes, Boiotia) which commenced in the years either side of 700 (Schäfer 1957; Cambitoglou 1981; Simandoni-Bournia 1990).

Massimo Nafissi has recently suggested (1991, 338–41) that the development of Spartiate funerary practice before 550 should be set in the context of the transformation of a seventh-century aristocratic society into the classical Spartan polis. He concurs that the practice of grand aristocratic funerals was incorporated within the ethic of the heroic military death on behalf of the community. He argues, however, that this ideology failed to restrain the actions of leading families, who were able to exploit the heroisation of their dead for the promotion of their lineages. Only from the mid-sixth century, in his view, with the reforming work of the ephor Chilon, were their funerary activities brought under official control.

This analysis, however, perhaps exaggerates the possibilities open to leading families in the last years of this period. Certainly, the existence of highly visible funerary rites in the later seventh century is suggested by both the evidence of Tyrtaios and the iconographical evidence of the two *prothesis* scenes on the ivory plaques. However, these *prothesis* scenes quickly disappear from the artistic repertoire. Outside Lakonia similar scenes are common until the 530s; but they never recur at Sparta, either in the ivory reliefs, which continue in some density until the mid-sixth century, or in any other medium. The disappearance of the depiction of the *prothesis* may indicate that such scenes had lost their prestige value due to the extension of prominent rituals to dead warriors from ordinary families. Furthermore, the highly visible funerary rituals have not produced burials rich in grave goods. Overall, the early Spartan burial evidence is disappointing in both quantity and quality; and it falls away markedly in the century before 550. The disappearance of the pithos cremations with their metal grave goods is especially suggestive of a degree of sumptuary control. The Spartan burial record contrasts markedly with the much fuller cemetery evidence from Aegean and eastern mainland Greece. In this period it has far more in common with other areas of western mainland Greece, where the rarity of archaic graves is also evident in Achaia, Aitolia, Arkadia, Elis, Messenia, and elsewhere in Lakonia (Morris 1997, 54).[24] It is true that the large and elaborately decorated relief amphoras may represent an attempt by the wealthy to establish prominent markers for their family graves by utilising an iconography in keeping with the new Tyrtaian ideology. If so, early sixth-century burial practice was far from egalitarian. Nevertheless, such markers constituted only a limited form of display, especially in the absence of any written indication of the identity of the deceased. Unlike several states in central Greece (Wallace 1970), archaic Sparta lacks any funerary monuments with inscribed verse epitaphs.[25] The indications are that already before 550 Spartan funerary expenditure and display were relatively restrained.

After 550
The evidence
All the evidence suggests that after 550 this restraint was considerably extended. It must be stressed from the start that there is one big gap in this evidence. No burials have yet been discovered in Sparta that are securely datable to the three and a half centuries between 550 and 200 BC.[26] The funerary restraint discussed below, which included the prohibition of grave goods, is no doubt itself a major factor in the archaeological invisibility of classical burials; and it is not of course impossible that some of the undated burials without grave goods mentioned earlier are of classical date. Even if all these undated tombs were indeed from our period, however, we would still have an astonishing archaeological lacuna whose full explanation is far from clear. With the exception of a single extant burial of Spartan soldiers abroad, the following analysis must consequently rest solely upon the evidence of the literary sources, epigraphy and iconography.

Before outlining the relevant evidence, we must rule out of consideration one particular class of artefact: a much-debated series of stone or marble Lakonian 'hero-reliefs', which are found both at Sparta and elsewhere in Lakonia from the mid-sixth century to the hellenistic period (Tod and Wace 1906, 102–13). These reliefs typically depict a seated couple or single male holding a wine cup and accompanied by a snake and sometimes other chthonic objects. Occasionally, miniature worshippers are shown approaching the seated figure(s). Opinions concerning the identity of the persons depicted and the purpose of the reliefs have differed widely.[27] One view sees the seated figures as heroes, although within this view there is divergence between those who view the figures as mythological heroes, such as Helen and Menelaos, and others who interpret them as the heroised dead, including family ancestors. Another interpretation holds that the reliefs were dedicated to chthonian deities, such as Hades, Dionysos or Demeter (e.g. Stibbe 1991). Proponents of this latter view normally accept that some of the reliefs may relate to heroes, but would exclude any connection with the heroised dead. In recent years interpretation of the stone reliefs as monuments to mythological heroes has been boosted by the discovery of around a thousand similar terracotta plaques at the shrine of Agamemnon and Alexandra/Cassandra at Agia Paraskevi near Amyklai[28] This find augments smaller numbers of similar plaques already known from other shrines such as the Heroon by the Eurotas (Wace 1905/6; Hibler 1992; 1993; Salapata 1993).²⁹ Since the reliefs concern mythological heroes, they do not appear to be relevant to the question of Spartan families' treatment of their dead. It has, admittedly, been suggested that a change on the stone reliefs from depictions of a seated couple to depiction of a single male, which occurs early in the fifth century, may signify a shift in their character towards a funerary purpose or towards their use as votives to the recently deceased (Hibler 1993, 200–1). This suggestion, however, is somewhat undermined by the fact that seated couples subsequently reappear on the more numerous terracotta plaques. The variations between couples and single figures (which include terracottas depicting single *women*) are more plausibly ascribed to the depiction of different heroes or heroines, who were represented singly or as couples according to their individual stories (Salapata 1993). It is true that certain real-life Spartiates were sometimes given such hero worship after their death, to judge from a late sixth-century relief bearing the inscription [..]ΙΛΩΝ, which has been interpreted as a reference to the famous ephor and sage Chilon.³⁰ It has been suggested that Chilon, like Brasidas in Amphipolis over a century later (Thuc. 5.11), was honoured with a heroon around his tomb, with the relief being erected over his actual grave (Wace 1937, 220; Cartledge 1987, 339). This, however, was an example of communal, not specifically family, worship. This is also the case with another, late archaic, relief from Magoula (the ancient Spartan village of Pitana), depicting a standing youth holding a cake or fruit and his spear, which bears the inscription, 'The *koroi* [dedicate this image of] Theokles son of Nam[-]'.³¹ The 'hero-reliefs' can, consequently, be left aside in our consideration of the use of private family wealth.

There are no synoptic accounts of funerary practices for non-royal Spartiate citizens before the late fourth century. The earliest account is a brief statement in a passage of Herakleides Lembos (373.13 Dilts), which derives from the Aristotelian *Polity of the Lakedaimonians* (*Lak. Pol.*, = 611.13 Rose), that, 'Graves are modest and the same for all.'

Next come two accounts which bear obvious resemblances. First, the hellenistic *Instituta Laconica* (no. 18 = Plut. *Mor.* 238d):

> Lykourgos removed all superstition concerning burials, granting the right to bury the dead in the polis and to have the *mnēmeia* near the sacred places. He also abolished pollutions. He permitted them to bury nothing with the body; but, all treating it alike, to enfold it in a *phoinikis* and olive leaves. He did away with inscriptions on *mnēmeia*, except for those who had died in war, and also with mourning (*penthē*) and lamentations (*odyrmous*).

Secondly, Plutarch's *Life of Lykourgos* (27.1–2):

> Furthermore, he [sc. Lykourgos] made excellent arrangements for their burials. First, removing all superstition, he did not prevent them from burying the dead within the polis and having the *mnēmata* near the sacred places, thus making the youth

Ch. 8. Restrictions on the deployment of wealth: burial and funerary practice

familiar with such sights and accustomed to them, so that they were not disturbed by them and had no horror of death as polluting those who touched a corpse or walked among graves. Next, he allowed them to bury nothing with the body; instead they enfolded it in a *phoinikis* and olive leaves when they laid it away. When they buried it, it was not permitted to inscribe the name of the deceased, except for a man who died in war and a holy woman/woman in childbirth [*text disputed**]. He fixed a short period of mourning (*penthous*), eleven days; on the twelfth they had to sacrifice to Demeter and end their grieving.

[* πλὴν ἀνδρὸς ἐν πολέμῳ καὶ γυναικὸς τῶν ἱερῶς (vel ἱερῶν) ἀποθανόντων. K. Latte, followed by a number of recent editors (Ziegler, Flacelière, Manfredini and Piccirilli), would amend the final words to (τῶν) λεχοῦς ἀποθανόντων.]

Besides these accounts of ordinary burials in Sparta, Aelian (*Varia Historia* 6.6) gives a synoptic account of the burial of fallen soldiers:

> Those fighting nobly and dying are crowned/bound[32] with olive and other branches and carried (off) with praises; those who were supremely brave were wrapped in their *phoinikis* and buried with special honours.

In addition, the evidence of a number of literary and epigraphic sources which refer to the burial of particular (groups of) dead warriors will be considered below.

Although these sources are largely post-classical in date, there is nevertheless reason for thinking that most of their information relates to an earlier period, especially as the details in the *Instituta Laconica* and Plutarch's *Lykourgos* largely elaborate the essence of the message in the late fourth-century Aristotelian *Lak. Pol.* On one particular point, their reference to intra-mural burial, their evidence is in line with the archaeological record of burials in the vicinity of the Spartan villages during both the pre- and post-classical periods. There are other respects too, as we shall see, in which their testimony matches archaic or classical evidence either from Sparta itself or from elsewhere in Greece.

The significance of the funerary measures mentioned in the above texts can best be viewed in the light of legislation attested from other poleis which was designed partly to ensure a proper despatch of the dead into the next world, but also to control the divisiveness and factionalism produced by elaborate and expensive burial practices and the potential influence derived by leading families from their conduct of private funerary rituals (Garland 1989; cf. Ampolo 1984; Toher 1991). Although sometimes subjected to social control, significant expenditure on funeral expenses was otherwise common practice in many Greek states. Even the comparatively austere funerary practices advocated in Plato's *Laws* (958d–960c), which were specifically designed to avoid extravagant spending, permitted an expenditure of one mina (100 drachmas) – a hundred times the daily wage of a skilled craftsman – for those in the lowest property class, rising to five minas (500 drachmas) for those in the highest property class. Plato's assumption of differential expenditures according to wealth speaks volumes for the opportunities which the death of a family member offered for families to engage in the conspicuous consumption and destruction of wealth. The Spartan restrictions detailed above were partly designed to prevent the use of wealth in various aspects of funerary ritual.

Restriction of public mourning

Public mourning was a significant part of archaic Spartan funerary practice. As we have seen, the poems of Tyrtaios twice emphasize the importance of public lamentation (frs. 7; 12.27), and this message is reinforced by the ivory plaques which depict open lamentation during the *prothesis*. In contrast, the *Instituta Laconica* and Plutarch both indicate severe restrictions upon public mourning.[33] How precisely was the restraint on mourning applied? At first sight, the two accounts seem mutually contradictory. At the end of its remarks concerning the prohibition of inscribed monuments, the *Instituta* abruptly adds that so also were mourning (*penthē*) and lamentations (*odyrmoi*). Plutarch, however, states that mourning was permitted only for the brief period of eleven days. Although Plutarch sometimes invents plausible detail to fill out information provided by his sources, the precision of his account, including the circumstantial reference to the sacrifice to Demeter on the twelfth day, argues for its authenticity. In fact, the two accounts can be reconciled. Plutarch's comments clearly relate to the overall period of transition during which rituals performed by the family effected the passage of the deceased from the land of the living. This was an invariable feature of Greek treatment of the dead, whatever controls were placed on the ceremonies and behaviour through which it was articulated. When the *Instituta* comments that mourning was prohibited, neither the original author of the remark nor the hellenistic compiler of the *Instituta* can surely have thought that Spartans had no period or rituals of transition. Its comments, with their stress on the prohibition of lamentations, therefore probably relate to outward and audible expressions of grief. Xenophon provides a historical instance of this compulsory restraint, when the ephors ordered female relatives of the dead at Leuktra not to cry out but to bear their grief in silence (*Hell.* 6.4.16). When King Kleomenes III in the late third century maintained his normal outward bearing on the death of his wife, but nevertheless engaged in the appropriate mourning with his kinsfolk, he was not merely displaying personal high-mindedness, as Plutarch claims (*Kleom.* 22.1–3), but following traditional Spartan precedent.

It is instructive to compare Spartan practice with legislation attested elsewhere. The prohibition of lamentation was allegedly advocated by the archaic lawgiver Charondas of Catana (Stobaios 44.40 = 4.153, Hense) and is also attributed to Epizephyrian Locri (Herakleides Lembos 383.60, Dilts = Arist. fr. 611.60, Rose). Solonian legislation is said to have prohibited female mourners from lacerating their cheeks, singing prepared dirges or engaging in lamentation during the funeral procession; and only those closely related to the deceased could engage in lamentation at the grave (Cicero, *De Legibus* 2.59, 64;

Plut. *Solon* 21.4). A similar restriction of lamentation until after the funerary procession reached the grave was enacted *c.* 400 BC by the Labyad phratry at Delphi (Sokolowski 1969, no. 77; Garland 1989, 9). If the *Instituta Laconica*'s brief statement should indeed be interpreted as a complete prohibition of lamentation, Spartan restraint went further than in most other poleis. So also its curtailment of the period of mourning to eleven days is briefer than the thirty days current in classical Athens, and far shorter than the limits specified in the third-century law at Gambreion, near Pergamon, which stated that ceremonies for the deceased were to be concluded within three months and that men and women should cease their mourning, respectively, in the fourth and fifth months (Garland 1989, 10). There is, however, an even tougher law from Thasos of *c.* 350 BC, which limits mourning to as little as five days (Pouilloux 1954, 371). In sum, the prohibition of lamentation and severe curtailment of the period of mourning limited the extent to which families could engage in self-promotion through the advertisement of their loss of distinguished kin. The former provision also automatically removed the tendency for lamentations to be made not just for the person recently dead but for other deceased kin, thereby publicising the lineage of the family concerned.

Equality of burial

A second restrictive aspect of Spartiate funerary practice concerned the burial itself. The fragment deriving from the Aristotelian *Lak. Pol.* insists that Spartiate graves were both modest in character and the same for all. The passage from the *Instituta Laconica*, which may have been influenced by the Aristotelian *Lak. Pol.* (see ch. 2), concurs that every deceased Spartiate was treated alike. Both the *Instituta* and Plutarch's *Lykourgos* state that grave goods were not permitted and that the body was simply enfolded in a military cloak, the *phoinikis*, and in olive leaves.

Before placing Spartiate practice in the context of practice elsewhere, we must correct one recent misinterpretation of the above evidence. Nafissi (1991, 291) has argued that Plutarch has confused two different circumstances of burial: that into an account of the modest burial accorded to Spartan dead in general he has inserted details of the obsequies for fallen warriors. In reality, Nafissi claims, burial in the *phoinikis* and olive leaves was reserved for those who died in battle. He cites in support Aelian's statement that those who died bravely were 'crowned' with olive and other plants and that burial in the *phoinikis* was reserved to those of special distinction. The crown of olive, he suggests, was linked to the military prize of *aristeia*. This interpretation, however, is misguided. First, Aelian's evidence is implausible: it is unbelievable that the *phoinikis*, the standard garment of every Spartan soldier, was denied in death, not only to citizens who died peacefully, having worn it without dishonour in life, but even to many fallen soldiers who had died wearing it in battle. The implication that those who died during peacetime were less deserving is contradicted by attested Spartan ideology (Loraux 1977, 110). Tyrtaios (frs. 10.27–9; 11.11–13; 12.35–42) and Xenophon (*Lak. Pol.* 9.2–3) insist on the honour of the brave soldier who survives and portray escape from premature death as an inseparable companion of Spartan valour.[34] Moreover, prizes of *aristeia* were not reserved for fallen combatants, but were given also to living victors. Eurybiades, who led the Greek fleet at Salamis, was given the victor's crown of olive. To the best of our knowledge, he finally died in peacetime; but he was still honoured with a prominent memorial (Hdt. 8.124; Paus. 3.16.6). Secondly, there is no reason to believe that Plutarch has confusedly inserted details of military burials into his account. He clearly refers to Spartiate burials in general; indeed, his following sentence, which mentions a specific exception for fallen warriors, indicates the non-military context of the overall passage. This peacetime context is even clearer in the *Instituta Laconica*.[35] Thirdly, even if Aelian's verb (ἀνεδοῦντο) should be translated as 'crowned' rather than the more prosaic 'bound' (cf. n. 32), his idea that the olive leaves in the burial constituted a crown bears no relation to the evidence of the *Instituta Laconica* or of Plutarch's *Lykourgos*. In both these passages the olive leaves enfold the body (τὸ σῶμα περιστέλλειν/τὸ σῶμα περιέστελλον) in the same manner as the *phoinikis*; they do not crown the head. In sum, except for Aelian's dubious evidence, it is clear that burial in the *phoinikis* and olive leaves refers simply to normal peacetime burials. There is no doubt that the evidence of the Aristotelian *Lak. Pol.*, the *Instituta Laconica* and Plutarch's *Lykourgos* each relates not to military burials but to Spartiate burials in general.

All these sources insist that Spartiate rich and poor received the same modest burial, with no opportunities for the rich to utilise their wealth. The expenditure of sizeable sums on items placed in the tomb was a source of concern to many classical communities; and Sparta was not alone in imposing restrictions. The ordinance of the Labyad phratry at Delphi, for example, limited items deposited in the tomb to no more than 35 drachmas' worth of new purchases or of items removed from the house. Restriction of grave goods is also evident in the archaeological record. Indeed, surviving grave goods are very poor at most excavated cemeteries throughout central Greece and the Aegean after 700. There are indications of richer offerings in the later sixth century; but the fifth century witnessed the onset of austerity in grave goods throughout the Greek world, though the situation changes somewhat after 400 (Morris 1992, 128–55; 1997). Outside Sparta, however, austerity in grave goods does not signify their total absence, even if the surviving contents often consist of no more than two or three modest pots. If the sources are correct in asserting that Spartiate graves held no grave goods at all, Spartan practice was – as in other spheres – an extreme version of general trends.

It is important, moreover, not to confine our attention to the imperishable – or less perishable – grave goods, such as pottery or metal objects, most typically found in excavated burials. We must also take into account essential but perishable accoutrements for the deceased, such as clothing, coverings and pillows. These too could involve significant expenditure which communities often attempted to limit. The Labyad ordinance at Delphi ordered that only one biercloth could be placed under the deceased's body and only one pillow under his head. Solonian legislation at Athens specified that the dead could not be buried with more than three cloaks (*himatia*: Plut. *Solon* 21.5). A law of the later fifth century from Iulis on the island of Keos also imposed a limit of three *hematia*, though their cost was permitted to be as high as 300 drachmas (*IG* xii.5.593; Garland 1989, 11). In specifying that the sole coverings should be olive leaves and a single *phoinikis*, Spartan restrictions on expenditure were again much more severe than laws attested elsewhere.[36] The key point is the absence of scope, not just for differential expenditure, but equally for the sending of social signals by differential choices of grave goods. As Ian Morris has demonstrated, although the comparatively modest grave goods of fifth-century Athens talk a common language of restraint, divergences in the precise goods deposited in different burials score highly on a statistical coefficient of inequality (Morris 1992, 106–18).[37] In contrast, the absence of permissable variation in the deposition of grave goods was the distinctive mark of Spartiate practice.

Memorials, inscriptions and the burial of fallen warriors

Similar conclusions can be drawn concerning the other main potential cause of expenditure, the above-ground grave marker. First, however, we need to clarify the evidence on this issue, beginning with the two relevant literary sources, the *Instituta Laconica* and Plutarch's *Lykourgos*. According to the earlier source, the *Instituta*, Spartiates were permitted two things: to bury their dead within the polis and to have the *mnēmeia* near sacred places. Plutarch follows this account, with some variations in phrasing, except that for *mnēmeia* he substitutes the term *mnēmata*. How should we interpret the second of these provisions, to have the *mnēmeia* / *mnēmata* near sacred places? In its earliest usage the word *mnēma* signified the function of memorialisation performed by an object designed to perpetuate the memory of a dead (or a living) person (Simondon 1982, 81–94). Subsequently, it increasingly came to refer to the object, or memorial, itself. Archaic and early classical funerary inscriptions, however, typically continue to distinguish the *mnēma*, or commemorative stēlē, from the actual tomb or grave. In the fourth century this distinction tended to disappear. Hence the words *mnēmeia* and *mnēmata* are often translated by modern commentators as 'tombs', thus implying that the second provision referred to above was simply a closer specification of the first, to the effect that the general permission for intra-mural burial applied even in the vicinity of sacred places. The older signification of 'memorial', in the sense of a commemorative stēlē, however, never entirely disappeared; and this is clearly the meaning intended in the *Instituta*, since the word *mnēmeia* recurs later in the passage, signifying objects with the potential to carry inscriptions. This intimation of a distinction between the tomb and the memorial is already present at the start of the same passage, in the very separation of Lykourgos' measures into two distinct provisions: a generic provision that *burials* could be made within the polis and a more precise provision concerning permissible locations for *mnēmeia*. On this reading, the second provision is not a closer specification of the first, but makes an additional point about funerary monuments. Note also that, although *mnēmeion* most frequently signifies a grave marker erected over the deceased's grave, it can signify a memorial erected to a person buried elsewhere.[38] I shall argue shortly that this broader interpretation fits better with the evidence of one significant group of monuments, the ΕΝ ΠΟΛΕΜΟΙ stēlai, which were not associated with the grave of the deceased.

These points have a direct bearing on a conflict of evidence between the *Instituta* and Plutarch's *Lykourgos*. Both sources agree that inscriptions commemorating deceased Spartan males were prohibited, except in the case of those who died in battle.[39] They differ, however, regarding the nature and location of such commemorative inscriptions. The *Instituta* refers to inscriptions on *mnēmeia*, without specifying their relation to the grave of the person commemorated. Plutarch's account diverges from the earlier text by entirely rephrasing the sentence and, in particular, by adding the word θάψαντας ('when they buried [it]'): ἐπιγράψαι δὲ τοὔνομα θάψαντας οὐκ ἐξῆν τοῦ νεκροῦ. Through this addition Plutarch links the statement back to the previous sentence, which referred to burial of the body, thereby associating the regulation concerning inscriptions with the act and place of burial in a way that the *Instituta* does not. It should be stressed that the overall structure of Plutarch's account clearly derives from the *Instituta*, covering the topics of intra-mural burial, memorials in the vicinity of sacred places, the absence of pollution, burial practice and the regulations concerning inscriptions and mourning in precisely the same sequence as the earlier source. At various points, however, he rephrases and expands the earlier account to produce more elegant and convincing prose. In this instance, Plutarch's addition of the reference back to the previous sentence is a transparent literary device to produce an impression of greater coherence; but it changes the meaning of the passage by artificially restricting commemorative inscriptions to the time and place of burial.

On this issue the account of the *Instituta* accords better with our other evidence, especially with a special body of epigraphic evidence from Lakonia: the ΕΝ ΠΟΛΕΜΟΙ stēlai. With one exception, these monuments, 19 in number, consist of a simple undecorated, roughly-worked stēlē surmounted by a small plain pediment.[40] All but three bear simply the name of the deceased, followed by the words ΕΝ or ΕΜ ΠΟΛΕΜΟΙ or ΠΟΛΕΜΩΙ or ΠΟΛΕΜΩΙ, i.e 'X. [died] in battle'.[41] Leaving aside a few of unknown provenance, just over half come from the region of the five Spartiate villages. All the others (barring one found in Tegean territory) come from other parts of Lakonia, including two from the neighbourhood of Sellasia.[42] Dating is often difficult, though there is agreement among specialist epigraphers that the earlier stēlai are of classical date.[43] Tod and Wace (1906, 25) assigned individual stēlai to a range of dates, mainly from the fifth to third centuries. Jeffery (1990, 197) concludes on the grounds of the continued use of specific archaic letter forms that 'several typical grave-inscriptions may be attributed with confidence to the Peloponnesian War'.[44] Guarducci (1974, 173) would even date one of these (*IG* v.1.701) to the early fifth century. In some cases the classical dating is capable of additional proof. Whereas most of the stēlai read ΠΟΛΕΜΩΙ, four (possibly five) bear the reading ΠΟΛΕΜΟΙ, with an omikron instead of an omega for the penultimate letter.[45] The absence of the omega is typical of Lakonian inscriptions before the mid-fourth century;[46] and the considerable overlap between these inscriptions and the ones which Jeffery assigns on other grounds to the late fifth century is additional confirmation of their classical date.[47] Further support for this dating is that one of the omikron inscriptions proclaims the death of a certain Eualkes at Mantineia: the famous battle in 418 BC is an obvious candidate. Like the class of monuments as a whole, the known provenances of the omikron stēlai are split evenly between Sparta itself and perioikic territory.

The ΕΝ ΠΟΛΕΜΟΙ stēlai provide tangible support for the statements in the sources that the right to a commemorative inscription was reserved to those who died in battle. The question, however, is: did these stēlai mark the graves of fallen soldiers, as Plutarch's *Lykourgos* implies, or were they memorials unconnected with the place of burial, as one might deduce from the *Instituta Laconica*? All the late archaic and classical evidence argues in favour of the latter view and demonstrates that a major change had taken place since the time of Tyrtaios. Tyrtaios clearly implies that fallen warriors were buried at home with great public honours and that their tombs remained visible to subsequent generations. Sometime during the sixth century, however, practice changed dramatically. The historical sources down to the third century are unanimous that the bodies of non-royal Spartiates who died abroad, whether in battle or through other causes, were not returned to Sparta but buried abroad (Pritchett 1974–91, iv.243–6; Cartledge 1987, 337). Burials of fallen warriors took place either close to the battlefield or (if necessary) in friendly neighbouring territory. This practice was already in force at the 'Battle of the Champions' at Thyrea *c.* 545, where Pausanias later saw the tombs of the 300 Spartan 'Champions' (2.38.5; cf. Pritchett 1974–91, iv.160–1 no. 5).[48] Similarly, Archias, who died heroically during the expedition to Samos *c.* 525, was buried with public honours by the Samians (Hdt. 3.55). The tomb of Anchimolios, who led the Spartan expedition to Attica in *c.* 510, was visible in Alopekai in Herodotus' day (Hdt. 5.63). After Plataia in 479 the Spartans buried all their dead upon the battlefield (Hdt. 9.85). In 422 Brasidas was buried in Amphipolis (Thuc. 5.11). After the battle of Mantineia in 418 the Lakedaimonians buried their dead in neighbouring Tegea (Thuc. 5.74). When Lichas, the non-combatant leader of the Spartan supervisory commission, died of illness at Miletos in

Rich citizens and the use of private wealth

411, a dispute arose between the Spartans and Milesians over exactly where in Miletos he should be buried (Thuc. 8.84; cf. Gomme et al. 1945–81, v.280). After Haliartos in 395 Lysander's body was carried over the Boiotian border for burial in friendly Panopeos, where his memorial was seen several centuries later by Plutarch (*Lys.* 29.3).[49] After Leuktra in 371 the Spartan dead were buried within Boiotian territory (Paus. 9.13.11).

A further contrast with the evidence of Tyrtaios is that fallen warriors were typically buried not singly but in a collective tomb, or *polyandreion*. This practice is attested archaeologically by the impressive collective tomb in the Kerameikos cemetery in Athens, which contained the Lakedaimonian dead from King Pausanias' Athenian expedition of 403 (*Fig.* 12).[50] Collective graves are also attested on earlier occasions in the literary evidence: for example,

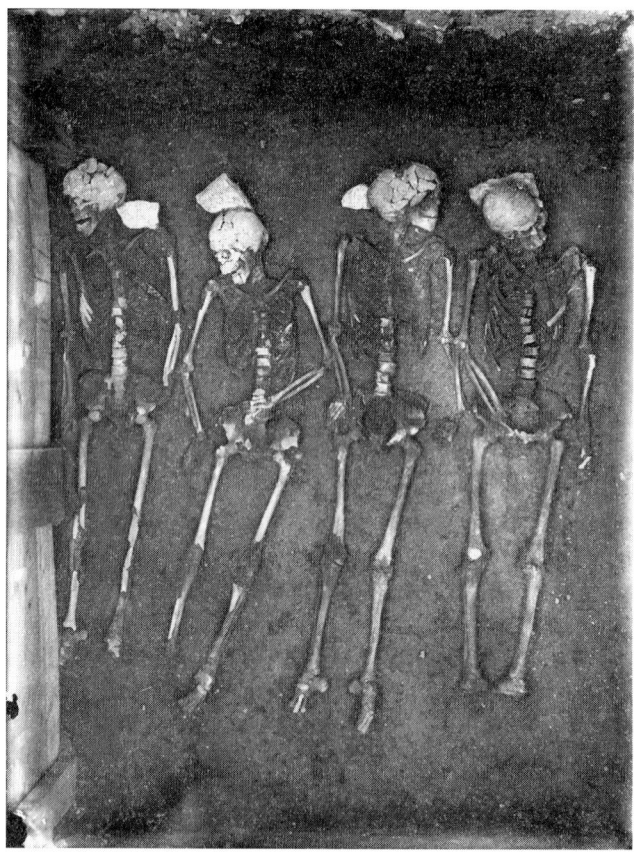

Fig. 12. Fallen Lakedaimonian soldiers from King Pausanias' Athenian expedition in 403 BC, buried in a *polyandreion* in the Kerameikos cemetery in Athens (photo courtesy of Deutsches Archäologisches Institut, Athens). The photograph shows four out of five soldiers in one of the flanking chambers.

Ch. 8. Restrictions on the deployment of wealth: burial and funerary practice

after Thermopylai and Plataia (Hdt. 7.228; 9.85). There was apparently also a *polyandreion* at Selinous in Sicily for the Lakedaimonians who accompanied the late sixth-century Spartiate adventurer Euryleon.[51] On other occasions of military burials the evidence, though unspecific, is consistent with collective rather than individual burial.[52]

Since, apart from the helot revolt of the 460s and the brief foreign invasions of 370/69 and 362, all Sparta's wars in the classical period took place outside Lakonia, the obvious conclusion is that few, if any, of the ΕΝ ΠΟΛΕΜΟΙ stēlai from Lakonia were erected over the actual graves of the warriors they commemorate. They must, as suggested long ago by Roehl (1876, 230–1), be commemorative monuments for soldiers buried elsewhere.[53] Indeed, one stēlē provides explicit confirmation. The stēlē of Eualkes mentioned above (*IG* v.1.1124), which is exceptional in stating where he died, states that he died in battle at Mantineia. The stēlē itself was found at the perioikic polis of Geronthrai, whereas (as we have seen) the Lakedaimonian dead from that battle were buried at Tegea.

Despite the strength of these arguments, there remains a persistent scholarly desire to view the ΕΝ ΠΟΛΕΜΟΙ stēlai as actual grave monuments. It has been suggested that they could be gravestones for soldiers who died of war wounds after their return home (Roberts 1887, 266–7); but this is surely special pleading (cf. Missoni 1986, 72–3 n. 36). More seriously, Nafissi (1991, 294–301) uses the stēlai to argue that during the fifth century the Spartans made a limited reintroduction of the practice of home burial for certain of the bravest fallen warriors, a change which he claims was utilised to their own advantage by the elite families. To the evidence of the stēlai he adds a passage of Aelian (*VH* 12.21), which claims that Spartan mothers who learned of their sons' death used to inspect their wounds. Those with more frontal wounds would be carried home to their ancestral tombs; those with more back wounds were abandoned to a communal tomb or brought to the family graves in secret. He also adduces an apophthegm in the *Apophthegmata Lakonika* (Anon. no. 51 = Plut. *Mor.* 235a), which quotes an epigram about a fallen warrior carried home on his shield, as well as certain apophthegms in the *Lakainōn Apophthegmata*, which include references to mothers burying their sons with pride (*Anon*. nos. 2; 8 = 241a; 241c) and the famous injunction of the Spartan mother who said as she handed her son his shield, 'either this [shield] or upon this' (*Anon*. no. 16 = 241f). Similar *exempla* are found in other late sources of Roman Imperial and Byzantine date (Hammond 1979/80). Finally, there are three hellenistic epigrams which claim to be local funerary epitaphs commemorating deeds of Spartan heroism (e.g. *Greek Anthology* 7.229, 434–5; cf. Gow and Page 1965, i.90–1, 147; ii.261–3, 424).

None of this evidence, however, provides any strong support for Nafissi's thesis. His main ground for interpreting the ΕΝ ΠΟΛΕΜΟΙ stēlai as grave markers is the text of Plutarch's *Lykourgos*; but we have already seen that

Plutarch's text introduces for literary purposes an entirely artificial connection between burials and commemorative inscriptions which distorts the evidence of its source. The evidence of Aelian once again runs counter to attested classical Spartan usage.[54] The idea that mothers could have visited a battlefield, which before 370 were all outside Spartan territory, is untenable. Furthermore, the implication that a communal grave was the lot of the ignoble is contradicted by the communal burial of the heroes of Thermopylai and Plataia or the impressive tomb of the Lakedaimonians in the Kerameikos. Similarly, in two of the epigrams – one from the *Apophthegmata Lakonika*, the other from the *Greek Anthology* (7.435) – the dead warriors are cremated, a practice never attested in any of the classical evidence. The evidence of the *Lakainōn Apophthegmata* is obviously infected by its archetypal presentation of the tough, patriotic Spartan mother, an image which is utterly post-classical in inspiration. What better illustration of this image could there be than the mother who positively glories in her son's death? Despite Nafissi's efforts to relate these apophthegms to some historical reality (1991, 296–300), recent studies have clearly demonstrated both the non-Spartan origin and the fictitious, pseudo-historical nature of these hellenistic anecdotes. Similarly, the post-classical epigrams should not be regarded as authentic epitaphs on Spartiate tombs.[55] None of this evidence can be read as proof that in the classical period exceptional warriors were specially privileged with a home burial. The fallen Spartiate soldier was buried abroad, regardless of his family's wealth or importance.

In fact, the foreign burial of fallen warriors is in itself the strongest reason for the existence of the ΕΝ ΠΟΛΕΜΟΙ stēlai, since these models of exemplary citizen conduct, who were buried in visible tombs abroad, would otherwise have been without any tangible memorial inside Sparta itself. Indeed, they might otherwise be the *only* deceased citizens without a mark of their existence. It is sometimes assumed that citizens who died outside battle received no grave marker at all. Robert Parker (1989, 150), for example, refers to 'unmarked, unhonoured graves' (cf. Toher 1991, 171; Richer 1994, 57 n. 30) and suggests that a major element of religious piety, the regular visiting of the tombs of one's deceased relatives, may have been absent from Spartiate society. If so, an important reinforcement of the ties of family and kin would thereby have been removed. The suggestion, however, is extreme.[56] Neither the *Instituta Laconica* nor Plutarch says that grave markers were forbidden; both say only that commemorative inscriptions were prohibited. This is hardly surprising, since, as Kurtz and Boardman (1971, 218) note, even an unostentatious pile of surplus earth over the grave could function as a marker. Moreover, given the practice of intra-mural burial, even the simplest of graves would probably have been distinguishable by a man's children and grandchildren. Subsequently, the individual grave may have faded into anonymity; but that would hardly be a phenomenon peculiar to Sparta. Even the magnificent family peribolos tombs (groups of graves surrounded by an enclosure wall) of late classical

Ch. 8. Restrictions on the deployment of wealth: burial and funerary practice

Athens exhibit a low generational depth: rarely is there evidence for tomb-groupings extending over more than three generations (Humphreys 1980, 114–20; Garland 1985, 106–7). The same limited generational depth is also apparent elsewhere in Greece and in other parts of the ancient world (Ian Morris, pers. comm.). This phenomenon was rooted in the demographic reality facing all pre-industrial societies, that in every generation typically about 40% of families lacked a direct male heir, thereby entailing a drastic disruption of most lineages every two or three generations. The probability that Spartiates honoured the tombs of their deceased in the same way as other Greeks makes it perfectly understandable that special inscribed stēlai were permitted for fallen warriors whose tombs lay abroad. Perhaps these stēlai were the *mnēmeia* 'near the sacred places' mentioned in the *Instituta Laconica*, placed in a sanctuary where they would be visible not just to family members but to all citizens.

Despite these hints that simple grave markers and some element of public display of commemorative memorials were still retained, Spartiate funerary display was clearly much less ostentatious than elsewhere. The contrast is not absolute, since other poleis also experienced periods of restraint. Before *c.* 550 there is a general paucity of notable grave monuments in many parts of central Greece and the Peloponnese. The fifth century witnessed a thoroughgoing 'collapse of monumental burial' throughout mainland and eastern Greece, including an almost complete disappearance of grave monuments in Attica between 500 and 425 (Morris 1997, 32, 73). At other times and places, however, the contrast between Sparta and other poleis stands out boldly: for example, in the later sixth century, which witnessed a widespread increase in grave monuments elsewhere in the precise period when restraint was being applied in Sparta with the move to foreign military burials. In the fourth century, moreover, the general restraint evident in fifth-century Greece breaks down almost everywhere, with widespread signs of increasing monumental funerary display (Morris 1992, 128–46). Even the comparatively austere world of Plato's *Laws* (958e) exemplifies this trend in permitting the construction of a mound such as could be made by five men in five days and a stone monument capable of bearing an inscription four heroic lines in length.

The contrast between Spartiate burial practice and that of Athens (outside her temporary period of restraint between 500 and 425) is especially marked. Attic archaeology has revealed a wide variety of more or less costly grave markers which Athenians gave to their dead both before 500 and after 425: large earth or plastered earth mounds; built tombs of stone or mud brick decorated with painted terracotta plaques; peribolos tombs; stone or marble kouroi and korai; relief and decorated stēlai of various sorts; columns and stone vases – to name but the more prominent types (Kurtz and Boardman 1971, 79–91, 105–8, 121–41, 218–46). The scale of expenditure involved could be considerable. Diogeton is said to have spent 2,500 drachmas on his brother's tomb in 409 and to have made the fraudulent, but presumably plausible, claim that the

Rich citizens and the use of private wealth

real expense was double that amount (Lysias 32.21). In 349 another Athenian is claimed, perhaps exaggeratedly but again not implausibly, to have spent over 12,000 drachmas on a grave monument for a woman he had formerly seduced (Demosthenes 45.79). The key point is not that these costly tombs or monuments were typical of the mass of citizen burials; but, quite the reverse, that they were exceptional works of the wealthy elite. This comes across clearly in the speech of Thrasyboulos before the battle of Munychia in 403: 'Happy is he who is slain; for no one, however rich he may be, will gain a monument (*mnēmeion*) so glorious' (Xen. *Hell.* 2.4.17). The evidence for fourth-century Athens indicates that only a small group of persons were buried in peribolos tombs, whilst most Athenian graves had only a simple inscribed stēlē.[57]

The other relevant comparison for classical Spartiate burial practice is with practice in Sparta itself in the last two centuries BC. After 200 the funerary practices established in the sixth century were finally abandoned: 'monumental masons now for the first time began to produce grave reliefs of the usual Greek type' (Cartledge and Spawforth 1989, 72; cf. Tod and Wace 1906, 127, with nos. 257, 294). Moreover, excavations south of the Acropolis have revealed a group of four built chamber tombs of dressed stone, containing grave-goods of gold and silver jewellery, the earliest of which dates to the period 200–150 BC.[58]

In contrast, though recognisable to immediate kin, the tombs of classical Spartiates who died outside combat, even those from the wealthiest families, displayed minimal visibility to other citizens. This denial of the opportunity for advertising the family's prominence also extended of course to funerary inscriptions. Once again the Spartan situation is not entirely singular: use of the verse epitaph, for example, was rare in several parts of the Greek world. Nevertheless, unlike citizens in certain poleis, especially those in central Greece, no recently-deceased Spartiate could be vaunted by his heirs for his hospitality or athletic success, for his personal qualities or high esteem (Wallace 1970; Sourvinou-Inwood 1995, 172). The sole criterion for epigraphic commemoration in Sparta was death in battle.

Differential honours among fallen warriors
Of course, even the commemoration of fallen warriors was hardly prominent. The ΕΝ ΠΟΛΕΜΟΙ stēlai are mostly unimposing monuments, extremely plain with minimal decoration and a height ranging from a modest 90 cm down to a minuscule 11 cm. They embody only the most limited individualisation of the deceased, containing neither reference to his lineage nor praise of his valour or stirring deeds, but simply a bald statement that X. had died in battle. Moreover, although the fallen warrior's kin could take pride in his noble death, looking 'bright and happy' at the news (Xen. *Hell.* 6.4.16), even going about 'like prizewinners' (4.5.10), although they could erect a simple memorial, they were unable to advertise his glory any further by burying him at home. The state's appropriation of the burial of fallen warriors, made in front of their comrades,

Ch. 8. Restrictions on the deployment of wealth: burial and funerary practice

but in a collective tomb away from their families at home and the other citizens, placed a strict limit on the extent to which even a man's noble death could boost the prestige and influence of his lineage.

Complete equality did not, however, always prevail among the noble dead. There were certain fallen warriors from time to time who received more than the basic funerary honours. Some received special commemoration in Sparta itself. The Spartan polis did not normally hold public ceremonies for its dead soldiers, as did classical Athens with its well-known public oration and funeral games (Pritchett 1974–91, iv.106–241). Special commemorations were, however, given to certain groups of warriors who gave their lives on specially important military occasions. Hymns were sung at the festival of the Gymnopaidiai in honour of the 300 who died in the 'Battle of the Champions' (Bölte 1929b, 130 n. 6; Wade-Gery 1949, 80 n. 4).[59] The 300 at Thermopylai were also commemorated annually, probably from a date soon after the event (Ball 1976). The stēlē listing the 300 even included the names of their fathers (Paus. 3.14.1). Moreover, extra-special honours or cult were given to certain outstanding individuals from Thermopylai. A certain Dienekes was said to have gained the most distinction, and after him the brothers Maron and Alpheios, the sons of Orsiphantos; back in Sparta the brothers were honoured with a heroon (Hdt. 7.226–7; Paus. 3.12.9).[60] Brasidas, the celebrated commander of the 420s, was also given a special cenotaph in Sparta (Paus. 3.14.1).[61]

Other soldiers were given special burials abroad. After Plataia three fallen warriors – Poseidonios, Amompharetos and Philokyon – were adjudged to have gained the highest distinction (Hdt. 9.71). They were included in a separate, select tomb, along with a certain Kallikrates, 'the most beautiful man in the Greek camp', who was killed by an arrow before battle began (9.72, 85).[62] The tomb in the Kerameikos for the fallen soldiers in Pausanias' Athenian expedition in 403 also suggests a priority given to certain of the dead. The tomb was not fully published by the original excavators and is now being restudied as part of current re-excavations in the Kerameikos.[63] Preliminary reports, however, indicate that it contained 13 skeletons placed in three chambers. The central chamber contained only three bodies, as against five in each of the flanking chambers. (*Fig. 12*, on page 252, shows four of the bodies in one of the flanking chambers.) These three bodies were given more room than the others and were laid out more carefully and more evenly spaced. Their heads were also better supported upon two stones, as against a single stone for the other bodies. The trio concerned were accorded somewhat higher burial honours than their comrades.[64] In certain other cases too the sources mention the commander's tomb without reference to that of his troops: for example, the tombs of Anchimolios at Alopeke (Hdt. 5.63) and of Lysander at Panopeos (Plut. *Lys.* 29.3). Although, as Pritchett argues, the sources' focus on leading individuals probably obscures the existence of a communal grave,[65] it signifies that the commander's burial was somewhat more special than that of his troops.

Although the above privileges in burial were given not by the men's relatives but by the polis, it has been suggested that their subsequent posthumous honours may owe something to the recipients' superior social or inherited status (Richer 1994, 59–60). Certainly, the case of Thermopylai offers a striking reversal of priority. Although Dienekes was judged to have gained most distinction (Hdt. 7.226–7), he is not attested as having received the hero-shrine at Sparta which was given to the brothers Maron and Alpheios. By the time of Pausanias Dienekes' role had been forgotten and contemporary opinion accorded the prime honour, after King Leonidas, to the brothers (Paus. 3.12.9). That Herodotus gives a patronymic for the brothers, but not for Dienekes, has been adduced as evidence that they were from an elite family; hence, it is claimed, their receipt of cult. However, it is not certain that superior social status was the reason for this reversal. The key factor might equally be the brothers' fraternity (Richer 1994, 96), which evoked memories of the Dioskouroi and was a fitting complement to the heroisation of King Leonidas, given the intimate association between the Dioskouroi and the dual kingship. Their fraternity would also explain Herodotus' naming of their father, who was its *fons et origo*. In contrast, Dienekes did not need a patronymic, since his fame derived from his personal qualities, exemplified by his jocular sayings in the face of death.

Similarly, after Plataia, it is unclear that the separation of Spartan soldiers into two tombs was on the basis of inherited status. There is disagreement concerning the correct reading of the text which describes the occupants of the more select tomb. The manuscript of Herodotus 9.85 reads ἱρέες (*irees*, usually translated as 'priests'). Many editors emend ἱρέες to ἰρένες (*irenes*), a term which some regard as a reference to the position of *eirēn*, supposedly the term for Spartan youths aged 20 (Plut. *Lyk.* 17.2). However, the emendation is by no means secure;[66] and the very existence of the term *eirēn* in classical times has recently been called into question (Kennell 1995, 16–17). Some scholars suggest that by *irenes* Herodotus means the elite *hippeis*;[67] if so, this would be a question of acquired rather than inherited status, since the *hippeis* were apparently selected on merit (Xen. *Lak. Pol.* 4.3). In fact, there is good reason to retain the manuscript reading, though the term *irees* should be understood more in the sense of 'heroes' than as 'priests' (Richer 1994, 66). The persons known to have been included among this select group possess a certain coherence as men chosen for their extraordinary personal qualities: Kallikrates for his beauty; and Poseidonios, Amompharetos and Philokyon for their military exploits (Richer 1994, 64–8). On this hypothesis too it is a question of status earned, not inherited.

In the case of the Lakedaimonian tomb in Athens, the essential issue is the identity of the trio in the central chamber. There are two clues. First, the tomb is mentioned by Xenophon (*Hell.* 2.4.33), who states,

And there died Chairon and Thibrachos, both polemarchs, and Lakrates the Olympic victor and other Lakedaimonians who lie buried in front of the city gates in the Kerameikos.

Secondly, there is the inscription on the tomb itself, of which only the beginning of the text (written retrograde) survives. The inscription was laid out such that the names of the deceased were interspersed with individual letters of the word ΛΑΚΕΔΑΙΜΟΝΙΟΙ (i.e. 'Lakedaimonioi'), which was inscribed in significantly larger letters. The surviving text reads (translating the retrograde text into left-to-right format)

THIBRAKOS POLEMARCHOS L CHAIRON POLEMARCHOS A

followed by the initial letter of a third name.

The priority given to the polemarchs in both texts suggests that they formed two of the central trio. Military, not social, status was consequently the key. Whose was the third body? Xenophon's text suggests that it was Lakrates, who as Olympic victor would have fought in King Pausanias' bodyguard (Plut. *Lyk.* 22.4; cf. *Mor.* 639e), and whose renown may have entitled him to privileged burial. Whether the inscription supports this suggestion is unclear. The initial letter of the third name is normally read as an 'M' (Willemsen 1977, 136); but this reading is challenged by Pritchett (1974–91, iv.134 n. 123), who sees 'only two joining diagonal strokes as for the upper part of an alpha, delta, or lambda'. Hence the third name *might* be that of Lakrates, though this is uncertain.[68] If so, however, it is again a matter of acquired status, since Xenophon's description 'suggests a personal triumph rather than a victory in a chariot race' (Ste Croix 1972, 354) and only athletic victors fought in the royal bodyguard.

In none of these cases, therefore, are there grounds for believing that privileges in burial or subsequent honours were specifically channelled to warriors from the leading families. Inherited status may, however, have provided indirect advantage. Although success in the Spartiate upbringing was in principle based upon merit, it is likely that boys from privileged families fared better in the selection procedures by which the future military leaders were chosen. Although we do not know the backgrounds of the polemarchs Chairon and Thibrakos, nor that of Amompharetos, who is described as commander of the Pitanate *lochos* at Plataia (Hdt. 9.53),[69] there is evidence that most of the commanders prominent in Sparta's foreign campaigns in the late fifth and early fourth centuries came from elite families (Hodkinson 1983, 260–5; 1993, 157–9). Although it is unclear whether the sources are correct in implying that these commanders often received separate burials, the fact that their tombs could be identified by later generations implies that they were at least marked by a prominent inscription. Hence citizens from the wealthy elite were at least to some degree differentially honoured in foreign military burials. In this sense at least there may have been a chink in the egalitarian procedures which otherwise marked Spartiate funerary customs.

Rich citizens and the use of private wealth

The burial of Spartan women

As with many aspects of women's lives, we suffer from a dearth of information about their burials. True, the eighth-century pithos cremation burial from Mesoa mentioned above was female (Raftopoulou 1998a, 276–8), to judge by the character of its metal grave goods (six spiral rings and several cylinders). The fact that this pithos burial ranks among the richest in grave goods, alongside the warrior burial from Limnai, indicates something about the honours with which certain women might be buried in this early period. However, the adult female grave in the tumulus grave-group excavated by Christou cannot now be treated as reliable evidence for the burial of women alongside their menfolk and children in our period, given the serious doubts about the dating of the group. Otherwise, direct evidence is almost completely lacking. Tyrtaios is concerned only with male burials, as are the ivory plaque *prothesis* scenes. The figured scenes on the relief amphoras relate solely to male activities. Finally, except on one controversial point, the passages of the *Instituta Laconica* and Plutarch's *Lykourgos* make no explicit mention of female burials. Of course, their near-silence concerning special funerary practices for women may in itself constitute mute testimony. Although one piece of information – concerning burial in the *phoinikis* – implicitly relates only to men, the remainder of their evidence is gender-neutral. Hence we should probably assume that, like their menfolk, Spartiate women of whatever social background were buried in simple graves without grave goods other than the simplest of coverings and with the same restricted period of mourning.

The one point at which female burials are explicitly mentioned concerns the question of funerary inscriptions. As we have seen, both the *Instituta* and the *Lykourgos* indicate that for most Spartans – again we should assume women as well as men – such inscriptions were not permitted. The sole exception mentioned in the *Instituta* is a soldier who died in battle. The manuscripts of Plutarch, *Lykourgos* 27.2, however, add a second exception, 'a woman from among the *hieraí* (γυναικὸς τῶν ἱερῶς [vel ἱερῶν]). This text has been amended by Kurt Latte to read γυναικὸς [τῶν] λεχοῦς 'a woman who died in childbirth'. The emendation has been followed by most subsequent editors and historians.[70] If accepted, it would confirm that wealth and inherited status had no influence on funerary practices for Spartan women. However, the emendation has no foundation in any of the manuscripts: even its proponents concede its arbitrary character and the difficulty of explaining how λεχοῦς could have become doubly corrupted to both ἱερῶν and ἱερῶς. The main reason why many scholars prefer the emendation is to bring Spartan practice into line with the parallel drawn in some Greek writings between male involvement in war and female involvement in marriage and childbirth, an equivalence which has recently had an especial appeal to structuralist historians (cf. Vernant (ed.) 1968, 15; Loraux 1981).

The sole evidential ground for Latte's emendation is the existence of four funerary inscriptions, two from the region of Sparta itself, two from elsewhere in Lakonia, which refer to women who died in childbirth. These inscriptions, however, do not provide as strong support for the emendation as is often supposed, still less for the idea that it describes the position in classical times. There are three difficulties. First, none of the inscriptions is certainly classical in date. One (*IG* v.1.714), which reads, ΑΓΙΠΠΙΑ ΛΕΧΟΙ ('Agippia in childbirth') is probably hellenistic (Guarducci 1974, 173; Richer 1994, 54 n.18). The date of another (*IG* v.1.713), written retrograde, ΙΟΧΕΛ..., with the deceased's name now lost, is uncertain: opinions differ as to whether it too is post-classical (MacDowell 1986, 121) or somewhat earlier (Guarducci 1974, 173 n.1). Yet another (*IG* v.1.1128), which reads ΟΝΑC[ΙΑ] ΛΕΧΟΙ ΧΑΙΡΕ, is surely Roman. The last inscription (*IG* v.1.1277) is also late, as it includes a late form of the letter Alpha. Hence, even if these inscriptions do support the emendation of Plutarch's text, they do not prove that the terms of that emendation operated in classical times. A second difficulty is that only the first two inscriptions come from the vicinity of Sparta. The other two come, respectively, from Geronthrai and the Tainaron peninsula, areas of Lakonia which were politically independent from Sparta for most of the hellenistic and Roman periods. One might argue that continuing cultural interaction led to similar practices throughout Lakonia. However, the evidence of the Tainaron inscription in fact runs counter to Latte's emendation. The inscription lists at least seven deceased women: three names are followed by the word ΛΕΧΟΙ, but the others have no such indication. The inclusion of both women who died in childbirth and those who did not indicates that death in childbirth was not a special criterion for a commemorative inscription. This leads us to a third difficulty, acutely pointed out by Wallace (1970, 99 n.11). The ΛΕΧΟΙ inscriptions cannot logically be adduced as support for Latte's emendation, since Plutarch's statement 'determines only who may have epitaphs, not what they may be'. The fact that certain women received inscriptions indicating that they died in childbirth need not signify that their death in childbirth was what entitled them to receive that inscription. The Tainaron inscription is a perfect illustration of that point.

However attractive an emendation, it remains in principle hazardous methodology to alter a manuscript reading, unless it can be demonstrated that it is a corruption of the original text and in itself devoid of sense. In this case neither criterion is fulfilled: we have already noted the difficulty in explaining how the postulated corruption took place, and the manuscript reading is perfectly defensible. It is important, however, not to choose the wrong grounds for defence. The noun *hierai* is sometimes translated as 'priestesses' (e.g. Cartledge 1981, 95 n.72). This translation, however, is somewhat dubious. The normal word for priestess is *hiereia* (MacDowell 1986, 121). The word *hierai*, in contrast, is cognate, not with the masculine singular for 'priest', *hiereus*, but with the term *hieros*. The existence in classical Lakedaimon of individuals called *hieroi* is attested by a fifth-century epitaph from Gerenia which reads, in Lakonian dialect, '[hi]aros Agehipolis' (*IG* v.1.1338). The term *hieros* in its primary sense indicates someone 'consecrated', made 'sacred' or 'holy', signifying not so much a juridical status as a property or condition of a specific individual (Debord 1982, 78–82; Richer 1994, 53–4; cf. Le Roy 1961, 231 n. 4). This connotation finds further support from the evidence of Lakonian inscriptions which make mention of *hieroi* and *hierai* attached to local cults. It has been suggested that their position was akin to the *hieroi* and *hierai* known from the cult of the Mysteries at Andania in Messenia – a cult marked by strong Spartan influences – who were chosen each year by lot, exercising their functions on a purely temporary basis (Le Roy 1961, 230–2; Sokolowski 1969, no. 65, 117–32). If this is correct, the sense of the manuscript reading, that 'women among the *hierai*' were permitted a funerary epitaph would imply, not an hereditary elite of priestesses, but rather a more fluid and open group of women.

In sum, it is uncertain whether Plutarch's statement that women 'from among the *hierai*' were entitled to a funerary inscription describes the classical situation, since the statement does not appear in the passage from the *Instituta Laconica* and none of the ΛΕΧΟΙ inscriptions is certainly of classical date. Even if it does, the criterion does not imply any significant discrimination in favour of wealthier women.

The burial of Spartiate kings

The outstanding exceptions to the egalitarian funerary practices discussed above were the two kings. First, unlike ordinary Spartiates, the bodies of kings who died abroad were brought back to Sparta for burial. We are specifically informed that this occurred in the cases of King Agesipolis, who died of fever while on campaign in 381 (Xen. *Hell.* 5.3.19), and of Agesilaos II, who died of old age in Libya in 360 (Plut. *Ages.* 40.3). Admittedly, there is some uncertainty concerning kings who died in war (Richer 1994, 70–1). According to Herodotus (6.58), if a king died in battle, an image (*eidōlon*) was made of him for the purpose of the funeral procession at Sparta. On its own, this implies that a fallen king was interred on the field of battle. Plutarch, however, describing the return of the body of Agesilaos, comments that the bodies of kings who died abroad were brought home, making no distinction between death in battle or in other circumstances. Either Plutarch was ignorant of this distinction or Herodotus' comment refers only to circumstances in which the king's body was not retrieved from enemy hands. Unfortunately, no narrative source provides any information about the burial of particular kings who died in battle in the classical and hellenistic periods. Since, however, all but one of these deaths are reported by Plutarch, he apparently did not know of any occasion which contradicted his general comment (Richer 1994, 72–3). It is also possible that Herodotus' account was coloured by the prominent occasion of the death of Leonidas, whose body was in Persian hands and whose burial must therefore have required an *eidōlon* (Schaefer 1957). Accordingly, it is probable that the

Ch. 8. Restrictions on the deployment of wealth: burial and funerary practice

bodies of kings who died in battle were brought home for burial in the same way as kings who died abroad of other causes (Pritchett 1974–91, iv.241–2; Cartledge 1987, 333–4).

A king's funerary rites at home contrasted markedly with those of other citizens.[71] For Herodotus, indeed, the rites contrasted with normal Greek customs in general, being more reminiscent of barbarian customs. One essential difference was the public nature of the rites, which contrasts with the general tendency throughout Greece to restrict involvement to certain degrees of kin. On the death of a king, the *agora* was sprinkled with chaff and all sales ceased for three days (Herakleides Lembos 372.11 = Aristotelian *Lak. Pol.* 611.11). There was a public proclamation of his death throughout the length and breadth of Lakonia, accompanied by a beating of kettles throughout Sparta itself by the women. At this signal, two free persons from every household had to put on mourning. At the burial attendance was compulsory not only for Spartiates but for perioikoi and helots too, men and women, all striking their foreheads, weeping and wailing ceaselessly, and proclaiming that their last king was the best. By the classical period, therefore, the kings alone retained the funeral devotions from the servile population which had once been the preserve of all Spartiates. We are ill-informed about the details of the treatment of the body; but it has been suggested that before the burial there was a public lying-in-state. The time required for the helots and perioikoi to assemble implies that its period was extended. The burial normally took place in one of the two royal cemeteries, for kings of the Agiad house in the village of Pitana, for the Eurypontids in Limnai (Paus. 3.12.8). After the burial public mourning continued and public business was suspended for a full ten days.

The overall impression of a royal burial is vividly conveyed by Xenophon's comment concerning the funeral of King Agis II that 'he received a more splendid burial than belongs to a man' (Xen. *Hell.* 3.3.1), a remark he clarifies elsewhere by saying that the funerary rites were 'intended to show that the kings of the Lakedaimonians are honoured not as men but as heroes' (*Lak. Pol.* 15.9).[72] The impact of these elaborate mortuary rites on public perception of the surviving members of the royal house, especially the deceased king's successor, has rightly been stressed. They established the new king as a man of charismatic status who would himself one day accede to the position of a hero and, as Cartledge (1987, 340) notes, 'served to express the legitimacy of the hereditary kingship as the exclusive preserve of the Agiad and Eurypontid houses'. This narrowly exclusive aspect is worth stressing. Whereas in the early archaic period comparable funerary celebrations might once have been the aspiration of a number of high-born families, their burials were now reduced to the level of ordinary citizens (Nafissi 1991, 290). The royal houses now stood alone as the recipients of the vicarious prestige which accrued from highly-visible funerary rights. In subsequent chapters we shall view other spheres in which the kings stood at the head of, but also apart from, Spartiate social life.

Rich citizens and the use of private wealth

Notes

[1] Cf. Toher 1991, 160; Nafissi 1991, 278–9, with references to earlier studies from these different perspectives. Note, especially, recent debate about whether changes in funerary practice in the archaic and classical periods should be ascribed to significant changes in collective perceptions of and attitudes to death (Sourvinou-Inwood 1981; 1983; 1995; Morris 1989; 1995).

[2] Indeed, the earliest funerary laws are the most socio-political in tone (Toher 1991, 168).

[3] We have no evidence concerning the burial of Spartan children, apart from a single child grave in the dubiously 'archaic' grave group discussed below.

[4] The word *despotas* shows that our source for this passage, Pausanias (4.14.4–5), is mistaken in associating it with the funeral rites of the Spartan kings and other magistrates (Hdt. 6.58; Ducat 1990a, 60).

[5] In theory, this passage might signify that the helots at large mourned the death of every Spartiate; but such regular widespread lamentation seems implausible, especially as this scale of display was – as we shall see – the prerogative of the kings.

[6] Dawkins (ed.) 1929, pl. CII, nos. 2–3; Marangou 1969, 50–3, nos. 23–4, pls. 38–9; Carter 1985, 147–8, figs. 46–7; Förtsch 1998, fig. 13 [Athens, National Mus. nos. 15518, 16432].

[7] Steinhauer 1972, 245, pl. 179 ; *JHS, AR* (1978) 30; Raftopoulou 1998a, 273, 277 figs. 2–3, 278; 1998b, 133 and fig. 12.14.

[8] Pithos cremations with metal grave goods: Steinhauer 1972, 244–5; *JHS, AR* (1978) 30; Raftopoulou 1998a, 275–8 and figs. 4–6; 1998b, 133 and 134 figs. 12.15–16. The other pithos cremations are undated: *BSA* 12 (1905–6) 281, 293; cf. Nafissi 1991, 328 with n. 233.

[9] *AD* 23 (1968) B.1, *Chronika*, 151 ff.; *AD* 24 (1969) B.1 *Chronika*, 134 ff.; cf. Nafissi 1991, 329, 332–3.

[10] Steinhauer 1972, 246–8, pl. 183; *JHS, AR* (1978) 30–1; cf. Nafissi 1991, 332.

[11] Note, for example, the find of a tomb on the left bank of the Eurotas in early British excavations. The contents included three archaic bone plaques (cf. Marangou 1969, figs. 147–8, 150), along with pieces of mirrors, coins, broken ornaments and cone-shaped objects of gilded metal. In the excavators' judgement, 'we have before us probably older objects which found their way into a later grave' (*JHS* 12, 1892, 41).

[12] *CVA, Oxford* 2 (*Great Britain* 9 (1931)) 59–60, nos. 3, 10, 13–14, 16–18.

[13] Raftopoulou (1998b, 134) claims that two-storey tombs were typical of Sparta and continued into the hellenistic period. Apart from the building discussed in the main text, however, she cites no pre-hellenistic evidence to support this claim.

[14] Christou 1964a; cf. *BCH* 85 (1961) 682–4.

[15] In the English summary of the excavation report the bone horse statuette is said to be archaic, but this dating appears to be absent from the report's main text (Christou 1964a, 142, 283).

[16] Cf. the list in Christou 1964b, 172–5.

[17] For the longer chronological range, Christou 1964b; Andersen 1977, 62; Stibbe 1989, 142 n. 248; for the briefer time span, based upon the opinion that even the earliest examples are Lakonian III work, Lauter-Bufe 1974, 89; Fitzhardinge 1980, 54.

[18] Whether this was a sanctuary area in the archaic period is, however, uncertain, since the construction date of the Great Altar is apparently not precisely known: *BSA* 12 (1905–6) 302. The amphoras from this area are nos. III, X, XI, XII in Christou's list.

Ch. 8. Restrictions on the deployment of wealth: burial and funerary practice

19 In Christou's list nos. II, V, IX, XIII and XX are said to be from the Heroon; no. VIII is from the Acropolis. Fragments similar to no. XXI were reportedly found at the Heroon, on the Acropolis and at the Orthia sanctuary. Cf. also the report in *BSA* 27 (1925–26) 201 that 'other pieces of pithoi, of similar date, but small dimensions, have come to light in our excavations on the Acropolis in the past three years, and will be published when opportunity offers'; to my knowledge, such publication has never taken place.

20 Nos. I and XV, respectively, in Christou's list; cf. also *BSA* 27 (1925–26) 199–200; Fitzhardinge 1980, 52. Another possible example of an amphora with fragments in diverse places is no. XVII. The amphora in the post-archaic burial tumulus discussed above may have arrived there through reuse.

21 The evidence is summarised in Nafissi 1991, 327–41.

22 On their one-sided decoration, Fitzhardinge 1980, 52; *BSA* 27 (1925–26) 199–200; Christou 1964b, pls. 78–81. The photograph of no. IX in *BSA* 12 (1905–6) pl. 9, reprinted in Dawkins (ed.) 1929, pl. 15, also shows a lack of decoration to the right of the handle.

23 Compare fr. 11 (West), lines 35–8, with *Fig.* 11 (Dawkins (ed.) 1929 pl. 16 = Christou 1964b, 173 no. 9 and pls. 84 and 99). Note the archer on the extreme left of the upper zone.

24 In one respect, divergence from western mainland patterns may be evident. The dating of the attested warrior burial before rather than after 700 sets Sparta apart from other western regions, where warrior burials become more prominent in the seventh century, and puts her more in line with Aegean and eastern mainland trends, which witnessed their disappearance (Morris 1998, 19, 54–5). However, one should be cautious of drawing wide-reaching conclusions from a single burial.

25 Wallace 1970, 99–100 n. 13. *IG* v.1.238, *c.* 500–475, from Magoula, labelled in Tod and Wace (1906, 25 and 73 no. 611) as a metrical epitaph, is judged to be an athletic dedication by Jeffery (1990, 195 and 201 no. 48). *IG* v.1.699 from the Menelaion is probably a mason's mark: Boring 1979, 102 no. 37. *IG* v.1.720–2 are unlikely to be sepulchral epigrams, as is sometimes alleged: Jeffery 1990, 193–4; 200 no. 31; Wallace 1970, 99–100 n. 13 and 103.

26 Raftopoulou 1998b, 135, mentions 'a group of simple burials without offerings… covered with fill of late fifth–early fourth century BC', but notes that 'this layer can be used only as a *terminus ante quem*…and the lack of offerings deprives us of any more reliable and specific dating'.

27 The following summary draws upon the accounts of Salapata 1993, 189 and Hibler 1993, 121; both give references to earlier studies.

28 References to preliminary reports of the excavations in Salapata 1993, 195 n. 13.

29 Further support for the hero cult interpretation comes from the resemblances of the Lakonian reliefs to the Totenmahl reliefs from such places as Tegea, Thasos, Paros and Attica and from the fact that several of the common attributes on the reliefs, such as the snake, the kantharos and the horse, are more characteristic of heroic cult than of cult of the dead (Larson 1995, 43–55).

30 *IG* v.1.244; Jeffery 1990, 200 no. 26.

31 *IG* v.1.457; Jeffery 1990, 200 no. 29. Another relief which Kennell (1995, 140, with 212 n. 164) associates with the Theokles relief does not appear to be Spartan, since it was reportedly found at Charouda in the Mani: Stibbe 1991, 41 C.2; Hibler 1993, 202 fig. 6, 204 n. 36.

32 I give the alternative translations of the Greek ἀνεδοῦντο by N.G. Wilson [Loeb] and J.G. DeVoto [Ares]. The former translation is also adopted by Nafissi 1991, 291.

33 Aelian's reference to processions to the tomb amidst praises does not contradict this image, since he refers to the different context of military burials outside Sparta, where it is also a question not of lamentations but of praises, which came not from the deceased's relatives but from his fellow soldiers.

34 Cf. the apophthegms expressing the Spartan preference for cocks that kill over those that die fighting: Plut. *Mor.* 191e–f; 224c; *Lyk.* 20.6.

35 Indeed, if the *Inst. Lac.* were referring to military burials, its insistence that all bodies were treated alike would blatantly contradict Aelian's allegedly differential burials.

36 It has even been suggested that the body was simply placed in the earth without a coffin (Toher 1991, 171).

37 I here consciously reverse the emphasis placed on these phenomena by Morris himself; but I agree with his argument that patterns of grave goods cannot be treated as a simple index of the general importance of wealth. Later chapters will demonstrate how the use of wealth, although restricted in the sphere of funerary practice, played a powerful role in other areas of Spartiate life.

38 For the translation as 'tombs', cf. the Loeb and Budé editions of the *Moralia* and the Penguin and Budé editions of the *Lykourgos*; also Richer 1994, 52. The translation 'memorials' is given in the Loeb trans. of the *Lykourgos* and by Michell 1964, 62; Garland too (1989, 13) writes of 'grave-monuments'. The only other use of *mnēmeion* in an apophthegm in the *Moralia* relating to a Spartan is 191d, where the reference is also to a monument, though of unspecified location. Some references elsewhere in the *Moralia* clearly refer to memorials set up in places other than the grave itself (e.g. 330f; 821e). There is also a notable classical Spartan example of this usage: Tod 1948, no. 120, the inscription on the monument set up at Delphi *c.* 380 by the exiled King Pausanias for his son Agesipolis, who had been buried in Sparta (Xen. *Hell.* 5.3.19). The inscription describes the monument as a [μν]αμεῖόν. Plutarch sometimes uses *mnēma* of a tomb (e.g. *Sol.* 21.5; *Pel.* 21.1; *Sert.* 9.3; *Brut.* 28.1; *Ant.* 22.4), but equally often seems to be thinking of the monument associated with a tomb (*Arist.* 19.7; *Kim.* 4.2; 19.4; *Arat.* 53.1; *Cat. Maj.* 5.4; *Cat. Min.* 11.2; *Otho* 18.1). The reason for his choice of a different word from that used in the *Instituta Laconica* appears to be personal preference rather than an intention to signal a particular meaning, since he uses *mnēma* 21 times elsewhere in his *Parallel Lives* as against only 6 uses of *mnēmeion*. His usage of the two words seems not to differ significantly: although he sometimes uses *mnēmeion* of the monument (e.g. *Lys.* 29.3; *Sul.* 38.4; *Luc.* 29.10), elsewhere the tomb is clearly included in the reference (*Phok.* 22.1; *Alex.* 69.4).

39 Some scholars also mistakenly allege a difference between the two sources regarding the definition of the exceptions who were permitted commemorative inscriptions. This allegation arises from the fact that, whereas the *Instituta* clearly states that it was 'those who died in war', Plutarch's account is more complicated: inscriptions were not permitted, πλὴν ἀνδρὸς ἐν πολέμῳ καὶ γυναικὸς τῶν ἱερῶς (vel ἱερῶν) ἀποθανόντων. Here it is necessary to anticipate briefly my discussion below of the dispute concerning the question of inscriptions for deceased women, a dispute which arises out of Latte's emendation of Plutarch's final words to (τῶν) λεχοῦς ἀποθανόντων. On Latte's emendation, the text's meaning is straightforward: those entitled to inscriptions were men dying in battle and women in childbirth. I shall argue below, however, that Latte's emendation should be

rejected. Some scholars who concur in retaining the manuscript reading think that the phrase τῶν ἱερῶς (vel ἱερῶν) relates not only to γυναικός but to ἀνδρός as well (den Boer 1954, 294–300; Wallace 1970, 99; cf. MacDowell 1986, 121). On this view, Plutarch is saying that not all fallen warriors, but only those who were also *hieroi*, could receive an inscription. In my view, however, the application of the phrase should be restricted to Spartan women as a balancing phrase to ἐν πολέμῳ, which is likewise restricted to Spartan men. This brings Plutarch's evidence into line with the *Instituta*. Both agree that inscriptions were permitted for anyone who died in battle, without further qualification.

40 *IG* v.1.701–10, 918, 921, 1124–5; 1320; 1591; v.2.251; Papanikolaou 1976; one unpublished example for a certain Gorgopas in the Sparta Museum. Le Bohec (1993, 446) provides a convenient list of the stēlai. However, she omits *IG* v.2.251 and also v.1.1124, which is the one aberrant example, consisting of a base which apparently supported some sort of cippus. At least two stēlai (*IG* v.1.701, 703 = Tod and Wace 1906, nos. 377, 385) bear a circular hole near the top; I have seen no explanation of its purpose. Steinhauer 1992, 241 n. 8, mentions another unpublished stēlē from the first century BC, which, unlike the other stēlai, bears a representation of a hoplite.

41 One exception is the aforementioned aberrant monument of Eualkes which adds that he died 'at Mantinea' (EN MANTINEAI). Another is *IG* v.1.708, which is unusual in containing the names of two deceased warriors, one of whom is said to have been an Olympic victor (ΟΛΥΜΠΙΟΝΙΚΑΣ). The third (*IG* v.1.1320) concludes with the parting greeting ΧΑΙΡΕ, 'farewell'. There is also a fragmentary metrical inscription (*IG* v.1.721) ending in the letters …ΑΓΡΑΙ which has been interpreted – perhaps somewhat speculatively – as an epitaph to a soldier killed at the battle of Tanagra in 457 (Boring 1979, 110 no. 111).

42 The provenances given by Le Bohec do not always accord with the information in *IG* v.1, which is followed here. From Sparta and its immediate vicinity or from Amyklai: *IG* v.1.701, 702, 703, 704, 706, 707, 710, and probably 708, 709. From elsewhere in Lakonia: *IG* v.1.918, 921, 1124, 1125, 1320, 1591; Papanikolaou 1976–77. Provenance uncertain: *IG* v.1.705; the unpublished example in the Sparta Museum.

43 Le Bohec claims that the entire group dates by letter forms to the third century BC and that – with one exception (*IG* v.1.1124) which explicitly states that the deceased, a certain Eualkes, died in battle at Mantineia – they could relate to the battle of Sellasia in 222 BC. This blanket assertion is over-confident, since no epigraphic detail is provided to justify this uniform dating and no argument made against the datings by specialist epigraphers detailed in the main text. MacDowell (1986, 121) also assigns the inscriptions to 'a later period' on grounds which he does not explain. Kelly too (1981, 33–4 n. 9) asserts, without either reasoned justification or reference to epigraphic studies, that they are 'all from the fourth century BC, or later, *as not much can be expected earlier*' (my italics).

44 Her catalogue (1990, 201–2 nos. 57–60) makes specific reference to *IG* v.1.701, 702, 1124, 1125.

45 *IG* v.1.701, 707, 1124, 1125; and possibly 706, the correct reading of which is unclear from Fourmont's copy, on which we are dependent.

46 Cf. the table of Lakonian letter forms in Jeffery 1990, 183; with Ducat 1990b, 177–180.

47 Jeffery (1990, 184) conceded the appearance of a rather primitive 'stray *omega*' (alongside ten omikrons) in a manumission inscription from Tainaron (*IG* v.1.1230)

which she dated to the third quarter of the fifth century. The manumission took place during the ephorate of Aristeus, who may (or may not) be identical to the ephor in the final extant section of the famous Damonon inscription (*IG* v.1.213). More recently, however, Jeffery herself suggested that the Damonon inscription should be downdated to the early fourth century (1988; cf. 1990, 448). Ducat's recent detailed study (1990b, 180) also places *IG* v.1.1230 around 380 BC.

[48] A well-known Lakonian cup by the Hunt Painter made around the time of Thyrea depicts a procession in which pairs of soldiers are carrying fallen comrades over their shoulders (Berlin, Staat. Mus. 3404 = *CVA, Berlin* 4, *Deutschland* 33 (1971), pl. 183.1 = Stibbe 1972, no. 218 = Fitzhardinge 1980, 43 no. 26); Nafissi (1991, 304–5) suggests that it may even commemorate the burial procession of the 300 Champions themselves. Scholarly assumptions that the bodies are being carried home to Sparta (Kurtz and Boardman 1971, 191; Richer 1994, 72) ignore the obvious interpretation, that the cup depicts a procession to a battlefield grave (Pritchett 1974–91, iv.104; Clairmont 1983, 253 n. 2; Nafissi 1991, 294 n. 73). As Pritchett points out, a pair of men could never have carried a corpse far on ancient Greek roads without use of a cart. Moreover, several Attic vases depict similar scenes of removal from the battlefield, especially involving dead Amazons whose return home was inconceivable (von Bothmer 1957, 40, 44, 95–7).

[49] Cf. also *Apophth. Lak.*, Anon. no. 20 (= Plut. *Mor.* 233c); Diod. 15.52.5; Frontinus, *Strategemata* 1.12.5; Plut. *Ages.* 31.6; 40.3; Paus. 2.38.5; *SIG*³ 826e, col. III lines 32–3. On the corrupt text of Pausanias (3.16.4), which some commentators have taken to signify the return of the ashes of dead Spartans from Sicily, see the detailed discussion and agnostic conclusion of Pritchett (1974–91, iv.161–3, with *Apophth. Lak.*, Areus no. 2 (= Plut. *Mor.* 217f) and Plut. *Lyk.* 20.5); cf. Page 1981, 404–5.

[50] Xen. *Hell.* 2.4.33; van Hook 1932; Tod 1933; Kurtz and Boardman 1971, 110; Willemsen 1977.

[51] Hdt. 5.46; Peek 1955, 10 no. 23; Page 1981, 404–5 no. 100, with *Apophth. Lak.*, Areus 2 = Plut. *Mor.* 217f; Pritchett 1974–91, iv.161–3 no. 7; cf. n. 47, above.

[52] Pritchett 1974–91, iv.159 no. 2; 160 no. 5; 161–3 no. 7; 163 no. 8; 168–73 no. 15; 195 no. 49; 208 no. 66; 211–12 no. 78; 230–1 no. 99. As he notes (ibid. 164), the fact that the sources sometimes mention only the burial of the commander is a function of their focus on leading individuals; it is unclear whether it signifies a separate burial.

[53] Cartledge 1987, 235, suggests that the stēlē for Ainesias (*IG* v.1.703) may have derived from his death during the invasion of 370/69, but he adduces no supporting arguments for this idea.

[54] The attempt of Robertson (1983, 89–90) to argue, on the basis of the *Lakainōn Apophthegmata*, that this was indeed Spartan practice ignores the bulk of the classical evidence cited above.

[55] Hammond 1979/80; Gow and Page 1965, ii.262, 424; Page, 1981, 440; cf. Pritchett 1974–91, iv.243 n. 427.

[56] Similarly, I see no grounds for Raftopoulou's speculation (1998b, 135–6) that 'during the period of the Lycurgan so-called "austerity", there were no individual burials in the city and the dead were deposited at the Apothetai, the well known Kaiadas and other caves with precipices on mount Taygetos'. (Note that in her article the last nine lines of the left column on p. 136 have become transposed; they rightly belong at the top of the column.) The idea runs directly counter to the literary sources for 'Lykourgan' Sparta, which explicitly insist upon intra-mural burial. Moreover, it is inconceivable that deceased

Ch. 8. Restrictions on the deployment of wealth: burial and funerary practice

Spartan citizens were disposed of in the same places as sickly or deformed infants and convicted criminals (cf. Plut. *Lyk.* 16.1–2; Thuc. 1.134).

57 Morris 1992, 134–8, with references. Whilst the number of attested periboloi remains probably less than 200, known numbers of inscribed stelai reach as high as five figures.

58 *BSA* 13 (1906–7) 155–68; cf. Cartledge and Spawforth 1989, 72, 132, 222 no. 45. For other hellenistic and Roman funerary finds, Tod and Wace 1906, 235 no. 549; 240 no. 685; Steinhauer 1972, 242–5; Raftopoulou 1998b, 134, 136; cf. Nafissi 1991, 328–9.

59 Robertson (1983, 90–1) suggests that the festival of the Ariontia was likewise devoted to a *polyandreion* of fallen Spartans at Phigaleia, notwithstanding later identification of the occupants of the tomb as Arkadians (Paus. 8.39.4–5, 41.1; cf. Polyainos 6.27.2).

60 According to Nafissi (1991, 31 n. 148), the peripheral location of their heroon suggests that it was situated in a family necropolis. This, however, is unprovable and its very existence must imply official sanction. Whether the cult was founded immediately after Thermopylai or only later is unknown, since it is not mentioned before Pausanias' account.

61 It is not impossible that Brasidas' cenotaph owed its survival, if not its construction, to the Roman family of the Claudii Brasidae (cf. Musti and Torelli 1991, ad loc.; Bradford 1977, 91–2). This possibility would support my argument below that soldiers from high-status families did not receive privileged burial or subsequent honours *during the classical period*.

62 The three men mentioned above were awarded their honours during a post-battle discussion among the Spartans concerning 'who had distinguished himself most'. Herodotus' words here (ὃς γένοιτο αὐτῶν ἄριστος: 9.71.3) are closely similar to those he uses to describe the distinctions gained at Thermopylai (ἀνὴρ ἄριστος γενέσθαι: 7.226.1; ἀριστεῦσαι…Λακεδαιμόνιοι δύο ἀδελφεοί: 7.227), though in the latter case – with no Spartans remaining alive on the battlefield – the forum for discussion must have been different. It has been suggested that such discussions and awarding of honours were a regular occurrence after every battle (Richer 1994, 59).

63 I am grateful to the director of the new excavations, Dr Jutta Stroszeck of the Deutsches Archäologisches Institut in Athens, for helpful information about the tombs and the plans for their full publication.

64 Willemsen 1997, 132; cf. van Hook 1932; Tod 1933; Kurtz and Boardman 1971, 110. Some non-royal commanders abroad may have been buried separately from their troops. This was certainly true of Brasidas, of whom we learn that his funeral at Amphipolis 'took place at public expense in front of what is now the *agora*. The people of Amphipolis made an enclosure round his tomb, and for the future they sacrificed to him as to a hero and honoured him by holding games and making annual offerings to him' (Thuc. 5.11). As a burial conducted not by Spartans but by another polis, this was obviously a special case, as was the special burial given by the Samians to Archias, who was separated from the main army inside the walls of Samos (Hdt. 3.55).

65 Cf. n. 52, above. In Lysander's case, Pritchett's argument receives some support from Xenophon's evidence that the other fallen Lakedaimonians were also, like their commander, carried outside Boiotia (Xen. *Hell.* 3.5.24). One Spartan who did receive a solitary burial abroad was a certain 'Hippokles the Lakedaimonian', whose simple funerary stēlē was found at Thespiai in Boiotia (*IG* vii.1904). His death has been

connected to the Spartan garrison in Thespiai during the 370s; but this is merely speculation. There is no indication that he possessed any military rank and it may be that the individual character of his tomb resulted from his death through illness rather than in battle, as in the case of Lichas at Miletos (Thuc. 8.84). The early fifth-century funeral *stēlē* from Eretria commemorating the Spartan-born Pleistias (*IG* xii.9.286, Suppl. p. 186; Peek 1955, i.862; Page 1981, no. 440; Jeffery 1990, 86, 88 no. 17) is irrelevant to this discussion, since he apparently left Sparta in his childhood.

66 The justification claimed for it is the appearance of the word *eirēn* in a glossary of unusual words found in Herodotus (*Lexeis Herodotou*, s.v. *eirēn*, in Stein (ed.)1871, 465). Its only certain appearance, however, is in *recensio* B of the glossary, a version which, although based on the better *recensio* A, also contains many words which are not to be found in Herodotus' text (den Boer 1954, 288–300). Since the final part of *recensio* A covering Book IX is lost (Nafissi 1991, 302 n. 108), it remains uncertain whether or not the word *eirēn* was in Herodotus' text.

67 e.g. Kelly 1981, 33–6; Nafissi 1991, 302. Some would amend the text directly to read *hippees*: e.g. Jeanmaire 1939, 545; Lazenby 1985, 181 n. 16.

68 Note that Xenophon names the polemarchs in a different order from that on the stone. Willemsen (1977, 136) uses this to argue that Lakrates was not a Spartan but should be identified with an Athenian athlete found buried 50 m from the Lakedaimonian monument. He hypothesises that Xenophon gives the polemarchs' names from left to right and that Lakrates' name was therefore not on the inscription, since, if his name had been to the left, Xenophon would have given it before the polemarchs. It is unclear, however, how closely Xenophon's account was based upon the inscription, since he spells the name 'Thibrachos' with a chi for the antepenultimate letter, whereas the inscription uses a kappa. Moreover, Willemsen's hypothesis contradicts the obvious sense of Xenophon's words which, in sandwiching Lakrates' name between the polemarchs and the 'other Lakedaimonians', clearly identify him as one of the Lakedaimonians buried in the tomb.

69 I eschew engagement in the controversy over the nature and existence of the Pitanate *lochos* (cf. Thuc. 1.20).

70 Cf. the editions of Ziegler (Teubner), Flacelière (Budé), Manfredini and Piccirilli (Valla). Among historians, cf. Flacelière 1948, 403–5; Le Roy 1961, 231 n. 4; Pomeroy 1976, 36 and n. 8; Loraux 1981, 37; MacDowell 1986, 121–2; R. Parker 1989, 150; Nafissi 1991, 295 n. 77. The emendation has been resisted by den Boer 1954, 288–300; Wallace 1970, 99 n. 11; Richer 1994, 52–5.

71 My discussion draws upon the excellent study of royal funerary rites by Cartledge 1987, 331–43. The source for unattributed statements in the present paragraph is Hdt. 6.58.

72 For the controversy regarding the significance of this phrase for the *post mortem* status of kings, R. Parker 1988; 1989, 169 n. 51; Cartledge 1988b.

Chapter 9

MATERIAL AND RELIGIOUS INVESTMENT:
BRONZE DEDICATIONS AT SPARTA AND ABROAD

The previous two chapters have examined aspects of Spartiate life and death in which there were certain restrictions upon the private deployment of wealth. In those chapters the testimony of the literary sources has been augmented, where possible, by archaeological and iconographical evidence. There are, however, important areas of social life in the Greek polis on which we are almost completely reliant upon the archaeological record. This chapter will address the use of wealth, and restrictions on that use, in one sphere of Spartiate life in which the record of material culture stands independently of written evidence.

For much of the twentieth century it has been claimed that the history of Lakonian artistic production provides a compelling illustration of the way in which the use of wealth was brought under strict control during the late archaic and classical periods. The quality and quantity of artefacts (both imported and locally-made) found at early levels during the excavation of the sanctuary of Artemis Orthia by the British School at Athens between 1906 and 1910 made it clear that early Sparta and Lakonia before the mid-sixth century was an 'open' society marked by considerable private wealth and artistic production (Dawkins (ed.) 1929). This picture has since been extended by detailed studies of work in a range of artistic media – ivory-carving, painted pottery, bronzework and so on – which have discussed the 'rise' of Lakonian art to a peak of high-quality production in the late seventh and early sixth centuries.[1] This was followed by a subsequent diminution of artistic activity – the so-called 'decline' of Lakonian art. According to several scholars, the cause of this decline was the transformation of Spartiate society into an increasingly austere, barrack-like culture which, along with official restrictions on the use of wealth, led to a decay in patronage of the arts and hence to the decline of craft activity.[2]

I have argued elsewhere, however, that the alleged link between changes in artistic production and internal socio-political developments is far from clear (Hodkinson 1998a). Although there was undoubtedly less native Lakonian artistic production in the fourth century than in the sixth, unqualified talk of a general 'decline' gives a misleading impression. There is little correlation between the histories of different media and art-forms: some ended suddenly, but at different dates; some fell away gradually over an extended period; whilst certain others even commenced in classical times. These diverse trajectories do not constitute evidence for an increasingly barrack-like culture, since it is mainly the more export-oriented products which tailed away first, and those more geared to local consumption which continued longer. Furthermore, the patterns of Lakonian production in the late archaic and classical periods are paralleled elsewhere in Greece. As Richard Catling (1996, 88) has aptly remarked, they were part of a long-term process of artistic convergence, through which by the end of the classical period Lakonia had become 'a producer of provincial versions of types widespread in much of the Greek world'. The most fundamental point, however, is that, since the Spartiates themselves were (with perhaps a few, unimportant exceptions) not responsible for the production of Lakonian art and much of it was directed at external consumers, patterns of artistic production are hardly a meaningful indicator of restrictions on Spartiate use of wealth or changes in the character of their culture. To shed direct light on these issues through the archaeological record, we should examine the surviving material evidence, not for production, but for Spartiate expenditure and investment.

Ideally, one would examine the material evidence for expenditures in several spheres of Spartiate life; but the extremely patchy coverage of current archaeological research renders this unfeasible. There are few excavated burial sites from Sparta or its environs and no complete Spartiate house from our period has yet been excavated. On the other hand, the wealth of excavated evidence which has long existed from the major Spartan sanctuaries – Artemis Orthia, the sanctuaries on the Acropolis, the sanctuary of Menelaos and Helen at Therapne (the Menelaion), and that of Apollo at Amyklai (the Amyklaion) – could potentially provide a significant body of data about Spartiate expenditures on religious offerings, a sphere in which we might test the material record for evidence of the use of wealth and for signs of restrictions on that use.[3] Dedicatory practices at sanctuaries are, moreover, a sphere of activity rarely discussed in the literary evidence, one which only the archaeological record can illuminate.

The socio-political significance of this sphere of expenditure cannot be underestimated. The development of sanctuaries and the construction of monumental temples were fundamental constitutive elements of the formation of polis communities in early Greece (Snodgrass 1977; de Polignac 1995; Osborne 1996, 88–104). At most sanctuaries the eighth and seventh centuries witnessed an exponential growth in votive offerings (Snodgrass 1980, 52–4; Osborne 1996, 92–5). In many poleis, especially in central and eastern Greece, the sanctuary took the place of the funeral and the grave as the primary location where the rich put expensive goods out of commission through dedicating them to the deity. In early Sparta too, as we saw in chapter 8, the archaeological record of rich burials is minimal in comparison with the wealth of finds mentioned above from the sanctuary of Artemis Orthia. Although this shift of expenditure from a familial to a communal context may have represented a degree of public control upon the activities of the wealthy, the making of costly votive offerings presented an opportunity for the rich to indulge in public display, to engage in competition for status, and to emphasize their special connection to the divine. The social importance of expensive votive offerings is also shown by the high percentage of Orientalising artefacts among metal dedications of the late eighth and seventh centuries, gifts which added an extra layer of meaning by evoking the dedicator's privileged links to the Near East (Morris 1997). This last phenomenon is evident in early dedications at Spartan sanctuaries, which contain many Orientalising votives, ivories and Phoenician imports.[4] The subsequent history of votive offerings in the late archaic and classical periods is, consequently, a major issue in any examination of the use of private wealth.

Examination of the full range of votive offerings lies beyond the scope of this chapter, partly because, due to the novelty of this type of approach, little advance groundwork is available in the form of systematic inventories of finds. I shall therefore focus on one particular medium, the votives in bronze. My selection is influenced by the status of bronze as a precious metal, which – unlike silver and gold – survives in reasonable quantities and whose votive use indicates a not insignificant material investment; and by the fact that bronze dedications come in the form of a variety of offerings, large and small, 'raw' and 'converted', reflecting a wide range of expenditures.[5] Another advantage of studying the bronzes is that they include dedications by women as well as men, thus giving access to the sphere of female expenditure which is often poorly represented in the literary evidence. In addition to examining the bronze votives at Spartan sanctuaries, I will conclude the chapter by considering the evidence for Spartiate bronze dedications at foreign shrines.

Bronze votives at Spartan sanctuaries

Obstacles to a quantified approach

Although the votive offerings at Sparta's main sanctuaries constitute the most extensive range of evidence available within the field of Spartiate material culture, the construction of a satisfactory database of bronze votives, on which to found cogent historical conclusions, faces serious obstacles. First, although bronze survives in greater quantities than more expensive metals, the material record of bronze dedications at Spartan sanctuaries, as elsewhere in Greece, is seriously depleted by several post-depositional factors. The intrinsic value of bronze frequently led temple officials to melt down earlier dedications for refashioning into larger, more impressive objects. Plundering of temples, especially disused ones, became increasingly frequent from the late classical period onwards. Bronze is also subject to corrosion and disintegration in damp climatic conditions, such as those at Artemis Orthia, where metal dedications from unsealed classical and later levels have suffered heavily from the site's low-lying situation by the flood-prone River Eurotas.[6] The numbers of excavated bronzes are therefore a minimum to be multiplied many times over in any estimation of the original level of dedications. An even greater problem, however, is not so much the global depletion of original dedications as the differential impact upon votives of different types and periods. Objects in sheet metal, being more easily melted down and corroded, have typically suffered more than cast objects, a phenomenon only partly compensated by the finds of handles and ornaments of bronze vessels whose bodies no longer survive. (For an example, see *Fig.* 13.) Conditions have also often been more conducive to the preservation of archaic than classical material. At Artemis Orthia the Spartans covered the sanctuary with a layer of sand in the early sixth century; this created a sealed deposit which enabled earlier votives to escape the worst effects of the humidity which affected later bronzes. At the Menelaion, too, bronzes buried in the 'Great Pit' sometime in the sixth century had more favourable conditions for survival than later metal votives, which may have become badly depleted in the disturbed times of the hellenistic period when the shrine seems to have fallen at least partly into eclipse.[7]

The incomplete and differential survival of the original dedications is compounded by a further difficulty: the incomplete publication of those finds which have been excavated. The fundamental requirement for a thorough study of expenditure and investment in votive offerings is a complete inventory or database of the finds from the sanctuaries in question, in order to permit quantification of the numbers of dedications of various types of artefact in different periods. Unfortunately, few of the excavation reports display an interest in quantification of the bronze finds; indeed, many of the excavated bronzes remain unpublished.[8] The incomplete publication of the metal finds from Tsountas's 1890 excavations at the Amyklaion has recently been detailed by Calligas (1992), and the publication record of the early British excavations was little better. Published comments on the Artemis Orthia bronzes evinced the most desultory interest in the overall assemblage of finds:

> Even at the date of the excavation the bronze objects found at the site of Orthia could hardly have been expected to win very much attention, for the interest of such things had been largely exhausted by former excavations... (Droop 1929, 196).

Fig. 13. Figurine of a running figure (front and back), which once ornamented a bronze vessel, from the sanctuary of Athena Chalkioikos on the Spartan Acropolis, c. 550–525 BC (reproduced with permission of the British School at Athens).

Ch. 9. Material and religious investment: bronze dedications at Sparta and abroad

The published bronzes were hence confined to selected artefacts and biased towards finds from earlier periods (Droop 1906/7; 1929; Lamb 1926/7b). The bronzes from certain years of the 1920s Acropolis excavations received somewhat fuller treatment from Winifred Lamb, whose published comments (1926/7a, 83) evince some realisation of the importance of systematic documentation. Her coverage, nevertheless, was still biased towards objects of artistic significance, with other finds mentioned in such generic fashion (for example, 'handles of various types') as to lack statistical value. She did not, moreover, attempt to re-study the bronzes from the earlier Acropolis excavations which had received much less satisfactory coverage.[9] The early reports from the Menelaion excavations were similarly inadequate, providing little discussion of individual artefacts or indication of numbers of bronzes.[10] Published reports from the more recent Menelaion excavations are as yet preliminary, and hence also partial in coverage of the bronze finds.[11]

The state of the published evidence is, consequently, far from satisfactory, providing only a selective coverage of the finds governed by considerations of archaeological distinctiveness or artistic quality rather than by concern for the assemblage as a whole. Ultimately, a complete study of the bronze votives will need to go back beyond the published reports to a comprehensive re-examination of all the finds, including the many finds currently unpublished. At present such a task has been achieved only for one particular type of artefact: bronze, iron and silver pins, whose finds throughout the entire Peloponnese from prehistoric to archaic times have been fully catalogued by Imma Kilian-Dirlmeier (1984). For other votives such an inventory remains a major desideratum for the future. For the present, an essential preliminary exercise is to bring some order to the current haphazard state of the published evidence, scattered over numerous excavation reports, by compiling a database of all the bronzes mentioned (however inadequately) in publications to date.

The outcome of that exercise is set out in TABLES 6, 8a–c and 9a–d, which present the data in quantitative form, covering the period *c.* 650–*c.* 350 BC.[12] (Pins which are itemised in the excavation reports are included; but other pins catalogued by Kilian-Dirlmeier are excluded from the tables, on the grounds that inclusion of this exhaustive set of data, including hundreds of unpublished examples, would misleadingly skew the statistics and undermine the character of the tables as a representation of the current state of published excavation reports. Instead, the statistics from Kilian-Dirlmeier's study will be considered separately.) These tables, naturally, bear many marks of the deficiencies in the excavation reports mentioned above. The frequent appearance of the signs 'Ind(efinite)' and '+' indicate, for example, the large number of cases in which the reports fail to specify the precise number of artefacts. Problems with dating are also evident. The large number of objects with unhelpful labels like 'DNG' (Date Not Given) or 'archaic' reflects the fact that existing reports often provide either no information or only vague indications concerning the dating of finds.

Rich citizens and the use of private wealth

This lack is clearly most serious in the case of the Amyklaion where – as TABLE 6 makes clear – fully 80% of the finds are undated.

Following the catalogue of deficiencies rehearsed above, it might be questioned whether the data in the tables can shed any serious light upon Spartiate expenditures on bronze votives. I would argue, however, that even the current flawed database may suggest significant hypotheses for future, more comprehensive study, especially when set besides similar data from elsewhere in Greece. The following sections will attempt to put some flesh on the bones of that proposition.

Overall patterns of bronze dedications

TABLE 6 presents the global statistics of published bronze finds from the four main sanctuary areas in the period *c.* 650–*c.* 350 BC. TABLES 8a–c (on p. 281) then provide a more detailed breakdown of the dedication of the most common types of surviving bronze votives (vessels, jewellery, statuettes and figurines) across the range of sanctuaries, whilst TABLES 9a–d (on p. 282) examine the range of votive offerings at each sanctuary. What conclusions do the tables suggest? For a start, they provide unambiguous confirmation that in the period to *c.* 550, and even down to *c.* 500, Spartiates expended their resources on a range of metal votive offerings. Fitzhardinge's claim (1980, 123) that, 'to judge from the extant remains, the use of precious metals was not common at Sparta at any time' is definitively disproved, especially given that the present statistics represent only a fraction of the original bronze votives. It has been suggested that 'the relative luxury displayed by the sixth-century Laconian should not mislead us

TABLE 6. Published bronze finds from Spartan sanctuaries, *c.* 650–*c.* 350 BC.

	Orthia	Acropolis	Menelaion	Amyklaion	Total
c. 650–*c.* 600	40+	3	24+	5+	72+
c. 600–*c.* 550	22	7/8	21+	4+	54+
c. 550–*c.* 500	6	15–18	6+	8/9	35+
c. 500–*c.* 450	2	10–14	1+	1/2	14+
c. 450–*c.* 400	1	5–7	Ind	0/1	7+
c. 400–*c.* 350	-	1	-	-	1
Early archaic	1	-	-	-	1
Archaic	13	-	Ind	5	19+
Late archaic	-	-	-	3	3
Lak. III–V and later	-	-	11+	-	11+
DNG	3	74+	3+	115+	195+

Key: DNG = Date Not Given
The signs '+' and 'Ind' signify the existence of an indefinite number of artefacts whose limit is not specified in the relevant excavation reports.

Ch. 9. Material and religious investment: bronze dedications at Sparta and abroad

into placing Sparta on the same level as the cities of the north-east Peloponnese or Athens' (Rolley 1986a, 107). True though that may be, it should not lead us to minimize the significance of the available evidence. For example, Rolley's judgement (1982, 76–7) that Lakonian-made vessels were very rarely dedicated in sanctuaries in Lakonia itself can be seen, on the strength of TABLES 8a–c, to underestimate the scale of domestic vessel offerings, as is attested by the survival of their ornamented handles and attachments.[13] The published bronze record attests a number of relatively grandiose objects – such as vessels, furniture with metal attachments, armour, and decorative plaques – as well as more modest statuettes, and personal and dress items.

In the period after *c.* 550, as TABLE 6 shows, there is a clear decline in the total number of bronze finds. At first sight this might seem to suggest the growth of restrictions on this use of wealth; but the picture is in reality more complex. Between *c.* 550 and *c.* 500 bronze finds actually increase on the Acropolis, and possibly also at the Amyklaion. There is also more continuity into the fifth century than might at first be apparent. On the Acropolis, dedications maintained their higher levels on into the early fifth century. Even in the later fifth century they are still at a level comparable with that of the early sixth century, and higher than that of the later seventh century. In fact, there is cause to think that the fifth-century figures might be significantly increased. The Acropolis finds include between 40 and 50 bronze bells; but only five of these – those which bear inscriptions – have been individually itemised and dated in the excavation reports. (*Fig.* 14 shows one example.) The remainder are mentioned only in passing.[14] All the inscribed bells were dated by the excavators to the fifth century. If similar dates should apply to the other 40 or so (currently included among the category of 'Date Not Given'), then the fifth-century Acropolis bronzes would clearly outnumber finds of earlier periods by a considerable margin.

It is only at Artemis Orthia and the Menelaion that the figures suggest a marked decline in bronze votives from the second half of the sixth century. Since it is precisely at these two sanctuaries that we have already noted the existence of post-depositional factors which led to the differential survival of archaic over classical bronzes, the perceived decline at these shrines may not be

Fig. 14. Drawing of inscribed bronze bell dedicated by Enpedoklees to Athena, from the sanctuary of Athena Chalkioikos, early fifth century (reproduced with permission of the British School at Athens).

TABLE 7. Finds of lead figurines from Artemis Orthia.

	Period	Number	No. per annum
Lead 0	(? –650)	23	-
Lead I	(650–620)	5719	191
Lead II	(620–580)	9548	239
Lead III–IV	(580–500)	68822	860
Lead V	(500–425)	10617	152
Lead VI	(425–250)	4773	27

as sharp as the present figures appear to suggest. Indeed, preliminary reports of the recent excavations at the Menelaion refer to fragments of several major dedications from the early fifth century onwards which I have not been able to include in the current statistics (H.W. Catling 1976/7, 33). We should probably accept, however, the reality of some degree of decline.

It might still be argued that even a limited decline confined to Artemis Orthia and the Menelaion betokens some degree of restriction on the use of wealth, in that these two shrines have also produced the largest numbers of cheap lead votive figurines.[15] These leads are sometimes cited as proof of the Spartiates' increasing disdain for more precious metals which, it is argued, led them to opt instead for cheaper votives (e.g. Wace 1929, 250). TABLE 7 documents the increasing votive use of leads at the sanctuary of Artemis Orthia from the later seventh century, rising to a dramatic peak in the sixth century, followed by a decline in numbers during the fifth century and later.[16] The chronological trajectory of the less well published Menelaion leads is apparently similar. Comparison of TABLES 6 and 7 indicates that there is a certain overlap in the sixth century between the decline in bronze votives and the peak of the leads. The leads, however, had begun increasing in popularity as early as the later seventh century before the decline in bronze dedications at either Artemis Orthia or the Menelaion. Moreover, the leads themselves went into decline early in the fifth century, in parallel with the further fall in bronze votives. The absence of any clear inverse synchronism between the chronological trajectories of the bronzes and the leads, along with the gross numerical disparity between the numbers of votives in the two media, suggests that the decline of bronze dedications at Artemis Orthia and the Menelaion cannot be ascribed to restrictions involving a switch to the use of cheaper lead figurines. Indeed, it is questionable whether the leads should be viewed primarily as performing the role of 'cheaper', alternative votive offering to more precious metals. Certainly, the less costly material, their minute size, the immense numbers dedicated and some of the motifs depicted, especially those of hoplite warriors (cf. *Fig. 8*, on p. 223), indicate that their dedicants came from a wide spectrum of the citizen population. The wide range of motifs, together with the high artistic quality of many of the figurines, especially in Leads II–IV, suggests, however,

Ch. 9. Material and religious investment: bronze dedications at Sparta and abroad

that they served a distinctive purpose of their own. The enormous care taken to depict elaborate patterns on the model textiles and dresses of the female figurines, whose ornateness seems to evoke the sumptuous clothing worn by their dedicants on ritual occasions (such as that represented in Alkman's *Partheneion*: cf. 1.67–8, Page), hardly matches the image of a more austere, alternative form of votive (cf. Foxhall 1998, 304–5; Foxhall and Stears 2000). Indeed, the decline of lead votives in classical times is probably connected to the parallel decline of bronze dedications.

In sum, the present evidence indicates divergent trends between different Spartan sanctuaries and offers little material support for any idea of a general imposition of restrictions on votive offerings in the late sixth or fifth centuries. Despite an overall decline in numbers of dedications, a sizeable number of Spartiates were still expending their wealth on bronze votives in the central polis sanctuaries on the Acropolis down to the end of the fifth century. Only in the early fourth century do votive expenditures apparently cease in their entirety.

Can one conclude, then, that a general restriction on votive expenditures was finally imposed in the years around 400? To answer this question, it is instructive to compare Spartan dedications with those at sanctuaries elsewhere in Greece. Such a comparison reveals that the patterns of Spartiate bronze votive offerings revealed in TABLE 6 are not unique. It has long been noted that the sixth and fifth centuries witness a significant decline in the quantity of small votives excavated at many Greek sanctuaries, including a marked decrease in surviving bronze dedications.[17] Snodgrass (1989/90) has argued that this phenomenon reflects major changes in the nature and role of votive offerings following from a profound change in religious practice – a further sign that we should not interpret Spartan patterns purely in terms of local restrictions. As the relatively small number of statistical case-studies cited in Snodgrass's study shows, there is need for more work on the nature and chronology of this phenomenon. A survey of published reports from a number of sites suggests, however, that the timing of the decline in votives, both of bronze and in other media, varies from sanctuary to sanctuary, at some places beginning early in the sixth century, at others not until the fifth. On Crete several shrines show a major decline in votives during the sixth century (Morris 1998, 62–3). At the sanctuary of Hermes and Aphrodite at Symi Viannou on Crete, for instance, the bronze relief plaques which have been published in detail decline markedly from 61 finds from the seventh century to only 13 from the sixth and just two from the fifth (Lembesi 1985). Similarly, at the harbour sanctuary at Emporio on Chios, few of the wide variety of bronze finds were dated later than Period IV, which terminates *c.* 600 (Boardman 1967, xii, 205–9, 257). On the acropolis at Lindos on Rhodes the decline took hold somewhat later in the sixth century, to judge from the absence of bronzes ascribed to the period 525–400 BC (Blinkenberg 1931). At the shrine of Artemis on Samos votive deposits peak in the third quarter of the sixth century and start to decline thereafter; whereas at the sanctuary of Hera the decline is delayed until the fifth century (Kyrieleis 1993, 129). (Note this further example of differences between sanctuaries within the same polis.) At Olympia the decline in helmet and jewellery dedications also takes place mainly in the early fifth century (Kunze 1958, 118–51; 1961, 56–137; 1967, 111–83; Philipp 1981, 8–10), though other bronzes continue until the onset of a major rupture around 450 (Gauer 1991, 169; cf. Rolley 1993, 394–5). At the sanctuary of Poseidon at the Isthmos of Corinth, the peak of arms and armour dedications comes in the period after *c.* 550, only to be terminated abruptly with the destruction of the archaic temple of Poseidon around 470 (Jackson 1992, 141–4). The following period also witnesses a comparative paucity of other valuable dedications (Broneer 1959, 339).

The above evidence suggests several points: first, that there was a sharp general decline in votive offerings at sanctuaries throughout Greece during the sixth and fifth centuries; secondly, that there are considerable variations in the timing of that decline; thirdly, that the decline appears to begin earlier in local polis sanctuaries, taking effect somewhat later at those shrines (Olympia, Isthmia and the Heraion on Samos) which attracted frequent votives from foreign dedicants; fourthly, that even at these shrines the decline had set in by 400 BC. Hence Spartiate dedication patterns appear to conform to the general Greek norm, both in the general decline in bronze votives and in the variations between different Spartan sanctuaries in the precise timing of that decline. In comparison with elsewhere, the decline in Spartiate votives is, if anything, a little delayed. In particular, the pattern of dedications on the Spartan Acropolis – a particularly *Spartan* cult area, which included the shrine of Sparta's guardian deity, Athena Poliouchos, and which is completely lacking in foreign dedications – comes close to the pattern observed at panhellenic sanctuaries. I have argued elsewhere (Hodkinson 1998b) that the broad similarities of Spartan trends to those elsewhere means that the decline of votive offerings cannot be seen as reflecting the growth of a uniquely austere society. These similarities do not necessarily, however, preclude an interpretation in terms of restrictions on the use of wealth. It has been suggested that the universal decline in votive offerings was part of a wider collapse of elitist ideology in the late archaic period, involving the decline of Orientalising art, of elitist literary activity and of wealthy self-advertisement in burials and dress (Morris 1997, 43). The delay in the decline at panhellenic sanctuaries could reflect the activities of the wealthy in circumventing restrictions in their home poleis through dedications abroad. Evidence that Spartan votive trends were part of this wider development might be sought in signs that celebrations of Spartiate Olympic success were likewise confined to Olympia and excluded from Sparta itself (Hodkinson 1999, 167–76; cf. ch. 10, below). The continuation of dedications on the Acropolis does not fit this pattern, however, and it is noteworthy that commemorations of local agonistic success also continued on the Acropolis down to the years around 400 (Hodkinson 1999, 152–5).

Ch. 9. Material and religious investment: bronze dedications at Sparta and abroad

TABLE 8a. Published bronze vessels from Spartan sanctuaries.

	Orthia	Acropolis	Menelaion	Amyklaion	Total
c. 650–c. 600	6+	-	6+	4	16+
c. 600–c. 550	8	5	10+	2	25+
c. 550–c. 500	1	5/6	2+	1	9+
c. 500–c. 450	0/1	0/1	-	-	0–2
c. 450–c. 400	0/1	-	-	-	0/1
c. 400–c. 350	-	-	-	-	-
DNG or Vague	7	5+	1+	12+	25+

TABLE 8b. Published bronze jewellery from Spartan sanctuaries.

	Orthia	Acropolis	Menelaion	Amyklaion	Total
c. 650–c. 600	18	3	Ind	-	22+
c. 600–c. 550	11	-	Ind	-	12+
c. 550–c. 500	1	-	-	-	1
c. 500–c. 450	-	-	-	-	-
c. 450–c. 400	-	-	-	-	-
c. 400–c. 350	-	-	-	-	-
DNG or Vague	1	6	3+	75	85+

TABLE 8c. Published bronze statuettes/figurines from Spartan sanctuaries.

	Orthia	Acropolis	Menelaion	Amyklaion	Total
c. 650–c. 600	1	-	Ind	-	2+
c. 600–c. 550	2	2/3	0/1	0/1	4–7
c. 550–c. 500	2	7–9	-	6/7	15–18
c. 500–c. 450	2	6–8	1	1/2	10–13
c. 450–c. 400	1	3/4	-	0/1	4–6
c. 400–c. 350	-	1	-	-	1
DNG or Vague	-	9+	1	12+	22+

Trends in the use of different types of votives

To investigate more closely the expenditure of wealth on religious dedications, it is important to go beyond the general trends revealed in TABLE 6 to the more detailed breakdown provided in TABLES 8a–c and TABLES 9a–d, which give specific figures for the three main types of votives: vessels, jewellery and free-standing statuettes/figurines. The picture of specific rather than global decline emerges still more clearly from these statistics. As TABLES 9a–d indicate, jewellery and vessels formed the most frequent bronze dedications in the period down to *c.* 550. After *c.* 550 jewellery votives then fall away (TABLE 8b). The

Rich citizens and the use of private wealth

TABLE 9a. Categories of published bronze finds: Artemis Orthia

	Vessels	Jewellery	Statuettes	Other
c. 650–c. 600	6+	18	1	15
c. 600–c. 550	8	11	2	1
c. 550–c. 500	1	1	2	2
c. 500–c. 450	-	-	2	-
c. 450–c. 400	-	-	1	-
c. 400–c. 350	-	-	-	-
DNG or Vague	7	1	-	9
Total	22+	31	8	27

TABLE 9b. Categories of published bronze finds: Acropolis

	Vessels	Jewellery	Statuettes	Other
c. 650–c. 600	-	3	-	-
c. 600–c. 550	5	-	2/3	-
c. 550–c. 500	5/6	-	7–9	3
c. 500–c. 450	0/1	-	6–8	4/5
c. 450–c. 400	-	-	3/4	2/3
c. 400–c. 350	-	-	1	1
DNG or Vague	5+	6	9+	54+
Total	15+	9	28+	64+

TABLE 9c. Categories of published bronze finds: Menelaion

	Vessels	Jewellery	Statuettes	Other
c. 650–c. 600	8+	Ind	Ind	14+
c. 600–c. 550	11+	Ind	1	9+
c. 550–c. 500	2+	1	-	3+
c. 500–c. 450	-	-	1	Ind
c. 450–c. 400	-	-	-	Ind
c. 400–c. 350	-	-	-	-
DNG or Vague	Ind	3+	1	14+
Total	22+	6+	4+	42+

TABLE 9d. Categories of published bronze finds: Amyklaion

	Vessels	Jewellery	Statuettes	Other
c. 650–c. 600	4	-	-	Ind
c. 600–c. 550	2	-	0/1	Ind
c. 550–c. 500	1	-	6/7	1
c. 500–c. 450	-	-	1/2	-
c. 450–c. 400	-	-	0/1	-
c. 400–c. 350	-	-	-	-
DNG or Vague	12+	75	12+	37+
Total	19+	75	19+	40+

bronze vessels also decline after *c.* 550, except on the Acropolis where they continue into the later sixth century (TABLE 8a). Free-standing statuettes and figurines, in contrast, increase in number after *c.* 550 and become the most common votive between 550 and 500 (TABLES 8c; 9b). At the Amyklaion they decline in the early fifth century; but they remain prominent on the Acropolis until the later fifth century. (For one example, see *Fig.* 15.)

The decline in jewellery dedications is also evident from Kilian-Dirlmeier's study of the pins (1984). At the sanctuary of Artemis Orthia no fewer than 927 pins were found in association with late Geometric pottery of the late eighth and early seventh centuries. A rather smaller, though still sizeable, number (374 pins) were found with Lakonian I or II pottery (*c.* 650–*c.* 580 BC), below the early sixth-century layer of sand. The strata above the sand, however, were marked by a complete absence of pins (Kilian-Dirlmeier 1984, 12).

These changes were not confined to the bronzes. Jewellery motifs among the leads dedicated at both Artemis Orthia and the Menelaion declined significantly in numbers of both types and varieties after *c.* 580 (the period of Leads III–IV), subsequently disappearing entirely in the fifth century. At Artemis Orthia the textile motifs, which may represent the items of clothing, perhaps especially those worn on ritual occasions, with which dedications of jewellery were often associated, also cease after the end of Lead II (*c.* 620–580).[18] Similarly, the upward trend of bronze statuettes and figurines finds some parallel among the leads, although at a somewhat earlier date: leads depicting human and animal figures (real or mythical) are very few in Lead I (*c.* 650–620), but increase and exceed jewellery motifs from Lead II (*c.* 620–580) onwards (Wace 1929, 280–1).

In interpreting these changes, we need once again to ask whether they mirror developments elsewhere in Greece. The frequency of Spartan jewellery dedications in the early part of our period matches the general pattern at archaic sanctuaries throughout the Greek world (Simon 1986, 198). The subsequent decline of jewellery votives also occurs at other sanctuaries, although difficulties in the dating of metal jewellery types – many of which have a long life without much development –

Fig. 15. Bronze figurine of Athena, from the Spartan Acropolis, *c.* 450 or later fifth century BC (reproduced with permission of the British School at Athens).

Rich citizens and the use of private wealth

without secure stratigraphic and pottery contexts often makes for a lack of precision about dating in excavation reports (Simon 1986, 174). Hence how closely the chronology of the sixth-century decline of jewellery at Spartan sanctuaries matches trends elsewhere remains a little uncertain. The Spartan timing, however, is paralleled at the sanctuary of Hera Akraia at Perachora, where the numerous seventh-century jewellery finds at the so-called 'temple of Hera Limenia' on the upper, Eastern terrace fall markedly in the sixth century.[19] Likewise, at the harbour sanctuary at Emporio, as we have seen, the decline in jewellery, as with the other bronze finds, begins in the early part of the same century. At the extramural sanctuary of Demeter and Persephone at Cyrene, however, the decline comes somewhat later, after the archaic and early classical periods (Warden 1990, 14, 40). At Olympia too, as might be expected, the decline is largely a phenomenon of the early fifth century, and even then finger rings remain relatively numerous in the classical period after a comparatively undistinguished showing in earlier centuries (Philipp 1981, 8–10).

Another ground for viewing the Spartan decline in jewellery dedications in a panhellenic context is the fact that jewellery is also generally less common in classical graves than in those of earlier periods (Kurtz and Boardman 1971, 61–2, 101, 207). This general decline may be related to an increasing simplicity in the ornamentation of female dress which is observable in depictions of women on monuments (Bonfante and Jaunzems 1988, 1390–91). Herodotus (5.87–8) recounts a story in which the Athenian women murdered the sole survivor of a disastrous expedition against Aigina by stabbing him with the brooches from their dresses. Following this incident, he claims, the women were compelled to adopt the Ionian-style broochless dress in place of their former Doric-style dress, which required a fastening and which had formerly been worn by all Greek women. The tale itself and the alleged former universality of Doric-style dress are doubtless invented – dresses without fastenings are attested iconographically from earlier periods (Pekridou-Gorecki 1989, 72). Moreover, Herodotus himself notes that women in Argos and Epidauros, and apparently also in Corinth, still dressed in the Doric style. His comments, however, do at least indicate that the broochless female dress was in widespread use in his day. Simplicity of female dress in classical Sparta is, as we have seen (ch. 7), intimated by the evidence of the late fourth-century Aristotelian *Polity of the Lakedaimonians* (*ap.* Herakleides Lembos 373.13, Dilts) that women were not permitted to wear ornaments.

As regards statuettes and figurines, Spartan dedication patterns in the early part of our period (*c.* 650–*c.* 550 BC) display a certain idiosyncrasy in the infrequency of votives in comparison with dedications elsewhere.[20] This phenomenon coincides with a considerable gap in local production, which lasted from the termination of a longstanding series of Geometric horse figurines early in the seventh century until the emergence of statuette production in the early sixth.[21] After 550, however, although detailed studies of other Greek sanctuaries

Ch. 9. Material and religious investment: bronze dedications at Sparta and abroad

are again urgently needed, Spartan patterns appear to follow general trends. At the extramural sanctuary of Demeter and Persephone at Cyrene bronze figurines are prominent during the archaic period, but decline significantly afterwards (Warden 1990, 12). At Delphi too the number of published bronze statuettes drops from nearly 30 from the sixth and early fifth centuries to a mere seven from the remainder of the fifth century.[22] At the Kabeirion in Boiotia stylistic dating of bronze and lead oxen statuettes (Schmaltz 1980) suggested a huge drop from 122 later archaic dedications to only six in the classical period. Subsequent epigraphic dating of the 37 inscribed statuettes from this group, however, suggests a general lowering of dates (22 archaic, 12 classical and 3 hellenistic bronzes) and a less sharp decline, focused mainly on the early fifth century (Roesch 1985; Rolley 1986b). General surveys of Greek bronze statuettes suggest a staggered decline in votives comparable to that in TABLE 8c, occurring at some shrines in the early fifth century, as at the Amyklaion, but at most places in the years after 450, as on the Acropolis (Lamb 1969, 106; Rolley 1986a, 169).

The decline in Spartan bronze vessel dedications raises further issues for future research. At first sight, it is tempting to explain this decline in local terms by connecting it with the end of Lakonian bronze vessel production *c.* 530–520 (Rolley 1982, 75–8); but the link is not strong, since (apart from on the Acropolis) the decline in dedications starts earlier, around 550. So, once again, the question is whether it was part of more widespread changes in the role of bronze vessels. Modern discussions of the panhellenic decline of bronze dedications tend to focus on smaller dedications; but there are indications that larger objects were also affected. At Olympia vessel dedications reach their peak in the sixth and early fifth centuries, but then share in the general decline of bronze votives after *c.* 450 (Gauer 1991, 1, 169). Rolley (1986a, 169) has suggested that there was a widespread shift in the period 450–300 BC towards the use of bronze vessels as funerary objects and items of display in private houses. (It is tempting to recall the episode in which foreign invaders plundering Spartan houses in 370 BC found them full of many valuables: Xen. *Hell.* 6.5.27.) If this is so, one issue requiring particular clarification is whether the declining use of bronze vessels as sanctuary offerings is connected with the emergence of the life-size bronze statue during the late sixth and early fifth centuries as the most prestigious dedicatory object (Mattusch 1988, 58–118). At Spartan sanctuaries there is at present no archaeological evidence that statue dedications did replace offerings of vessels. Since very few bronze statues survive from anywhere in the Greek world, their absence from the Spartan material record is unsurprising; but evidence is also lacking for the more durable stone bases on which such statues would once have stood.[23] A similar picture emerges from the literary evidence, which attests a number of bronze statues dedicated by the Spartan polis, but no private statue dedications until the mid-fourth century at the earliest.[24] There are, for example, no attested personal statues of living

285

athletic or equestrian victors at Sparta itself before the mid-fourth century (see further, ch. 10). Similarly, Lysander's celebrations of his victory at Aigospotamoi in 405 included a grandiose group of statues of himself and his commanders at Delphi (Paus. 10.9.7–10; ML no. 95), but no statues of living humans in Sparta itself.[25] In contrast, Konon's comparable victory at Knidos in 394 was commemorated with statues at Athens as well as abroad (Paus. 1.3.2; 6.3.16). Further research is needed on sanctuaries elsewhere to determine a wider context for the Spartan archaeological record. But present evidence suggests that, although there were no general restrictions on votive offerings, a more limited restriction may have been imposed upon statue dedications inside Sparta as a means of controlling the display of wealth and status in front of fellow citizens.

Raw and converted offerings

The relationship of these changes in numbers and types of votive offerings to issues of expenditure and material investment can be explored further by framing them within another context. Snodgrass (1989/90, 291–4) has suggested that the broad votive changes under discussion stemmed, at least in part, from a widespread shift from 'raw' to 'converted' offerings which took place around the end of the archaic period. To quote his definition of these terms,

> A 'raw' dedication is something like a weapon of war, a brooch, an ear-ring, a shield or a jumping-weight, which is an unmodified object of real, secular use. Its dedication involved no more than the simple act of surrender… Often the owner, or someone else, will have used it for a considerable time before its dedication. By contrast, a statue or statuette, though equally direct in expressing the piety of the dedicant, does so in a different way: it is a *conversion* of a part of his or her wealth…and in most cases it has been produced for the specific purpose of dedication (ibid. 291).

Snodgrass argues that this shift not only represented a more sophisticated religious attitude but also had an important economic aspect which is reflected in the decline in numbers of surviving votives from the late archaic period onwards. First, since the 'converted' dedication was typically more costly than the 'raw', the change in votive patterns involved 'a simultaneous decrease in the *frequency* of dedication, together with a general rise in the *value* of each separate dedication'.[26] Secondly, the greater value of converted offerings made them more prone to subsequent looting and expropriation. Although the archaeological record for these expensive offerings is mute, they are amply attested in a number of temple inventories from the classical and early hellenistic periods.[27] One reason for the greater value of offerings was, in Snodgrass's view, increased social differentiation within the poleis of classical Greece.

To what extent do these hypotheses hold good for Sparta? In the absence of temple inventories, we must rely entirely upon the material record. TABLE 10 indicates the changing numbers of 'raw' and 'converted' bronze votives at

Ch. 9. Material and religious investment: bronze dedications at Sparta and abroad

TABLE 10. The character of bronze votives at Spartan sanctuaries.

	ARTEMIS ORTHIA		ACROPOLIS	
	Raw	Converted	Raw	Converted
c.650–c.600	24	10	3	0
c.600–c.550	12	2	0	2–3
c.550–c.500	2	3	1	9–11
c.500–c.450	0	2	0–1	7–9
c.450–c.400	0	1	0–1	3–4
c.400–c.350	0	0	0	1
DNG	2	0	11+	24+
Total	40	18	15+	46+

Artemis Orthia and the Acropolis during our period.[28] The figures show a reasonable degree of fit with the claimed trend from 'raw' to 'converted' offerings. At Artemis Orthia there is a clear preponderance of 'raw' dedications before c. 550, which subsequently fades away and is even marginally reversed; although after c. 550 the overall numbers of finds are, admittedly, very small. The figures for the Acropolis illustrate the other side of the coin. Numbers of 'converted' offerings are few before c. 550, but increase thereafter. The other notable phenomenon is the paucity of dated 'raw' offerings of any period on the Acropolis, a point to which I shall return below.

If the evidence provides some support for the notion of a shift from 'raw' to 'converted' dedications, does it also support the idea of a rise in their individual value and the associated implication of the development of a more differentiated society? To a certain extent it might. The specially-produced statuettes and bronze bells, which predominate among later sixth- and fifth-century votives, were more expensive items than the small pieces of jewellery, such as pins or brooches, which were dedicated in earlier periods. (Compare *Figs.* 14 and 15, on pp. 277, 283, with *Fig.* 16 on p. 288.) There are certainly other grounds for believing that fifth-century Sparta witnessed growing inequalities in wealth and an increasing tendency on the part of rich citizens to use that wealth to acquire extra status and prestige (Hodkinson 1989; 1993; 1997; see chs.10–13, below). The growth in statuette dedications and the increasing focus on the central sanctuaries of the Acropolis might suggest that this tendency was reflected to some degree in the sphere of votive offerings. On the other hand, a statuette was a cheaper votive than the ornamented vessel, which all but disappears from the archaeological record in the fifth century. As already noted, the lack of larger offerings might suggest the imposition of certain limited restrictions in an attempt to minimise the visibility of differential status within a citizen body which continued to maintain the rhetoric of a community of 'Peers'. This brings us back to the question posed earlier: whether the current archaeological record accurately reflects the original extent of classical dedications, or whether

Rich citizens and the use of private wealth

Fig. 16. Small votives, mainly pins (c, d, l, m) and brooches (a, e, f, g), from the sanctuary of Artemis Orthia, late seventh and early sixth century BC (reproduced with permission of the British School at Athens).

the fragments of major classical dedications mentioned in preliminary reports of the recent Menelaion excavations constitute a truer representation of the real patterns of private dedications in the latter part of our period. Until those excavations are fully published the question of the relationship between the change from 'raw' to 'converted' offerings and changes in character of classical Spartiate society must remain open.

Variations between sanctuaries and the gender of Spartan votive offerings
To conclude this study of dedications at Spartan sanctuaries, it is important to view the material record from two interrelated further perspectives which are closely connected to the chronological variations in types of votive offerings. The first perspective is the marked differences in types of votives between the various sanctuaries. As TABLES 8a–c indicate, vessels are found in reasonable numbers at all four sanctuaries. Jewellery votives, however, are much more prominent at Artemis Orthia and at the Amyklaion than on the Acropolis. (There are also significant, though unspecified, numbers of jewellery dedications at the Menelaion.) Statuettes and figurines, in contrast, are most frequent on the Acropolis and quite common at the Amyklaion, but less frequent at Artemis Orthia and the Menelaion. It is these differences in types of dedications which

underlie the divergent votive chronologies of the various sanctuaries evidenced in TABLE 6. This divergence is especially marked in the case of Artemis Orthia, whose bronze votives drop away sharply after *c.* 550, and the Acropolis, whose offerings increase – or at least continue – in the same period. The decline in votives at Artemis Orthia is especially startling because there is no reason to think that the cult suffered any decay in the classical period. Indeed, the decline takes place shortly after the sanctuary underwent a major remodelling in the early sixth century, involving the raising and levelling of the precinct, a new temple and an enlarged enclosure wall (Dawkins 1929a, 19–25).

The second perspective is that of gender. Thus far, I have discussed Spartan patterns of votive offerings without explicit consideration of the gender or personal circumstances of their dedicants. Yet the prominence of both male and female dedicants is evident from temple inventories (Aleshire 1989; Harris 1995, 223–8). Moreover, Christopher Simon's detailed study of Ionian votive offerings and cults has concluded that the most critical factors in determining the type of votive offerings were the needs and status of the person making the dedication (1986, 414). This observation suggests that close study of votive types might illuminate the changing votive trends under discussion by shedding light on the kinds of persons who dedicated at each sanctuary and the purposes for which they did so, thereby providing a rare insight into gender-related uses of wealth.

Given the paucity of published votives from the Menelaion and Amyklaion, my remarks will focus upon Artemis Orthia and the Acropolis. At Artemis Orthia, besides the vessels which are common to all four sanctuaries, the early votives are dominated by jewellery types. Jewellery votives were not always dedicated by women. For example, some Ionian men wore finger- and ear-rings; and jewellery dedications by men are mentioned occasionally in temple inventories from Ionia (Simon 1986, 199–202, 415). Male dedications of rings also appear among the treasures of the Hekatompedon in Athens (Harris 1995, nos. 131, 149, 152, 155). However, the absence of published rings of any sort from the post-Geometric bronze finds at Artemis Orthia suggests that, as at other sanctuaries (e.g. Aleshire 1989), women were responsible for the bulk of jewellery dedications. Temple inventories elsewhere indicate that votive jewellery (especially pins and fibulae, which are the most common jewellery types at Artemis Orthia) were frequently dedicated in the context in which they were used in everyday life, attached to items of personal clothing. These garments, which of course no longer survive, were often dedicated at moments of transition in the dedicant's life, the most common occasions being marriage and childbirth. These observations fit well with the existence of a cult of Eileithyia, the goddess of childbirth, situated, according to Pausanias (3.17.1), 'not far' from Artemis Orthia, perhaps within the temenos itself. The link between the cults of Artemis and of Eileithyia is attested by finds at the sanctuary of an inscribed bronze pin-head and die, both *c.* 625–600 BC. The pin-head is dedicated to 'Eleuthia', the bronze die jointly to 'Eleuthias' and 'Orthia'.[29]

Rich citizens and the use of private wealth

The subsequent decline in jewellery dedications during the sixth century was, consequently, a phenomenon closely connected with the votive activities of Spartan women. As already noted, the decline is paralleled among the lead figurines, whose jewellery motifs decrease markedly, with the female textile motifs apparently ceasing entirely. Although the decline in jewellery votives is part of a wider development affecting Greek sanctuaries generally, its comparatively early timing may suggest the additional presence of local factors. Wace (1929, 282–3) has argued that it was part of a significant change in the nature of the cult, by which the goddess Orthia became identified with, and perhaps even eclipsed by, Artemis.[30] Certainly, among the leads, this period sees the appearance of Artemis-like goddesses armed with a bow and of a new animal type, the deer, the favourite of Artemis. In contrast, other animal types decrease and ultimately disappear. Quite why the increasing importance of Artemis should entail the decline of jewellery votives is, however, unclear, especially given her role throughout Greece as a guardian at times of life-crisis (Schachter 1992, 49–51).

We should therefore ask whether the decline in female dedications might be connected to other factors affecting the shrine. Two obvious candidates here are the early sixth-century remodelling of the sanctuary and its acquisition of a central role in the male public upbringing.[31] To what extent the two are interconnected is unclear. Certainly, the period after the remodelling witnesses a fourfold increase in finds of lead figurines to a phenomenal 68,822 votives in the period of Lead III–IV (*c.* 580–500 BC). Among these figurines, votives depicting hoplite warriors, although present already before the remodelling, increase markedly, with a proliferation of different types and shield designs (Wace 1929, 269, 274–6). For Kennell (1995, 136), this upsurge is a direct reflection of the sanctuary's role in the upbringing: 'hoplite figurines would have made appropriate dedications for those who had endured or were about to endure the rites of passage that would transform them into warriors'. Support for this hypothesis might be sought among the votive clay masks, which likewise increase from hundreds of fragments before the sanctuary's remodelling to thousands in the period immediately following (Dickins 1929, 164). Although most of the masks are grotesque in character, two types have a normal human appearance: one type which represents bearded adult males ('warriors') and another that represents unbearded male youths. The former type commenced before the remodelling of the sanctuary, but became more prominent during the sixth century; the latter commenced around 550 and continued into the fifth century (Dickins 1929, 167, 177).

It might seem, then, that the new association between the sanctuary and the boys' upbringing led to a differently gendered orientation of votive offerings, marked by increasing male and decreasing female involvement in dedications. Certain qualifications, however, are in order. First, the public upbringing, although focused upon boys, was not confined to them; as we saw in chapter 7,

Ch. 9. Material and religious investment: bronze dedications at Sparta and abroad

girls had their own form of public training. The absence of any direct evidence in literary sources for a link between this training and the Artemis Orthia sanctuary may stem simply from the sheer paucity of information about female life. Secondly, after the sanctuary's remodelling and throughout the rest of the sixth century (the period of Leads III–IV), the varieties of lead figurines depicting warriors are exceeded in number by those depicting human women (not including deities). During the fifth and fourth centuries, moreover, dedications of warrior figurines decline, as do all the leads. Thirdly, among the bronzes from the sanctuary, there are few signs of the connection with the male upbringing. With the exception of two spear heads found with Lakonian I and II pottery (Droop 1929, 201 and pls. 87h and 88g) – i.e. before the remodelling – none of the small number of published bronze votives shows any sign of military or other themes which might suggest a connection with the upbringing.

The patterns of published votive offerings on the Acropolis are, as we have seen, markedly different, with few 'raw' offerings such as jewellery and a comparatively greater number of 'converted' votives such as the statuettes, whose dedication reaches a peak in the sixth century and continues into the fifth. This difference in the nature and timing of votive types reflects in part the character of the deities worshipped. The Acropolis contained several shrines (Paus. 3.17.4–5). The centrepiece was the sanctuary of Athena Poliouchos ('Defender of the Polis') or Chalkioikos ('the Bronze House'). In addition, there was a sanctuary of Athena Ergane ('Worker'), a shrine of the Muses, and temples of Zeus Kosmetas ('Orderer') and Aphrodite Areia ('Warlike'). Each of these shrines was closely linked to the official life of the polis. Hence it is understandable that dedications on the Acropolis reach their peak, not in the eighth or seventh centuries as in most other Greek sanctuaries, but during the period of the 'sixth-century revolution', when the Spartan polis was developing into a more thoroughly integrated entity, with centralised institutions which were forming a pervasive control over social practices previously more voluntaristic in character (cf. Hodkinson 1997a). It is understandable, also, that the Acropolis, which was less closely linked than Artemis Orthia to the personal lives of Spartan citizens (cf. Cartledge 1979, 358), should be marked by a greater formality of offerings.

Several of the published votives on the Acropolis can be directly linked to the status of dedicants and the capacity in which they will have visited its shrines. This is clearest in the case of the votives with military connections. The military associations of the Acropolis sanctuaries were manifold. The various epithets of Athena expressed her military role. As 'Poliouchos', she was depicted standing in rigid pose with helmet, aegis, shield and spear.[32] Her titles 'Erganē' (expressing her patronage of crafts) and 'Chalkioikos' ('Bronze House', a reference to her bronze-plated temple) suggest a role as patroness of the makers of bronze armour (Piccirilli 1984). Aphrodite was worshipped in her link with Ares; and the Muses for the military function of music (Paus. 3.17.5; cf. Thuc. 5.70).

Rich citizens and the use of private wealth

The temenos of Athena Chalkioikos was used as a place of assembly for men of military age and as the destination of an ancient procession of young men in arms (Plb. 4.22.8, 35.2). In keeping with these warlike associations, there are a number of votive offerings with a military reference made by men affirming their hoplite status: an inscribed miniature breastplate of *c.* 530–520 (*Fig.* 17); a fifth-century inscribed bronze mid-rib of an iron blade; a rim fragment of a votive shield; a cheek piece of a helmet; a small vessel in the form of a miniature helmet; also an early fifth-century armed statuette of Athena Promachos and a late fifth-century statuette of Athena wearing an inscribed helmet.[33] The military associations of the Acropolis also made it an appropriate place for the most grandiose personal dedication known from the sanctuary: the two statues of Nike, goddess of Victory, each resting on an eagle, placed in the western stoa by Lysander to commemorate his victories at Notion and Aigospotamoi (Pausanias 3.17.4).

It is also relevant to note the prominence at the sanctuary of dedications in other media advertising another area of male achievement: success in athletic and equestrian contests.[34] The votives range from modest items, such as two late archaic inscribed marble jumping weights, through several late archaic Panathenaic prize amphoras dedicated by Spartan victors at the Athenian games, to a series of inscribed marble stēlai, spanning the late sixth to early fourth centuries, which record the dedicants' victories in local games.[35] Some of these stēlai (including the famous Damonon stēlē, to be discussed in ch. 10) specifically associate their victories with Athena by including a verse dedication to the goddess alongside their list of successes. These athletic dedications thus exhibit a range of types of offerings: from 'raw' objects used in the contest itself, through prizes given for victory, to special monuments sculpted specifically for the dedication and designed to display the victor's achievements to greatest effect.

The greater formality of votives on the Acropolis in comparison with Artemis Orthia is indicated, accordingly, both by the higher proportion of 'converted' offerings and by the prominence given to dedicatory inscriptions. This latter phenomenon is also clearly evident in the bronze votives. In all, inscribed bronzes from the Acropolis outnumber those from Artemis Orthia

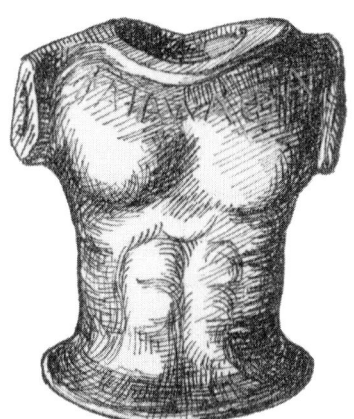

Fig. 17. Inscribed miniature breastplate dedicated to Athena, from the Spartan Acropolis, c. 530–520 BC (reproduced with permission of the British School at Athens).

Ch. 9. Material and religious investment: bronze dedications at Sparta and abroad

by ten to four. Their chronological distribution also differs markedly: all the inscribed bronzes from Artemis Orthia date to the archaic period; whereas eight or nine of the total of ten from the Acropolis date to the fifth century.[36] The fact that such a high proportion of the inscribed bronzes from the Acropolis dates to the fifth century is particularly striking. It reinforces the indications above regarding the increased prominence of more formal offerings in classical times.

The votive features of the Acropolis sanctuaries so far adduced – their official military associations, the celebration of male agonistic success, the degree of formality – might appear to imply that the dedicants were primarily male. However, Athena's epithet Erganē could reflect her patronage of female as well as male crafts (Villing 1998, 154–9). Of the ten inscribed bronzes mentioned above, four bear the names of their dedicants: a mirror and three bronze bells. Of these four votives, three were dedicated by women.[37] Female dedication of a feminine personal possession like a mirror is unsurprising. The fact that two of the three bells were dedicated by women, however, is noteworthy for two reasons. First, it would otherwise be tempting to interpret the bells as another military dedication due to their attested use in Greek warfare.[38] A considerable proportion of the bells bear the unusual feature of small 'feet' attached to their lower edge (see *Fig.* 14 on p. 277), and it may be that they were objects of cultic, perhaps musical, use. Secondly, it raises the possibility that a considerable proportion of the large number of *uninscribed* bells dedicated at the sanctuary – more than 40 bronze examples and about 80 in terracotta – were also dedicated by women.[39] If so, then the Acropolis finds provide an indication that certain Spartiate women in the fifth century were expending not insignificant sums on specially commissioned votive offerings at the central shrine of the polis: an activity symbolic perhaps of their increasing importance within Spartan society which I shall discuss in chapter 13.

It should be emphasized again that the study of patterns of votive offerings offered in this chapter is a provisional one, dependent upon the current state of publication of finds in just one medium, which themselves constitute only a small sample of the total of excavated votives. The present chapter has been merely a toe dipped in the ocean of the material record of archaic and classical Lakonian votive practice. The need now is for a more systematic investigation of unpublished votives in various media at a range of sanctuaries. Such an investigation also requires both a better awareness of comparative developments and trends across the Greek world, based upon a detailed analysis of the specific patterns and varying contexts of dedications at individual sanctuaries. In our current state of partial and limited understanding we are not always in a position to comprehend the precise impulses behind the making of specific types of votive offerings. It is nonetheless clear that patterns of material investment in religious dedications at particular sanctuaries were significantly dependent upon a range of non-material factors and needs. The manner in which the expenditure and use of wealth were intimately connected to wider societal factors will be examined further in different contexts in the following two chapters.

Spartiate bronze dedications at sanctuaries abroad

Spartiate private expenditure on bronze votive offerings was not limited to sanctuaries in Sparta itself, but extended to certain shrines outside Spartan territory. To develop that general statement into an examination of the scale of foreign dedications in different periods by individual Spartiates is, however, problematic. Let us begin with the archaeological evidence. Whereas it is a reasonable assumption that the vast majority of votives found at Spartan sanctuaries were offered by Spartiate men or women, at foreign sanctuaries that assumption obviously does not apply. How, then, can one identify the donor of a particular offering as a Spartiate? The most certain evidence is provided by those offerings which bear a dedicatory inscription in which the donor positively identifies himself or herself as a Spartiate (*Spartiatēs*) or a Lakedaimonian (*Lakedaimonios*) or as a person known to be a Spartiate from other evidence. A further reasonable indicator is an inscription which, whilst not providing direct affirmation of the person's status, is written in Lakonian script. In such cases it can normally be assumed that the dedicator was of Lakedaimonian, and very probably of Spartiate, status. Using these criteria, we can identify some 19 bronze votives dedicated at various foreign sanctuaries: seven at Olympia (plus one from nearby Mazi in Elis), seven at Delphi, two at the sanctuary of Athena Alea at Tegea, one at the sanctuary of Hera on Samos and another found at Lebadeia, possibly a votive at the important local shrine of Trophonios.[40] Of these 19, nine dedicators specifically identify themselves as Spartiates or Lakedaimonians or are known to be Spartiate from other evidence.[41] The earliest example is a certain Eumnastos, who around 550 BC placed his dedicatory inscription ('Eumnastos to Hera a Spartiate') on the collar of a recumbent bronze lion, which once ornamented the rim of a large vessel found at the Samian Heraion (see *Fig.* 21, on p. 343 below).

The evidence of these inscribed dedications shows that certain Spartiates devoted significant expenditures upon votive offerings at sanctuaries abroad. As Cartledge (1982, 256) has commented about Eumnastos, 'that he was a wealthy man is implicit in the expense both of the offering itself and of the travel needed to dedicate it in far-away Samos', travel probably undertaken as a visit to a Samian guest-friend. The donors mentioned by name include persons from the highest level of Spartiate society. They include prominent persons known to us from the literary sources for Spartan history: Lysander, who dedicated at Delphi the so-called 'Navarchs' Monument', a grandiose group of 39 or 40 bronze statues, to celebrate his victory at Aigospotamoi in 405 (ML 95; Paus. 10.9.7–10; cf. ch. 13); Kyniska, daughter of King Archidamos II, whose statue groups were dedicated to celebrate her Olympic victories in the 390s

Ch. 9. Material and religious investment: bronze dedications at Sparta and abroad

(see, further, ch. 10); and the exiled king Pausanias, whose statue dedication at Delphi *c.* 380 commemorated his dead son, King Agesipolis.[42] With the exception of Kyniska, all the named dedicators are male.

The geographical distribution of these dedications fits other evidence for the religious and socio-political activities of leading Spartiates. Sparta's connections with nearby Olympia and with the oracle at Delphi are well attested. Leading Spartiates also maintained close links with neighbouring Tegea after her subjugation around the mid-sixth century (cf. Hdt. 1.66–8; 6.72; 9.9, 26–8, 61), as also with the aristocracy on Samos (Cartledge 1982). Also noteworthy, in view of our earlier discussion of dedications at Spartan sanctuaries, are the types and dating of these votives. Twelve of the votives date to the sixth century: six bronze vessels of various sorts, three statuettes, two dedications of armour and a probable statue. The remaining six votives all date to the very end of the fifth century and first half of the fourth century: four statues or statue-groups and two statuettes. The votive pattern for the bronze vessels is hence very similar to that observed inside Sparta in being concentrated entirely in the sixth century and not extending into the fifth. So too, to an extent, is the pattern of dedications of statuettes, which first come into use in the second half of the sixth century and, after an apparent gap in the fifth century, continue during the early fourth. There is, however, one notable difference: namely, the existence of dedications of expensive bronze statues, which are so conspicuously absent from the record of votives inside Sparta. The material record, therefore, gives support to the idea already mooted above that wealthy and powerful Spartiates used foreign sanctuaries to advance their reputations by making expenditures on an exalted scale not possible at home. Further support for this proposition comes from Herodotus' account of the dedicatory practices of the regent Pausanias. He seized the opportunity of his foreign commands to dedicate a huge bronze bowl at the mouth of the Black Sea and to attempt to turn the golden tripod and bronze snake dedicated at Delphi out of Persian spoils into his own personal votive offering (Hdt. 4.81; 9.81; Thuc. 1.132).

Whilst the evidence of inscribed dedications illuminates certain positive features of Spartiate votive practices abroad, the small number of inscribed artefacts inevitably limits the strength of any broader conclusions suggested by the material. For example, the paucity of statuette and armour dedications compared with more expensive dedications of vessels and statues, along with the presence of donations by eminent Spartiates, might suggest that votive offerings at foreign sanctuaries were generally made by persons from a higher level of society than dedications inside Sparta. To substantiate this suggestion, however, we need to examine whether the preponderance of more expensive offerings is evident not just among the limited sample of inscribed votives but also among the much larger number of uninscribed dedications.

The difficulty in taking uninscribed votives into account stems from the obvious problem of determining the ethnic affiliation of the dedicant. How might we identify Spartiate donors of uninscribed votives? The key issue is whether votives of Lakonian manufacture can be used as evidence of Spartiate dedications. Would it be correct to assume that the majority, at least, of votives made by Lakonian craftsmen were dedicated by Spartan citizens? It is true that some Lakonian artefacts may have been used as votives by *perioikoi* rather than by Spartiates, especially as Lakonian bronze production is thought to have taken place throughout perioikic territory (Leon 1968; Rolley 1982, 76). Others could have been dedicated by foreigners, since archaeological evidence of metal-working at sanctuary sites suggests that during major festivals craftsmen from different regions would set up temporary workshops which could be patronised by all and sundry (Risberg 1992). Nevertheless, it is commonly accepted that at panhellenic sanctuaries there is often a link between the place of origin of a bronze artefact and the ethnic affiliation of its dedicant. This is most obviously the case with the statuettes, the type of bronze most closely linked to local consumption (Rolley 1982, 76; 1986a, 33, 107, 114); but it has been judged to be true of larger vessels too, at least in the case of finds at sanctuaries frequented by Spartiates (as opposed to more distant locations such as the Celtic world or Magna Graecia).[43] Support for this judgement comes from the six Lakonian-made vessels already discussed, which were inscribed with dedications in Lakonian script, including, in the case of Eumnastos, an explicit statement of Spartiate identity.

It is, therefore, worth considering the evidence of published Lakonian bronze votives found at certain important sanctuaries in mainland and Aegean Greece. TABLES 11a–b present evidence for dedications of the two main types of Lakonian-made votives, the vessels and statuettes, at the four shrines where they appear most frequently, Olympia, Delphi, Dodona and the sanctuary of Hera on Samos.[44] (The more spasmodic evidence from other sanctuaries will be cited at relevant points in the argument.) The period covered in the tables ends at *c.* 500 BC because production of vessels by Lakonian workshops appears to end in the later sixth century and because, although production of statuettes carries on into the fifth century, there are no published finds of Lakonian-made statuettes from the sanctuaries in question during that period.

The statistics in TABLES 11a–b should be used with caution. For example, the figures suggest that considerably more dedications of Lakonian artefacts were made at Olympia than at other major shrines. The modest showing of distant Dodona is to be expected; but the limited record from Delphi may seem surprising, given its close connections with Sparta.[45] It has been suggested that Delphi was visited less frequently than Olympia by Spartiates on private, as opposed to public, business (Rolley and Chamoux 1991, 161); and clearly Olympia was more easily accessible from Sparta. Allowance, however, needs to be made for the German Institute's particularly systematic publication of the Olympia finds and for more favourable conditions of preservation. Whereas Olympia has been buried for over a millennium under metres of alluvium,

TABLE 11a. Published Lakonian bronze vessels from major foreign sanctuaries.

	Olympia	Delphi	Dodona	Samos
c.650–c.600	4	-	-	-
c.600–c.550	16	2	1	-
c.550–c.500	12	5	6	2
DNG	6	2	1	1
Total	38	9	8	3

TABLE 11b. Published Lakonian bronze statuettes/figurines from major foreign sanctuaries

	Olympia	Delphi	Dodona	Samos
c.650–c.600	-	-	-	-
c.600–c.550	3	-	-	-
c.550–c.500	5	3	2	1
DNG	1	-	1	-
Total	9	3	3	1

preservation of metal artefacts at Delphi has suffered from its being a site of habitation until 1892, from its high altitude hillslope location and from its seasonally alternating climatic conditions of humidity and dryness.

Despite such limitations, however, the record of Lakonian artefacts at sanctuaries abroad suggests certain significant points which link in with other evidence. First, they provide further illuminating hints of the range of foreign sanctuaries patronised by Spartiates. They give material support to literary evidence for Spartan connections with the sanctuary of Zeus at Dodona.[46] Indeed, the independent statuettes and decorative figurines on bronze vessels found at the sanctuary express a close connection with the character of Spartiate life, several of them representing figures of hoplites and one a figure of a running Spartiate girl.[47] Nearer home, finds of two sixth-century Lakonian statuettes at or near the sanctuary of Zeus Lykaios in southwestern Arkadia also connect with later literary evidence for Spartan links with the shrine (Herfort-Koch 1986, K32, 93; Thuc. 5.19). The position of the Heraion at Samos as a significant recipient of Spartiate votives is suggested by the evidence of several Lakonian-made artefacts, besides the Eumnastos dedication already discussed: a bronze hoplite figurine, 'one of only two of this class found outside the Greek mainland' (Cartledge 1982, 255), which may have served as a vessel ornament; a bronze mirror handle in the shape of a young woman; and possibly a vessel handle in the form of a lion which is said to come from Samos.[48]

Secondly, the preponderance of vessel dedications over statuettes, at the major foreign shrines throughout the period covered, presents a certain contrast with the situation inside Sparta, where statuettes outnumber vessels at Artemis Orthia, the Acropolis and the Amyklaion in the period c. 550–c. 500. This

Rich citizens and the use of private wealth

supports the suggestion mooted above that dedicants at these foreign sanctuaries were generally from a higher level of Spartiate society, persons better able to afford the expense of a large bronze vessel ornamented with figurines and elaborate decoration. The evidence of votive offerings from foreign sanctuaries thus alerts us to a certain separation of activities within the Spartan citizen body: between the mass of Spartiates whose dedicatory activities were largely confined to Sparta itself and a wealthy few whose votive offerings were also made on a more elevated, panhellenic plane. The following chapters will pursue this point further through an examination of the foreign equestrian pursuits, relationships of *xenia* and military commands undertaken by the wealthy elite.

Notes

1 For a convenient synopsis, Fitzhardinge 1980.

2 Different forms of this theory have been elaborated, with increasing degrees of sophistication, by Dickins 1908; Wade Gery 1925; Ehrenberg 1929; Holladay 1977; Cartledge 1979, 156; Förtsch 1998.

3 Cf. esp. the original excavations from 1906 to 1910 at Artemis Orthia, the Acropolis and the Menelaion reported in *BSA* 12 (1905/6) – 16 (1909/10) and in Dawkins (ed.) 1929. Subsequent years of work in the 1920s were reported in *BSA* 26 (1923/4) – 30 (1928/9). The more recent Menelaion excavations have received preliminary reports in *JHS*, *AR* 23 (1977) 24–42 and in *Lakonikai Spoudai* 2 (1975) 258–69; 3 (1977) 408–16; 8 (1986) 205–16. Greek and German work at the Amyklaion was reported in *AE* (1892) 1–26; *MDAI(A)* 52 (1927) 1–85; cf. also Calligas 1992.

4 Dawkins (ed.) 1929; Carter 1985, esp. 91–7, 125–32, 151–7, 287–92; 1987.

5 Although not every sanctuary find is necessarily a votive offering *sensu stricto* (most notably, utensils and vessels used in cult rituals and feasting), such objects were often gifts by worshippers intended for general use in connection with the cult (cf. Tomlinson 1992, 336–7, 345–9). As such they constitute good evidence for private expenditure and religious investment. Cf. the comments of Kyrieleis 1993, 139–40, on the marginal distinction between votive offerings and the food and equipment brought to the sanctuary by participants in ritual banquets.

6 Note the comments of Droop that the humidity 'has wrought such havoc with these offerings that only in the most massive is any solid core of metal preserved. Most of them are mere masses of corrosion' (1929, 196).

7 H.W. Catling 1976/7, 42; 1977, 414. The 'Great Pit' was apparently refilled in two stages, the second taking place 'much later in the life of the shrine'; but details of the date of this second refilling and the finds which it preserved have yet to be published.

8 Spartan excavation reports are of course not the only ones to suffer from these deficiencies; cf. Simon 1986, 175, on Ionian sanctuary sites.

9 *BSA* 13 (1906/7) 146–50; 14 (1907/8) 145; 26 (1923–5) 266–74.

10 *BSA* 15 (1908/9) 144–50.

11 For references, see n. 3.

12 The chronological focus reflects partly the historical period central to this book, partly the vague classification of earlier finds in the excavation reports: typical labels such as 'Geometric' are too imprecise for the finer chronological specification required.

Ch. 9. Material and religious investment: bronze dedications at Sparta and abroad

[13] e.g., from Artemis Orthia, four female protomes (Droop 1929, pl. 89f, g, k, l), three lion's paw supports (pl. 88c, e, f), three handles (pl. 90f, g; Herfort-Koch 1986, K169) and two cow ornaments (Lamb 1926/7b, 103 and fig. 5.21). From the Acropolis, five further female protomes (Lamb 1926/7a, 92 nos. 24–8 with pl. 10) and various ornaments (Herfort-Koch 1986, K109, 131, 158). From the Menelaion, a number of handles and pendant attachments to handles, and more protomes: *BSA* 15 (1908/9) 146–50; H.W. Catling 1976/7, 38–9 fig. 36; R. Catling 1986, 211. From the Amyklaion, various attachments to lebetes and yet more protomes: Calligas 1992, 36 and n. 41, 47 and n. 108; Herfort-Koch 1986, K17, 165. The reports also mention numerous fragments of vessel bodies: Droop 1929, 201; H.W. Catling 1977, 414 fig. 36; R. Catling 1986, 211.

[14] The five itemised examples are discussed in *BSA* 24 (1919–21) 118 nos. 66–8; 26 (1923–25) 273–4 no. 7; 30 (1928–30) 252 no. 5. The passing mention of *c*. 40 other bells comes in *BSA* 30 (1928–30) 273.

[15] Wace, Thompson and Droop 1908/9; Wace 1929; Cavanagh and Laxton 1984.

[16] TABLE 7 is based upon the figures in Wace (1929, 251–2), but with a revised chronology. The excavators based their classifications of the leads upon their chronology for Lakonian I–VI pottery. The chronology used here is a compromise between that of the excavators, the revision proposed by Boardman (1963) and the recent reconsideration by Cavanagh and Laxton (1984).

[17] Payne, 1940, 93; Tomlinson 1976, 23; Kyrieleis 1993, 129; Simon 1986, 106; Morris 1998, 32–3, 55, 62–3. I am grateful to Susan Cole, Catherine Morgan, Ian Morris, Christopher Simon, Anthony Snodgrass and Alexandra Villing for their advice concerning comparative patterns of votive offerings within and outside Sparta.

[18] Wace 1929, esp. 279–82; Wace, Thompson and Droop 1908/9, 127. Wace himself did not recognise the textile motifs for what they were, terming them 'pendant plaques' and 'decorative plates (pendants?)': 1929, 255–6, 264–5, 270. I owe this point to Lin Foxhall.

[19] Payne 1940, 124, 168. Tomlinson (1977; 1992, 327–9) argues that the rectangular structure which the excavators called a temple was in fact a hestiatorion for ritual feasting; but he does not exclude the dedication of offerings on this upper terrace. The decline in jewellery finds seems to antedate the abandonment of the buildings on the terrace in the latter part of the sixth century.

[20] Contrast the position at Olympia and at the Kabeirion sanctuary at Thebes, where statuette and figurine dedications continue at a good level from the Geometric period through the seventh century (Heilmeyer 1979; Schmaltz 1980). The trend at Delphi, however, though not as extreme as at Sparta, does indicate a marked decline in numbers of free-standing human and animal statuettes from over a hundred in Geometric times to fewer than twenty in the seventh century (Rolley 1969).

[21] Zimmermann 1989, 171–5; Herrmann 1964; Rolley 1982, 39, 76 n. 201.

[22] Personal calculations from the catalogue of Rolley 1969. The raw figures are: 16 from the seventh century; 9 from the sixth and early fifth, plus 21 fragmentary statuettes, most of which are sixth-century or 'archaic' in date; 7 from the rest of the fifth century.

[23] I presume that references to inscribed statuette bases of the fourth or third centuries in preliminary reports of the recent Menelaion excavations (H.W. Catling 1976/7, 41) refer to rather smaller objects.

[24] Most attested public statues were those of deities: e.g. Athena and Zeus Hypatos on the Acropolis (Paus. 3.17.2, 6); Apollo at Amyklai (3.19.2); Apollo Pythaios at

Thornax (3.10.8). But there were also statues of deceased humans: e.g. the Olympic victors Hipposthenes and Hetoimokles (Paus. 3.13.9, 15.7); and two statues of the regent Pausanias at the sanctuary of Athena Chalkioikos (Thuc. 1.134; Paus. 3.17.7–9).

[25] Votives arising from his victory at Sparta were limited to two eagles bearing figures of Nike on the roof of the Western stoa on the Acropolis and two bronze tripods at the Amyklaion (Paus. 3.17.4, 18.7–8).

[26] Cf. also Tomlinson 1976, 23: 'perhaps the true impression is that the offerings in general were more valuable than in previous centuries'.

[27] Aleshire 1989; Harris 1995; Linders 1988.

[28] I have omitted the bronze bells from the Acropolis, since it is unclear whether they were items of secular use or objects custom-made for use in the cult rituals (cf. the discussion in Simon 1986, 293–5). I have also omitted the bronze vessels from my calculations since, as Snodgrass notes, several of these occupy an intermediate status, simulating everyday objects, but often produced in an ornate style expressly for sanctuary usage. He has since suggested (*pers. comm.*) that, tripods apart, the vessels may have had a use in real life and hence could count as raw dedications. Given the fragmentary nature of the vessel remains, however, it is frequently difficult to identify the precise type of vessel from the available published details. Since tripods probably represent a minority of vessels, the inclusion of vessels would accentuate rather than blur the change from raw to converted votives discussed in the text, making the decline in 'raw' votives at Artemis Orthia more dramatic and supplying a greater number of 'raw' votives on the Acropolis before *c.* 500, and probably a preponderance before *c.* 550.

[29] Kilian 1978, pl. 6.1, 3; cf. Lamb 1926/7b, 103–4 no. 26, fig. 5; Droop 1929, 202; Woodward 1929, 370, no. 169.24; Lazzarini 1976, no. 479; Jeffery 1990, 447 no. A. Alkman's *Partheneion* has often been regarded as a hymn to Artemis Orthia, thus providing literary evidence for the connection between the goddess and the transition of Spartan girls into adulthood and marriage; but it is uncertain whether the critical line 61 is in fact a reference to Orthia or to some other deity (Bowra 1961, 51–2).

[30] It has been argued (Carter 1987, 374–5) that the association of Orthia with Artemis was a late phenomenon, on the grounds that the first dedicatory inscription that refers to Artemis Orthia, rather than to Orthia alone, dates only from the first century AD; but, as Pipili (1987, 44) notes, their association as early as the sixth century BC is effectively demonstrated by the lead figurines depicting a goddess with a bow or a deer, both attributes of Artemis, not Orthia.

[31] Kennell 1995, 126–9, 135–8, 142; cf. Xenophon's reference in the early fourth century to contemporary performance of the cheese-stealing rite at the sanctuary (*Lak. Pol.* 2.9) and the fourth-century victory dedication of Arexippos for victory in 'the gathering of boys' (*IG* v.1.255; Woodward 1929, 296–7 no. 1; Kennell 1995, 127 pl. 9).

[32] Cf. her representation on a Lakonian copy of a Panathenaic amphora (*BSA* 28, 1926/7, 78 fig. 18) and her description as *pammachon* in Aristop. *Lysistrata* 1320.

[33] Breastplate: Herfort-Koch 1986, K146 fig. 19.8; Lamb 1926/7a, 91 no. 22 pl. 8. Bronze mid-rib: Woodward 1928–30, 252–3 no. 8 fig. 7. Shield rim: Woodward 1923–25, 274 fig. 5.13, with p. 247. Helmet cheek-piece: Lamb 1926/7a, 93 no. 29 fig. 6. Helmet vessel: Lamb 1926/7a, 92 no. 23 pl. 8.23. Athena Promachos: Lamb 1926/7a, 86 no. 7 pl. 8.7; Niemeyer 1960, 61 pl. 5 figs. 17–18; *BCH* 99 (1975) 350 fig. 23–4. Athena with helmet: Steinhauer n. d., 34 fig. 9; Lamb 1926/7a, 87 no. 8 pl. 9.8.

[34] Hodkinson 1999, 153–5; and ch. 10, below.

35 Jumping-weights: references in Hodkinson 1999, 179 n. 15. Panathenaic amphoras: *BSA* 13 (1906/7) 150–3; 14 (1907/8) 145; others were also dedicated at the Menelaion. Marble stēlai: refs. in Hodkinson 1999, 178–9 nn. 10, 16–18.

36 Inscribed bronzes from Artemis Orthia: the bronze pin and die referenced in n. 29, both dating to the late seventh century; cow, probably a vessel attachment, dedicated by Alkinadas, *c.* 550–525 (Herfort-Koch 1986, K175); die, early sixth century, found in the layer of sand (Lazzarini 1976 no. 424; Kilian 1978, 221 pl. 6.2). From the Acropolis: miniature breastplate, *c.* 530–520 (Herfort-Koch 1986, K146; Lazzarini 1976, no. 425); bull statuette, late sixth/early fifth century (Herfort-Koch 1986, K174; Lazzarini 1976, no. 481); cow, start of fifth century? (*BSA* 24, 1919–21, 118 no. 69; Herfort-Koch 1986, K174); bronze mid-rib of iron blade, fifth century (Woodward 1928–30, 252–3 no. 8; Lazzarini 1976, no. 354); 2 inscribed bells, fifth century (*BSA* 24, 1919–21, 118 nos. 67–8); the inscribed mirror and 3 bells cited in n. 37.

37 Female dedications: inscribed mirror dedicated by Euonyma (*BSA* 1923–25, 271–2 no. 5; Lazzarini 1976, no. 91); inscribed bell dedicated by Eirana (*BSA* 24, 1919–21, 117 no. 66); inscribed bell dedicated by Kalikratia (*BSA* 30, 1928–30, 252 no. 5). Male dedication: inscribed bell dedicated by Enpedokles (*Fig.* 14, on p. 277 above; *BSA* 26, 1923–25, 273–4 no. 7; Lazzarini 1976, no. 92).

38 Aischylos (*Sept.* 385–6 and 399) and Euripides (*Rhes.* 308 and 383) mention the use of bells as shield-attachments and horse-trappings intended to frighten the enemy. Bells were also carried by guards on patrol (Thuc. 4.135).

39 The Acropolis bells are now in process of study by Alexandra Villing, upon whose information and references my comments depend.

40 Under the rubric 'bronze votives' I include marble and stone bases which once held bronze votives which are now lost. For convenience I give, where possible, the catalogue numbers in Herfort-Koch 1986 [K] and Jeffery 1990, 198–202, 446–8 [J], who provide references to earlier works. *Olympia dedications*: J nos. 12, 19, 64; *IvO* 160, 274, 634. *Mazi*: K45 = J no. 67. *Delphi*: J nos. 11, 47a, 65, and H; Tod 1948, no. 120; ML no. 95; *IG* v.1.1565a, 1561. *Tegea*: K43, K116. *Samos*: K163a = J no. 16a. *Lebadeia*: K1 = J no. 7. I have excluded the dedication of a bronze figurine of a ram made by a certain Xenoklees at a sanctuary of Poseidon somewhere in Arkadia (Cartledge 2000). Cartledge suggests that Xenoklees may be a Spartiate; but this cannot be confirmed on the criteria outlined in the text, since no ethnic is given and the lettering of the inscription is probably Arkadian.

41 J nos. 12, 19; *IvO* 160, 634; Tod 1948, no. 120; K163a = J no. 16a; ML no. 95; *IG* v.1.1565a.

42 Other possible prominent persons: (i) the person named ΘΙΑΡΩΝΑΝ, who appears on a statue base at Olympia (*IvO* 274) has been identified, through emendation of the text to ΙΑΡΩΝ, with Hieron, the Spartiate who commanded the mercenaries at Leuktra in 371 (Xen. *Hell.* 6.4.9; Pomtow 1909, 181–2; Flacelière 1937, 67); (ii) Landridas the Lakedaimonian, whose name appears on a round marble base (*FdD* iii.4 no. 196; *IG* v.1.1565a) has been identified with the exiled Spartiate who fought on the Theban side at Leuktra (Diod. 14.54.1).

43 Cf. the comments of Rolley (1982, 39) concerning the different functions of two Lakonian vessels (Herfort-Koch 1986, K2–3), one found at Olympia, the other at Gela, whose female heads at the base of their vertical handles were made from the same mould: 'A Olympie, sanctuaire fréquenté par les Spartiates, le vase est une offrande, au même

titre que les statuettes. A Gela, il y a réellement exportation… Nous avons là les deux destinations possibles pour ces vases.'

44 These statistics are mainly based on published artefacts recorded in the systematic catalogues in Herfort-Koch 1986; Pipili 1987; Gauer 1991.

45 Cf. the episodes recorded by Hdt. 1.66–7; 5.63; 6.66; Thuc. 1.103; 1.118; 3.92; 5.16. The oracular officials who assisted the kings were called Pythioi (Hdt. 6.57) and the Spartans held the right of first consultation, *promanteia*, for at least part of our period (Pritchett 1974–91, iii.296).

46 e.g. Plut. *Lys.* 25.3; Diod. 14.13.4; *Apophth. Lak.* 208f; Cicero, *De Divinatione* 1.34.76; 2.32.69.

47 Hoplites: Herfort-Koch 1986, K136–9, 141. Running girl: K49.

48 Hoplite: Herfort-Koch 1986, K132; Cartledge 1982, 255 n.62. Mirror handle: Congdon 1981, no.124; Cartledge 1982, 255 n.63. Lion handle: Gabelmann 1965, no.73. Cf. also the ivory and terracotta dedications at the shrine referenced by Cartledge ibid.

Chapter 10

EQUESTRIAN COMPETITION: PARTICIPATION AND EXPENDITURE

One specific type of dedication noted in the discussion of votive offerings in chapter 9 was dedications made to commemorate success in athletic and equestrian competitions. These competitions were significant events in archaic and classical Greek society, an important means by which aspiring individuals engaged in the *agōn* (or 'contest'), which was a defining characteristic of Greek culture.[1] The importance of sporting success as a determinant of status made it a central preoccupation of the Greek elite. Leading Spartans were no exception. In a study of Spartiate participation in athletic contests both at home and abroad (Hodkinson 1999) I have argued that, despite certain local idiosyncrasies, Spartan citizens, both individually and collectively, accorded a high valuation to engagement and success in the athletic *agōn*. The present chapter aims to extend that study to Spartiate participation in equestrian competition. As the most expensive of agonistic activities, within the financial reach only of the richest persons, equestrian contests merit special attention as a sphere of expenditure engaged in by wealthy Spartiates.

Equestrian competition within Spartan territory

Our knowledge of the practice of equestrian competition within Sparta's home territory depends upon a single, rich piece of evidence: the well-known stēlē dedicated by a certain Damonon in the sanctuary of Athena on the Spartan acropolis (*Figs*. 18–19).[2]

> Damonon dedicated this to Athena Poliachos, having gained these victories in a manner unparalleled among those now living.

> Damonon won the following victories with his own four-horse chariot and himself driving: in the games of the Earth-Holder four times, and at the games of Athena four times, and at the Eleusinian games four times. Damonon also won at the games of Poseidon at Helos, at the same time winning the race on horseback, himself driving, seven times with colts bred from his own mares and his own stallion. And Damonon also won at the games of Poseidon at Thouria eight times, himself driving, with colts bred from his own mares and his own stallion. And at the games of Ariontia Damonon won eight times, himself driving, with colts bred from his own mares and his own stallion, and he won the race on horseback at the same time. Damonon also won the Eleusinian games four times, himself driving, with his colts.

Enymakratidas won the following victories: ... [*text of uncertain reading*], the long race and the race on horseback on the same day. And at the games of Ariontia Enymakratidas won ... [*break of uncertain length between the two extant parts of the stone*]. And at the Parparonian games Enymakratidas won the boys' stade race, the two stades and the long race, and the race on horseback on the same day.

And Damonon as a boy won the stade and the two stades at the games of the Earth-Holder. And Damonon as a boy won the stade and the two stades at the Lithesian games. Damonon also as a boy won the stade and the two stades at the Lithesian games. And Damonon as a boy won the stade and the two stades at the Parparonian games, and the stade at the games of Athena.

In the ephorate of Echemenes Damonon won the following victories: at the games of Athena with his colts, himself driving, and the race on horseback on the same day, and his son won the stade at the same time. In the ephorate of Euippos Damonon won the following victories: at the games of Athena with his colts, himself driving, and the race on horseback on the same day, and his son won the stade at the same time. In the ephorate of Aristeus Damonon won the following victories: at the games of the Earth-Holder with his colts, himself driving, and the race on horseback on the same day, and on the same day his son won the stade and the two stades and the long race, all winning at the same time. In the ephorate of Echemenes Damonon won the following victories: at the games of the Earth-Holder with his colts, himself driving, and his son won the stade and...

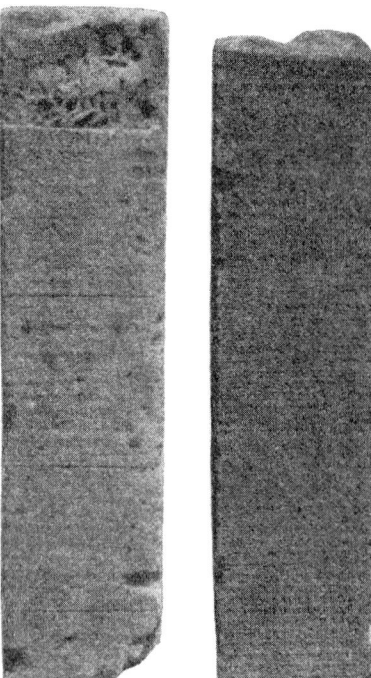

Fig. 18. Two parts of an inscribed marble victory stēlē dedicated by Damonon to Athena, from the Spartan acropolis, shortly before or after the Peloponnesian war (Sparta Museum 440; reproduced with permission of the British School at Athens).

Fig. 19. Detail of the sculpted relief on the Damonon stēlē, depicting a four-horse chariot in motion (photo courtesy of Deutsches Archäologisches Institut, Athens).

Ch. 10. Equestrian competition: participation and expenditure

The stēlē lists a large number of athletic and equestrian victories won at contests within Spartan territory by Damonon and his son Enymakratidas. It presents several significant features. Despite the inclusion of the athletic victories, the stēlē was clearly intended primarily as a celebration of equestrian success. The inscription is crowned with a sculpted relief depicting a four-horse chariot in motion (see *Fig.* 19); and within the inscription itself equestrian victories are given pride of place, listed first after the opening dedication to Athena. In total, the inscription records a minimum of 43 four-horse chariot race and 21 horse race victories.[3] Damonon himself was responsible for all these equestrian victories, except for three of the horse races which were won by Enymakratidas. Damonon's equestrian victories were achieved over a period of at least eleven years,[4] all of them coming during his adulthood, in contrast to his athletic victories, which were confined to his boyhood. The chronological pattern of Enymakratidas' victories is somewhat different, in that some of his athletic and horse race victories were achieved in parallel. The first recorded set of Enymakratidas' running and horse race victories – immediately before the lacuna in the text caused by the breaking of the stone into two halves (see *Fig.* 18) – seem to have been gained while he was a young man in his 20s;[5] whilst those mentioned immediately after the lacuna are explicitly dated to his boyhood. Then in the final part of the inscription he appears several times as victor in men's running events.

The stēlē also provides evidence of a range of festivals within Spartan territory which included equestrian contests. Chariot and/or horse racing contests are recorded at seven of the nine festivals mentioned. These festivals were spread over a broad geographical area. Some took place at Sparta itself, such as those of Athena and the Earth-Holder (Poseidon Gaiaochos).[6] Other festivals were held in more distant parts, such as the Parparonia, which took place at Thyrea near the Argive border, the games of Poseidon at Helos in southern Lakonia, and the games of Poseidon at Thouria in eastern Messenia.[7]

The multiplicity of attested festivals suggests the existence of a regular circuit of annual games at which horse-owning Spartiates could pursue equestrian competition. Furthermore, the fact that Damonon was able to dedicate his stēlē on the Acropolis in the central sanctuary of Sparta's guardian deity might appear to suggest both the acceptability of equestrian contests as an activity for Spartan citizens and the prestige to be gained from equestrian success. There is a problem, however, in that Damonon's dedication is unique among our surviving evidence. Whereas the archaeological record from Spartan sanctuaries includes several dedications by victors in local athletic contests (Hodkinson 1999, 152–6), Damonon's is the only dedication specifically concerned with victories in equestrian events.[8] Obviously, its unique survival does not necessarily imply that the stēlē was unique at the time of its dedication; but the severe imbalance in surviving dedications raises the question whether equestrian victors were normally discouraged or prevented from overt celebration of their success. There is, moreover, a possible reason why Damonon's dedication may, exceptionally, have been permitted. Equestrian competition did not normally involve the personal participation of the horses' owner, who typically procured the services of a specialist rider or charioteer. Damonon's stēlē emphasizes, however, that he personally drove his own chariot and rode his own horses. The fact that his equestrian successes were equivalent to the personal achievements of athletic victors – and note that Damonon also includes his own athletic victories on the stēlē – provides a plausible explanation why he, and he alone, may have been allowed to celebrate them through a public dedication on the Acropolis, alongside the victory dedications of local athletes.

If there was indeed a restriction against the celebration of vicarious equestrian success, one factor in that restriction may have been a policy of minimising the display of achievement that derived from the possession of wealth. Yet, if so, Damonon's stēlē flouts such a policy blatantly, since he openly advertises his status as a wealthy breeder of horses. Three times he asserts that he won his victories with colts bred from his own mares and his own stallion. In fact, Damonon comes across as a classic example of a social type recently identified by Mark Golden (1998, 117–23): the wealthy man able to prolong the athletic successes of his youth through switching to equestrian pursuits. It is true that Enymakratidas does not fit so neatly into this mould, in that he achieved some of his running and horse race victories in parallel as both boy and young man. But he is given no credit for any of the chariot race victories; and the final part of the inscription, which records only his athletic triumphs, gives the distinct impression that only after he was older and had inherited his father's stables would Enymakratidas be able to engage in chariot racing.

The inscription, consequently, provides an excellent picture of a wealthy Spartiate family successfully employing its considerable wealth in equestrian pursuits. Damonon was clearly a past master of the sport, at least in local terms. This observation, however, raises the question of his apparent lack of achievement at more prestigious and competitive foreign games. At first glance, the obvious explanations are either that he abstained from foreign competition through recognition of the limits of his ability or that he competed abroad without success. Yet these explanations would have rendered Damonon's assertion that his victories were unparalleled among his contemporaries absurd to his fellow citizens, in view of the outstanding record of Spartiate foreign equestrian success to be discussed below – unless we can interpret his claim simply as a reference to his personal participation. There is, however, one further possibility worth consideration. The date of the dedication is uncertain. It cannot belong to the period of the Peloponnesian war, since none of the ephors mentioned in the inscription appear in the list of eponymous ephors for the years 432/1–404/3 which appears in Xenophon's *Hellenika* (2.3.8–9). Scholars, however, are divided between a date immediately preceding or immediately following the war.[9] If the latter dating is correct, much of Damonon's chariot-racing career detailed in the early part of the inscription may have fallen during the last years of the fifth century, the one period when Spartiates were least able to participate abroad. They were banned from the Olympics from 420 until 400 or 396;[10] and participation in the Panathenaic games would also have been impossible during the Dekeleian/Ionian war of 414–404. This singular set of circumstances would provide a plausible scenario in which Damonon could, exceptionally, boast of his victories inside Lakonia without the stigma of a lack of foreign success.

Equestrian competition abroad
The growth of Spartiate Olympic success

In comparison with the situation within Spartan territory, the evidence for equestrian activity abroad is both more varied and covers a wider chronological range. Our most informative body of evidence concerns Spartiate victories at Olympia (TABLE 12), though there is also a limited amount of information relating to victories at the other 'Crown' games at Delphi, Nemea and the Isthmos of Corinth, as well as to the Panathenaic games at Athens. Regarding TABLE 12, it should be stressed that, although the approximate chronology of Spartiate victories at Olympia is reasonably certain, the *precise* dates of individual victories are uncertain, due to the vagueness or lateness of the evidence and conflicts between different sources. The one exception is the victory of Lichas in 420, securely dated by Thucydides (5.50). Although the painstaking work of Moretti (1957; 1970; 1992) and Hönle (1972) has established a generally plausible catalogue of victories assigned to particular Olympiads, there are sometimes grounds for disagreement with their dating of particular Spartiate victories. Hence, in TABLE 12 I have added my own altered dating of Spartiate equestrian victories to that of Moretti and Hönle, giving the grounds for my suggested alterations in the footnotes.

It is evident from TABLE 12 that Spartiate equestrian success at Olympia is heavily concentrated in the second half of the fifth and the early fourth centuries. Although the four-horse chariot race was instituted at Olympia in 680, we know the names of very few victors in the seventh century and there are no Spartiates among them. It was not until the first third of the sixth century that the main expansion of interest in panhellenic chariot racing took place, with the formation of a regular circuit (or *periodos*) of contests at the 'Crown games' at Olympia, Delphi, Nemea and the Isthmos and the creation of other significant festivals such as the Panathenaia *c.* 566. The victories of Euagoras and of King Damaratos provide evidence of Spartiate success at the highest level during the second half of the sixth century. Euagoras' triple success is testimony to the value which a leading citizen might place upon Olympic victories; his record, as Herodotus (6.103) says, was equalled by only one other man, Kimon of Athens. The participation of a Spartan king speaks volumes in itself. Nevertheless, we should not exaggerate the degree of Spartiate involvement in

TABLE 12. Spartiate equestrian victories in the Olympic games.[11]

Date	Victor (Moretti/Hönle)	Victor (Hodkinson)
Four-horse chariot race		
548	Euagoras	Euagoras
544	Euagoras	Euagoras
540	Euagoras	Euagoras
504	Damaratos	Damaratos
484	Polypeithes	Polypeithes
448	Arkesilaos	Arkesilaos
444	Arkesilaos	Arkesilaos
440	Polykles	Leon[12]
432	Lykinos	Xenarkes (?)[13]
428	Anaxandros	Anaxandros
424	Leon	Polykles (?)[14]
420	Lichas	Lichas
396	Kyniska	Kyniska
392	Kyniska	Kyniska
388	Xenarkes (?)	
384 or later	-	Lykinos[15]
Four-horse chariot race for foals		
384	Eurybiades	Eurybiades
Two-horse chariot race		
368	Euryleonis	Euryleonis

equestrian activity. It is sometimes claimed that the beginning of chariot-race victories was linked to a decline in Spartiate athletic victories during the later sixth century (e.g. Ste Croix 1972, 354–5). However, as I have already argued (Hodkinson 1999, 161–3), the connection is far from clear. The decline in athletic victories had begun already in the 580s or 570s (cf. A. Powell 1998, 139); and the real concentration of chariot victories at Olympia did not occur until the later fifth century. That said, a steadily growing involvement in chariot racing is corroborated by evidence from the Panathenaic games. The sanctuaries of Athena Chalkioikos and the Menelaion have produced tens of fragments of Panathenaic prize amphoras, several of which have been loosely dated to the later sixth and early fifth centuries.[16] Unfortunately, only seven of the amphoras, all from Athena Chalkioikos, have been individually published; of these, only three are diagnostic, but all show chariot-racing scenes.[17] The most complete example, dated to *c.* 525–500, depicting a four-horse chariot, is illustrated in *Fig. 20*.[18] The dedication of these fruits of foreign equestrian victories in local Spartan sanctuaries is itself a noteworthy sign of contemporary attitudes.[19]

Despite this growing involvement in equestrian contests, in the period from

Ch. 10. Equestrian competition: participation and expenditure

550 to 450 Sparta had as many Olympic victories in athletics (five in number) as in chariot racing. Pausanias (6.1.7) claimed that after the Persian wars the Lakedaimonians became the most ambitious horse breeders in all Greece; but there is no record of any definite Spartiate Olympic victories over the following generation. From the long-range perspective of the second century AD, the Persian wars were an obvious generic chronological marker; and we should not over-interpret Pausanias' words as specifying a precise timetable for the development of Spartiate equestrian activity. As TABLE 12 makes clear, the sudden upsurge of Spartiate success is a phenomenon of the 440s and 430s.

How can we explain this development? Leslie Kurke (1993, 153) has recently attempted to connect it with the phenomenon of athletic heroisation, which occurred in the early fifth century in several poleis, including Sparta, where divine honours were given to the late seventh-century wrestler Hipposthenes (Paus. 3.15.7). In her view, athletic heroisation was a response made by beleaguered aristocracies faced by threats to their position, an attempt to renew their power by laying claim to a new form of charismatic authority derived from athletic success. She links this attempt with John Davies' interpretation of the increased participation of the Athenian aristocracy in chariot racing in the sixth and fifth centuries. Davies viewed this phenomenon as the aristocracy's attempt to deploy property power to substitute for its declining cult authority (1981, 88–131). This model, Kurke suggests, can also be applied in Sparta, where,

> the kings and certain aristocrats who opposed the ephors were very active in chariot-racing competition… In this context it is worth noting that one of the latest-known victor-heroes is Kyniska of Sparta, daughter and sister of Spartan kings, who, according to Plutarch (*Ages.* 20) was encouraged in her horse-racing proclivities by her brother, King Agesilaos. Do her competition and heroization reflect a final bid for renewed talismanic authority by the Spartan kingship in the face of the encroaching power of the Ephorate? (1993, 162–3 n. 87).

Fig. 20. Drawing of a Panathenaic amphora dedicated to Athena, depicting a four-horse chariot in motion, from the sanctuary of Athena Chalkioikos, *c.* 525–500 BC (Sparta Museum; reproduced with permission of the British School at Athens).

There are difficulties, however, with Kurke's account. First, it is improbable that, in a polis which stressed the ethic of personal effort, the cult of the wrestler Hipposthenes could have served as a charter for chariot racing, which did not normally involve personal participation. Second, the idea that Spartan politics centred on a conflict between kings and ephors or that the fifth and fourth centuries witnessed the growing power of the ephorate at the expense of the kings has long since been abandoned by historians (Andrewes 1966, 8–10; Ste Croix 1972, 138–49; Cartledge 1987, 125–9). Thirdly, there are no grounds for believing that fifth-century Sparta was characterised by an aristocracy under threat; on the contrary, with the developing concentration of landholdings (see ch. 13), there is every indication that the power of the traditional wealthy elite was increasing. Finally, with the exception of King Damaratos, Spartan kings were not active in chariot racing – and for very good reasons, as we shall shortly see. Kyniska's involvement did not entail that of Agesilaos, who encouraged her participation precisely to discredit the sport, which he conspicuously disdained (Xen. *Ages.* 9.6; Plut. *Ages.* 20.1). Agesilaos' power was based on other factors, especially that of patronage (see ch. 11). None of this is to deny that chariot racing was pre-eminently the pursuit of wealthy Spartiates or that victories brought with them a talismanic authority; but, as I shall argue below, the exploitation of this source of power represented, not the reactionary tactic of an embattled aristocracy, but a rather more destabilising phenomenon.

The upsurge of Spartan equestrian success is better explained in terms of a response to new developments and opportunities open to wealthy Spartiates which provided them with both the resources and the stimulus to engage in this most expensive and prestigious of sports. The most fundamental development (given the huge resources required for horse keeping) was the growth in inequalities of landholding within the citizen body. As I have argued elsewhere (Hodkinson 1989, 82–9; cf. ch. 13, below), the increasing inequalities in wealth which had been emerging throughout the archaic period were markedly intensified by the economic impact of the great earthquake of *c.* 464 BC. The huge loss of life will have accelerated the normal process of property devolution, giving many Spartiates, and especially wealthy families, sizeable additional inheritances which would not otherwise have come their way, thus increasing the number of citizens with the resources for equestrian pursuits.

Certain other contingent factors also increased the importance of wealth as a determinant of status and encouraged the deployment of property power through chariot racing in a manner akin to that highlighted by Davies in classical Athens. One factor was the greater numbers of wealthier heiresses produced by the earthquake, which will have stimulated increased competition for advantageous marriages, in which the display of wealth and status through horsebreeding and participation in equestrian contests was no doubt a valuable attraction. A second factor arose out of the longstanding ties of guest-friendship (*xenia*) which many wealthy Spartiate families maintained with leading families from other states (cf. ch. 11, below). It is notable that the victories of Arkesilaos which opened the run of Spartiate chariot-racing successes came a mere 12 years after the four-horse chariot victory of his namesake, King Arkesilaos IV of Cyrene (Moretti 1957, no. 268). Connections between Sparta and Cyrene are well attested (e.g. Nafissi 1985; Schaus 1985). The Spartan lineage to which Arkesilaos belonged was a old-established one with many external connections (cf. Hdt. 1.67–8; Thuc. 5.50, 76; Xen. *Mem.* 1.2.61; Plut. *Kimon* 10.6), and identity of name is frequently a sign of ties of *xenia* (Herman 1990). It seems probable, therefore, that a relationship of *xenia* existed between the Spartan and Cyrenean families and that it was in emulation of his royal guest-friend that the Spartiate Arkesilaos was impelled to deploy his considerable wealth in pursuit of Olympic success – his double victory then triggering a competitive chain reaction among other wealthy Spartiates.[20] A third factor came with the start of the Peloponnesian war and the emergence of attractive new overseas commands, access to which – as we shall see below – could sometimes be gained through the prestige of equestrian success.

The convergence of these various developments was, I suggest, responsible for the unparalleled series of four-horse chariot victories achieved by Spartan citizens in the Olympiads between 448 and 420. Neither was this merely a temporary phenomenon. The Spartiates' run of success might have continued even longer, had they not been banned from competing at Olympia in 420. The resumption of Spartiate participation in the games in 400 or 396 was quickly followed by several further victories in a variety of equestrian events, as recorded in TABLE 12. The extent of leading Spartiates' commitment to horsebreeding and chariot racing throughout the later fifth and early fourth centuries can be gauged from other indicators. First, Spartiate victories were not confined to Olympia. At least two of the Olympic chariot race victors, Polykles and Xenarkes, also won at the other Crown games at Delphi, the Isthmos and Nemea, thus completing the ancient equivalent of a 'Grand Slam' and earning the coveted title of *periodonikēs* (Paus. 6.1.7, 2.1–2). Secondly, Kyniska's involvement in chariot racing in the 390s was reportedly encouraged by her brother, King Agesilaos II, in order to discredit the activity.[21] However, not even the strictures of Agesilaos could stem the tide of Spartiate equestrian preoccupations. According to the words which Isokrates (6.55) puts into the mouth of Agesilaos' son, Archidamos, Spartiates were still devoting their resources to 'feeding teams of ravenous horses', even when Sparta was in dire straits after the liberation of Messenia.[22]

Indeed, Spartiate equestrian preoccupations in this period were not restricted to agonistic contests, but were also stimulated by another new development. In 424 the Spartans created for the first time a native Lakedaimonian cavalry force (Thuc. 4.55). Initially some 400 strong, by the early fourth century it probably numbered some 720 horse, organized into regimental units called *morai* corresponding to the infantry *morai* (Xen. *Hell.* 4.2.16; *Lak. Pol.* 11.4; cf.

Lazenby 1985, 11–12). The responsibility for providing horses for the cavalry fell upon the 'very rich' (Xen. *Hell.* 6.4.11). This was a task which King Agesilaos apparently took to with relish: spurning the breeding of chariot horses, 'he adorned his estate with works and possessions worthy of a man, keeping many hounds and war horses' (*Ages.* 9.6). No doubt the conversations about horses which he reportedly shared with his fellow-king Agesipolis included much talk about the qualities of their respective herds of cavalry chargers (Xen. *Hell.* 5.3.20).[23]

The significant amount of landed resources devoted to horse-rearing as a consequence of the combination of agonistic and military demands is reflected in the way that the glowing retrospective comments of the pseudo-Platonic dialogue *Alkibiades I* (122d), on the wealth of Spartiate estates, single out the horses for special mention among all the livestock which grazed in Messenia. We must recall, however, that the writer, like the other sources cited, is referring, not to Spartiates in general, but to the estates of wealthy Spartiates. The fact that the right to use another's horses is included among the property borrowing mechanisms described by Xenophon (*Lak. Pol.* 6.3) is clear evidence that many Spartiates could not afford to own them and that the possession of herds of horses marked a clear differentiation within the citizen body. This picture of an activity that was increasingly prevalent among rich Spartiates, but still restricted to a privileged few, is confirmed by the fact that the number of known male Spartiates with names incorporating the words *hippos* (horse) or *polos* (foal) increases from less than 4% in the period from *c.* 600 to 433 to almost 8% in the period from 432 to 362.[24] The increase is impressive, but the eight per cent of persons whose parents gave them 'horsey' names still represents a distinct minority of the entire citizen body.

The economic implications of equestrian activity

What were the economic implications of the maintenance of horses? Some basic distinctions need to be made. First, we should distinguish the horses used for chariot racing and for cavalry service. Although in pre-classical Greece the same type of horse seems to have been used for both driving and riding, the heavy-bodied war horse 'is already differentiated from the light and elegant race horse in the fourth century BC.' (Anderson 1961, 19–20). The passage of Xenophon's *Agesilaos* (9.6) quoted above makes a clear distinction between war horses and chariot horses.[25] Any wealthy citizen who had the responsibility for providing war horses and also wished to participate in equestrian sports would have had to sustain a double economic burden in keeping two different types of animals. The continued involvement of many rich families in chariot racing in the early fourth century is, consequently, an indication of their considerable wealth.

A second distinction is that between simple horse *keeping* and genuine *breeding*. Evidence from classical Athens indicates that there was a significant financial gulf between the few very rich families who could afford to breed horses and the mass of horseowners who maintained the minimum number of animals and simply purchased new ones when required (Davies 1981, appendix; Bugh 1988, 38–74; Burford 1993, 73–4). Not that the Spartan situation was completely identical. Since leading Spartiates possessed on average rather larger estates, situated in more favourable horse rearing territory, than their Athenian counterparts ([Plato], *Alkibiades I* 122e; cf. ch. 4, above), a greater proportion of horseowners may have been breeders. So, for example, whereas many Athenian cavalrymen were simply horseowners, the 'very rich' who provided Sparta's cavalry surely bred the horses themselves. The evidence regarding the chariot race victors, however, reveals a mixed picture. Some victors were clearly breeders. The victories of Arkesilaos and his son Lichas, although separated by almost 25 years, probably resulted from continuity of breeding, especially as this family was one of the wealthiest and most distinguished in Sparta (Xen. *Mem.* 1.2.61; Plut. *Kimon* 10.6). That Lykinos also bred his own horses is suggested by the fact that he initially entered his team in the competition for foals (Paus. 6.2.2). In the case of Damonon, as we have seen, we are left in no doubt. Other chariot victors, however, appear to have been mere owners. Euagoras won his three successive Olympic victories with the same team of four horses (Hdt. 6.103): as Burford (1993, 74) says of Kimon of Athens, who achieved the same feat a few years later, 'if he had been a serious horse *breeder*, he should have been able to enter other, younger horses'. In the case of Leon, we are told explicitly by the inscription on his victory monument that he gained his success with 'Enetic horses', from the region of the Veneti around the northern Adriatic (see n. 12, above). Although Enetic horses are mentioned as early as *c.* 600 by the poet Alkman (fr. 1, Page, lines 50–1; fr. 172), this should not mislead us into thinking that a foreign breed had been maintained in Sparta for almost two centuries. Normal ancient usage apparently differed from modern usage, in that such a reference indicated not a breed but the region from which the horses themselves came (Anderson 1961, 38). Hence Leon's Enetic horses will have been acquired from the Adriatic region, not bred in Spartan territory. Finally, given the circumstances of the victories of Kyniska, urged to engage in chariot racing by her brother Agesilaos, her horses too were probably acquired for the purpose, not produced by breeding.[26]

We should therefore envisage two different levels of horse-keeping costs. The long-term breeder will have owned permanent herds with a substantial number of horses. He will have needed to devote considerable areas of private land each year for pasture and fodder crops, even if there were also certain regions available for public grazing. The breeder could, however, perhaps recoup part of his outlay through sale of surplus horses to citizens without permanent herds. Even simple horse-keeping was not a cheap affair. The purchase of a top-class team of chariot horses could involve considerable outlay. The only surviving figure from Greek antiquity is the five or eight talents (the sources disagree about the sum) which the Athenian Teisias of Kephale claimed to have given Alkibiades in 416 for the purchase of the four-horse team of the state chariot of Argos (Isok. 16.46; Diod. 13.74.3; Davies 1971, xxv, 501–2). As Davies notes, the costs of selection and training of this specialist team adequately explain the magnitude of the purchase price compared with recorded prices for Athenian cavalry mounts, which most commonly stood at some 500 drachmas, though they could rise to as much as 1,200 drachmas. At fourth-century Athenian prices, a sum of 500 drachmas would have provided between one and two years' supply of grain for a family of six (Spence 1993, 274–80). The Argive state chariot may have been a special case, but any Spartiate who wished to acquire a chariot team would still have had to expend significant economic – or social – resources. Once the horses were acquired, moreover, their owner began to incur, albeit on a lesser scale, the same kind of maintenance costs as the regular breeder. The ancient sources consistently imply that competitive *hippotrophia* (a word which could refer as much to simple keeping of horses as to their breeding) was a most expensive activity, potentially ruinous to its devotees (Davies 1971, xv–xvi n. 7).

To quantify the costs of feeding a team of chariot horses is difficult, since there is only one piece of evidence concerning ancient food rations for horses in the centuries before Christ: Polybius' information concerning rations in the Roman Republican army (6.39.13–14). According to Polybius, a Roman cavalryman was given a monthly ration of 2 Attic *medimnoi* of wheat and 7 *medimnoi* of barley, and an allied cavalryman 1⅓ *medimnoi* of wheat and 5 *medimnoi* of barley. The barley was probably for animal consumption and the wheat for the cavalryman and his attendant(s). This works out at a daily ration of 11.2 Attic *choinikes* of barley available to the Roman cavalryman and 8 *choinikes* to his allied counterpart. Most scholars assume that these figures cover the feeding of two horses, one each for the cavalryman and his mounted groom (Walbank 1957, 722; Anderson 1961, 94, 137; Spence 1993, 280–4). The most recent treatment, that by Spence, suggests a general rule of thumb of 4 *choinikes* (or about 3 kg) of barley per horse per day, based on the smaller allied rations – a figure comparable with the prescribed rations of the small horse or mounted infantry pony in the early twentieth-century British army.

The chariot horses of wealthy Spartiates probably required rations at least as high as, if not higher than, these war horses: note Isokrates' comment on 'teams of ravenous horses'.[27] The slow travel at human marching speed required of a cavalry horse would not burn up as much energy as chariot racing, which required high speed over distances as long as 12 km, punctuated by frequent bursts of quick acceleration after rounding the marker posts at each end of the stadium. The stresses of the racetrack probably also caused many injuries. Hence chariot horses would require high levels of starch for energy and protein for muscle and tissue repair (Hyland 1990, 44). That the allied horse ration mentioned by Polybius was itself only a basic ration for a military horse is suggested by the larger ration available to Roman cavalrymen. Moreover, to enable their chariot horses to perform at optimal levels in highly competitive contests, Spartiate chariot owners would surely have had to feed their teams not just barley, but a wider variety of high-protein fodder crops, such as lucerne (or alfalfa, *Medicago sativa*), which had been introduced to Greece in the early fifth century and was well-known as being particularly valuable for horses (cf. Hodkinson 1988, 44–5). We should, therefore, treat the Roman Republican allied cavalry horse ration as indicating the minimum fodder requirements for the keeping of chariot horses in classical Sparta.

The size of this ration can be appreciated in two ways. First, we can compare it with human consumption requirements. It may be compared with the ration of ⅔ *medimnos* of wheat per month, or 1.06 *choinikes* per day, received by Roman and allied infantrymen, an amount which is approximately equal to the 'standard ration' revealed in evidence from the Greek world.[28] Since the calorific value of a given volume of whole, hulled barley is about half that of an equivalent volume of wheat (all ancient grain figures are measurements of *volume*),[29] it can be calculated that the horse was expected to consume almost twice the amount of calories in grain as a Roman or allied soldier. The grain consumption of a team of four chariot horses would therefore be 7½ times the calories consumed by an adult human male and over four times the calorific value of the contribution of barley meal (*alphita*) which a citizen made to the common messes.[30] A second way of appreciating the significance of the horse ration is in terms of the land required for its production. At 3 kg per horse per day, a four-horse chariot team would require some 4,380 kg of barley per year. On the basis of attested annual yields of barley of about 640 kg/ha in Lakonia and Messenia between 1911 and 1950 (Gallant 1991, 77), this would require nearly 7 ha of cereal land, not to mention additional land needed for grazing territory and for growing other fodder crops. The fact that 7 ha is more than the size of a typical hoplite farm in ancient Greece (some 3.6–5.4 ha: Burford Cooper 1977/8; Gallant 1991, 86–7) is a good indication of the heavy burden of horse rearing.

The expenses of horsekeeping were not, of course, exhausted by costs of purchase and feeding. To these one must add the expenses of maintaining a stable and a groom and the costs of riding tackle. For chariot racing there were also costs associated with the competition itself. One such item was the cost of the chariot, which, although of slender construction and relatively simple in design (Swaddling 1980, 69–70; Decker 1992, esp. pls. 59–60), had to be commissioned from a wood- and metalworker and would require regular maintenance, not to mention repair or replacement given the frequent crashes and accidents associated with the sport.[31] To these costs we should add the costs of the logistical and operational support necessary for competing at foreign games (Decker 1992). Although the 30-day Olympic training period probably did not apply to equestrian competitors (Crowther 1991, 165), the horses would require some period of training on the spot to bring them into peak condition after their journey. A successful chariot team, if it were not to rely upon local artisans, would also need to take its own support personnel: a stable hand and a trainer with medical experience, a wheelwright and chariot builder, a cook and other auxiliary personnel to deal with the practicalities of life in temporary accommodation.

The other requirement was, naturally, the charioteer. It was by no means ignoble to drive one's own chariot, and some wealthy men did so (cf. Pindar, *Isthmian I*; Lefkowitz, 1984, 41–2). For a variety of reasons, however – age, the impossibility of a ruler's leaving his territory, the contest's inherent danger – most owners left this task to others. Sometimes the charioteer was a close kinsman, as was Karrhotos, the brother-in-law of King Arkesilaos of Cyrene, or Thrasyboulos, the son of Xenokrates (*Pythian V* and *VI*). Sometimes he might even be a slave ([Dem.] 61.23). Unfortunately, the status of the charioteers who achieved the Spartiate victories at Olympia is unknown. In certain cases the owner certainly did not drive. Kyniska, as a woman, could not enter Olympia during the festival. Due to the prohibition of Spartan participation, Lichas in 420 had to enter by subterfuge under the name of the public chariot of the Boiotians; he revealed his presence only after his chariot had won (Thuc. 5.50). In any case, he was already an old man (Xen. *Hell.* 3.2.21), as his father Arkesilaos will therefore have been at the time of his own victories a quarter of a century earlier. It is likely that Lichas' subterfuge implies the use of a Boiotian charioteer; but whether the favour which the Boiotian authorities did for Lichas involved an economic or purely social transaction is unknown. This case apart, Spartiate owners may have normally preferred a charioteer familiar with the team of horses, perhaps one of their own helots; but we cannot support this hypothesis with hard evidence.

The final economic aspect of Spartiate equestrian activity is the material rewards of victory. The victory prize at Olympia was no more than a wreath of olive (Hdt. 8.26) and prizes at the other 'Crown' games were similarly symbolic. For competitors from several other poleis, however, a victory in one of these major games might bring other forms of material reward. Some poleis provided various gifts of money for their Olympic victors or free meals at public expense (Young 1984, 128–41; Kyle 1996, 115–16). Sparta, in contrast, abstained from this practice. There was, however, one avenue to material rewards open to Spartiate competitors: namely, through competing at those non-Crown games which offered material prizes, such as the Athenian Panathenaia. As we have seen, dedications of late sixth- and early fifth-century Panathenaic amphoras at Spartan sanctuaries provide evidence of Spartiate equestrian victories. A partially-preserved Athenian inscription from the early fourth century provides details of the prizes awarded.[32] Unfortunately, the prizes given for the four-horse chariot race are missing, but those for the two-horse chariot race are preserved. The winner of the race for full-grown animals received 140 amphoras of olive oil, the highest recorded prize on the entire inscription, with 40 amphoras going to second placed finisher. The prizes for the more prestigious four-horse races were probably even higher. The value of the 140 amphoras of oil has been calculated (in Athenian terms), at between 1,680 and 2,520 drachmas, equivalent to between 2½ and 3½ years' wages for a skilled worker or the cost of a festival liturgy (a typical comic or dithyrambic chorus cost 1,500–2,000 drachmas).[33] Admittedly, these figures cannot be applied directly to the Spartan evidence, since there is a time gap of 100 years and over between the date of this inscription and the Panathenaic amphoras attested at Spartan sanctuaries. (Thorough study of the incompletely-published amphoras may of course reveal a wider range of dates.) It has been argued that the size of Panathenaic prizes may have increased in the early fourth century (Valavanis 1987, 489–90). Whatever the truth of this, the prizes were probably already sizeable in the late archaic period. Our main area of ignorance, however, concerns the ways in which Spartiate victors utilised their prizes of olive oil. In modern Greece farmers have frequently used surplus olive oil as a commodity to be stored and sold for cash at times when the price was right or a significant financial outlay was required (Forbes and Foxhall 1978, 37). Despite Sparta's role as a regional market, however, she lacked anything approaching the modern demand for olive oil stemming from large non-landowning urban populations.

Celebrations of equestrian success
The absence of epinician
In spite of the material prizes of the Panathenaia, victory at the Crown games was always the achievement most desired by any competitor; and the most important reward of victory was the panhellenic glory which it brought. The magnitude of the chariot victor's renown is attested in a fragment of Kritias (fr. 8, Diels-Kranz, *ap.* Plut. *Kimon* 10.6) in which he prays for 'the wealth of the Skopadai, the magnanimity of Kimon and the victories of Arkesilaos the Lakedaimonian'. To have more than a transient effect, however, the victor's glory had to be broadcast publicly in such a way as to perpetuate the public memory of his achievement. The two main means attested in late archaic and classical Greece were through a victory song and a victory monument.

The earlier of these two methods was the victory song (or *epinikion*), a poem 'written on commission for victors at athletic games and usually performed at the site of the games or at the victor's home in the context of a victory celebration'. It emerged shortly before the mid-sixth century, not long after the development of the *periodos* of Crown games (Barron 1984, 19–22; Jenner 1986; Bernadini 1992, 969–71; Golden 1998, 77), and continued until the 440s. Despite recent controversy, it seems that the initial recital was usually performed 'by a chorus of his fellow citizens before an audience that would include many of his countrymen',[34] sometimes in the context of a polis festival (Bernadini 1992, 969). Subsequently, the ode 'was chiefly reperformed at symposia, sung by a solo singer who accompanied himself on the lyre'; but these private occasions often spilled over into further, more public, celebrations during the *kōmos*, an outdoor processionary revel following the end of the *symposion*.[35] The content of epinician often focused not just upon the individual victor but also upon his lineage and his native polis.

The wide diffusion of the *epinikion* is shown by the fact that the 40 or so epinician odes in the Pindaric corpus alone were commissioned for victors from no fewer than 16 different states, including several Peloponnesian poleis. With one possible exception, however, there are no known epinicians for Spartiate victors in either athletic or equestrian contests. The possible exception is an early one, a fragmentary poem of Ibykos *c.* 550 BC which may celebrate a Spartiate running and wrestling victor at the games at Sikyon.[36] After this, the record is blank. It is true that there are relatively few known Spartiate victors in the Crown games during the peak years of epinician. But there were some; and since all the three major epinician poets (Simonides, Bacchylides and Pindar) wrote other works for a Spartan audience,[37] the absence of epinician odes looks like a phenomenon of Spartan society.

At one level, the explanation surely lies in the essentially public and pedagogic role of music within Spartan society and in the state's control over occasions at which epinician odes might otherwise have been sung. Choral singing was undoubtedly a major feature of Spartiate life; but our extant evidence, at least for the classical period, suggests that Spartan choruses were thoroughly state-controlled affairs, in which all citizens were expected to participate, often collectively in their age classes, in roles structured hierarchically to reflect and define their status.[38] The attested content of choral songs at state festivals reinforced approved behavioural norms of military valour and civic conformity. Such festivals clearly had no room for individual celebration, let alone for the advertisement of family lineage.

Similar considerations apply to sympotic re-performance of the *epinikion*. Music was undoubtedly part of the luxurious *symposia* and *kōmoi* depicted on archaic Lakonian pottery (A. Powell 1998, 122–3); but solo singing is completely absent from the sources' accounts of the practices of classical Spartan non-royal messes, which placed less emphasis than did *symposia* elsewhere on the stage of drinking, when musical performance typically took place.[39] Ewen Bowie (1990) has, it is true, argued for a continuing sympotic tradition in classical Sparta, in order to explain late fourth-century evidence for the competitive individual singing of the poems of Tyrtaios in the royal *syssition* on campaign (Philochoros, *FGrH* 328F216; Lykourgos, *Against Leokrates* 107). But, even if one can extrapolate such performances beyond their immediate royal and military context to the mass of ordinary *syssitia* in Sparta, the sentiments expressed in Tyrtaian martial elegy, with its overt depreciation of athletic prowess, were hardly conducive to positive reception of the ideology of individual glory expressed in the epinician ode. Indeed, the very organisation and ethos of the Spartan messes – with their military connections, their composition cutting across family and generational ties, their ethic of collective solidarity, and their control of drunkenness and hybristic behaviour – were a hostile environment for the solo re-performance of epinician and its associated komastic celebrations.

Behind the factors so far adduced lies the fundamental point that the rise of epinician seems to have represented an attempted revival of the very social forces which the Spartans' recent transformation of their society – their 'sixth-century revolution' – had been designed to escape. Kurke (1991, 258–9) has suggested that 'the impetus behind epinikian performance represents a kind of counter-revolution on the part of the aristocracy. Constrained by sumptuary legislation, the aristocracy uses epinikion as a new outlet for prestige displays' – displays of the kind that many sixth-century poleis had been seeking to control. The local Spartan context for these general developments is, unfortunately, obscure; but the suggestion that one Spartiate victor may have led the way in the rise of epinician indicates the possibility that prestige displays of victory celebration may once have been commonplace in 'pre-revolution' Sparta. For classical Sparta such displays would have been dangerous affairs. As Plato (*Laws* 802a) was later to warn, in a comment which has been linked to Spartiate practice (A. Powell 1994, 294), 'it is unsafe to honour those still living with encomia and hymns'. At all events, the absence of epinician in the later sixth and early fifth centuries is a mark of the success of the Spartan revolution in eradicating such displays in a manner that many other poleis could not.

The use of victory monuments
In contrast to their abstention from the victory song, Spartiate equestrian victors did make use of the other main means of perpetuating the memory of their success: through the erection of a victory monument by the victor himself or by his family. From the 440s onwards the monument came to supplant the victory song throughout Greece as the primary form for the celebration of agonistic success; but its lineage was in fact much older than that. From Euagoras in the 540s to Euryleonis in the 360s, all Sparta's equestrian victors, bar two, are recorded as having dedicated some kind of victory monument. In one respect, Spartiate victors' use of the monument to celebrate their success fits with the absence of the *epinikion* at Sparta, since before the fourth century all the monumental commemorations of equestrian success were located not at Sparta but at the site of the games themselves. Mark Golden (1998, 86) has observed that victory monuments were primarily

> messages to the victors' own kind, those Greeks who had the leisure and means to visit with some regularity the precincts where they stood. From this perspective, the abandonment of epinician, the shift from song to statue, reflects the closure of one channel of communication between mass and elite in Greek society. No doubt it occurred earliest in communities where elite competition had itself lost some of its lustre, such as at Athens.

Rich citizens and the use of private wealth

At Sparta, where elite competition had been a cause for circumspection for even longer, this channel of communication had almost never been open. The polis tolerated monumental commemorations abroad which were not permitted in front of the mass of citizens at home.

It is instructive to consider the development of Spartiate equestrian monuments at Olympia in comparison with those erected by other Greeks. The available information is summarised in TABLE 13 (cf. also Herrmann 1988). We should note that the information is dependent upon the account of the monuments at Olympia given in Book VI of Pausanias' *Guide to Greece* and that, although Pausanias' account is skewed towards inclusion of monuments from our period, the absence of a reference to a victory monument need not always mean that none ever existed.[40]

The earliest known Spartiate equestrian monument, that of Euagoras in the 540s, consisted simply of a bronze chariot without a statue (Paus. 6.10.8).[41]

TABLE 13. Olympic victory monuments for the four-horse chariot race (Spartiate victors in CAPITALS).

Date	Victor	Statue	Chariot	Driver	Horses	Other	Sculptor
560	Miltiades of Athens					Ivory horn	
548/4/0	EUAGORAS		X				
516	Kleosthenes of Epidamnos	X	X	X	X		Ageladas
488	Gelon of Gela	X	X				Glaukias
484	POLYPEITHES		X			Statue of father	
468	Hieron of Syracuse		X	X		(Dedicated by son)	Onatas
464	Kratisthenes of Cyrene	X	X			Statue of Nike	
448	ARKESILAOS	X					Myron
444	ARKESILAOS	X					Myron
440	LEON	X					
432 (?)	XENARKES	X					
428	ANAXANDROS	X					
424 (?)	POLYKLES	X				Statues of two boys	
420	LICHAS	X				(Posthumous dedication c. 400)	
400	Timon of Elis	X	X			Statue of Nike on chariot	Daidalos
396/2	KYNISKA	X	X	X	X	Miniature horses	Apelles
384	LYKINOS	X					
372	Troilos of Elis	X					Lysippos
364	Eubotas of Cyrene	X					

Although relatively modest by later standards, it was by no means out of place compared with the ivory horn dedicated a few years earlier by Miltiades the Athenian. Already in the 540s and 530s certain victors in athletic contests were beginning to dedicate life-size statues of themselves (Paus. 6.18.7). It was not apparently until a generation later, in 516, however, that this practice first spread to equestrian victors, when Kleosthenes of Epidamnos erected a grandiose monument in the form of a statue group consisting of a life-size personal bronze statue and a statue of his charioteer, along with his chariot and horses. The immediate impact of Kleosthenes' monument is unclear due to a gap in our information, a gap which includes the victory of King Damaratos in 504. During the first half of the fifth century, however, at least three non-Spartiate equestrian victories were commemorated with a statue and chariot. In two of these cases the person figured was the chariot owner himself; in another – the victory of the tyrant Hieron – the person figured was not Hieron himself but his charioteer. The monument dedicated by the Spartiate Polypeithes in 484 falls in between these alternatives. Polypeithes dedicated a representation of his father Kalliteles, in commemoration of the latter's wrestling victory, but contented himself with a small chariot in honour of his own success.[42]

Up until 450, therefore, no Spartiate equestrian victor had, to our knowledge, dedicated a victory monument including a personal statue. From the 440s onwards Spartiate practice changed markedly, with almost every victor dedicating his or her own statue. Few of the monuments of Spartiate victors, however, included more than that: hence in comparison with previous attested practice most Spartiate victory monuments appear comparatively modest. Two monuments, however, were out of the ordinary. The first was that of Polykles. According to Pausanias (6.1.7), his monument consisted of a statue of himself holding a ribbon, together with figures of two boys (his sons?), one asking for the ribbon, the other holding a wheel. Polykles was an exceptionally dedicated chariot-race owner, a winner also at the three other Crown games. He received the punning nickname 'Polychalkos' ('rich in bronze' or perhaps even 'much-bronzed'), a reference to the number of his bronze victory statues at the various sanctuaries. Polykles' monument, however, was outdone at the start of the fourth century by that of Kyniska, who in fact made two dedications. One was erected outdoors in the Altis, the heart of the Olympic sanctuary. It contained a personal statue, one of her charioteer, her chariot and team of horses (Paus. 6.1.6). Part of the limestone base which supported the statue of Kyniska herself survives, bearing the outline of the toes of her over-life-size right foot, positioned in a such a way as to indicate that the statue was turned to look towards the chariot team and its driver.[43] The other dedication was a set of less than life-size bronze horses placed in the pronaos of the temple of Zeus, where the partially-preserved marble base which supported them was found during the German excavations, bearing the signature of the famous sculptor Apelles of Megara.[44]

Several aspects of these monuments merit attention. First, there is the level of expenditure involved. In fourth-century Athens the cost of a life-size bronze statue was 3,000 drachmas, or half a talent (Diogenes Laertius 6.2.35; *IG* ii².555). Normally one might be cautious about translating into Spartan terms cash figures from a markedly different market-oriented economic context. In this case, however, the men responsible for the bronze statues at Olympia were foreign sculptors working in a panhellenic market. We can identify two of the sculptors who made Spartiate monuments: Myron of Eleutherai, who produced the two statues of Arkesilaos (cf. n.15, on p.330), and Apelles of Megara, who sculpted the victory group of Kyniska. It is probable that such sculptors worked for Spartiate victors on the same terms as for their other clients, receiving payment in silver (coined or uncoined), whose legal possession by Spartan citizens was established in chapter 5. It follows that even a single statue would represent a significant cash outlay, on a par with many state liturgies in contemporary Athens. The significant level of expense required perhaps helps explain the relatively modest nature of most Spartiate dedications. As for the more grandiose monuments, the statue group of Lykinos must have cost well over a talent (and he probably also had monuments at Delphi, Nemea and the Isthmos). The main monument of Kyniska, which involved no fewer than seven bronze figures (including the horses and chariot), may have involved a greater expenditure, perhaps as much as three talents.

A second significant aspect of the monuments is their epigraphic content. Kurke (1993, 141–9) has recently highlighted the role of the victor's statue as providing, metaphorically, a 'script' for the reenactment of the victory. There was also, however, a script that was not merely metaphorical but real, since most, if not all, of the monuments bore commemorative inscriptions. Even the simplest inscription, by identifying the victor, performed the fundamental role of immortalizing his or her name. But several of the recorded Spartiate equestrian inscriptions do much more than that, displaying what Pleket (1975, 79) has termed 'the tendency to add…a "surplus-value" to that of the victory itself', by emphasizing some special feature which gave it extra distinction. We have already seen that, within a local context, Damonon claimed that his victories were 'unparalleled among those now living'. Among the Olympic victors, the monument of Polypeithes evidently included an inscription reminding passers-by of his father's wrestling victory. Anaxandros' monument also focused on his lineage, announcing that he was the first of his family to gain an Olympic chariot victory but that his paternal grandfather had previously won the pentathlon (Paus. 6.1.7). Pausanias' information about the victories of Polykles and Xenarkes in the other three Crown games probably came from the inscriptions on their Olympic monuments (6.1.7, 2.1–2). The special feature stressed by Leon's inscription was his use of Enetic horses. (The text of Polemon which preserves a record of the inscription adds that he was the first to win with such horses.) For adding 'surplus value', however, all other Spartiate inscriptions pale before the celebratory epigram on the base of the statue-group of Kyniska (*IG* v.1.1564a; *Palatine Anthology* 13.16; Ebert 1972, no. 33):

> Kings of Sparta are my father and brothers.
> Kyniska, conquering with a chariot of fleet-footed steeds,
> Set up this statue. And I declare myself the only woman
> In all Hellas to have gained this crown.

In this, as in the grandeur of her monument, she outstripped the bragging of her male predecessors with a singular claim of royalty and precedence.

A final important aspect is the physical placing of Spartiate equestrian monuments within the sanctuary of Olympia. By identifying Pausanias' route around the Altis (the central place of the Olympic cult) and noting the order in which the various dedications are described, one can locate their positions with a reasonable degree of confidence (Hyde 1912; 1921, 339–53; Herrmann 1988, 132–4). Spartiate victor monuments, both equestrian and athletic, of the sixth and early fifth centuries were apparently placed among those from other poleis in the southern part of the Altis, either in the area later occupied by the temple of Zeus or immediately to the south-east.[45] The equestrian monuments of the later fifth and early fourth centuries, on the other hand, were placed all together in a group or row close to the heart of the Altis, either along the southern flank of the temple of Hera or in the area between the south-east corner of the temple, the ancient shrine of Pelops and the Great Altar of Zeus. Their positioning in a near-exclusive enclave close to the nub of cult activity has significant implications. It probably reflects competitive rivalry and emulation among the victors themselves; but it also ensured both the prominence of each individual monument to the eyes of visiting Greeks and a dominating collective Spartiate presence at the very centre of Olympia.

The effectiveness of the efforts that Spartiate equestrian victors made to immortalise themselves and their successes through their inscribed victory monuments can be measured by the very fact of their inclusion over five centuries later in Pausanias' account of Olympia. Pausanias' coverage was avowedly selective: 'I shall not even record all those whose statues have been set up… Those only will be mentioned who themselves gained some distinction, or whose statues happened to be better made than the others' (6.1.2). That as many as nine of the thirteen known Spartiate equestrian victors satisfied these elitist criteria says much for the high quality of the monuments of Spartiate equestrian victors and the enduring nature of their panhellenic renown.

The socio-political implications of equestrian victories

The contemporary audience at Olympia consisted largely, as has been noted, of men from other poleis. It is uncertain how many Spartan citizens will have visited the sanctuary to be personally impressed by the memorials of their fellow-citizens' achievements. No doubt boasting, rumour and hearsay had some effect at home. Nevertheless, the question remains: what impact did equestrian victories have upon society and politics inside Sparta itself?

Answers to this question can be approached from different angles, dependent upon the perspective from which one views the role of the sporting *agōn* within Greek society. One perspective views the *agōn* as a safety-valve against the explosion of political strife within the polis, as an acceptable channel for the competitive instincts of ambitious citizens (cf. Poliakoff 1987, 105, 112–15). Another current perspective focuses upon the effect of agonistic success in accentuating existing socio-political differentiation within the citizen body. Examples of this approach are Kurke's portrayal of agonistic activity as a tactic of the aristocracy (1993, 153) and Davies' aforementioned study of classical Athens (1981, 88–131), which emphasizes how wealthy families sought to use expenditure upon chariot racing as a means of translating large-scale property ownership into political power. Both perspectives can help to illuminate the effects of equestrian activity on Spartiate society. In one sense, equestrian contests served a stabilizing function by enabling rich citizens to deploy their wealth and achieve prestige outside Sparta, whilst living in a society which, unlike other poleis, restricted the opportunities for communal patronage, engagement in liturgies or conspicuous consumption at home. From another angle, the fact that only the rich could participate in equestrian contests was surely a differentiating factor *per se* which set them above ordinary citizens. When their participation was crowned with success, it could bring great political advantage, as I discuss shortly.

Before doing so, however, I would add a third perspective. This focuses upon the role of equestrian success as an agent of socio-political mobility within the wealthy elite, a factor with the potential to destabilise existing hierarchies. In Athens, for example, Kimon's three Olympic chariot-race victories in the later sixth century raised him to such a position of prestige that the Peisistratid tyrants became fearful of his position and had him killed (Hdt. 6.103). Similarly, Alkibiades' extraordinary performance in entering seven chariot teams at Olympia in 416 and finishing first, second and fourth was his primary justification for claiming military command in Sicily against older and more experienced generals (Thuc. 6.16).

We have already seen that within the Spartiate chariot-racing elite there are signs of economic disparity between the very rich who could afford to be long-term breeders with permanent herds of horses and those who owned just a single team. Some of the latter, although clearly rich, were probably not among the very wealthiest of families. Some may only recently have come into the wealth required for equestrian pursuits – perhaps following the acquisition of unexpected inheritances after the earthquake of *c.* 464. I have suggested elsewhere (1989, 96–100) that, although chariot racing was by no means a novel way for the richest Spartiates to deploy their wealth, what was new from the mid-fifth century onwards was that participation became more intensive and widespread. The involvement of new families who may not previously have specialised in horse keeping can also be detected from the evidence of victors like Polypeithes and Anaxandros, whose father and grandfather (respectively) had won Olympic athletic victories, but who themselves turned from athletic to equestrian competition. Men from such families among the 'lesser rich' could now compete for the highest renown of Olympic success. The enormous wealth of the richest Spartiates might tilt the odds in their favour, but an aspiring man of lesser wealth could still win through the acquisition of a single high-quality team or a skilled charioteer, or through sheer good fortune during the mêlée of the race itself. Chariot races could be chaotic affairs, in which accidents and multiple collisions might ruin the chances of the wealthiest, most favoured competitors. An important consequence of the growth of chariot racing was to increase the element of chance in the achievement of prestige and renown.

The impact of chariot racing as an agent of social mobility at the highest levels of society was intensified by the fact that, with the single exception of Damaratos (to whom I shall presently return), it was an activity which did not involve the Spartan kings. For most kings, whose authority rested on the exploitation of more certain, distinctive and enduring advantages (their birth and wealth, their military and religious leadership), chariot racing offered little advantage and much potential loss in case of defeat. Hence most kings wisely eschewed the sport. In doing so, however, they left the field open for non-royal Spartiates to obtain access to a powerful alternative type of prestige. The importance of this potential threat to the power of the Spartan kings will be discussed below.

How significant was the impact of an Olympic victory? Such a victory was regarded as a gift of the gods (e.g. Pindar, *Pythian V* 122–3; *X* 10). Recent research has rightly emphasized that the victor was seen as someone in their special favour, an auspicious person who possessed an aura of invincibility. As such, he was an ideal person to be associated with the leadership of major state enterprises (Kurke 1993, 136–7). The Spartans themselves shared this belief. Spartiate *athletic* victors were given a special place in the king's bodyguard (Plut. *Lyk.* 22.4; *Mor.* 639e; cf. Xen. *Hell.* 2.4.33), being used as special auxiliaries to assist the established military leadership (Hodkinson 1999, 168–9). The position, however, was somewhat different with equestrian victors. Being for the most part older men whose victories were not the result of personal prowess, they were not, to our knowledge, incorporated among the young *hippeis* who formed the king's bodyguard. Some equestrian victors were over 60, and hence remained totally apart from the traditional military chain of authority under the king. There were, however, other official roles – not auxiliary positions, but ones of leadership – to which their Olympic victory gave them a powerful claim.

One such role was diplomatic. Consider the case of Lichas and his dramatic acquisition of prominence in Spartan political life in the years following his victory in 420. As son of Arkesilaos, Lichas came from an important and wealthy family. By 420, as we have seen, he was already a man of great maturity, over age 60 (Xen. *Hell.* 3.2.21). Yet, when he makes his first appearance in the historical record only the previous year, as an envoy sent to Argos in 421, he apparently plays second fiddle, only the second-named envoy after his otherwise unknown colleague Ampelidas (Thuc. 5.22). Following his Olympic victory, everything changes. In 418 he is the sole member of another embassy sent to Argos; and Thucydides now reveals that he was the Argives' official *proxenos* (5.76; see further, ch. 11). This last piece of information suggests two interesting alternatives. Either Lichas had already been *proxenos* at the time of the earlier embassy in 421, in which case his apparent subordination suggests a relative lack of prestige before his chariot victory; or his appointment to the proxeny followed and should be ascribed to his Olympic success. Lichas' career then reaches its climax in 412–411, with his appointment as leader of the supervisory commission sent to oversee the war in the Eastern Aegean. In this capacity he directed the course of Spartan diplomacy in the region up until his death.[46]

There were also military roles outside the orbit of the traditional Lakedaimonian army which developed during the period of Sparta's empire in the late fifth and early fourth centuries (Parke 1930; Hodkinson 1993). As we have already seen (n. 12, on p. 329), the Leon whom the Spartans chose in 426 to lead the foundation of their colony at Herakleia Trachinia is probably identical with the Olympic chariot-race victor of 440 BC. He was clearly an important man, for he is named ahead of a man named Alkidas, who had recently been admiral of the Spartan navy. The obvious conclusion is that Leon was given the position as primary oikist of the colony because of his specially auspicious position as Olympic victor – and who more appropriate for the foundation of a polis named after Herakles, wearer of the lion skin, than a man whose name meant 'lion'? After this office Leon's career developed into other official roles, as ambassador to Athens in 420 and eponymous ephor in 419/18 (Thuc. 5.44; Xen. *Hell.* 2.3.10).[47]

A chariot victory could help a man to leapfrog above his former status into positions of leadership he would not otherwise have gained. From this perspective we can explain why King Damaratos, unlike other kings, sought his chariot-racing victory. For most kings, who could expect to share the hereditary generalship, chariot racing offered no advantage. Damaratos, however, was in a unique position, as a king accustomed to a share in command, but suddenly excluded by the influence of his fellow king Kleomenes, following the state's decision in 506 that henceforth only one king should command the army (Hdt. 5.75; cf. Carlier 1977, 76–8). His chariot victory – which (following Moretti) is conventionally placed in 504, but which could equally have been in a subsequent Olympiad – was surely a bid to regain access to the generalship through the acquisition of the divine aura of invincibility that came with Olympic success.

Of course, Damaratos' bid was a failure. In the toughest of political struggles his chariot-racing victory was insufficient against the grip which Kleomenes had on Spartan policy-making. Yet the struggle between equestrian success and royal power was still in progress a century later. The clearest indication of the prestige and influence which chariot-racing victories could bring is the opposition it aroused from King Agesilaos II, as seen retrospectively in Xenophon's encomium of the king:

> Surely, too, he did what was seemly and dignified when he adorned his own estate with works and possessions worthy of a man, keeping hounds and war horses, but persuaded his sister Kyniska to breed chariot horses, and showed by her victory that such a stud is a mark not of manliness but of wealth. How clearly his true nobility comes out in his opinion that a victory in the chariot race over private citizens would add nothing to his renown… (Xen. *Ages*. 9.6)

The strength of Agesilaos' determination to undermine the impact of chariot racing is the most convincing evidence of the perceived threat which it posed to a Spartan king. A notable aspect of the passage is its gendered conception of different types of horsebreeding. Rearing war horses (and hounds) is an attribute of manliness, whereas breeding successful chariot teams is by implication something even a woman can do, dependent not on personal merit but on wealth. (The additional implication that the deployment of wealth was itself a womanly activity neatly sidesteps the fact that wealth was equally necessary for Agesilaos' rearing of hounds and war horses.) Later in the same work Agesilaos' polemic against the trappings of equestrian victories is extended still further, in the comment that he refused to allow statues to be made of himself, deeming them to be appropriate to rich rather than to good men (Xen. *Ages*. 11.7; cf. Plut. *Ages*. 2.2).

Agesilaos thus expressed his opposition in terms of chariot racing's incompatibility with the 'traditional' Spartan ethic of personal merit; but his own reaction can be seen to rupture existing norms. Agesilaos' grounds for abstention express an elitist conception of the kingship whose novelty, in terms of Spartan thought, cannot be overemphasized. Redolent of fourth-century monarchical ideas, it stands besides the advice to the tyrant Hieron which Xenophon put into the mouth of Simonides – that it was misguided for a tyrant to compete in chariot-racing against ordinary citizens (*Hieron* 11.6). It foreshadows the famous remark of Alexander that he would run at Olympia 'provided my adversaries are kings' (Plutarch, *Alexander* 4). The challenge posed by chariot racing thus played its part in stimulating Agesilaos' attempt to place himself as king in a different category from his fellow citizens (see further ch. 11).

A similar destabilisation of Spartiate norms resulted from Agesilaos' promotion of Kyniska's success. The *kudos* of Olympic success now extended beyond the bounds of the male 'Peers' to a woman, whose celebrations of her success broke new ground in comparison with those of her predecessors, with

Rich citizens and the use of private wealth

a dedication whose grandeur exceeded anything that had gone before and the most boastful of victory epigrams. But Kyniska's victory also broke the mould in another respect. Commemoration of her victories extended beyond Olympia into Sparta itself, for a hero-shrine to her was erected, presumably after her death, in the centre of the polis at the Platanistas (Paus. 3.15.1). The placing of the shrine is significant, as Ducat has noted: close to the Dromos, where the young girls ran; close to the sanctuary of Helen, model for the young female Spartiate; close to the tomb of Alkman, the educator of young girls. The polis hence held Kyniska up to the young girls as the model of a woman who had gained *aristeia* (Ducat 1999, 168). Local commemoration of Kyniska's success and the connection with Helen seems, in fact, to have preceded her death. Part of a small Doric capital and abacus has been found at the Menelaion. Inscribed with Kyniska's name, it probably once supported a dedication to Helen (*IG* v.1.235; Woodward 1908/9, 86–7). This dedication suggests that, unlike previous Olympic victors, she was permitted to celebrate her success in front of the citizen audience at home – though at the peripheral sanctuary of the Menelaion rather than at Athena Chalkioikos on the acropolis where Damonon's dedication was made.[48]

Within a few years the rupture of traditional norms was extended still further. According to Pausanias (3.8.1), after Kyniska a number of other women won Olympic victories, especially women of Lakedaimon. One of these female victors, Euryleonis (winner of the Olympic two-horse chariot race in 368), went even further than Kyniska in being commemorated with a statue on the Acropolis itself, close to the temple of Athena Chalkioikos (Paus. 3.17.6). In his attempt to use his sister to oppose the challenge of chariot victories to the hierarchy of the kingship, Agesilaos thus opened the door to yet new forms of agonistic culture, forms which were even more inimical to the traditional norms of the male-centred polis and which foreshadowed, in the prominent social role of wealthy women, the character of a very different Sparta in the hellenistic age.

Notes

[1] See most recently, Golden 1998. The phenomenon was stressed long ago in Burckhardt 1902, though he largely restricted its application to the archaic period.

[2] *IG* v.1.213; *CEG* I.378; incomplete translation in Sweet 1987, 145–6.

[3] The full number of victories was probably somewhat higher, since the stēlē is incomplete in two respects. First, the stone has subsequently been broken roughly horizontally into two parts (see *Fig.* 18), leaving a lacuna of uncertain length in the midst of the list of Enymakratidas' victories. Secondly, the lower stone is broken off at the bottom before the end of the listing of Damonon's victories during various ephoral years.

[4] I have calculated the minimum period of eleven years by adding the eight victories at the games of Ariontia and of Poseidon at Thouria to the three distinct ephoral years in the final section. (For a possible explanation of the change of presentation in the

inscription, Jeffery 1990, 196.) Note that the two separate references to the ephorate of Echemenes should refer to the same year, since iteration in holding the ephorate was not permitted (Westlake 1976).

⁵ Cf. the restoration of the phrase *kai hēbōn* in line 39, just before the lacuna, by Schwartz 1976.

⁶ The games of Athena were presumably those of Athena Poliachos herself. The racecourse of the Earth-Holder was just south of Sparta (Xen. *Hell.* 6.5.30; Paus. 3.20.2).

⁷ Parparonia: *Anecd. Graec.* 1408, s.v. Parparos [Bekker]; Hesychios, s.v. Parparos; cf. Pliny, *NH* 4.17. Helos: Paus. 3.20.6. The Eleusinian games may be those of Eleusinian Demeter on the slopes of Mt. Taygetos (Paus. 3.20.5).

⁸ Although Jeffery (1990, 196) claims that the Damonon stēlē is 'the crowning example of the type of victory-list of which we have reviewed so many incomplete examples', none of the other lists which she mentions definitely relates to equestrian events.

⁹ Cf. the different opinions expressed at various times by Jeffery (1988; 1990, 196, 201 no. 52, 448).

¹⁰ Thuc. 5.50; Xen. *Hell.* 3.2.21; Diod. 14.17.4 The terminal date depends upon the chronology of Sparta's war against Elis. According to the chronology adopted by Funke (1980) and Cartledge (1987), the Elean war was completed by spring/summer 400, in time for Spartiates to compete that year. According to Hamilton (1982), it was partly Elis' continued refusal to permit Spartiate participation in 400 which caused the war to *start* in that year; on this chronology they were not readmitted until 396.

¹¹ I have omitted the four-horse chariot victory of Diaktoridas in 456 (Moretti 1957, no. 278). Moretti suggests that he may have been Spartiate owing to the identity of his name with that of the father of King Leotychidas' second wife. His state of origin, however, is not known and the name is also found in Thessaly and elsewhere.

¹² Our evidence for Leon's victory comes in a fragment of Polemon Periegetes (fr. 19 Preller; Müller, *FHG* iii.122) preserved in a scholion on Euripides, *Hippolytos* 231, which places his victory in the 89th Olympiad (424 BC). The version of the same scholion given by the medieval deacon Eustathios (*ap. Iliad* 2.852), however, puts the victory in the 85th Olympiad (440 BC), the date preferred by Poralla (1985, no. 482). Although certainty is impossible, the earlier date seems preferable on grounds of the probable identification of this Leon with the Leon chosen as the primary oikist of the colony at Herakleia Trachinia in 426 (Thuc. 3.92). The fact that the latter Leon was the first-named oikist out of three suggests a man of some seniority, especially as his second-named colleague, Alkidas, had recently been Sparta's *nauarchos*. Yet the above-mentioned fragment of Polemon quotes a victory inscription (Λέων Λακεδαιμόνιος ἵπποισι νικῶν Ἐνέταις, Ἀντικλείδα πατήρ) which implies that at the time of his chariot-race victory Leon was still a relatively young man. (This is so, whichever of the two most plausible emendations of the last two words is adopted: Ἀντικλείδα<ς> πατήρ, proud father Antikleidas commemorates his son's victory; or Ἀντικλείδα πατ<ρός>, father Antikleidas as owner of the horses. On this passage, see Ebert 1972, no. 28; Whitehead 1979, 193.) Accordingly, it seems better to assume a gap of 14 years between Leon's victory and his appointment as oikist, rather than that the appointment preceded his victory.

¹³ Moretti's original catalogue (1957, no. 386) placed Xenarkes' victory in 388 on the grounds that the list of victors in the four-horse chariot race was full from the Persian wars until 392. Subsequently (1970; 1992), he acknowledged the doubts raised by Hönle

in her dissertation of 1968 (1972, 154 n. 3). Hönle argued that an earlier date would better suit the context of Pausanias' reference to Xenarkes and that, since Pausanias does not state which equestrian event he won, it need not have been the four-horse chariot race but could have been one of the other contests of 428, such as the horse race. Since the victory of Lykinos should probably be re-dated from Moretti's date of 432 to one of 384 or later (see n. 15), that would create a space before the Peloponnesian war into which Xenarkes' victory could plausibly be placed. It seems more likely, however, that Xenarkes' success was in the four-horse chariot race than in any other event. In Pausanias' text (6.2.1–2) his name stands at the head of a group of known chariot-race victors. In common with the other men, Xenarkes is called a horsebreeder, an appellation which would better suit someone who could produce a team of horses than just a single mount.

14 I have altered the date of Polykles' victory, in order to place Leon's victory in 440 (see n. 12). C. Robert (1900, 176) placed the victory in 428 or 424, though he admitted that it could equally belong to the early fourth century, a date also advocated by Nafissi (1991, 102 n. 11, 163, 172 n. 82).

15 My altered date for Lykinos' victory derives from the statement of Pausanias (6.2.1–2) that he won the chariot race for full-grown horses after one of his animals had been disqualified from entering the race for teams of foals; this race was not introduced until 384 (Paus. 5.8.10). The *communis opinio* (e.g. Frazer 1898, i.588; iv.4; Hyde 1921, 24, 259–60), followed by Moretti, has been to dismiss Pausanias' statement on the grounds that he also says that there were two statues of Lykinos sculpted by Myron the Athenian. Moretti's date for Lykinos' victory is therefore aligned with Myron's *floruit* around the mid-fifth century. The difficulty with the *communis opinio* is why Lykinos should have had two personal statues for a single victory. The answer sometimes given is that he should be identified with a certain Lyk(e)inos who won the hoplite race in 448 (Moretti 1957, no. 448; *P. Oxy.* 222, col. II.34). This identification, however, is most uncertain (Ste Croix 1972, 354 n. 2; cf. the criticisms of Grenfell and Hunt 1899, 95). Lyk(e)inos' ethnic is unknown and Pausanias does not mention Lykinos' supposedly prior athletic victory, as he does in other cases (e.g. Eubotas of Cyrene: 6.8.3). There is a simpler solution. The passage in which Pausanias refers to Lykinos' victory and statues is quite complex: first, he mentions the statues of four Spartiate equestrian victors (Xenarkes, Lykinos, Arkesilaos and Lichas); then he relates a brief anecdote concerning the sporting history of each man. It is in the latter part of his anecdote about Lykinos that the reference to two statues appears. The relevant clause, however, is structured by a verb (ἀνέθηκε) without a named subject; it contains no reference to Lykinos by name. In the following sentence Pausanias mentions the two victories won by Arkesilaos, victories whose mid-fifth-century date is assured by independent evidence (Kritias fr. 8, Diels-Kranz, *ap.* Plut. *Kimon* 10; cf. his son Lichas, who was over 60 when he won his victory in 420: Thuc. 5.50; Xen. *Hell.* 3.2.21). As has been noted by various translators of Pausanias (cf. the Loeb and Penguin editions), it is likely that the previous clause concerning the two statues should logically relate not to Lykinos but to Arkesilaos. Either Arkesilaos' name has slipped out of the text or Pausanias himself has become confused; his confusion hereabouts is evident earlier in the same chapter where he repeats the name Xenarkes for both the Spartan equestrian victor and a pankratiast from Akarnania. Once the two statues by Myron are ascribed to Arkesilaos, there is no obstacle to accepting Pausanias' anecdote regarding the disqualification of Lykinos' horses and to placing his victory in or after 384.

[16] *BSA* 13 (1906/7) 150–3; 14 (1907/8) 145; 15 (1908/9) 114; H.W. Catling 1976/7, 41.

[17] *BSA* 13 (1906/7) 150–3, nos. 1, 3, 7.

[18] Beazley 1956, 369, 'Leagros group' no. 112; Brandt 1978, no. 72.

[19] It is possible that the base of a monument containing a dedication to Apollo at Delphi by a certain Alkibiadas (*IG* i².272; *SEG* xxvii.135; Daux 1977; Jeffery 1990, 78 no. 39, with 447 no. 47a, 448), and dated *c.* 525–500, may be part of a commemoration of a chariot-race victory; but considerable uncertainty surrounds this dedication. The inscription, formerly thought to be Athenian, is now seen as Lakonian. The dedicator was surely the ancestor of the well-known diplomat and ephor, Endios, guest-friend of Alkibiades, and an early member of the well-born Spartan family whose longstanding connection with the prominent Athenian lineage goes back to 550 or even earlier (Davies 1971, 12, 15–16). The suggestion that the monument in question was for a chariot-race victory was made by Davies (1971, 15) based upon Daux's original restoration (1922, 441–3) of the words [Πύ]θια πρ[ῶτος]. In his later 1977 article, however, Daux, corrected the restoration above, in such a way as to remove any indication as to the occasion of the dedication. The nature of the monument which the base supported is also apparently uncertain.

[20] I follow Chamoux (1953, 206–9) in placing the overthrow and death of King Arkesilaos IV around 440 rather than in the mid-late 450s.

[21] Xen. *Ages*. 9.6; *Apophth. Lak.*, *Agesilaos* no. 49 = Plut. *Mor.* 212b; Plut. *Ages*. 20.1.

[22] The dramatic date of the work is *c.* 366 BC.

[23] Note also the story of Agesilaos playing pretend horse-riding games with his children (Plut. *Ages*. 25.5; *Mor.* 213e; Aelian, *VH* 12.15).

[24] The idea of quantifying the increasing use of *hippos* names was prompted by the stimulating remarks of A. Powell 1988, 227. There are twenty-two examples out of *c.* 285 names of Spartiates mentioned in contexts falling with reasonable certainty within the period 432–362; only four out of 110 within the period *c.* 600–433. A man whose life spans the two periods is allocated to the earlier period. Statistics from Poralla 1985. The names from the period 432–362 are nos. 16, 53, 103, 196, 292, 304, 347, 349, 372, 386, 389, 390, 391, 393, 394, 456, 506, 522, 538, 582, 591, 653. Those from *c.* 600–433 are nos. 389a, 392, 521, 725. (Note also nos. 66, 114, 120, 387, 480, 603 and 666 of either uncertain date or legendary status; no. 395 from the period before *c.* 600; nos. 197, 388, 598 and 776 from the period after 362; the female names nos. 52, 312, 313; and the perioikoi represented by nos. 227 and 724.)

[25] The distinction is also implicit in Xenophon's *On the Art of Horsemanship*, which stresses more than once that his concern is with the war horse (1.2; 3.7).

[26] This is especially so if Kyniska's first victory was achieved as early as 396, the year to which it is normally ascribed. The verb Xenophon uses to describe Kyniska's activities, ἁρματοτροφεῖν, is often translated as 'to breed chariot horses' (e.g. the Loeb and Penguin translations), but could refer to either breeding or simple keeping.

[27] I am grateful to Philippa Nickson for her expert advice on horse nutrition.

[28] Foxhall and Forbes 1982. The higher rations of 2 *medimnoi* per month for Roman cavalrymen and 1⅓ for allied cavalrymen are simply multiplications of the infantryman's ration designed to feed the cavalrymen's attendants.

[29] My calculations of the calorific value of barley and wheat are based on the figures in Foxhall and Forbes (1982, 43–6). According to their estimates, whole, hulled barley contains 2,158 calories per kg, with a weight of about 0.6 kg per litre. (This last figure is

Rich citizens and the use of private wealth

a compromise between the different figures they provide in the table on p. 43.) Wheat is said to contain 3,340 calories per kg, with a weight of 0.7772 kg per litre. Hence, the number of calories per litre may be calculated at 1294.8 for barley and 2595.85 for wheat.

[30] The comparison between the horse rations and mess contributions, both of which are given as monthly amounts, is calculated as follows. Following the estimates of Foxhall and Forbes, *alphita* at 3,320 calories per kg, with a weight of 0.643 kg per litre, contains 2,134.74 calories per litre, compared with the figure of 1,294.8 calories per equivalent volume of whole, unhulled barley: a ratio of 1.65:1. The figure in the text is then produced by taking into account the respective volumes of the mess contributions and of the cavalry horses' rations (1½ as against 2½ Attic *medimnoi*).

[31] *Iliad* 23.382–97; Pindar, *Pythian V* 49–51; Sophokles, *Elektra* 713–48; Aristop. *Knights* 556–68; *Peace* 899–904; [Dem.] 61.29.

[32] *IG* ii².2311, translated in Miller 1991, no.84.

[33] For the calculations, Young 1984, 116, with Golden 1998, 165.

[34] Quotations from Kurke 1991, 3 and 5.

[35] Quotation from Morgan (1993, 11), who provides a convenient summary of recent debates, reaffirmation of the traditional view that the initial context for the performance of (Pindaric) epinician involved choral rather than solo singing, and discussion of the relationship between epinician and the *kōmos*.

[36] Ibykos (S 166), as interpreted by Barron 1984, 20–1.

[37] Simonides fr. 531, Campbell, ap. Diod. 11.11.6; fr. XXII(b); Bacchylides, fr. 20, Campbell; Pindar, frs. 112 and 199, Maehler, ap. Athen. 631c and Plut. *Lyk.* 21.4, respectively.

[38] R. Parker 1989, 149; Xen. *Lak. Pol.* 9.5; *Ages.* 2.17; *Hell.* 6.4.16; Plut. *Lyk.* 14.3; 21.1–2; *Mor.* 149a; 208d–e; 219e; Athen. 555c.

[39] The only mention of song and dance comes in a fragment of the early fifth-century poet Ion of Chios (fr. 27 West; cf. West 1985) which may relate to the entertainment of foreign visitors in the Spartan royal mess.

[40] One monument not attested by Pausanias is that of Leon. The evidence for his monument (see n. 12, above) does not indicate where it was dedicated, but Olympia is the most probable place.

[41] Pausanias does not explicitly indicate that this or most of the other monuments mentioned below were made of bronze. Since his normal practice, however, is to point out monuments made of wood or marble, we can assume that monuments on which he does not comment were of bronze.

[42] On the debate about the exact nature of this monument (a pillar bearing a free-standing statue and miniature chariot or simply a sculpted relief), Hodkinson 1999, 180 n. 35.

[43] *IvO* 160, currently in the Olympia Museum. For a detailed discussion of the base, Serwint 1987, 432–3.

[44] Paus. 5.12.5; *IvO* 634; Serwint 1987, 431–2.

[45] When the Zeus temple was constructed (it was completed in 457), monuments in the former area were moved either to the south or south-west of the temple, near the southern terrace wall, or possibly slightly outside the Altis, below and south of the terrace wall.

[46] Thuc. 8.39, 42–3, 52, 57–8, 84, 87. From Thuc. 8.84 it is evident that he died in Asia Minor in 411 or shortly afterwards. The attempt of Pouilloux and Salviat (1983)

to extend Lichas' life down to the 390s, on the grounds that a certain Lichas appears as archon in Thasos in those years, betrays a fundamental ignorance of processes of name diffusion in Greek antiquity and should be firmly resisted (cf. Cartledge 1984; Herman 1987, 20–1; 1990).

[47] Admittedly, Leon was only second-named ambassador to Athens. But, since the man named first, Philocharidas, had recently been one of the 15 non-royal Spartans (possibly members of the *gerousia*) who had sworn the oaths of peace and alliance with Athens in the previous year (Thuc. 5.19, 24), he was an unavoidable choice as leader of an embassy whose purpose was to restore the fragile relationship between the two states. That Leon was named ahead of the third-named envoy, the important Endios, *xenos* of Alkibiades, is a measure of his position.

[48] Cf. also *IG* v.1.1567, a marble fragment bearing the name KYN… along with a reference to the shrine of Hyakinthos at Amyklai.

Chapter 11

THE USE OF WEALTH IN PERSONAL AND POLITICAL RELATIONS

Early one day in spring 378 Archidamos, the son of King Agesilaos II, was facing a nerve-racking task. He had promised his beloved Kleonymos that he would ask his father the king to intercede on behalf of Kleonymos' father, a certain Sphodrias, who was on trial for his life following an act of military misconduct. We can follow Xenophon's account of the day's events (*Hell.* 5.4.28):

> He got up at dawn and watched to be sure that he did not miss his father when he left the house. But when he did see him on his way out, he first of all gave way to any citizen who happened to be there and wanting to speak to Agesilaos; next he stood aside for any foreigner (*xenos*), and then even for any of his servants (*therapontes*) who had a request to make. Finally, when Agesilaos came back from the [River] Eurotas and went indoors again, Archidamos went away without even having come near him. On the next day too he acted in the very same way.

The continuation of this story is well known to historians: when Archidamos did finally pluck up courage to speak to his father, Agesilaos used his influence with his friends among the trial judges to secure Sphodrias' unexpected acquittal. For our purposes, however, the primary interest lies in Xenophon's description of the details of what was evidently a typical day for Agesilaos – above all, in the picture of a king surrounded by a string of petitioners (citizens, foreigners and even servile attendants) who approached him as a patron.[1] At first sight, this episode might appear to limit patronage to the role of the kings; but another part of the story indicates that kings were by no means the only patrons. When first asked to approach his father, Archidamos had initially demurred, 'Kleonymos, I must tell you that I myself do not dare to look my father in the face; if I want to get something done in the polis, I go with my request to anyone rather than to him' (5.4.27). Other men too evidently exercised such personal influence over the course of affairs that even the son of a king might need their assistance.

Sparta is thus revealed as a place in which patron-client relationships played an essential role. The question to be asked in this chapter is: to what extent did the exercise of patronage rest on the possession and use of property and wealth, and what were the effects on Spartan society and politics? I shall examine this question by considering in turn the men of various statuses who approached Agesilaos.

Patronage over non-citizen dependants

In the episode above, Agesilaos was approached by his servants (*therapontes*) who had requests to make. As noted in chapter 7, the sources indicate that all Spartiate households possessed male and female attendants to perform domestic work and personal service. Although referred to by the standard terms in use elsewhere (e.g. *doulos*, *oiketēs*), most were probably helots, with perhaps a sprinkling of chattel slaves ([Plato], *Alk. I* 122d; Plut. *Comp. Lyk.-Numa* 2.4; cf. Hodkinson 1997b, 47–8).

The sources frequently indicate the close and enduring character of the personal relationship between Spartiate households and their servants. Male servants accompanied their masters as batmen on campaign and probably also on their daily round of activities (Hodkinson 1997b, 50). In many cases this may have been the continuation of a relationship that began in childhood. Several sources refer to a category of servile Lakonians called *mothōnes* who were brought up alongside (*paratrephomenoi*) the free children.[2] It has been plausibly argued that these *mothōnes* were helot children reared as attendants of Spartiate boys.[3] This ties in with Plato's description of the *krypteia* (*Laws* 633b–c), which, in emphasizing that the youths were sent out without attendants, suggests that they would normally be attended by a personal servant. The connection between a Spartan citizen and his helot attendant may, therefore, have been a lifelong affair. Indeed, one source (*Etym. Magn.*, s.v. *mothōn*) describes the *mothōn* as a slave born within the household, a further indication of the intimate link between the helot servant and the household which he served. The connections of female domestics to their household were more intimate still. Female servants wet-nursed and cared for Spartiate children and are depicted as sharing the most intimate sexual secrets of a Spartan queen.[4] Some had sexual intercourse with their Spartiate masters. The sons of such women were partly integrated into the institutions of Spartan life. The forces which King Agesipolis took against Olynthos in 381 included 'bastards (*nothoi*) of the Spartiates, men of very good appearance and not without experience of the life of honour in the polis' (Xen. *Hell*. 5.3.9).[5]

We must be careful not to romanticize the relations between Spartiates and their household servants, which must often have involved much exploitation, degradation and brutality. Whether for good or ill, however, the closeness of this relationship suggests some important implications. There must have been a deal of prestige in the possession of a significant retinue of personal servants. The retinue of a king was no doubt considerable, and Agesilaos surrounded by all his helot petitioners will have been an impressive sight. Similarly, the siring of a number of *nothoi* is likely to have been a source of prestige, especially as a contribution of much-needed manpower to the polis. However, as we shall see in more detail in chapter 12, the maintenance of such persons will not have been cheap. It is uncertain whether poorer Spartiate households could have afforded to provide separate attendants for their sons. The upkeep of a *nothos* will have been particularly onerous, especially if – as seems likely – his integration into Spartan military life involved inclusion in the upbringing and in a mess group. Probably only the wealthy possessed the resources to maintain a large household personnel. The great disparities in the capacity of citizen households to maintain household servants, *mothōnes* and *nothoi* were therefore surely a potent source of social differentiation, a distinction evident both on a daily basis and on certain special occasions in Spartiate life. On the second day of the annual festival of the Hyakinthia, we are told, 'the citizens entertain to dinner all their acquaintances, including their own personal slaves' (Polykrates, *ap.* Athen. 139f). On this day the wealthy Spartiate who appeared surrounded by the large retinue of the *nothoi* he had sired and the helot servants he maintained will have cut a far more impressive figure than his poorer 'Peers'.

A rich Spartiate's retinue at the Hyakinthia, however, was not limited to those of servile status, but included his free acquaintances too. We should, therefore, examine the evidence for the patronal relations that wealthy citizens could establish among other men of free status. I shall start with the question of foreign friends.

Relations with foreigners

Spartiate involvement in *xeniai*

'The elites of the ancient world were not confined to their immediate communities… On the contrary, they participated at one and the same time both in [foreign] networks and in their immediate communities.' Gabriel Herman's statement (1987, 8) reflects a growing appreciation in recent years of the importance of links between leading men from different states in ancient Greek society and politics. The presence of foreigners among the groups of persons who approached Agesilaos is a sign that Herman's statement applies as much to classical Sparta as to other Greek poleis; and, above all, that Sparta's reputation for the practice of *xenēlasia* (the expulsion of foreigners) did not entail the permanent absence of foreigners from the polis.[6]

In fact, a range of evidence indicates that Spartiates were thoroughly implicated in the bonds of solidarity between individuals from different poleis known as *xenia* (pl. *xeniai*), guest- or ritualised friendship. Note, for example, the personal relationships which underlay Sparta's expedition against Samos in *c.* 525, the range of poleis whose intimate links engendered fictitious claims to be Spartan colonies, and the number of 'special relationships' between poleis whose common denominator is a close connection with Sparta.[7] These varied phenomena show that leading Spartiates stood at the centre of a network of *xeniai* which gives a real meaning to the part-title of Irad Malkin's recent book (1994), 'the Spartan Mediterranean'. The importance of such *xeniai* throughout the classical period is demonstrated by an abundance of literary references to particular relationships involving Spartan citizens (TABLE 14). In Herman's catalogue of explicit references to *xeniai* (1987, 166–75), almost a quarter (23

TABLE 14. Relationships of *xeniai* involving Spartiates.

Date	Spartiate xenos	Foreign xenos	Principal Source	Remarks
Late 6c	(Unnamed)	The Peisistratidai [Athens]	Hdt. 5.63, 90	
510	King Kleomenes I	Isagoras [Athens]	Hdt. 5.70	
5c	Eurypontid house	Kyniskos [Mantineia]	(Cf. Tuplin 1977)	
479	(Unnamed)	Chileos [Tegea]	Hdt. 9.9	
479	Pausanias	Hegetorides [Kos]	Hdt. 9.76	
470s	Pausanias	Xerxes [Persia]	Thuc. 1.128-30	
Mid-5c	Aristokritos	Libys [area around Siwah]	Diod. 14.13.5	
Mid-5c	King Archidamos	Faction of Podanemos [Phleious]	Xen. *Hell.* 5.3.13	
431	King Archidamos	Perikles [Athens]	Thuc. 2.13	
424	Brasidas	Panairos et al. [Pharsalos]	Thuc. 4.78	
412	Endios	Alkibiades [Athens]	Thuc. 8.6	Ancestral
405	Lysander	Kyros [Persia]	Xen. *Hell.* 2.1.14	
405	Lysander	(Unnamed) [Miletos]	Plut. *Lys.* 8.1	
403	Lysander	(Unnamed) [throughout Aegean]	Plut. *Lys.* 19.1	
403	Lysander	Libys [area around Siwah]	Diod. 14.13.5	Ancestral
403	King Pausanias	Diognetos [Athens]	Lys. 18.10	Ancestral
402	King Agis	Xenias [Elis]	Paus. 3.2.27	
410	Cheirisophos	Kyros [Persia]	Xen. *Anab.* 1.4.3	
390s	(Unnamed)	Lykophron [Pherai]	Xen. *Hell.* 6.4.24	
390s	Phylopidas	Xenophon [Athenian exile]	Diog. Laert. 2.53	
395	King Agesilaos	Apollophanes [Kyzikos]	Xen. *Hell.* 4.1.29	
394	King Agesilaos	Son of Pharnabazos [Persia]	Xen. *Hell.* 4.1.39	
388	Antalkidas	Tiribazos [Persia]	Xen. *Hell.* 5.1.6	
388	Antalkidas	King Artaxerxes [Persia]	Plut. *Artax.* 22.3	
387	Antalkidas	Ariobarzanes [Persia]	Xen. *Hell.* 5.1.28	Ancestral
381	King Agesilaos	Prokles et al. [Phleious]	Xen. *Hell.* 5.3.13	
370	King Agesilaos	(Unnamed) [Mantineia]	Xen. *Hell.* 6.5.4	Ancestral
370	King Agesilaos	(Unnamed) [Tegea]	Xen. *Ages.* 2.23	
c. 365	King Agesilaos	Mausolos [Karia]	Xen. *Ages.* 2.27	Ancestral

Notes: (1) Exiled Spartiates are excluded.
(2) Some other possible cases of *xeniai* have been omitted due to uncertainties in the evidence.

out of just over 100) of his historical, pre-hellenistic cases of *xeniai* involve a Spartiate partner. (I exclude his Homeric and fictional references.) Similarly, in his catalogue of networks of *xeniai* during the Peloponnesian war (ibid. 180–4) a Spartan connection appears in as many as 20 out of 90 entries.

Besides the evidence of explicitly attested *xeniai*, indications of yet further relationships can be detected from the names which certain Spartiate parents gave their sons. Some such names were modelled on foreign places; others were homonyms of those used by foreign families (TABLES 15–16). Some of these *xeniai* had been inherited from earlier generations and were actively maintained by their descendants. The classic example is the *xenia* attested in 412 between Endios and the Athenian Alkibiades (Thuc. 8.6). This relationship must have been some 150 years old, since the Athenian lineage took the name Alkibiades from their Spartan *xenoi* and the earliest attested Athenian Alkibiades was born around 550 or even earlier (Davies 1971, 12, 15–16). Other *xeniai* were more recent; indeed, new *xeniai* were contracted by leading Spartiates throughout the fifth and fourth centuries (e.g. Xen. *Hell.* 4.1.29; 39–40).

Closely connected to ties of *xenia* was the institution of *proxenia*, whereby a chosen person acted within his own polis as diplomatic representative for the citizens of another polis. Sparta made as much use of this institution as did other poleis. According to Herodotus (6.57), the appointment of *proxenoi* was one of the privileges of the kings. This particular mechanism of appointment is something of a peculiarity, since *proxenoi* were ordinarily chosen by the polis

TABLE 15. Spartiate names modelled on foreign places.

Date	Spartiate name	Supporting evidence for xenia
Late 6c	Samios (P658)	Named following father's glorious death and burial at Samos
c. 510	Thessalos (P367)	-
423	Athenaios (P32)	Both Athenaios and father, Perikleidas, envoys to Athens
421	Akanthos (P47)	-
419	Knidis (P449)	-
412	Chalkideus (P743)	-
408	Boiotios (P175)	-
402	Samios (P659)	-
395	Skythes (P668)	-
370	Olontheus (P576)	-

Key: P = Number in the Lakedaimonian prosopography of Poralla 1985.

TABLE 16. Spartiate names shared with homonyms in other poleis.

Date	Spartiate name	Homonym elsewhere
*c.*525	[Al]kibiad[as] (P59a)	Alkibiades lineage in Athens (cf. Davies 1971, 12 15–16)
479	Aeimnestos (P31)	Aeimnestos of Plataia, father of Lakon (Thuc. 3.52)
440s	Arkesilaos (P141)	King Arkesilaos IV of Kyrene (cf. ch. 10)
420	Lichas Arkesilaou (P492)	Lichas Arkesilaou, archon at Thasos, 398 (cf. Herman 1987, 20)
403	Libys (P490)	Libys, ruler of area around Siwah (Diod. 14.13.5)

whose interests they represented. The kings' privilege, however, should not be interpreted as an exclusive one, but intended 'to supplement, not to take the place of, arrangements made by other states' (Mosley 1971, 435). Indeed, there is evidence that certain poleis made their own choice of Spartiate *proxenoi* in the normal way (*IG* ii².106 = Tod 1948, no. 135). Although the evidence is not as extensive as for ties of *xenia*, we know the names of several Spartiates who acted as *proxenoi* for other poleis (TABLE 17).[8]

TABLE 17. Spartiates acting as *proxenoi* for other poleis.

Date	*Spartiate* proxenos	Polis represented	Principal source
c. 550	Gorgos	Elis	*SEG* xi.1180a
c. 500	Euanios	Elis	*SEG* xxvi.476
418	Lichas	Argos	Thuc. 5.76
410	Klearchos	Byzantion	Xen. *Hell.* 1.1.35
390	Pharax	Boiotia	Xen. *Hell.* 4.5.6
367	Koroibos	Athens	*IG* ii².106
Mid-4c	Megillos	Athens	Plato, *Laws* 642b

TABLE 18. Foreigners acting as *proxenoi* for Sparta

Date	*Foreign* proxenos	Native polis	Principal source(s)
Late 6c	Alkibiades (I)	Athens	Thuc. 5.43; 6.89
Late 6c	Hipponikos (I), son of Kallias (I)	Athens	Xen. *Hell.* 6.3.4
Early 5c	Kleinias (I), son of Alkibiades (I)	Athens	Thuc. 5.43; 6.89
Early 5c	Kallias (II), son of Hipponikos (I)	Athens	Xen. *Hell.* 6.3.4
Early 5c	Arimnestos/Aeimnestos	Plataia	Hdt. 9.72; Thuc. 3.52
Mid-5c	Alkibiades (II), son of Kleinias (I)	Athens	Thuc. 5.43; 6.89
Mid-5c	Kimon	Athens	Plut. *Kimon* 14.3
427	Lakon, son of Aeimnestos	Plataia	Thuc. 3.52
Later 5c	Hipponikos (II), son of Kallias (II)	Athens	Xen. *Hell.* 6.3.4
Later 5c	Alkibiades (III), son of Kleinias (II)	Athens	Thuc. 5.43; 6.89
418	Alkiphron	Argos	Thuc. 5.59
402	Xenias	Elis	Paus. 3.2.27
Early 4c	Xenophon	(Skillous)	Diog. Laert. 2.51
375	Polydamas	Pharsalos	Xen. *Hell.* 6.1.4
371	Kallias (III), son of Hipponikos (II)	Athens	Xen. *Hell.* 6.3.4
371	Iason	Pherai	Xen. *Hell.* 6.4.24

Equally significantly, the sources attest a number of foreigners who acted as *proxenoi* on behalf of Sparta in their native poleis (TABLE 18) and others noted for their friendliness to Sparta.[9] The total number of foreigners acting as *proxenoi* for Sparta throughout the Greek world was probably considerable. As is evident from TABLE 18, in fifth-century Athens alone there were two, and at one time three, Athenian families who regarded themselves as *proxenoi* of

Sparta. Foreign *proxenoi* were often – though not always – men who already had personal relations of *xenia* with leading citizens from the foreign polis in question (Herman 1987, 138–42; Mitchell 1997, 33–5). Hence *proxenoi* were frequently employed by their native polis to conduct diplomatic negotiations with the foreign polis whose interests they represented. The foreigners who appear as petitioners of Agesilaos in spring 378 were surely primarily men of this sort, individuals with strong personal links with leading Spartiates, including the king himself, men known as having worked on behalf of Sparta in the past who could therefore approach him about their own private affairs and those of their polis.

Xeniai and the role of wealth

For our purposes, the essential point is that the possession and deployment of wealth was integral to participation in these high-level friendships (Herman 1987, 58–61, 73–115; Mitchell 1997, 18–21). It was wealthy men who had the resources to circulate privately in panhellenic circles, and who were attractive as potential *xenoi*. Men of wealth were the persons typically chosen for state enterprises, whether military or diplomatic, where shared command or occasions of hospitality might give rise to new *xeniai*. The ritual which initiated a *xenia* included an exchange of precious gifts. Subsequently, the services rendered between *xenoi* frequently included not just intangible favours but also the provision of material resources, such as natural products, money and other valuables, troops, land and slaves.

Several of these material transactions can be exemplified in cases of *xeniai* involving Spartiates. There are several instances of Spartiate adherence to the material aspects of the initiatory ritual. In 395, when King Agesilaos accepted an offer of *xenia* from the son of the Persian satrap Pharnabazos, he gave the boy a splendid set of horse trappings in return for a beautiful javelin (Xen. *Hell.* 4.1.39). A few years earlier, during his expedition to Athens in 403, King Pausanias had been approached by two competing groups. The first came from the Thirty, who wished to initiate a bond of *xenia*. The other came from the relatives of the deceased Athenian general Nikias, who wished to renew an older *xenia*, which probably derived from the collaboration of Nikias with Pausanias' father, King Pleistoanax, over the peace treaty and alliance of 421. Pausanias' reaction was to accept the latter approach. As part of their approach, both sides offered gifts to Pausanias; and in keeping with his decision, 'Pausanias rejected the gifts of the Thirty, and accepted ours' (Lysias 18.12). In acting as they did, Agesilaos and Pausanias were following the behaviour of the Spartan polis itself almost a century and a half earlier. When initiating a bond of *xenia* and alliance with King Croesus of Lydia, the polis had itself sent a huge decorated bronze krater in return for a gift of gold (Hdt. 1.69–70).

There are also suggestions of material exchanges between existing *xenoi*. The gift of slave prisoners of war sent to Xenophon by the Spartiate Phylopidas

(Diog. Laert. 2.53) probably derived from a *xenia* which the two men had contracted as comrades in Asia Minor. The hospitality at dinner which Lichas provided for foreigners visiting the festival of the Gymnopaidiai was presumably intended particularly for his existing *xenoi*, as well as for the purpose of acquiring new bonds of *xenia*.[10] Similarly, his *xenoi* will have been among the men who benefited from Agesilaos' belief that 'the generous man is…required to spend his own in the service of others' (Xen. *Ages*. 11.8; cf. 4.1). Another aspect of *xenia* relationships with material implications was that a *xenos* would sometimes act as foster-parent to his partner's children, subsidising their upbringing in his own household (Herman 1987, 22–6). Spartiate *xenoi* practised a variant of this practice, as is revealed by Xenophon's reference to the '*xenoi* among the so-called foster-children' (*xenoi tōn trophimōn kaloumenōn*) – clearly a sizeable body of men – who participated in King Agesipolis' expedition against Olynthos in 381 (Xen. *Hell*. 5.3.9). These foreign 'foster-children' were the children of Spartan admirers who had put their sons through the Spartiate upbringing.[11] The term *trophimoi* implies that they participated in the upbringing under the sponsorship of a Spartiate family which subsidised the costs of their upbringing.[12] No doubt these foreign boys were another group among the retinue of wealthy Spartiates on public occasions such as the festival of the Hyakinthia.

The mute material record of uninscribed Lakonian artefacts found outside Spartan territory discussed in chapter 9 may also conceal instances of Spartiate gift-giving in connection with *xenia* relationships. One wonders how many of the numerous bronze vessels, mirrors and figurines found in diverse parts of the Greek and non-Greek world originally travelled from Lakonia as a result of Spartiate *xeniai*. Precisely this argument has been made concerning several later seventh- and sixth-century bronzes and ivories found at the sanctuary of Hera on Samos, whose leading men maintained close ties of *xenia* with leading Spartiates. These artefacts are 'the kind of *objets* that a Samian aristocrat might have received from his host on a visit to Sparta…or that a Spartan aristocrat might have dedicated to Hera while visiting his Samian *xenos*' (Cartledge 1982, 255). Indeed, one of the objects from the sanctuary is far from mute, but speaks out boldly through its dedicatory inscription. A couchant lion ornament, dated *c.* 550 BC, which once decorated the rim of a large bronze vessel, bears the dedicatory inscription 'Eumnastos, a Spartiate, to Hera' (*Fig.* 21).[13] As Cartledge notes (ibid. 256), the wealth of Eumnastos 'is implicit in the expense both of the offering itself and of the travel needed to dedicate it in far-away Samos'. At around the same period another Spartiate – a certain Gorgos – commemorated his position as *proxenos* of the people of Elis by installing in the stadium at Olympia his own personal inscribed marble seat from which he could watch the games from a privileged position (*Fig.* 22).[14] Half a century later, *c*. 500, Gorgos' action was emulated by a subsequent *proxenos*, a certain Euanios.[15]

Besides the use of personal wealth, the evidence also indicates ways in which Spartiate commanders could exploit their influence over the disposal of public

Ch. 11. The use of wealth in personal and political relations

Fig. 21. Inscribed figurine of a bronze lion dedicated by Eumnastos to Hera, from the Heraion on Samos, *c.* 550 BC (Vathy Museum B3; photo courtesy of Deutsches Archäologisches Institut, Athens).

Fig. 22. Inscribed marble seat installed by Gorgos, proxenos of the Eleans, in the stadium at Olympia, *c.* 550 BC (Olympia Museum; photo courtesy of Deutsches Archäologisches Institut, Athens).

resources for the material benefit of foreign friends. King Agesilaos on his Asian campaign of 396–394 was a keen dispenser of this kind of asset. Noting that there was a large amount of booty in the hands of the official booty-sellers and that prices were at rock bottom, Agesilaos advised his friends to buy and ordered the booty-sellers to sell upon terms of credit. He then took his army down to the coast, where there was a large market, and all his friends were able to sell their goods for 'a prodigious amount of money' (Xen. *Ages.* 1.18). In addition, whenever deserters informed him of sources of plunder, he ensured that it was captured by his friends, so that they could gain both wealth and prestige (Xen. *Ages.* 1.19).[16] As Xenophon records, 'the immediate result of this was that his friendship was ardently wooed by large numbers of people'. The significance of the material aspects of *xeniai* could hardly be clearer.

The advantages of *xeniai*

What kind of advantages could wealthy Spartiates derive from their foreign connections? They can be categorised under three headings: selection for posts; assistance and benefits in post; and influence over policy-making.

343

Rich citizens and the use of private wealth

Selection for posts
The possession of personal connections considerably improved one's chances of selection for official posts. For example, it was probably his Spartiate *xenos* Endios who secured the Athenian Alkibiades' safe entry into Sparta in 415, and it was surely on the strength of the latter's initial popularity and success that Endios was elected ephor in 413/12 (Herman 1987, 149). It is most often in relation to positions abroad, however, that foreign connections were an asset. Lynette Mitchell (1997, 73–89) has recently calculated that about 34% of attested appointments of Spartan ambassadors and 17% of attested appointments of harmosts and archons were made on the basis of a personal connection with the polis or region where the person was appointed to serve. These percentages would surely be higher still if fuller family and personal information were available about each appointee. To select just a couple of examples, the appointment of Aneristos and Nikolaos as ambassadors to Persia in 430 surely derived from the personal ties which their fathers, Sperthias and Boulis, had contracted on their meetings with King Xerxes and the satrap Hydarnes fifty years earlier. Notably, their families were both wealthy and high-born, precisely the kind of persons most likely to contract such foreign *xeniai* (Hdt. 7.137–7; Thuc. 2.67). Similarly, Klearchos was appointed to several military commands in the Hellespont and at Byzantion due to his being *proxenos* of the Byzantines (Mitchell 1987, 82–3). Such foreign postings were, moreover, self-perpetuating for the families involved, in that during his spell abroad an envoy or commander would frequently contract new *xeniai* in the course of local diplomatic or military collaboration, ties which would pass down to his descendants. Consequently, the Spartans frequently selected the descendants of previous ambassadors to represent them in diplomatic negotiations with particular states (Mosley 1973, 50–4).

Assistance and benefits in post
Once a Spartiate was in post, collaboration with his *xenoi* could greatly enhance his chances of success in the policies he wished to pursue. Brasidas in 424, for example, was aided in the difficult task of taking his troops through Thessaly to Northern Greece by his *xenoi* from Pharsalos (Thuc. 4.78). Sometimes the help given by *xenoi* was even more direct. Alkibiades' personal influence was crucial in ensuring that the Spartan war effort was directed against Ionia and organised from Sparta by Endios and his fellow ephors rather than by King Agis at Dekeleia, thus – as he said privately to Endios – bringing the prestige to his *xenos* rather than to the king. Not only was Alkibiades instrumental in deciding the target of Sparta's war-effort and initiating the enterprise, he also helped lead it and ensured its early success (Thuc. 8.6–17).

In the cases just mentioned the apparent benefits to the Spartiate partner were largely political. However, it is important to note that military success itself could have important economic ramifications, since it was standard practice that victorious commanders received a special share of the booty (Pritchett 1974–91, v.398–401). In some cases the close inter-connections between political and material benefits are clear.[17] Although not specifically labelled a *xenia* in the sources, the developing relationship between Pausanias the Regent and the Persian king Xerxes is instructive. In return for Pausanias' generosity in freeing certain friends and kinsmen of the King, Xerxes promised him unlimited money and troops to bring Greece under Persian control. As Herman remarks (1987, 42), it was surely Xerxes' gifts which enabled Pausanias subsequently to indulge in costly Persian-style clothing and banquets, not to mention a Persian bodyguard. In this case, however, the political gains he hoped to achieve with Persian support did not follow, because his outrageous behaviour so alienated his fellow-Greeks that he was recalled to Sparta.[18]

The relationship in which the political and material benefits to the Spartiate partner can be traced in the most complete manner is the *xenia* between Lysander and Cyrus, son of the Persian king Darius II.[19] The association between Cyrus and Lysander began at their first meeting in 407, when over dinner Cyrus asked how he could gratify the Spartan. At this stage Lysander could have requested a personal gift; but, instead, looking to his longer-term advantage, he asked Cyrus for a pay increase for the rowers in his fleet, over and above the rate of pay officially agreed by the King (Xen. *Hell*. 1.5.1–7). At the end of his command Lysander returned all the remaining money to Cyrus, as if it were a personal gift (1.6.10). In 405 Cyrus joined Lysander's Greek *xenoi* in asking for his reappointment to command of the Peloponnesian navy, thereby persuading the Spartans to bend their normal rule against iteration of the nauarchy (2.1.6–7). Cyrus also gave Lysander additional money for the fleet – apparently out of his personal resources, since the King's money had now been spent (2.1.11–12). Subsequently, Cyrus even assigned to Lysander the future right to all the tribute to which he was personally entitled from the Greek poleis, along with all the current balance in hand (*Hell*. 2.1.14). It was these resources that underpinned Lysander's victory at Aigospotamoi which raised him and Sparta to pre-eminence. Up to this point Lysander had used all these gifts of *xenia* for public purposes. Now, however, the private benefits became evident with the immense prestige at home and power abroad which accrued from his victory. There were also material benefits. To celebrate Aigospotamoi, Cyrus sent him a gold and ivory model of a trireme, a gift which Lysander then converted into religious prestige by depositing it in the treasury of Brasidas and the Akanthians at Delphi. According to the local (probably third-century) Delphian writer, Anaxandrides, Lysander also deposited there almost two talents of silver, money which probably came from the tribute assigned to him by Cyrus (Plut. *Lys*. 18.1–2). Cyrus' money may also have paid for the personal statue which the same treasury also held (*Lys*. 1.1; *Mor*. 397f).

Cyrus was not the only *xenos* to offer Lysander gifts after Aigospotamoi. Crowns of victory and other gifts were offered to him by many Aegean poleis:

some of them perhaps from those without established ties with the new master of the seas and intended to win his goodwill, but others surely from his grateful *xenoi* now established in positions of power. Many of these personal gifts Lysander apparently sent back to Sparta to become public property (Xen. *Hell.* 2.3.8; Diod. 13.106.8; Plut. *Lys.* 16.1). But not all, since local inventories of temple treasures indicate that Lysander dedicated a golden crown on the Athenian acropolis and three more crowns at the temple of Apollo at Delos (Bommelaer 1981, 11–12 nos. 10–11). The Athenian crown was presumably a gift to him from his friends among the Thirty (Bommelaer 1981, 11–12 nos. 10–11; Harris 1995, v.428). Besides these personal gifts, Lysander's grateful *xenoi* also dedicated bronze statues in his honour: the Samians at Olympia and the Ephesians in their own polis in their sanctuary of Artemis (Paus. 6.3.14–16; Bommelaer 1981, 13 nos. 12–13). The makers of these dedications were the two most devoted groups of Lysander's friends: from Ephesos, which he had used as his centre of operations in Ionia (Xen. *Hell.* 1.51; Plut. *Lys.* 3.2–3), and from Samos, where he had rescued his associates from the most fervent of democracies (Cartledge 1982, 263–4). The depth of the latter's gratitude is conclusively demonstrated by their institution of divine cults in Lysander's honour.[20]

Sometimes *xeniai* were a means by which Spartiate commanders could obtain not just the money to hire troops but the troops themselves. In 387 the nauarch Antalkidas was sent 20 ships from the satrap Ariobarzanes on the strength of their ancestral *xenia*, ships which helped him to enforce the decisive blockade in the Hellespont which ended the Corinthian war (Xen. *Hell.* 5.1.28–29). Other ships also came to Antalkidas from another satrap, Tiribazos. Since the Spartans had appointed Antalkidas as *nauarchos* precisely in order to gratify Tiribazos, it seems that these two men were also *xenoi*, a relationship probably started during their collaboration in the peace talks of 393/2 (Mitchell 1997, 126). Behind this assistance from the Persian satraps lay the *xenia* Antalkidas seems to have contracted with the Persian king Artaxerxes shortly before, during his negotiations of 388/7 which resulted in the subsequent peace treaty of 387/6, known (alternatively and appropriately) as the King's Peace or the Peace of Antalkidas.[21] Antalkidas' *xeniai* were, consequently, a crucial asset in the success of his nauarchy.

The practice of using *xeniai* to obtain military assistance for the Spartan polis was, however, not a new phenomenon of Sparta's imperial age, nor was it confined to commanders abroad. It had long been implicit in the make-up of the Peloponnesian league. Recent research has emphasized that the very structure of Spartan power within the Peloponnese rested on *xeniai* between important Spartiates, especially those from the royal houses, and their oligarchic friends within the Peloponnesian league (Tuplin 1977; Cartledge 1987, 243–6). Several examples of these *xeniai* are recorded in TABLE 14. The provision of troops was the primary means by which her *xenoi* in Peloponnesian allies rendered service to Sparta. This is not to argue that the league rested solely or even primarily upon *xeniai*. It could not be guaranteed that a person or group with Spartiate *xenoi* would be dominant in every allied polis; some, after all, were democracies. Hence Sparta's allies were bound to her by sworn treaties in which they undertook 'to follow the Lakedaimonians whithersoever they may lead' (Xen. *Hell.* 2.2.20; 5.3.26; cf. Ste Croix 1972, 106–7). Even treaty obligations, however, were often ignored when it was in the interests of a supposedly allied polis. In these circumstances it was often the relationship and obligations of *xeniai* which helped keep an ally loyal. Indeed, as Mitchell (1997, 111–33) has pointed out, the obligations of *xenia* typically had a more powerful and enduring impact among the Greek friends of poleis like Sparta, who viewed it as an exchange of services among equals, than among their Persian *xenoi*, who viewed the relationship as a hierarchical one from which they could withdraw their services when dictated by self-interest or the weakness of the Greek party. Hence in the negotiations of 367, during the nadir of Spartan power, Antalkidas was so neglected by King Artaxerxes in favour of Sparta's enemies that he apparently starved himself to death for fear of the reaction of the ephors (Plut. *Pelop.* 30.4–5; *Artax.* 22.3–4).

Contrast the case of Sparta's *xenoi* at Mantineia. A striking feature of Mantineian policy in the 470s and 460s was her loyalty to Sparta in a period of serious revolts by many other Arkadian poleis (Andrewes 1952). She abstained from the anti-Spartan alliance of Tegea and Argos at the battle of Tegea and from the battle of Dipaieis when Sparta had to fight 'against all the Arkadians, except the Mantineians' (Hdt. 9.35). Then during the great helot revolt of the 460s the Mantineians, we are told, rendered the Eurypontid king Archidamos II many services in the wars against the Messenians (Xen. *Hell.* 5.2.3). The key to this outstanding loyalty is probably the *xenia* which the Eurypontid house (to which Archidamos belonged) maintained with one of the leading Mantineian lineages, the family of Kyniskos (Tuplin 1977). Later in the century, however, Mantineia became a democracy and began to pursue a consistently independent, anti-Spartan policy. Even when brought to heel after 418 and officially sworn to provide military support, we learn that by the late 390s and early 380s the Mantineians were in the habit of excusing themselves from campaigns or serving badly and unwillingly when they did participate (Xen. *Hell.* 5.2.2). In 385, however, Sparta intervened to install an oligarchy, probably dominated by the hereditary *xenoi* of King Archidamos' son, Agesilaos (5.2.3; 6.5.4). Immediately, we learn, the Mantineians 'came in from their villages to join the army much more willingly than they did when they were under a democracy' (5.2.7; cf. 6.4.18). A parallel example of a polis providing military forces to Sparta, at a time when others were turning against her, is the case of Phleious between 379 and 365. The reason, once again, was that Phleious was dominated by the *xenoi* of Agesilaos (Xen. *Hell.* 5.2.1–23). Through their *xeniai* with leading Mantineians and Phleiasians, the Eurypontid house was therefore able to secure the loyalty of important allies, thereby increasing its own political importance inside Sparta.

Among the Eurypontid kings, Agesilaos himself was the past master in the exploitation of *xeniai* for both his own and Sparta's military and political advantage, as Xenophon indicates:

> Is it not a striking proof of his freedom from avarice that he was able to get money for others, whenever he wanted, for the purpose of rendering financial assistance to the polis or his friends (*philoi*)? For had he been in the habit of selling his favours or taking payment for his benefactions, no one would have felt that he owed him anything. It is the recipient of unbought, gratuitous benefits who is always glad to oblige his benefactor in return for the kindness he has received... (Xen. *Ages*. 4.3–4).

In other words, Agesilaos developed a network of friends by bestowing favours and, in return, was able to call upon those friends for money which would then enable him to render financial assistance to others. One example of this comes in the mid-360s, when Agesilaos was able to use his ancestral ties of *xenia* with Mausolos of Caria (ties probably contracted with Mausolos' father Hekatomnos during Agesilaos' campaign in Caria in 395) to persuade him to abandon the siege of Sestos and Assos and to contribute money to Sparta (*Ages*. 2.27). In this case the polis was the ultimate beneficiary of Agesilaos' *xenia*, and his ability to gain access to outside resources otherwise inaccessible to the community made him a benefactor of his fellow citizens. Note, however, that Xenophon openly admits that some of Agesilaos' fund-raising was for private purposes, for rendering financial assistance to his *philoi*. These *philoi* would then be in debt to him and obligated in due course to return the favour. Such *philoi* could, of course, be Spartiates as well as non-Spartiates. Hence the exploitation of *xenia* could become a means of creating not only a generic but also a direct personal influence over one's fellow citizens.

Influence over policy-making

The third advantage the possession of foreign connections brought was the capacity to exercise greater influence over the making of policy, especially when the interests of one's *xenoi* were at stake. This was the *quid pro quo* for the support which those *xenoi* provided to Sparta. Often the influence of *xeniai* on policy-making is most easily detectable in the case of policy towards more distant regions, such as the Eastern Aegean or Asia Minor, where other reasons for military involvement (such as a threat to Sparta's internal security) were less obviously pressing. For example, Sparta's campaign against Polykrates *c.* 525 BC – which Herodotus (3.56) called 'the first expedition to Asia by Lakedaimonian Dorians' – is, as Cartledge (1982) has shown, only explicable as an act of assistance by leading Spartiates to their aristocratic *xenoi* from Samos. Similarly, a century and a quarter later, Sparta's settlement of affairs in the northern and eastern Aegean after Aigospotamoi was clearly conditioned by Lysander's determination to instal his '*philoi* and *xenoi*' in power through the notorious dekarchies.[22] The case of Sparta's policy towards her greatest benefactor in the Ionian war, Cyrus, is particularly interesting. After the war, Cyrus appealed to the Spartans 'to show themselves as good friends to him as he had been to them in their war with the Athenians' (Xen. *Hell*. 3.1.1) by helping his expedition to gain the Persian throne. The ephors, seeing the justice of his request for the return of favours, ordered that military help should be sent. Modern commentators are surely right to see the hand of Cyrus' *xenos* Lysander behind this decision (Xen. *Hell*. 3.1.1; *Anab*. 1.4.2–3; Hamilton 1979, 105). There may also have been a second *xenia* at work. The forces sent included 700 Peloponnesian hoplite mercenaries, commanded by the Spartan Cheirisophos, who became full participants in Cyrus' expedition. According to Xenophon, Cheirisophos was personally sent for by Cyrus (μετάπεμπτος ὑπὸ Κύρου: *Anab*. 1.4.3); moreover, he 'responded to Cyrus' private summons…precisely as did some other of Cyrus' *xenoi*' (Herman 1987, 100). It seems, therefore, that Cheirisophos used the opportunity of official Spartan support for Cyrus to fulfil his obligations to his *xenos* by supplying and commanding this mercenary contingent.

The supply of military aid to Cyrus has its unusual aspects, especially in that the troops involved were mercenaries commanded by a citizen other than a king; but it was not in principle different from the help that had long been supplied to *xenoi* of leading Spartiates within the Peloponnesian league by the regular forces of the Lakedaimonians and their allies. As Thucydides (1.19) remarks, the Spartans 'saw to it that they [their allies] were governed by oligarchies who would work in their interests'. The annals of Spartan history are full of instances of military intervention which altered the political complexion of other Peloponnesian poleis (Ste Croix 1954/5, 20 n. 5). Often the sources fail to specify the detailed background to Spartan intervention, especially the persons installed in power and the precise nature of their Spartiate connections.[23] At other times, however, the picture is clear. Sparta's intervention against Elis in the 400s was prompted and commanded by King Agis on behalf of the oligarchic faction led by his *xenos*, Xenias, who was also the Spartan *proxenos* (Xen. *Hell*. 3.2.21–31; Paus. 3.8.4–5). Her intervention against Phleious in 381–379 was inspired and led by King Agesilaos on behalf of his *xenoi* in the faction of Prokles and his father's *xenoi* in the faction of Podanemos (Xen. *Hell*. 5.3.10–25). Similarly, Agesilaos' campaign against Tegea in 370 was aimed at restoring his exiled 'friends (*philoi*) and *xenoi*' (Xen. *Ages*. 2.23; *Hell*. 6.5.10–21). In the light of this history of assistance for Sparta's friends abroad, it is not surprising that foreigners were among the petitioners who approached Agesilaos in spring 378; nor that when the other king, Agesipolis, marched out against Olynthos in 381, he was joined by volunteers from allied states and cavalrymen from Thessaly who 'wanted to become known' to him (Xen. *Hell*. 5.3.9).

It is important, however, to stress the significant role which foreign *xenoi* themselves played in enabling leading Spartiates, including even the kings, to mobilise military aid. After 506, when it was decided that henceforth only one king should lead the army in the field, the kings no longer had the right to mobilise the army on their own account (Hdt. 5.75; Carlier 1977). Military expeditions could be authorised only through the official decision-making procedures of the Gerousia and assembly. Several scholars have remarked upon the frequency with which Sparta's foreign policies appear to emerge in response to outside requests (e.g. Andrewes 1966; W.E. Thompson 1973; Hodkinson 1983, 276–8). The historical sources are full of direct or indirectly-reported speeches made by foreigners (sometimes official ambassadors, sometimes private individuals) in Sparta, appealing for action on their behalf. This phenomenon has sometimes been interpreted as a sign of the relatively open and democratic character of the Spartan political process: 'we frequently find the assembly in Xenophon acting independently, responding not to the dictates of their leaders but to the arguments of foreign ambassadors' (W.E. Thompson 1973, 55). The distinction drawn here between the influence of internal leaders and of foreign ambassadors is, however, largely illusory. Rather, I suggest, they were often working together; and the public appeal of foreign speakers and the influence of leading Spartiates were two parts of the same process. The prominence of foreign speakers in the assembly is hardly surprising, since this was the arena in which foreigners had to appear in order to initiate the process of obtaining military help. This applied as much to *xenoi* who already had private links with leading Spartiates as to those outside such networks. Conversely, the public appeal made by a suppliant *xenos* was an essential trigger which enabled his friends in Sparta to start using their personal influence in support of their preferred policy.

To illustrate this point, consider the case of Spartan intervention in Phleious in 381–379 on behalf of the Phleiasian exiles. Before Sparta ordered this military intervention, the exiles and their associates had had to come to Sparta twice to ask for help, despite the fact that they already had a double bond of *xenia* with King Agesilaos, the most powerful man in Sparta (Xen. *Hell.* 5.2.8–9, 3.11–13; cf. Cartledge 1987, 264–5). One might imagine that a man of Agesilaos' influence could have proposed military intervention to the ephors and assembly and secured it through his own efforts; but in practice the appeal of his Phleiasian friends was as necessary to him as his support was to them. For, although Agesilaos could on occasions simply exert his influence to fix things as he wanted, it was necessary for him to limit his use of such naked control in order to escape the inevitable criticism and opposition which the continual exercise of direct influence would have provoked. Less than a year after the end of the Phleiasian affair, Agesilaos felt compelled to decline the military command against his old enemies the Thebans because he feared the adverse reaction of the citizens (Xen. *Hell.* 5.4.13; cf. Plut. *Ages.* 24.3). In this case, notably, there had been no appeal for help from suppliant *xenoi* from Thebes which Agesilaos could use to justify his personal intervention.

Ch. 11. The use of wealth in personal and political relations

The involvement of *xenoi*, making their pleas for help in the Spartan assembly, was, consequently, an essential means by which a leading Spartiate could affect particular decisions without appearing over-mighty. Indeed, the appearance of a suppliant *xenos* gave his Spartiate friend a legitimate reason to intervene; an obligation, indeed, which would be acknowledged and even applauded by other citizens. It was through this means that Agesilaos and, before him, other leading Spartiates, were able to guide Spartan decision-making so effectively in favour of the policies desired by themselves and their *xenoi* abroad. Note, also, that Spartan military intervention against Phleious came only after the Phleiasian authorities had imposed a fine on some of its citizens for going to Sparta as suppliants without official authorisation. As the suppliants themselves commented, 'their aim is that no-one in future will dare to come here to tell you what is going on in our polis'. In effect, the Phleiasian authorities were threatening the essential link through which upper-class Phleiasians and their Spartiate *xenoi* could mobilise the Spartan decision-making process into action on their behalf. The interruption of this link would have endangered the entire informal sub-structure of the Peloponnesian league. No wonder the Spartan reaction was a prompt and implacable military campaign.

The observations in the preceding paragraph prompt some particular comments on the position of the kings and other public officials. As TABLE 14 indicates, a large proportion of attested Spartiate *xeniai* were long-term hereditary connections involving the two royal houses. The kings were clearly in a privileged position for the attraction of *xeniai*, given the permanent and influential place which they occupied within the Spartan decision-making structure. Moreover, as we have seen, collaboration with *xenoi* played an essential role in creating the conditions in which the kings could best deploy their influence inside Sparta. Similar considerations apply to other public officials. Regarding the ephorate, it was above all wealthy ephors with foreign connections who could best use the opportunities offered by their position. As Mitchell's analysis has made clear, the ephors for 421/20, Xenares and Kleoboulos, who wished to overturn the peace of Nikias, attempted to do so, not by going publicly through official channels, but through private negotiations with the Boiotian and Corinthian ambassadors in collaboration with their other friends in Sparta.[24] (Note that the name of Xenares' father, Knidis, 'the Knidian', suggests that this was a family endowed with foreign connections.) Hence, although public office counted for a lot, only when allied to personal connections, which depended *inter alia* on the possession of wealth, could it be exploited to its fullest extent. The further implication is that the influence which the possession and use of *xeniai* could bring was open also to wealthy men not in public office. As can be seen from TABLES 14–18, personal connections abroad are attested for many leading Spartiates besides the kings. The fact that much of our source material, especially that of Xenophon, is orientated towards the royal houses should not blind us to the way in which foreign connections

Rich citizens and the use of private wealth

could be used by other leading men. This is shown clearly during the period of Sparta's overseas empire, in particular, when powerful new positions abroad became available on a significant scale to such men.

Xeniai were of course sometimes controversial affairs which could backfire, provoking accusations of putting private connections above the good of the polis. A fine and other sanctions were imposed upon King Agis II for withdrawing the army from battle against Argos, following his private negotiations with two Argives, one of whom was a Spartan *proxenos* and probably a *xenos* of Agis himself (Thuc. 5.59–63; Herman 1987, 145–6). Agesilaos was criticised for excessive zeal in helping his Phleiasian and Theban friends. It is instructive that Agesilaos wisely declined an offer of *xenia* from the Persian king Artaxerxes, which might have saddled him with politically embarrassing obligations to a *xenos* whom many Spartans regarded with mistrust. As Xenophon intimates, in his critical reference to a ruler of superior wealth setting himself above his rival, Artaxerxes' superior capacity to bestow material benefits would have left Agesilaos permanently in his debt (Xen. *Ages.* 8.3–4; Plut. *Ages.* 23.6). The Spartiates' very sensitivity to the subversive potential of *xeniai* is yet another reminder of their significance as an instrument of power, in which a crucial element was the deployment of wealth.

Patronage over *perioikoi*

Before discussing the third group of Agesilaos' petitioners – his fellow citizens – we should first consider a group of persons whom Xenophon conspicuously does not mention, the free inhabitants of Lakonia and Messenia known as the *perioikoi*. This omission is typical of their neglect by ancient authors (G. Shipley 1992, 211–12); but it is also surprising, in that if any group of free non-Spartiates stood potentially to gain from royal patronage it was surely the *perioikoi*, who were fellow-members, along with the Spartiates, of the Lakedaimonian polis. By the year 378, better-off *perioikoi* of hoplite status had long since been integrated into the formerly exclusively Spartiate regiments of the Lakedaimonian army (Cartledge 1987, 40–3). Some *perioikoi* had been entrusted with positions of considerable responsibility, as in 412 when a certain Phrynis was sent as an agent to Chios to check on the Chians' naval power and another *perioikos*, Deiniadas, was given command of the allied fleet against Lesbos (Thuc. 8.6, 22). The connection between the royal houses and the *perioikoi* was longstanding. According to the pseudo-Platonic dialogue *Alkibiades I* (123b), there existed a 'royal tribute of no slight amount which the Lakedaimonians pay to their kings'. Another ancestral privilege of the kings was their ownership of choice land within the territories of many perioikic poleis (Xen. *Lak. Pol.* 15.3). It is not surprising then that some members of their elite, the so-called '*kaloi kagathoi* among the *perioikoi*' took steps to ingratiate themselves with King Agesipolis I by volunteering for his expedition to Olynthos in 381 (Xen. *Hell.* 5.3.9).

The position of wealthy *perioikoi* was in certain respects parallel to that of

Sparta's *xenoi* in poleis within the Peloponnese. Indeed, Cartledge has argued that the relations developed by Sparta with its perioikic 'allies' foreshadowed the system of imperialistic domination which she later evolved outside Lakonia, according to which she ensured that the regions under her hegemony 'were controlled by the wealthy and ideologically pliant few' (1987, 16; cf. 1979, 107–8). I suggest that the roots of this cooperation between leading Spartiates and leading *perioikoi* was founded, as with Sparta's *xenoi*, in the period of boyhood. Xenophon's description of the foreign boys as being 'among the so-called *trophimoi*' implies that there were other groups of *trophimoi* besides the sons of *xenoi*. If one is to look for a parallel category of boys who might also have temporarily left their natal families for a Spartiate foster-family, the group that comes most readily to mind is boys from prominent Lakonian and Messenian perioikic families. Such families no doubt possessed longstanding connections with the Spartiate foster-households and sent their sons into the upbringing in preparation for a lifetime of military service and to enable them to establish personal links with leading Spartiates.[25] The patronal relationships thus established probably continued into adulthood. The former foster-boy might, for example, receive privileged invitations to dine at the common messes (Fisher 1989, 34–6). Or he might be incorporated into army units where his members of his patron family held officerships and given positions of responsibility within the perioikic *enōmotiai*. Through such means leading Spartiate families could extend their roles as patrons into the central institutions of polis life.

Patronage over fellow citizens

According to Spartan ideology, all Spartiate citizens were *homoioi*, 'Peers' who shared a fundamental uniformity of treatment, rights and obligations, regardless of personal diversity in background and wealth (e.g. Hdt. 7.234; Xen. *Lak. Pol.* 10.7). In chapter 7 we examined a variety of mechanisms which operated within the communal spheres of citizen life to minimise the importance of differences of wealth. We also saw that certain aspects of the socio-economic structure of the polis – such as the basic minimum of land originally possessed by each household and the absence of communal patronage – reduced the scope for the development of patron-client relationships. Yet in the opening paragraph of this chapter we witnessed a scene in which Spartan citizens were foremost among those who stepped forward to approach King Agesilaos when he came outdoors to bathe. Although the verb used (διαλέγεσθαι, 'to converse with') is neutral in connotation, the context of an influential man holding his daily audience suggests that many of the citizens were there to petition the king as clients to a patron.

One might object that the contrast between the ideology of the *homoioi* and the practice of royal patronage is more apparent than real. Possessed of a hereditary position which provided automatic privileges and exempt (if they were immediate heirs) from the public upbringing, Spartan kings were not members of the *homoioi*, but stood over and above the mass of their fellow citizens. Yet, as we have seen, Xenophon indicates that Agesilaos was not the only dispenser of patronage: his practices were typical of other important men. It seems, then, that a social system whose organisation and practices encouraged horizontal, egalitarian relations of solidarity had come by the early fourth century – if not before – to be infiltrated by asymmetrical, vertical bonds of patronage and clientism.

Consideration of all the non-material manifestations of patronage within the Spartiate citizen body goes beyond the scope of this study. My concern is rather to examine its material aspects, the ways in which patronal ties stemmed from inequalities in property and wealth. As Cartledge (1987, 140) has noted, in a patron-client relationship the patron's offerings are often solidly material, a point made in Aristotle's remarks on the reciprocity of unequal friendships: 'the superior friend should get more honour and the needy friend more gain' (*EN* 1163b1–3; cf. 1163b13–15). I shall argue that, in spite of the constraints highlighted above, there remained a number of avenues for the employment of wealth in interpersonal and social relations between citizens. I shall focus first on avenues which existed within the specific context of the public institutions of the upbringing, the common messes and the army, before turning my attention to the more general sphere of social and political life.

The upbringing

Although the public upbringing was one of the most important institutional constraints upon the influence of wealth, its operation was nevertheless far from egalitarian. On the contrary, as Finley (1986, 166) has commented, 'there were leaders, elites at all levels, and the primary principles of selection were appointment and co-optation'. Hence the current generation of leaders could exercise a significant influence over the men who were going to replace them, a situation ripe for the deployment of patronage. Yet none of this necessarily contained a material element, except in so far as wealthy men in positions of power might give preferment to youths from their own class over the sons of poorer citizens. The institution of pederasty offers more fertile ground for speculation. The episode of Archidamos and Kleonymos with which the chapter started demonstrates the patronal role that the senior lover (*erastēs*) could adopt on behalf of his beloved (*erōmenos*). Lysander played a similar role towards his beloved Agesilaos in helping the latter to secure the kingship and his subsequent command in Asia.[26] Among the services performed by an *erastēs* for his *erōmenos* was the supply of the household necessities required by the latter's household during the period up to the age of 30 when he was married but not allowed to enter the *agora* (Plut. *Lyk.* 25.1). The *erastēs* shared this task with the kinsfolk of the *erōmenos*. It is unclear whether the role of the *erastēs* was to provide economic support for his beloved's household out of his own resources or

Ch. 11. The use of wealth in personal and political relations

simply to act as joint-manager of his beloved's resources in market transactions. Even if it were merely the latter, it would still represent a temporary breach of the economic independence of the citizen *oikos*.

This temporary period of economic dependence affected the household of every young Spartiate who married under age 30; but there were some future citizens who were subject to a much lengthier period of material clientage during their upbringing. We have already seen that well-connected Spartiates frequently sponsored the sons of *xenoi* through the upbringing. There is evidence for a similar procedure in the case of the group of disadvantaged Spartans known as the *mothakes*. The most reliable evidence concerning their position is provided by Phylarchos and Aelian:

> The *mothakes* are foster-brothers (*syntrophoi*) of the Lakedaimonians. Each of the boys of citizen status, according as their private means suffice,[27] make some boys their foster-brothers – some one, others two, and some more. The *mothakes* are free, though not Lakedaimonians, but they share all the same upbringing (*paideias*). They say that one of these was Lysander, who defeated the Athenian navy after he had been made a citizen for his courage (Phylarchos, *FGrH* 81F43, *ap*. Athen. 271e–f).

> Kallikratidas, Gylippos and Lysander in Lakedaimon were called *mothakes*. This was the name of the <foster-brothers (*syntrophois*)> of the affluent,[28] whom their fathers sent with them to compete with them in the gymnasia. The man who made this arrangement, Lykourgos, granted Lakonian citizenship to those who kept to the boys' *agōgē* (Aelian, *VH* 12.43).

The precise status of the *mothakes* has been the subject of considerable debate.[29] Since I have discussed the issues fully elsewhere (Hodkinson 1997b, 55–62), I summarise here the conclusions of my earlier study.[30] There is good reason to believe that, late sources though they are, Phylarchos and Aelian are both describing a status which existed as part of the Spartan upbringing of the classical period. In contrast to certain modern notions, the *mothakes* were neither of servile origin nor a 'catch-all' group embracing youths from various backgrounds (including sons of foreigners and *perioikoi*, *nothoi*, and also privileged sons of helots). They were free-born youths comprising sons of poor or disfranchised Spartiate families. This ties in with the claim that Kallikratidas, Gylippos and Lysander were *mothakes*, since Gylippos was the son of an exile condemned to death for treason (Plut. *Per*. 22.2; cf. Thuc. 6.104) and Lysander is said to have been raised in poverty (Plut. *Lys*. 2.1).

Two essential points emerge from the evidence of Phylarchos and Aelian. First, Spartiate families could sponsor boys who were free but not of full citizen status and put them through the upbringing together with, and as foster-brothers of, their own sons. Secondly, such boys could acquire Spartiate citizenship. Phylarchos and Aelian appear to disagree whether the acquisition of citizenship was automatic on completion of the upbringing or at the discretion of the authorities. Automatic or not, *mothakes* were only in a position to acquire citizenship due to the support of their sponsor household. The most significant aspect of this support was material. It is explicitly stated by Aelian that it was wealthy families who engaged in this practice; and Phylarchos indicates that the number of boys sponsored was a function of wealth. In Lysander's case, it has been plausibly suggested that his support through the upbringing came from an associate of the Eurypontid royal house, with which he was allied later in his career (Cartledge 1987, 28–9).

During their adult lives men like Lysander and Gylippos were able to establish through their own achievements a degree of personal prestige which released them from a state of dependence upon their sponsor households. But such exceptional individuals, both from previously elite backgrounds, were hardly typical of the run of *mothakes*, who surely came from more lowly backgrounds. Most poor *mothakes* will surely have lived their citizen lives as members of the entourage of their foster-brothers, thereby adding to the reputation and influence of their sponsor household. In addition, those *mothakes* who had gained citizen status but were still burdened by the difficulties of inherited poverty would have continued in a state of lifelong material dependence, relying upon their sponsor household for subsistence help to provide their mess contributions and feed their families. The *mothax* origins of certain citizens may, consequently, have opened up a serious breach in the nominal equality of Spartiate citizens, especially from the late fifth century onwards when there was a large increase in the number of poor and disfranchised citizen families from which the *mothakes* were recruited.

The common messes
As we saw in chapters 6 and 7, every Spartiate belonged to a common mess, in which strict uniformity between messmates was enforced in terms of equality of their compulsory contributions and of their consumption of food. Nevertheless, as in the upbringing, personal relationships within the messes were inescapably hierarchical. Whilst some of these hierarchies arose from non-material differences, such as seniority or differences in personal ability (Hodkinson 1983, 251–4), others were connected with the deployment of wealth. The first point of interest is the extra, voluntary donations of foodstuffs which were made over and above the compulsory contributions and which formed an additional course to the meal, termed the *epaiklon* by most of the sources.[31] These extra donations are first attested by Xenophon (*Lak. Pol.* 5.3), who notes that 'many unexpected additions come from hunting and the rich in turn contribute wheat bread (*arton*)'. Dikaiarchos, writing later in the fourth century, also indicates (*ap.* Athen. 141b) that the messmates 'may even get something especially added, a fish or a hare or a ring-dove or something similar'.

In my first discussion of this subject (Hodkinson 1983, 254), I assimilated this fourth-century evidence to several passages from later sources excerpted by Athenaios in his *Deipnosophistai* composed around AD 200. According to

Sphairos, the late third-century adviser of King Kleomenes III,

> Sometimes the common people bring whatever is caught in the chase; but the rich contribute wheat bread and anything from the fields which the season permits (Athen. 141c–d).

According to another Hellenistic writer, Molpis,

> they contribute [the *epaiklon*]…to give evidence of their own prowess in the hunt. Many of them, too, who keep flocks, give a liberal share of the offspring. So the dish may consist of ring-doves, geese, turtle-doves, thrushes, blackbirds, hares, lambs and kids. The cooks announce to the company the names of those who bring in anything for the occasion, in order that all may realize the labour spent upon the chase and the zeal manifested for themselves (Athen. 141d–e).

Finally, Athenaios himself, drawing upon an unidentified but probably late source, claims that the *epaikla* for the men's messes were

> prepared from certain definite animals which are given as a present to messmates by one, sometimes even several, rich members (140e).

There is clearly much in common between the fourth-century and later evidence; but there is one potentially significant difference concerning the origins of the additional meat dishes. According to Xenophon and Dikaiarchos, the meat donations were game obtained from the wild by hunting or fishing.[32] In contrast, Molpis and the unidentified source depict rich men as also contributing meat from animals reared on their private estates. Although the fourth-century evidence may simply be incomplete, we may be dealing with a genuine change of practice.

The wealthy clearly had an advantage over their poorer messmates in their capacity to make these extra donations. Although talent at hunting was not wealth-dependent, it was the rich who could afford to own packs of hunting-dogs. Although poorer citizens were permitted to borrow the hunting-dogs of wealthier men (Xen. *Lak. Pol.* 6.3), their capacity to hunt may, nevertheless, have been more limited. As the sources indicate, it was the rich alone who could donate bread made from wheat, a superior cereal to the barley meal which formed the staple of the compulsory mess contributions.[33] Owing to its lesser reliability as a subsistence crop, wheat could be grown only by those who had surplus lands not required for ensuring a sufficient barley harvest.[34] Depending upon how one interprets the silence of Xenophon and Dikaiarchos, it is possible that in the classical period wealthy citizens were restrained from exploiting their private herds of animals for donations to the *epaikla*. Another aspect mentioned only by the later sources is the explicit announcement of the name of the person who had made the extra donation, which appears in the evidence of Molpis and also of the early second-century writer Polemon (*ap.* Athen. 139b–c).[35] In this case the silence of the fourth-century sources is less significant, since neither is concerned with the details of procedures. But, whether ceremonially announced or not, the identity of the donor will hardly have been lost upon his messmates.

The function served by these voluntary distributions of food is nicely expressed by Fisher (1989, 31–2): 'the idea is that any surplus wealth or extra good things should be shared with one's closest and permanent companions, and one main effect is to reward, with honour and powers of patronage, the donors, who are those who have achieved success in this intensely competitive, narrow world'. The greater range and degree of largesse which richer messmates were able to bestow upon their less well-off companions must have had a pronounced effect upon relations between messmates. Its impact may have been further intensified by interaction with the ethic of deference to seniors and with the patronal relationship between *erastēs* and *erōmenos*, since it is probable that an *erōmenos* normally joined his *erastēs'* mess (Hodkinson 1983, 253; Fisher 1989, 33). It is likely that the youngest messmates below age 30 – who were still within the upbringing and unable to take full charge of their economic affairs – will have been largely recipients rather than donors of largesse. Their semi-permanent state of indebtedness will have worked in combination with the avowed ethic of the messes 'that the younger might learn from the experience of those older' (Xen. *Lak. Pol.* 5.5) to ensure the subservient relationship of the young to other messmates.

The messes also gave scope for a particular kind of patronage by the kings. Each king received a double portion with which he could honour other individuals by inviting them to share it at the royal mess (Hdt. 6.57; Xen. *Lak. Pol.* 15.4). Typically, Agesilaos used to forego both his portions in order to honour two men at once (Xen. *Ages.* 5.1). The material element here is of course trivial compared with the honorific, but in other situations it may have been more prominent. The kings each chose two citizens to be the Pythioi who conducted Sparta's relations with Delphi; all four became permanent members of the royal mess (Hdt. 6.57; Xen. *Lak. Pol.* 15.5). For the men selected as Pythioi this was a considerable material reward, since they were maintained at public expense (Hdt. 6.57.2) and were therefore presumably relieved of the obligation to make mess contributions.

The army

Like the upbringing and the messes, the traditional Spartan army, with its remarkable degree of stratification comprising over 150 senior and junior officerships graded into four ranks below the king – 'officers serving under other officers', as Thucydides (5.66) put it – must have provided many opportunities for patronage in the allocation of these positions.[36] In contrast to the situation in the upbringing and the messes, however, the scope for a material element to this patronage was limited. The most important potential opportunity for the distribution of wealth was in the disposal of booty. Pritchett's recent detailed examination (1974–91, v.375–416) has shown, however, that in principle

Spartan commanders had no direct control over the distribution of booty after it was collected. It was typically handed over to officials known as the *laphyropōlai*, who conducted its sale and ensured that the receipts went to the treasury. On traditional, short campaigns within southern and central Greece, in which the army typically returned when its supplies were exhausted, that would normally have been the end of the matter. No source mentions any use of booty for the needs of the regular army in the field and the only references to plundering relate to the activities of non-Spartiate volunteers or contingents acting independently of the main force (Xen. *Hell.* 3.2.26; 4.7.6). On longer foreign expeditions matters were slightly different. A commander could divert the proceeds from the sale of booty to provide pay and sustenance for his troops (e.g. Xen. *Hell.* 3.1.28; 5.1.24; *Hell. Oxy.* 22.4), and no doubt such successful commanders gained in reputation and support. These distributions seem, however, to have been restricted to what was necessary for maintenance of the entire army, rather than providing profit for favoured friends or clients. This last point is demonstrated by the incident considered earlier in which Agesilaos gave his friends access to privileged information gained from deserters to enable them to gain private spoils. Had the booty been captured by the main army, Agesilaos would not have been able to allocate the spoils to his friends. During naval expeditions, commanders are sometimes recorded as explicitly allowing their troops to engage in private plunder, especially of captured hostile settlements (Thuc. 8.28; Xen. *Hell.* 1.6.14; 2.1.19). It is possible that the small number of Spartiates on these expeditions (besides the commander, there were usually a few supporting staff and Spartiate trierarchs of Lakonian ships) may have shared in such plunder; but this too was part of a concession allowed to the troops in general, not targeted patronage.

General social and political life

To what extent did the deployment of wealth in inter-personal relations extend beyond the institutional contexts discussed above into Spartiate political and social life in general? The first aspect to consider is material transactions which might influence the behaviour of persons holding public office, and first among these is the question of bribery. According to Aristotle, Spartan magistrates exhibited a high degree of susceptibility to taking bribes. Of the ephorate, Aristotle claims that,

> Its members come from among all the people, with the result that often men who are very poor find themselves on this board, and due to their lack of means they were open to bribery. There have been many demonstrations of this in the past; and in our own day we have the affair of the Andrians, in which certain ephors have been so corrupted by gifts of money that it is no thanks to them if their state was not utterly ruined (1270b8–13).[37]

As for the Gerousia,

> It is known that those who have taken on a share in this office conduct much public

business by taking bribes and showing favouritism... But the lawgiver, in a way that is clearly typical of his whole approach to the constitution, begins by making the citizens ambitious and then uses their ambition as a means of getting the Elders elected; for no one who is not ambitious would ask to hold office. Yet the truth is that men's ambition and their desire to make money are among the most frequent causes of deliberate acts of injustice (1271a3–5, 13–18).

These are remarkable judgements in that in general Aristotle apparently viewed bribery as of little significance in Greek political life (Harvey 1985, 99). He is silent, for example, about the use of bribery in Athens, despite the fact that allegations are rife in the forensic speeches. He even omits bribery from his account of causes of the downfall of states in *Politics* Book V – in marked contrast with his comments on the effects of bribery during the Andrian affair. Aristotle clearly judged the bribery of officials to be significant at Sparta in a way that it was not in other poleis.

It is difficult to substantiate this judgement by reference to precise incidents. Of the 36 alleged incidents of bribery involving Spartiates catalogued in Noethlichs' study of the subject (1987), only two relate to the bribery of one citizen by another (nos. 31 and 33). One is Thucydides' report that, when Pausanias the Regent returned to Sparta under threat from the ephors, he felt confident of being able to clear himself through the use of money (1.131; cf. Nepos, *Paus.* 3.5). The other is the incident in which, according to Xenophon (*Hell.* 2.4.29), King Pausanias in 403, desiring to overturn Lysander's policy in Athens, was able to lead out the army, 'having persuaded three of the ephors'. In the latter case, moreover, the term 'having persuaded' (πείσας) is formally ambiguous: it could signify persuasion either by money or by words (Harvey 1985, 78–9). However, the paucity of bribery allegations involving only citizens compared with those involving foreigners is not a reliable indicator, since the former were normally less visible and less intrinsically interesting to our non-Spartan sources, whose preponderant concern lies with foreign relations. The former episode is especially interesting in Pausanias the Regent's assumption (or that of Thucydides' source) that bribery was a tactic which he could employ with success. In the event, though Pausanias was initially thrown into prison by the ephors, he subsequently managed to secure his release. Unfortunately, we are not told how.

Were the incidents of bribery referred to by Aristotle typically purely instrumental in character, arising solely out of the immediate political situation – what sociologists have variously termed 'negative reciprocity', 'simplex bonds' or 'casual friendships' (cf. Gallant 1991, 150–1), that is, without any necessary implications of an enduring personal interaction? Or were they part of a longer-term social relationship involving multiple material exchanges? In the case of Pausanias, Thucydides' account indicates that, even after his guilt had been proven beyond doubt, one of the ephors remained so friendly to him that 'out of goodwill' he gave Pausanias a secret sign which enabled the Regent to escape arrest (Thuc. 1.134). The evidence does not permit us, however, to do more than speculate on the background to the ephor's partiality. In general, one might expect that the ephors, being often just ordinary citizens and in office for only a year, would be less likely to attract enduring social relationships with wealthy citizens than would the 28 non-royal members of the Gerousia, who were typically from upper-class families and held office for life (Arist. *Pol.* 1270b23–5, 38–40; 1294b29–31; 1306a18–19; Ste Croix 1972, 353–4).

Of all Sparta's major political institutions, the Gerousia is the least mentioned in the historical sources. During the episode with which this chapter started, however, the trial of Sphodrias in 378 (Xen. *Hell.* 5.4.24–33), we are given an insight into the social relationships in which its members were implicated.[38] In assessing the views of the judges before the trial, Xenophon comments (5.4.25),

> Now the friends (*philoi*) of [King] Kleombrotos were comrades (*hetairoi*) of Sphodrias, and were therefore inclined to acquit him; but they feared [King] Agesilaos and his friends (*philoi*), and also those in the middle.

In other words, a large number of the Elders (though not all) were attached to one or the other of the two kings. As the episode unfolded, the nature of their attachment became clear. It was assumed before the trial that Agesilaos would wish to condemn Sphodrias. However, as we saw earlier, the pederastic relationship between Sphodrias' son Kleonymos and Agesilaos' son Archidamos led Kleonymos to ask Archidamos to approach his father with a request to save Sphodrias. Both Kleonymos and Archidamos assumed that it was within Agesilaos' power to save Sphodrias through his influence over his friends in the court; and so it proved to be. The reality of the relationship between Agesilaos and his friends became apparent during a conversation between one of Sphodrias' friends and a friend of Agesilaos who was one of the judges – a certain Etymokles, an influential man twice chosen as an ambassador to Athens (Xen. *Hell.* 5.4.22; 6.5.33):

> Now one of the friends of Sphodrias, in conversation with Etymokles, said to him, 'I suppose' said he, 'that you friends of Agesilaos are all for putting Sphodrias to death.' And Etymokles replied, 'By Zeus, then we shall not be following the same course as Agesilaos, for he says to all with whom he has conversed the same thing, that…it is a hard thing to put to death one who as a boy, youth and young man has consistently acted well and honourably, for Sparta has need of such soldiers.' The man, then, upon hearing this, reported it to Kleonymos. And he, filled with joy, went at once to Archidamos and said, 'We know now that you have a care for us…' (5.4.32–3).

Etymokles' remarks show, first, that Agesilaos had been making known his personal view among his various contacts and, secondly, that in the view of Agesilaos' friends it would be most extraordinary for them to vote differently from the king. On hearing the news, Kleonymos could safely assume that his father would be acquitted, since the votes of Agesilaos and his friends when added to those of King Kleombrotos and his friends evidently far outnumbered those of the judges not committed to either group.

How was it that the two kings could between them have established such bonds of friendship over a majority of the Elders? Part of the answer may come in Herodotus' list of the prerogatives of the kings, which notes that in the absence of one of the kings from the Gerousia, his vote was cast by his nearest kinsman among the Elders (Hdt. 6.57). This suggests that the Gerousia often included relatives of the kings. Plutarch supplies further elucidation in revealing that Agesilaos used to send a cloak and an ox as a mark of honour to each newly-elected member of the Gerousia (Plut. *Ages.* 4.3; *Mor.* 482c–d) – a good example of the use of material gifts to woo a powerful official. This single action cannot, however, provide a full explanation: after all, several of the Elders thus solicited remained outside Agesilaos' circle of friends, some even joining (or remaining in) the circle of the other king. Indeed, Plutarch's use of the verb ἔπεμπε suggests a gift sent via an intermediary rather than given in person, perhaps an indication that this was sometimes a restrained first step in attempting to forge a new personal bond. Certainly, as regards those Elders within Agesilaos' circle, the gifts in question must have been part of a longer-term process of solicitation, whether commencing before or after their election.

Although the paucity of evidence about relations between the kings and Gerousia precludes further specific discussion, some progress may perhaps be made by viewing these relations within a broader perspective. It is clear that the role of friendship in Spartan social and political life was considerable. The works of Xenophon enable us to view it most clearly in relation to the kings, and especially to Agesilaos. For example, towards the end of Agesilaos' siege of Phleious in 379, the Phleiasians attempted to bypass the king by sending an embassy to surrender their city into the hands of the authorities in Sparta. Agesilaos, however, 'sent to his friends at home and arranged that the decision about Phleious should be left to him'. (*Hell.* 5.3.24). Such political friendships, however, were not merely confined to networks surrounding the kings. In 420 it was 'those in the circle of the ephor Xenares' (the very man whose foreign *xeniai* we glimpsed earlier) who ensured that the Spartans rebuffed the Athenian embassy led by Nikias (Thuc. 5.46). Xenares was able to sway this decision, despite the fact that Nikias must surely have had the backing of King Pausanias, who had collaborated with him over the peace treaty and alliance of 421. Similarly, Lysander is said to have developed a large *hetaireia*, or group of comrades, by the time of his death in 395 (Plut. *Ages.* 20.2).[39] No doubt the creation and maintenance of a circle of friends, comrades and supporters will have been a fact of life for most important and influential Spartiates. By the time he gained election to the Gerousia at age 60 or more, an Elder will long have been enmeshed in a web of personal relationships acquired during his upbringing, as a pederastic partner, in his mess, and in other social interactions over the course of 30 years as a full citizen. We get a glimpse of the multiplicity of these relationships in two passages from the sources. The first of the two Xenophon passages quoted above reveals that several of the Elders were *hetairoi* of Sphodrias himself, besides being friends of Kleombrotos.[40] Secondly, Plutarch's account of the celebrations following the election of a new Elder (*Lyk.* 26.3–4) reveals that he was served a meal by each of his *epitēdeioi* (comrades), even before he visited his mess. Clearly, an Elder's comrades were accepted as being intimately concerned with his new position.

For details of how a leading Spartiate might deploy his wealth to create and maintain a circle of adherents, however, we are limited to the evidence that Xenophon supplies about the methods of patronage practised by Agesilaos – methods already exhaustively analysed by Paul Cartledge (1987, 143–59), to whose penetrating discussion the following comments are indebted. During his final summation of Agesilaos' personal qualities in his encomium of the king (*Ages.* 11.13) Xenophon provides an invaluable list of the range of those personally indebted to Agesilaos' good offices:

> By his relatives (*syggeneis*) he was described as 'attached to his family', by his close associates (*chrōmenoi*) as 'unhesitatingly devoted', by those who served him (*hypourgēsantes*) as 'ever mindful', by those who were wronged or treated unjustly as a 'champion', and by those who endured dangers with him as a 'saviour second only to the gods'.

Of these, the first three groups are most worthy of attention. Agesilaos took care to cement firm bonds of friendship with his relatives and to use them as his agents in positions of responsibility, making his brother-in-law Peisandros *nauarchos* in 394 (Xen. *Hell.* 3.4.29) and obtaining a range of military commands for his younger half-brother Teleutias (Poralla 1985, no. 689), who was the product of the second marriage of Agesilaos' mother Eupolia, following the death of King Archidamos II. The support of Teleutias was achieved, above all, by material means. On being pronounced king as successor to his half-brother King Agis II, Agesilaos also inherited all Agis' property; of this 'he gave half to his mother's kinsfolk because he saw that they were in want' (Xen. *Ages.* 4.5; cf. Plut. *Ages.* 4.1).

As for his 'close associates', these were probably high-ranking men of Agesilaos' own social class: men important politically, such as his *philoi* within the Gerousia and those who had been able to arrange matters for him regarding Phleious; also prominent military commanders and envoys who carried out his policies.[41] They will have included the *philoi* to whom Agesilaos distributed the meat from the sacrificial animals before the battle of Koroneia in 394 (Plut. *Ages.* 17.3). This group of men are mentioned several times under a variety of names in Xenophon's encomium of the king. They are the *hetairoi* for whom he showed such zeal (*Ages.* 6.4), and whom he served alongside his fatherland (9.7;

cf. 11.10). They are 'his own people' (τῶν ἑαυτοῦ), for whom Agesilaos thought 'the generous man is required to spend his own goods' (11.8). Such people probably included the harmost Phoibidas, put on trial for seizing the Theban acropolis, an act which Agesilaos pointedly declined to condemn (Xen. *Hell.* 5.2.31). Agesilaos is said to have 'saved Phoibidas' (Plut. *Ages.* 23.7), perhaps by paying the crippling fine imposed upon him (Ste Croix 1972, 135–6; Cartledge 1987, 156). Indeed, the provision of financial help for men subject to official fines may have been a common means of material patronage in Sparta, to judge from an anecdote in the *Apophthegmata Lakōnika* (Plut. *Mor.* 221f). A certain Thektamenes, questioned as to why he was smiling after receiving a sentence of death, reportedly replied, 'I rejoice to think that I must pay this penalty myself without begging or borrowing anything from anybody' (cf. Cicero, *Tusc. Disp.* 1.42 [100]). One incident reminds us, however, that – as with Agesilaos' foreign *xenoi* – transfers of material resources were not always one way. As we saw in chapter 5, in 362 the king drew loans and contributions from his friends in the polis to finance Sparta's military campaigns (Plut. *Ages.* 35.3).

The third group, 'those who served him', were probably ordinary citizens, the sort of men who approached Agesilaos during his daily appearance in public and whose service to the king would include voting for his policies and candidates in the assembly. Agesilaos' material patronage of such citizens is suggested by Xenophon's comment that 'he rejoiced to see the avaricious poor and to enrich the upright' (11.3). Hints that ordinary citizens might often need financial support comes in passages already noted in chapter 5: Herodotus' reference (6.59) to debts owing to the kings and a reference to the Spartans' use of tally-sticks as a record of loans (Dioskourides, *ap.* Photios *Lexikon*, s.v. *skytalē*). One possible circumstance for such loans by the time of Agesilaos' reign was the need for subsistence help as many citizen families became increasingly impoverished. There was hence considerable opportunity for wealthy Spartiates like Agesilaos to establish a permanent clientship over poor citizens through the ongoing provision of foodstuffs or through direct payment of their mess dues. Agesilaos' donation of land to his poor relations shows his awareness of the problem and in their case his willingness to provide a permanent solution. Unfortunately, lack of evidence prevents us from turning these speculations into a firm understanding of the significance of subsistence help in Agesilaos' practice of patronal politics.

According to Xenophon, Agesilaos was a man 'who delighted to give away his own for the sake of others' and of whom 'many acknowledged that they had received many benefits from him' (*Ages.* 4.1). Plutarch's comment (*Ages.* 4.2) that the ephors laid a fine on the king on the grounds that he had made public citizens his private property, though probably invented, captures the essence of his policy. How typical was Agesilaos, both of his own time and of earlier generations? Clearly, as king he had many advantages of position and wealth over even the wealthiest of non-royal citizens. Yet, although our evidence is

Ch. 11. The use of wealth in personal and political relations

sketchy on the point, there are sufficient indications of the practice of patronage by other wealthy Spartiates to suggest that Agesilaos' methods were not unique. As regards earlier periods, though our evidence is woefully inadequate, there are hints (such as in Herodotus' aforementioned reference to debts owed to the kings) that Agesilaos was developing methods already pioneered by his predecessors. What is clear, however, is that, with the new opportunities of the Spartan empire and the increasing degree of economic stratification in Spartiate society, conditions in Agesilaos' day were especially ripe for the deployment of material patronage; and that Agesilaos exploited them for all they were worth. The extent and causes of that increasing economic stratification will be the subject of the final part of this volume.

Notes

[1] Although different verbs are used to describe the purposes for which the citizens and the servants approached Agesilaos (διαλέγεσθαι, 'to converse with', in contrast to τῷ δεομένῳ), the context of an influential man holding his daily audience ('glad to make himself accessible to all…best pleased when he could dismiss his petitioners quickly with their requests granted', as Xenophon put it elsewhere: *Ages.* 9.2) suggests that the difference of terminology is largely an ideological reflection of their respective statuses: a citizen's approach is represented as a different matter from that of a servile attendant.

[2] Harpokration, s.v. *mothōn*; Schol. *ap.* Aristop., *Wealth* 279; Schol. *ap.* Aristop. *Knights* 634; Hesychios, s.v. *mothōnas*. Full texts in Lotze 1962, 427.

[3] Cantarelli 1890, 472; Bruni 1979, 21–4; Ducat 1990a, 166–8. Against the doubts of Paradiso 1991, 48–9, see Hodkinson 1997b, 51 n. 12.

[4] Hdt. 6.61; Plut. *Lyk.* 16, 2–3; *Alk.* 1.2; *Ages.* 3.1.

[5] Sons born of helot women are also mentioned in a fragment from the later third-century Cynic philosopher Teles (*Peri phygēs, ap.* Stobaios 3.40.8). He too indicates that they participated in the upbringing. His statement that the Spartans honoured such men 'on a par with the best' is vague in its implications (cf. Ogden 1996, 221), but should not be interpreted as proving that they became full citizens. The phraseology of Xenophon, a contemporary source, indicates that *nothoi* were partly, not fully, integrated into Spartiate life.

[6] In fact, the sources' uniform use of the plural form of the word, *xenēlasiai*, suggests that they were occasional and temporary expulsions rather than a longstanding exclusion: Thuc. 1.144; 2.39; Aristop. *Birds* 1012–13; Xen. *Lak. Pol.* 14.4; Plato, *Protagoras* 342c; *Laws* 950b; 953e; cf. Rebenich 1998.

[7] Sparta and Samos: Cartledge 1982, esp. 244, 249. Fictitious 'colonies': Knidos (Hdt. 1.174); Thera (Hdt. 4.145–50; Pindar, *Pythian V* 256–9); Melos (Thuc. 4.112); Kythera (7.57). 'Special relationships': Knidos and Taras; Thera and Samos; Kyrene and Samos (Hdt. 3.138; 4.152).

[8] There are also other Spartiates who, though not explicitly attested as *proxenoi*, are recorded as possessing good relations with particular foreign poleis: e.g. Philocharidas and Leon, said to be friends of Athens in 420 (Thuc. 5.44).

[9] e.g. Eustrophos and Aison of Argos in 420 BC (Thuc. 5.40).

Rich citizens and the use of private wealth

¹⁰ Xen. *Mem.* 1.2.61: the word *xenoi* in this text seems to bear its generic sense of 'foreigners'; cf. also Plut. *Kimon* 10.6.

¹¹ Hodkinson 1997b, 62–5. Xenophon and Phokion are both said to have sent their son(s) to be brought up in Sparta (Diog. Laert. 2.54; Plut. *Ages.* 20.2; *Phokion* 20.2), though doubt has been expressed about the authenticity of the information regarding Xenophon's sons (Higgins 1977, 160 n. 46).

¹² Cf. the term *syntrophoi tōn Lakedaimoniōn* used with reference to the Spartan *mothakes* discussed later in this chapter, men not of full citizen status, who were sponsored through the upbringing by wealthy citizens (Phylarchos, *FGrH* 81F43, *ap.* Athen. 271e–f; cf. Aelian, *VH* 12.43).

¹³ Herfort-Koch 1986, no. 163a; Jeffery 1990, 446 no. 16a.

¹⁴ *SEG* xi.1180a; Kunze and Schleif 1944, 164–6; Jeffery 1990, 199 no. 15, 448. The use of Lakonian script and the fact that the marble used was probably from the southern Peloponnese argue against the view of Mosley (1971, 435) that the monument was dedicated for Gorgos by the Eleans.

¹⁵ *AD* 27, *Chron.* B.1 (1972), 275 and pl. 212a; *SEG* xxvi.476.

¹⁶ By mounting 'unofficial' raiding parties Agesilaos' friends were presumably able to keep any booty, whereas had it been seized in regular army action it would have been commandeered by the official booty-sellers. Elsewhere (*Hell.* 4.1.20–8) Xenophon recounts an occasion when the thin dividing-line between official and unofficial military action led to dispute between Sparta's native Asian allies, who claimed their plunder as private spoils, and one of Agesilaos' officers, who had it seized from them as state property. The native allies were so insulted that they deserted to the enemy; they were evidently used to being allowed by Agesilaos to keep their plunder.

¹⁷ In what follows I leave aside references to the bribery of Spartiate officials, despite the connection between allegations of bribe-taking and the practice of gift-giving between *xenoi* which is observable in the classical Athenian evidence (Perlman 1976; Harvey 1985; Herman 1987, 73–81; Mitchell 1997, 181–6). In contrast, none of the references to incidents of alleged Spartiate bribe-taking (assembled by Noethlichs 1987, nos. 9–11, 13, 15–23, 25–7) sets it in the context of *xenia* relationships. Moreover, Aristotle's criticism of the ephors' susceptibility to bribery (*Pol.* 1270b8–13) is explained in terms of their poverty. Such poor citizens were not the sort of men typically involved in *xeniai*.

¹⁸ Thuc. 1.128–30; Diod. 11.44.4. Although recent scholarship has been inclined to locate Pausanias' pro-Persian activities within the context of his second period abroad, rather than his first as Thucydides claims (e.g. Fornara 1966, 263–6; Rhodes 1970, 389, 391), their existence is not usually doubted.

¹⁹ Note that, although Lysander was apparently raised in poverty (Plut. *Lys.* 2.1), and hence may seem to disprove my argument that the possession of wealth was a key requirement for participation in *xeniai*, his circumstances were somewhat exceptional. Although Lysander's rise to prominence probably owed much to his sponsorship by the Eurypontid royal house and his *xenia* with Cyrus stemmed from his position as *nauarchos*, his family was well-born and his father had been a man involved in *xeniai* (Diod. 14.13.6). Without this background in the recent family past, Lysander's sponsorship by the Eurypontids and subsequent official command would have been unlikely.

²⁰ Douris, *FGrH* 76F26, 71, *ap.* Plut. *Lys.* 18.3–4; *AA* 1965, 440.

²¹ Although the existence of their *xenia* is not recorded in the sources until negotiations of subsequent years (Plut. *Pelop.* 30.4), it surely originated at their first face-to-face

22 Cf esp. Xen. *Hell.* 2.3.6–14; Lysias 12.71–6; Diod. 13.70.3–4, 107; Plut. *Lys.*, esp. 5.3–5; 7.1; 9.1–2; 13.3–4; 19.1–3.

23 e.g. Thucydides' account of the Spartans' installation of oligarchies in Sikyon and Argos after Mantineia in 418 (5.81; cf. 76).

24 Thuc. 5.36–7; Mitchell 1997, 52–3.

25 It might asked, in criticism of my suggestion, why the *perioikoi* are not mentioned among the *trophimoi* in Xenophon's list of Agesipolis' forces: the upper-class *perioikoi* (τῶν περιοίκων…καλοὶ κἀγαθοί) are listed instead as a special category of volunteers. There are two obvious reasons. One is that Xenophon was not writing a systematic account of Spartan social structure and he preferred instead to stress different attributes of the social categories which he mentioned. In the case of the *perioikoi*, he was concerned to stress the fact that – unlike the other groups – they were volunteers and that – unlike a normal perioikic levy – the men involved were all of the highest status. The other reason is that the perioikic contingent consisted of adults and hence were no longer *trophimoi*, whereas all the sons of *xenoi* must by definition have belonged to that category.

26 On their pederastic relationship, Plut. *Ages.* 2.1. On Lysander's assistance to Agesilaos regarding the kingship and Asian campaign, cf. esp. Xen. *Hell.* 3.3.1–4, 4.1–3; Plut. *Ages.* 3.3–5; 6.1–3; *Lys.* 22.5–6; 23.1–2.

27 ὡς ἂν καὶ τὰ ἴδια ἐκποιῶσιν: the authenticity of this clause, deemed corrupt by some editors, is defended by C.B. Gulick (Loeb edition of Athenaios, ad loc.).

28 Insertion of the word '*syntrophois*' is proposed by Lotze 1962, 429.

29 e.g. Lotze 1962; Michell 1964, 40–1; MacDowell 1986, 46–51. Besides Phylarchos and Aelian, the *mothakes* are also mentioned in several other less reliable pieces of evidence (Plut. *Kleom.* 8.1; Hesychios, μ 1538; [Herakleitos], *Epist.* 9.2). For the weaknesses of their accounts, Hodkinson 1997b, 56–60.

30 The treatment of *mothakes* by Daniel Ogden (1996, 218–24) had not yet appeared at the time my article was written; but I cannot agree with his approach. He argues that *mothakes* were the equivalent of *nothoi*, bastard sons of helot women, on the grounds that Aelian's reference to Kallikratidas, Gylippos and Lysander comes 'in the context of a chapter which is otherwise devoted to famous men reputed to be *nothoi* or low-born' (ibid. 218). Since, however, he concedes that several of the famous men mentioned elsewhere in the chapter were not *nothoi*, there is no reason to ascribe that status to the three Spartans. His subsequent discussion of these three men (222–3) produces no evidence for their bastardy, beyond the unsubstantiated speculation of Bommelaer (1981, 36–8) that Phylarchos' 'they say' might imply that Leotychidas, whose claim to the throne in 400 was hindered by his alleged bastardy, may have paid Lysander back in kind with a similar allegation following the latter's support for Agesilaos.

31 Polemon (*ap.* Athen. 139b–c), however, calls it 'the so-called *aiklon*'.

32 The term *phatta* (ring-dove or wood pigeon) used by Dikaiarchos usually signifies a wild bird (D.W. Thompson 1895, 177–9; Pollard 1977, 57).

33 As noted in chapter 7, Link (1998, 100–1) has suggested that the infamous 'black broth' was typically the poor man's contribution of *epaiklon*.

34 Wheat is less suited than barley to thin limestone soil, more susceptible to drought while germinating and more prone to disease in its longer period of maturation (Braun 1995, 25–6). In classical Attica even wealthy estates had to concentrate their cereal production exclusively or mainly on barley (Sallares 1991, 314, 477–8 n.65).

³⁵ My previous attribution of this latter passage to the late archaic poet Epicharmos (Hodkinson 1983, 254) represented a misreading of Athenaios' text.

³⁶ From Thucydides' description of the army structure at Mantineia in 418, it can be calculated that there were 154 officers (5.68). Similar calculations from the generic account of Xenophon (*Lak. Pol.* 11.4) give the number as 174. If one were to double the number of *enōmotiai* at Mantineia, as has been mooted (Gomme et al. 1945–81, iv.116), the number of officers would increase to around 270.

³⁷ The affair of the Andrians is otherwise unknown to us.

³⁸ Admittedly, the Gerousia is never mentioned by name in Xenophon's account of the affair; but we know from other evidence that it judged all major trials, with or without the addition of the five ephors (Ste Croix 1972, 132–3, with references).

³⁹ It is not necessary to believe Plutarch's claim that this *hetaireia* had been built up only in the brief period after Lysander's return from Asia or for the sole purpose of opposing Agesilaos (cf. D.R. Shipley 1997, 252–3).

⁴⁰ As Cartledge (1987, 151) remarks, although *hetairoi* in other poleis were typically age peers, 'friendship groupings composed of men equal in age…could not formally exist in Sparta, where the common messes were specifically designed to cut across age-grouping in the interests of promoting trans-generational solidarity'. Hence there is nothing unusual in Sphodrias, a commander perhaps in his 40s or early 50s (in view of his teenage son), having *hetairoi* in their 60s or above.

⁴¹ e.g. men like Xenokles, Skythes and Herippidas (Poralla 1985, nos. 569, 668, 349; cf. Cartledge 1987, 154).

PART IV

PROPERTY AND THE SPARTAN CRISIS

Chapter 12

SPARTIATE HOUSEHOLD ECONOMIES: TOWARDS AN ESTIMATE OF A BALANCE-SHEET

It is well known that, following her victory in the Peloponnesian war and acquisition of an unprecedented empire in mainland and Aegean Greece, Sparta's power underwent a rapid decline during the opening 35 years of the fourth century. This period saw the abandonment of her overseas empire, the collapse of her efforts to dominate the Greek mainland, and (above all) her loss of control over Messenia following its liberation during the enemy invasion of winter 370/69. Although some scholars would explain the decline of Spartan power in purely military terms, a more general consensus is that Sparta's military weakness was grounded in a shortage of citizen manpower – a shortage connected with increasing inequality of property ownership and the inability of poor Spartiates to pay the mess dues which were a requirement of citizenship (Arist. *Pol.* 1270a34–6). However, although the outlines of Sparta's problems have been generally recognised, the manifold connections between changes in the sphere of property and the growth of Sparta's internal crisis have not hitherto been explored in detail.

In Part III of this book it became clear that, despite the existence of a common lifestyle and commemoration of death, there remained an important gulf between ordinary citizens and an elite whose possession of significant surplus wealth enabled them to engage in a range of socio-political activities beyond the reach of the average Spartiate. In Part IV I shall examine how this gulf developed considerably during the course of the fifth and early fourth centuries and how it contributed to the Spartan crisis. In chapter 13 I will discuss the historical development of property concentration and the impoverishment of citizen households. The current chapter will explore the economic context for those developments.

The main obstacle to understanding this economic context is the difficulty of quantifying the economic demands upon citizen households, and how well they could meet those demands through the agricultural exploitation of their estates. The basic problem is our lack of statistical information concerning most of the critical variables, such as the size and consumption needs of citizen households, the extent of their estates, the number of helot labourers, and the productivity of Spartiate holdings. These difficulties have led some scholars to despair at the possibility of a quantitative approach and to question the value of the exercise (e.g. Michell 1964, 227–8). Certainly, any attempt at quantification must necessarily contain many points of uncertainty. It is impossible to draw up an exact balance-sheet of the production and outgoings of a 'typical' Spartiate household. But it may at least be possible to specify more closely than in previous studies the factors which require consideration, and to suggest some plausible estimates which, however hypothetical, would enable us to bring the economic circumstances of Spartiate households into sharper focus.

Demands upon citizen household economies

An initial step must be to specify the economic demands faced by citizen households. We should start with the question of food requirements. On this subject we can utilise recent studies (Foxhall and Forbes 1982; Gallant 1991) which have examined the evidence for ancient food rations in the light of modern estimates of human consumption requirements. This, however, immediately raises the question of the nature and extent of the Spartan household. How many and what group of persons did a citizen household comprise?

The composition and size of Spartiate households

First, we must consider those household members of citizen status. The composition of a Greek citizen household was dependent upon several variables. Most citizen households in ancient Greece constituted what historical demographers term the 'simple family household', comprising a nuclear family of a couple and their children (Gallant 1991, 22–6; Sallares 1991, 195–7). At any given point in time, however, there was also a significant minority of 'extended family households', which included other close kin – an ageing (usually female) parent, a younger unmarried sibling or other relatives such as orphaned cousins. This prevailing pattern of domestic co-residence was the product of a number of critical demographic parameters, such as age at and order of marriage, infant mortality rates and adult life expectancy (Gallant 1991, 17–22). Ancient Greece appears by and large to have shared what demographers of more recent periods have termed a 'Mediterranean marriage pattern', characterised by a high age of male marriage (around the late 20s or early 30s), a somewhat lower age for women (in the mid- to late teens) and a tendency for the marriages of men to be delayed until all or most of their sisters had been married off (Hajnal 1965; Cox 1988, 386). High rates of infant mortality have been predicated for ancient Greece as for many other pre-industrial societies.[1] The average age of death of those who survived into adulthood has been estimated at about 44 years for men and 36 for women, or perhaps a little higher (Angel 1969, 429; Sallares 1991, 109–16). The implication is that many parents – and especially fathers, given the late male age of marriage – died before their surviving children reached adulthood and marriage.

As for household size, comparative studies of human populations from a number of different times and places indicate that the most common mean household size is around 4–5 persons (e.g. Laslett 1972, 61 table 1.3, 76 table 1.6). Calculations based upon information about (mainly elite) families in classical Attica suggest that the residential and demographic parameters mentioned above produced a similar mean figure (Raepset 1973; Gallant 1991, 23–4). Of course, within any population there is at any given moment considerable variation around this mean, due to the effects of differential reproduction and the varying incidence and timing of child and adult mortalities. The fact of differential reproduction and completed family size within contemporary Greek poleis was taken for granted by Aristotle.[2] There are also variations in household size during the life-history of any individual household as it increases or decreases through childbearing, the marrying-out of its children and the death of parents and grandparents. Furthermore, any given household size may conceal significant differences in family composition. A five-person household of a couple, two infants and an aged grandparent, for example, is very different both in character and in food requirements from one comprising a lone surviving spouse and four adolescents.

How did the size and composition of Spartiate citizen households compare with these general Greek patterns? Spartan households apparently shared the nuclear orientation of other Greek households. This is the implication of Herodotus' comment (5.40) on the double-marriage of King Anaxandridas that 'henceforth he lived with two wives in two separate houses', as also of Xenophon's remark (*Lak. Pol.* 1.9) that the attraction of wife-sharing arrangements to Spartan women was that it enabled them to take charge of two households. It is notable that, even in the case of wife-sharing, where two men procreated through the same woman and the children of the second man were considered to belong to the *genos* of the original husband, the two men did not join together to form what demographers term a 'multiple – or joint – family unit', comprising two co-resident conjugal families. In fact, Spartiate residence arrangements followed inheritance rights. Separate nuclear households were retained under wife-sharing because each man's property went only to the children he had personally sired. Similarly, Anaxandridas' two wives will have passed on their personal property separately to their own offspring. No doubt, as in other poleis, many nuclear households came at some point(s) during their life-cycle to embrace elderly parents or unmarried minors.[3] Although the sparse literary evidence provides no attested examples of 'extended family households' during the classical period itself, the household in which the mid-third-century king, Agis IV, was reared apparently included his grandmother Archidamia (Plut. *Agis* 4.1).

The fact that most Spartiate households shared the widespread basic alternation between 'simple family' and 'extended family' structure may imply that the mean household size of between 4 and 5 persons applied in Sparta as much as elsewhere.[4] Nevertheless, Spartiate households do display some significant differences from households elsewhere. Although there is no reason to doubt that Sparta shared many of the general features of the 'Mediterranean marriage pattern', the mean age of marriage was a little different. The female age of marriage lay at the upper end of general Greek norms, in the late teens (Xen. *Lak. Pol.* 1.6; Plut. *Lyk.* 15.3; Cartledge 1981, 94–5; MacDowell 1986, 72–3). In contrast, by the fourth century, at least, all Spartiate men were legally obliged to marry by age 30; hence most men probably married slightly younger than elsewhere, in their late 20s (Cartledge 1981, 94–5; Hodkinson 1989, 109). Consequently, more fathers probably survived into their children's adulthood than elsewhere in Greece, implying a somewhat larger proportion of extended family households. The incentives offered by the polis to men with three or more sons may also have produced some larger family sizes.[5] The practice of adelphic polyandry – that is, of several brothers sharing a single wife – attested by Polybius (12.6b.8) also presumably involved larger household units. Although Polybius does not specify the precise residential arrangements, the several men and their joint wife probably lived under the same roof.[6] On the other hand, in some families the practice of wife-sharing will have limited household size. Under this arrangement both the woman's husband and the man with whom she subsequently cohabited retained their separate households, and one woman's fertility was spread between both. The implication of these local peculiarities is that Spartiate households probably displayed even more diversity in size and composition than did households in other poleis, due to greater variation in the size of completed families, in the composition of the adult membership and in the age spans covered by extended family households.

A second group of persons to consider is the servile labour force. As we have seen (ch. 7; cf. Hodkinson 1997b), the literary sources suggest that all Spartiate households possessed servile attendants, indeed that they had a greater dependence upon servile labour for their domestic activities than did citizen households in other poleis. We have no direct evidence regarding numbers of household servants. Some intimation of minimum numbers may be derived from the range of tasks they fulfilled. Female servants are depicted as serving the female members of the household: attending their mistress, caring for her children, and performing domestic work (Plut. *Ages.* 3.1; Hdt. 6.61; Xen. *Lak. Pol.* 1.3–4). Male servants are mentioned in public contexts: sometimes with their masters, for example, as batmen on campaign;[7] sometimes on their own (Xen. *Lak. Pol.* 6.3). The implication is that both master and mistress required at least one servant each in their separate public and domestic lives. At times in the household's life-cycle the demands of child-rearing may have necessitated more female servants. Wealthier households no doubt had higher numbers of household staff: Timaia, the wife of Agis II, had several maids (Plut. *Ages.* 3.1); and the groom with whom King Damaratos' mother was rumoured to have had intercourse (Hdt. 6.68) was doubtless a specialised servant typical among horse-rearing households. As we saw in chapter 11, the sons of wealthy families had their own personal servants too, the *mothōnes*, boys of servile origin brought up alongside the citizen boys as their attendants.

In the same chapter we noted that there were also other economically-dependent persons attached to certain Spartiate households, youths of intermediate status between slave and citizen: the *nothoi*, bastard sons of Spartiates and helot women;[8] the *mothakes*, sons of disfranchised citizens; and the foreign *trophimoi* or foster-children, who were sons of the *xenoi* of leading Spartiates (Xen. *Hell.* 5.3.9). The economic responsibility of the Spartiate host household to all these youths was above all to subsidise their participation in the public upbringing.

The most striking point to emerge from this analysis is the variety in the size and composition of Spartiate households, due to socio-economic differentiation, varying marriage practices and natural demographic diversity. The consequent differences in the food requirements of these diverse households were further exacerbated by official policy and established social practice: as we saw in chapter 7, Spartan girls were typically fed more generously than in other poleis; whereas the food provided for the boys in the upbringing was abnormally sparse. Most importantly, the food requirements of households containing adult males were markedly increased by the mess dues, which were significantly higher than normal subsistence requirements (see ch. 6).

Estimated food requirements: two model Spartiate households

Given this diversity, it is clearly impossible to identify a 'standard' Spartan household whose food requirements we could conveniently estimate. The best one can do is to outline some estimates for various permutations of household size and composition. My especial concern in this chapter is to illuminate the position of 'ordinary' Spartiate households and of somewhat poorer households facing economic difficulties. I have therefore constructed, as illustrative case-studies, the hypothetical life cycles of two attested forms of Spartiate households: a 'normal' monogamous household; and a polyandrous household, as detailed by Polybius, in which three brothers pooled their scant resources by sharing a single wife. The life cycle of the monogamous household is based upon the hypothetical ancient Greek household life cycle constructed in the study by Gallant (1991, 27–30), with some modification to take account of the comparatively late age of female marriage in Sparta and somewhat earlier age of male marriage. That of the polyandrous household is constructed upon similar lines. To the composition of these households at each stage of their life cycles,

Property and the Spartan crisis

I have applied the daily calorific consumption requirements by gender and age suggested by Gallant on the basis of a range of scientific and comparative evidence (1991, 62–75, esp. table 4.5). The outcome of these calculations is given in TABLES 19 and 20. Once again, certain modifications have been made to take account of factors peculiar to Sparta. The adult male 'consumption requirement' is based upon the daily 6,420 calories of foodstuffs that they contributed to their common mess (ch. 6) and has been rounded up to 7,000 calories to account for additional food consumed outside the mess. In contrast, due to the attested sparse diet of Spartan boys, I have recorded the food contributions of households for their teenage boys at the low figure of 2,600 calories, the figure for 10–12 year old males in Gallant's table.[9] Finally, since Gallant records no figure for the calorific needs of children under age 4, I have

TABLE 19. Monogamous household: composition and daily calorific requirements of citizen members.

			HOUSEHOLD COMPOSITION				
Year	Husb	Wife	Widow	Sib	Child 1	Child 2	Child 3	Bride
0	AM	F16–19	AF	AM				
3	AM	APF	AF	AM	M0–3			
6	AM	APF	AF		M4–6	F0–3		
9	AM	APF			M7–9	F4–6	M0–3	
12	AM	AF			M10–12	F7–9	M4–6	
15	AM	AF			M13–15	F10–12	M7–9	
18	AM	AF			M16–19	F13–15	M10–12	
21	AM	AF			AM		M13–15	
24		AF			AM		M16–19	
27		AF			AM		AM	F16–19

			DAILY CALORIE REQUIREMENTS					
Year	Husb	Wife	Widow	Sib	Child 1	Child 2	Child 3	Bride	Total
0	7000 +	2310 +	2200 +	7000					18510
3	7000 +	2500 +	2200 +	7000 +	1000				19700
6	7000 +	2500 +	2200 +		1830 +	1000			14530
9	7000 +	2500 +			2190 +	1830 +	1000		14520
12	7000 +	2200 +			2600 +	2190 +	1830		15820
15	7000 +	2200 +			2600 +	2350 +	2190		16340
18	7000 +	2200 +			2600 +	2490 +	2600		16890
21	7000 +	2200 +			7000 +		2600		18800
24		2200 +			7000 +		2600		11800
27		2200 +			7000 +		7000 +	2310	18510

Key: AM = Adult Male; AF = Adult Female; APF = Adult Pregnant or Breastfeeding Female; M/F4–6 etc. = Male/Female aged 4–6 years and so on.

Ch. 12. Spartiate household economies: towards an estimate of a balance-sheet

used the low figure of 1,000 calories per day for this group, partly on the assumption that the younger among them, at least, would obtain much of their nutritional needs through breastfeeding.

A few words about the development of these household life cycles are in order. The monogamous household in TABLE 19 is viewed initially in the first triennium after the marriage of the couple (Year 0), when the groom is in his mid–late 20s and the bride in her high teens. The members of the household at this stage include the groom's widowed mother and an unmarried, adolescent younger brother in his early 20s. (Owing to the Spartiate upbringing, the two male members are of course not physically resident in the household, but the household is responsible for the payment of their mess dues.) By the second triennium (Year 3) the couple have a nursing infant male; hence the demands

TABLE 20. Polyandrous household: composition and daily calorific requirements of citizen members

HOUSEHOLD COMPOSITION

Year	Husb	Husb	Husb	Wife	Widow	Child 1	Child 2	Child 3	Bride
0	AM	AM	AM	F16–19	AF				
3	AM	AM	AM	APF	AF	M0–3			
6	AM	AM	AM	APF		M4–6	F0–3		
9	AM	AM	AM	APF		M7–9	F4–6	M0–3	
12	AM	AM	AM	AF		M10–12	F7–9	M4–6	
15	AM	AM	AM	AF		M13–15	F10–12	M7–9	
18	AM	AM	AM	AF		M16–19	F13–15	M10–12	
21		AM	AM	AF		AM		M13–15	
24		AM	AM	AF		AM		M16–19	
27			AM	AF		AM		AM	F16–19

DAILY CALORIE REQUIREMENTS

Year	Husb	Husb	Husb	Wife	Widow	Child 1	Child 2	Child 3	Bride	Total
0	7000 +	7000 +	7000 +	2310 +	2200					25510
3	7000 +	7000 +	7000 +	2500 +	2200 +	1000				26700
6	7000 +	7000 +	7000 +	2500 +		1830 +	1000			26330
9	7000 +	7000 +	7000 +	2500 +		2190 +	1830 +	1000		28520
12	7000 +	7000 +	7000 +	2200 +		2600 +	2190 +	1830		29820
15	7000 +	7000 +	7000 +	2200 +		2600 +	2350 +	2190		30340
18	7000 +	7000 +	7000 +	2200 +		2600 +	2490 +	2600		30890
21		7000 +	7000 +	2200 +		7000 +		2600		25800
24		7000 +	7000 +	2200 +		7000 +		2600		25800
27			7000 +	2200 +		7000 +		7000 +	2310	25510

Key: AM = Adult Male; AF = Adult Female; APF = Adult Pregnant or Breastfeeding Female; M/F4–6 etc. = Male/Female aged 4–6 years and so on.

on the household's food supply now reach a peak of some 19,700 calories per day. By the third triennium (Year 6) these demands have declined due to the death of the elderly widow and the marriage of the younger brother. The household is now purely a 'simple family household', consisting of the couple and their children. Over the following four triennia (Years 9–18) this household grows to include three surviving children (boy–girl–boy). As the children grow up, the household's calorific requirements increase. They reach a secondary peak in the seventh triennium (Year 21), despite the departure of the daughter in marriage, owing to the elder son's acquisition of adulthood and responsibility for mess dues. They decline sharply in the eighth triennium (Year 24) due to the death of the household head, only to rise equally sharply by Year 27 when the younger son reaches adulthood and the elder son marries. The household now returns to its original composition as in Year 0. It is worth noting, however, that, had the father survived into the adulthood of his two sons (as a sizeable number of Spartiate fathers no doubt did), the demands on the household would at this stage have grown to the highest peak in the entire cycle, at some 25,510 daily calories.

The development of the polyandrous household can be followed in similar terms. The hypothesis underlying the construction of its life cycle is that the brothers in question, faced with a serious diminution in their individual holdings should they split the parental inheritance, decide to share a wife as a means of stabilising their properties and reducing the number of their heirs. The household is first viewed at this point (Year 0). The brothers are all in their 20s, with the eldest already approaching the age of 30, by which time he was legally obliged to marry. (One difference from the case of the monogamous household is that it is assumed that the timing of the joint marriage had been delayed until the youngest son had reached adulthood and become legally entitled to marry; hence the widowed mother also survives a shorter time into the period of marriage.) At this point (Year 0), as they support their widowed mother and all three brothers are responsible for mess dues, their daily food requirement, at 25,510 calories, is some 38% higher than that of the monogamous household. Between the third and seventh triennia (Years 6–18) the gap between the food requirements of the two households increases dramatically to between 81% and 96% Whereas the monogamous household drops markedly in size with the marriage of the younger brother and death of the mother, the polyandrous household retains all its adult male members and increases in size with the birth and growth of its children, reaching a peak daily food requirement of 30,890 calories in Year 18. Finally, however, in the eighth to tenth triennia (Years 21–27) demand begins to fall steadily, with the deaths of two of the three brothers outweighing the adulthood of the household's two sons. The survival of the youngest brother, however, ensures that food requirements remain (at least temporarily) quite high. At this stage the two adult sons face the choice whether they should emulate their fathers by taking a shared bride or marry individually, thereby dividing their resources and each assuming the burden of maintaining a separate household.

To the calorific requirements of the citizen members of these households, we need to add those of its household servants. Since neither household is wealthy, I shall assume the minimum level of staffing for each household's needs. In the case of the monogamous household, we may set the minimum household staff at one male and one female servant. The household would also need to consider whether it could afford additional female servants to help with child-rearing and additional male attendants, *mothōnes*, for its boys. Perhaps many households which could only just afford an extra servant might employ an additional female servant when its children were young, switching to an additional male attendant as its sons left the home at age 7 to enter the public upbringing. (I assume that these servants could be drawn from and returned to the helot farming families who worked the household's landholdings.) For the polyandrous household, the need for male attendants will have been even greater since, although the three brothers might conceivably have shared an attendant during peacetime at home, on campaign each would have required a personal batman. For the purposes of calculation, I have compromised by postulating a minimum of two male servants.

At what level to set the calorific demands of helot servants is a difficult problem since, despite their high levels of physical activity, they may often have been underfed, especially in households with limited resources. On Sphakteria in 425 the rations of the attendants of Lakedaimonian troops were only half those of their masters (Thuc. 4.16). I have set the calorific requirements of helot servants at a (perhaps somewhat generous) two-thirds of the rations of citizens of an equivalent age. As for the age of helot servants, I adopt the working hypothesis that the primary attendants of the husband and wife were normally of similar ages to their master and mistress. The male attendant may have started as a young *mothōn* attendant brought up alongside his master in the upbringing. Similarly, if the primary female servant was required to act as a wet-nurse, she too would ideally be of similar childbearing age to her mistress. Otherwise, a second female servant may have been an adolescent girl, of a suitable age for accompanying citizen daughters out of doors.

On the basis of these considerations TABLES 21 and 22 set out the additional calorific requirements hypothetically implied by the presence of household servants. It was clearly not insignificant. In the monogamous household, servants account for between about 19% and 45% of overall consumption requirements; in the polyandrous household between about 21% and 30%. For richer households who maintained a larger domestic staff and also a sizeable group of *nothoi*, *mothakes* and sons of *xenoi*, we must envisage much higher figures for calorific demands.

Property and the Spartan crisis

TABLE 21. Monogamous household: composition and daily calorific needs of household servants (minimum staffing), with calculation of total household needs

Year	Composition				Daily rations			
0	AM	F16–19			2000 +	1540		
3	AM	APF	F13–15		2000 +	1667 +	1660	
6	AM	APF	F16–19		2000 +	1667 +	1540	
9	AM	APF	AF	M7–9	2000 +	1667 +	1467 +	1460
12	AM	AF		M10–12	2000 +	1467 +		1733
15	AM	AF		M13–15	2000 +	1467 +		1933
18	AM	AF		M16–19	2000 +	1467 +		2047
21	AM	AF		AM	2000 +	1467 +		2000
24		AF		AM		1467 +		2000
27		AF		AM		1467 +		2000

Year	Servant calories	Citizen calories	Total calories
0	3540	18510	22050
3	5327	19700	25027
6	5207	14530	19737
9	6594	14520	21114
12	5200	15820	21020
15	5400	16340	21740
18	5514	16890	22404
21	5467	18800	24267
24	3467	11800	15267
27	3467	18510	21977

Key: AM = Adult Male; AF = Adult Female; APF = Adult Pregnant or Breastfeeding Female; M/F13–15 etc. = Male/Female aged 13–15 years and so on.

The above calculations provide some indication of the basic food requirements of certain types of Spartiate households. Note, however, that no household will have been content merely to provide itself with the minimum of subsistence. Literary, epigraphic and archaeological evidence from ancient Greece itself concurs with comparative evidence from around the globe that households in agrarian societies typically aim to produce a significant annual surplus of crops over and above the minimum subsistence requirements in order to build up a sizeable store of foodstuffs – frequently in the range of 10–16 months' worth – upon which they could fall back in years of crop failure or other deprivation.[10] These considerations apply as much to Spartiate households as to those of subsistence peasants, since the socio-political consequences of failure to meet one's mess dues or – in the case of richer households – to maintain one's retinue of dependants were sufficiently severe for the accumulation of surplus foodstuffs to be a vital household strategy.

Ch. 12. Spartiate household economies: towards an estimate of a balance-sheet

TABLE 22. Polyandrous household: composition and daily calorific needs of household servants (minimum staffing) with calculation of total household needs.

Year	Composition					Daily rations
0	AM	AM	F16–19			2000 + 2000 + 1540
3	AM	AM	APF	F13–15		2000 + 2000 + 1667 + 1660
6	AM	AM	APF	F16–19		2000 + 2000 + 1667 + 1540
9	AM	AM	APF	AF	M7–9	2000 + 2000 + 1667 + 1467 + 1460
12	AM	AM	AF		M10–12	2000 + 2000 + 1467 + 1733
15	AM	AM	AF		M13–15	2000 + 2000 + 1467 + 1933
18	AM	AM	AF		M16–19	2000 + 2000 + 1467 + 2047
21	AM	AM	AF		AM	2000 + 2000 + 1467 + 2000
24	AM	AM	AF		AM	2000 + 2000 + 1467 + 2000
27		AM	AF		AM	2000 + 1467 + 2000

Year	Servant calories	Citizen calories	Total calories
0	5540	25510	31050
3	7327	26700	34027
6	7207	26330	33537
9	8594	28520	37114
12	7200	29820	37020
15	7400	30340	37740
18	7514	30890	38404
21	7467	25800	33267
24	7467	25800	33267
27	5467	25510	30977

Key: AM = Adult Male; AF = Adult Female; APF = Adult Pregnant or Breastfeeding Female; M/F13–15 etc. = Male/Female aged 13–15 years and so on.

Other expenditures

The provision of food of course by no means exhausted the demands on household resources. In an agrarian society most households face other necessary expenses which cannot be supplied from their own resources. The funds for these have to be provided out of surplus agricultural production. These expenses may be either economic or social in character – what Eric Wolf in his general study of peasants (1966, 6–7) has termed, respectively, 'replacement' and 'ceremonial' fund. In the former category, Gallant (1991, 92–3) identifies four main capital demands on ancient Greek peasants – building timbers, livestock, metal and agricultural tools, and terracotta products – besides more regular expenditures on items such as salt, charcoal, wood and honey. How applicable were these demands to Spartiate households?

One item which requires significant qualification is the classification of livestock as a capital drain. It is perhaps true that large livestock, such as plough oxen, had to be acquired by purchase or other form of exchange, since probably only wealthier households were in a position to breed cattle. The opposite, however, was surely true of sheep and goats, which were less expensive to maintain and whose reproductive growth rate is considerably higher (Dahl and Hjort 1976, 232–4). As we shall see, the majority of Spartiates, at least before the later fifth century, probably owned estates of a size to support herds of a sufficient size for breeding to be feasible, not only for replacement purposes, but also for the generation of surplus animals. Despite the high disease risks of pastoral activity before the advent of modern veterinary medicine, which sometimes led to the sudden decimation of herds, it is unlikely that the purchase of additional small livestock was a regular drain on the household economy. On the contrary, the possession of livestock obviated one major potential drain on household resources omitted by Gallant – the supply of clothing. Although, as we saw in chapter 7, Spartan dress was relatively simple in character, the supply of clothing for an entire household, including helots and dependants, would have been a significant regular expense, were it necessary to purchase in the market rather than make the clothes within the household using wool from one's own flocks.

The position regarding the other economic expenses is unclear. Most of Gallant's evidence derives from classical Athens, which possessed a significant non-agrarian sector. At Athens a sizeable number of households (non-citizen as well as citizen) lacked the capacity to acquire raw materials from their own resources or to produce their own agricultural equipment. They were, consequently, reliant on purchase in the market. Clearly, some considerable adjustment is needed, given the overwhelmingly agrarian basis of Spartan household economies. As was seen in chapter 5, there is no reason to deny absolutely the role of the market in the supply of some household necessities. The problem is rather to define the extent of that role and to identify those products for which most Spartiate households were (and were not) reliant upon market supply. Regarding the items mentioned by Gallant, it is likely that more households than elsewhere in Greece had access to timber supplies for building and fuel on or near to their country estates.[11] We should surely envisage a similar situation also for products such as honey. The situation regarding manufactured products, such as metal tools and terracotta vessels, involves two further issues which both suggest that we should not expect uniform practice by all citizen households. First, there is the uncertainty noted in chapter 5 whether the prohibition from banausic activities precluded citizen households from setting up their own craft workshops manned by their helots. However, such sponsorship of craft activity, if it existed, would surely have been largely restricted to wealthier households. The presence at Sparta of an iron market containing tools for agriculture, forestry and stonework (Xen. *Hell.* 3.3.7) suggests that many citizen households were reliant upon it for manufactured

Ch. 12. Spartiate household economies: towards an estimate of a balance-sheet

metal products. Secondly, there is the question whether responsibility for the supply of agricultural equipment lay with Spartiate households or their helot cultivators. In chapter 4 I suggested the probability of considerable variation from one farm to the next, according to geographical distance from Sparta and the extent of direct citizen management of the estate. Spartiate owners who personally supervised their estates in the Eurotas valley may have taken responsibility for the provision of farming tools. Conversely, it is unlikely that helot cultivators of distant landholdings were dependent upon infrequent provision from an absentee landowner. No doubt the helot farming communities of Messenia, and perhaps the further regions of Lakonia, will have possessed their own small-scale pottery and metal workshops which supplied local needs independently of the rentier master class. In general, then, it seems that Spartiate households, although not exempt from 'replacement fund' expenditures for the maintenance and running of their homes and estates, incurred them at a lower level than citizen households in Athens.

The same was probably also true of necessary social expenditures. (Here I would emphasize the word 'necessary'.) We have seen in recent chapters a variety of spheres in which wealthier Spartiates could deploy their surplus wealth. It is clear, however, that the social expenses of ordinary citizens were on a much lower plane. In several key areas of Spartiate life – the upbringing, dress and equipment, marriage, funerary practice – no more than a limited outlay was necessary to fulfil the requirements of citizenship. The high degree of public control over other critical moments of transition, such as birth and the passage into adulthood, suggests that these too involved minimal household celebrations and expenditures.[12] To these reduced ceremonial expenses we can add that the provisions for the communal use of private property, though limited in scope, did give ordinary citizens access to some additional items belonging to wealthier Spartiates, especially dogs for the civic activity of hunting, without the expense of personal ownership.

Overall, therefore, the necessary extra-household expenditures of Spartiate families were significantly lower than those of their counterparts in other poleis. Hence, whereas Gallant suggested adding an extra 10% of costs for the household's replacement and ceremonial fund on top of its essential food requirements, for Spartiate households a more conservative figure of 5% will be used in my calculations. Although these extra-household expenditures are different in character from the food consumption requirements earlier, the justification for expressing them in terms of calorific requirements – quite apart from the convenience of a single standard of measure – is that such costs had to be met out of surplus agricultural production. In TABLES 23 and 24 the figure of 5% is applied to the daily calorific requirements of the hypothetical monogamous and polyandrous households calculated in TABLES 21 and 22 to produce an overall estimate of the level of daily calorie production required to sustain these households.

Property and the Spartan crisis

TABLE 23. Monogamous household: daily food and non-food calorific demands.

Year	Food needs (calories)	Other costs (5%)	Total demands (calories)
0	22050	1103	23153
3	25027	1251	26278
6	19737	987	20724
9	21114	1056	22170
12	21020	1051	22071
15	21740	1087	22827
18	22404	1120	23524
21	24267	1213	25480
24	15267	763	16030
27	21977	1099	23076

TABLE 24. Polyandrous household: daily food and non-food calorific demands.

Year	Food needs (calories)	Other costs (5%)	Total demands (calories)
0	31050	1553	32603
3	34027	1701	34728
6	33537	1677	35214
9	37114	1856	38970
12	37020	1851	38871
15	37740	1887	39627
18	38404	1920	40324
21	33267	1663	34930
24	33267	1663	34930
27	30977	1549	32526

The size of Spartiate estates

Having made some estimate of the production demands faced by Spartiate households, our next step is to examine the landed resources which were available to meet those burdens. First, however, we must face the question: is it possible to make any estimates of the size of Spartiate estates? Certainly, there have been numerous previous attempts to do so. Before examining previous calculations, or making our own, some general considerations need to be taken into account.

The most fundamental issue is whether there was ever such an entity as an 'average' citizen estate or whether we must reckon with utter diversity in the landholdings belonging to different households. As we have already seen in chapters 3 and 4, the answer to this question must be mixed. The creation of a citizen body of full-time warriors in the archaic period must have entailed giving poorer citizen households additional land to that which they already possessed, in order to bring their holdings up to a basic minimum which, when half the produce was delivered by the helot labourers, would provide each household with a tolerably secure subsistence. We cannot be certain whether this allocation of additional land was made in piecemeal fashion or through a general assignment to all citizens of a share of newly-conquered territory, such as that in Messenia. It is clear, however, that, despite the later myth, there was no global *re*-distribution of existing landholdings into equal plots. It was not until the 220s that King Kleomenes III enforced Sparta's first-ever pooling and egalitarian redistribution of landed property (Plut. *Kleom.* 11.1–2). Consequently, whilst there may have existed at some point in the archaic period a notional minimum quantity of land which was used as the basis for establishing citizens as full-time warriors, certain households will even then have

Ch. 12. Spartiate household economies: towards an estimate of a balance-sheet

possessed amounts above the minimum. Moreover, even the newly-distributed holdings will not have remained intact in subsequent generations, but will have been subject to the normal processes of fragmentation and concentration stemming from the prevailing system of partible inheritance.

These considerations suggest that the foundations of many past attempts to calculate the size of classical Spartiate estates are insecure. Several scholars have used as their starting point the statement of Plutarch (*Lyk.* 8.3–4) that each of 9,000 Spartiate households was allocated an equal *klēros* from which its helot cultivators were obliged to deliver an *apophora* consisting of an annual 82 – presumably Lakonian – *medimnoi* of barley (70 *medimnoi* for their master and 12 for his wife), with proportionate quantities of 'fresh produce'.[13] These figures, however, cannot be used directly as the basis for estimating estate sizes in the classical period, since – as seen in chapter 4 – they are inextricably linked to the unhistorical notion of permanently equal Spartiate *klēroi*. These equal *klēroi*, as we saw in chapter 3, bore no relation to the reality of land tenure in the archaic or classical periods, but formed part of the programme of Agis and Kleomenes in the later third century who artificially retrojected them into earlier periods.

A different method of estimating the size of classical citizen estates, one which focuses exclusively upon the contemporary archaic and classical situation, is via an estimation of the area of cultivable land available for Spartiate use in Lakonia and Messenia. I suggested in chapter 4 that about 90,000 ha were available in Messenia and something under 50,000 ha in Lakonia. For the purposes of calculation, I shall use 45,000 ha for the latter figure, thus making a total of some 135,000 ha of cultivable land. If we divide this figure by the highest trustworthy figure for the number of Spartiates, the 8,000 citizens in the year 480 indicated by Herodotus (7.234), the result is a mean landholding size per *person* of 16.88 ha. In fact, however, the mean size of landholding per *household* should work out somewhat higher, since by no means all 8,000 citizens will have been the heads of separate households. As we saw above, during certain stages of its life cycle even a monogamous household could contain two, three or even more adult citizens, due to the presence of unmarried adult siblings or sons. In a plausible model life table such as the Princeton Model South, Mortality Level 3, Growth Rate 0 (Coale and Demeny 1983, 449), men aged 20–24 account for some 14.4% of the adult male population and men aged 25–29 a further 13.4%. On the assumption (given a mean male age of marriage in the late 20s) that all the 20–24 year olds and a third of the 25–29 year olds were as yet unmarried, the number of households in a citizen population of 8,000 would be of the order of 6,500.[14] A figure of 6,500 households would imply a mean landholding size of 20.77 ha per household.

This mean estate size does not of course tell us the average size of the holding of an 'ordinary' Spartan citizen, since landholding was always unequal. How much allowance we should make for landed inequalities is a matter of debate; but it has been estimated that in classical Attica some 9% of citizen households owned about 40% of the usable land (Foxhall 1992, 157). If we apply these figures to the cultivable territory of Lakonia, the original heartland of Spartan territory, some 585 out of 6500 Spartiate households would have owned 18,000 ha out of a total of 45,000 ha, with the remaining 5915 households sharing the remaining 27,000 ha. This is equivalent to an average estate size of 30.77 ha for the elite and only 4.56 ha for other Spartiates.[15] On the assumption that the territory of Messenia, in contrast, was originally distributed more equitably (whatever its distribution in later times), its 90,000 ha, shared between the entire citizen body of 6,500 households, would amount to some 13.85 ha per household. The mean size of the landholdings of ordinary citizens would thus be some 18.41 ha and those of the elite some 44.62 ha.

Obviously, we should not press these figures too hard. The calculation, however, does at least provide a plausible indication of the situation whilst Spartiate citizen numbers stood at the high level indicated by Herodotus, before their decline later in the fifth century. In fact, my figure of 18.41 ha for the mean size of ordinary citizen landholdings provides a reasonable match with recent calculations by other scholars. It is not far above Figueira's estimate (1984, 104) of a standard Spartiate *klēros* of some 15.4 ha and very near to Jameson's suggestion (1992, 137) that the size of a Spartiate farm was probably close to 18 ha (cf. also Cartledge 1987, 173).

Spartiate holdings of this size would also make sense in terms of evidence from elsewhere in Greece. Recent scholarship is agreed that a 'typical' subsistence family farm in classical and hellenistic Greece was generally of the order of around 3.6–5.4 ha, or 40–60 *plethra* in ancient Greek units of measure (Burford Cooper 1977/8; Gallant 1991, 86–7). In this context, a mean ordinary Spartiate estate size of the order of 18.4 ha, or 204 *plethra*, would be quite realistic, given that half the estate had to support the helot labour force. An effective holding of some 9.2 ha would fit with the likelihood that the 'basic minimum' of land given to ordinary households must have been set relatively high, so as to ensure some reasonable margin against inevitable fluctuations in annual crop production, since a Spartiate's status depended upon his delivery of produce to the mess. My estimates also accord with recent assessments of the size of wealthy estates in Athens. According to the evidence of [Plato], *Alkibiades I* (122d) – quoted in chapter 3 – Spartiate estates were larger than the holdings even of wealthy landowners in Athens. Foxhall's recent study has estimated that of the top 2,000 Athenian households, a half possessed holdings between 10 and 20 ha, and the other half estates between 20 and 50 ha (1992, 157). My figure of 18.4 ha for the average size of an 'ordinary' Spartiate citizen estate fits well with Foxhall's estimates in that it is higher than the holdings of all but the richest Athenians, precisely as the *Alkibiades I* states. Similarly, my calculation that, at 44.62 ha, the *average* property holding of wealthy Spartiates exceeded those of most rich Athenians accords well with the passage's

Ch. 12. Spartiate household economies: towards an estimate of a balance-sheet

somewhat exaggerated claim that 'not one of our estates could compare with theirs in extent'.

Agricultural production on citizen estates

Thus far I have attempted to estimate, first, the size and economic requirements of Spartiate households and, secondly, the size of Spartiate estates. I shall now attempt to close the circle by estimating the productive capacity of citizen estates, in order to assess how well they could meet the economic demands placed upon them. In this, as earlier in the chapter, I shall draw – with certain modifications – upon the methods used by Thomas Gallant in his widely-acclaimed study of citizen farming households in ancient Greece (1991, 60–112).

Helot population and agriculture

First, however, we need to take account of one important difference between Spartiate households and the households analysed by Gallant. In his study Gallant developed a simulation which assessed the interaction of ongoing changes in the consumption needs, labour availability and landholding size of a model citizen farming household. In his simulation each of the above factors fluctuates according to a single variable: namely, the household's changing composition. This kind of unified model simulation, however, is not appropriate to the Spartan situation, since Spartiate households were rentier landowners whose holdings were cultivated by the helots. Hence, although the consumption needs and holdings of Spartiate households fluctuated according to their changing composition, as in other poleis, the availability of labour depended upon a different and largely independent variable, namely, the life cycles of the helot households who farmed their landholdings.[16] Analysis of the productive capacity of Spartiate estates must start from the angle of helot farming households, partly because they supplied the necessary labour, partly because, given the prevailing 50/50 sharecropping relationship, the disparity of helot numbers over those of Spartan citizens meant that, in so far as Spartiate–helot landholdings were geared to the production of basic foodstuffs, the critical subsistence pressures fell upon the helots.

We do not know the exact size of the helot farming population. As noted in chapter 4, modern estimates range from 140,000 to 375,000. The literary evidence relates to only one moment in time. Herodotus (9.10, 28–9) informs us that each of 5,000 Spartiates at the battle of Plataia in 479 BC was accompanied by seven helots; so the number of adult male helots at that time must have been at least 35,000. However, at least one of the seven helots attached to each citizen will have been his personal household servant. Hence the number of helot *farmers* at Plataia will have been 30,000 at most. This is clearly only a minimum figure for the total number of helot farmers, since the Spartans are unlikely to have committed their entire workforce to the battle.

The difficulty is to know how far above this minimum figure we should go. The Spartans often operated their military recruitment on the basis of a two-thirds levy. Indeed, Figueira (1986, 167–8) has suggested that this was levy of Spartan citizens at Plataia.[17] If this was the proportion of helot *farmers* recruited for Plataia, it would imply a total of 45,000 adult male helot farmers between ages 20 and 60. On the model life table used earlier (Princeton Model South, Mortality Level 3, Growth Rate 0), this would imply a total adult male helot farming population of about 52,000.[18] On the assumption that about 20% of these would be young unmarried men, this would imply some 41,600 helot families.[19] On the standard multiplier of 4½ persons per family, this would mean an overall farming population of about 187,000. Alternatively, it is often suggested that the 7:1 ratio at Plataia may reflect the Spartans' perception of the overall ratio of adult male numbers within the respective populations (Jameson 1992, 136–7). Application of this ratio to the figure of 8,000 citizens given by Herodotus (7.234) would yield a global figure of 56,000 adult male helots, or (once household servants are deducted) 48,000 adult males in the helot farming population. If 20% of these were young unmarried men, this would yield some 36,000 helot farming families. Application of the standard multiplier of 4½ persons per family would indicate a total farming population of some 162,000. This calculation, consequently, provides a result of the same order of magnitude as that reached on the assumption of a two-thirds levy. My estimates of some 162,000–187,000 helots are also not far from the estimate of 175,000–200,000 suggested by Cartledge (1987, 174).

Although my estimates stand towards the lower end of the range of modern estimates, for a helot population of even this size to support itself off 135,000 ha of available land in Lakonia and Messenia would still have entailed considerable hardship, given that half the produce had to be delivered to the Spartiate owner. To reduce the figures to a more human scale, a figure of 36,000–41,600 helot families implies that a family will have had to support itself off half the produce from an average holding of only 3.25–3.75 ha. The helots' situation can usefully be compared with evidence from modern Mediterranean peasant societies which indicates that holdings of 3 ha are generally considered the absolute minimum for subsistence (Gallant 1991, 82–6). Nevertheless, many households do own less than this minimum and are often able to achieve a precarious survival through use of additional expedients, such as renting extra land, performing wage labour, pooling resources with kinsmen, and borrowing. This suggests that, *mutatis mutandis*, there were ways through which helot families could have eked out a bare living in their parlous land-poor circumstances.

Indeed, analogues for some of the expedients adopted by modern peasants can be identified as potentially open to helot cultivators. First, one form of pooling of resources among kinsmen is the co-residence of multiple families in a single household and their joint cultivation of particular landholdings. The possibility of this kind of household arrangement has been suggested already in chapter 4; it is supported by the evidence mentioned there that

Messenian helots, at least, resided in nucleated settlements rather than scattered farmsteads. This practice has been found to produce economies of scale among sharecropping households in nineteenth-century Italy (Kertzer 1984, 36). Also, in so far as the different co-resident families are at somewhat different stages of their life cycles, the arrangement can iron out some of the periodic troughs in labour supply which cause difficulties for the capacity of single family households to maintain intensive production (Gallant 1991, 89).[20] If some Spartiate landlords were able under certain circumstances to move helot families or households between different holdings, as also suggested earlier, this too could have helped avoid the worst of imbalances between household size and availability of land. Secondly, although wage labour was doubtless not an available option among the helot population, we have already seen (ch. 4) that helot society was not undifferentiated and that certain privileged helot households may have been able to accumulate cultivation 'rights' over larger holdings than were manageable by their available family labour. Consequently, there were probably opportunities for members of the poorest families to find employment as labourers or sub-tenant cultivators of richer neighbours. Likewise, many of the herdsman of the large Spartiate herds and flocks were probably men from helot households on the brink of subsistence. Thirdly, social relations both between Spartiate masters and helot cultivators and within the helot population may have involved relations of paternalism and dependency which included the provision of subsistence help at times of food shortage (Hodkinson n. d.). Indeed, in so far as food shortage was an endemic feature of the daily existence of the bulk of helot farmers, one might plausibly view it as a structural feature which held the society together by binding a large subject population to a minority master class upon which it was dependent for the material assistance critical to its physical survival.

Besides these various expedients open to poor helot families, we should not forget the potential to exploit a range of non-arable resources. As noted in chapter 5, the value of modest domestic herds of animals – which could have been kept alongside livestock belonging to their Spartiate masters – has long been acknowledged by students of traditional farming as a multi-purpose nutritional resource, as a provider of manure, as a means of transforming otherwise indigestible plant material for human use and as an emergency store of food in time of famine (cf. Hodkinson 1988, 60). Another option was the exploitation of marine resources. Note Thucydides' account (4.26) of the Spartans' use of helot boat owners to bring supplies to their soldiers trapped on the island of Sphakteria in 425:

> There were many ready to take the risk of doing so, and particularly the helots, who put to sea from various parts of the Peloponnese and brought their boats in by night to the side of the island facing the open sea…the helots had had their boats valued and ran them ashore without minding whether they were damaged…

These helots had clearly invested resources in fishing boats for the exploitation of inshore and offshore waters. Although a recent study has attempted to minimise the potential productivity of fishing in antiquity (Gallant 1985), the latest research suggests a more optimistic assessment (Curtis 1991; de Souza, n.d.). To fishing we should add the hunting of game and the gathering of wild flora – including greens, mushrooms, nuts and dried seeds – from the uncultivated landscape, a resource whose potential importance in antiquity has until recently been unjustly neglected (Gallant 1991, 116–20; Forbes 1996).

Clearly, there were methods by which helot households could ensure their physical survival by supplementing the meagre subsistence derived from cultivation of the Spartiates' estates. With what degree of success a household could exploit these opportunities must, however, have varied widely, according to a host of diverse personal circumstances, social relations with potential patrons and fluctuating climatic conditions. Although the overall viability of the helots' efforts at subsistence is demonstrated, at the most basic and generic level, by their continued existence as a self-reproducing population over a period of several centuries, such a general perspective does not exclude the likelihood that the fate of many individual helot households was far more grave. Even when exploited to their fullest extent, moreover, the methods outlined above, though critical to survival, will have been merely supplemental to the foodstuffs produced through arable cultivation. Consequently, as observed in chapter 4, helot farmers will typically have had to labour at maximum intensity to produce their subsistence. The existence of significant pressure upon arable resources indeed seems confirmed by the fact that during the later fifth and early fourth centuries several thousand helots could be diverted off the land for service in Sparta's armies (see further, ch. 13).

In forcing the helots to labour intensively for their own subsistence, the 'whip of hunger' should in principle have ensured that, on a 50/50 sharecropping arrangement, they produced more than was necessary to meet the economic demands upon Spartiate households. According to my estimations above, a 'typical' 18.4 ha Spartiate estate will have contained on average about five helot families. In supplying their own subsistence, these helot families should, in normal circumstances, have comfortably supplied the needs of a single citizen household plus its domestic servants.

The productive capacity of citizen estates

I shall now attempt to put some flesh on the bare bones of this last proposition by estimating the productivity of the hypothetical, average 'ordinary' citizen estate and relating it to the economic demands on citizen households discussed above. Since a similar set of calculations has already recently been undertaken with considerable methodological sophistication in Gallant's general study of free Greek peasants, my exploration will follow the broad lines of his enquiry, drawing where appropriate upon the statistical data which he has assembled.

At certain points, however, it will be necessary to query some of the values employed in his calculations.

By way of explanation of the grounds underlying Gallant's (and my own) figures, it should be emphasized that his study aligns itself with recent revisionist evaluations of the character of ancient Greek agriculture (e.g. Jameson 1977/8; Halstead 1987; Garnsey 1988; Hodkinson 1988; Wells (ed.) 1992). Older accounts tended to view Greek agriculture as operating in a rather static and uniform manner, strictly constrained by the dry Mediterranean physical environment and by a comparatively primitive technology (e.g. Semple 1922; 1932; Jardé 1925). This view stressed the dominance of cereal crops cultivated under a regime of biennial fallow ploughed bare in the spring, with rotation systems involving legumes and pulses being a relative rarity. This method of farming, it was argued, was accompanied by a near-universal divorce between arable culture and animal husbandry. The lack of available lowland summer grazing, combined with the summer heat, enforced the seasonal transhumance of herds and flocks to mountain pastures, with a consequent loss of their manure for half the year. The productive capacity of ancient Greek agriculture was viewed as comparatively limited and fixed under these ineluctable constraints. In contrast, more recent approaches have, with certain exceptions (Isager and Skydsgaard 1992), stressed the ways in which ancient farming shared 'the considerable elasticity of productivity which is a feature of almost all agricultural systems. Land does not have a fixed carrying capacity, but will produce larger or smaller amounts depending on the amount of labour invested and the techniques and crops used' (Foxhall 1992, 156). Within the overall constraints of environment and technology, a variety of subsistence strategies – such as those suggested above for helot households – was open to ancient farmers, as well as considerable flexibility in the way these strategies were put into effect in response to the changing circumstances of each year. Along with this newer approach goes an emphasis upon the prevalence of small-scale, intensive, mixed farming, which employed larger quantities of a wider range of crops than envisaged in older accounts. Particular stress is given to crop rotation systems involving legumes, which fix nitrogen in the soil, thereby increasing its fertility. So too is the close integration of arable farming with the all-year-round herding of animals on or near the cultivated fields. The availability of animal manure throughout both winter and summer, along with the use of human dung, contributed to the potential for increases in productivity.

Building upon these newer perspectives, Gallant has cogently demonstrated the range of measures which subsistence farmers in antiquity could adopt to minimise the risk of crop failure and maximise the overall range of food resources available: crop diversification, intercropping of different plants, intensive weeding and hand tillage of the soil, annual cropping or multicropping in place of biennial fallow, the keeping of animals and intensive collection and spreading of their manure (1991, 36–57).

The essential requirements for the implementation of these practices are twofold: the availability of ample labour and the capacity to direct that labour to the desired practices. In the case of farming on Spartiate estates, the former requirement was clearly satisfied. The latter requirement needs a little discussion. As a dependent population farming their masters' land, helots clearly did not have unfettered control over choice of crops and methods of cultivation or even over the disposition of their labour. Spartan citizens are attested supervising the cultivation of their estates close to Sparta (Xen. *Hell.* 3.3.5), though whether this personal intervention was feasible on more distant estates is doubtful. The key question is whether Spartiate landowners will typically have insisted upon choices of cropping and uses of labour which limited the flexibility needed for the optimal use of the land. Certainly, Spartan male landowners must have insisted that an appropriate proportion of their estates be devoted to producing the necessary supply of barley meal, wine, cheese and figs demanded by the compulsory mess dues. These, however, were items which helot households themselves needed for their own subsistence. The range of foodstuffs covered by these dues itself indicates a certain degree of diversification, and an even more diverse range was apparently grown for use in the voluntary prepared dishes contributed towards the *epaikla*.[21] In any case, there is no reason to believe that the foodstuffs eaten at the mess exhausted the range grown for consumption in Spartan households or on other occasions.[22] It is impossible, given the limited available information, to do full justice to the doubtless complex interaction of interests between the Spartiates and their helot cultivators. But there are no strong grounds for believing that Spartiate landowners would normally have had cause to restrict the diversified husbandry which was surely the helots' own preferred agricultural option. On the contrary, Spartan citizens will surely have desired the gains in productivity achieved by the helots' intensive farming. As already argued in chapter 4, there are good grounds for thinking that the agricultural exploitation of Spartiate estates was characterised by the intensive and diversified farming practices recently suggested for Greek agriculture in general.

It seems, then, that the agriculture practised by helot farmers was similar to that practised by the peasant farmers studied by Gallant. The next issue is how to translate these general perspectives into plausible estimates of levels of production. There are two aspects to this problem. The first is how to weight the relative significance of different crops in the ancient diet. Drawing upon a variety of ancient and modern evidence, Gallant suggests a dietary regime whereby 65% of the calories came from cereals, 25% from fruits, pulses and vegetables, and 10% from oil and wine (1991, 62–8, 72–33). The second is what levels of yield to assign to each of these crops. In contrast to previous studies which have based their production estimates on short time series whose representativeness is suspect due to high levels of interannual variability in crop yields, Gallant presents data for mean yields of various crops from different regions of Greece over a forty-year period from 1911 to 1950, then converts the overall mean yield of each crop from Greece as a whole into a figure indicating its mean calorific yield per ha (1991, 77, table 4.7). He then combines these crop yields with the proportionate role of each crop in the ancient diet, presenting the integrated data in a series of tables and figures intended to demonstrate the calories required from each group of crops in fulfilling the consumption requirements of his model peasant household and the areas of land required to produce those calories.[23] Subsequently, he applies coefficients of variation in yields to take account of crop yield variability. He then builds all these calculations into a series of simulations (the last of which incorporates a 33% increase in yields to account for the subsistence farmer's intensification of cultivation) which measure the resulting crop yield in relation to household subsistence needs.[24] The results, Gallant argues, 'demonstrate the highly precarious position of the ancient Greek peasantry' (1991, 110).

Whilst the theoretical basis of these calculations is unexceptionable, it should be noted that there are certain problems with the actual figures used in Gallant's tables and graphs.[25] First, whereas his text argues that the respective proportions of calories derived from cereals and pulses/vegetables should be set at 65% and 25%, the proportions actually used in his calculations (given numerically in his tables 4.6 and 4.8 and displayed graphically in his figure 4.3) are, for an unexplained reason, altered to the less realistic proportions of 60% and 30%.[26] Since, on Gallant's figures, pulses and vegetables are considerably less productive in calories per hectare than cereals, this unexplained discrepancy significantly increases the area required to feed his hypothetical peasant household, inflating its value by some 6–7%.[27] This inflationary error is apparently continued into Gallant's subsequent calculations, with a consequent over-estimation of the peasant household's subsistence difficulties.

Secondly, the figures for the calorific yield of the various groups of crops given in his tables 4.6 and 4.8 also appear to vary inexplicably from their values as calculated from his forty-year series of data presented in his table 4.7. For example, although in table 4.7 the mean yields of wheat and barley are given, respectively, as 2,088,036 and 1,903,642 calories per ha, the calculations in tables 4.6 and 4.8 appear to be based upon a reduced yield of around only 1,800,000 calories per ha. Similarly, in table 4.7 the mean yields of broad beans and lentils are given, respectively, as 806,346 and 946,120 calories per ha; but the calculations in tables 4.6 and 4.8 appear to be based upon a yield of around only 620,000 calories per ha.[28] (Some of this latter reduction may be accounted for by the inclusion of fruit and vegetables, but this is not explicitly stated.) These reductions of yield per ha have a further inflationary effect upon Gallant's calculations of the required area of land – which, once again, appear to feed into his subsequent calculations.

Overall, the combined inflationary effects of the unexplained change of crop ratios and the reductions in calorific yields are of the order of some 15–16%.

Property and the Spartan crisis

For example, under his tables 4.6 and 4.8, Life Cycle 0, application of the original ratios of 65%–25%–10%, respectively, for cereals, pulses/vegetables and oil/wine, together with calorific yields per ha more closely in line with the data series in his table 4.7, suggests that the household's landholding needs would be only 2.83 ha, instead of the 3.36 ha claimed by Gallant.[29] The precariousness of the position of the ancient Greek peasantry, though undoubtedly real, is consequently somewhat overdrawn.

My estimates of the productivity of Spartiate estates, accordingly, follow the principles of Gallant's methodology, but with some significant modifications. I adopt his suggested ratios of 65%–25%–10% for the proportions of calories derived from the different categories of foodstuffs; but I utilise crop yield figures derived directly from the modern statistical evidence which he presents, rather than the figures which appear in his calculations. Since Sparta's cereal crop was mainly barley, I base my calculations of cereal productivity upon an average of the mean figures for barley production in Lakonia and Messenia between 1911 and 1950: namely, 639.9 kg per ha.[30] At a conversion rate of 2,650 calories per kg (Gallant 1991, 77), this works out at 1,695,735 calories per ha, which I round up to 1,700,000. For pulses/vegetables I adopt the figure of 800,000 calories per ha; for oil/wine Gallant's own figure of 2,500,000 calories per ha.[31] In addition to calculations made from these figures, I have also, following Gallant (1991, 107–10), made further calculations based upon calorie yields one-third higher, to take account of achievable levels of agricultural intensification probably practised by helot households.[32] Using these figures, TABLE 25 indicates the estimated number of calories per annum and per day produced by arable farming and arboriculture on an 'ordinary' Spartiate 18.4 ha estate. It also indicates the share – expressed in terms of calories per day – of those calories which belonged to the Spartiate household, calculated on a 50/50 share of the crops. In TABLE 26 that share is then set beside the minimum and peak daily calorific requirements of the monogamous and polyandrous households, as calculated in TABLES 19–24.

The comparison of calorific production and demands in TABLE 26 suggests that, even when farmed unintensively, an average Spartiate estate of around 18 ha was more than ample for the calorific needs of most citizen households. The Spartiate share of 34,329 calories per day exceeds the peak demand upon the hypothetical monogamous household (26,278 calories) by over 30% and the minimum demands by a generous 214%. Surplus production on this scale would have enabled the household to amass ample stores of foodstuffs against bad years, to offer subsistence help to less-favoured kinsmen or to hard-pressed helots, and to convert part of the produce into other forms of wealth for non-subsistence use. From this perspective, the capacity of Spartiate households to generate the large-scale donation of votive offerings, such as the lead and terracotta figurines found in their thousands at the sanctuary of Artemis Orthia, becomes readily intelligible. The position of the polyandrous household (whose

Ch. 12. Spartiate household economies: towards an estimate of a balance-sheet

TABLE 25. Calories produced through agriculture and arboriculture on an 18.4 ha Spartiate estate.

	MEAN CALORIES PER ANNUM				MEAN CALS PER DAY	
	Cereals (Area used)	Pulse/Veg (Area used)	Oil/Wine (Area used)	Total (Area used)	Total	Spartiate share
Unintensive farming	16,320,000 (9.6 ha)	6,240,000 (7.8 ha)	2,500,000 (1.0 ha)	25,060,000 (18.4 ha)	68,657	34,329
Intensive farming	21,760,000 (9.6 ha)	8,320,000 (7.8 ha)	3,333,333 (1.0 ha)	33,413,333 (18.4 ha)	91,543	45,772

The proportions of calories supplied by the various crops are as follows:
Cereals 65%; Pulses/Vegetables 25%; Oil/Wine 10%.
Under unintensive farming, calories produced per ha are as follows:
Cereals 1,700,000; Pulses/Veg. 800,000; Oil/Wine 2,500,000.
Under intensive farming, productivity is increased by one-third.

TABLE 26. Comparison of mean calories produced and required per day.

	CALORIES PRODUCED	CALORIES REQUIRED					
		Monogamous household			Polyandrous household		
	Spartiate share	Minimum demand	Mean demand	Peak demand	Minimum demand	Mean demand	Peak demand
Unintensive farming	34,329	16,030	22,533	26,278	32,526	36,272	40,324
Intensive farming	45,772	16,030	22,533	26,278	32,526	36,272	40,324

minimum and peak demands vary between 32,526 and 40,324 calories per day) is evidently less assured. When farmed intensively, however, the 45,772 daily calories produced on average from its 18.4 ha estate would have provided a sufficient surplus to build up a decent-sized store of food against difficult years.

On the assumption that most Spartiate estates were – as I have suggested – of the order of 18 ha, we should conclude from this analysis that the Spartiate system of land ownership was in principle fundamentally viable. This conclusion should occasion no surprise, since we know historically that the system operated successfully for the best part of two centuries. Established at some point in the later seventh or early sixth centuries, it supported as many as 8,000 citizens in 480 BC and did not run into serious difficulties until later in the century. The system's medium-term robustness is further illustrated if we consider the position regarding landholdings smaller than 18 ha. From the figures in TABLES 25–26, we can calculate that the monogamous household would have been able, through intensive farming, to produce sufficient calories to meet its food requirements, even in its year of peak demand, providing its landholdings remained above 10.6 ha. Only when they dropped as low as 9 ha would its mean production fall below its mean calorific requirements. Even the hard-pressed polyandrous household would have been able to produce sufficient calories to meet its peak requirements, as long as its landholdings remained above 16.2 ha. Its mean production would have been able to supply its mean calorific requirements, as long as its holdings remained above 14.6 ha. Even then, however, regular shortfalls need not necessarily be assumed, since the production figures in TABLE 25 take no account of the significant additional calories which could be obtained from pastoral products deriving from animal husbandry, or from fishing, hunting or gathering. Even with only 9 ha and 14.6 ha, respectively, the monogamous and polyandrous households might still hope to remain economically viable, especially with the application of domestic economies.

The weak points of this fundamentally robust system of landholding lay, I suggest, at the margins and in the long-term. The family sizes of the hypothetical households considered in this chapter were purposely placed in the middle of the range, in order better to represent the experience of the majority of Spartiate households. Throughout the population as a whole, however, there will in each generation have been a significant minority of households which had to support more persons than the norm – households whose production capabilities were consequently placed under greater pressure. In cases where the additional burden resulted from the extended survival of aged parents or the need to care for other kinsfolk, that pressure will have been temporary. In others, however, where the burden was due to a large number of surviving children, the pressure will have intensified in the following generation through the system of partible inheritance, which will have led to a greater than normal division of the parental property. In cases where the households of those children were themselves burdened by a large number of children or the need to support other additional persons, the pressure of demands upon resources will have been more intense still. Owing to the greater difficulty which such households will have had in amassing stores of food in reserve, they would have been particularly vulnerable to the large degree of interannual variation in crop yields characteristic of Mediterranean agriculture (Gallant 1991, 102–3).

Hence, whilst for much of the archaic and classical periods the majority of Spartiate households may have maintained themselves comfortably, in each generation a minority of households with diminished landholdings probably struggled to maintain their subsistence and, above all, their compulsory food contributions to the common messes. In each generation some of these struggling households will have defaulted on those contributions and lost citizen status. Over a period of time, a growing number of Spartiate households may have found their estates declining into the category of smaller holdings in which

Ch. 12. Spartiate household economies: towards an estimate of a balance-sheet

particularly adverse circumstances could put their citizen status under threat. In the final chapter of this volume I shall examine in detail the socio-economic causes and other contributory factors behind the increasing impoverishment of poor citizens and the shortage of citizen manpower that, according to Aristotle (*Pol.* 1270a33–4), destroyed the might of classical Sparta.

Notes

[1] Whether natural infant mortality was aided by the frequent practice of selective (female) infanticide is a controversial subject: see the references listed by Gallant (1991, 21), to which add Sallares (1991, 134–60), who doubts that it was practised extensively before the Hellenistic period.

[2] *Pol.* 1265a38–b1, as correctly interpreted by Sallares 1991, 194.

[3] There is no clear evidence concerning the residential practice of newly-weds. No firm conclusion can be drawn from the statement of Plut. *Lyk.* 25.1 that those under 30 (and still within the upbringing) had their household necessities supplied by their kinsfolk and *erastai*. It could signify either the existence of a separate marital home or provisioning for the bride within the home of the young man's parents.

[4] It might be questioned whether the mean was as high as this during the period when Sparta's citizen population was in decline. But it is unclear to what extent her *oliganthrōpia* was due to demographic as well as economic factors; and, as noted below, household sizes may have been raised by certain official incentives in force during this period.

[5] Arist. *Pol.* 1270a39–b6. Aristotle's criticism of the harmful effect of these incentives in pauperising the children may imply that a significant number of couples had responded to them.

[6] This would accord with the principle that residential arrangements tracked those of inheritance, since the purpose of polyandry was to pass on the brothers' property holdings to a single set of heirs. Even were it possible to identify their individual biological paternity, the children will have been regarded as the common offspring of all the men.

[7] Hdt. 7.229; Thuc. 4.8, 16; Xen. *Hell.* 4.5.14; 8.39; Kritias fr. 37, Diels-Kranz, *ap.* Libanius, *Orations* 25.63. Kings and other generals on campaign had multiple attendants (e.g. Hdt. 6.80–1; Xen. *Hell.* 3.1.27); but this is not relevant to ordinary citizen soldiers. The fact that at Plataia in 479 each Spartiate was given seven helot attendants is also not indicative of his normal retinue, since the presence of such a large number was due to the polis' exceptional need for light-armed troops (Hdt. 9.10, 28–9). Although these helots probably attended the Spartiate to whom they were already attached in peacetime (cf. Ducat 1990a, 157–8), the majority were surely agricultural labourers.

[8] The sources are silent about daughters born of such unions. If allowed to survive after birth, they would perhaps have been reared as the next generation of household servants.

[9] I have not made any upward adjustment for the diet of Spartan girls, since even if it was relatively fuller than the sparser diet of (some) upper-class girls in Athens, it is unclear that it was large in comparison with the diet attested by comparative evidence from other societies. As noted in ch. 7, there was no doubt considerable variation in female diet from one household to the next.

[10] Forbes 1982, esp. 234–5; Gallant 1991, 94–8, with references. For the purpose of his calculations Gallant suggests the inclusion of an additional demand of 30% to take

Property and the Spartan crisis

account of this factor. I shall not follow his procedure, since my concern is to examine the unavoidable demands of subsistence and citizen life.

11 Cf. Forbes 1996, 79–87, who notes the apparent contrast in Aristophanes, *Acharnians* (33–6) between the market-purchase of charcoal by Athenian town-dwellers and its non-market acquisition in the countryside.

12 For the public scrutiny of newborn males, Plut. *Lyk.* 16.1; on the initiation ceremonies of the classical upbringing, Kennell 1995, 115–42.

13 Figueira (1984, 98–9 n. 33) argues that, unlike the measures Plutarch gives for the messes in *Lyk.* 12, these measures are Attic. His arguments are that these measures come from Dikaiarchos and that use of Lakonian measures would so inflate the total amount of land needed for the *klēroi* that they would entail unacceptably radical conclusions for the tradition of 9,000 *klēroi*, for Herodotus' figures for Spartiate numbers in 480 and for Tyrtaios' evidence that the helots' rent was 50% of the produce. None of these arguments are cogent. Since I have shown (ch. 4) that Plutarch's *apophora* relates only to the third-century reforms, it follows that they cannot come from Dikaiarchos and that they carry no implications for the evidence of Herodotus and Tyrtaios regarding earlier periods. As shown in ch. 2, moreover, the tradition of 9,000 *klēroi* is fictional. The only consideration, in my opinion, is whether Plutarch's measures make sense in terms of the distribution of 4,500 *klēroi* planned by Agis IV or that of 4,000 *klēroi* effected by Kleomenes III.

14 If one adds to this the fact of polyandrous households, which involved co-residence of mature adult citizens aged over 30, and the probable co-residence of a number of elderly citizens in the households of their married sons, the number of separate households might fall as low as 6000.

15 On these figures, incidentally, it would be readily intelligible both why Sparta put such energy into the expansion of territorial control into neighbouring Messenia and why ordinary citizens felt ground down by the Second Messenian war when they were deprived of access to their landholdings outside Lakonia.

16 The changing composition of the citizen household did, admittedly, have an indirect relationship to certain changes in the helot labour supply, in so far as the number and identity of the helot cultivators working for a given household altered according to the devolution of landholdings between the generations, which was closely related to changes in citizen household composition.

17 5,000 recruited out of the total of 8,000 citizens (allowing for 500 citizens unfit or too old for military service). The two-thirds levy is attested for the Peloponnesian forces during the Archidamian war (Thuc. 2.10, 47; 3.15).

18 On this model life table, men aged 20–59 form 86.88% of the adult male population.

19 As noted earlier in the text, under the model life table used in this chapter men aged 20–24 account for some 14.4%, and men aged 25–29 some 13.4%, of the adult male population. I base my estimate of 20% unmarried men on the assumption that under a Mediterranean marriage pattern characterised by male marriage in the late 20s or early 30s, none of 20–24 year-olds and about a half of the 20–29 year-olds would be married. In this paragraph I use the term helot 'families' rather than 'households', since in my discussion of helot household structure (cf. ch. 4 and this chapter, below) I envisage the possibility of multiple family households. The existence of such co-residential households, however, need not imply a markedly different size of total population from that produced under a pattern of single family households.

Ch. 12. Spartiate household economies: towards an estimate of a balance-sheet

[20] In the parish of Bertalia near Bologna studied by Kertzer, the mean size of multiple family households in the year 1880 was 8.0 persons with a typical holding size of 10 ha (1984, 25, 74 table 3.8). In the nearby communes of Borgo Panigale and Zola Predosa in the mid-nineteenth century, households with a mean size as high as 13.4 persons were supported off farms of only 7.68–9.6 ha (ibid. 75, 214 n. 15 with refs.).

[21] Cf. the use of (olive) oil mentioned in Athen. 140d–f, citing Polemon and Molpis.

[22] For example, the food eaten at the festival known as Kopis ('the Cleaver') included green cheese, paunch, sausage, broad beans (*kuamoi*), green beans (*phasēloi chlōroi*), sucking-pigs, according to Polemon (*ap.* Athen. 139a); barley-cake, wheaten bread, meat, raw greens (*lachanon ōmon*), broth, figs, dried fruits (*tragēma*) and lupine (*thermos*), according to Molpis (140b).

[23] Gallant 1991, table 4.6 (p. 73): *Dietary and land-holding needs over the life cycle*; fig. 4.3 (p. 74): *Dietary needs over the life cycle*; table 4.8 (p. 79): *Required and available labor over the life cycle* (the first part of this table reproduces the information in table 4.6, but giving the hectarage required to one rather than two decimal points); fig. 4.6 (p. 83): *Land required to produce subsistence minimum*.

[24] Gallant 1991, figures 4.11–16 on pp. 103, 105–6, 108–9, 111–12.

[25] These problems have not, to my knowledge, previously been noticed in print. Cf., however, the review of Gallant's book by Frost (1992, 192), who notes 'the alarming profusion of misprints, transposed characters, and unfortunate spellings…it remains mistake-ridden to the point of distraction and could leave one wondering about the accuracy of Gallant's many tables crammed with numerals, where mistakes would not be as readily apparent'.

[26] Cereals surely accounted for more than 60% of the calories in the average Greek diet (Foxhall and Forbes 1982). Note also that there are other specific errors in tables 4.6 and 4.8 as printed. In table 4.6, under Life Cycle 3, the hectarage required for cereals and oil/wine should, on Gallant's calculations, read not 0.44 and 0.10 but, respectively, 1.44 and 0.17, as given in table 4.8. In both tables 4.6 and 4.8, under Life Cycle 21, the hectarage required for oil/wine should read, not 0.06, but 0.12. Under Life Cycle 24, the calories for oil/wine (at a proportion of 10%) and the hectarage required should read, not 144,500 and 0.04, but 192,355 and 0.08.

[27] For example, in tables 4.6 and 4.8, Life Cycle 0, the total amount of land really required (if cereals account for 65% of the calories and pulses/vegetables 25%) is only 3.16 ha, not the 3.36 ha given in the tables.

[28] I write '*appear* to be based', since the calorific yields per ha used in his tables 4.6 and 4.8 are nowhere specifically stated. The reader is left to calculate them from the data in the tables. Similarly, I write '*around* only 1,800,000 calories' etc. since, on the basis of such calculations, the precise calorific yields per ha appear not to be uniform but to fluctuate worryingly within a range of values. For example, the values used for cereals fluctuate between 1,783,523 and 1,905,487 calories per ha.

[29] This calculation is based upon a yield for cereals of 1,995,839 calories per ha (the average of the values for wheat and barley given in table 4.7) and a more plausible, though still conservative, figure of 700,000 calories per ha for pulses/vegetables. The calculation is as follows: 65% cereals = 2,550,437 kcals @ 1,995,839 kcals per ha = 1.28 ha; 25% pulses/vegetables = 980,938 kcals @ 700,000 kcals per ha = 1.40 ha; 10% oil/wine = 392,375 kcals = 0.15 ha (as per Gallant's tables 4.6 and 4.8). Total required hectarage = 2.83 ha.

[30] The separate figures for Lakonia and for Messenia (more precisely, the region of Kalamata) are, respectively, 627.7 kg and 650.9 kg per ha (Gallant 1991, 77 table 4.7).

[31] This figure is slightly lower than the modern figures for the calorie yield of broad beans (806,346 calories) and much lower than that of lentils (946,120 calories). My downward adjustment to take account of the inclusion of less calorific vegetables is somewhat smaller than that made by Gallant.

[32] These intensified yields bring the calorific productivity of barley within the same order of magnitude as the 2,465,000 calories per ha proposed by Sarpaki (1992, 74). She also suggests a much higher calorific yield for pulses of some 2,375,000, based partly upon the study of Charles (1985, 56–7; cf. 42), who gives modern kg/ha yields from the Mediterranean and Eurasia markedly higher than those of Gallant. The nature of the agricultural regimes which produced these last figures is, however, unclear.

Chapter 13

PROPERTY CONCENTRATION AND THE EMERGENCE OF A PLUTOCRATIC SOCIETY

The archaic and classical sources, as we have seen, consistently attest the unequal distribution of property among Spartan citizens. Most of these sources are concerned only to reflect the state of affairs in their own day and do not comment upon changes over time. Aristotle, however, states clearly that by the fourth century the rich had become richer and the poor poorer:

> The defects of the arrangements concerning women seem, as was said earlier… to contribute something to the greed for money; for after the points just made one could attack practice in respect of the uneven levels of property. For we find that some have come to possess (συμβέβηκε κεκτῆσθαι) far too much, others very little indeed; hence the land has fallen into the hands of a few (εἰς ὀλίγους ἥκεν) (*Pol*. 1270a11–18).

Through his reference to greed and his use of the perfect tense Aristotle indicates that the gross inequalities in question were developing and increasing. He reiterates these developmental perspectives elsewhere: first, in his comments on the division of landholdings that 'if many are born and the land is divided accordingly, many inevitably become poor' (1270b4–6); secondly, in his reference at 1307a34–6 to 'Sparta, where properties keep coming into the hands of a few'.

Another indicator of increasing inequalities in property ownership is the evidence for a sharp decline in the number of citizens. In 480 BC the number of Spartiate *homoioi* was said to be 8,000 (Hdt. 7.234). At the battle of Plataia in the following year Sparta was able to field an army of 5,000 citizens (Hdt. 9.10). By contrast, even on the most generous estimates, the 700 Spartiates who fought at the battle of Leuktra in 371 (Xen. *Hell*. 6.4.15) indicate a total army size of not much more than 1,200.[1] Aristotle (*Pol*. 1270a29–31) comments that, although the territory was sufficient to support 1,500 cavalry and 30,000 hoplites, the number fell to below 1,000; he is probably referring to the period shortly after Leuktra, at which 400 Spartiates were killed (Xen. *Hell*. 6.4.15). This decline in citizen numbers had already started during the fifth century. Thucydides' figures (5.68) for the Lakedaimonian contingent at the battle of Mantineia in 418 have been the subject of considerable controversy. But, even if we follow those scholars who believe that his figures should be doubled, the Spartiate contingent will have numbered 3,000–3,500 at most, implying a total available manpower of no more than 4,200.[2] Although – as we shall see – there were several contributory causes to this decline, one of the most significant was widespread impoverishment within the citizen body, since those who were too poor to contribute their mess dues were excluded from citizenship (Arist. *Pol.* 1271a26–36).

In this final chapter my aim will be to study the processes through which the robust system of property distribution examined in chapter 12 was progressively undermined through the increasing concentration of land in the hands of a few. I shall also explore the effects of property concentration on Spartiate society, especially its role in the crisis of Sparta in the early fourth century and in the emergence of a plutocratic society, which enshrined the dominance of rich Spartiates over their poorer fellow citizens.

Structural tendencies towards property concentration: demography and partible inheritance

In chapter 3 we saw that Spartiate private property was passed on between the generations by means of partible inheritance. The evidence indicates that each son received an equal share of the inheritance. In the absence of sons (either natural or adopted), the parental property was inherited by any surviving daughters (known as *patrouchoi*); but it is clear from the evidence of Aristotle (*Pol.* 1270a23–5) that even daughters with living brothers received large allocations of the family property, including land. Aristotle calls these allocations 'dowries'; but I suggested that, although typically given on marriage, they were in fact a *pre-mortem* inheritance which reflected a daughter's right to a share of the parental property one-half the size of a son's share. I described this as 'universal female inheritance', on the grounds that every daughter could expect some share of the inheritance. Whether one accepts my particular interpretation of Aristotle's comments or not, it is clear that Sparta's inheritance system was characterised by what anthropologists call 'diverging devolution' (Goody 1976a): that is, property could devolve between the sexes, from a male owner to either a male or a female heir or to a combination of the two, and similarly in the case of a female owner.

Aristotle himself implicates Sparta's system of partible inheritance as a source of growing inequalities, linking it with demographic factors in his comments (quoted above) on the impoverishment of children born into large families. It seems worth while, therefore, to undertake by means of computer simulation a more systematic examination of the combined effect of demography and partible inheritance upon the distribution of land.[3]

The algorithm (that is, the set of procedural statements specifying the operations to be performed by the computer) behind the simulation postulates a model population of 10,000 married couples, in which each couple initially owns one unit of land in what I shall call Generation One.[4] This initial equal distribution of land is an entirely fictional construct whose sole purpose is to depict in sharper relief the degree of inequality generated by the Spartiate inheritance system. The algorithm also employs a Family Composition Distribution Model, which specifies the numbers of *surviving* sons and daughters produced by each of the 10,000 couples, beginning with couples with no sons or daughters and continuing through the various permutations up to a maximum of four sons and four daughters.[5] The precise numbers of couples producing each permutation of sons and daughters was calculated (by means of binomial expansion) on the simplifying assumptions of a stationary population with an equal sex ratio in which the replacement of all members of one generation by the next takes place simultaneously and in which each child born has a 0.5 chance of surviving beyond the deaths of its parents.[6]

On the basis of this Family Composition Distribution Model, each family's single unit of land is divided among their surviving children according to the rules of two specified inheritance systems (on which, see below). Land belonging to families with no surviving children is reallocated as an indirect inheritance to some of the other families on a 'selective proportional basis'. (The families are categorised according to their permutations of sons and daughters; an equal proportion of families within each category receives an additional unit of land.[7]) This additional land is then also divided among the children of those families.

The individual men and women who form Generation Two of the model population are now grouped (separately) into different *male* and *female* 'landholding sets', each set comprising those persons holding identical amounts of land. These men and women are then paired off to form Generation Two families. This pairing is also performed on a selective proportional basis. In order to examine the inherent implications of the inheritance system, it is necessary to avoid the 'real-life' tendency towards marriages between persons of similar wealth. Therefore, the men within any given male landholding set are married among women from *all* the female landholding sets. The number of men who marry into each female landholding set is determined by the size of that landholding set in relation to the total female population. It is then possible to calculate the combined landholdings of each new Generation Two family and to group these families into *family* landholding sets, each set comprising families of identical wealth. The cycle now recommences with the application of the Family Composition Distribution Model, again on a selective proportional basis, to each of these family landholding sets, in order to produce the individual men and women of Generation Three. (Within each family landholding set there is an identical distribution of the permutations of numbers of surviving sons and daughters.) The personal landholdings of these Generation Three men and women are then calculated, and they are ranked in landholding sets and paired off into couples as before.

For the purposes of the simulation, I have run the program using two different systems of partible inheritance. The first is the system of 'universal

Property and the Spartan crisis

female inheritance' which I have advocated, according to which daughters inherited the entire property in the absence of sons and, when there were sons, a share calculated at half a son's share. The second is a system which I term 'residual female inheritance', in which daughters inherit only as residual heirs in the absence of sons; in the presence of sons they inherit nothing at all. I have employed this second system for comparative purposes, to counter scepticism about my interpretation of female property rights. It simulates what would have happened to the distribution of property, if daughters had inherited as heiresses (*patrouchoi*) but there had been no dowries of land given to other daughters on marriage.

The graphs in *Figs.* 23–24 show the outcome of the simulation for the distribution of landholdings by the stage of Generation Seven. *Fig.* 23 shows for the two inheritance systems the number of families (on the horizontal axis) who possess holdings *equal to or less than* the units of land indicated on the vertical axis. (For sake of clarity, the graphs are restricted to landholdings of two units in size or below.) It shows that, although all Generation One families started with equal holdings comprising one unit of land, by Generation Seven severe inequalities have become firmly established. Under both systems of inheritance the vast majority of families own holdings smaller, many *much* smaller, than the one unit held by their ancestors. In contrast, at the other end of the scale a sizeable minority of families are wealthier, and a tiny minority (those off the top of the graph) *much* wealthier, than their ancestors.

Note, however, that there are significant differences in the extent of inequality

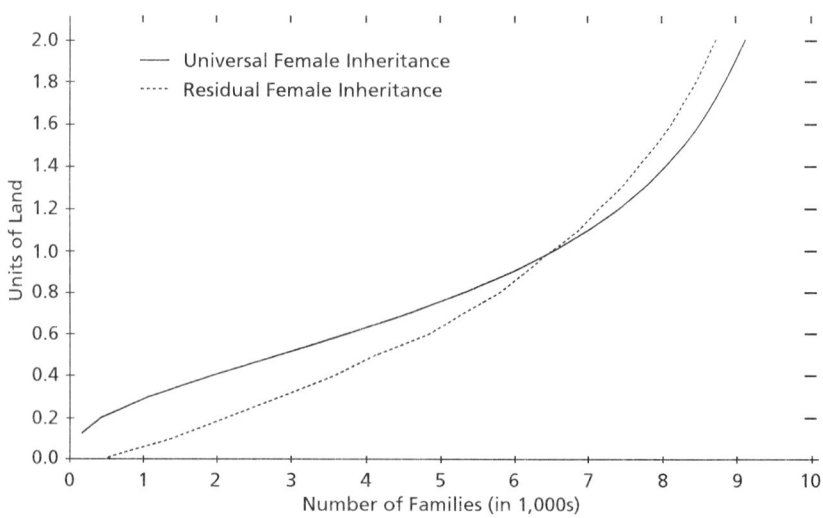

Fig. 23. Family landholding in Generation Seven.

Ch. 13. Property concentration and the emergence of a plutocratic society

and property concentration under the two different inheritance systems. The higher starting-point and the flatter graph produced by the system of universal female inheritance indicates a less unequal distribution of land than the sharply-rising one of residual inheritance only. The differences between the effects of the two systems are especially noticeable at the low end of the landholding scale. Under the system of residual female inheritance as many as 4,120 families, over 41% of the entire population, own landholdings a half or less the size of the landholdings formerly owned by their Generation 1 ancestors. Under universal female inheritance the comparable figure is much smaller: 2,837 families, or slightly over 28% of the population. At yet lower levels of landholding the differences are even more marked. There are 3,572 families with only 0.4 units of land or less under residual female inheritance compared with only 1,927 under universal female inheritance. In terms of the average 'ordinary' 18.4 ha citizen estate hypothesised in chapter 12, a landholding reduced to 0.4 of the original estate would be only 7.36 ha, a level at which the family would experience considerable difficulties in sustaining its citizen status. Significant differences between the two inheritance systems can be seen elsewhere on the landholding scale. At the top end of the scale there are more wealthy families under residual female inheritance. For example, some 201 families own 4 or more units of land under residual female inheritance, compared with only 68 families under universal female inheritance. Conversely, under universal female inheritance there are more 'middling' families whose holdings lie between 0.5 and 1.5 units: 5,462 families as against 4,354 under

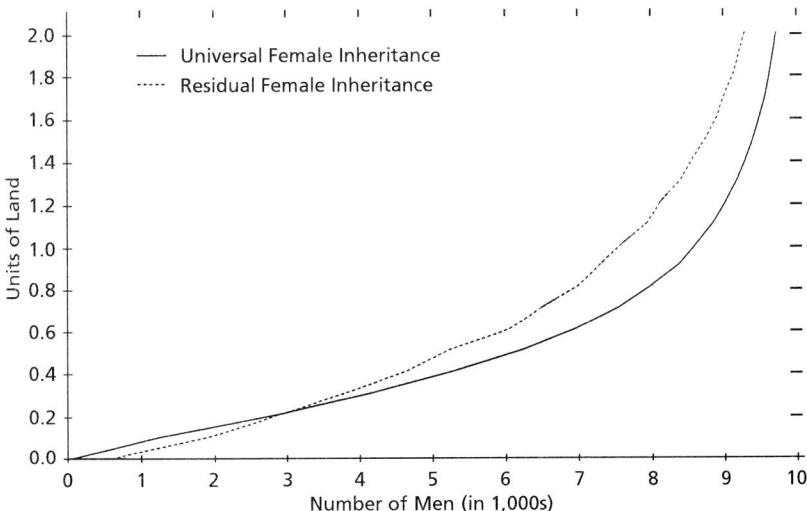

Fig. 24. Male Landholding in Generation Seven.

residual female inheritance. The reason for these differences is that under residual female inheritance a minority of daughters inherit entire estates, but the rest nothing: the effect is that significant differences of wealth are passed down to the next generation. In contrast, when all daughters, as well as sons, inherit at least some land, it is divided more evenly among more persons. Collectively, those daughters on marriage contribute a more even balance of property holdings to the next generation of families.

This comparison between the two systems is reinforced by the evidence of *Fig.* 24 which shows that among the *male* portion of the population (considered alone) universal female inheritance produces not only less *relative* inequality, but also fewer very poor men in *absolute* terms. There are, in fact, only 74 men with 0.1 unit or less and 1,288 men with 0.2 units or less under universal female inheritance compared with 590 and 1,927 men, respectively, under residual female inheritance. This outcome is at first sight unexpected, since under universal female inheritance males own considerably less land overall: 57.6% of the total as against 74.9%. The key to this paradox is that, among the poorer sections of the population, under universal female inheritance men generally gain more land through inheritance from their mothers (most of whom own no property at all under residual female inheritance) than they lose by sharing the parental holdings with their sisters.

Although a simulation is a fiction, 'like a good fictional story…it does claim to be understandable in terms of the real world and to be useful in shedding light on the operation of that world' (J.E. Smith 1987, 250). We can draw two conclusions from the simulation. First, the significant inequalities produced under *both* inheritance systems suggest that there was an inherent trend towards the concentration of property in the operation of the Spartiate system of partible inheritance. When families have different numbers of surviving children to share their property holdings, the inevitable result is the development of considerable inequalities in wealth.

Secondly, the fact that the system of universal female inheritance produces a lesser degree of inequality than residual female inheritance supports my hypothesis that this was the inheritance system practised in classical Sparta. Acceptance of my hypothesis would contribute to the solution of a puzzling feature of Spartiate socio-economic trends: namely, the comparatively lengthy timescale that it took for the phenomenon of impoverishment to develop into a serious problem. As we shall see below, from the late seventh or early sixth century the Spartiate property system apparently operated without observed ill-effects for a century or more before property concentration and the decline in citizen numbers became serious problems in the fifth century. My argument is that the practice of universal female inheritance, which tends to produce fewer poor and rich families and a larger number of families with moderate amounts of property, may help to explain this phenomenon. Conversely, the simulation helps to disprove the idea that daughters inherited only in the absence of sons.

Given the results of the simulation, it would be hard to explain why, under this system, the unequal distribution of property did not become serious until the late fifth and early fourth centuries.

These observations lead to a further point which may at first seem surprising. The system of universal female inheritance used in the simulation represents (as noted above) my interpretation of Aristotle's statement concerning the giving of large landed dowries. Even if one rejects my particular interpretation, the fact is that the more prevalent the practice of giving dowries was, the nearer it approached a system of universal female inheritance. Here we meet an apparent contradiction, in that Aristotle included the giving of large dowries as one of the causes of Spartiate citizen manpower shortage and the concentration of property, whereas the simulation indicates that universal female inheritance in itself has a more levelling effect. The resolution of this contradiction is that within the simulation the marriages of wealthy daughters are arranged in a controlled impartial fashion without regard to their wealth: heiresses and daughters with large dowries are paired as much with poor and 'middling' men as with rich ones. Aristotle's criticism, in contrast – focusing his attention on heiresses, but the same was no doubt true of dowried daughters – was that their marriages were *not* subject to control.

> But, as it is, one may give an *epiklēros* in marriage to any person one wishes; and, if a man dies without making a will, the man he leaves as *klēronomos* gives her to whomever he likes (*Pol.* 1270a26–9).

Heiresses could be given outside the kin group to any one whatsoever, with the implication that wealth tended to marry wealth. In this way the beneficial tendencies of universal female inheritance could be thwarted by the self-interested marriage practices of Spartiate families.

Diverging devolution and Spartiate marriage practices

Following Aristotle's lead, let us examine the evidence for Spartiate marriage practices in the context of the system of inheritance. As noted above, whether one prefers my hypothesis of a system of universal female inheritance or an interpretation whereby Aristotle's 'dowries' were simply voluntary marriage gifts, the Spartiate system was clearly one of 'diverging devolution', whereby property (including landed property) could pass down not just to heirs of the same sex as the owner but also between the sexes. Historical demographers have observed that one notable effect of such a mode of inheritance is considerable and continuous *short-term* instability in landholding. When not only men inherit land, but women also, and those women receive property on marriage, land changes hands both down the generations and between the sexes at the majority of adult deaths and at every marriage (Goody 1976b, 10). The ownership of specific holdings is drastically reorganized every generation and may be continually reallocated from one lineage to another, because daughters are constantly

Property and the Spartan crisis

receiving land from both father and mother and ultimately bequeathing it to children whose father may be from an entirely different lineage.

In addition, when daughters receive landed property even in the presence of sons, the parental landholdings are subject to far greater division. The precise effects vary considerably from family to family, according to the ratio of sons to daughters. For example, the grandchildren of couples with only sons stand to gain increased inheritances as those sons marry propertied wives without losing any of the parental property to sisters; whereas families with more daughters than sons give away more land with those daughters than is brought in by the wives of their sons.

These phenomena must have been important preoccupations for Spartiate families. There was, however, a lack of direct mechanisms for remedying their most serious effects. As we saw in chapter 3, there is no evidence that the kings, in adjudicating between claimants to unbetrothed heiresses, allocated such women to sons from larger families; nor was there a reservoir of public land for such sons to exploit. Only through adoption (Hdt. 6.57.5) could some evening-out of property be achieved; although, since an heirless person would normally adopt a fellow kinsman (cf. Rubinstein 1993, 22–8), this operated largely within kin groups rather than between them. Consequently, it was primarily in the sphere of marriage that Spartiate families had to seek solutions to their problems.

The anthropologist Jack Goody (1976a), in a statistical analysis of several hundred societies, has noted a high degree of association between inheritance systems of diverging devolution and specific kinds of marriage practices which are designed, from the viewpoint of individual households, to minimize the various difficulties described above. Spartiate marriage customs accord well with the general pattern observed by Goody. He notes the frequent co-existence of diverging devolution with the practices of male monogamy and polyandry, as opposed to polygyny.[8] Herodotus (5.39-40) indicates that male monogamy was normal Spartiate practice, in commenting that, when King Anaxandridas II in the mid-sixth century took a second wife *in addition to* his first one, it was a very un-Spartan practice, which he undertook only as a measure of last resort. When Anaxandridas' fellow king, Ariston, voluntarily took another wife, he adopted the more usual practice of divorcing his existing spouse (Hdt. 6.63). Polyandry is attested by Polybius (12.6b.8), who says that it was a longstanding custom and quite usual for three, four or even more brothers to have one wife.[9]

Both monogamy and polyandry can be interpreted as practices designed to limit the number of legitimate children that a man sired and hence the division of the inheritance. Other Spartiate customs tended in the same direction. As noted in chapter 12, women typically married at a later age than in most Greek states, in their late teens, thus reducing their years of potential fertility. The Spartiates also practised a form of wife-sharing, in which a man could request to borrow the wife of another citizen in order to sire children of his own.[10] This practice enabled one woman's fertility to be divided between two men. Polybius (12.6b.8) specifically remarks that it was when a man had begotten sufficient children by his wife that he would give her to a friend. Xenophon too comments that it enabled men to get additional brothers for their sons without increasing the number of claims on their property (*Lak. Pol.* 1.9).

Goody also notes a significant correlation between diverging devolution and a high degree of control over female marriage aimed at ensuring that one's womenfolk marry persons of similar status (the practice of homogamy). When women are holders of property, it is important for families that their son or daughter does not marry someone of markedly inferior wealth. Control over female marriage and a strong tendency towards homogamy is evident in Sparta. A woman's marriage was decided by her male *kyrios*, or legal guardian (Hdt. 6.57.4; Arist. *Pol.* 1270a26–9). As we saw in chapter 3, although matrimonial rites may have included a symbolic marriage by capture (Plut. *Lyk.* 15.3–5), normally marriages were preceded by a betrothal arranged by the bride's parents or next of kin (Cartledge 1981, 99–100; MacDowell 1986, 77–82; Ducat 1998, 396). The tendency towards homogamy can be seen through a variety of evidence. One illustration is the episode (Plut. *Lys.* 30.6; *Mor.* 230a; Aelian, *VH* 6.4; 10.5) in which Lysander's daughters were deserted by their suitors when the poverty of their inheritance became known. Such a marriage would have entailed such a disparity in wealth for the suitors that it apparently outweighed Lysander's former prestige and influence. Homogamy can also be seen in the practice of wife-borrowing. Xenophon's remarks (*Lak. Pol.* 1.8) about the kind of wife a man would request to borrow imply that she would be of similar status. Furthermore, Philo (*On Special Laws* 3.4.22) informs us that the Spartiates permitted marriage between uterine half-siblings (*homomētrioi*, children of the same mother but of different fathers). This would have allowed the woman's sons and daughters by her different partners to be exchanged in marriage. The whole complex is clearly one of homogamy, with the added bonus of concentrating the parents' properties for the benefit of their grandchildren.

The practice of marriage between close kin, exemplified in its closest form by uterine half-sibling marriage, is of course another form of homogamy. Philo's statement implies that marriage between *homomētrioi* was practised throughout the Spartan citizen population, and the same was no doubt true of other forms of close-kin marriage. For specific examples, however, we must turn to marriages attested within the royal houses: the marriages of Anaxandridas II to his sister's daughter (Hdt. 5.39); of Kleomenes I's daughter, Gorgo, to her step-uncle Leonidas (Hdt. 7.205.1); and of Archidamos II to his aunt Lampito (Hdt. 6.71). Close-kin marriage (also known as endogamy) had the advantage that not only did it ensure that the amount of property brought by the bride was consonant with the status and wealth of the groom and his parents, but it also retained the property of a kinswoman within the kin. Endogamy was especially important to the royal houses, which were the richest and most prestigious lineages in Sparta. It was often their best option to avoid marriages below their station and the dispersal of their property and therefore their power. Often, of course, endogamy was not possible. In those circumstances the royal houses typically contracted marriages with spouses from leading non-royal families. When King Ariston in the mid-sixth century wanted to replace his wife, he selected a woman from a prosperous family who was the spouse of his closest friend (Hdt. 6.61–2). Similarly, the future king Agesilaos II was married to Kleora, daughter of Aristomenidas, a leading Spartiate with connections in Boiotia (Paus. 3.9.3).

Such matches were attractive propositions for the leading families concerned. The mid-sixth-century episode mentioned above, in which King Anaxandridas II was compelled to take an additional wife, provides a vivid illustration of the passion with which an alliance with the royal houses was sought and jealously guarded by the girl's kin. Anaxandridas' first wife was his own niece (his sister's daughter); but his second wife came from a different lineage, being the daughter of Prinetadas and granddaughter of a certain Demarmenos. The second wife produced a male child, but then the first wife straightaway became pregnant; whereupon the kinsfolk of the second wife expressed such doubts about her conception of a prospective rival for the throne after several years of barrenness that the ephors were obliged to attend the birth to guarantee the authenticity of her pregnancy. The value this same kin group put upon achieving distinguished marriages for their womenfolk is further indicated by the fact that another granddaughter of Demarmenos, Perkalos, daughter of Chilon, was betrothed to Leotychidas, the leading member of the junior branch of the Eurypontid royal house (Hdt. 6.65). Perkalos was indeed such an attractive match that Leotychidas' senior kinsman, King Damaratos, seized her for himself before the marriage was consummated. Here we see a leading Spartiate lineage attempting to further the status of its descendants by marrying two of its womenfolk into the two royal houses, and two royal males keen to establish a liaison with a prominent family apparently related to the famous ephor Chilon.[11]

In sum, the evidence shows Spartiate families adopting marriage practices which limited the number of heirs and the division of the inheritance, which concentrated their property among close kin, or which brought in a sizeable landholding from a spouse from another lineage. The practice of close-kin marriage might appear to conflict with Aristotle's statement (quoted earlier), which implies that heiresses were freely married outside the kin group to any one whatsoever. A better interpretation, however, would be to view the practice of endogamy and exogamy as mutually complementary, as a means by which a household could balance the need to maintain the coherence of the kindred and its property holdings with the need to develop advantageous alliances with other lineages.[12] The marriage practices of the royal houses, noted above, are a good illustration. Cheryl Cox has, indeed, observed precisely this balancing act in operation among classical Athenian households: 'once nonkinsmen had been absorbed into the kin group, these relationships could be reaffirmed by kinship endogamy…or by repeated alliances into the native deme or into the deme of one's affines' (1998, 18).

Aristotle's comments on the marriage of heiresses outside the kin have prompted Cynthia Patterson (1998, 102–3) to suggest that – in contrast to Athens (where there existed a long sequence of related kindred, the *anchisteia*, with the right to marry an *epiklēros*) – the network of related kindred in Sparta was comparatively weak. This suggestion is, however, perhaps somewhat premature. Aristotle is outlining what was *permissible* regarding the marriage of heiresses, not the full range of social practice. Levi-Strauss has suggested that the practice of uterine half-sibling marriage, such as practised at Sparta, is symptomatic of a society in which the givers of brides have more prestige than the takers (1983, 127–40; cf. Bresson 1990, 55 n. 13). If so, the possession of an heiress, the wealthiest kind of bride, will have provided a golden opportunity for her relatives to exercise their prestige through an alliance with another lineage, rather than lock it up through an endogamous marriage. Hence the fact that the kinsman left as *klēronomos* could use the heiress as an instrument of alliance, rather than being compelled to marry her himself, could indicate, not the weakness of the network of *anchisteia*, but its capacity to extend its strength.

These suggestions receive support from Alain Bresson's perceptive elucidation (1990) of Plutarch's comment – made *à propos* of the fine imposed upon the suitors who withdrew their engagement to Lysander's daughters – that there was a penalty for making a bad marriage and that this measure was aimed against those who sought marital alliance with the wealthy rather than with good men and with their kinsfolk (*Lys.* 30.5). This measure, which punished men who neglected their female relatives in order to grasp after rich heiresses from other lineages, makes perfect sense as an official attempt to restrain acquisitive behaviour, in a context in which many lineages were seeking to marry their heiresses outside the kin. As Bresson notes, its effect was probably to reinforce the kind of balanced strategy outlined above, whereby many marriages were contracted either with close kin or between families already closely linked by friendship and intermarriage.

The establishment of a socio-economic elite

The conclusions of Bresson's study chime with my own observations in a previous study (Hodkinson 1989, 113) regarding the social implications of Spartiate marriage patterns, especially the emphasis upon homogamy and the exchange of sons and daughters in the context of wife-sharing and uterine half-sibling marriage. Here we can contrast the situation in modern mainland Greece where, as in ancient Sparta, children of both sexes inherit from both father and mother and daughters typically receive their portion at marriage. In modern Greece, however, the rules against incestuous marriage promulgated by the Orthodox

Church and by the Civil Code of the Greek state have the effect of prohibiting exchange marriages; and this prohibition 'prevents the transfer of property at marriage from resulting in either a series of equal exchanges between two sets of kin groups or in a regular pattern of circulation through several generations among particular sets of such groups' (Friedl 1962, 64–5). In Sparta, as in many other societies which lacked such restrictions, the opposite probably occurred, with landholdings circulating among networks of friendly families who became closely interlinked through exchange marriages. A necessary implication of such a pattern of marriages was a tendency for wealth to marry wealth. Hence the effect was surely to harden existing economic inequalities by adding an extra layer of social differentiation, thus exacerbating the trends towards the concentration of property inherent in the inheritance system. The resulting social and economic distance between rich and poor is graphically expressed (albeit in extreme form) in Plato's *Republic* (551d). His account of the degeneration of his Spartan-inspired timocratic state into a condition of oligarchy envisages the division of the citizen body into two poleis, a polis of the rich and a polis of the poor. As Plato implies, classical Spartan society contained the seeds of such a division, even if its ultimate realisation did not come into effect until after the end of the classical period.

Ideally, one would attempt to confirm these general observations through a statistical analysis of the marital histories of Spartiate lineages and kin groups. The expected broad overall picture would be one in which (chance exceptions aside) a minority of wealthy lineages successfully maintained and increased their wealth and high status over the generations at the expense of the mass of other citizens. The paucity of prosopographical information for Spartan citizens, especially before the late fifth century, however, makes such an analysis impossible. The best one can do is to highlight individual cases of prominent lineages about which sufficient information survives to indicate their continued prominence from one century to the next.

The prime cases are the two royal houses, some of whose marital manoeuvres have already been mentioned. I start with the Agiad house (*Fig.* 25). Our first detailed insights into Agiad family history come around 550 BC, in the time of King Anaxandridas II. His first marriage, to his sister's daughter, was a typical example of royal endogamy to consolidate the family holdings (Hdt. 5.39). Notably, when urged to divorce his niece for another, more fertile, wife, Anaxandridas refused to do so. He consented to taking another wife only as an addition to his niece. Here too his choice of spouse showed economic good sense: his new bride came from one of the most distinguished, and no doubt wealthy, lineages in Sparta, related (as we have seen) to the famous ephor Chilon (Hdt. 5.41). These two marriages between them produced four sons: his first wife produced Dorieus, Leonidas and Kleombrotos; his second wife bore the future King Kleomenes I. The resulting division of Anaxandridas' property holdings will have left each son with a considerably reduced inheritance.

Ch. 13. Property concentration and the emergence of a plutocratic society

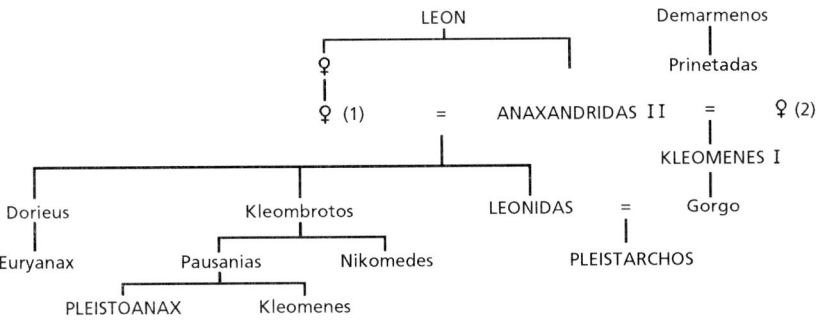

Fig. 25. Family tree of the Agiad house, later sixth and fifth centuries (kings given in CAPITALS).

A step was taken to remedy this problem, however, when (sometime before 491 BC) Kleomenes married his only daughter and sole heiress, Gorgo, to his half-brother, Leonidas (Hdt. 7.205). Their son, Pleistarchos, thus became heir to both Leonidas' and Kleomenes' property. Fate then intervened favourably for the Agiad house. Pleistarchos himself died in 458 BC without known heirs and his entire property probably devolved to the lineage of Kleombrotos, the youngest of the sons of Anaxandridas and apparently the only one of the four brothers whose line survived. Kleombrotos' lineage was hence heir to some three-quarters, at least, of the combined properties of Anaxandridas and his two wives.[13] This large property holding would at this point have been shared between Kleombrotos' younger son, Nikomedes, and his grandchildren, King Pleistoanax and Kleomenes, through his deceased eldest son, Pausanias.[14] Beyond this point the paucity of information about the marital and reproductive history of the Agiad house hinders further informed commentary. The lineage continued uninterruptedly, however, down to the later third century.

The marital history of the Eurypontid royal house can be traced over a longer period. As with the Agiads, details first come to light with the tales told to Herodotus about events *c.* 550, when King Ariston, having failed to produce children through two previous wives, acquired the beautiful wife of his closest friend, Agetos son of Alkidas, through an act of trickery. The woman brought with her more than her beauty, since she came from a wealthy family (Hdt. 6.61). As it turned out, Ariston's trickery backfired. His new wife produced a son, Damaratos, through a premature birth less than nine months after her remarriage to Ariston. Although initially accepted as heir and subsequently king, Damaratos was later deposed as not being Ariston's son. The throne passed to his kinsman Leotychidas, along presumably with Ariston's former property (6.65–6).

Even before his accession, Leotychidas had shown himself astute in his marital negotiations, having contracted a betrothal to a girl called Perkalos,

Property and the Spartan crisis

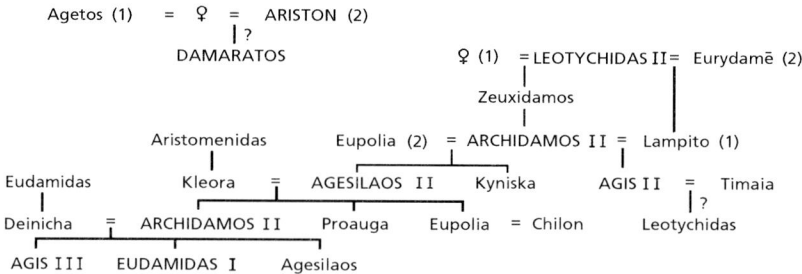

Fig. 26. Family tree of the Eurypontid house, fifth and fourth centuries (kings given in CAPITALS).

whose distinguished lineage is indicated by the names of both her father, Chilon, and her grandfather, Demarmenos – the man whose other granddaughter had married King Anaxandridas. Unfortunately for Leotychidas, however, Perkalos had been seized by King Damaratos before her marriage to Leotychidas had been consummated (Hdt. 6.65). We lack information about the wife whom Leotychidas subsequently married; but we know that this marriage produced a son, Zeuxidamos, who in turn fathered a son of his own, the future King Archidamos II, before dying prematurely. Following Zeuxidamos' death, Leotychidas married again to a certain Eurydamē. Although Herodotus is vague about the precise status of Eurydamē's family, the manner in which he names her brother Menios and father Diaktorides suggests that they were people of note who needed no further introduction to his audience (Hdt. 6.71).[15] This second marriage produced an only daughter, Lampito, whom Leotychidas then married to Archidamos, his grandson and heir to the throne. He thus ensured that Archidamos' and Lampito's future children would inherit both all his own property and everything belonging to his two wives.

In the following generation King Archidamos produced a son through Lampito, the future King Agis II. He then married again to a certain Eupolia, through whom he had a further son, Agesilaos, and a daughter, Kyniska (Plut. *Ages.* 1.1; Cartledge 1987, 145). Although this remarriage implied a division of Archidamos' own landholdings, it was surely a necessary strategy to ensure a future heir in case of Agis' unexpected death (no doubt Archidamos recalled his own father's premature demise). It was a reasonable strategy in material terms, too, in that Agis was assured of inheriting all Lampito's personal property. Moreover, the equine connotations of Eupolia's name (from *polos*, foal) suggest that Archidamos took care to marry a woman of wealth, thus ensuring that the children of his second marriage were reasonably provided for. In the event, the division of most of Archidamos' property lasted barely a quarter of a century after his death in 427. On Agis II's death *c.* 400 BC, his half-brother Agesilaos successfully challenged the legitimacy of Leotychidas, Agis' reputed son, and gained not only the kingship but also all Agis' property: that is, not merely

Agis' share of Archidamos' former holdings, but also the property he had inherited from Lampito.

The immense scale of Agesilaos' property at this point is indicated by the fact that (as discussed in ch. 11) he now gave away half of his inheritance from Agis. The beneficiaries of his generosity were his mother Eupolia's new kinsfolk, acquired through her remarriage following Archidamos' death. As we have seen, Agesilaos thereby tied these distant relations into his personal faction (Xen. *Ages.* 4.5; cf. Plut. *Ages.* 4.1). Another reason why Agesilaos could afford to be generous at the expense of his own children and future heirs was that they could expect a sizeable inheritance from their mother; for Agesilaos had married a daughter of a prominent citizen family, Kleora, daughter of Aristomenidas, a man with foreign connections in Boiotia (Paus. 3.9.3). Subsequently, Agesilaos was also assiduous in arranging profitable marriages for his own children. His son, the future King Archidamos III, was married to a certain Deinicha, a woman whose name suggests descent from an established Spartan family (see below), and who was quite possibly the daughter of the prominent commander Eudamidas. One of his two daughters was married to a certain Chilon, probably another descendant of the famous ephor (Cartledge 1987, 147–9). Thus Agesilaos ensured that his descendants were well established with property holdings. It is no surprise to find that in the mid-third century the Eurypontid house contained the richest men and women in Sparta (Plut. *Agis* 4.1; 6.6; 9.3; 13.2).

The royal houses provide clear examples of wealthy families who perpetuated and enhanced their socio-economic position over the generations through the judicious combination of endogamous unions and advantageous marriages with other rich families. We lack comparable generation-by-generation details of the history of other Spartiate families; but in a number of cases sufficient hints survive to suggest that a select group of non-royal wealthy lineages pursued similar strategies with equal long-term success. One case is the lineage of Endios, the influential ephor and foreign ambassador during the Peloponnesian war, who was *xenos* of Alkibiades of Athens (Poralla 1985, no. 264). Since the Athenian family derived the name 'Alkibiades' from the Spartan family (Thuc. 8.6), we can deduce that the influence and wealth of Endios' ancestors goes back at least to the time when the earliest-known Athenian Alkibiades received his name, that is, to around 550 BC or possibly even earlier (Davies 1971, 15–16).

In other cases, hints of the long-term perpetuation of a lineage's elite socio-economic status are provided by the evidence of Spartiate nomenclature, in particular by the tendency for names to recur within a lineage, most often in alternate generations. One example is the lineage of Chilon, the famous ephor of *c.* 550 BC. As we have seen, his kinsfolk were powerful enough to establish marriage alliances with both royal houses during the later sixth century; and over 150 years later, in the early fourth century, a man named Chilon (probably a descendant) was sufficiently prominent to marry into the Eurypontid house. Another elite lineage already mentioned above is that of Alkidas, the father of

Agetos, the close friend duped by King Ariston. The family's elite status in the mid-sixth century is shown both by its royal friendship and by Agetos' marriage to a girl from a wealthy family. Over 100 years later, another Alkidas appears as admiral of the fleet in 427 (Poralla 1995, no. 62). His elite status is suggested by the fact that, despite his patent incompetence, he was nonetheless 'rewarded with an easy post in the aristocratic manner' (Gomme et al. 1945–81, iii.395) as co-founder of the colony at Herakleia Trachinia in 426. David Whitehead (1979) has noted the evidence for Alkidas' personal friendship with his fellow oikist at Herakleia, the Olympic victor Leon, father of the famous diplomat Antalkidas, whose elite foreign connections were noted in chapter 11. Leon's friendship with Alkidas was so close that, in choosing his son's name, he apparently made a conscious alteration from his own father's name 'Antikleidas' to 'Antalkidas' in honour of his friend and colleague. This is not the last we hear of this prominent lineage, since another Alkidas appears as Spartan admiral in the year 374/3 (Diod. 15.46.1–3).

A further probable example of longstanding membership of the Spartiate elite is the wealthy family of Lichas and Arkesilaos, whose horsebreeding activities in the mid-late fifth century were discussed in chapter 10. It is likely that their lineage goes back to Lichas, the prominent mid-sixth century Spartan, an 'Agathoergos' and ex-member of the elite *hippeis*, who famously acquired the 'Bones of Orestes' from Tegea, thereby inaugurating a new direction in Spartan foreign policy (Hdt. 1.67; cf. Leahy 1955). Similarly, the Samios who was appointed admiral in 402/1 was surely a descendant of the famous Archias, who died a glorious death at Samos *c.* 525, and whose grandson Herodotus spoke with in the smart Spartan village of Pitana (Hdt. 3.55; Poralla 1985, nos. 151–2, 658–9).[16] Cartledge (1982, 250–1) has plausibly suggested that the Samian *proxenia* ran in this Spartan lineage; hence the posthumous honours which Archias received from the Samians.

Other examples of homonyms provide us with less certain, but still plausible, cases of lineages which retained their importance over a period of a century or more. It is possible that Deinicha, wife of King Archidamos III in the mid-fourth century, is descended from the Deinis whose dedication *c.* 600 BC of a fine inscribed bronze perfume flask at the sanctuary of the Menelaion marks him out as a man of wealth and status.[17] Equally, Euryleonis, the female owner of the victorious team in the Olympic two-horse chariot race for foals in 368, may be a descendant of Euryleon, companion of Dorieus on his western Greek adventures in the late sixth century (Poralla 1985, nos. 327–8). Likewise, the Eurybiades who commanded the Greek fleet at Artemision in 480 may be an ancestor of Eurybiades, winner of the Olympic four-horse chariot race for foals in 384. Finally, the lineage of Polypeithes, victor of the Olympic four-horse chariot race in 484, apparently remained prominent into the mid-fourth century, to judge from his namesake who was a *prostatēs* of the Naopoioi at Delphi in autumn 352 (*CID II* 31, 61–2).

Ch. 13. Property concentration and the emergence of a plutocratic society

In the cases considered so far, we can trace the continued prominence of these lineages in different centuries due to the chance survival of information from the poorly-attested periods of the sixth and early fifth centuries. There are an even greater number of cases of lineages which are unattested in the scant evidence for these early periods, but whose prominence can be traced over shorter lengths of time during the better-attested periods of the later fifth and fourth centuries.[18] For example, Pharax, adviser (probably as an old man) to King Agis in 418, had a son, Styphon, who commanded the troops on Sphakteria in 425. Another Pharax (Styphon's son?) pursued a long and distinguished military and diplomatic career – partly as *proxenos* of the Boiotians – from the 400s down to 370/69 BC. Subsequently, yet another Pharax fought as a mercenary commander in Sicily in 355.[19] Timokrates, the leader of an advisory commission in 429, was followed in office sixty years later by his namesake (probably his grandson) who was an ambassador to Athens (Poralla 1985, nos. 70–1). Thibron, the commander of the early 390s, was also succeeded by a namesake (probably again a grandson) in the 320s who was sufficiently important to become lieutenant of the Macedonian noble Harpalos and to acquire personal control of the Pentapolis in Cyrenaica (Poralla 1985, nos. 374–6).

Although no collection of individual examples can provide definitive proof, the cases considered above do put some flesh upon the bare bones of the proposition that classical Spartiate society was dominated by a restricted group of wealthy lineages which for the most part successfully perpetuated their elite position from generation to generation. As the decline in citizen numbers accelerated during the classical period, members of these successful lineages were even better able to secure the high offices detailed in the case studies above. There must, of course, have been cases of rich lineages which died out through failures of reproduction or high child mortality, or which suffered a decline in wealth and status. One example is the lineage of Lysander.[20] His family was of noble birth, claiming descent from the sons of Herakles. His father Aristokritos was sufficiently well-off to maintain a close relationship of *xenia* with the local king in the region of the Oasis of Siwah in north Africa, a friendship which led to Lysander's brother being given the name 'Libys'. Yet somehow the family's wealth became so dispersed that (as we saw in chapter 11) Lysander was brought up in poverty as a *mothax* and was probably able to gain full citizen status and pursue his outstanding career only with the material support of an associate of the Eurypontid royal house. Moreover, due to his personal abstention from wealth, Lysander died a poor man; and after his death his daughters, as we have seen, were spurned by their suitors. Other leading lineages could fall away for other reasons. The enforced exile of Kleandridas, adviser to King Pleistoanax in 446, seems to have demoted his son Gylippos to *mothax* status (Plut. *Per.* 22.2; cf. Thuc. 6.104; Aelian *VH* 12.43).

Despite these exceptions, the trends mainly worked the other way. Indeed, the episode of the suitors confirms not only the exceptional nature of Lysander's behaviour – the suitors clearly expected that his military success would have made him a wealthy man – but also the normal marital pattern of wealth marrying wealth. (Note, moreover, that although they were fined, the suitors were not apparently compelled to marry the poverty-stricken girls.) The consequence was the increasing concentration of property and the social differentiation between rich and poor lineages whose outlines have been sketched above.

Contingent developments: the fifth century and the earthquake of 464 BC

Thus far I have considered the concentration of property in terms of the structural factors of demography and inheritance practices and of long-term marital practices, several of which are visible as early as the sixth century. It is also important, however, to consider the role played by historical developments during the classical period. The patterns of marital behaviour considered above should not be viewed as fixed patterns of behaviour impervious to historical circumstance. Given the high degree of association which Goody has detected between economic stratification and several of the marriage practices discussed earlier, it is plausible to suggest that they increased in frequency over time with the increasing inequalities in wealth.

This point is reinforced by the evidence that the marked decline in Spartiate numbers, accompanied by public concern about citizen manpower shortage (*oliganthrōpia*), only became apparent during the fifth century. As Figueira (1986, 178) has noted, Spartiate population trends up to the Persian wars appear relatively buoyant, and official perceptions correspondingly confident. Herodotus (1.66) connects the Spartans' campaign against Tegea in the early sixth century with their strength in numbers. The campaign's purpose was to divide Tegean territory among themselves, a policy probably later put into effect when Sparta gained the Thyreatis c. 545. In the 'Battle of the Champions', during this latter campaign, the Spartiates willingly accepted the loss of 300 warriors in a heroic fight to the death (Hdt. 1.82). Then, c. 520, Dorieus was permitted to take citizens with him on his colonial expedition (Hdt. 5.42). All this evidence suggests a need for additional land; and, although this may be an indication that impoverishment of poorer families was perceived as at least a potential danger, there is no hint of worries about *oliganthrōpia*.[21] In 480 the Spartiates sent to Thermopylai 300 men, whom they were willing to sacrifice in battle (Hdt. 7.205). The selection of only men with sons shows a desire to preserve lineages from extinction, but again no evident concern about declining citizen numbers. In 480, after all, they stood at the healthy level of 8,000. Only during the course of the fifth century does that concern become apparent with the evident onset of *oliganthrōpia*. Although this decline may be rooted in longer-term developments, we should consider whether short-term developments may have exacerbated the impact of longer-term trends.[22]

Ch. 13. Property concentration and the emergence of a plutocratic society

Scholars have frequently noted that the quarter century commencing with the Persian wars was an extremely difficult period militarily, during which there were probably severe losses in battle. After the loss of almost 300 men at Thermopylai, 91 Spartiates were killed the following year at Plataia (Hdt. 9.70). At some time during the 470s and 460s, in addition to a campaign in Thessaly (Hdt. 6.72), the Spartans had to meet two serious challenges in the battles of Tegea and Dipaieis (Hdt. 9.35). At Dipaieis they fought against great odds – in a single line, according to the exaggerated account of Isokrates (6.99) – against almost all the Arkadians; although victorious, they may have suffered significant losses. Then in the helot and Messenian revolt of the 460s at least one contingent of 300 men was wiped out and there was a major battle at 'the Isthmos', or Ithome (Hdt. 9.35, 64). Finally, there were great losses at the battle of Tanagra in which 1,500 Lakedaimonian troops were involved (Thuc. 1.107–8).

In addition, there was the great earthquake that struck Sparta *c.* 464. Several scholars have seen this event as a turning-point in Spartan demographic history, arguing that Spartiate losses were so large that they caused a permanent drop in citizen numbers (e.g. Toynbee 1969, 346–52; Lane Fox 1985, 220–1; Figueira 1986, 177–83); though other accounts have tended to minimize its importance (Ste Croix 1972, 331–2; Cartledge 1979, 307–17; Cozzoli 1979, 59–73). Jean Ducat (1984) has identified three different traditions among the sources for this event. Thucydides (1.128; 3.54; cf. 1.101; 2.27; 4.56), followed by Pausanias (4.24), suggests that the earthquake had a major impact, but is restrained concerning details of the casualties. Diodorus (11.63; 15.66.4), probably following Ephorus, claims that more than 20,000 Lakedaimonians perished, including most of the male citizens, many of them through the collapse of their homes during the course of a prolonged series of shocks. Plutarch (*Kimon* 16.4–5), following a source also used by Cicero (*De div.* 1.112) and Pliny (*NH* 2.191), states that only five houses remained undemolished and narrates a story in which the *neaniskoi* fortuitously escaped the deaths suffered by the *ephēboi* through dashing out in pursuit of a hare just before the collapse of the stoa inside which they had been exercising. He claims that a collective tomb called Seismatias, which held those who died in the earthquake, was still evident in his own day.

In my original discussion of this subject (Hodkinson 1989, 103–5), I attempted to model statistically the possible impact of deaths in the earthquake and in the following helot revolt upon subsequent Spartiate demographic trends. Assuming, in particular, the elimination of the 18–19 year old *ephēboi* and heavy casualties among women, girls and boys under age seven trapped in their homes while their menfolk outdoors, I concluded that the extent of disruption of fecundable marriages would have caused future fertility levels to be appreciably lower than mortality levels, thus fixing a considerably lower ceiling for Spartiate numbers.

I am now, however, less sanguine concerning the feasibility and fruitfulness of that exercise, partly on empirical, partly on theoretical grounds. My empirical doubts concern both the extent of the loss of life caused by the earthquake and the difficulty of knowing which sections of the population were most affected. Although the loss of life was doubtless severe, Diodorus' figure of 20,000 deaths seems an exaggeratedly round number. Moreover, Plutarch's story of the fortunate escape of the *neaniskoi* and deaths of the *ephēboi* is suspiciously dramatic. As Ducat has pointed out, its ethical paradox (the saving of the undisciplined *neaniskoi*, who acted contrary to Spartiate standards) and the implausible presence of a hellenistic-style gymnasium in fifth-century Sparta, plus the use of non-classical terms for the age classes, point to subsequent invention. Although the collective tomb mentioned by Plutarch presumably did exist, that it contained an entire age class of *ephēboi*, as he claimed, is open to doubt. No less problematic than the elimination of the *ephēboi* are the supposedly heavier-than-average casualties among females and young boys; these are not mentioned in any ancient evidence and are a product of modern guesswork. Plutarch makes no mention at all of persons being trapped in their homes. Diodorus, who does, fails to specify precisely whom and writes in general only of the large number of deaths among adult males. Our ignorance of the precise categories of persons most affected means, consequently, that previous attempts at model calculations, including my own, are built upon sand.

Theoretically, too, there are problems in utilizing presumed earthquake deaths to deduce the parameters for subsequent Spartiate demographic trends. This is not just because model life tables are static constructs, which can be used to make only linear predictions, whereas the dynamics of human populations are inherently non-linear (Sallares 1991, 415–16). Even more fundamentally, the determining factor in human population dynamics is not levels of mortality but rates of fertility, and these latter may change rapidly in response to altered conditions (Sallares 1991, 114–15); hence the correct observation that 'populations recover quickly from such natural disasters unless there are inherent factors independently causing decline' (Ste Croix 1972, 332; cf. Le Bras 1969). This means that, if one is to argue that the deaths caused during the earthquake and subsequent helot revolt had a lasting impact upon Spartiate population levels, one must identify ways in which those mortalities could have hindered the expected acceleration of fertility and birth rates following these disasters. In his examination of the Athenian epidemic of 430–27 BC, Robert Sallares (1991, 258–62) was able to argue for a link with fertility rates, owing to the known effects of smallpox in causing high rates of spontaneous abortions, miscarriages and damage to male reproductive organs. In spite of these effects, Athenian population levels relatively soon recovered, although with some short-term distortions of age structure (Thuc. 6.26.2, qualified by Sallares ibid., 259–60). Sparta's earthquake and battle casualties will have had no such direct impact upon fertility rates.

Ch. 13. Property concentration and the emergence of a plutocratic society

If one is to discover a long-lasting impact of the increased mortalities of the 460s, it must be sought in their effect on the distribution of property. Thucydides (2.53) comments that during the Athenian epidemic,

> Seeing how quick and abrupt were the changes of fortune which came to the rich who suddenly died and to those who had previously had nothing but now inherited their wealth, people now began openly to venture upon acts of self-indulgence which before then they used to keep dark.

In his concern to delineate the moral decline caused by the epidemic, Thucydides concentrates upon public perceptions, which, as usual, focused upon the exceptional rather than the ordinary event. But the passage draws attention to the effect that increased and unexpected mortality has in accelerating the normal process of property devolution and in doing so abruptly and prematurely, often before property owners have had chance to found families or make planned arrangements for the disposition of their property.

So, too, in the late 460s many Spartiates will have inherited additional land which would not otherwise have come their way. Many will have gained larger inheritances, either immediately or later, through, for example, the sudden death of siblings, nephews or nieces who would have been entitled to a share in the parental property or of parents who would otherwise have produced more children. The effect was probably to accelerate the gradual development of inequalities discussed earlier. First, although citizens of all levels of wealth will have benefited from such random mortality, the overall result will have been increased economic differentiation. Richer persons with deceased relatives will have gained considerably more property, in comparison, not only with those whose relatives survived, but also with beneficiaries from poorer backgrounds, because their deceased relatives will themselves generally have had a greater actual or potential inheritance. No doubt there were some exceptionally fortunate poor men who inherited great wealth, as in Athens; but, in general, the greater cohesion of the wealthy elite in Sparta's more exclusively land-based economy is likely to have reduced the frequency of this phenomenon. Secondly, there will have been an increased number of wealthy heiresses. This is likely to have stimulated both a higher level of movement of wealth between different lineages and greater than normal opportunities for securing profitable marriages – to the advantage, doubtless, of the rich.

It is within this changed economic context that the earthquake may have affected future levels of fertility. I have suggested elsewhere (Hodkinson 1989, 95–100) that one effect of the higher levels of land-ownership enjoyed by many citizens was a significant increase in the importance of wealth as a determinant of status as against other, non-material, criteria of ranking. This phenomenon is evident, above all, in the efforts of rich Spartiates to translate their larger landholdings into enhanced socio-political status through participation in the expensive pursuit of chariot-racing. It is notable, as observed in chapter 10, that the Spartiates' near-monopoly of victories in the Olympic four-horse chariot-race occurs precisely in the generation after the earthquake, following a long period of no more than minimal success in the event. As we saw in the previous section, the elite status of several of the known chariot-racing lineages – those of Arkesilaos/Lichas, Eurybiades and Euryleonis – probably goes back into earlier periods. Yet only after the earthquake is there evidence that they turned to equestrian competition. This period too was when Anaxandros deserted the pentathlon event of his paternal grandfather for participation in chariot racing (Paus. 6.1.7).

This changed socio-economic context, I suggest, may have led to the increasing significance of the marriage practices discussed earlier (homogamy, close-kin marriage, wife-sharing, uterine half-sibling marriage and polyandry). These were all means by which wealthy families could maintain their descendants' property, in a society in which their status increasingly depended upon it; or by which poor families could avoid slipping into further impoverishment, in an age in which marriage above one's station was probably harder than ever to achieve. In this context one might also plausibly suggest, with Lane Fox (1985, 221), a decline in marital fertility: 'many enjoyed bigger estates in the wake of the disaster and they did not wish to ruin them by reproducing too freely'. The practices of wife-sharing and polyandry would have had the inherent effect of restricting fertility, and they may well have been supplemented by more direct efforts at family limitation. The very fact that there were official incentives for Spartiates to bear additional sons (Arist. *Pol.* 1270a39–b6) may suggest a perception by the authorities of a general tendency to limit family sizes. There is also the possibility that, among some families struggling on the borderline of citizen status, the need to give priority to maintaining their mess contributions led to a decline in nutritional provision for female and younger members of the household, which may have affected rates of fertility and child mortality.

When added to the long-term effects of the inheritance system and the dramatic short-term increase in mortality of the 460s, these developments may have made a major contribution to Sparta's demographic problems. Wrigley (1978, 149) has pointed out that, at normal rates of mortality in pre-industrial communities, a society

> would run into great difficulties if any significant proportion of the population was so moved by concern for solving its immediate problems of heirship that it kept family sizes down to a level that appeared rational in the local context of the immediate nuclear family.

Among the Spartiates, a closed elite with virtually no recruitment from outside and an economic qualification for continued membership, the difficulties created by the combination of factors referred to above may have been considerably more serious than even those posited by Wrigley.[23]

It is not surprising, consequently, that *oliganthrōpia* became evident, both in reality and in Spartiate consciousness, by the last quarter of the fifth century. The episode of the 420 Lakedaimonian troops trapped on Sphakteria in 425 BC provides two indications of the seriousness of the problem. First, there is the desperate concern shown by the authorities to preserve the troops' lives from the moment of their entrapment and throughout their imprisonment in Athens (e.g. Thuc. 4.15, 108, 117; 5.15). This concern even extended to offering freedom to helots who carried in supplies and to permitting the troops to make a dubious act of surrender, an act so contrary to the Spartiate norm of fighting to the death that it subsequently led to their temporary exclusion from citizen rights (4.26, 38–40; 5.34). Secondly, there is the evidence that the units of the Lakedaimonian army on the island were no longer wholly Spartiate in composition. Whereas at Plataia the Spartiates had fought in a separate contingent from the *perioikoi*, by the time of Sphakteria the previously all-citizen contingents had evidently been bulked out by the addition of non-Spartiates. Out of 292 troops taken prisoner at the end of their siege, only about 120 were Spartiate (Thuc. 4.38). Hence, even if most of the 128 troops who had died in battle were citizens, they will hardly have formed more than about half of the original contingent. Such a heavy dilution of the Spartiate contingents is a clear symptom of the serious onset of *oliganthrōpia*.

The severity of its development is confirmed by the figures for the Lakedaimonian forces at Mantineia in 418. Thucydides' figures for the six main Lakedaimonian *lochoi* at the battle (excluding the seventh *lochos* of Brasideioi and *neodamōdeis*) amount to only c. 3,072 men, to whom one should possibly add the 300 *hippeis* and a few more Lakedaimonians on the extreme right wing (5.67). As already noted, scholars are divided as to whether these figures ought to be augmented by a further 3,000 or so troops, on the grounds that Thucydides may unwittingly have omitted to enumerate half the Lakedaimonian army.[24] Given the attested ratio of Spartiates to non-Spartiates on Sphakteria, the proportion of citizens at Mantineia is unlikely to have been more than 50%. Since the force at Mantineia was some ⅚ths of the total levy (Thuc. 5.64.1), the total available Spartiate military manpower in 418 will, consequently, have been approximately 2,400 or 4,200, depending upon one's view of Thucydides' figures. Either figure represents a significant fall from the 8,000 *homoioi* in 480 BC.

A final military indicator of the concentration of property and decline in citizen numbers is provided by the fact that, during the later fifth and early fourth centuries, several thousands of helots were moved by the polis out of agricultural production, mainly for recruitment into army service. There was the offer of freedom to collaborating helots in 425, the notorious murder of 2,000 helots at some unspecified date, the recruitment of 700 helots for Brasidas' campaign in 424, and (above all) the creation – sometime between 424 and 421 – of the force of ex-helots known as *neodamōdeis*, who formed an important element in Sparta's armies abroad down to the 370s. Finally, more than 6,000 helots were freed to defend Sparta against enemy invasion in 370 BC.[25] The commencement of these initiatives came, moreover, barely more than a generation after the polis had been compelled to let a large body of Messenian rebels depart into freedom – with their wives and their children – at the end of the 460s revolt (Thuc. 1.101). That so many helots – presumably primarily young men without settled families – could be spared from farming implies that their labour was surplus to the needs of agricultural production. The reasons, I suggest, were twofold. First, a smaller number of Spartiate families now required supporting from the land. Secondly, a greater proportion of the territory now lay in the hands of wealthier citizens who, once their needs for arable crops were met, used their remaining lands for the less labour-intensive, but more prestigious and more profitable, raising of livestock. One recalls the comments of the pseudo-Platonic dialogue, *Alkibiades I* (122d), whose overriding recollection of wealthy Spartiate estates was of the number of horses and other livestock that grazed in Messene.

The polis' concern about declining citizen numbers is evident, not only in its incorporation of non-citizens into the army, but also in two measures which it introduced in an attempt to increase the birthrate. First, the institutional controls upon the timing of male marriage seem to have been altered. In the fourth century Spartan males normally married in their twenties; but until age 30 they were severely restricted in performing the normal roles of a husband. They could not reside with their wives, meetings were limited and furtive, and they were prohibited from entering the market to obtain their family's household necessities (Xen. *Lak. Pol.* 1.5; Plut. *Lyk.* 15.4; 25.1). These restrictions derived, I suggest, from an earlier period when men were not permitted to marry until age 30, when they left the upbringing and became fully adult (cf. Sallares 1991, 176). At some point in Sparta's history, therefore, the male age of marriage was lowered. In addition, the polis imposed an *upper* age limit (perhaps 30) before which men had to marry.[26] Compulsory marriage – or, perhaps more accurately, compulsory *procreation* (Xen. *Lak. Pol.* 1.8) – was now enforced by elaborate official sanctions against offenders.[27] Secondly, incentives were introduced to encourage greater numbers of sons. Fathers of three sons were given exemption from military service and fathers of four exemption from all public duties (Arist. *Pol.* 1270a39–b6). In addition, older men with younger wives were permitted, and probably encouraged, to bring in younger men for the purpose of procreation (Xen. *Lak. Pol.* 1.8; Plut. *Lyk.* 15.7). Even the practice of wife-borrowing may have been officially encouraged as a device to ensure that, when a couple had decided to have no more children, the woman's remaining fertile years should not be wasted.

No source indicates the date(s) at which these various changes were introduced. Daube (1977), followed by Cartledge (1979, 309–10), suggested the period around 500 as the time when Sparta took legal steps to stimulate the procreation of embryonic warriors. Their view has been criticized by MacDowell (1986, 76); but his argument that the sources almost invariably attribute these measures to Lykourgos is no reason for ascribing them to a much earlier date. Sallares (1991, 171) also argues for an early date, on the grounds that a stigma on bachelorhood may arise within an age class system when most members of a class have married and pressure grows upon bachelors to rectify their anomalous position. Such a stigma, he suggests, could have existed long before any fear of manpower shortage. Sallares' view, however, is dependent upon a 'survivalist' approach to Spartan historical development which I have criticised elsewhere, a view which treats Sparta's age classes as primeval social entities independent of the polis under whose aegis they developed (Hodkinson 1992d, 380–1; 1997a, 89–92). There is an important difference, moreover, between social pressure, however strong, and the state-imposed penalties attested in classical times; it is the introduction of the latter which we need to explain. The years around 500 suggested by Daube and Cartledge certainly provide a plausible context. In the late sixth century Sparta several times had to recognize the limitations of her capacity to campaign abroad (Hdt. 3.148; 5.49; 6.84; cf. also 6.108; Thuc. 3.68). I would suggest, however, that an even more plausible context is the mid-fifth century, the period when official concern about declining numbers is unequivocally attested by the military reforms detailed above.

The measures introduced by the polis, however, attacked only the symptoms of the malaise and ultimately failed. The incentives for fathers of several sons were, as Aristotle (*Pol.* 1270b4–6) pointed out, positively harmful, since they led to greater division of holdings and consequent impoverishment. The practice of wife-sharing could, as we have seen, be turned into an instrument of family limitation and property concentration. Even the sanctions against failure to marry could be ignored, as is shown by the case of Derkylidas (Poralla 1985, no. 228). Between 411 and 389 BC he was abroad on campaign for at least 14 out of 22 years, and thereby neglected to sire a child. Plutarch (*Lyk.* 15.2) records an incident in which he was criticised for this by a younger citizen, who refused to give up his seat, as was normal practice towards an older man. Nevertheless, Derkylidas did not forfeit his prestigious overseas commands. His military ability, embodied especially in his reputation for wiliness (Xen. *Hell.* 3.1.8) and in the indispensable service he rendered in keeping the Spartan cause alive in Asia Minor after the battle of Knidos (ibid. 4.8.3–5), ensured that he was able to pursue a distinguished military career, regardless of his neglect of his reproductive duty.

Contingent developments: the Peloponnesian war and Spartan empire

As we saw in chapters 1 and 2, the Peloponnesian war and Sparta's subsequent acquisition of empire have traditionally been viewed as fundamental causes of her socio-economic crisis. Indeed, the majority of ancient writers treat Sparta's crisis as an exclusively fourth-century affair. Her acquisition of empire, they claim, stimulated an unprecedented and uncontrolled desire for wealth among her citizens, in place of the former ethic of austerity and disdain for material possessions. Within this general perspective we can detect two versions which, although they occasionally coalesced, represent essentially distinct strands of thought about the Spartan crisis. Some writers, such as Isokrates and (to a large extent) Xenophon, focused on the greed of Spartiate commanders abroad.[28] This version, however, was overshadowed by a more influential version, according to which it was the growing desire for wealth among the citizen body inside Sparta itself which corrupted her previously well-ordered society. This second version is the one found in the writings of Diodorus and Plutarch. It seems to have originated with Ephorus and, to a lesser extent, Theopompos.[29] This second approach is often followed by modern scholars (e.g. David 1981).

As we have seen (chapter 2), there are two main strands to this second approach. One strand is embodied in the claim that Sparta's victory over Athens in 404 led to the breakdown of a traditional prohibition of gold and silver currency, after it was agreed to admit the booty sent home by Lysander into the polis for public, though not for private, use:

> in the reign of Agis coinage first flowed into Sparta, and with coinage greed and a desire for wealth prevailed through the agency of Lysander, who, though incorruptible himself, filled his country with the love of riches and with luxury, thus subverting the laws of Lykourgos (Plut. *Lyk*. 30.1 cf. *Lys*. 17; Diod. 7.12.8).

The other strand represents a subsequent development of the first one by the propagandists of the late third-century revolution:

> the affairs of the Lakedaimonians began to suffer distemper and corruption soon after its subversion of the Athenian supremacy filled it with gold and silver. However, since the number of households instituted by Lykourgos was still preserved in the transmission of lots (*klēroi*), and father left to son his inheritance, to some extent the continuation of this order and equality sustained the polis in spite of its errors in other respects. But when a certain powerful man, Epitadeus by name, who was headstrong and of a violent temper, came to be ephor, he had a quarrel with his son and introduced a *rhētra* which permitted a man during his lifetime to give his household (*oikos*) and lot (*klēros*) to any one he wished, or to bequeath it in his will. This man, then, satisfied a private grudge of his own in introducing the law; but his fellow citizens welcomed it out of greed, made it valid, and so destroyed the most excellent of institutions. For the men of power and influence at once began to acquire estates without scruple, ejecting the rightful heirs from their inheritances; and speedily wealth streamed into the hands of a few and poverty ruled the polis… Consequently, there were [sc. by the mid-third century] left no more than 700 Spartiates, and of these there were only 100 who possessed land and a *klēros* (Plut. *Agis* 5.1–4).

Note that, although the introduction of the *rhētra* is ascribed solely to Epitadeus, the passing of the new law and its adverse consequences are ascribed to the greed of the citizen body, which implicitly derived from the corrupting effects of the influx of imperial wealth.

Ch. 13. Property concentration and the emergence of a plutocratic society

The historicity of both these strands has already been challenged in earlier chapters. In chapter 3 we saw that, contrary to the claims of the *Life of Agis*, landed property was always privately held and unequally distributed throughout the archaic and classical periods; and that gift, and probably also bequest, of land was already practised before the earliest possible date for Epitadeus' legislation. As Schütrumpf (1987) has demonstrated, Plutarch's account of Epitadeus and his *rhētra* is a third-century fiction. The notion that an early fourth-century change of law created the inequalities of late classical and hellenistic Sparta is both untenable and fails to explain the considerable inequalities in wealth and consequent decline in Spartiate numbers evident already in the fifth century. Similarly, in chapter 5 we examined evidence which suggests that precious metal foreign coinage and uncoined bullion were present in Sparta in both public and private use long before 404. The cumulative weight of this evidence makes the notion of an alleged ban on private possession and use of coinage difficult to sustain. The decision to admit the coinage sent home by Lysander for public but not for private use represented, therefore, not a relaxation but a restriction of previous practice. Indeed, Plutarch's claims about the corrupting effects of this public-private compromise are effectively undermined by Plato, who recommended exactly the same compromise for his model Cretan state (*Laws* 742a).

The fundamental error of the above notions is their insistence that Sparta's socio-economic problems arose only in the fourth century, an error already exposed by the penetrating contemporary analyses of Plato (*Republic* 547a–551b) and Aristotle (*Politics* 2.9). As we saw in chapter 2, both commentators agree that love of wealth was central to the problems of Spartan society; but neither portrays it as the product of recent corruption. For Plato, the secret love of money was part of the very essence of his Spartan-based timarchy (548a–c; 549b), and the decline of timarchy through the personal accumulation of wealth resulted from inherent weaknesses in its essential character (550d–551b). For Aristotle, Sparta's failings in the sphere of property and wealth were long-established characteristics which derived from errors of her original lawgiver (Schütrumpf 1994). I would not deny that the Peloponnesian war and Spartan empire played an important role in the development of the Spartan crisis. But, as I have argued elsewhere (Hodkinson 1996, 94–7), most of the changes which they stimulated had their roots in the prior developments examined earlier in this chapter.

Indeed, the very character of Sparta's involvement in war and empire, and therefore of its contribution to the development of her social crisis, was influenced by the fact that the twin constituents of the crisis, property concentration and *oliganthrōpia*, were already significantly advanced before the late fifth century. Throughout most of the period of war and empire, from the 420s down to the 370s, Sparta conducted all her overseas campaigns and many of those in distant parts of the Greek mainland in such a way as to commit abroad only a minority of Spartiates, who acted as commanders or staff officers (cf. Parke 1930). As I have highlighted in a previous study (Hodkinson 1993, 152–61), the persons selected for these foreign commands were predominantly men from the leading families, from lineages whose wealth is shown by indicators such as their connections with the Spartan royal houses, their horse-breeding backgrounds, their ambassadorships, or their *xeniai* with foreign elites. Sparta's organisation of foreign commands and selection of commanders were themselves the product of a declining citizen body dominated by a wealthy elite.

That said, prolonged engagement in foreign warfare was a new factor in Spartiate society, which significantly exacerbated existing socio-economic trends. We may distinguish two broad groups of effects. The first relates to the very experience of overseas campaigning. Although a minority within the society as a whole, Sparta's foreign commanders must have represented a significant proportion of the elite of their generation. Although we do not know the exact number of men involved, during each of the peak decades of overseas engagement (the 400s and 390s) some 30 or so individual foreign commanders are known to us by name. I have estimated that we perhaps need to triple these numbers to about 100, to take account of the large number of unnamed officers and unattested commands in the many theatres of war poorly covered by the literary sources (Hodkinson 1993, 154–5). Despite some younger exceptions, foreign commanders were mostly men in their 40s or 50s (Hodkinson 1983, 251 and n. 28). In a plausible model life table (Princeton Model South, mortality level 3, growth rate zero: Coale and Demeny 1983, 449), men aged 40–59 form about 35% of the adult male population. Within a citizen body of 3000 men (I choose the number as lying in between the different estimates for Spartiate strength in 418), men aged 40–59 would therefore constitute some 1,050 citizens. On these calculations Sparta's foreign commanders would have accounted for about 10% of their peer group, surely embracing the majority of wealthy households with men of that age. It would be surprising if the exposure of such a large proportion of leading citizens to foreign commands had no significant impact.

One direct impact was the opening of access to new means of acquiring wealth. Given their dominant positions in control of military forces superior to those of the local populations among whom they were stationed, Spartiate officers – especially those placed in positions of sole responsibility as harmosts in particular poleis – must have had considerable opportunities for private gain. Xenophon (*Lak. Pol.* 14.2–3) comments that,

> I know that formerly the Lakedaimonians preferred to live together at home with moderate possessions rather than to be corrupted by flattery as harmosts in the poleis. And I know that in the past they were afraid to appear to have gold, whereas nowadays there are some who even pride themselves in possessing it.

Although Xenophon prefers the vague phraseology that harmosts in foreign poleis were 'corrupted by flattery', the contrast he draws between life abroad and life at home with moderate possessions implies that material gain was an integral part of their corruption. Moreover, although his assertion about the boastful possession of gold may refer to citizens at home as well as abroad, he implicitly identifies this corruption as originating with commanders abroad – a point confirmed by the fact that his following remarks return to the ambition of leading citizens to serve as harmosts abroad (cf. Flower 1991, 91).

Xenophon's comments idealise the situation in former days; but there is no reason to doubt his judgement of contemporary behaviour, which can be confirmed by particular examples. Note the case of Thorax, who was executed for his possession of silver (Plut. *Lys.* 19.4). This episode apparently took place shortly after Thorax's return from a three-year spell abroad between 406 and 403 (Poralla 1985, no. 380). His acquisition of the silver probably took place either from the spoils of Aigospotamoi or during his time at Samos among the fanatical pro-Spartan oligarchs notorious for their extreme idolisation of Lysander. Another example is Gylippos' theft of 30 talents from the booty entrusted to him by Lysander (Plut. *Lys.* 16; *Nik.* 28.3; Diod. 13.106.8–9). As noted in chapter 5, the fact that Gylippos evidently expected to be able to use such a large amount without suspicion implies that he was someone already rich in silver coin, money perhaps acquired during his time in Sicily in 414–13, when the Syracusans had accused him of avarice (Timaios, *FGrH* 566F100b, *ap.* Plut. *Nik.* 28.3). Agesilaos' manipulation of the price of booty to make profits for his friends is a further indication of what other commanders could do for their own benefit (Xen. *Ages.* 1.17–19). Besides these attested cases, there are also several allegations of commanders' receipt of bribes (Noethlichs 1987, nos. 22–6) – allegations which, as we have seen (ch. 5), can rarely be proved in any individual case, but which cumulatively demonstrate the expectation of contemporaries that Spartiate commanders were prone to personal profiteering.

Ironically, the commander whose career shows most clearly the possibilities for the acquisition of wealth is the person most renowned for incorruptibility: Lysander, who scrupulously sent home to Sparta the immense amount of public monies and private gifts in his possession after Aigospotamoi, even enclosing a written note of the sum enclosed in each sack, which enabled the ephors to detect the peculation of Gylippos. We have already noted the disappointed expectations on the part of the suitors of Lysander's daughters, who were clearly surprised that his military success had not made him wealthy. Lysander himself, however, was not immune to acquiring wealth for his private use. He retained control of sufficient funds to make expensive religious dedications at Delphi to celebrate his victories: for example, the 'Navarchs' Monument' discussed below and the golden stars representing the Dioskouroi (Plut. *Lys.* 18.1; cf. *Mor.* 397f). According to one source (Anaxandrides of Delphi, cited in Plut. *Lys.* 18.1), Lysander even secretly salted away a large deposit of one talent, fifty-two minas and eleven staters in the treasury of the Akanthians.

Property and the Spartan crisis

Lysander's career also shows that, even if a commander abstained from more dubious means of acquiring wealth, the ties of *xenia* which such men will have contracted with local elites could involve the receipt of material goods. As we saw in chapter 11, after Aigospotamoi he received golden crowns and other personal gifts from his associates in various Greek poleis (Xen. *Hell.* 2.3.8; Diod. 13.106.8; Plut. *Lys.* 16.1). His closest *xenos*, Cyrus, gave Lysander a model of a trireme two cubits long, made of gold and ivory (Plut. *Lys.* 18.1). Many of these personal gifts he donated to the Spartan polis; but others he retained in order to make personal dedications in foreign sanctuaries. Cyrus' gift was deposited at Delphi in the treasury of Brasidas and the Akanthians. Some of his crowns were given to other sanctuaries. Inventories of the treasures of the Hekatompedon on the Athenian acropolis between 401/0 and 385/4 BC record 'a golden crown, which Lysander the Lakedaimonian, son of Aristokritos, dedicated to Athena; weight 66 drachmas 5 obols' (Harris 1995, 192 no. 428). Three further golden crowns, also dedicated by Lysander, are recorded in various inventories of the temple of Apollo at Delos.[30] Lysander, moreover, was not alone in the receipt and dedication of gifts following Aigospotamoi. A golden crown of laurel leaves dedicated by his subordinate commander, Pharax, is recorded several times in third- and second-century inventories of the temple of Apollo at Delos (Bommelaer 1981, 178 n. 32, with references).

As the evidence in the previous paragraph suggests, the making of religious dedications abroad was an important means by which Spartiate commanders could deploy their newly-acquired possessions. In chapter 10 we saw that in the period after 450 BC Spartiate chariot victors at Olympia began to erect costly victory monuments centred on a personal bronze statue. The sphere of foreign commands now gave certain other leading citizens the opportunity to make monumental celebrations of their personal achievements in the military sphere, using the sanctuary of Delphi as an alternative place of display. The crowning glory was the so-called 'Navarchs' Monument' dedicated by Lysander at Delphi (Paus. 10.9.7–10; ML no. 95; Plut. *Lys.* 18.1). It comprised a large group of 39–40 bronze statues disposed in two rows, each resting on a huge oblong base, situated just inside the entrance to the sanctuary of Apollo on the left of the Sacred Way. In the foreground stood several divinities: the Dioskouroi, Zeus, Apollo, Artemis, and Poseidon placing a crown on Lysander, who was flanked by his seer and his steersman. Behind these were 29 or 30 (Pausanias mistakenly says 28) statues of subordinate commanders who fought at Aigospotamoi, arrayed as if in line of battle. The statue of Arakos, Sparta's official *nauarchos*, stood at the right-hand end (left from the spectator's viewpoint) and those of two other Spartiates, Epikydidas and Eteonikos, at the other end. The monument bore an inscribed epigram in praise of Lysander written by Ion of Samos.[31] The expense of the monument must have been immense: at 3,000 drachmas per statue (cf. ch. 10), around some 20 talents.[32]

Discussion of the 'Navarchs' Monument' leads us to the second group of effects distinguished above, which concern the impact of overseas campaigning on the character of Spartiate society. The most immediate and noticeable impact came in the form of reaction: the adverse attitude taken by 'the wisest of the Spartans' and by certain of the ephors against the corrupting effects of the booty sent home to Sparta by Lysander (Plut. *Lys.* 17.1–2). I have argued (ch. 5) that private possession of foreign precious metal currency was nothing new in 404. What was new, however, was the vast scale of monetary wealth becoming available to leading citizens from their overseas commands. The enormous amount of booty sent home by Lysander – some 1,000 or 1,500 talents, according to different sources[33] – must have raised fears of the even deeper penetration of monetary wealth into Spartiate society. The motives which the sources ascribe to the opponents of the influx of imperial wealth are entirely altruistic. But there must also have been a self-interested concern, on the part of leading Spartans who at the time had no access to foreign posts (for example, members of the Gerousia and households without men of the right age), that their more traditional forms of wealth would be overshadowed by the immense new resources potentially open to Sparta's commanders abroad. Hence their introduction, for the first time, of a prohibition against private ownership of precious metal currency and its immediate rigorous enforcement against the hapless Thorax. Lysander's conspicuous abstinence from financial gain, which earned him such a high reputation in Sparta (cf. Plut. *Lys.* 30.1), was probably a political tactic to avoid envy and opposition from such men.

In the long run, the prohibition of precious metal currency, as we have seen (ch. 5), proved incapable of enforcement. But, even in the short run, it did not restrain expenditures by leading citizens. It did not prevent Lysander's commissioning of the Navarchs' monument; nor did it curtail the impact of that extraordinary monument upon the dedicatory activities of other leading Spartiates, especially upon his political rivals. Its grandeur may have influenced the elaborate Olympic monument of Kyniska, sister of King Agesilaos, whose expense exceeded any previous victory dedication. It certainly prompted King Agis II, who had commanded the Peloponnesian forces at Dekeleia, to erect his own counter-monument at Delphi, challenging Lysander's claims by calling himself 'king of land and sea' (Plut. *Mor.* 467f; cf. Athen. 543b). Agis' monument may in turn have prompted the exiled former king Pausanias to erect, shortly after 381 – at Delphi again – a statue of his deceased son, King Agesipolis I, made by the well-known sculptor Kleon of Sikyon. Its inscription proudly announces that 'Hellas proclaims his excellence with one voice' (*IG* v.1.1565; Tod 1948, no. 120). Another Spartiate, a certain Hieron, who commanded the corps of mercenaries at Leuktra, apparently went even further by commissioning personal statues at both Delphi and Olympia (Plut. *Mor.* 397e; *IvO* no. 274).[34] It was in this context of both Olympic victors' and military leaders' proclaiming their successes through conspicuous expenditure upon personal statues that the arch-conservative King Agesilaos II ostentatiously refused a statue for himself,

Property and the Spartan crisis

scorning them as appropriate to wealthy rather than to good men (Xen. *Ages.* 11.7). The vehemence of Agesilaos' reaction suggests that the cases of personal statues attested in the surviving evidence were merely part of a much wider trend towards personal glorification.

All the above dedications were made outside Sparta, in line with our suggestion in chapters 9 and 10 that the dedication of personal statues inside Sparta was restricted in order to control the display of wealth and status in front of fellow citizens. Yet Lysander was able to make lesser, but still impressive, dedications at home. In the western stoa on the Spartan acropolis he dedicated two eagles, each bearing a statue of the goddess Nike (Victory), in celebration of his twin victories at Notion and Aigospotamoi (Paus. 3.17.4). At the sanctuary of the Graces at Amyklai two bronze tripods each supported by a female figure (Sparta and Aphrodite) were dedicated from the spoils of Aigospotamoi, works of Aristandros of Paros and Polykleitos of Argos (Paus. 3.18.7–8). As Cartledge (1987, 82–3) has observed, 'it was unprecedented for a Spartan to erect a memorial of 'his' (not Sparta's) victories at Sparta in his lifetime'. As with his foreign dedications, Lysander's offerings in Sparta may have paved the way for further celebrations of personal achievement inside the polis, in the form of the monuments celebrating the Olympic successes of Kyniska and Euryleonis discussed in chapter 10.

As the comments of Agesilaos show, the capacity to make dedications of the sort just discussed depended upon the possession of significant amounts of surplus wealth. The advent of foreign commands increased the significance of wealth within Spartiate society in other respects too. Selection to these commands rested not on popular election, as with the posts of the ephorate and Gerousia, but on appointment and cooptation (cf. Finley 1986, 166). As I have outlined elsewhere, an important part in these appointments was played by patronage, personal influence and the cultivation of connections – social networking in which the possession of wealth was an essential ingredient (Hodkinson 1993, 159–61). The role of wealth and inherited social status in appointments to foreign commands were further increased by the fact that commanders were typically much younger than the candidates who competed for the traditional peak of a Spartiate's career, membership of the Gerousia. Family influence upon elections to the Gerousia was limited by the fact that a candidate aged over 60 would only rarely have elder relatives alive to provide support. In contrast, supporting senior relatives will have been available far more frequently for men in their 40s or 50s competing for foreign positions. The element of competition must often have been considerable, for two reasons. First, there were a larger number of families involved in the competition for foreign commands than for election to the Gerousia, since considerably more families will have had members aged 40–59 than over age 60. (In the model life table used above men aged 40–59 are over two and a half times as numerous as those over 60.) Secondly, despite the range of available commands, their status

Ch. 13. Property concentration and the emergence of a plutocratic society

and importance varied considerably, from major posts such as the nauarchy or regional harmostships (such as held by Brasidas in Thrace or by Thibron and Derkylidas in Asia Minor) to relatively minor positions such as subordinate staff officer. The more prestigious posts generally contained greater potential for independent initiative and more opportunities for self-enrichment. The competition, moreover, was not simply to gain a single foreign posting, but to hold on to it for a lengthy period or to join the distinguished elite group of commanders re-appointed to two, three or even more commands (Hodkinson 1993, 155–7).

For all these reasons there was a built-in incentive for would-be commanders and their patrons to place a high priority on the acquisition of additional property at home, in order to enhance their influence and their capacity to participate in the competitive networking which underpinned the allocation of foreign commands. The lack of popular election to these posts also meant the lessening of constraints upon the acquisition of property at the expense of poorer citizens. The traditional ambition of leading men to gain election to the Gerousia must have restrained their behaviour towards the mass of poorer Spartiates, since it was upon such men that their election depended. In contrast, the ambition for foreign posts could be pursued without regard for one's fellow citizens, as long as one possessed the necessary personal influence or a patron's goodwill. Furthermore, the fact that, once in post, the success of most commanders' campaigns (and their chances of reappointment) depended not on citizen troops but on non-citizen soldiers or rowers probably added to the perception that ordinary citizens were irrelevant and dispensable in the scramble for high positions.

A final respect in which Sparta's extended involvement in warfare and empire increased the role of property and wealth was through the impetus it gave to the development of factional groupings. The desire for control over policy-making had no doubt often previously led to conflict between leading men, especially between the two kings, with their groups of friends and supporters. The dramatic growth of Spartan power to an unprecedented position of hegemony in mainland and Aegean Greece, however, raised both the stakes and the temperature of political conflict. As Cartledge (1987, 140–1) has reminded us, social scientists have often observed that at times of change and crisis existing networks of patron–client relationships tend to coalesce into more solid factions. Lysander's efforts to consolidate the temporary power gained by his naval victories into an enduring personal authority involved the creation of a band of supporters among his fellow commanders, whose cohesion was apparently so firm that they were perceived as a potential threat even after his death (Xen. *Hell.* 1.6.4–6; Plut. *Ages.* 20). In response, the Eurypontid king Agesilaos II used the base of the kingship to develop his own permanent faction, which enabled him to dominate Spartan policy-making for almost 40 years. Agesilaos' patronal politics have been thoroughly analysed elsewhere (Cartledge

Property and the Spartan crisis

1987, 139–59). Here it is simply necessary to re-emphasize the point already made in chapter 11 regarding the extent to which his faction-building was based upon the large-scale deployment of material resources (Xen. *Ages.* 4; 11.8; Plut. *Ages.* 4). Agesilaos was not alone. We are poorly informed about the activities of the other royal house; but it is evident from the episode of Sphodrias that by 378, if not before, it could count upon the support of a similarly firm – if somewhat less numerous – body of support among the highest ranking citizens within the Gerousia (Xen. *Hell.* 5.4.25).

Fourth- and early third-century Sparta: a plutocratic society

It is evident that, by the fourth century, Sparta was rapidly becoming a plutocracy – a society dominated by the rich, whose ambitions increasingly distanced them from ordinary Spartiates. This society was very different from the Sparta of earlier times described by Thucydides (1.6), in which 'those who had great possessions adopted a lifestyle that was as much as possible like that of the many'. It is true that during his long reign King Agesilaos actively promoted the traditional virtues of personal austerity and abstention from excessive display, setting an example by leading his own life according to the principles outlined by Thucydides (Xen. *Ages.* 5.1–3; 8.6–8; 9.3–7). His criticisms of expenditure on chariot racing and personal statues contrasted these uses of wealth with the qualities of manliness and personal merit (ibid. 9.7; 11.7). The ordinariness of Agesilaos' personal lifestyle, however, was undermined by other, more elitist aspects of his behaviour. His practice of economic patronage set him well above ordinary Spartiates. And, though he eschewed breeding chariot horses, he exploited his massive landholdings to the fullest extent: 'he adorned his own estate, breeding many hunting dogs and war horses' (ibid. 9.6), thereby establishing himself as a public benefactor by supplying the animals required for maintaining military fitness and for the cavalry (Xen. *Lak. Pol.* 4.7; *Hell.* 6.4.11).

The indications are that other leading Spartiates followed Agesilaos' exploitation of wealth, whilst failing to observe his personal restraint. The fourth-century evidence paints a consistent picture of a society dominated by a wealthy elite engaged in the uncontrolled pursuit and exploitation of material resources. The exploitation of wealth by leading citizens for such things as equestrian pursuits, religious dedications and personal patronage has already been viewed in this and in earlier chapters. Their relentless pursuit of additional landholdings is vividly attested by Aristotle during his discussion of deviations from justice in constitutions. He observes that aristocracies lean towards oligarchy and are unstable because 'those who have the advantage of riches, if they enjoy a preponderance in the constitution, seek to ill-treat others and enhance their own fortunes' (*Pol.* 1307a19–20). After giving the example of Thourioi, where the notables illegally got possession of all the land due to the advantage they possessed within a constitution biased towards oligarchy (29–31), Aristotle then turns to Sparta:

> A further consequence of the fact that all aristocratic constitutions are oligarchic in character is that the notables are more grasping (μᾶλλον πλεονεκτοῦσιν): for example, at Sparta, where properties keep coming into the hands of a few (34–6).

For Aristotle, Sparta was a classic example of a polis whose wealthy citizens accumulated property at the expense of the poor.

Elsewhere Aristotle provides further evidence of the selfish economic behaviour of wealthy citizens in his comments upon Spartan public finance (1271b10–17):

> Public finance is another thing badly managed by the Spartiates. They are obliged to undertake large wars, but there is never any money in the public treasury. Also they are very bad at paying the *eisphorai*, for as most of the land is the property of the Spartiates themselves, they do not inquire too closely into each other's *eisphorai*.

Aristotle provides a notable insight into the depth of resistance of Spartiate landowners – no doubt especially the wealthiest citizens – to the taxation of their private property for public purposes. His remarks chime with Plato's judgment concerning the failings of oligarchies, that 'they are too grasping to want to pay the expenses of a war' (*Republic* 551e). Another intimation of this problem appears in the speech ascribed to King Archidamos in the debate in Sparta in 432: 'we neither have public funds nor do we readily (ἑτοίμως) contribute from our private resources' (Thuc. 1.80).[35] Neither was the resistance to payment simply a private affair: Aristotle also emphasizes the inadequate scrutiny of payments. Although he eschews comment on the officials responsible for checking the assessment and payment of *eisphorai*, the polis authorities were evidently unable, or unwilling, to compel their fellow citizens to pay the correct *eisphorai*. The lack of enquiry into the payments made suggests corruption and abdication of responsibility at the highest levels of Spartiate society (Saunders 1995, 158).

This lack of enforcement is also evident in the failure of the prohibition of private ownership of gold and silver currency. As we saw in chapter 5, this prohibition introduced in 404 was soon flouted by leading Spartiates and became a dead letter after barely more than a generation. By the late fourth century the pseudo-Platonic dialogue *Alkibiades I* (122e) could portray Sparta as a polis in which there was more gold and silver privately held than in all Greece. We may speculate that the prohibition's failure relates to the potential role of precious metal currency in the acquisition of landed property: as a lubricator of transactions through which wealthy families could acquire additional holdings by manipulating ordinary citizens' rights of gift and bequest and the freedom of guardians to choose a husband for an heiress. Fourth-century Sparta, consequently, presents us with the paradox of a polis whose authorities reputedly wielded well-nigh tyrannical powers against misconduct by its citizens (Xen. *Lak. Pol.* 8.3–4), yet which proved incapable of controlling the acquisitive behaviour of its wealthy elite.

Property and the Spartan crisis

The reason for this absence of control was the grip which this elite had come by the fourth century to exercise over the most important positions of power – a grip illustrated by Aristotle's comment (*Pol.* 1306a18–19) that the choice of members of the Gerousia, though conducted through popular acclamation, was 'dynastic', *dynasteutikē*, working in favour of a narrow range of families. From their entrenched position Sparta's wealthy families began to abandon the long-standing social compact between rich and poor citizens outlined by Thucydides, which their ancestors had constructed during the archaic period. The later fourth and early third centuries witnessed the undermining of key public institutions which had maintained Spartiate citizens, both rich and poor, as a uniform body of Peers. One indication of this is the number of prominent Spartiates in this period who absented themselves, not on state campaigns as their predecessors during Sparta's period of empire, but on private mercenary ventures abroad: Agesilaos II in Asia and Egypt in the 360s; Gastron and Lamios in Egypt *c.* 350; Archidamos III in Crete and Italy in the 340s and 330s; Thibron in Athens and Crete in the late 320s; Akrotatos in Sicily in 315; Kleonymos in Italy and Corcyra in the late 300s; Xanthippos in Carthage in 255.[36] Some of these ventures took place with official permission, others without; but they all involved opting out of the public way of life, which by implication had now become a less essential element of Spartiate citizenship.

The decline of Sparta's public institutions is especially evident in the third century. Although the public upbringing appears to have survived into the early century,[37] Agis IV is said to have declared its restoration as one of his prime objectives (Plut. *Agis* 4). So too Kleomenes III in the early 220s set about arranging afresh 'the *paideia* of the young men and the so-called *agōgē*' (Plut. *Kleom.* 11.2; cf. 18.4). The implication is that by the middle of the century the classical upbringing had fallen into desuetude (Cartledge and Spawforth 1989, 42; Kennell 1995, 11–14). Changes to the common messes appear somewhat earlier in the century. According to Phylarchos (*FGrH* 81F44, *ap.* Athen. 141f–142b), 'the Lakedaimonians desisted from going to the common messes (*phiditia*) in the traditional fashion'. When they did go, they relaxed on generous and richly-embroidered couch-coverings,

> indulging in the display of many cups and in the service of food dressed in every variety, and what is more, rare unguents and wines and desserts likewise. And these practices were begun by Areus (309–265 BC) and Akrotatos (264–259? BC), who reigned a little while before Kleomenes; yet even they in their turn were so far outdone in their own magnificence by certain private citizens of their generation in Sparta…

Despite the propagandistic embellishment to be expected from a supporter of Kleomenes III's more frugal reforms, it is hard to believe that the passage, with its precise chronology of change, is total invention. The messes had evidently become like voluntary *symposia* in other poleis, serving 'more as forums for luxurious display by the sympotic rich than as arenas of political...solidarity for the citizenry as a whole' (Cartledge and Spawforth 1989, 42).

The reign of King Areus, mentioned by Phylarchos above, provides further signs of the decline of Sparta's former uniform, military lifestyle: the victory of a Spartan comic actor at the festival of the Soteria at Delphi and the construction of a theatre of normal hellenistic type for the staging of plays.[38] Finally, there was Areus' introduction of Sparta's first silver coinage (Grunauer-von Hoerschelmann 1978). Although not of any great economic significance (they were minted outside Sparta and intended mainly for international, propagandist purposes), these coins symbolised the increasing identification of Spartan kings with other hellenistic monarchies as opposed to the traditional dual kingship of Sparta's classical past.

Several of the above developments were not new in origin. As I have commented elsewhere, during the period of her internal transformation 'Spartan social trends exhibit a strong degree of continuity with those evident in earlier periods' (Hodkinson 1996, 97). Departure abroad for private mercenary activity goes back to the activities of Klearchos in the late 400s (Xen. *Anabasis* 2.6.1–5; Diod. 14.12). Differentiation between different messes probably existed in classical times (Hodkinson 1983, 254). The monarchic tendencies of the kingship became evident in the reign of Agesilaos (see ch. 10, p. 327). The growth of a plutocratic Spartiate society had its roots in the increasing use which rich citizens were able to make of their private wealth during the classical period, when the concept of a body of citizen 'Peers' was still a living reality.

These internal transformations were implicated in the dramatic decline of Spartan power abroad (Cartledge 1987; Cartledge and Spawforth 1989, 3–37). It is hardly surprising that Sparta's authorities failed to tackle the roots of the malaise which led to the downfall of her hegemony: the economic difficulties facing poorer families that underlay the decline of Spartiate citizen numbers. The problem required a radical collective solution involving some material sacrifice by the rich: a redistribution of land, or a restructuring of the economic basis of the common messes to alleviate the contributions required from poorer citizens, or a dissolution of the link between mess membership and citizenship. These fundamental solutions were never embraced; the authorities avoided such tough choices. Instead, they opted for cosmetic solutions which papered over the cracks but could not prevent the edifice from falling apart: measures such as trying to stimulate the birth rate or drafting non-Spartiates into the army. On a personal level, wealthy Spartiates sponsored individual *mothakes* through the upbringing, thereby enabling them to regain citizen status. Possibly – though evidence is lacking – some also gave poorer messmates material assistance to meet their food contributions. In both cases, however, the generosity was self-interested, gaining the donor patronal deference and prestige and entrenching the growing social differentiation which lay at the heart of Sparta's problems. The polis failed to address the difficulties of its poor citizens because not to do so suited the narrow self-interest of the dominant wealthy elite, who were determined to avoid public regulation of their acquisitive behaviour.

Unlike their archaic forbears, moreover, poorer Spartiates themselves no longer possessed the collective political clout to compel the rich to address their difficulties. In the seventh century the deleterious effects of the Second Messenian war had apparently stimulated a concerted protest which could not be ignored. By the fourth century the erosion of the economic position of poorer Spartiates had diminished both their status and their numbers. In contrast to the body of several thousand citizens which had emerged from the social compact of the archaic period, the figures for the battle of Leuktra in 371 indicate, as we saw earlier, a total army size of not much more than 1,200. Earlier in the fourth century, in his account of the conspiracy of Kinadon *c.* 398, Xenophon (*Hell.* 3.3.6) mentions the existence of a body of disfranchised former Spartiates, the *hypomeiones* ('Inferiors'). They are listed alongside other numerically significant groups – the helots, *neodamōdeis* and *perioikoi* – who were potential supporters of the conspiracy. Since there were tens of thousands of helots and *perioikoi* and even the *neodamōdeis* numbered several thousand (cf. *Hell.* 3.4.2), the implication is that the Inferiors too were a numerically significant group whose numbers may have approached or even exceeded the number of full Spartiates. A more dramatic illustration of the parlous economic conditions within Spartan society can hardly be imagined.

As we have seen, recent developments had emphasized the social marginalisation of those ordinary Spartiates who retained their citizen rights – excluded, as they were, from the international arena which many leading citizens now viewed as their prime focus of activity, whether as equestrian competitors or as military commanders. Yet there are no signs of any united reaction by such poor Spartiates or of any solidarity with their disfranchised former comrades. An indication of the disunity of the two groups is provided by Kinadon's conspiracy (Xen. *Hell.* 3.3.4–11). Although led by an Inferior who had close contacts with the full citizens (ibid. 5, 8–9, 11; Arist. *Pol.* 1306b34–5), the forces it hoped to enlist were entirely non-Spartiate. There is no suggestion of the possible involvement of ordinary Spartiates, who are treated as the enemy on a par with the leading magistrates.[39] Plutarch does record two further conspiracies in 370/69 BC. Although the first was apparently a conspiracy of non-citizens, the second involved Spartiates (*Ages.* 32.3–7). It is unlikely, however, that the conspirators, who met in a single house, were very many in number;[40] and there is no suggestion that the leaders were ordinary citizens rather than more prominent Spartiates who wished to exploit Agesilaos' current unpopularity to secure his deposition (cf. *Ages.* 30.1; 31.4; 34.1; Flower 1991, 87). Note also that this conspiracy was not coordinated with the first conspiracy of non-citizens. In general, the very fact that the only attested reactions of groups disadvantaged by contemporary economic developments took the form of easily suppressed conspiracies, rather than widespread popular opposition, is a clear sign of the helplessness of poor current and former Spartiates in the face of the domination of the wealthy elite.

The consequence was that the later fourth and early third centuries witnessed a further decline in the fortunes and numbers of ordinary citizens. Unfortunately, lack of evidence prevents us from tracing precise economic developments during this period. One major factor was the loss of Messenia in 370/69, which deprived the citizen body of most of its territory: some 90,000 ha, according to my calculations in chapter 4, leaving the Spartiates with less than 50,000 ha in Lakonia. We can only guess at the far-reaching socio-economic effects of the loss of about two-thirds of citizen land. All social levels will have been affected, but the poor probably more seriously than the rich. Wealthy citizens will have lost their large estates in Messenia on which they grazed their herds of livestock ([Plato], *Alk. I* 122d). Nevertheless, Isokrates' reference (6.55) to the continued horsebreeding activities of wealthy citizens, in a work explicitly dated after the loss of Messenia, indicates that many rich Spartiates retained ample estates in Lakonia. In contrast, any ordinary citizen household which had a sizeable portion of its holdings in Messenia would have suffered a loss of sufficient magnitude to threaten its capacity to meet its mess dues. Hence the loss of Messenia probably made a significant contribution to the impoverishment of ordinary citizens.[41]

As a consequence, Spartiate numbers continued to fall. As noted earlier, according to Aristotle (*Pol.* 1270a29–31), the number of Spartiates fell to below 1,000, probably after the loss of 400 citizens at the battle of Leuktra in 371. Citizen numbers were now so worryingly low that the authorities declined to impose the normal penalty of *atimia* upon those accused of cowardice, both after this battle and after the defeat at Megalopolis 40 years later (Plut. *Ages.* 30.6; Diod. 19.70.5). By the 240s the number of Spartiates had fallen still further to not more than 700 citizens (Plut. *Agis* 5.4). Although this may seem a relatively modest decline after the even sharper falls of the fifth and early fourth centuries, it was accompanied by dramatic economic differentiation. Plutarch states that of the 700 citizens only one hundred possessed land and a *klēros* (γῆν κεκτημένοι καὶ κλῆρον), whilst the remainder were without resources or civic rights (ἄπορος καὶ ἄτιμος ἐν τῇ πόλει). The correct interpretation of this statement is a matter of debate (cf. Fuks 1962b). Plutarch's comment that the poorer Spartiates were *atimoi* may appear to conflict with their subsequent participation in the citizen assembly (*Agis* 9.1–11). Hence it has been suggested that they must have retained at least a sufficient minimum landholding to remain as citizens. An alternative interpretation is that these citizens were so heavily indebted to the rich landowners that many had had to mortgage their holdings (Cartledge and Spawforth 1989, 42). Whichever was the case, it represents a further significant downturn in the fortunes of poor citizens since the early fourth century.

One facet of the marginalisation and impoverishment of poor male citizens was the increased importance of wealthy women. The important role of Spartiate women in the sphere of property has been evident at various points during this study: for example, as owners and inheritors of land and other property and as dedicants of valuable offerings at religious sanctuaries. This is not the place to enter into recent debates about the overall role of women within the classical Spartan polis.[42] The significant role that married women played within the household is, however, sufficiently clear. Although I would question the tendency in certain recent studies to view the Spartan household as an exclusively female sphere from which Spartiate men with their extensive public duties were largely excluded,[43] the reality of female influence should not be rejected. Plato (*Laws* 805e) refers to their role in household management; and Xenophon (*Lak. Pol.* 1.9) comments, *à propos* of the wife-sharing arrangements, that 'the women want to take charge of two households'. Comparative evidence from classical Athens, where women had fewer property rights than their Spartan counterparts, indicates the significant initiative and influence in household affairs that could nevertheless be exercised by well-dowried women.[44] In Sparta, where (on my view) all women inherited and retained ownership of some landed property, one would expect wives (and widowed mothers) to have exercised an even greater leverage. This is precisely the role that Euripides in his *Andromache* gives to the wealthy Spartan princess Hermione: her possessions are said to secure her freedom of speech and she is criticised for lording it over her husband (ll. 147–53, 211, 940). As Ellen Greenstein Millender (1999, 370) has noted, 'Beneath its biased and hostile portrayal of Spartan women, Euripides' *Andromache* provides an important kernel of information concerning the[ir] economic position.' Certain aspects of Spartiate marriage practices also enhanced the wife's influence. Her relatively late age of marriage, combined with the lowering of the male age of marriage, made her less unequal in age to her husband. The practice of wife-sharing and of polyandry gave certain women an extended household management role over the affairs of multiple men. Within a wife-sharing arrangement the woman became the central focus uniting both families, especially if her children by her different partners subsequently intermarried. The economic background to a polyandrous marriage must often have been that the woman was wealthier than each of her male partners.

The influence of women over the affairs of their households was not in itself problematic. Recent work has rightly noted the important role played by women in the stable functioning of Spartan society (e.g. Redfield 1977/8; Ducat 1998). Women had a direct interest in their menfolk's observance of the established Spartiate code of behaviour, in that the public performance of its males affected the prestige of the household, including the status of its female members, and its capacity to contract socially and materially advantageous marriages for its children. Traditionally, therefore, there was an identity of purpose between the interests of the polis and those of women in the well-being and success of their households.

Ch. 13. Property concentration and the emergence of a plutocratic society

This identity of purpose, however, may have been seriously weakened by growing economic differentiation and the increasing importance of wealth as a determinant of a household's status. I have suggested elsewhere (1989, 106) that this happened precisely at a time when the influence of women was increasing due to the greater frequency of marital practices, such as wife-sharing and polyandry, which served to retain land within the kin group and/or limit the number of heirs. These twin developments were probably closely linked, since greater economic differentiation stimulated the changes in marriage practices which increased female influence; and, for the benefit of their children, women (or at least wealthy ones) probably supported these new practices, which themselves fuelled the growth of economic differentiation. Aristotle was apparently aware of this link when he highlighted the connection between female influence and the esteem given to wealth (*Pol.* 1269b23–4). Wealthy women now had both the motive for promoting the interests of their own households to the detriment of poorer families and also more opportunity to make their wishes effective through their greater influence within the household. This is precisely what Aristotle complained about in his rhetorical question: 'what difference does it make whether the women rule or the rulers are ruled by women?' (*Pol.* 1269b32–4).

Ducat (1983, 164) has suggested that one consequence of the citizen manpower shortage will have been a proportionally increased rate of Spartiate mortality in war. (Note the death of 400 out of 700 Spartiates at Leuktra: Xen. *Hell.* 6.4.15.) As a result, both of this and of the increased frequency of polyandry and wife-sharing, a greater number of propertied women may have remained unmarried or become widows, thereby gaining a freer rein for independent economic activity. Our evidence for fourth-century Sparta is inadequate to provide detailed substantiation of the above suggestions; but there are certain significant hints. As we saw in chapter 10, some wealthy women – Kyniska, Euryleonis, and others too (Paus. 3.8.10) – deployed their wealth for their own personal prestige through chariot racing. As noted in chapter 5, the accounts of the Naopoioi at Delphi show one woman, a certain Philostratis, who visited the sanctuary and made her own personal donation on equal terms with Spartiate men (*CID II* 4.1,55–6; TABLE 3). Theopompos supplies a tantalising account of an episode of conflict (probably during the early 370s) between King Agesilaos and a certain Lysanoridas. The outcome was Lysanoridas' exile, followed by the execution of his mother Xenopeithia and her sister Chrysē. The episode suggests that Xenopeithia and Chrysē were two elderly matrons (probably widows, given the lack of reference to their husbands) who were Lysanoridas' chief supporters among his kindred. Their political prominence was presumably accompanied by a comparable influence over the economic affairs of their families.[45]

By the mid-late third century the powerful economic role of Spartan women is attested even more clearly. In Plutarch's *Lives of Agis and Kleomenes* we view two further elderly women, Agesistrata and Archidamia, mother and grandmother of King Agis IV, both of them independent widows, who are depicted as wielding considerable economic power. They were apparently the richest persons in Sparta (*Agis* 4.1). Archidamia possessed many male dependants, friends and debtors whom she could influence (ibid. 6.4; 7.3). Plutarch also mentions another independent wealthy matron, Kratesikleia, mother of King Kleomenes III, who provided her son with 'unstinting subsidies'. It is emphasized that Kratesikleia was 'in no need of marriage', though she voluntarily chose to remarry in order to further Kleomenes' political ambitions. (*Kleom.* 6.1). These royal women stood at the peak of Spartan society; but they were merely the tip of an iceberg. There were many other rich women, who lived lives of luxury and enjoyed much honour and influence in consequence of their wealth (*Agis* 7.3–5).

By the mid-third century, therefore, the united Spartiate citizen body, composed of men who could realistically be described as 'Peers', had ceased to exist. It had been replaced by a plutocracy of wealthy men and women who were implacably opposed to the egalitarian economic changes – especially the redistribution of land – proposed by Kings Agis and Kleomenes.

The opposition between an entrenched plutocracy and egalitarian revolutionary kings in mid-third-century Sparta brings us full circle back to the beginning of this volume. As we saw in Part I (chs. 1–2), in order to justify their reforms in the face of fierce opposition, the revolutionaries claimed that their plans for egalitarian reform were simply a restoration of measures implemented by Lykourgos which had operated during Sparta's classical past. Pre-existing processes of myth-making about the Spartan property system were thereby given a decisive new momentum. Through the agency of Plutarch, this 'invented tradition' of an egalitarian (and even communitarian) economic system – in which male citizens lived an austere military life, in possession of equal landholdings which reverted to the state on their death – became Sparta's major contribution to modern social and political thought.

The purpose of this book has been to argue that the reality of classical Spartan property and wealth was very different. My examination of the anatomy of the property system in Part II (chs. 3–6) concluded that Spartiate property-holding was fundamentally private in character and always distributed unequally. Landed property was passed down within the family by means of partible inheritance, with daughters inheriting as well as sons. Inequality of land ownership brought with it unequal access to the servile labour force of the helots, who were largely fixed to the holdings they cultivated. Richer Spartiates with larger estates and greater numbers of helots could cultivate a wider range of crops and build up large herds of animals. Contrary to the claims of certain ancient writers, Spartiates could also possess the full range of items of movable wealth, including precious metal bullion and foreign coinage. The right to participate in market

Ch. 13. Property concentration and the emergence of a plutocratic society

exchange was a central privilege of citizenship. The private character of property ownership was moderated by the existence of certain communal rights over individually-held property and over the produce from their estates; but none of these rights had a significant redistributive effect.

In Part III (chs. 7–11) we saw that the Spartan polis ensured that inequality of property was squared with the ideology of a community of citizen Peers through restrictions on the use of wealth. Structural impediments to the deployment of communal patronage were reinforced by the imposition of a common public lifestyle, which involved a basic uniformity of education, food and dress, supplemented by specific restrictions upon male and female personal expenditures. This was matched by a parallel uniformity of funerary and burial practices, which were kept simple and austere. Only deceased kings and, to a lesser degree, fallen warriors received any differential commemoration in death. There remained certain spheres, however, in which surplus wealth could be used. For most of our period Spartan men and women dedicated religious votives involving varying degrees of personal expenditure and display at sanctuaries both at home and abroad. The wealthiest citizens bred or kept horses, especially for participation in chariot racing. Successful owners dedicated costly victory monuments, although before the fourth century these monuments were excluded from Sparta itself. Rich Spartiates were also able to employ their wealth to establish and maintain a variety of patronal relationships – with non-citizen dependants, foreign guest-friends, *perioikoi*, and even with fellow citizens.

Finally, in Part IV (chs. 12–13), we have seen how a fundamentally robust system of property-holding, which initially gave most Spartiates sufficient land to feed their families and maintain their compulsory contributions to the common messes, was progressively undermined over time by the increasing concentration of wealth in the hands of a few. Sparta's citizen manpower declined sharply to fewer than 1,000 men as impoverished Spartiates forfeited their citizen rights. By the fourth and early third centuries the community of male citizen Peers, created during the archaic period as a solution to Sparta's chronic internal strife, had been replaced by a plutocratic society dominated by wealthy men and women. The unity and identity of purpose among Spartan citizens, based on the social compact between rich and poor, had been thoroughly undermined. Their disappearance removed the essential foundation of Sparta's foreign influence and hegemony. The consequence was the dramatic decline of Spartan power within the wider Greek world.

Notes

[1] Since the call-up included four of the six *morai* and 35 of the 40 year classes (Xen. *Hell.* 6.1.1, 4.17), the 700 Spartiates, if spread evenly across the *morai*, would indicate a complement of 200 citizens per *mora*. We also need to add a few men to take account

Property and the Spartan crisis

of those left behind in Sparta owing to their official duties (6.4.17). Forrest (1968, 134) believes that Xenophon's 700 should be emended to 1,700; this would indicate a complement of about 500 Spartiates per *mora* and a total army size of 3,000, still well below Herodotus' figure for Plataia.

² The evidence for this conclusion is discussed in more detail on p. 421.

³ For a fuller explanation of the following simulation, including discussion of the theoretical and programming issues, Hodkinson 1992c. I am grateful to my colleague Sarah Davnall of Manchester Computing for constructing and running the computer program.

⁴ The figure of 10,000 couples is simply a convenient round number of the approximate order of magnitude for the size of the Spartiate citizen body at its apogee, being the factor of 10 closest to the figure of 8,000 *homoioi* given by Herodotus (7.234). It does not imply belief in the veracity of the figure of 10,000 Spartiates, which some fourth-century writers mentioned with reference to former times (Arist. *Pol.* 1270a36–7).

⁵ For a table showing the Family Composition Distribution model, Hodkinson 1989, 85; 1992c, 29.

⁶ The distribution used in this study derives from the work of E.A. Wrigley and R.M. Smith, who have produced a number of distribution tables employing varying assumptions regarding fertility and mortality rates and rising, stationary and declining populations (Wrigley 1978, 140–1 tables 3.1–3.3; R.M. Smith 1984, 44–52, tables 1.2–1.7). *Fig.* 23 represents my own extrapolation from these published tables, which I have extended to cover combinations of surviving daughters as well as sons. This extrapolation has been cross-checked against similar, unpublished calculations made by Smith, then subjected to minor adjustments to render the population stationary. I am grateful to my colleague, Dr Theo Balderston, for his help with the mathematical calculations required to extend the work of Wrigley and Smith.

⁷ There are 2,126 units of such land to be distributed among 7,874 families with surviving children; consequently, 27% (2126/7874 = 0.27) of these families each receive one extra unit. So, for example, there are 16 families with 4 sons and 4 daughters; of these, four families receive an extra unit of land in addition to their original holding (16 x 0.27 = 4.32). Similarly, there are 1,028 families with one son and one daughter; of these, 278 families receive an extra unit of land (1028 x 0.27 = 277.56).

⁸ On the association of polyandry with 'systems in which women as well as men are the bearers of property-rights', see also Leach 1955, 185.

⁹ As I have pointed out (Hodkinson 1987, 232), MacDowell (1986, 86) confuses Polybius' attestation of polyandry with the practice of wife-sharing, which is mentioned immediately afterwards. MacDowell is consequently wrong to state that Polybius' evidence should be rejected.

¹⁰ Xen. *Lak. Pol.* 1.8–9; *Lakainōn Apophthegmata*, Anon. no. 23 (= Plut. *Mor.* 242b); Plb. 12.6b.8; Plut. *Lyk.* 15.7; *Comp. Lyk.-Numa* 3.3.

¹¹ Every typical pattern has its exceptions, and one probable example is the second marriage of Eupolia, daughter of Melesippidas, to an otherwise unknown Theodoros (*Palatine Anthology* 7.426). Since Eupolia's first marriage had been to King Archidamos II (Plut. *Ages.* 1.1) and her new kinsfolk were poor (Xen. *Ages.* 4.5; Plut. *Ages.* 4.1), Eupolia clearly remarried down the economic scale – although probably still within the social elite, since the name of a son of the marriage, Teleutias, suggests a link with the family of the well-born commander Pedaritos (Cartledge 1987, 145). As an eminent widow,

Eupolia was probably subject to less family control than an unmarried girl. Nevertheless, her son from her first marriage, Agesilaos, on becoming king, was sufficiently sensitive about the economic imbalance that he gave his mother's kin half the property he had inherited with the kingship. (There is no evidence for the assumption of Hamilton (1991, 13) that Eupolia herself was from a poor background; Xenophon states that it was her *kinsmen* who were poor.)

12 I purposely omit consideration of possible genetic motives for balancing endogamy and exogamy, since we lack adequate knowledge of contemporary perceptions of the effects of human inbreeding. My concern here is with socio-economic motivation.

13 The position regarding the lineage of Anaxandridas' second son, Dorieus, is unclear. Although Dorieus departed abroad, he apparently left a legitimate son, Euryanax, who was a figure of sufficient importance for the regent Pausanias (the son of Kleombrotos) to take him into joint command at Plataia (Hdt. 9.10). Despite being descended from the second eldest son of Anaxandridas, Euryanax was not chosen as king or even as regent for Leonidas' son Pleistarchos, who was a minor. It is unknown whether he had any descendants or what happened to whatever property belonged to Dorieus or himself.

14 The text of Thucydides 5.71.3 appears to mention a third son of Pausanias named Aristokles; but his existence is open to doubt (Gomme et al. 1945–81, iv.120).

15 Some scholars have viewed the Diaktorides who won the Olympic four-horse chariot race in 456 as a member of this Spartan family, but the identification is uncertain (Moretti 1957, no. 278).

16 Pitana held the burial ground of the Agiad royal house (Paus. 3.15.2–3). On its status, cf. also Pindar, *Ol.* 6.28; Eur. *Tro.* 112 ff.; Plut. *Mor.* 601b.

17 Cartledge 1987, 147; Catling and Cavanagh 1976, 147–52. The aryballos itself was probably made *c.* 650, but its dedicatory inscription is apparently not earlier than *c.* 600 (Jeffery 1990, 446 no. 3, 448).

18 One example from an earlier period is the Amompharetos, commander of the Pitanate *lochos* at Plataia (Hdt. 9.53–7), who is surely a descendant of his namesake who was one of the Spartan arbitrators in the Atheno-Megarian dispute over Salamis (Plut. *Solon* 10). Unfortunately, controversy over the date of this arbitration makes it uncertain how long this lineage had been prominent. Earlier scholars dated the arbitration to 610 (Busolt 1893–1904, ii.217 n.2, 247). Legon (1981, 138) argues for the 560s or early 550s. Piccirilli (1973, 52–3) and others would downdate it to 519/18, making the two men (probably) grandfather and grandson.

19 The sources are given by Poralla 1985, nos. 716–18; but for a more accurate assessment of the careers of the various Pharax-es, see Mosley 1963.

20 The sources for what follows are Plut. *Lys.* 2.1, 30.5; Diod. 14.13.5–6; Phylarchos, *FGrH* 81F43, *ap.* Athen. 271e–f; Aelian, *VH* 12.43; cf. Cartledge 1987, 28–9.

21 Sallares (1991, 213–14; cf. 170–1) has criticized the idea of a buoyant citizen population in archaic Sparta on the grounds that the relatively late ages of male and female marriage dictated by her age class system always restricted population growth. However, as he notes (ibid. 150–1), Sparta's marriage pattern (late marriage for males, early marriage – relatively – for females), imposed, from a cross-cultural perspective, no more than an intermediate level of demographic restriction. It was less restrictive than the prevailing patterns in early modern England and France, which produced an average completed family size as high as 8.42 children for women who married at age 20. As he emphasizes, it was the *combination* of a regulatory marriage pattern with

limitations of resources (in Sparta's case owing to excessive property concentration) which led to population decline, not the former alone. In the lengthy period before property concentration had a serious impact upon poor Spartiates, there was potential for moderate demographic growth.

22 Such a combination of 'raisons accidentales' and 'raisons permanentes' has already been suggested by Andreades 1931.

23 In an earlier discussion (Hodkinson 1989, 107–9) I suggested that the above difficulties were compounded by higher child mortality and (I might have added) reduced fertility, deriving from the deleterious effects of increased levels of inbreeding entailed in some of the marriage practices mentioned above. This analysis, however, requires modification. The reliability of certain earlier studies which I cited has been questioned, due to the inadequacy of their control groups, somewhat arbitrary modelling and failure to apply appropriate statistical techniques (Bittles and Makov 1988, 164). Other studies of the demographic impact of inbred marriages have shown divergent results (Khlat 1988). Some report a significant reduction in fertility compared with non-consanguineous marriages; but others show elevated levels of fertility, and yet others no significant pattern. Similarly, although some studies have indicated higher child mortality, others have reported no difference. Population genetics theory in fact predicts that progressive elimination of deleterious genes – and consequently a diminished impact of inbreeding – will occur when there are prolonged high levels of inbreeding (Cavalli-Sforza and Bodmer 1971, 341–3). Finally, the fact that recent studies (e.g. Khoury et al. 1987, 259–61; Khlat 1988, 188) stress the variable effects of inbreeding on different populations, according to varying genetic constitutions or environmental conditions, indicates that one cannot securely extrapolate from the theoretical possibility of deleterious genetic effects to their *actuality* in classical Sparta (cf. Sallares 1991, 235).

24 The most complete discussion is that of Andrewes in Gomme et al. 1945–81, iv.110–17.

25 For the first three episodes, Thuc. 4.26, 80. On the *neodamōdeis*, Thuc. 5.34, with the other references discussed *ad loc.* in Gomme et al. iv.35–6. For the freed helots of 370, Xen. *Hell.* 6.5.28–9; Diod. 15.65.6, however, numbers them at only 1,000.

26 Xen. *Lak. Pol.* 1.6; Plut. *Lys.* 30.4; *Moralia* 228a; Pollux 3.48; 8.40; cf. MacDowell 1986, 74–5.

27 Xen. *Lak. Pol.* 9.5; Klearchos, fr. 73, Wehrli; *Apophth. Lak.*, *Lykourgos* no. 14 = *Mor.* 227f; Plut. *Lyk.* 15.1–2; cf. Cartledge 1979, 310.

28 Isok. *Peace* 95–100; *Panathenaikos* 225; Xen. *Lak. Pol.* 14.

29 Diod. 7.12.8, derived from Ephorus; Plut. *Lyk.* 30.1; *Lys.* 17, citing Theopompos and Ephorus.

30 Bommelaer 1981, 11–12 no. 11a–c, with references to the original inscriptions.

31 There were also two epigrams for the Dioskouroi. In their present state none of the inscribed epigrams are epigraphically contemporary with the monument, but date to the fourth century. Scholars disagree as to whether they are later creations or merely later re-cuttings of the original inscriptions.

32 Plutarch (*Mor.* 397f) mentions a stone statue of Lysander at Delphi; but he is probably referring to the marble statue in the sanctuary of Brasidas and the Akanthians which he discusses in his *Life of Lysander* (1.1), not to Lysander's statue in the Navarchs' Monument.

33 Plut. *Nik.* 28.3, citing Timaios, *FGrH* 566F100b; Diod. 13.106.8–9.

³⁴ Cf. ch. 9, n. 42. I was mistaken in suggesting (in Hodkinson 1996, 96 n. 35) that the marble base dedicated *c.* 400–350 BC at Delphi by a Spartiate named Landridas (*IG* v.1.1565a) may also have borne a personal statue. Subsequent autopsy has shown that the object it held must have been somewhat smaller.

³⁵ On the precise import of ἑτοίμως Gomme (1945–81, i.247) quotes approvingly the interpretation of Classen: 'ἑτοίμως nicht *bereitwillig*, sondern mit *Leichtigkeit*, nämlich von bereit daliegenden Mitteln'; but this interpretation depends on the mistaken notion that Spartiates were deficient in liquid assets. In view of Aristotle's comments, the translation given in the text is more likely.

³⁶ Discussion and references in Lazenby 1985, 169–170; Cartledge and Spawforth 1989, 12, 27.

³⁷ Note Pyrrhos of Epeiros' avowed intention in 274 to send his younger sons to be brought up in the 'Lakonian customs' (Plut. *Pyrrh.* 26.10) and Polybius' comment that Xanthippos was 'a Spartan who had taken part in the *agōgē*' (1.32).

³⁸ *SGDI* 2565.59; Dilke 1950, 48–51; Piper 1986, 185, 223 n. 20; Cartledge and Spawforth 1989, 37.

³⁹ Lazenby (1997, 438 n. 8) explores the possibility that an important Spartiate like Lysander was implicated in the plot; and the involvement of the seer Tisamenos – presumably a descendant of the man granted citizenship in the early fifth century – is intriguing. These, however, were exceptional Spartiates, not ordinary citizens.

⁴⁰ Plutarch refers to this conspiracy as being *meidzōn* in comparison with the first conspiracy of non-citizens which involved 200 persons. *Pace* Lazenby (1997, 441, n. 17) and most modern translators, *meidzōn* probably means 'more serious' rather than 'larger'. As Flower (1991, 87 n. 46) notes, 'given that…the Spartiate population had dropped to as few as 800, it is *prima facie* impossible that more than 200 Spartiates were involved in this second conspiracy', especially as the conspirators were all executed.

⁴¹ Cartledge has suggested that a comment of Aristotle concerning abstention from agricultural labour (ὅπερ καὶ νῦν Λακεδαιμόνιοι ποιεῖν ἐπιχειροῦσιν: *Pol.* 1264a9–10) signifies that the Spartans in his day were attempting to introduce such a measure, with the implication that some poor citizens were now finding it necessary to farm their own lands (Cartledge 1987, 172; Cartledge and Spawforth 1989, 15). This interpretation of Aristotle's remark, however, is by no means certain, as can be seen from even a cursory glance at various modern translations. Is Aristotle saying that abstention from agricultural labour is 'the rule which the Lacedaemonians are now trying to introduce' (T.A. Sinclair and T.J. Saunders, Penguin Classics) or the exact opposite: cf. 'even that is a rule which the Spartans already attempt to follow' (E. Barker, OUP); 'a prohibition which the Lakedaimonians try to enforce already' (B. Jowett, Clarendon Press); 'yet the Lacedaemonians attempt to do this even now' (C. Lord, University of Chicago Press); 'règle que précisément les Lacédémoniens s'efforcent de suivre' (J. Aubonnet, Budé)?

⁴² Cartledge 1981; Kunstler 1987; Dettenhofer 1993; 1994; Ducat 1998; Greenstein Millender 1999; Thommen 1999.

⁴³ Kunstler 1987; Dettenhofer 1993; 1994. This view is rightly criticised by Greenstein Millender (1999, 372) and Thommen (1999, 144–6).

⁴⁴ Schaps 1979, 76–7; Gould 1980, 49–50; Foxhall 1989.

⁴⁵ Theopompos, *FGrH* 115F240, *ap.* Athen. 609b; cf. A. Powell 1999, 409–10.

BIBLIOGRAPHY

Aalders, G.J.D.
    1982   *Plutarch's Political Thought*, Amsterdam, Oxford and New York.
Africa, T.W.
    1961   *Phylarchos and the Spartan Revolution*, Berkeley and Los Angeles.
    1979   'Thomas More and the Spartan mirage', *Historical Reflections* 6, 343–52.
Alcock, S.E.
    1991   'Tomb cult and the post-classical polis', *AJA* 95, 447–67.
    forthcoming   'A simple case of exploitation: the helots of Messenia', in P. Cartledge, L. Foxhall and E. Cohen (eds.) *Money, labour and land in ancient Greece*, London.
Alcock, S.E., Berlin, A., Harrison, A., Heath, S., Spencer, N. and Stone, D.
    in prep.   'The Pylos Regional Archaeological Project. Part IV: Historic Messenia, Geometric to Late Roman', *Hesperia*.
Aleshire, S.B.
    1989   *The Athenian Asklepieion*, Amsterdam.
Alessandrì, S.
    1985   'Le civette di Gilippo (Plut. *Lys.* 16–17)', *ASNP*, ser. III, 15, 1081–93.
Allen, T.W.
    1936   'Adversaria III', *RPhil*, 3 sér., 10, 201–8.
Ampolo, C.
    1984   'Il lusso nelle società arcaiche', *AION* 6, 71–102.
Andersen, L.H.
    1977   'Relief pithoi from the Archaic period of Greek art', Diss. Ann Arbor.
Anderson, J.K.
    1961   *Ancient Greek Horsemanship*, Berkeley and Los Angeles.
    1970   *Military Theory and Practice in the Age of Xenophon*, Berkeley and Los Angeles.
Andreades, A.M.
    1931   'La mort de Sparte et ses causes démographiques', *Metron* 9, 99–105.
    1933   *A History of Greek Public Finance*, Cambridge, Mass.
Andreev, J.V.
    1975   'Sparta als Typ einer Polis', *Klio* 57, 73–82.
Andrewes, A.
    1952   'Sparta and Arcadia in the early fifth century', *Phoenix* 6, 1–5.
    1956   *The Greek Tyrants*, London.
    1966   'The government of classical Sparta', in E. Badian (ed.) *Ancient Society and Institutions: Studies presented to Victor Ehrenberg on his 75th birthday*, Oxford, 1–20.
Andronikos, M.
    1956   'Λακωνικά ἀνάγλυφα', *Peloponnesiaka* 1, 253–314.

Bibliography

Angel, J.L.
    1969   'The bases of palaeodemography', *American Journal of Physical Anthropology* 30, 427–38.

Armstrong, P., Cavanagh, W.G. and Shipley, G.
    1992   'Crossing the river: observations on routes and bridges in Laconia from the archaic to the Byzantine periods', *BSA* 87, 293–310.

Asheri, D.
    1961   'Sulla legge di Epitadeo', *Athenaeum* 39, 45–68.
    1963   'Laws of inheritance, distribution of land and political constitutions in ancient Greece', *Historia* 12, 1–21.
    1966   *Distribuzioni di Terre nell'Antica Grecia*, Torino.

Ashton, R.
    1993   'A revised arrangement for the earliest coinages of Rhodes', in M. Price et al. (eds.) *Essays in Honour of Robert Carson and Kenneth Jenkins*, London, 9–16.

Austin, M.M.
    1993   'Alexander and the Macedonian invasion of Asia: aspects of the historiography of war and empire in antiquity', in Rich and Shipley (eds.) *War and Society*, 197–223.

Ball, R.
    1976   'Herodotos' list of the Spartans who died at Thermopylai', *Museum Africum* 5, 1–8.

Barber, G.L.
    1935   *The Historian Ephorus*, Cambridge.

Barello, F.
    1993   'Il rifiuto della moneta coniata nel mondo Greco. Da Sparta a Locri Epizefiri', *Rivista Italiana di Numismatica e Scienze Affini* 95, 103–11.

Barker, G., Lloyd, J. and Reynolds J. (eds.)
    1985   *Cyrenaica in Antiquity*, BAR Int. Ser. 236, Oxford.

Barron, J.P.
    1984   'Ibycus: *Gorgias* and other poems', *BICS* 31, 13–24.

Bauslaugh, R.A.
    1990   'Messenian dialect and dedications of the "Methanioi"', *Hesperia* 59, 661–8.

Beazley, J.D.
    1956   *Attic Black-Figure Vase-Painters*, Oxford.

Beck, F.A.G.
    1964   *Greek Education, 450–350 BC*, London.

Beloch, K.J.
    1912–27   *Griechische Geschichte*, 2nd edn, Berlin and Leipzig.

Bentley, J.W.
    1987   'Economic and ecological approaches to land fragmentation: in defense of a much-maligned phenomenon', *Annual Review of Anthropology* 16, 31–67.

Bergquist, B.
    1990   'Sympotic space: a functional aspect of Greek dining rooms', in Murray (ed.) *Sympotica*, 37–65.

Bernadini, P.A.
    1992   'La storia dell'epinicio: aspetti socio-economici', *Studi Italiani di Filologia Classica*, ser. 3, 10, 965–79.

Berry, E.G.
- 1961 *Emerson's Plutarch*, Cambridge, Mass.

Berthiaume, G.
- 1976 'Citoyens spécialistes à Sparte', *Mnemosyne* 29, 360–4.

Berve, H.
- 1937 *Sparta*, Leipzig.
- 1941 'Vier Spartabücher', *Gnomon* 17, 1–11.

Bintliff, J.L.
- 1977 *Natural Environment and Human Settlement in Prehistoric Greece*, 2 vols., BAR Suppl. Series 28, Oxford.

Bittles, A.H. and Makov, E.
- 1980 'Inbreeding in human populations: an assessment of the costs', in C.G.N. Mascie-Taylor and A.J. Boyce (eds.) *Human Mating Patterns*, Cambridge, 153–68.

Blinkenberg, C.
- 1926 Review of Laum 1924 and 1925, *Gnomon* 2, 102–9.
- 1931 *Lindos: Fouilles de l'acropole 1902–1914, I. Les Petits Objects*, Berlin.

Bloesch, H.
- 1959 'Spartanische Krieger', *Museum Helveticum* 16, 249–56.

Blundell, S.
- 1995 *Women in Ancient Greece*, London.

Boardman, J.
- 1963 'Artemis Orthia and chronology', *BSA* 58, 1–7.
- 1967 *Excavations in Chios 1952–55: Greek Emporio*, BSA Suppl. Vol. 6, London.

Bockisch, G.
- 1981 'Die Helotisierung der Messenier: ein Interpretationsversuch zu Pausanias IV 14,4f.', in *Antiken Abhängigskeitsformen in den griechischen Gebieten ohne Polisstruktur und den römischen Provinzen*, Actes du colloque sur l'esclavage, Iena 1981, Berlin, 29–48.

Bodin, J.
- 1606 *The Six Bookes of a Commonweale*, London; translation of the French original, 1576, by R. Knolles.

Boeckh, A.
- 1828 *Corpus Inscriptionum Graecarum I*, Berlin.

Bölte, F.
- 1929a 'Sparta: Geographie', RE^2 III, cols. 1294–1373.
- 1929b 'Zu lakonischen Festen', *RhM* 78, 124–43.

Bolgar, R.R. (ed.)
- 1979 *Classical Influences on Western Thought, AD 1650–1870*, Cambridge.

Bommelaer, J.-F.
- 1981 *Lysandre de Sparte: Histoire et traditions*, Athens.

Bonfante, L. and Jaunzems, E.
- 1988 'Clothing and ornament' in Grant and Kitzinger (eds.) *Civilization of the Ancient Mediterranean*, iii.1385–1413

Boring, T.A.
- 1979 *Literacy in Ancient Sparta*, Leiden.

Bowie, E.
　1990　'*Miles Ludens*: the problem of martial exhortation in early Greek elegy', in Murray (ed.) *Sympotica*, 221–9.
Bowra, C.M.
　1961　*Greek Lyric Poetry*, 2nd edn, Oxford.
Bradford, A.S.
　1977　*A Prosopography of Lacedaemonians from the Death of Alexander the Great, 323 BC, to the Sack of Sparta by Alaric, AD 396*, Vestigia 27, Munich.
Brandt, J.R.
　1978　'Archaeologia Panathenaica I: Panathenaic prize-amphorae from the sixth century BC', *Acta ad archaeologiam et artium historiam pertinentia* 8, 1–24.
Braun, T.
　1995　'Barley cakes and emmer bread', in Wilkins et al. (eds.) *Food in Antiquity*, 25–37.
Bravo, B.
　1974　'Une lettre de plomb de Berezan: colonisation et modes de contact dans le Pont', *DHA* 1, 111–87.
　1977　'Remarques sur les assises sociales, les formes d'organisation et la terminologie du commerce maritime grec à l'époque archaïque', *DHA* 3, 1–59.
　1984　'Commerce et noblesse en Grèce archaïque', *DHA* 10, 98–160.
Bremmer, J.
　1990　'Adolescents, symposion, and pederasty', in Murray (ed.) *Sympotica*, 135–48.
Bresson, A.
　1990　'Le cercle des οἰκεῖοι à Sparte', in M.-M. Mactoux and E. Geny (eds.) *Mélanges Pierre Lévêque, V. Anthropologie et Société*, Besançon, 53–9.
Broneer, O.
　1959　'Excavations at Isthmia', *Hesperia* 28, 298–343.
Brown, W.L.
　1950　'Pheidon's alleged Aeginetan coinage', *NC* 10, 177–204.
Bruni, G.B.
　1979　'*Mothakes, neodamōdeis, Brasideioi*', in *Schiavitù, Manomissione e Classi Dipendenti nel Mondo Antico*, Pubbl. Ist. di Storia Antica, Univ. di Padova 13, 21–31.
Buckler, J.
　1977　'Land and money in the Spartan economy – a hypothesis', *Research in Economic History* 2, 249–79.
Bugh, G.R.
　1988　*The Horsemen of Athens*, Princeton.
Burckhardt, J.
　1902　*Griechische Kulturgeschichte, IV*, Stuttgart and Berlin; English translation of the 1930 edition in *The Greeks and Greek Civilization*, London 1998, 127–363.
Burelli Bergese, L.
　1986　'Sparta, il denaro e i depositi in Arcadia', *ASNP*, ser. III, 16, 603–19.
Burford (Cooper), A.
　1969　*The Greek Temple Builders at Epidauros*, Liverpool.
　1977/8　'The family farm in Greece', *CJ* 73, 162–75.
　1993　*Land and Labor in the Greek World*, Baltimore and London.

Burnett, A.
    1976   *Coinage in the Roman World*, London.
Busolt, G.
    1893–1904   *Griechische Geschichte*, 2nd edn, Gotha.
Busolt, G. and Swoboda, H.
    1920–26   *Griechische Staatskunde*, 3rd edn, Munich.
Byres, T.J. (ed.)
    1983   *Sharecropping and Sharecroppers*, London = *Journal of Peasant Studies* 10.
Calligas, P.G.
    1980   'The sanctuary of Apollo Hyperteleateas in Laconia', *LS* 5, 10–30 (in Greek; English summary).
    1992   'From the Amyklaion', in Sanders (ed.) ΦΙΛΟΛΑΚΟΝ, 31–48.
Cambitoglou, A.
    1981   *Archaeological Museum of Andros*, Athens.
Cantarelli, L.
    1890   'I mothakes spartani', *RFIC*, 18, 465–84.
Carlier, P.
    1977   'La vie politique à Sparte sous le règne de Cléomène 1er. Essai d'interprétation', *Ktema* 2, 65–84.
    1984   *La Royauté en Grèce avant Alexandre*, Strasbourg.
Carradice, I. and Price, M.
    1988   *Coinage in the Greek World*, London.
Carter, J.B.
    1985   *Greek Ivory-Carving in the Orientalizing and Archaic Periods*, New York and London.
    1987   'The masks of Ortheia', *AJA* 91, 355–83.
Cartledge, P.A.
    1976   'Did Spartan citizens ever practise a manual *tekhne*?', *LCM* 1, 115–19.
    1977   'Hoplites and heroes: Sparta's contribution to the technique of ancient warfare', *JHS* 97, 11–27.
    1979   *Sparta and Lakonia: A regional history, 1300–362 BC*, London.
    1981   'Spartan wives: liberation or licence?', *CQ* n. s. 31, 84–105.
    1982   'Sparta and Samos: a "special relationship"?', *CQ* n. s. 32, 243–65.
    1983   '"Trade and politics" revisited: archaic Greece', in P. Garnsey, K. Hopkins and C.R. Whittaker (eds.) *Trade in the Ancient Economy*, London, 1–15.
    1984   'A new lease of life for Lichas son of Arkesilas?', *LCM* 9, 98–102.
    1985a   'Rebels and sambos in classical Greece: a comparative view', in Cartledge and Harvey (eds.) *Crux*, 16–46.
    1985b   Review of Rolley 1982, *JHS* 105, 238–40.
    1987   *Agesilaos and the Crisis of Sparta*, London.
    1988a   'Serfdom in classical Greece', in L. Archer (ed.) *Slavery and Other Forms of Unfree Labour*, London, 33–41.
    1988b   'Yes, Spartan kings were heroized', *LCM* 13, 43–4.
    1993a   *The Greeks: A portrait of self and others*, Oxford and New York.
    1993b   'Classical Greek agriculture: recent work and alternative views', *Journal of Peasant Studies* 21, 127–36.
    1998   'The economy (economies) of ancient Greece', *Dialogos* 5, 4–24.

- 1999 'The Socratics' Sparta and Rousseau's', in Hodkinson and Powell (eds.) *Sparta: New perspectives*, 311–37.
- 2000 '"To Poseidon the driver": an Arkado-Lakonian ram dedication', in G.R. Tsetskhladze, A.J.N.W. Prag and A.M. Snodgrass (eds.) *Periplous: Papers on classical art and archaeology presented to Sir John Boardman*, London.

Cartledge, P. and Harvey, F.D. (eds.)
- 1985 *Crux: Essays presented to G.E.M. de Ste Croix on his 75th birthday* (= *History of Political Thought* 6.1/2), Exeter and London.

Cartledge, P. and Spawforth A.
- 1989 *Hellenistic and Roman Sparta: A tale of two cities*, London and New York.

Carvalho Gomes, C.H. de
- 1995 'Xouthias, son of Philakhaios: on *IG* V.2.159 and its possible historical placement', *ZPE* 108, 103–6.

Catling, H.W.
- 1976/7 'Excavations at the Menelaion, Sparta, 1973–76', *JHS, AR* 23, 24–42.
- 1977 'Excavations at the Menelaion 1976–77', *LS* 3, 408–16.

Catling, H.W. and Cavanagh, W.G.
- 1976 'Two inscribed bronzes from the Menelaion, Sparta', *Kadmos* 15, 145–57.

Catling, R.
- 1986 'Excavations at the Menelaion: 1985', *LS* 8, 205–16.
- 1996 'The archaic and classical periods', in Cavanagh et al., *Laconia Survey*, II, 33–89.

Cavaignac, E.
- 1948 *Sparte*, Paris.

Cavalli-Sforza, L.L. and Bodmer, W.F.
- 1971 *The Genetics of Human Populations*, San Francisco.

Cavanagh, W., Crouwel, J., Catling R.W.V. and Shipley, G.
- 1996 *The Laconia Survey, II: Archaeological data*, London.
- forthcoming *The Laconia Survey, I: Methodology and interpretation*, London.

Cavanagh, W.G. and Laxton, R.
- 1984 'Lead figurines from the Menelaion and seriation', *BSA* 79, 23–36.

Cavanagh, W.G. and Walker, S.E.C. (eds.)
- 1998 *Sparta in Laconia: The archaeology of a city and its countryside*, Proceedings of the 19th British Museum classical colloquium, British School at Athens Studies 4, London.

Cawkwell, G.L.
- 1983 'The decline of Sparta', *CQ* n.s. 33, 385–400.

Chamoux, F.
- 1953 *Cyrène sous la monarchie des Battiades*, Paris.

Chantraine, H.
- 1956 'Peloponnes', *Jahrbuch für Numismatik und Geldgeschichte* 7, 59–120.

Charles, M.P.
- 1985 'An introduction to the legumes and oil plants of Mesopotamia', *Bulletin on Sumerian Agriculture* 2, 39–61.

Cheung, S.N.S.
- 1969 *The Theory of Share Tenancy*, Chicago and London.

Chrimes, K.M.T.
   1949   *Ancient Sparta: A re-examination of the evidence*, Manchester; 2nd edn, 1952.

Christ, K.
   1986   'Spartaforschung und Spartabild', in K. Christ (ed.) *Sparta*, Darmstadt, 1–72; repr. in his *Griechische Geschichte und Wissenschaftsgeschichte*, Historia Einzelschriften 106, Stuttgart 1996, 9–57.

Christien, J.
   1974   'La loi d'Epitadeus: un aspect de l'histoire économique et sociale à Sparte', *RD* 52, 197–221.

Christou, C.
   1964a   'Archaic graves in Sparta and a Laconian funeral figured relief amphora', *AD* 19 A´, 123–63 [in Greek]; 283–5 [English summary].
   1964b   'The new amphora from Sparta: the other amphorae with reliefs of Laconian manufacture', *AD* 19 A´, 164–265 [in Greek]; 285–8 [English summary].

Clairmont, C.W.
   1983   *Patrios Nomos: Public Burial in Athens during the fifth and fourth centuries BC, I–II*, BAR Int. Ser. 161, Oxford.

Clauss, M.
   1983   *Sparta: eine Einführung in seine Geschichte und Zivilisation*, Munich.

Coale, A.J. and Demeny P.
   1983   *Regional Model Life Tables and Stable Populations*, 2nd edn, New York.

Coldstream, J.N.
   1976   'Hero-cults in the age of Homer', *JHS* 96, 8–17.

Comstock, M.B. and Vermeule, C.C.
   1976   *Sculpture in Stone: The Greek, Roman and Etruscan collections of the Museum of Fine Arts, Boston*, Boston, Mass.

Congdon, L.O. Keene
   1981   *Caryatid Mirrors of Ancient Greece*, Mainz am Rhein.

Cope, E.M.
   1877   *The Rhetoric of Aristotle*, revised by J.E. Sandys, Cambridge.

Coulson, W.D.E. and Kyrieleis, H. (eds.)
   1992   *Proceedings of an International Symposium on the Olympic Games*, Athens.

Coulson, W.D.E. and Wilkie, N.C.
   1983   'Archaic to Roman times: the site and environs', in W.A. McDonald, W.D.E. Coulson and J. Rosser (eds.) *Excavations at Nichoria in Southwest Greece, III: Dark Age and Byzantine occupation*, Minneapolis, 332–50.

Courbin, P.
   1959   'Dans la Grèce archaïque: valeur comparée du fer et de l'argent lors de l'introduction du monnayage', *Annales ESC* 14, 209–33.

Cox, C.A.
   1988   'Sibling relationships in classical Athens', *Journal of Family History* 13, 377–95.
   1998   *Household Interests: Family, property, marriage strategies, and family dynamics in ancient Athens*, Princeton.

Cozzoli, U.
   1978   'I fondamenti del ΚΟΣΜΟΣ licurgico nel pensiero di Plutarco', *Cultura e Scuola* 66, 84–93.

Bibliography

1979 *Proprietà Fondiaria ed Esercito nello Stato Spartano dell'Età Classica*, Rome.
Crawford, M.H.
  1982 'Sidareoi at Byzantium', *Athenaeum* n. s. 60, 276.
Crawford, M.H. and Whitehead, D.
  1983 *Archaic and Classical Greece: A selection of ancient sources in translation*, Cambridge.
Crowther, N.B.
  1991 'The Olympic training period', *Nikephoros* 4, 161–6.
Curtis, R.I.
  1991 *Garum and Salsamenta: Production and commerce in materia medica*, Leiden.
Curtius, E.
  1858 *Griechische Geschichte, I*, 2nd edn, Berlin.
Däubler, T.
  1923 *Sparta. Ein Versuch*, Leipzig.
Dahl, G. and Hjort, A.
  1976 *Having Herds: Pastoral herd growth and household economy*, Stockholm.
Darré, R.W.
  1937 *Das Bauerntum als Lebensquell der Nordischen Rasse*, 6th edn, München.
Daube, D.
  1977 'The duty of procreation', *Proceedings of the Classical Association* 74, 10–25; also published as a separate pamphlet by Edinburgh University Press.
Daux, G.
  1922 'Inscriptions de Delphes', *BCH* 46, 439–66.
  1977 'Repentirs et mises au point', in *Études Delphiques*, *BCH* Supplément IV, Paris, 49–66.
David, E.
  1979a 'The pamphlet of Pausanias', *PdP* 34, 94–116.
  1979b 'The influx of money into Sparta at the end of the fifth century BC', *Scripta Classica Israelica* 5, 30–45.
  1981 *Sparta between Empire and Revolution, 404–243 BC*, New York.
  1982/83 'Aristotle and Sparta', *AncSoc* 13/14, 67–103.
  1989 'Dress in Spartan society', *Ancient World* 19, 3–13.
  1992 'Sparta's social hair', *Eranos* 90, 11–21.
Davies, J.K.
  1967 'Demosthenes on liturgies: a note', *JHS* 87, 33–40.
  1971 *Athenian Propertied Families 600–300 BC*, Oxford.
  1981 *Wealth and the Power of Wealth in Classical Athens*, New York.
Davis, J.L., Alcock, S.E., Bennet, J., Lolos, Y.G. and Shelmerdine, C.W.
  1997 'The Pylos Regional Archaeological Project. Part I: Overview and archaeological survey', *Hesperia* 66, 391–494.
Dawkins, R.M.
  1929a 'The history of the sanctuary' in Dawkins (ed.) *Sanctuary of Artemis Orthia*, 1–51.
  1929b 'Gold and silver jewellery', in Dawkins (ed.) *Sanctuary of Artemis Orthia*, 381–4.
  1930 'Artemis Orthia: some additions and a correction', *JHS* 50, 298–9.
Dawkins, R.M. (ed.)
  1929 *The Sanctuary of Artemis Orthia at Sparta*, Society for the Promotion of

Hellenic Studies, Suppl. Paper 5, London.

de Polignac, F.
 1995 *Cults, Territory and the Origins of the Greek City-State*, Chicago; trans. of French original, Paris 1984.

de Ridder, A.
 1894 *Catalogue des Bronzes de la Société Archéologique d'Athènes*, Bibliothèque des Écoles Françaises d'Athènes et de Rome, fasc. 69, Paris.

de Romilly, J.
 1977 *The Rise and Fall of States according to Greek Authors*, Ann Arbor.

de Souza, P.
 n.d. 'Fish and fishing in the ancient economy', unpublished paper delivered at the Leicester–Nottingham seminar on 'The Productive Past', March 1997.

Debord, P.
 1982 *Aspects sociaux et économiques de la vie religieuse dans l'Anatolie gréco-romaine*, Leiden.

Decker, W.
 1992 'Zum Wagenrennen in Olympia – Probleme der Forschung', in Coulson and Kyrielis (eds.) *Proceedings*, 129–39.

del Corno, D.
 1996 'Introduzione', to G. Zanetto (ed.) *Plutarco, Le Virtù di Sparta*, Milano.

Delano Smith, C.
 1979 *Western Mediterranean Europe*, London and New York.

den Boer, W.
 1954 *Laconian Studies*, Amsterdam.

Dettenhofer, M.H.
 1993 'Die Frauen von Sparta: Gesellschaftliche Position und politische Relevanz', *Klio* 75, 61–75.
 1994 'Die Frauen von Sparta: Ökonomische Kompetenz und politische Relevanz', in M.H. Dettenhofer (ed.) *Reine Männersache? Frauen in Männerdomänen der antiken Welt*, Köln, Weimar and Wien, 15–40.

Dickins, G.
 1908 'The art of Sparta', *The Burlington Magazine* 14, 66–84.
 1929 'The masks', in Dawkins (ed.) *Sanctuary of Artemis Orthia*, 163–86.

Diels, H. and Kranz, W.
 1959 *Die Fragmente der Vorsokratiker II*, Berlin.

Diesner, H.-J.
 1953/4 'Sparta und das Helotproblem', *Wissenschaftliche Zeitschrift Greifswald* 3, 219–25.

Dilke, O.A.W.
 1950 'Details and chronology of Greek theatre caveas', *BSA* 45, 21–62.

Dilts, M.R. (ed.)
 1971 *Heraclidis Lembi Excerpta Politiarum*, Greek, Roman and Byzantine Studies Monographs 5, Durham, N.C.

Dover, K.J.
 1974 *Greek Popular Morality in the time of Plato and Aristotle*, Oxford.

Droop, J.P.
 1906/7 'Laconia. Excavations at Sparta, 1907, 5. The early bronzes', *BSA* 13, 109–117.

1929	'Bronzes', in Dawkins (ed.) *Sanctuary of Artemis Orthia*, 196–202.

Ducat, J.
1978	'Aspects de l'hilotisme', *AncSoc* 9, 5–46.
1983	'Le citoyen et le sol à Sparte à l'époque classique', in *Hommage à Maurice Bordes, Annales de la Faculté des Lettres et Sciences Humaines de Nice* 45, 143–66.
1984	'Le tremblement de terre de 464 et l'histoire de Sparte', in *IVe rencontres internationales d'archéologie et d'histoire d'Antibes: tremblements de terre, histoire et archéologie, 2.3.4 Nov. 1983*, Valbonne.
1990a	*Les hilotes*, BCH Supplément XX, Paris.
1990b	'Esclaves au Ténare', in M.-M. Mactoux and E. Geny (eds.) *Mélanges Pierre Lévêque, IV. Religion*, Besançon, 173–93.
1998	'La femme de Sparte et la cité', *Ktema* 23, 385–406.
1999	'La femme de Sparte et la guerre', *Pallas* 51, 159–71.

Duncker, M.
1887	'Über die Hufen des Spartiaten', in his *Abhandlungen aus der Griechischen Geschichte*, Leipzig; originally published in *Ber. d. Berl. Akad.* 1881.

Ebert, J.
1972	*Griechische Epigramme auf Sieger an gymnischen und hippischen Agonen*, Abhandlungen der Sächsischen Akademie der Wissenschaften zu Leipzig, Philologisch-historische Klasse 63.2, Berlin.

Ehrenberg, V.
1924	'Spartiaten und Lakedaimonier', *Hermes* 59, 23–72; repr. in his *Polis und Imperium*, Zurich 1965, 161–201.
1929	'Sparta (Geschichte)', *RE* III, A.2, 1373–1453.

Eryomin, A.
1996	'Stephen Hodkinson and the problems of the Spartan polis', in *Istoria i istoriografia zarubezhnogo mira v litsakh* (*Prominent Figures in Foreign History and Historiography*), Samara, 150–6 [in Russian].

Evans, M.M. and Abrahams, E.B.
1964	*Ancient Greek Dress*, London.

Farquharson, J.
1976	*The Plough and the Swastika: The NSDAP and agriculture in Germany, 1928–45*, London and Beverly Hills.

Figueira, T.J.
1984	'Mess contributions and subsistence at Sparta', *TAPhA* 114, 87–109.
1986	'Population patterns in late archaic and classical Sparta', *TAPhA* 116, 165–213.
1993	'Athenians, Aiginetans, and the Solonian crisis', in his *Excursions in Epichoric History: Aiginetan essays*, 61–86.
1998	*The Power of Money: Coinage and politics in the Athenian empire*, Philadelphia.
1999	'The evolution of the Messenian identity', in Hodkinson and Powell (eds.) *Sparta: New perspectives*, 211–44.

Finley, M.I.
1985	*The Ancient Economy*, 2nd edn, London.
1986	'Sparta', in *The Use and Abuse of History*, 2nd edn, London, 161–78 = *Economy and Society in Ancient Greece*, B.D. Shaw and R.P. Saller (eds.), London 1981,

24–40 = Vernant (ed.) *Problèmes de la Guerre*, 143–60.

Fisher, N.R.E.
- 1988 'Greek associations, symposia and clubs', in Grant and Kitzinger (eds.) *Civilization of the Ancient Mediterranean*, ii.1167–97.
- 1989 'Drink, *hybris* and the promotion of harmony in Sparta', in Powell (ed.) *Classical Sparta*, 26–50.
- 1994 'Sparta re(de)valued: some Athenian public attitudes to Sparta between Leuctra and the Lamian war', in Powell and Hodkinson (eds.) *Shadow of Sparta*, 347–400.

Fisher, N.R.E. and van Wees, H. (eds.)
- 1998 *Archaic Greece: New approaches and new evidence*, London and Oakville, Conn.

Fitzhardinge, L.F.
- 1980 *The Spartans*, London; unchanged reprint, 1985.

Flacelière, R.
- 1937 *Plutarque, sur les oracles de la Pythie*, Paris.
- 1948 'Sur quelques passages des *Vies* de Plutarque', *REG* 61, 67–103 and 391–429.

Flower, M.A.
- 1988 'Agesilaos and the origins of the ruler cult', *CQ* n. s. 38, 123–34.
- 1991 'Revolutionary agitation and social change in classical Sparta', in Flower and Toher (eds.) *Georgica*, 78–97.
- 1994 *Theopompus of Chios: History and rhetoric in the fourth century BC*, Oxford.

Flower, M.A. and Toher, M. (eds.)
- 1991 *Georgica: Greek studies in honour of George Cawkwell*, Institute of Classical Studies, Bulletin Suppl. 58, London.

Förtsch, R.
- 1998 'Spartan art: its many different deaths', in Cavanagh and Walker (eds.) *Sparta in Laconia*, 48–54.

Forbes, H.A.
- 1982 'Strategies and soils: technology, production and environment in the peninsula of Methana, Greece', Diss. Pennsylvania.
- 1995 'The identification of pastoralist sites within the context of estate-based agriculture in ancient Greece: beyond the "transhumance versus agro-pastoralism" debate', *BSA* 90, 325–38.
- 1996 'The uses of the uncultivated landscape in modern Greece: a pointer to the value of the wilderness in antiquity?', in G. Shipley and J. Salmon (eds.) *Human Landscapes in Classical Antiquity*, London and New York, 68–97.

Forbes, H.A. and Foxhall, L.
- 1978 '"The queen of all trees": preliminary notes on the archaeology of the olive', *Expedition* 21, 37–47.

Fornara, C.W.
- 1966 'Some aspects of the career of Pausanias the Regent', *Historia* 15, 257–71.

Forrest, W.G.
- 1968 *A History of Sparta 950–192 BC*, London.

Fortenbaugh, W.W., Huby, P.M., Sharples, R.W. and Gutas, D.
- 1992 *Theophrastus of Eresus: Sources for his life, writings, thought and influence*, Leiden, New York and Köln.

Foxhall, L.
- 1989 'Household, gender and property in classical Athens', *CQ* n.s. 39, 22–44.
- 1992 'The control of the Attic landscape', in Wells (ed.) *Agriculture*, 155–60.
- 1998 'Cargoes of the heart's desire: the character of trade in the archaic Mediterranean world', in Fisher and van Wees (eds.) *Archaic Greece*, 295–309.

Foxhall, L. and Forbes, H.A.
- 1982 'Σιτομετρεία: the role of grain as a staple food in classical antiquity', *Chiron* 12, 41–90.

Foxhall, L. and Stears, K.
- 2000 'Redressing the balance: dedications of clothing to Artemis and the order of life stages', in M. McDonald and L. Hurcombe (eds.) *Gender and Material Culture*, London.

Frazer, J.G.
- 1898 *Pausanias's Description of Greece*, London.

Freeman, K.
- 1946 *The Pre-Socratic Philosophers*, Oxford.

Friedl, E.
- 1962 *Vasilika: a village in modern Greece*, New York.

Frost, F.J.
- 1992 'Staying alive on the ancient Greek farm', *AHB* 6, 187–95.

Fuhrmann, F.
- 1988 *Plutarque. Oeuvres Morales, III*, Paris.

Fuks, A.
- 1962a 'Non-Phylarchean tradition of the programme of Agis IV', *CQ* n.s. 12, 118–21.
- 1962b 'The Spartan citizen-body in the mid-third century and its enlargement proposed by Agis IV', *Athenaeum* 40, 244–63; reprinted in his *Social Conflicts in Ancient Greece*, Jerusalem and Leiden 1984, 230–49.

Funke, P.
- 1980 *Homonoia und Arche: Athen und die griechische Staatenwelt vom Ende des Peloponnesischen Krieges bis zum Königsfrieden (404/3–387/6 v. Chr.)*, Wiesbaden.

Fuqua, C.
- 1981 'Tyrtaeus and the cult of heroes', *GRBS* 22, 215–26.

Furtwängler, A.
- 1980 'Zur Deutung der Obeloi im Lichte Samischer Neufunde', in A. Cahn and E. Simon (eds.) *Tainia. Roland Hampe zum 70. Geburtstag*, Mainz, 81–98.

Fustel de Coulanges, N.D.
- 1891 'Etude sur la propriété à Sparte', in *Nouvelles Recherches sur Quelques Problèmes d'Histoire*, ed. C. Jullian, Paris, 52–118; originally published in *Mémoires de l'Académie des Sciences Morales et Politiques de l'Institut de France* 16 (1988) 835–930.

Gabba, E.
- 1957 'Studi su Filarco', *Athenaeum* 35, 3–55 and 193–239.

Gabelmann, H.
- 1965 *Studien zum frühgriechischen Löwenbild*, Berlin.

Gabrielsen, V.
- 1994 *Financing the Athenian Fleet: Public taxation and social relations*, Baltimore and London.

Gallant, T.W.
- 1985 *A Fisherman's Tale. An analysis of the potential productivity of fishing in the ancient world*, Miscellanea Graeca 7, Gent.
- 1989 'Crisis and response: risk-buffering behavior in Hellenistic Greek communities', *Journal of Interdisciplinary History* 19, 393–414.
- 1991 *Risk and Survival in Ancient Greece*, Cambridge.

Gansiniec, Z.
- 1956 'The iron money of the Spartans and the origin of the obolos currency', *Archaeologia* 8, 367–413 [in Polish, with English summary].

Garlan, Y.
- 1988 *Slavery in Ancient Greece*, Ithaca and London; English trans. of *Les Esclaves en Grèce Ancienne*, Paris 1982.

Garland, R.
- 1985 *The Greek Way of Death*, London.
- 1989 'The well-ordered corpse: an investigation into the motives behind Greek funerary legislation', *BICS* 36, 1–15.

Garnsey, P.
- 1988 *Famine and Food Supply in the Graeco-Roman World*, Cambridge.

Gauer, W.
- 1991 *Die Bronzegefässe von Olympia, I*, Olympische Forschungen 21, Berlin and New York.

Gemoll, W.
- 1924 *Das Apophthegma: Literarhistorische Studien*, Wien and Leipzig.

Gentili, B. and Prato, C. (eds.)
- 1979 *Poetae Elegiaci: Testimonia et fragmenta*, Leipzig.

Gilbert, G.
- 1872 *Studien zur altspartanischen Geschichte*, Göttingen.

Gill, D.
- 1983 'Tuscan sharecropping in united Italy: the myth of class collaboration destroyed', in Byres (ed.) *Sharecropping and Sharecroppers*, 146–69.

Glotz, G.
- 1925 *Histoire Ancienne II. Histoire Grecque, I*, Paris.

Golden, M.
- 1990 *Children and Childhood in Classical Athens*, Baltimore and London.
- 1998 *Sport and Society in Ancient Greece*, Cambridge.

Gomme, A.W., Andrewes, A. and Dover, K.J.
- 1945–81 *A Historical Commentary on Thucydides*, 5 vols., Oxford.

Goody, J.
- 1973 'Bridewealth and dowry in Africa and Eurasia' in J. Goody and S.J. Tambiah, *Bridewealth and Dowry*, Cambridge, 1–58.
- 1976a *Production and Reproduction*, Cambridge.
- 1976b 'Inheritance, property and women: some comparative considerations', in J. Goody, J. Thirsk and E.P. Thompson (eds.) *Family and Inheritance: Rural society in western Europe, 1200–1800*, Cambridge, 10–36.

Bibliography

Goody, J. and Harrison, G.A.
    1973   'The probability of family distributions', Appendix (pp. 16–18) to J. Goody, 'Strategies of heirship', *CSSH* 15, 3–20.

Gould, J.
    1980   'Law, custom and myth: aspects of the social position of women in classical Athens', *JHS* 100, 35–59.

Gow, A.S.F. and Page, D.L.
    1965   *The Greek Anthology: Hellenistic epigrams*, 2 vols., Cambridge.

Granger-Taylor, H.
    1996   'Dress', in *OCD*^{3}, 497–8.

Grant, M. and Kitzinger, R. (eds.)
    1988   *Civilization of the Ancient Mediterranean: Greece and Rome*, 3 vols., New York.

Greenstein Millender, E.
    1996   '"The Teacher of Hellas": Athenian democratic ideology and the "barbarization" of Sparta in fifth-century Greek thought', Diss. Pennsylvania.
    1999   'Athenian ideology and the empowered Spartan woman', in Hodkinson and Powell (eds.) *Sparta: New perspectives*, 355–91.

Grell, C.
    1995   *Le dix-huitième siècle et l'antiquité*, 2 vols., Oxford.

Grenfell, R.P. and Hunt, A.S.
    1899   *The Oxyrhynchus Papyri, II*, London.

Griffiths, A.H.
    1972   'Alcman's *Partheneion*: the morning after the night before', *QUCC* 14, 1–30.

Grote, G.
    1862   *A History of Greece*, new edn, 8 vols., London.

Grunauer-von Hoerschelmann, S.
    1978   *Die Münzprägung der Lakedaimonier*, Berlin and New York.

Gschnitzer, F.
    1964–76   *Studien zur griechischen Terminologie der Sklaverei*, Mainz.

Guarducci, M.
    1974   *Epigrafia Greca, III*, Rome.

Guerci, L.
    1979   'L'immagine di Sparta e Atene in Mably e nei fisiocratici', *Quaderni di Storia* 9, 71–108.

Habicht, C.
    1985   *Pausanias' Guide to Greece*, Berkeley, Los Angeles and London.

Hajnal, J.
    1965   'European marriage patterns in perspective', in D.V. Glass and D.E.C. Eversley (eds.) *Population in History: Essays in historical demography*, London, 101–43.

Halstead, P.
    1987   'Traditional and ancient rural economy in Mediterranean Europe: plus ça change?', *JHS* 107, 77–87.

Hamilton, C.D.
    1979   *Sparta's Bitter Victories: Politics and diplomacy in the Corinthian war*, Ithaca and London.
    1982   'Étude chronologique sur le règne d'Agésilas', *Ktema* 7, 281–96.

1991 *Agesilaos and the Failure of the Spartan Hegemony*, Ithaca and London.

Hammond, M.
1979/80 'A famous *exemplum* of Spartan toughness', *CJ* 75, 97–109.

Hampl, F.
1937 'Die Lakedämonischen Periöken', *Hermes* 72, 1–49.

Hanson, V.D.
1989 *The Western Way of War*, London.

Harris, D.
1995 *The Treasures of the Parthenon and Erechtheion*, Oxford.

Harrison, A.B. and Spencer, N.
1998 'After the palace: the early "history" of Messenia', in J.L. Davis (ed.) *Sandy Pylos: An archaeological history from Nestor to Navarino*, Austin, 147–78.

Harrison, A.R.W.
1968–71 *The Law of Athens*, Oxford; new edn, London and Indianapolis, 1998.

Harvey, F.D.
1985 '*Dona ferentes*: some aspects of bribery in Greek politics', in Cartledge and Harvey (eds.) *Crux*, 76–117.
1994 'Lacomica: Aristophanes and the Spartans', in Powell and Hodkinson (eds.) *Shadow of Sparta*, 35–58.

Head, B.V.
1911 *Historia Numorum*, Oxford.

Heilmeyer, W.-D.
1979 *Frühe Olympische Bronzefiguren: Die Tiervotive*, Olympische Forschungen XII, Berlin.

Herfort-Koch, M.
1986 *Archaische Bronzeplastik Lakoniens*, Boreas: Münstersche Beiträge zur Archäologie, Beiheft 4, Münster.

Herman, G.
1980–81 'The "friends" of the early Hellenistic rulers: servants or officials?', *Talanta* 12–13, 103–49.
1987 *Ritualised Friendship and the Greek City*, Cambridge.
1990 'Patterns of name diffusion within the Greek world and beyond', *CQ* n.s. 40, 349–63.

Herring, R.J.
1983 *Land to the Tiller: The political economy of land reform in south Asia*, New Haven.
1984 'Chayanovian versus neoclassical perspectives on land tenure and productivity interactions', in E.P. Durrenberger (ed.) *Chayanov, Peasants and Economic Anthropology*, London, 133–49.

Herrmann, H.V.
1964 'Werkstätten geometrischer Bronzeplastik', *JdI* 79, 17–71.
1988 'Die Siegerstatuen von Olympia', *Nikephoros* 1, 119–83.

Herzfeld, M.
1980 'Social tension and inheritance by lot in three Greek villages', *Anthropological Quarterly* 53, 91–100.

Hibler, D.
1992 'Three reliefs from Sparta', in Sanders (ed.) ΦΙΛΟΛΑΚΟΝ, 115–22.

Bibliography

- 1993 'The hero-reliefs of Lakonia: changes in form and function', in Palagia and Coulson (eds.) *Sculpture*, 199–204.

Hicks, E.L. and Hill, G.F.
- 1901 *A Manual of Greek Historical Inscriptions*, Oxford.

Higgins, W.E.
- 1977 *Xenophon the Athenian*, Albany.

Hirzel, R.
- 1912 *Plutarch*, Leipzig.

Hoch, S.L.
- 1986 *Serfdom and Social Control in Russia: Petrovskoe, a village in Tambov*, Chicago and London.

Hodkinson, S.
- 1983 'Social order and the conflict of values in classical Sparta', *Chiron* 13, 239–81.
- 1986 'Land tenure and inheritance in classical Sparta', *CQ* n. s. 36, 378–406.
- 1987 Review of MacDowell 1986, *JHS* 107, 231–2.
- 1988 'Animal husbandry in the Greek polis', in Whittaker (ed.) *Pastoral Economies*, 35–74.
- 1989 'Marriage, inheritance and demography: perspectives upon the success and decline of classical Sparta', in Powell (ed.) *Classical Sparta*, 79–121.
- 1990 'Politics as a determinant of pastoralism: the case of southern Greece, c. 800–300 BC', *Rivista di Studi Liguri* 16, 139–64.
- 1992a 'Sharecropping and Sparta's economic exploitation of the helots', in Sanders (ed.) ΦΙΛΟΛΑΚΩΝ, 123–34.
- 1992b 'Imperialist democracy and market-oriented pastoral production in classical Athens', in A. Grant (ed.) *Les Animaux et leurs Produits dans le Commerce et les Échanges* = special issue of *Anthropozoologica* 16, 53–60.
- 1992c 'Modelling the Spartan crisis: computer simulation of the impact of inheritance systems upon the distribution of landed property', *BJRL* 74, 27–38.
- 1992d Review of Sallares 1991, *CPh* 87, 376–81.
- 1993 'Warfare, wealth and the crisis of Spartiate society', in Rich and Shipley (eds.) *War and Society*, 146–76.
- 1994 '"Blind Ploutos"?: contemporary images of the role of wealth in classical Sparta', in Powell and Hodkinson (eds.) *Shadow of Sparta*, 183–222.
- 1996 'Spartan society in the fourth century: crisis and continuity', in P. Carlier (ed.) *Le IVᵉ Siècle av. J.-C.: Approches historiographiques*, Nancy, 85–101.
- 1997a 'The development of Spartan society and institutions in the archaic period', in L.G. Mitchell and P.J. Rhodes (eds.) *The Development of the Polis in Archaic Greece*, London and New York, 83–102.
- 1997b 'Servile and free dependants of the Spartan *oikos*', in Moggi and Cordiano (eds.) *Schiavi e Dipendenti*, 45–71.
- 1998a 'Lakonian artistic production and the problem of Spartan austerity', in Fisher and van Wees (eds.) *Archaic Greece*, 93–117.
- 1998b 'Patterns of bronze dedications at Spartan sanctuaries, c. 650–350 BC: towards a quantified database of material and religious investment', in Cavanagh and Walker (eds.) *Sparta in Laconia*, 55–63.
- 1999 'An agonistic culture?: athletic competition in archaic and classical Spartan

society', in Hodkinson and Powell (eds.) *Sparta: New perspectives*, 147–87.
n.d. 'Spartiates and helots: subsistence, patronage and communal organisation', unpublished paper.

Hodkinson, S. and Powell, A. eds.
1999 *Sparta: New perspectives*, London.

Holladay, A.J.
1977 'Spartan austerity', *CQ* n.s. 27, 111–26.

Holm, A.
1899 *The History of Greece*, 4 vols., London and New York; trans. of German original, 1886–94.

Hönle, A.
1972 *Olympia in der Politik der griechischen Staatenwelt von 776 bis zum Ende des 5. Jahrhunderts*. Bebenhausen; based on her dissertation, Tübingen 1968.

Hooker, J.T.
1980 *The Spartans*, London.

Hopkins, K.
1980 'Brother–sister marriage in Roman Egypt', *CSSH* 22, 303–54.

Hornblower, S.
1991 *A Commentary on Thucydides, I: Books I–III*, Oxford.

How, W.W. and Wells, J.
1912 *A Commentary on Herodotus*, 2 vols., Oxford.

Howard, M.W.
1970 *The Influence of Plutarch in the Major European Literatures of the Eighteenth Century*, Chapel Hill.

Howgego, C.
1990 'Why did ancient states strike coins?', *NC* 150, 1–25.
1995 *Ancient History from Coins*, London and New York.

Hultsch, F.
1882 *Griechische und Römische Metrologie*, Berlin.

Humble, N.M.
1997 'Xenophon's view of Sparta: a study of the *Anabasis*, *Hellenica* and *Respublica Lacedaemoniorum*', Diss. McMaster.
1999 '*Sophrosyne* and the Spartans', in Hodkinson and Powell (eds.) *Sparta: New perspectives*, 339–53.

Humphreys, S.C.
1980 'Family tombs and tomb cult in ancient Athens: tradition or traditionalism?', *JHS* 100, 96–126; reprinted in her *The Family, Women and Death*, London 1983, 79–129.

Hussey, E.L.
1985 'Thucydidean history and Democritean theory', in Cartledge and Harvey (eds.) *Crux*, 118–38.

Huxley, G.L.
1962 *Early Sparta*, London.

Hyde, W.W.
1912 'The position of victor statues at Olympia', *AJA* 16, 203–29.
1921 *Olympic Victor Monuments and Greek Athletic Art*, Washington.

Bibliography

Hyland, A.
   1990   *Equus: The horse in the Roman world*, London.
Instone, S.
   1989   Review of Poliakoff 1987, *JHS* 109, 256–7.
Isager, S.
   1988   'Once upon a time. On the interpretation of [Aristotle] Oikonomika ii', in A. Damsgaard-Madsen, E. Christiansen and E. Hallager (eds.) *Studies in Ancient History and Numismatics presented to Rudi Thomsen*, Aarhus, 77–83.
Isager, S. and Skydsgaard, J.E.
   1992   *Ancient Greek Agriculture: An introduction*, London and New York.
Jackson, A.H.
   1992   'Arms and armour at the panhellenic sanctuary of Poseidon at Isthmia', in Coulson and Kyrieleis (eds.) *Proceedings*, Athens, 141–4.
Jaeger, W.
   1948   *Aristotle: Fundamentals of the history of his development*, 2nd revised English edn, London.
Jameson, M.H.
   1977/8 'Agriculture and slavery in classical Athens', *CJ* 73, 122–45.
   1988   'Sacrifice and animal husbandry in classical Greece', in Whittaker (ed.) *Pastoral Economies*, 87–119.
   1992   'Agricultural labour in ancient Greece', in Wells (ed.) *Agriculture*, 135–46.
Janssen, A.J.
   1957   *Het antieke Tropaion*, Ledeberg and Gent.
Jardé, A.
   1925   *Les céréales dans l'antiquité grecque: la production*, Paris.
Jeanmaire, H.
   1939   *Couroi et courètes: essai sur l'éducation spartiate et sur les rites d'adolescence dans l'antiquité hellénique*, Lille.
Jeffery, L.H.
   1988   'The development of Lakonian lettering: a reconsideration', *BSA* 83, 179–81.
   1990   *The Local Scripts of Archaic Greece*, revised edn of the original 1961 edition, with a supplement by A.W. Johnston, Oxford.
Jenner, E.A.B.
   1986   'Further speculations on Ibycus and the epinician ode: S 220, S 176, and the "Bellerophon Ode"', *BICS* 33, 59–66.
Johnston, J.
   1934   'Solon's reform of weights and measures', *JHS* 54, 180–4.
Jones, A.H.M.
   1967   *Sparta*, Oxford.
   1974   'Taxation in antiquity', in his *The Roman Economy: Studies in ancient economic and administrative history*, ed. P.A. Brunt, Oxford, 151–86.
Jost, M.
   1974   'Statuettes de bronze provenant de Lykosoura', *BCH* 99, 355–63.
Kahil, L.
   1977   'L'Artémis de Brauron: rites et mystère', *Antike Kunst* 20, 86–98.

Kahrstedt, U.
    1919   'Die spartanische Agrarwirtschaft', *Hermes* 54, 279–94.
Kaltsas, N.
    1983   'Ἡ ἀρχαϊκὴ οἰκία στὸ Κοπανάκι τῆς Μεσσηνίας', *AE*, 207–37.
Karabélias, E.
    1982   'L'epiclérat à Sparte', *Studi in Onore di Arnaldo Biscardi, II*, Milan, 469–80.
Karwiese, S.
    1980   'Lysander as Herakliskos Drakonopnigon', *NC* 140, 1–2.
Kayser, B. et al. (eds.)
    1964   *Economic and Social Atlas of Greece*, Athens.
Keaney, J.J.
    1980   'Hignett's *HAC* and the authorship of the *Athēnaiōn Politeia*', *LCM* 5, 51–6.
Kelly, D.H.
    1981   'Thucydides and Herodotus on the Pitanate Lochos', *GRBS* 22, 31–8.
Kennell, N.M.
    1995   *The Gymnasium of Virtue: Education and culture in ancient Sparta*, Chapel Hill and London.
Kerferd, G.B.
    1981   *The Sophistic Movement*, Cambridge.
Kertzer, D.I.
    1984   *Family Life in Central Italy, 1880–1910*, New Brunswick.
Kessler, E.
    1910   *Plutarchs Leben des Lykurgos*, Berlin.
Khazanov, A.M.
    1984   *Nomads and the Outside World*, Cambridge; trans. from Russian original.
Khlat, M.
    1988   'Consanguineous marriage and reproduction in Beirut, Lebanon', *American Journal of Human Genetics* 43, 188–96.
Khoury, M.J., Cohen, B.H., Chase, G.A. and Diamond, E.L.
    1987   'An epidemiologic approach to the evaluation of the effect of inbreeding on pre-reproductive mortality', *American Journal of Epidemiology* 125, 251–62.
Kidd, I.G.
    1988   *Posidonius, II. The commentary*, Cambridge.
Kiechle, F.
    1959   *Messenische Studien*, Kallmunz.
    1963   *Lakonien und Sparta*, München.
Kilian(-Dirlmeier), I.
    1978   'Weihungen an Eileithyia und Artemis Orthia', *ZPE* 31, 219–22.
    1984   *Nadeln der frühhelladischen bis archaischen Zeit von der Peloponnes*, Prähistorischer Bronzefunde XIII.8, München.
Kim, H.S.
    1994   'Greek fractional coinage: a reassessment of the inception, development, prevalence and functions of small change during the late archaic and early classical periods', M.Phil. diss., Oxford.
Klees, H.
    1975   *Herren und Sklaven*, Wiesbaden.

Bibliography

Kolchin, P.
- 1987 *Unfree Labor: American slavery and Russian serfdom*, Cambridge, Massachusetts and London.

Kraay, C.M.
- 1976 *Archaic and Classical Greek Coins*, London.

Krentz, P.
- 1989 *Xenophon. Hellenika I–II.2.10*, Warminster.
- 1995 *Xenophon, Hellenika II.3.11–IV.2.8*, Warminster.

Kroll, J.H.
- 1998 'Silver in Solon's laws', in R. Ashton and S. Hurter (eds.) *Studies in Greek Numismatics in Memory of Martin Jessop Price*, London, 225–32.
- n.d. '"In economic terms, the introduction of coinage is not in itself of great significance"', unpublished paper given at the conference *Money and Culture in Ancient Greece*, University of Exeter, July 1999.

Kromayer, J. and Veith, G.
- 1928 *Heerwesen und Kriegführung der Griechen und Römer*, München.

Kunstler, B.L.
- 1983 'Women and the development of the Spartan polis', Diss. Boston.
- 1987 'Female dynamics and female power in ancient Sparta', in M. Skinner (ed.) *Rescuing Creusa: New methodological approaches to women in antiquity*, Lubbock, Texas, 31–48.

Kunze, E.
- 1958 *VI. Bericht über die Ausgrabungen in Olympia*, Berlin.
- 1961 *VII. Bericht über die Ausgrabungen in Olympia*, Berlin.
- 1967 *VIII. Bericht über die Ausgrabungen in Olympia*, Berlin.

Kunze, E. and Schleif, H.
- 1944 *IV. Bericht über die Ausgrabungen in Olympia*, Berlin.

Kurke, L.
- 1991 *The Traffic in Praise: Pindar and the poetics of social economy*, Ithaca and London.
- 1993 'The economy of kudos', in C. Dougherty and L. Kurke (eds.) *Cultural Poetics in Archaic Greece*, Cambridge, 131–63.
- 1995 'Herodotus and the language of metals', *Helios* 22, 36–64.

Kurtz, D.C. and Boardman, J.
- 1971 *Greek Burial Customs*, London.

Kyle, D.G.
- 1996 'Gifts and glory: Panathenaic and other Greek athletic prizes' in J. Neils (ed.) *Worshipping Athena: Panathenaia and Parthenon*, Madison, Wisconsin and London.

Kyrieleis, H.
- 1993 'The Heraion at Samos', in N. Marinatos and R. Hägg (eds.) *Greek Sanctuaries: New approaches*, London and New York, 125–54.

Lacey, W.K.
- 1968 *The Family in Ancient Greece*, London; reprinted, Auckland 1980.

Lamb, W.W.
- 1926/7a 'Bronzes from the Acropolis, 1924–27', *BSA* 28, 82–95.
- 1926/7b 'Notes on some bronzes from the Orthia site', *BSA* 28, 96–106.

1969	*Ancient Greek and Roman Bronzes*, Chicago; reprint with additions of the original 1929 edition.

Lane Fox, R.
    1985   'Aspects of inheritance in the Greek world', in Cartledge and Harvey (eds.) *Crux*, 208–232.

Larson, J.
    1995   *Greek Heroine Cults*, Madison.

Laslett, P.
    1972   'Introduction: the history of the family', in P. Laslett and R. Wall (eds.) *Household and Family in Past Time*, Cambridge, 1–89.

Laum, B.
    1924   *Heiliges Geld: Eine historische Untersuchung über der sakralen Ursprung des Geldes*, Tübingen.
    1925   *Das Eisengeld der Spartaner*, Braunsberg.

Lauter-Bufe, H.
    1974   'Fragment eines lakonischen Reliefpithos', *AK* 17, 89–91.

Lazenby, J.F.
    1985   *The Spartan Army*, Warminster.
    1994   'Logistics in classical Greek warfare', *War in History* 1, 3–18.
    1995   'The *archaia moira*: a suggestion', *CQ* n.s. 45, 87–91.
    1997   'The conspiracy of Kinadon reconsidered', *Athenaeum* n.s. 85, 437–47.

Lazzarini, M.L.
    1976   *Le Formule delle Dediche Votive nella Grecia Arcaica*, Atti della Accademia Nazionale dei Lincei, Memorie. Classe di Scienze morali, stor. e filol. 19, Rome, 45–354.

Le Bohec, S.
    1993   *Antigone Dōsōn, Roi de Macédoine*, Nancy.

Le Bras, H.
    1969   'Retour d'une population à l'état stable après une catastrophe', *Population* (Paris) 24, 861–96.

Le Roy, C.
    1961   'ΛΑΚΩΝΙΚΑ', *BCH* 85, 206–35.

Leach, E.R.
    1955   'Polyandry, inheritance and the definition of marriage', *Man* 55, 182–6; reprinted in J. Goody (ed.) *Kinship*, Harmondsworth 1971, 151–62.

Leahy, D.M.
    1955   'The bones of Tisamenus', *Historia* 4, 26–38.

Lefkowitz, M.R.
    1984   'Pindar's *Pythian* V', in A. Hurst (ed.) *Pindare*, Fondation Hardt. Entretiens sur l'Antiquité Classique 31, Vandoeuvres-Geneva, 33–69.

Legon, R.P.
    1981   *Megara: the political history of a Greek city-state to 336 BC*, Ithaca and London.

Lehmann, D.
    1984   Review of Byres (ed.) 1983, *Journal of Development Studies* 20, 263–5.

Lembesi, A.
    1985   Το Ιερό του Ερμή και της Αφροδίτης στη Σύμη Βιάννου, *I*. Χάλκινα Κρητικά Τορεύματα, Athens.

Leon, C.
    1968   'Statuette eines Kouros aus Messenien', *MDAI(A)* 83, 175–85.
Lévi-Strauss, C.
    1983   *Le regard éloigné*, Paris.
Lévy, E.
    1987   'La Sparte de Polybe', *Ktema* 13, 63–79.
Lewis, D.M.
    1959   'Law on the Lesser Panathenaia', *Hesperia* 28, 239–47.
Linders, T.
    1988   *Comptes et inventaires dans la cité grecque*, Neuchâtel.
Linders, T. and Alroth, B. (eds.)
    1992   *Economics of Cult in the Ancient Greek World*, Boreas 21, Uppsala.
Link, S.
    1991   *Landverteilung und sozialer Frieden im archaischen Griechenland*, Historia Einzelschriften 69, Stuttgart.
    1994   *Der Kosmos Sparta: Recht und Sitte in klassischer Zeit*, Darmstadt.
    1998   '"Durch diese Tür geht kein Wort hinaus!" (Plut. Lyk. 12, 8): Burgergemeinschaft und Syssitien in Sparta', *Laverna* 9, 82–112.
Littman, R.J.
    1988   'Greek taxation', in Grant and Kitzinger (eds.) *Civilization of the Ancient Mediterranean*, ii.795–808.
Loomis, W.T.
    1992   *The Spartan War Fund: IG V 1,1 and a new fragment*, Historia Einzelschriften 74, Stuttgart.
Loraux, N.
    1977   'La belle mort spartiate', *Ktema* 2, 105–120; reprinted as 'The Spartans' "Beautiful Death"' in Loraux 1995, 77–91.
    1981   'Le lit, la guerre', *L'Homme* 21, 36–67; reprinted as 'Bed and war', in Loraux 1995, 29–53.
    1995   *The Expériences of Tiresias: The feminine and the Greek man*, Princeton; translation of French original, Paris 1989.
Losemann, V.
    1977   *Nationalsozialismus und Antike: Studien zur Entwicklung des Faches Alte Geschichte 1933–1945*, Hamburg.
Lotze, D.
    1959   ΜΕΤΑΞΥ ΕΛΕΥΘΕΡΩΝ ΚΑΙ ΔΟΥΛΩΝ: *Studien zur Rechtsstellung unfreier Landbevölkerung in Griechenland bis zum 4. Jahrhundert. v. Chr.*, Berlin.
    1962   'ΜΟΘΑΚΕΣ', *Historia* 11, 427–35.
    1971   'Zu einigen Aspekten des spartanischen Agrarsystems', *Jahrbuch für Wirtschaftgeschichte*, 63–76.
Loy, W.G.
    1970   *The Land of Nestor: A physical geography of the southwest Peloponnese*, National Academy of Sciences, Office of Naval Research, Report No. 34, Washington, D.C.
Lüdemann, H.
    1939   *Sparta. Lebensordnung und Schicksal*, Leipzig.

Lukermann, F.E. and Moody, J.
   1978   'Nichoria and vicinity: settlement and circulation', in G.R. Rapp, Jr. and S.E. Aschenbrenner (eds.) *Excavations at Nichoria in Southwest Greece, I: Site, environs and techniques*, Minneapolis, 78–112.

Lupi, M.
   1997   'L'ordine delle generazioni: classi di età e costumi matrimoniali a Sparta', Diss. Napoli 'Federico II'.

Macan, R.W.
   1895   *Herodotus. The Fourth, Fifth and Sixth Books*, 2 vols., London and New York.

McCloskey, D.N.
   1975   'The persistence of English open fields', in W. Parker and E.L. Jones (eds.) *European Peasants and their Markets: Essays in agrarian economic history*, Princeton, 73–122.

McDonald, W.A. and Rapp, Jr., G.R. (eds.)
   1972   *The Minnesota Messenia Expedition: Reconstructing a Bronze Age regional environment*, Minneapolis.

McDonnell, M.
   1991   'The introduction of athletic nudity: Thucydides, Plato and the vases', *JHS* 111, 182–93.

MacDowell, D.M.
   1986   *Spartan Law*, Edinburgh.

McQueen, E.I.
   1980   'The Eurypontid house in Hellenistic Sparta', *Historia* 39, 163–81.

Malkin, I.
   1994   *Myth and Territory in the Spartan Mediterranean*, Cambridge.

Manfredini, M. and Piccirilli, L.
   1980   *Plutarco, Le Vite di Licurgo e di Numa*, Milan.

Manso, J.C.F.
   1800–05   *Sparta*, 3 vols., Leipzig.

Marangou, E.-L.
   1969   *Lakonische Elfenbein- und Beinschnitzerein*, Tübingen.

Marasco, G.
   1978a   'La leggenda di Polidoro e la redistribuzione di terre di Licurgo nella propaganda Spartana del III secolo', *Prometheus* 4, 115–27.
   1978b   'Aristotele come fonte di Plutarco nelle biografie di Agide e Cleomene', *Athenaeum* 56, 170–181.
   1979   'Cleomene III, i mercenari e gli iloti', *Prometheus* 5, 45–62.
   1980   'La Retra di Epitadeo e la situazione sociale di Sparta nel IV secolo', *AC* 49, 131–45.
   1981   *Commento alle Biographie Plutarchee di Agide e Cleomene*, 2 vols., Rome.

Marshall, A.
   1890   *Principles of Economics*, London.

Martin, T.R.
   1985   *Sovereignty and Coinage in Classical Greece*, Princeton.
   1996   'Why did the Greek *polis* originally need coins?', *Historia* 45, 261–83.

Matthaiou, A.P. and Pikoulas, G.A.
   1989   ' Ἔδον τοῖς Λακεδαιμονίοις ποττὸν πόλεμον', *Horos* 7, 77–124.

Bibliography

Mattingly, H.B.
   1989   Review of Carradice and Price 1988, *NC* 149, 228–32.

Mattusch, C.C.
   1988   *Greek Bronze Statuary*, Ithaca and London.

Melville Jones, J.R.
   1993   *Testimonia Numaria: Greek and Latin texts concerning ancient Greek coinage, I. Texts and Translations*, London.

Meier, T.
   1939   *Das Wesen der spartanischen Staatsordnung*, Leipzig.

Meyer, Ed.
   1892   *Forschungen zur Alten Geschichte, I*, Halle.

Meyer, Ernst
   1978   'Messenien', *RE, Suppl.* 15, 155–289.

Michell, H.
   1947   'The iron money of Sparta', *Phoenix*, Suppl. 1, 42–4.
   1964   *Sparta*; reprint of original 1952 edition, Cambridge.

Miller, S.G.
   1991   *Arete: Greek sports from ancient sources*, 2nd edn, Berkeley and Los Angeles.

Millett, P.
   1991   *Lending and Borrowing in Ancient Athens*, Cambridge.

Missoni, R.
   1986   'Idealità e prassi degli spartani circa i caduti in guerra', in *Decima Miscellanea Greca e Romana*, Rome, 62–81.

Mitchell, L.G.
   1997   *Greeks Bearing Gifts: The public use of private relationships in the Greek world, 435–323 BC*, Cambridge.

Moggi, M. and Cordiano, G. (eds.)
   1997   *Schiavi e Dipendenti nell'Ambito dell'Oikos e della Familia*, XXII Colloquio GIREA, Pisa.

Momigliano, A.
   1936   'Per l'unita logica della *Lakedaimoniōn Politeia* di Senofonte', *RFIC* 64, 170–3; reprinted in his *Terzo Contributo alla Storia degli Studi Classica e del Mondo Antico, I*, Rome 1966, 341–5.

Moore, J.M.
   1975   *Aristotle and Xenophon on Democracy and Oligarchy*, London.

Moretti, L.
   1957   *Olympionikai, i Vincitori negli Antichi Agoni Olimpici*, Atti della Accademia Nazionale dei Lincei, Classe di Scienze morali, stor. e filol., ser. 8, vol. 8, fasc. 2, Rome, 53–198.
   1970   'Supplemento al catalogo degli Olympionikai', *Klio* 52, 295–303.
   1992   'Nuovo supplemento al catalogo degli Olympionikai', in Coulson and Kyrieleis (eds.) *Proceedings*, 119–28.

Morgan, K.A.
   1993   'Pindar the professional and the rhetoric of the ΚΩΜΟΣ', *CPh* 88, 1–15.

Mørkholm, O.
   1991   *Early Hellenistic Coinage: From the accession of Alexander to the Peace of Apameia (336–188 BC)*, eds. P. Grierson and U. Westermark, Cambridge.

Morris, I.
- 1989 'Attitudes towards death in Archaic Greece', *CA* 8, 296–320.
- 1992 *Death-Ritual and Social Structure in Classical Antiquity*, Cambridge.
- 1995 'The meanings of death' [review article of Sourvinou-Inwood 1995], *Cambridge Archaeological Journal* 5, 331–3.
- 1997 'The art of citizenship', in S. Langdon (ed.) *New Light on a Dark Age*, Columbia and London.
- 1998 'Archaeology and archaic Greek history', in Fisher and van Wees (eds.) *Archaic Greece*, 1–91.

Morrisson, C.
- 1993 'Les usages monétaires du plus vil des métaux: le plomb', *Rivista Italiana di Numismatica e Scienze Affini* 95, 79–101.

Morrow, G.R.
- 1960 *Plato's Cretan City*, Princeton.

Mosley, D.J.
- 1963 'Pharax and the Spartan embassy to Athens in 370/69', *Historia* 12, 247–50.
- 1971 'Spartan kings and proxeny', *Athenaeum* n.s. 49, 433–5.
- 1973 *Envoys and Diplomacy in Ancient Greece*, Historia Einzelschriften 22, Wiesbaden.

Mossé, C.
- 1977 'Les périèques lacédémoniens: à propos d'Isocrate, Panathénaïque, 177 sqq.', *Ktema* 2, 121–4.
- 1991 'Women in the Spartan revolutions of the third century BC.', in S.B. Pomeroy (ed.) *Women's History and Ancient History*, Chapel Hill and London, 138–53.

Murray, O.
- 1990 'Cities of reason', in Murray and Price (eds.) *The Greek City*, 1–25.
- 1991 'War and the symposium', in W.J. Slater (ed.) *Dining in a Classical Context*, Ann Arbor, 83–103.
- 1993 *Early Greece*, 2nd edn, London.

Murray, O. (ed.)
- 1990 *Sympotica: A symposium on the Symposion*, Oxford.

Murray, O. and Price, S. (eds.)
- 1990 *The Greek City from Homer to Alexander*, Oxford.

Musti, D. and Torelli, M.
- 1990 *Pausania, Guida della Grecia, III. La Laconia*, Milan.

Nachstädt, W.
- 1935 'Das Verhältnis der Lykurgvita Plutarchs zu den Apophthegmata Lycurgi und den Instituta Laconica', *Bericht über die Sitzungen des Philologischen Vereins im Jahre 1935*, Berlin, 3–5.

Nachstädt, W., Sieveking, W. and Titchener, J.B.
- 1935 *Plutarchi Moralia, II*, Lipsiae.

Nafissi, M.
- 1985 'Battiadi ed Aigeidai: per la storia dei rapporti tra Cirene e Sparta in età arcaica', in Barker, Lloyd and Reynolds (eds.) *Cyrenaica*, 375–86.
- 1989 'Distribution and trade', in Stibbe, *Laconian Mixing Bowls*, 68–88.
- 1991 *La Nascita del Kosmos: Studi sulla storia e la società di Sparta*, Napoli.
- 1999 'From Sparta to Taras: *Nomima, ktisis* and relationships between colony and mother city', in Hodkinson and Powell (eds.) *Sparta: New perspectives*, 245–72.

National Statistical Service of Greece
  1978   *Results of the Agriculture–Livestock Census of March 14, 1971*, Athens.
Nenci, G.
  1968   'Considerazioni sulle origini della monetazione romana in Plinio (*Nat. Hist.*, XXXIII, 43–7)', *Athenaeum*, n. s. 46, 3–36.
  1974   'Considerazioni sulle monete di cuoio e di ferro nel bacino del Mediterraneo e sulla convenzionalità del loro valore', *ASNP*, ser. III, 4, 639–57.
Newman, W.L.
  1887–1902 *The Politics of Aristotle*, Oxford.
Niemeyer, H.
  1960   *Promachos: Untersuchungen zur Darstellung der bewaffneten Athena in archaischer Zeit*, Waldsassen/Bayern.
Nilsson, M.P.
  1912   'Die Grundlagen des spartanischen Lebens', *Klio* 12, 308–40; reprinted in his *Opuscula Selecta, II*, Lund 1952, 826–71.
Nixon, L. and Price, S.
  1990   'The size and resources of Greek cities', in Murray and Price (eds.) *The Greek City*, 137–70.
Noethlichs, K.L.
  1987   'Bestechung, Bestechlichkeit und die Rolle des Geldes in der spartanischen Aussen- und Innenpolitik vom 7. bis 2. Jh. v. Chr.' *Historia* 36, 129–70.
Oakley, J.H. and Sinos, R.H.
  1993   *The Wedding in Ancient Athens*, Madison.
Ogden, D.
  1996   *Greek Bastardy in the Classical and Hellenistic Periods*, Oxford.
Oeconomides, N.
  1992   'The *IGCH* 101 hoard and the circulation of the Tortoise in the Peloponnesus', in *Florilegium Numismaticum: Studia in honorem U. Westermark edita*, Stockholm 1992, 307–12.
  1993   '"Iron coins": a numismatic challenge', *Rivista Italiana di Numismatica e Scienze Affini* 95, 75–8.
Oliva, P.
  1971   *Sparta and her Social Problems*, Prague.
Ollier, F.
  1933–43 *Le mirage spartiate: étude sur l'idéalisation de Sparte dans l'antiquité grecque*, 2 vols., Paris.
  1934   *Xénophon, La République des Lacédémoniens*, Lyon.
Osborne, R.
  1987   *Classical Landscape with Figures: The ancient Greek city and its countryside*, London.
  1988   'Social and economic implications of the leasing of land and property in classical and hellenistic Greece', *Chiron* 18, 279–323.
  1991   'Pride and prejudice, sense and sensibility: exchange and society in the Greek city', in J. Rich and A. Wallace-Hadrill (eds.) *City and Country in the Ancient World*, London and New York, 119–46.
  1996   *Greece in the Making, 1200–479 BC*, London and New York.

Page, D.L.
   1981   *Further Greek Epigrams*, Cambridge.
Palagia, O. and Coulson, W. (eds.)
   1993   *Sculpture from Arcadia and Lakonia*, Oxford.
Papanikolaou, A.D.
   1976–77   'Epitymbion ex arkhaias Sellasias', *Athena* 76, 202–4 [in Greek].
Paradiso, A.
   1991   *Forme di Dipendenza nel Mondo Greco*, Bari.
   1997   'Gli iloti e l'*oikos*', in Moggi and Cordiano (eds.) *Schiavi e Dipendenti*, 73–90.
Pareti, L.
   1917   *Storia di Sparta Arcaica*, Florence.
Parke, H.W.
   1930   'The development of the Second Spartan Empire (405–371 BC)', *JHS* 50, 37–79.
Parke, H.W. and Wormell, D.E.
   1956   *The Delphic Oracle*, 2 vols., Oxford.
Parker, H.
   1937   *The Cult of Antiquity and the French Revolutionaries: A study in the development of the revolutionary spirit*, Chicago; repr. New York 1965.
Parker, R.
   1988   'Were Spartan kings heroized?', *LCM* 13, 9–10.
   1989   'Spartan religion', in Powell (ed.) *Classical Sparta*, 142–72.
Parker, R.A.C.
   1955/6   'Coke of Norfolk and the agrarian revolution', *Economic History Review*, 2nd ser., 8, 156–66.
Patterson, C.B.
   1998   *The Family in Greek History*, Cambridge, Mass. and London.
Payne, H.
   1940   *Perachora, I*, Oxford.
Pearson, L.
   1962   'The pseudo-history of Messenia and its authors', *Historia* 11, 397–426.
Peek, W.
   1955   *Griechische Vers-Inschriften, I. Grab-Epigramme*, Berlin.
Pekridou-Gorecki, A.
   1989   *Mode in antiken Griechenland*, München.
Pelling, C.B.R.
   1980   'Plutarch's adaptation of his source-material', *JHS* 100, 127–40.
   1988   *Plutarch, Life of Antony*, Cambridge.
   1990   'Truth and fiction in Plutarch's *Lives*', in D.A. Russell (ed.) *Antonine Literature*, Oxford, 19–52.
Perlman, S.
   1976   'On bribing Athenian ambassadors', *GRBS* 17, 223–33.
Pettersson, M.
   1992   *Cults of Apollo at Sparta: The Hyakinthia, the Gymnopaidiai and the Karneia*, Stockholm.

Philipp, H.
   1981   *Bronzeschmuck aus Olympia*, Olympische Forschungen 13, Berlin and New York.
Picard, O.
   1980   'Xénophon et la monnaie à Sparte (Constitution des Lacédémoniens, c. 7)', *REG* 90, xxv–xxvi.
   1989   'Innovations monétaires dans la Grèce du IVe siècle', *CRAI* 673–87.
Piccirilli, L.
   1973   *Gli Arbitrati Interstatali Greci, I. Dalle origini al 338 a.C.*, Pisa.
   1984   'Il santuario, la funzione guerriera della dea, la regalità: il caso di Atena Chalkioikos', in M. Sordi (ed.) *I Santuari e la Guerra nel Mondo Classico*, Milan, 3–19.
Piérart, M.
   1995   'Chios entre Athènes et Sparte. La contribution des exilés de Chios à l'effort de guerre lacédémonien pendant la Guerre du Péloponnèse', *BCH* 119, 253–82.
Piper, L.J.
   1986   *The Spartan Twilight*, New Rochelle.
Pipili, M.
   1987   *Laconian Iconography of the Sixth Century BC*, Oxford.
   1998   'Archaic Laconian vase-painting: some iconographic considerations', in Cavanagh and Walker (eds.) *Sparta in Laconia*, 82–96.
Pleket, H.W.
   1973   'Economic history of the ancient world and epigraphy', in *Akten des VI. Internationalen Kongresses für griechische und lateinische Epigraphie, München 1972*, Vestigia 17, München, 243–57.
   1975   'Games, prizes, athletes and ideology', *Stadion* 1, 49–89.
Poliakoff, M.B.
   1987   *Combat Sports in the Ancient World*, New Haven and London.
Pollard, J.
   1977   *Birds in Greek Life and Myth*, London.
Pomeroy, S.B.
   1976   *Goddesses, Whores, Wives and Slaves*, London.
Pomtow, H.
   1909   'Studien zu den Weihgeschenken und der Topographie von Delphi. V', *Klio* 9, 153–93.
Poole, W.
   1994   'Euripides and Sparta', in Powell and Hodkinson (eds.) *Shadow of Sparta*, 1–33.
Pope, R.
   1995   'Late Pleistocene to late Holocene alluvial fan development, the Sparti basin, Greece', Diss. Reading.
Popkin, S.L.
   1979   *The Rational Peasant: The political economy of rural society in Vietnam*, Berkeley.
Poralla, P.
   1985   *A Prosopography of Lacedaemonians from the Earliest Times to the Death of Alexander the Great (X–323 BC)*, 2nd revised edn, by A.S. Bradford, of the original 1914 edn, Chicago.

Pouilloux, J.
    1954   *Recherches sur l'histoire et les cultes de Thasos*, Études Thasiennes 3, Paris.

Pouilloux, J. and Salviat, F.
    1983   'Lichas, Lacédémonien, archonte à Thasos et le livre VIII de Thucydide', *CRAI*, 376–403.

Powell, A.
    1988   *Athens and Sparta: Constructing Greek political and social history from 478 BC*, London.
    1989   'Mendacity and Sparta's use of the visual', in Powell (ed.) *Classical Sparta*, 173–92.
    1994   'Plato and Sparta: modes of rule and of non-rational persuasion in the *Laws*', in Powell and Hodkinson (eds.) *Shadow of Sparta*, 273–321.
    1998   'Sixth-century Lakonian vase-painting: continuities and discontinuities with the "Lykourgan" ethos', in Fisher and van Wees (eds.) *Archaic Greece*, 119–46.
    1999   'Spartan women assertive in politics?: Plutarch's Lives of Agis and Kleomenes', in Hodkinson and Powell, *Sparta: New perspectives*, 393–419.

Powell, A. (ed.)
    1989   *Classical Sparta: Techniques behind her success*, London and Norman, Oklahoma.

Powell, A. and Hodkinson, S. (eds.)
    1994   *The Shadow of Sparta*, London and New York.

Powell, J.E.
    1960   *A Lexicon to Herodotus*, 2nd edn, Hildesheim.

Prato, C. (ed.)
    1968   *Tyrtaeus*, Rome.

Price, M.J.
    1968   'Early Greek bronze coinage', in C.M. Kraay and G.K. Jenkins (eds.) *Essays in Greek Coinage presented to Stanley Robinson*, Oxford, 90–104.

Pritchett, W.K.
    1974–91   *The Greek State at War*, 5 vols., Berkeley and Los Angeles.

Raepset, G.
    1973   'A propos de l'utilisation de statistique en démographie grecque: le nombre d'enfants par famille', *AC* 42, 536–43.

Raftopoulou, S.P.
    1998a   'Ταφες τῆς ἐποχης τοῦ Σιδήρου στὴ Σπάρτη', in ΠΡΑΚΤΙΚΑ ΤΟΥ Ε΄ ΔΙΕΘΝΟΥΣ ΣΥΝΕΔΡΙΟΥ ΠΕΛΟΠΟΝΝΗΣΙΑΚΩΝ ΣΠΟΥΔΩΝ, Β΄, ΑΘΗΝΑΙ, 272–81.
    1998b   'New finds from Sparta', in Cavanagh and Walker (eds.) *Sparta in Laconia*, 125–40.

Rawson, E.
    1969   *The Spartan Tradition in European Thought*, Oxford.

Rebenich, S.
    1998   'Fremdenfeindlichkeit in Sparta? Überlegungen zur Tradition der spartanischen Xenelasie', *Klio* 80, 336–59.

Rebenich, S. (ed.)
    1998   *Xenophon, Die Verfassung der Spartaner*, Darmstadt.

Redfield, J.
    1977/8   'The women of Sparta', *CJ* 73, 146–61.

  1985 'Herodotus the Tourist', *CPh* 80, 97–118.
Reed, C.M.
  1984 'Maritime traders in the archaic Greek world: a typology of those engaged in the long-distance transfer of goods by sea', *AncW* 10, 31–43.
Reid, Jr., J.D.
  1973 'Sharecropping as an understandable market response – the post-bellum South', *Journal of Economic History* 33, 106–30.
  1975/6 'Sharecropping and agricultural uncertainty', *Economic Development and Cultural Change* 24, 549–76.
  1977 'The theory of share tenancy revisited – again', *Journal of Political Economy* 85, 403–7.
Rhodes, P.J.
  1970 'Thucydides on Pausanias and Themistocles', *Historia* 19, 387–400.
  1982 'Problems in Athenian *eisphora* and liturgies', *AJAH* 7, 1–19.
Rich, J. and Shipley, G. (eds.)
  1993 *War and Society in the Greek World*, London.
Richer, N.
  1994 'Aspects des funérailles à Sparte', *Cahiers du Centre Gustave-Glotz* 5, 51–96.
  1998 *Les éphores*, Paris.
Risberg, C.
  1992 'Metal working in Greek sanctauries', in Linders and Alroth (eds.) *Economics of Cult*, 33–40.
Robert, C.
  1900 'Die Ordnung der olympischen Spiele und die sieger der 75.-85. Olympiade', *Hermes* 35, 141–95.
Robert, L.
  1938 *Études épigraphiques et philologiques*, Paris.
Roberts, E.S.
  1887 *Introduction to Greek Epigraphy*, Cambridge.
Robertson, N.
  1983 'The collective burial of fallen soldiers at Athens, Sparta and elsewhere: "ancestral custom" and modern misunderstandings', *EMC* 27, 78–92.
Rocha-Pereira, M.H. (ed.)
  1973 *Pausaniae Graeciae Descriptio*, Leipzig.
Roebuck, C.A.
  1941 *A History of Messenia from 369 to 146 BC*, Chicago.
  1945 'A note on Messenian economy and population', *CPh* 40, 149–65.
Roehl, H.
  1876 'Inschriften aus dem Peloponnes', *MDAI(A)* 1, 229–34.
Roesch, P.
  1982 *Études Béotiennes*, Paris.
  1985 'Les taureaux de bronze du Kabirion de Thèbes et l'écriture archaïque béotienne', in J.M. Fossey and H. Giroux (eds.) *Actes du III Congrès International sur la Béotie Antique, 1979*, Amsterdam, 135–52.
Rolley, C.
  1969 *Les statuettes de bronze*, Fouilles de Delphes V.2, Paris.
  1982 *Les vases de bronze de l'archaïsme récent en Grande-Grèce*, Bibliothèque de

l'Institut français de Naples, 2ᵉ sér., V, Naples.
- 1986a *Greek Bronzes*, London; translation of French original, Fribourg 1986.
- 1986b 'Les bronzes grecs: recherches récentes', *RA*, 377–91.
- 1993 'Les bronzes grecs et romains: recherches récentes', *RA*, 387–400.

Rolley, C. and Chamoux, F.
- 1991 'Les bronzes', in *Guide de Delphes. Le musée*, École Française d'Athènes. Sites et Monuments VI, Paris, 139–89.

Rose, H.J.
- 1929 'The cult of Orthia', in Dawkins (ed.) *Sanctuary of Artemis Orthia*, 399–407.
- 1941 'Greek rites of stealing', *Harvard Theological Review* 34, 1-6.

Roussel, P.
- 1939 *Sparte*, Paris; 2nd edn, 1960.

Rubinstein, L.
- 1993 *Adoption in IV. Century Athens*, Copenhagen.

Ruschenbusch, E.
- 1978 *Untersuchungen zu Staat und Politik in Griechenland vom 7.-4. Jh. v. Chr.*, Bamberg.

Rutter, N.K.
- 1987 'Herodotus I.94.1 and the "first finders" of coinage', in *Studi per Laura Breglia*, Supplement to *Bollettino di Numismatica* 4, 59–62.
- 1997 *The Greek Coinages of Southern Italy and Sicily*, London.

Ste Croix, G.E.M. de
- 1954/5 'The character of the Athenian empire', *Historia* 3, 1–41.
- 1972 *The Origins of the Peloponnesian War*, London.
- 1981 *The Class Struggle in the Ancient Greek World*, London; corrected paperback imprint, 1983.

Salapata, G.
- 1993 'The Laconian hero-reliefs in the light of the terracotta plaques', in Palagia and Coulson (eds.) *Sculpture*, 189–97.

Sallares, J.R.
- 1991 *The Ecology of the Ancient Greek World*, London and Ithaca.

Saller, R.P.
- 1984 'Roman dowry and the devolution of property in the Principate', *CQ* n.s. 34, 195–205.

Salviat, F.
- 1986 'Le vin de Thasos: amphores, vin et sources écrites', in J.-Y. Empereur and Y. Garlan (eds.) *Recherches sur les amphores grecques*, *BCH* Supplément XIII, Paris, 145–95.

Sanders, J.M. (ed.)
- 1992 ΦΙΛΟΛΑΚΩΝ. *Lakonian studies in honour of Hector Catling*, London.

Sansone, D.
- 1981 'Lysander and Dionysius (Plut. *Lys.* 2)', *CPh* 76, 202–6.

Santaniello, C.
- 1995 *Plutarcho, Detti dei Lacedemoni*, Napoli.

Sarpaki, A.
- 1992 'The Mediterranean triad or is it a quartet?', in Wells (ed.) *Agriculture*, 61–75.

Bibliography

Saunders, T.J.
 1981 Revised edn of T.A. Sinclair trans., *Aristotle, The Politics*, Harmondsworth.
 1995 *Aristotle, Politics: Books I and II*, Oxford.
Scanlon, T.F.
 1988 '*Virgineum Gymnasium*: Spartan females and early Greek athletics', in W.J. Raschke (ed.) *The Archaeology of the Olympics*, Wisconsin and London, 185–216.
Schachter, A.
 1992 'Policy, cult and the placing of Greek sanctuaries', in Schachter et al. *Sanctuaire Grec*, 1–64.
Schachter, A. et al.
 1992 *Le sanctuaire grec*, Fondation Hardt Entretiens sur l'Antiquité Classique 37, Vandoeuvres-Geneva.
Schaefer, H.
 1957 'Das Eidolon des Leonidas', in K. Schauenburg (ed) *Charites: Studien zur Altertumswissenschaft (Festschrift E. Langlotz)*, Bonn, 223–33.
Schäfer, J.
 1957 *Studien zu den griechischen Reliefpithoi des 8.–6. Jahrhunderts v. Chr. aus Kreta, Rhodos, Tenos und Boiotien*, Kallmunz.
Schaps, D.M.
 1979 *Economic Rights of Women in Ancient Greece*, Edinburgh.
Schaus, G.P.
 1985 'The Laconian element in Cyrenaican life', in Barker, Lloyd and Reynolds (eds.) *Cyrenaica*, 395–403.
Schmaltz, B.
 1980 *Metallfiguren aus dem Kabeirenheiligtum bei Theben*, Das Kabirenheiligtum bei Theben VI, Berlin.
Schütrumpf, E.
 1987 'The *rhetra* of Epitadeus: a Platonist's fiction', *GRBS* 28, 441–57.
 1991 *Aristoteles, Politik: Buch II und Buch III*, Berlin.
 1994 'Aristotle and Sparta', in Powell and Hodkinson (eds.) *Shadow of Sparta*, 323–45.
Schwartz, G.S.
 1976 'I.G. V.1, 213: the Damonon Stele – a new restoration for line 39', *ZPE* 22, 177–8.
Scott, J.C.
 1976 *The Moral Economy of the Peasant*, New Haven and London.
Seaford, R.
 1994 *Reciprocity and Ritual: Homer and tragedy in the developing city-state*, Oxford.
Sekunda, N.V.
 1998 *The Spartans*, Oxford.
Semple, E.C.
 1922 'The influence of geographic conditions upon ancient Mediterranean stockraising', *Annals of the Association of American Geographers* 12, 3–38.
 1932 *The Geography of the Mediterranean Region: Its relation to ancient history*, London.
Sen, A.
 1981 'Market failure and control of labour power: towards an explanation of

Serwint, N.J.
- 1987 'Greek athletic sculpture from the fifth and fourth centuries BC: an iconographic study', Diss. Princeton.

Shear, T.L.
- 1937a 'A Spartan shield from Pylos', *AE* 140–3.
- 1937b 'The campaign of 1936', *Hesperia* 6, 333–81.

Shipley, D.R.
- 1997 *Plutarch's Life of Agesilaos: Response to sources in the presentation of character*, Oxford.

Shipley, G.
- 1992 '*Perioikos*: the discovery of classical Lakonia', in Sanders (ed.) ΦΙΛΟΛΑΚΩΝ, 211–26.
- 1996 'Archaeological sites in Laconia and the Thyreatis', in Cavanagh et al., *Laconia Survey*, II, 235–62.
- 1997 '"The other Lakedaimonians": the dependent perioikic *poleis* of Laconia and Messenia', in M.H. Hansen (ed.) *The Polis as an Urban Centre and as a Political Community*, Acts of the Copenhagen Polis Centre, vol. 4, Copenhagen, 189–281.

Simandoni-Bournia, E.
- 1990 ΑΝΑΣΚΑΦΕΣ ΝΑΞΟΥ: ΟΙ ΑΝΑΓΛΥΦΟΙ ΠΙΘΟΙ, Athens.

Simon, C.G.
- 1986 'The archaic votive offerings and cults of Ionia', Diss. Berkeley.

Simondon, M.
- 1982 *La mémoire et l'oubli dans la pensée grecque jusqu'à la fin du Ve siècle avant J-C*, Paris.

Sinclair, R.K.
- 1988 *Democracy and Participation in Athens*, Cambridge.

Singor, H.W.
- 1993 'Spartan land lots and helot rents', in H. Sancisi-Weerdenburg et al. (eds.) *De Agricultura: In memoriam Pieter Willem de Neeve*, Amsterdam, 31–60.

Smith, J.E.
- 1987 'The computer simulation of kin sets and kin counts', in J. Bongaarts, K. Wachter and T.K. Burch (eds.) *Family Demography: Methods and their application*, Oxford, 249–66.

Smith, R.M.
- 1984 'Some issues concerning families and their property in rural England 1250–1800', in R.M. Smith (ed.) *Land, Kinship and Life Cycle*, Cambridge, 1–86.

Smith, T.J.
- 1998 'Dances, drinks and dedications: the archaic komos in Laconia', in Cavanagh and Walker (eds.) *Sparta in Laconia*, 75–81.

Snodgrass, A.M.
- 1967 *Arms and Armour of the Greeks*, London; reprinted Baltimore 1999.
- 1977 *Archaeology and the Rise of the Greek State*, Cambridge.
- 1980 *Archaic Greece: The age of experiment*, London.
- 1989/90 'The economics of dedication at Greek sanctuaries', in *Anathema: Regime*

delle Offerte e Vita dei Santuari nel Mediterraneo Antico, special issue of *Scienze dell'Antichità*, 3–4, 287–94.

Sokolowski, F.
   1969   *Lois sacrées des cités grecques*, Paris.
Solari, A.
   1947   *Lo Stato Spartano*, Genua.
Souilhé. J.
   1962   *Platon, Oeuvres complètes, XIII.3. Dialogues apocryphes*, 2nd edn, Paris.
Sourvinou-Inwood, C.
   1981   'To die and enter the house of Hades: Homer, before and after', in J. Whaley (ed.) *Mirrors of Mortality: Studies in the social history of death*, London, 15–39.
   1983   'A trauma in flux: death in the 8th century and after', in R. Hägg (ed.) *The Greek Renaissance of the Eighth Century BC: Tradition and innovation*, Stockholm, 33–48.
   1988   *Studies in Girls' Transitions: Aspects of the Arkteia and age representation in Attic iconography*, Athens.
   1995   *'Reading' Greek Death*, Oxford.
Sparks, B.A. and L. Talcott, *The Athenian Agora XII. Black and plain pottery*. Princeton.
Spawforth, A.J.S.
   1990   Review of Powell (ed.) 1989, *CR* n. s. 40, 345–7.
   1994   'Symbol of unity? The Persian-Wars tradition in the Roman Empire', in S. Hornblower (ed.) *Greek Historiography*, Oxford.
Spence, I.G.
   1993   *The Cavalry of Classical Greece*, Oxford.
Sprague, R.K. (ed.)
   1972   *The Older Sophists*, Columbia.
Starr, C.G.
   1965   'The credibility of early Spartan history', *Historia* 14, 257–72 = *Essays in Ancient History*, eds. A. Ferrill and T. Kelly, Leiden 1979, 145–59.
Stein, H. (ed.)
   1871   *Herodoti Historiae*, II. Berlin.
Steinhauer, G.
   n.d.   *Museum of Sparta*, Athens.
   1972   'ΑΡΧΑΙΟΤΗΤΕΣ ΚΑΙ ΜΝΗΜΕΙΑ ΛΑΚΩΝΙΑΣ', *AD* 27, B.1 *Chronika*, 242–8.
   1992   'An Illyrian mercenary in Sparta', in Sanders (ed.) ΦΙΛΟΛΑΚΩΝ, 239–45.
Stewart, A.F.
   1997   *Art, Desire, and the Body in Ancient Greece*, Cambridge.
Stibbe, C.M.
   1972   *Lakonische Vasenmaler des sechsten Jahrhunderts v. Chr.*, Amsterdam.
   1989   *Laconian Mixing Bowls: a History of the Krater Lakonikos from the seventh to the fifth century BC*, Amsterdam.
   1991   'Dionysos in Sparta', *BABesch* 64, 1–44.
   1994   'Between Babyka and Knakion', *BABesch* 69, 63–102.
Strøm, I.
   1992   'Obeloi of pre- or proto-monetary value in Greek sanctuaries' in Linders and

Alroth (eds.) *Economics of Cult*, 41–51.

Svoronos, I.N.
   1906   'ΜΑΘΗΜΑΤΑ ΝΟΜΙΣΜΑΤΙΚΗΣ', *Journal International d'Archéologie Numismatique* 9, 147–236 (in Greek); French trans. in *Revue Belge de Numismatique* 64–6 (1908–10); English trans. in *American Journal of Numismatics* 43–4 (1908–10).

Swaddling, J.
   1980   *The Ancient Olympic Games*, London.

Sweet, W.E.
   1987   *Sport and Recreation in Ancient Greece: a sourcebook*, New York and Oxford.

Talbert, R.J.A.
   1989   'The role of the helots in the class struggle at Sparta', *Historia* 38, 22–40.

Thiersch, F.
   1833   *De l'état actuel de la Grèce et des moyens d'arriver à sa restauration*, Leipzig.

Thirlwall, C.
   1835–44   *A History of Greece*, London.

Thommen, L.
   1996   *Lakedaimonion Politeia: Die Entstehung der spartanischen Verfassung*, Historia Einzelschriften 103, Stuttgart.
   1999   'Spartanische Frauen', *Museum Helveticum* 56, 129–49.

Thompson, D.W.
   1895   *A Glossary of Greek Birds*, Oxford.

Thompson, W.E.
   1973   'Observations on Spartan politics', *RSA* 3, 47–58.

Thomsen, R.
   1964   *Eisphora*, Copenhagen.

Thür, H. and Taeuber, H.
   1994   *Prozessrechtliche Inschriften der griechischen Poleis: Arkadien (IPArk)*, Wien.

Tigerstedt, E.N.
   1965–78   *The Legend of Sparta in Classical Antiquity*, 3 vols., Stockholm, Göteborg and Uppsala.

Tod, M.N.
   1933   'Greek inscriptions. IV. A Spartan grave on Attic soil', *G&R* 2, 108–11.
   1948   *A Selection of Greek Historical Inscriptions, II: From 403 to 323 BC*, Oxford.
   1946   'Epigraphical notes on Greek coinage, II. ΧΑΛΚΟΥΣ', *NC* 6, 47–62.

Tod, M.N. and Wace, A.J.B.
   1906   *A Catalogue of the Sparta Museum*, Oxford.

Toher, M.
   1991   'Greek funerary legislation and the two Spartan funerals', in Flower and Toher (eds.) *Georgica*, 159–75.

Tölle-Kastenbein, R.
   1980   *Frühklassische Peplosfiguren: Originale. Textband*, Mainz am Rhein.

Tomlinson, R.A.
   1976   *Greek Sanctuaries*, London.
   1977   'The upper terraces at Perachora', *BSA* 72, 179–202.
   1992   'Perachora', in Schachter et al., *Sanctuaire Grec*, 321–51.

Bibliography

Toynbee, A.J.
    1969   *Some Problems of Greek History*, London.

Tuplin, C.J.
    1977   'Kyniskos of Mantinea', *LCM* 2, 5–10.
    1993   *The Failings of Empire: a reading of Xenophon* Hellenica *2.3.11–7.5.27*, Historia Einzelschriften 76, Stuttgart.
    1994   'Xenophon, Sparta and the *Cyropaedia*', in Powell and Hodkinson (eds.) *Shadow of Sparta*, 127–82.

Valavanis, P.D.
    1987   'Säulen, Hähne, Niken und Archonten auf Panathenäischen Preisamphoren', *AA*, 467–80.

Valensi, L.
    1985   *Tunisian Peasants in the Eighteenth and Nineteenth Centuries*, Cambridge.

van Andel, T., Runnels, C. and Pope, K.O.
    1986   'Five thousand years of land use and abuse in the southern Argolid', *Hesperia* 55, 103–28.

van Hook, L.
    1932   'On the Lacedaemonians buried in the Kerameikos', *AJA* 36, 290–2.

van Wees, H.
    1999   'Tyrtaeus' *Eunomia*: nothing to do with the Great Rhetra', in Hodkinson and Powell (eds.) *Sparta: New perspectives*, 1–41.

van Wersch, H.J.
    1972   'The agricultural economy', in McDonald and Rapp (eds.) 1972, 177–87.

Vérilhac, A.-M. and Vial, C.
    1998   *Le mariage grec du VIe siècle av. J.-C. à l'époque d'Auguste*, *BCH* Supplément 32, Athens.

Vernant, J.-P. (ed.)
    1968   *Problèmes de la guerre en Grèce ancienne*, Paris.

Viedebantt, O.
    1917   *Forschungen zur Metrologie des Altertums*, Leipzig.

Villing, A.
    1998   'Athena as Ergane and Promachos: the iconography of Athena in archaic east Greece', in Fisher and van Wees (eds.) *Archaic Greece*, 147–68.

Vita-Finzi, C.
    1969   *The Mediterranean Valleys: Geological change in historical times*, Cambridge.

von Bothmer, D.
    1957   *Amazons in Greek Art*, Oxford.

von Holzinger, C.
    1894   'Aristoteles' und Herakleides' lakonische und kretische Politien', *Philologus* 52, 58–117.

von Massow, W.
    1926   'Die Stele des Ainetos', *MDAI(A)* 51, 41–7.

von Reden, S.
    1995   *Exchange in Ancient Greece*, London.
    1997   'Money, law and exchange: coinage in the Greek polis', *JHS* 117, 154–76.

Wace, A.J.B.
    1905/6   'The Heroon', *BSA* 12, 288–94.

    1929   'The lead figurines', in Dawkins (ed.) *Sanctuary of Artemis Orthia*, 249–84.
    1937   'A Spartan hero relief', *AE* 217–20.
Wace, A.J.B., Thompson, M.S. and Droop, J.P.
    1908/9   'Excavations at Sparta, 1909. The Menelaion', *BSA* 15, 108–57.
Wade-Gery, H.T.
    1925   'The growth of the Dorian states', *CAH, III*, 1st edn, Cambridge, 527–70.
    1949   'A note on the origin of the Spartan Gymnopaidiai', *CQ* 43, 79–81.
Wagstaff, J.M.
    1981   'Buried assumptions: some problems in the interpretation of the "Younger Fill" raised by recent data from Greece', *Journal of Archaeological Science* 8, 247–64.
Walbank, F.W.
    1957   *A Historical Commentary on Polybius, I*, Oxford.
Wallace, M.B.
    1970   'Notes on early Greek grave epigrams', *Phoenix* 24, 95–105.
Warden, P.G.
    1990   'Part I: The small finds', in D. White (ed.) *The Extramural Sanctuary of Demeter and Persephone at Cyrene, Libya. Final Reports IV*, University of Pennsylvania, University Museum Monograph 67, Philadelphia.
Warriner, D.
    1962   *Land Reform and Development in the Middle East*, 2nd edn, London.
Weil, R.
    1960   *Aristote et l'Histoire*, Paris.
Wells, B. (ed.)
    1992   *Agriculture in Ancient Greece*, Stockholm.
West, M.L.
    1985   'Ion of Chios', *BICS* 32, 71–8.
West, M.L. (ed.)
    1972   *Iambi et Elegi Graeci, II*, Oxford.
Westlake, H.D.
    1976   'Re-election to the ephorate?', *GRBS* 17, 343–52.
Whitby, M.
    1994   'Two shadows: images of Spartans and helots', in Powell and Hodkinson (eds.) *Shadow of Sparta*, 87–126.
Whitehead, D.
    1979   'Ant[i]alkidas, or the Case of the Intrusive Iota', *LCM* 4, 191–3.
Whittaker, C.R. (ed.)
    1988   *Pastoral Economies in Classical Antiquity*, *PCPhS*, Suppl. 14, Cambridge.
Wide, S.
    1893   *Lakonische Kulte*, Leipzig.
Wilamowitz-Moellendorff, U. von
    1924   'Lesefrüchte', *Hermes* 59, 249–73.
Wilkins, J., Harvey, D. and Dobson, M. (eds.)
    1995   *Food in Antiquity*, Exeter.
Wilkinson, K.
    1998   'Geoarchaeological studies of the Spartan acropolis and Evrotas valley: some preliminary conclusions', in Cavanagh and Walker (eds.) *Sparta in Laconia*, 149–56.

Willemsen, F.
   1977   'Zu den Lakedämoniergräbern im Kerameikos', *MDAI (A)* 92, 117–57.
Willetts, R.F.
   1967   *The Law Code of Gortyn*, Kadmos Suppl. 1, Berlin.
Wolf, E.R.
   1966   *Peasants*, Englewood Cliff, N.J.
Wolff, H.J.
   1957   'Proix', *RE* XXIII.1, 134–70.
Woodward, A.M.
   1908/9   'Excavations at Sparta, 1909. The inscriptions', *BSA* 15, 40–106.
   1923–25   'Excavations at Sparta, 1924–25. The Acropolis. The Finds', *BSA* 26, 253–77.
   1928–30   'Excavations at Sparta, 1924–27, II. Votive inscriptions from the Acropolis', *BSA* 30, 241–54.
   1929   'Inscriptions', in Dawkins (ed.) *Sanctuary of Artemis Orthia*, 285–377.
Wrightson, K. and Levine, D.
   1979   *Poverty and Piety in an English village: Terling 1525–1700*, New York and London.
Wrigley, E.A.
   1978   'Fertility strategy for the individual and the group', in C. Tilly (ed.) *Historical Studies of Changing Fertility*, Princeton, 135–54; reprinted in his *People, Cities and Wealth: The transformation of traditional society*, Oxford 1987, 197–214.
Young, D.C.
   1984   *The Olympic Myth of Greek Amateur Athletics*, Chicago.
Ziegler, K.
   1951   'Plutarchos von Chaironeia', in *RE* XLI.1, 636–962.
Ziehen, L.
   1933   'Das spartanische Bevölkerungsproblem', *Hermes* 68, 218–37.
Zimmermann, J.-L.
   1989   *Les chevaux de bronze dans l'art géometrique grec*, Mayence.

INDEX

The entries for ancient writers and works cover significant quotations, citations or discussions of their evidence; but they are not intended to include every single reference.

Achaia, 169, 242
Achaian league, 43, 50
acquisition of wealth, 91, 176–9, 427–9
  contempt for/disincentives against, 24, 29, 51
acquisitive behaviour: see 'greed'.
Acropolis, 222, 239, 240, 303–6, 328, 430
  bronze dedications, 274, 275, 276–7, 280–3, 286–7, 288–9, 291–3
  sanctuaries on, ch. 9 *passim*
adoption, 67, 82–3, 406
Aeimnestos, 339
Aelian, 99, 127, 220, 245, 247–8, 253–4, 355–6, 359
Agamemnon, 243
Agesilaos II, King, 24, 26, 37, 41–2, 172, 176, 224, 354, 408, 412–13, 431–2, 434, 439
  as patron, 83, 179, 211, 335, 353, 358, 361–5
  opposition to chariot-racing and other displays, 309–10, 327–8, 429–30, 432
  use of *xeniai*, 335, 341, 342, 343, 347–8, 349, 350–1, 352
  use of wealth, 25–6, 83, 152, 179, 312, 338
  Xenophon's encomium of, 25–6, 211, 213
Agesipolis I, King, 262, 295, 312, 336, 349, 352, 429
Agesistrata, 111–12 n. 74, 440
Agetos, 153, 179, 411, 414
Agiatis, 97
Agis II, King, 56–7, 170, 226, 338, 349, 352, 412–13, 424, 429
Agis IV, King, 43–5, 70, 139, 383, 434
agōn, 303, 324
agriculture,

agricultural potential, 135–8, 141, 142–4
character of production, 131–5, 389–90, 422
freedom/abstention from engagement in, 178, 216, 445 n. 41
produce, 190–3, 201
supply of equipment, 129.
See also 'animal(s), husbandry'; 'helots/helotage, agricultural tribute'.
Aigina/Aiginetans, 169, 173
  currency, Spartan use of, 169, 171, 173, 174–5
Aiginetic standard, Spartan use of, 46, 156, 163–4, 168, 191–2
Aigospotamoi, battle of (405 BC), 157, 170, 286, 292, 294, 345, 427, 428, 430
Akanthos 339
Akritas peninsula, 144
Alkaios, 2, 77
[Al]kibiad[as], 339
Alkibiades (Athenian), 324, 339, 344, 413
Alkidas, lineage of, 413–14
Alkman, 2, 217, 229, 279, 313
Amompharetos, 257, 258, 259
  lineage of, 443 n. 18
Amphipolis, 244, 251
Amyklaion (sanctuary of Apollo), bronze dedications at, 274, 276, 277, 283, 285, 288
Anaxandridas II, King, 101–2, 371, 406, 407, 408, 410
Anaxandros (Olympic victor), 308, 322, 325, 330, 420
Anchimolios, 251, 257
Andania, 262
Andokos, 175
Aneristos, 344
animal(s), 203, 432

485

Index

husbandry, 129, 133–4, 142, 151–2, 179, 357, 380, 387, 389, 440
representations of, 222, 241, 283, 290
sacrifice, 179, 211, 239, 363
shared use, 200–1.
See also 'equestrian competition'; 'horses'; 'hunting, dogs'; 'livestock, ownership of'.
Antalkidas, 338, 346, 347, 414
Antikrates, 190
Apelles, 321–2
Apophthegmata Lakōnika, 38–43, 45–8, 54–8, 98, 152, 156, 163–4, 181, 203–4, 253–4, 364
Arakos, 428
archaeological evidence,
burials, pre- and post-classical Sparta, 238–40, 256, 260
burials in other Greek poleis, 248, 254–5
coinage, 161–2, 173–4
from Spartan sanctuaries, 240–1, 243, 273–94
funerary monuments abroad, 252
funerary monuments at home, 250–4, 256, 258–9, 260–2
jewellery, 229, 281–4, 288
spits, 162
statuettes and figurines, 229, 281–3, 284–5, 342
survey settlement patterns, 125, 138–9, 141, 144
terracotta amphoras, 240–2
vessels, 281–2, 285–6
victory monuments, 292, 303–7, 319–23
votive offerings, ch. 9 *passim*, 342
Archias, 251
lineage of, 414
Archidamia, 111–12 n. 74, 372, 439–40
Archidamos II, King, 102, 338, 347, 407, 412, 433
Archidamos III, King, 27, 311, 335, 354, 361, 413, 434
Areus, King, 434–5
Argenson, Marquis d', 11
Argos, 159, 161, 284, 326, 347, 352
Ariobarzanes, 346
Aristokritos, 338, 415
Aristomenidas, 408, 413
Ariston, King, 77, 406, 408, 411
exchange of treasures with Agetos, 153, 179
Aristophanes, 20, 224
Aristotelian *Polity of the Lakedaimonians*, 36, 46, 49, 56, 68, 71–2, 86–8, 114, 164, 202, 204, 217, 229, 244, 247, 263, 284
Aristotle, 12, 13, 29, 30, 40
Politics, 2, 33–5, 36, 69, 71–2, 80–1, 83–4, 86–7, 91–3, 94, 95–7, 98–101, 115, 161, 181, 189–91, 200–1, 209, 214, 219, 226–7, 359–60, 399, 400, 405, 409, 425, 432–3, 434, 437, 439, 445 n. 41
[Aristotle], *Oikonomika*, 162, 182, 189, 211
Arkadia/Arkadians, 157, 167, 242, 297, 347, 417.
See also 'Mantineia'; 'Tegea'.
Arkesilaos (Olympic victor), 308, 311, 313, 316, 317, 320, 322, 339
Arkesilaos IV (king of Cyrene), 311, 316
army,
burial and commemoration of fallen warriors, 250–4, 256–9
cavalry, 78, 152, 213, 221, 311–12, 432
changes to, 421–2
dress and equipment, 221–6, 241–2
incorporation of non-Spartiates, 198
limitations on patronage within, 213, 358–9
polemarchs, 56–7, 197, 258–9
representations of warriors, 222
supplies, 197–8.
See also 'overseas commands/campaigns'.
art/artistic production, 2, 217, 222, ch. 9 *passim*, 318, 342
Artaxerxes II (Persian king), 346–7, 352
Artemis Orthia (sanctuary), 271, 273–5
bronze dedications, 276–8, 286–7, 288–93
cheese-stealing and flagellation rituals, 202–4
coins, 174
gender of dedicants, 288–91
iron spits, 162
ivory plaques, 238
lead figurines, 218, 222, 223, 229, 278–9, 283
pins, 283
sickles, 163
terracotta amphoras, 240

Asine, 144
Athena Chalkioikos (sanctuary), 291–2
  bronze dedications: see 'Acropolis'.
  Panathenaic amphoras, 308–9
  victory monuments, 292, 303–5
Athenaios (Spartiate), 339
Athenaios of Naukratis, *Deipnosophistai*, 153, 157, 356–7
Athens/Athenian(s)/Attica, 116, 141, 168, 225, 251, 252, 258–9, 284, 339, 340–1
  comparison with Sparta, 20, 22, 35, 79–80, 83, 94–6, 99, 101, 115, 133, 177, 180, 181, 189, 197, 211–12, 213, 214, 216, 219, 224–6, 230, 247, 249, 254–6, 257, 286, 289, 309–10, 312–13, 319–20, 321, 322, 324, 360, 371, 380–1, 384–5, 408–9, 418–19, 438
  representations of Sparta, 21, 26, 128, 220, 224–5, 226–7.
  See also 'Panathenaic games'.
athletic(s),
  female, 227–8
  heroisation, 309–10
  nudity, 219, 220–1
  victories, 258–9, 292, 303–6, 307–8, 318, 322, 325
atimia: see 'citizenship/citizen rights'.
Aulon, 144
austerity, 12, 20, 21–2, 26, 27, 33, 36, 41, 42, 43, 45, 49, 53, 57, 152, 209, 220, 432

'Battle of the Champions' (c.545 BC), 251, 257,
Bodin, Jean, 9–10
Boiotia, 285, 316, 408, 415
Boiotios, 339
booty, 19, 26, 153–4, 157, 169–70, 172, 173, 343, 345, 358–9, 424, 427, 429
Boulis, 77, 344
boys, 36, 58, 73, 212, 221, 226, 336
  and adult messes, 198
  foster-children, 342, 353
  mothakes, 198, 355–6, 415, 435
  theft of food, 201–5
  upbringing, 198, 214–16, 290, 354–6
Brasidas, 168, 244, 251, 257, 338, 344, 345, 421, 428, 431
bribery, 20, 33, 167, 172, 359–61
bronze dedications, ch. 9 *passim*

arms and armour, 292
bells, 277, 293
jewellery, 229, 275, 281, 282, 283–4, 288, 289–90
statues, 173, 285–6, 294, 295, 321–2, 346, 428
statuettes and figurines, 222, 226, 281, 282, 284–5, 295, 297
vessels, 274, 281–2, 285, 295, 430.
See also 'votive offerings'.
bullion/uncoined silver, 159, 160, 165, 168–72
burials, ch. 8 *passim*.
See also 'funerary practice'.
Butis, 175
Byzantion, 159, 160, 162, 344

cavalry: see 'horses, cavalry'.
Chairon, 258–9
Chalkedon, 159
Chalkideus, 339
chariot racing, 77–8, ch. 10 *passim*,
  and kings, 309–10, 325, 326–7
  charioteers, 241, 306, 316, 321, 325
  economics of, 312–17
  socio-political implications, 323–8
  Spartan participation abroad, 307–28
  Spartan victories at Olympia, 307–12
  Spartan victory monuments, 319–23
  within Sparta territory, 303–7.
  See also 'epinician poetry, absence of'.
Charmos, 175
Charondas of Catana, 246
Cheirisophos, 202, 338, 349
Chilon, 22, 242, 244, 408, 413
  lineage of, 410, 412, 413
Chios/Chians, 22, 115, 169, 279
choruses, 212, 318
Chrysapha, 139
Chrysē, 439
citizen estates,
  geographical extent, 131–45
  productive capacity, 130–1, 132–5, 138, 142–3, 151–2, 179, 388–95
  size, 382–5
citizen households: see 'household(s), citizen'; 'household economies'.
citizenship/citizen rights, 3, 33, 88, 89, 177, 189, 355–6, 434
  atimia (deprivation of rights), 84–5
  loss of, 24, 34, 81, 190–1, 369, 400
  right to buy and sell, 84–5, 180, 440–1

487

Index

clothing: see 'dress'.
coinage: see 'currency, precious metal'.
common messes, 3, 4, 22, 23–4, 33–4, 37, 55–7, 216–18, 318–19, 356–8
  additional contributions (*epaikla*), 218, 356–8
  black broth, 20, 50, 57, 218
  boys' messes, 198
  drink, restrictions on, 22, 218
  foodstuffs, 133, 151, 191, 217–18
  in hellenistic period, 434–5
  inclusion of non-Spartiates, 198–9
  introduction of boys, 198
  mess dues, 3, 4, 171, 190–3, 369, 400
  mess dues, use of surplus, 196–9
  patronage within, 356–8
  rations, size of, 193–6
  royal mess, 358
communal use of property, 199–201
communitarianism, images of, 11–14
comparative evidence/context: see 'Sparta (classical) in comparative context'
computer simulation, 400–5
conspiracies, 124, 173, 180, 436–7
corruption (alleged and real), 10, 25, 27–30, 31–2, 49, 58–9, 78, 83, 91, 155, 359–60, 424–5, 426–7, 433
crafts (*technai*)/craft activity, 22, 153, 178
  alleged abstention from/prohibition of, 31, 55, 152, 177–8
  sponsorship of, 179, 380
Cragius, Nicholas, 10
Crete, 279
  comparison with Sparta, 29–30, 68, 94–5, 99–100, 190–1, 221
Croesus (King of Lydia), 3, 10, 341
currency, iron, 10, 12, 46, 51, 54–5, 155–8, 160–5, 181
currency, precious metal (gold and silver), 154–76, 181, 182
  abstention from coining, 158–60
  alleged prohibition before 404 BC, 24–5, 28–9, 44, 165–7
  compromise decision in 404 BC, 27, 155–6, 165, 174, 425, 429
  demise of 404 prohibition, 174–6, 433
  influx after 404 BC, 14, 28, 58–9, 424–5, 429
  private ownership before and after 404 BC, 170–6
  Spartan hellenistic coinage, 435
  state ownership before 404 BC, 167–70
Cyrene, 316
  links with Sparta, 311
  sanctuary of Demeter and Persephone, 284, 285
Cyrus (son of Darius II), 345, 349, 428

Damaratos, King, 98, 307, 308, 326–7, 408, 411
Damonon stēlē, 303–7
Darré, Richard Walther, 14
death, ideology of, 19, 238, 242, 245, 248, 254, 256, 262
debts, 170, 181–2, 358, 364, 437, 440
  alleged abolition by Lykourgos, 43–4, 45, 55
decision-making: see 'politics/policy-making'
dedications: see 'bronze dedications'; 'lead figurines'; 'masks, clay'; 'votive offerings'.
Deinicha, 413, 414
Deinis, 414
Delos, temple of Apollo, 346, 428
Delphi,
  games at, 311, 322
  Labyad phratry, 247, 248, 249
  oracle, 29, 295, 358
  sanctuary of Apollo, 167, 285, 286, 296–7, 358, 414, 435
  Spartan contributions to fund of Naopoioi, 174–6, 439
  Spartan dedications at, 157, 286, 294–5, 296–7, 345, 427, 428, 429
Demarmenos, 408, 412
demography: see 'helots/helotage, population'; 'manpower shortage'.
Demosthenes, 220
Diaktorides, 329 n. 11, 412, 443 n. 15
Dienekes, 257, 258
diet, 390
  male, 2, 22, 36, 36–7, 41–2, 49, 53, 57, 133, 191–6, 201–5, 215, 217–18, 356–8
  female, 228.
  See also 'food'.
Dikaiarchos, 36–7, 56, 171, 191–2, 356, 357
Diodorus Siculus, 28, 156, 417, 418, 424
Dioskourides, 181–2, 364
Dioskouroi, 258, 427, 428
Dipaieis, battle of, 417

Dodona, Spartan dedications at, 226, 296–7
domestic architecture, simplicity of, 42, 46–7, 57–8, 152, 209, 214
Dorieus, 213, 410, 414, 416
dowries, 33, 80, 180, 400, 405
  alleged prohibition of, 47, 53
  and female inheritance, 98–103
dress,
  female, 228–30, 279, 284
  male, 20, 34, 49, 53, 77, 209–10, 218–26.
  See also 'army, dress and equipment'.
drink/drinking, 22–3, 46, 49, 57, 153, 179, 193, 195–6, 199, 216–17, 218
Duris of Samos, 220

earthquake of *c*. 464 BC, 310, 417–20
economic egalitarianism,
  ancient images of, 29–30, 43–8, 50–60, 98, 152
  modern images of, ch. 1 *passim*
Eileithyia, cult of, 289
eisphorai: see 'land/land-ownership, taxation of'.
Elis, 294, 342, 349
empire, Spartan, 33, 52, 326
  impact of, 27, 423–32.
  See also 'Peloponnesian war'.
Endios, 338, 339, 344
  lineage of, 413
Enpedoklees, 277
Enymakratidas: see 'Damonon stēlē'.
Ephesos/Ephesians, 169, 346
ephors/ephorate, 29, 30, 33, 56–7, 101, 114, 181, 197, 226, 242, 246, 304, 309–10, 326, 344, 349, 351, 359, 360–1, 362, 364, 429
Ephorus, 26–30, 68, 69, 99–100, 114, 115, 117–19, 155–6, 166, 417, 424
epigraphy: see 'inscriptions, evidence of'.
Epikydidas, 428
epinician poetry, absence of, 317–19
Epitadeus, alleged rhētra of, 10, 44–5, 67, 71–2, 74–5, 78, 83, 90–4, 96, 424–5
equestrian competition, ch. 10 *passim*.
  See also 'chariot racing'; 'horses, horse races'.
Eteonikos, 428
Etymokles, 361
Euagoras (Olympic victor), 307, 308, 313, 319, 320–1
Euanios, 340, 342
Eudamidas, 413
Eumnastos, 294, 342, 343
Eupolia, 363, 412–13, 442–3 n. 11
Euripides, 20, 133, 142, 227, 434
Eurybiades (admiral), 248, 414
Eurybiades (Olympic victor), 308, 414, 420
Eurydamē, 102, 412
Euryleon, 253, 414
Euryleonis (Olympic victrix), 102, 308, 319, 328, 414, 420, 430, 439
exchange, 51–2, 84–5, 133–4, 135, 161, 177, 179–82, 341–2, 360–3

factions, development of, 431–2
festivals, 78, 204, 211, 212, 216, 218, 221, 222, 228, 229, 303–5, 318
fines, 24, 56–7, 95, 170–1, 202, 352, 364
fishing, 357, 387–8
food, 2, 3, 22, 23, 41–2, 46, 53, 56, 56–7, 115, 133, 134, 151, 190, 191–205, 215, 216–18, 228, 356–8, 373–8, 387–8, 434, 435
foreigners: see *xeniai*.
French revolution, images of Spartan property, 12
funerary practice, ch. 8 *passim*,
  body coverings, 247–9
  burial, equality of, 247–9
  ΕΝ ΠΟΛΕΜΟΙ stēlai, 250–4
  excavated pre-classical burials, 238–40
  fallen warriors, 250–4, 256–60
  females, 260–2
  grave goods, 239, 260
    absence of, 247–8
  grave markers, 239, 254–5
  hellenistic Sparta, 256
  'hero-reliefs', 243–4
  heroisation, 237–8, 242
  inscriptions, 250–4
  kings, 262–3
  ΛΕΧΟΙ stēlai, 260–1
  memorials, 249–56
  mourning, restriction of, 246–7
  prothesis, scenes of, 238
  terracotta relief amphoras, 239–42

gainful activity (*chrēmatismos*), prohibition of, 23, 31, 177–9

Index

Gambreion, 247
geomorphology of Spartan territory, 135–9, 142
Geronthrai, 139, 253, 261
Gerousia (council of Elders), 3, 152, 359–63. 430–1, 434
gift-giving, 19, 179, 341–2, 345–6, 362, 428
Gillies, John, 12–13
gold and silver currency: see 'currency, precious metal'.
Gorgo, 95, 407, 411
Gorgos, 340, 342, 343
Gortyn Code, 94–5, 99–100
'Great Rhētra', 3, 29
greed, 2, 27, 33, 34, 49, 59, 75, 80, 156, 399, 424
Grote, George, 13, 82
guest-friendship/ritualised friendship; see 'xeniai'.
Gylippos, 167, 355, 415,
  theft of booty, 155–6, 157, 172, 427
Gymnopaidiai (festival), 78, 211, 212, 221, 257, 337, 342

hair/hairstyles, 42, 224, 226, 229, 230
Haliartos, battle of (395 BC), 252
Harrington, James, 10
hēbōntes (20–29 year olds), 84–5
heiresses (*patrouchoi*), 19, 33, 77, 80, 94–8, 310, 405, 409, 419
Hekatomnos, 348
Helen, 243, 272, 328.
  See also 'Menelaion (sanctuary of Helen and Menelaios)'.
Hellanikos, 69
Helos, 117, 303, 305
Helos plain, 132, 138, 139–40
  geomorphology and agricultural potential, 138–40
helots/helotage, 4, 42, 79, ch. 4 *passim*, 173, 226, 237–8, 263, 380–1, 421
  agricultural tribute, 50, 58, 88–90, 125–31
  agriculture and animal husbandry, 131–5, 151, 387, 389–90, 422
  batmen, 198
  communal use of, 199–201
  devolution of cultivation rights, 124–5
  domestic servants, 227, 336–7, 372–3, 377
  exploitation of non-arable resources, 387–8
  female, 336
  household structures, 125, 386–7
  in the common messes, 199
  internal socio-economic differentiation, 125, 387
  Lakonia, 113, 119, 120–1, 127–9
  manumission, 115, 117, 421–2
  Messenia, 128–9
  military recruitment, 213, 421–2
  notion of 'contract of servitude', 50
  notion of fixed rents, 50, 58, 125–6, 383
  origins, 119
  ownership of coinage and bullion, 173
  population, 134–5, 385–6
  relationship with Spartiate landowners, 113–31, 387
  revolt of 460s BC, 347, 417
  security of tenure, 117–19
  settlement patterns, 125
  sharecropping, 126–31
  status, 113–17
  subsistence, 386–8.
  See also *mothōnes*; *nothoi*.
Helvétius, Claude-Adrien, 11
Heraia, 161
Herakleides Lembos, 36, 68, 74, 85–9, 114, 180, 202, 217, 229, 244, 263, 284
Hermippos of Smyrna, 47, 70, 98
hero-reliefs: see 'funerary practice, hero-reliefs'.
Herodotus, 2, 19–20, 69, 77, 82–3, 94–7, 128, 153–4, 171–2, 178, 181, 193–5, 217, 218, 230, 257–8, 262–3, 284, 295, 339–40, 362, 371, 385, 406, 411–12, 414, 416
Hesychios, 125, 158, 163, 183 n. 8, 212
Hieron, 301 n. 42, 429
Hipposthenes (wrestler), cult of, 309–10
hoplites: see 'army'; 'visual evidence, hoplites'.
horses, 154
  breeding and maintenance of, 78, 79, 133, 152, 303–6, 312–16, 432
  cavalry, 152, 213, 221, 311–12, 313, 432
  chariot-racing, 102, ch. 10 *passim*
  communal use, 23, 199–201
  horse races, 303–5
  sacrifice, 239

490

statuettes, 239, 284
household(s), citizen,
  composition and size, 227, 336–7, 370–3
  female influence, 437–40
  hypothetical models, 373–7.
  See also 'marriage/marriage practices'.
household economies, ch. 12 *passim*
  demands upon, 181, 370–82
  economic and social expenditures, 379–82
  food requirements, 373–8
  income-generation, 151, 177–9
  labour force: see 'helots/helotage'
  low degree of liquidity, 177
  productive capacity, 388–95
  size of estates, 210, 382–5.
  See also 'land/land-ownership'; 'property'.
household possessions, alleged attempt to equalise, 45, 46, 47, 55
hunting, 23, 216, 218, 241, 356, 357, 388
  dogs, 23, 151, 199–201, 432
Hyakinthia (festival), 212, 216

Ibykos, 318
iconography: see 'visual evidence'
impoverishment of citizen households, 35, 75, 81, 400, ch. 13 *passim*.
inbreeding, effects of, 444 n. 23
Inferiors (*hypomeiones*), 124, 436
inheritance, 12, 13, 14, ch. 3, *passim*, 419
  alleged life tenure of holdings, 66–8, 70–1, 72–4, 75
  alleged system of unigeniture, 67–8, 71–2, 74–5, 90–1
  diverging devolution, 103, 400, 405–9
  female, 94–103, 400, 402–6
  partible inheritance, 81–2, 400.
  See also Epitadeus, alleged rhētra of.
inheritance system, impact of
  computer simulation of, 400–5
  on citizen households, 121–4, 400–6
  on helot households, 120–4
inscriptions, evidence of, 157, 167, 168–9, 170, 174–6, 178, 231 n. 2, 244, 250–4, 259, 260–2, 266 n. 38, 269–70 n. 65, 292–3, 294, 303–7, 316–17, 322–3, 342, 429
Instituta Laconica, 38–41, 48–50, 57, 58, 68, 85–90, 126, 203–4, 208 n. 26, 215, 244–7, 247–8, 249–55, 260
invention of tradition, 44, 78–9, 151, 165–6
Ionia, 289, 307, 346
Ionian war, 168, 349
iron currency: see 'currency, iron'
Isidas, 170–1
Isokrates, 26–7, 58, 69, 202–5, 311, 417, 424, 437
Isthmos of Corinth (sanctuary of Poseidon and games), 280, 311, 322
Ithome, Mt., 142, 417
ivories, 238, 242, 246, 271, 273, 342, 345, 428

Jaucourt, Chevalier de (*Encyclopédie*), 11
jewellery, 229, 256, 260, 281–4, 288–90
Justin, 52–3

Kallikrates, 257, 258
Kallikratidas, 168
Karneia (festival), 212
Kerameikos (Athenian cemetery), 252, 254, 257, 258–9
Kimon ([I] Athenian Olympic victor), 307, 313, 324
Kimon ([II] Athenian general), 211, 317
Kinadon, conspiracy of: see 'conspiracies'.
kings(hip), 181, 431, 435
  Agiad house, 263, 410–11
  Eurypontid house, 263, 338, 347–8, 356, 411–13, 415
  jurisdiction over adoptions, 82–3
  jurisdiction over marriage of heiresses, 94–7
  marriage strategies, 407–8, 410–13
  rations at home and mess, 193–6
  receipt of tribute, 188, 352
  use of patronage, 179, 335, 353–4, 358, 361–5
  use of *proxenia* and *xeniai*, 339–40, 347–8, 349–51
  See also 'chariot racing, and kings'; 'common messes, royal mess'; 'funerary practice, kings'; 'land-ownership, kings'; 'marriage' 'marriage practices, royal houses'; also entries under individual kings.
Klazomenai, 162
Kleandridas, 415
Klearchos (Spartiate), 340, 344, 435
Klearchos of Soloi (writer), 35–6

Index

Kleoboulos, 351
Kleombrotos (son of Anaxandridas II), 410–11
Kleombrotos I, King, 361–2, 363
Kleomenes I, King, 95, 153, 179, 326–7, 338, 407, 410–11
Kleomenes III, King, 30, 43–5, 54, 70, 97, 246, 382, 383, 434, 440
Kleonymos (son of Sphodrias), 335, 354, 361–2
Kleora, 408, 413
Knidis, 339, 351
kōmoi,
  classical prohibition of, 218
  in archaic Sparta, 217, 318
Kopanaki, 144, 146 n. 17
Koroibos, 340
Koryphasion/Pylos, 141
Kratesikleia, 440
Kritias, 21–2, 153, 195, 196, 199, 218, 228, 317
krypteia, 114, 336
Kyniska (Olympic victrix), 102, 294–5, 308, 309–10, 311, 313, 316, 320, 321–3, 327–8
Kythera, 173

Lakainōn Apophthegmata, 38–41, 47, 229, 233 n. 25, 253–4
Lakonia, 2, 5, 113, 161, 242, 250–1, 260–2
  distribution of land-ownership, 11, 12, 67, 69, 76, 122, 243–4, 384, 437
  extent of Spartiate holdings, 131–2, 138–41
  geomorphology and agricultural potential, 135–9, 140–1
Lakonian art/artistic production: see 'art/artistic production'
Lakonian bronze votives, ch. 9 *passim*
lakonophiles, 26, 153, 220
Lakrates (Olympic victor), 258–9
Lampito, 102, 407, 412–13
land/land-ownership, 3, 4, ch. 3 *passim*, 113, 315
  agricultural exploitation, 132–5, 389–90
  alleged communal character, 11–14, 66–75
  alleged (Lykourgan) equal distribution, ch. 1 *passim*, 29–30, 44–5, 51, 53, 54, 58, 66–75, 382–3

  'ancient portion' (*archaia moira*), 68, 74, 85–90
  bequest, right of, 58–9, 83, 90–4
  citizen estates: see 'citizen estates'
  exploitation of helots, ch. 4 *passim*, 385–8, 390
  female rights, 94–103
  fragmentation of holdings, 121–4
  gift, right of, 58–9, 83, 90–4
  in Lakonia, 11, 12, 67, 69, 76, 122, 243–4, 384, 437
  in Messenia, 142–5
  increasing concentration/inequalities, 34, 35, 91, ch. 13 *passim*
  kings, 78–9, 139, 352
  private character, 76–85
  redistribution in third-century revolution, 43–4, 139
  relationship with helot cultivators, 113–31
  sale and purchase, 83–5
  sharecropping, 125–31
  taxation of, 34, 170, 189–90, 205–6, 433
  unequal distribution, 76–81, 382–5.
  See also 'agriculture'; 'dowries'; 'Epitadeus, alleged rhētra of'; 'inheritance'.
Landridas, 301 n. 42
lead figurines, 218, 222, 225–6, 229, 278–9, 283, 290–1
Lebadeia, 294
Leon (Olympic victor), 308, 313, 320, 322, 326, 329 n. 12, 414
Leonidas I, King, 95, 258, 262, 407, 410–11
Leonidas II, King, 44, 97
Leotychidas II, King, 98, 102, 171, 408, 411–12
Leuktra, battle of (371 BC), 1–2, 246, 252, 399, 429, 436, 437, 439
Libys, 339, 415
Lichas (Olympic victor), 78, 211, 251, 307, 313, 316, 325–6, 342
  lineage of, 414
Lindos, 279
lineages, histories of prominent, 410–16.
  See also 'kings, Agiad house'; 'kings, Eurypontid house'.
liturgies, near-absence of, 160, 177, 212–13
livestock, ownership of, 35, 79, 133, 151–2, 182, 379–80, 387, 422.
  See also 'animal(s), husbandry'.

492

Locri Epizephyrii, 159, 160, 246
luxury, 20, 28, 32, 33, 58–9, 227, 276–7, 424, 440
  disdain for/prohibition of, 9, 10, 11, 23–4, 53, 55, 152, 218
Lykinos (Olympic victor), 308, 313, 320, 322
Lykourgan apophthegms within the *Apophthegmata Lakōnika*, 41, 45–8, 54–7, 98, 152, 156, 163–4
Lykourgos, alleged laws of, chs. 1–2 *passim*, 65–75, 90–4, 115, 126, 152–3, 154–8, 161, 166, 177, 193, 196, 199–203, 209, 244–5, 249–54, 260–2, 355, 424–5
Lysander, 35, 95, 252, 338, 354, 362, 407, 427–9
  alleged corruption of Spartan society, 10–11, 27–9, 155–6, 157, 166–7, 424–5, 428–9
  as *mothax*, 355–6, 415
  gifts received after Aigospotamoi, 345–6, 428–9
  lineage of, 415
  relationship with Cyrus, 345, 349
  sending of booty back to Sparta, 27, 155–6, 157, 429
  use of dedications, 286, 292, 294, 346, 427–8, 430
Lysanoridas, 439
Lysias, 20, 341

Mably, Gabriel Bonnot de, 11–12
Maiandrios (Samian), 153, 179
Makaria plain, 132, 142, 144
Malea peninsula, 139, 141
manpower shortage (*oliganthrōpia*), 33, 75, 369, 399–400, 416–23, 425–6, 435–7, 439
Manso, J.C.F., 1, 13
Mantineia, 225, 347–8
  battle of 418 BC, 251, 253, 399, 421
Mariandynoi of Herakleia Pontika, 118–19
market exchange, 84–5, 180–1, 380
Maron and Alpheios (brothers), 257, 258
marriage/marriage practices,
  age at, 370–2, 406, 422–3
  betrothal, 94–8, 407
  close-kin marriage/endogamy, 101–2, 123, 407–9, 410–13
  control over female, 407
  exogamy, 408–9, 410–13
  heiresses, 80, 94–8, 124, 310, 405, 409, 419
  homogamy, 407–8
  male monogamy, 406
  polyandry, 82, 103, 123, 372, 406, 438–9
  ritual, 98, 230
  royal houses, 407–8, 410–13
  strategies, 123, 405–13, 420
  uterine half-sibling marriage, 82, 123, 407, 409
  wife-sharing, 81–2, 123, 371, 372, 406–7, 420, 438–9.
  See also 'dowries'.
Marx, Karl, 14
masks, clay, 290
Mausolos (Carian), 348
Megillos, 340
Megyllias, 175
Melos/Melians, 169
Mende, 189
Menelaion (sanctuary of Helen and Menelaos),
  bronze dedications, 273–8, 281–3, 288, 414
  dedication by Kyniska, 328
  lead votive figurines, 279
  Panathenaic amphoras at, 308
Menon, 175
mercenaries, use of, 168, 176, 188, 222, 224, 349, 429
Messenia/Messenians, 2
  agriculture, 79
  conquest of, 2, 76, 119
  distribution of land, 76–7, 87
  geomorphology and agricultural potential, 142–4
  helots/helotage, 79, 116, 119, 125, 126–9
  loss of control over (370/69 BC), 437
  pseudo-historical tradition, 128
  revolt of 460s BC, 116, 128, 347, 417, 422
  Second Messenian war, 2, 10, 34, 76
  Spartiate holdings, extent, 131–3, 142–5
messes: see 'common messes'.
Methone, 144
Miletos, 251–2
Mindaros, 168
Minnesota Messenian Expedition,

Index

mirage, Spartan: see 'Sparta, mirage'.
 See also 'invention of tradition'.
Mitford, William, 13
model life tables, 73, 383, 386, 418, 426, 430
Molaoi plain, 139, 141
Molokros, 169, 170, 231 n. 2
Molpis, 357
monetary wealth, 167–76, 180–2
 acquisition of, 176–9, 429
 disdain for/measures against, 24, 29, 51, 53.
 See also 'acquisition of wealth'; 'acquisitive behaviour'; 'currency, precious metal'.
Montesquieu, Baron de, 11
More, Thomas, 9
mothakes, 198, 355–6, 415, 435
mothōnes, 336
movable property/wealth, 84–5, ch. 5 *passim*.
 See also 'animal(s), husbandry'; 'currency, precious metal'; 'household possessions'; 'valuables'.
Moyle, Walter, 11
Myron of Athens/Eleutherai (sculptor), 173, 320, 322
Myron of Priene (writer), 64 n. 48, 89, 114

Nausiadas, 175
navy, financing of, 168, 212–13, 359
Nazi Germany, images of Spartan property, 14
Neapolis plain, 141
Nemea, games at, 311, 322
Neville, Henry, 10–11
Nikias (Athenian), 226, 341, 362
Nikolaos, 344
Nikomedes, 411
nothoi, 336–7
Notion, battle of (407 BC), 292, 430
nudity, male, 220–1

'Old Academy', 35
Olenos, 169
Olontheus, 339
Olympia (sanctuary), 280, 284, 285, 295–7
 Spartiate dedications, 294
Olympic games,
 impact of victory at, 323–8

Spartan participation, 307–12
Spartan victories, 102, 258–9, 307–11
Spartan victory monuments, 319–23
overseas commands/campaigns, 311, 344–6, 423, 425–31
oxen, 151, 152, 179, 239, 362, 380

Panathenaic games, 316–17
 finds of prize amphoras in Sparta, 308–9
Partheniai, 76
patronage, ch. 11 *passim*
 and politics, 348–52, 359–65
 communal, 210–11
 material, 210, 435
 over ephors, 359–61
 over fellow-citizens, 353–65, 430
 over foreigners, 337–52
 over non-citizen dependants, 336–7
 over *perioikoi*, 352–3
 restrictions on, 211
 within Gerousia, 359–63.
 See also 'liturgies'; '*xeniai*'.
Pausanias, King, 166, 252, 257, 259, 295, 338, 341, 360, 429
 pamphlet on laws of Lykourgos, 28–9
Pausanias the Regent, 20, 153–4, 295, 338, 345, 360–1, 411
Pausanias the Traveller (writer), 102, 114, 127, 128, 251, 258, 289, 309, 320–3, 328, 417, 428
Pauw, Corneille de, 12
pederasty, 85, 358, 354
'Peers'/*homoioi*, 2, 221, 226, 287, 337, 353–4, 399, 434, 435, 440
Peisandros, 363
Peloponnesian league, 3, 346–8, 349–51
Peloponnesian war, 21, 167–9, 189, 224, 311, 338, 423–32.
 See also 'empire, Spartan'.
Perachora (sanctuary of Hera), 284
Perikleidas, 224
Perikles (Athenian), 21, 211
perioikoi, 5–6, 7 n. 5, 43, 67, 89, 190, 263, 296
 as clients, 352–3
 in the army, 198–9, 222, 421
 territory and settlements, 139, 141, 144
 tribute to kings, 188
Peripatos/Peripatetic philosophers, 35–7, 40, 43, 70–1
Perkalos, 408, 411–12

Persia/Persians, 20, 77, 153–4, 168–9, 172, 181, 218, 229, 295
  xeniai with Spartiates, 338, 341, 344, 345, 346, 347, 349, 352
Pharax, 340, 428
  lineage of, 415
Pharnabazos, 168, 341
Philo of Alexandria, 82, 407
Philokyon, 257, 258
Philostratis, 174, 175, 439
Phleious, 347–8, 349, 350, 351, 362
Phoibidas, 170–1, 364
phoinikis, 224, 244–5, 247–8
Phylarchos, 43, 54, 71, 355–6, 434
Phylopidas, 338, 341
Physiocrats, 11
Pindar, 318
Plataia, battle of, 153–4, 218, 222, 251, 257, 258, 385–6, 399, 417
Plato, 29–30, 35, 220
  influence on third-century revolutionaries, 44–5, 72, 93–4
  Laws, 32, 58, 69, 74, 218, 227, 245–6, 255, 319, 336, 425, 438
  Republic, 31–2, 155, 165, 166–7, 178, 220–1, 410, 425
  [Platonic] dialogue *Alkibiades I*, 79, 133, 176, 188, 312, 313, 336, 352, 433
  [Platonic] dialogue *Eryxias*, 157, 163
Pleistarchos, 411
Pleistoanax, King, 170, 341, 411, 415
P[lou]tos, 175
Plutarch, 26, 36–7, 47, 48–9, 220, 327
  influence of, ch. 1 *passim*
  Lakonian apophthegms, relationship to his *Lives*, 37–41
  Life of Agesilaos, 190, 262, 362, 363, 364, 436–7
  Life of Kimon, 417–18
  Life of Lykourgos, 23, 30, 54–60, 66–8, 70–1, 72–4, 75, 85, 126, 152–3, 161, 171, 180, 181, 191–2, 203–4, 209, 212, 215, 227, 244–5, 246, 247–8, 249–51, 253–4, 260–2, 383, 423, 424–5
  Life of Lysander, 27–8, 155–6, 163, 166, 167, 409
  Lives of Agis and Kleomenes, 43–5, 67–8, 71–2, 74–5, 83, 90–4, 97, 139, 424–5, 439–40
  manipulation of earlier sources, 53–60, 250.

See also *Apophthegmata Lakōnika*; *Instituta Laconica*; *Lakainōn Apophthegmata*; 'Lykourgan apophthegms within the *Apophthegmata Lakōnika*'.
plutocracy: see 'Sparta, growth of a plutocratic society'.
polemarchs, 56–7, 197, 258–9
politics/policy-making, 348–52, 359–65
Pollux, 71, 158, 163
Polybius, 29–30, 50–2, 68–70, 73, 74–5, 82, 87, 157–8, 314–15, 406–7
Polydoros, King, 44, 67
Polykles (Olympic victor), 308, 311, 320, 321, 322
Polypeithes (Olympic victor), 308, 320, 321, 322, 325
  lineage of, 414
Pompeius Trogus, 53
poor citizens/households, 2, 23, 34, 69, 76, 77, 80, 104, 123, 124, 129, 151, 190, 198, 199, 200, 205, 209, 210, 214, 215, 217, 218, 219, 227, 228, 248, 336–7, 354, 355, 356, 357, 359, 364, 373–95, 399, 410, 419, 420, 431, 432–3, 434, 435, 436–7, 439, 441
Poseidonios (Spartan), 257, 258
Poseidonios (writer), 118, 157, 167
pottery, 144, 240
  black-figure, 217, 239, 318
  Lakonian I, 283, 291
  Lakonian II, 283, 291
  late Geometric, 283
  Proto-Corinthian, 239
  Protogeometric, 238
property,
  communal use of, 23, 199–201
  landed: see 'land/land-ownership'.
  movable, ch. 5 *passim*
  taxation of, 187–90.
  See also 'women, rights of land-ownership and inheritance'.
proxenia, 339–41
public finance, 34, 187–90, 433
  expenditure, 187–8
  revenue, 188–190
public way of life, 3, 4, 43, 434
Pythioi, 197, 302 n. 45, 358

religious investment: see 'bronze dedications'; 'lead figurines'; 'masks, clay'; 'votive offerings'.

Index

reproduction, official attempts to boost, 33, 422–3
Rollin, Charles, 12
Rome, 48
    comparison with Sparta, 50–1, 84, 131, 161, 188–9, 211
Rousseau, Jean-Jacques, 12
royal houses: see 'kings(hip)'.

sacrifices, private, 56, 245
    inexpensiveness, 47, 58, 209
sacrifices, public, 193, 194, 211
Salamis battle of (480 BC), 248
Samios, lineage of, 339, 414
Samos/Samians, 251, 279–80, 295, 337, 346, 348, 414, 427, 428
    sanctuary of Hera, 279–80, 294, 297, 342, 343
sanctuaries, foreign,
    compared with Spartan, 229, 279–80, 283–6, 289–90
    Spartiate offerings at, 174–5, 294–8, 319–23, 342, 428
sanctuaries, Spartan, 229, ch. 9 *passim*, 240
    Agamemnon and Alexandra/Cassandra, 243
    Great Altar, 240
    Heroon by the Eurotas, 240–1.
    See also 'Acropolis', 'Amyklaion', 'Artemis Orthia', 'Athena Chalkioikos', 'Menelaion'.
Schiller, Friedrich von, 13
Selinous, 253
Sellasia, 139, 250
Sikyon, 135, 168, 318, 429
sixth-century 'revolution', 4, 291, 319
Skythes, 339
soldiers: see 'army'.
Solon/Solonian legislation, 246–7, 249
Soulima valley, 132, 144, 146 n. 17
Sparta/Spartan,
    citizen organisation, 2, 3
    decline of power, 1–2, 369, 435–6, 441
    decline of power, ancient representations of, 25, 26–36, 49, 58–9, 60, 67
    growth of a plutocratic society, 432–40
    'mirage', ch. 2 *passim*, 227
    modern reception, ch. 1 *passim*
Sparta (classical) in comparative context, 7, 9
    adoption, 82–3

agriculture and animal husbandry, 79, 132–5, 151, 388–90
Athens/Attica, 20, 22, 35, 79–80, 82–3, 94–6, 99, 101, 115, 133, 177, 180, 181, 189, 197, 211–12, 213, 214, 216, 219, 224–6, 230, 247, 249, 254–6, 257, 286, 289, 309–10, 312–13, 319–20, 321, 322, 324, 360, 366 n. 17, 371, 380–1, 384–5, 408–9, 418–19, 438
bribery, 20, 360, 366 n. 17
cavalry, 213
chariot-racing, socio-political implications, 324
common messes/commensality, 190, 196, 216–18, 434–5
Crete, 29–30, 68, 94–5, 99–100, 190–1, 221
currency and coinage, 158–62
debt, 181–2
dowries, 99–101
dress, female, 229
dress, male, 218–20
female athletics, 228
female influence, 438
female property and inheritance rights, 94–5, 99–101
funerary practice and legislation, 242–3, 245–9, 254–6
Gortyn, 94–5, 99–100
heiresses, 95–6
hellenistic Sparta, 181–2, 256
helotage, 116–17, 386–7
horse-keeping, 314–15
household composition and size, 371–2
household economic and social expenses, 379–81
inheritance system, 81–2, 103
Lakonia, 251–2, 261
landed estates, 79, 123, 384–5
landholdings, fragmentation of, 121–3, 133
liturgies, 212–13
Locri Epizephyrii, 159, 246
Mariandynoi, 118–19
market exchange, 177
marriage practices, 123
marriage ritual, 230
military dress and equipment, 224–6
modern data, 195
modern Greece, 122
monetary wealth, 177

496

navy, 212–13
nudity, male, 220–1
other Greek poleis/regions, 81–2, 123, 132–5, 158–62, 187–9, 191, 210–11, 212–13, 216–18, 228, 229, 245–9, 254–6, 279–80, 283–6, 289, 371–2, 379–81, 384–5, 388–90
other (Mediterranean) societies, 103, 121–3, 129–31, 372, 386
patronage, 210–12
Persia, 232 n. 10, 263
rations 192, 195
Roman Empire, 131, 188–9
Roman Republic, 84, 161, 211, 314
Roman Sparta, 52, 261
sharecropping, 129–31
size of estates, 384–5
taxation/*eisphorai*, 187–92
upbringing, 214–15, 232 n. 1
victory monuments, 320–1
votive offerings, patterns of, 272–3, 279–80, 283–6, 289
Sparta valley, geomorphology and agricultural potential, 135–9
Spartan villages,
 Amyklai, 154, 238–9
 Limnai, 238–9, 240, 263
 Mesoa, 239, 240, 260
 Pitana, 244, 259, 263, 414
Spartiate households: see 'households'.
Sperthias, 77, 344
Sphairos of Borysthenes, 49, 93, 357
Sphakteria, episode of (425 BC), 84–5, 115, 173, 180, 190, 224, 225, 377, 387, 415, 421
 rations, 193–9
Sphodrias, 363
 episode/trial of, 335, 361, 432
Stenyklaros plain, 132, 142, 144
Stoicism/Stoic philosophers, 49, 204
 See also Persaios, Sphairos, Zeno
Strabo, 28–9, 114, 117–19
Stubbe, Henry, 10, 15 n. 7
symposion, 196, 216–18, 239, 317–18, 434–5
syssitia; see common messes.

Tainaron (peninsula), 261
 manumission inscriptions, 145–6 n. 9
Tanagra, battle of (c. 457 BC), 417
taxation, 187–99, 433
Taygetos, Mt., 135, 136, 139, 173

Tegea, 157, 161, 250, 251, 253, 294, 295, 347, 349, 414, 416, 417
Teisamenos, 167
Teleutias, 363
terracottas,
 bells, 293
 plaques, 243–4
 relief amphoras, 239–42
Tertullian, 188–9
Thasos, 191, 247
Thebes/Thebans, 350
theft, legitimised, 201–5
Theophrastos, 36–7, 48, 50, 55
Theopompos, King, 29, 92
Theopompos (writer), 26–7, 29, 41–2, 155–6, 424, 439
Thermopylai, battle of (480 BC), 252–3, 257, 258, 416, 417
Thessalos, 339
Thibrachos/Thibrakos, 258–9
Thibron, lineage of, 415
third-century revolution: 43–4, 181, 440
 influence of, 43–8, 50–60, 69–75, 88–94, 98, 114, 118–19, 121, 126, 152, 424–5, 440
Thirlwall, Connop, 13
Thorax, 156, 172, 427
Thouria, 305
Thucydides, 2, 3, 20–1, 77, 84–5, 144, 145, 180, 193–9, 209–10, 219, 220–1, 225, 232–3 n. 22, 349, 358, 360–1, 387–8, 399–400, 417, 419, 421, 432
Thyrea, battle of (c. 545 BC), 42, 251, 305, 416
 See also 'Battle of the Champions'.
Timaia, 373
Timeas, 175
Timokrates, lineage of, 415
Turpin, François, 11
Tyrtaios, 2, 34, 71, 76–7, 126–9, 142, 222, 237–8, 241–2, 246, 248, 251, 318

upbringing/education,
 female, 227–8, 290–1
 male, 198, 201–5, 214–16, 290–1, 434
 patronage within, 336–7, 342, 353, 354–6, 373
utopian tradition, 9–11

valuables, ownership and exchange of,

Index

152–4, 179, 285
victory monuments,
visual evidence, 2, ch. 9 *passim*
  animals, 241
  female dress, 229, 284
  funerary practice, 238, 240–2
  hair, 226
  'hero-reliefs', 243–4
  hoplites, 222, 224–6, 242, 290–1
  hunting, 241
  military dress and equipment, 222–6, 242
  warfare, 241–2
Voltaire, François Marie Arouet de, 12
votive offerings, ch. 9 *passim*
  at foreign sanctuaries, 174–5, 294–8, 319–23, 342, 428
  at Spartan sanctuaries, 273–94
  athletic, 292
  chariot racing, 173, 303–7, 308, 319–23
  gender of, 288–93, 295
  military commanders, 428–9
  raw and converted, 286–8.
  See also 'bronze dedications'; 'Lakonian bronze votives'; 'lead figurines'; 'masks, clay'.

warfare/warriors: see 'army'.
wealth,
  acquisition of, 176–9, 399, 426–7, 432–3
  'Blind Ploutos', 48, 55, 209
  influx after Peloponnesian war, 12, 27–8, 58–9, 164, 424–5, 429
  restrictions on use of, chs. 7–8 *passim*, 285–6, 317–20
  use of, chs. 9–11 *passim*, 428–30, 432, 433
weddings: see 'marriage, ritual'.
weights and measures, 163–5, 191–2
women,
  athletics, 227–8
  chariot-racing victories, 102, 321–3, 327–8
  diet, 228
  dress and appearance, 28, 228–30, 279
  funerary practice and memorials, 260–2, 263
  helot, 336
  hierai, 261–2

influence of wealthy, 437–440
marriage, 80, 81–2, 94–102, 230, 371–2, 406–13
negative representations of, 20, 32, 33, 226–7
rights of land-ownership and inheritance, 77, 80, 94–103, 400–6
upbringing, 227–8
votive offerings, 283–4, 288–93, 294–5.
See also 'dowries'; 'heiresses; marriage'.
Wren, Matthew, 10

Xenares, 351, 362
Xenarkes (Olympic victor), 308, 311, 320, 322
xenēlasia, 337
xeniai,
  advantages of, 343–52
  and Spartan politics 348–52
  and the Peloponnesian league, 346–8, 349–51
  role of wealth, 341–3
  Spartiate involvement in, 77, 337–52
Xenopeithia, 439
Xenophon, 29–30
  Agesilaos, 25–6, 83, 179, 211, 213, 312, 327, 335, 343, 348, 352, 363–5
  Anabasis, 202, 205, 349
  Hellenika, 78, 141, 154, 173, 197, 221, 246, 258–9, 263, 342, 360, 361–2, 362
  Memorabilia 78
  Oikonomikos, 177–8
  Polity of the Lakedaimonians, 22–5, 49–50, 55, 69, 71, 78–9, 81–2, 114–15, 124, 155, 162, 163–4, 165–6, 174, 177, 178–9, 180, 193, 196, 199–200, 201–2, 204–5, 208 n. 21, 209, 213, 214–15, 219, 220, 227, 228, 230, 231 n. 6, 231–2 n. 9, 263, 312, 356–7, 371, 407, 426–7, 436, 438
  as historical agent, 341–2, 366 n. 11
Xerxes I (Persian king), 344, 345
Xouthias, son of Philachaios, 157, 167

Younger Pliny, 131

Zeno, 49
Zeuxidamos, 102, 412